The History of the Granville Family

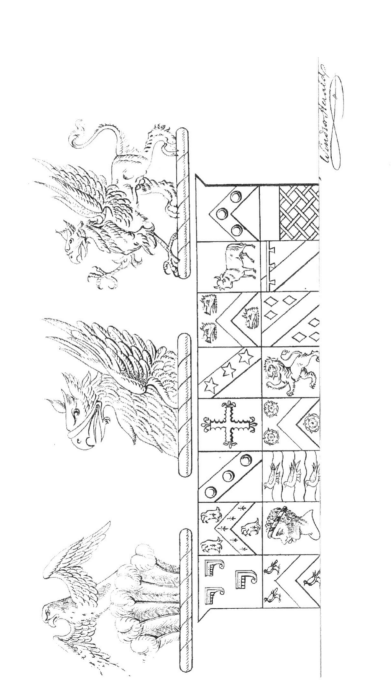

THE HISTORY

OF THE

GRANVILLE FAMILY.

Traced back to Rollo, First Duke of Normandy.

WITH PEDIGREES, ETC.

BY

ROGER GRANVILLE, M.A.,

RECTOR OF BIDEFORD.

Exeter :

WILLIAM POLLARD & CO., THE PRINTING WORKS, NORTH STREET.

1895.

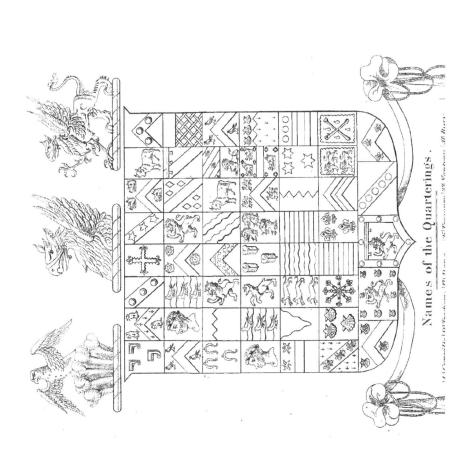

Names of the Quarterings.

THE HISTORY

OF THE

GRANVILLE FAMILY.

Traced back to Rollo, First Duke of Normandy.

WITH PEDIGREES, ETC.

BY

ROGER GRANVILLE, M.A.,

RECTOR OF BIDEFORD.

Exeter :
WILLIAM POLLARD & CO., THE PRINTING WORKS, NORTH STREET.
1895.

PREFACE.

THESE Memoirs were originally commenced by my late father, Mr Bernard Granville of Wellesbourne, who devoted much time in the latter years of his life to genealogical research, and left at his death two large volumes of manuscript notes as the result of his labours. Inheriting the same taste, and living on 'Granville' soil, I undertook to revise and complete what he began, and have been able to add a considerable amount of information, and, above all, by the kindness of Mr Ezekiel Rouse, of Bideford, and of Mr. Kemeys-Tynte and others, who possess the originals, or copies of them, have permission to print a large number of most interesting family letters in addition to those belonging to and collected by my father. The Kemeys-Tynte Collection has recently been privately printed, but few, I believe, of the others have seen daylight before. The story of their discovery is thus amusingly told in Mr. Baring Gould's "Life of the Rev. R. S. Hawker," the poet-priest of Morwenstow.

"One day, if indeed we may trust the story, Mrs Hawker, the first wife of the Vicar of Morwenstow, when lunching at Stowe, in the farm-house, noticed that a letter in old handwriting was wrapped around the mutton-bone that was brought on the table. Moved by curiosity she took the paper off and showed it to Mr. Hawker On examination it was found that the letter bore the signature of Sir Bevill Granville Mr Hawker at once instituted enquiries, and found a chest full of letters of different members of the Granville family in the sixteenth and seventeenth centuries. He at once communicated with Lord

Carteret, owner of Stowe, and the papers were removed, but by some unfortunate accident they were lost The only ones saved were a packet removed from the chest by Mr. Davies, Rector of Kilkhampton, previous to their being sent away from Stowe. These were copied by Miss Manning of Eastaway in Morwenstow, and her transcript together with some of the originals (I fear not all) is now in the possession of Ezekiel Rouse, Esq, of Bideford "

These letters were sent in six large packing cases, each nearly a yard square, to George, Lord Carteret, who died 22nd February, 1838, shortly after Mr. Hawker became Vicar of Morwenstow. Lord Carteret, when he next saw Mr Hawker, thanked him for the trouble he had taken, and said he had done the best thing he thought he could do with the documents, which was to commit them to the flames with the exception of two or three dozen letters What has become of these is not known. The late Mr Isaac Disraeli endeavoured, but unsuccessfully, to obtain permission to inspect them during the time he was completing his *Commentaries* on the reign of Charles I

It will be noticed that I have for the most part adhered to that spelling of the family surname which has been generally adopted since the Patent for the Earldom of Bath was made out for Sir John Grenvile after the Restoration, and in which he was styled " Baron Granville of Kilkhampton and Bideford, Viscount Granville of Lansdown and Earl of Bath " The name (as stated on p 1) has been variously spelt at various periods of the family's history but there can be little doubt that the correct manner is Granville as derived from the ancient Norman seigneury (see p 16)

My best thanks are due to Mrs Didham, of Middleton, Bideford, a lady devoted to Sir Bevill and Lady Grace Granville, for chronologically arranging the letters, and for

various useful comments and suggestions as to their contents
I have also to thank the Earl of St Germains for permission to
reprint several letters from the Port Eliot Collection ; and also
Mrs Coham-Fleming for allowing me access to the few in her
possession, including the very touching one addressed by Sir
Bevill to Sir John Eliot just before his death in the Tower
(see p. 182)

In a work of this kind originality cannot be expected. "I
have only made a nosegay of culled flowers, and brought
nothing of my own but the thread that ties them together.'
(Montaigne, Bk iii., ch 12). It only pretends to be a compilation
from the writings of well-known authors of established credi-
bility, thus giving in one book the descriptions and opinions
which appear in many Commenced originally with but little
idea of publication, I may not have been as careful as I ought
in quoting the sources of some of my information ; but I desire
to acknowledge my indebtedness to Mr. Tregellas, the author
of "Cornish Worthies," to Mr Robbins, the author of "Sir
Bevil Grenvill, the Knight of the West, a Biography in
outline;" to Mr. Cotton, the author of 'Barnstaple during
the Civil War," to Mr Julian Corbett for much relating to
George Monk, Duke of Albemarle, which I have taken from his
life of that chief actor in the Restoration in the "English Men
of Action" Series ; and last, but not least, to Mrs G. H Radford,
whose amusing account of the quarrels between Sir Richard
Granville, "the King's General in the West," and his wife
forms one of the papers in the "Transactions of the
Devonshire Association" for 1890

I regret that 'correcting proof' has proved a real stumbling-
block to me, and that therefore a too lengthy list of *corrigenda*
has to be annexed to the Volume, but these are nearly all cases of
misspelt words or grammatical slips ; the accuracy of dates and
facts is, I hope, quite correct At any rate my effort such as it
is, must now remain in its present condition, and I can only

trust that the original purpose I had in view, when I commenced
the task, may not be in vain, viz., to remind all who hold, or
shall hereafter hold, the honoured name of Granville, that they

> "   .   fetch their life and being
> From men of royal siege,"

and that realizing this, they may endeavour to uphold their
ancestral traditions, and to walk worthily in the steps of their
renowned forefathers

ROGER GRANVILLE.

The Rectory, Bideford,
        Christmas, 1895

LIST OF ILLUSTRATIONS.

THE HISTORY

OF THE

GRANVILLE FAMILY.

CHAPTER I

"THE most lasting families" says Dr Borlase, 'have only
their seasons more or less of a certain constitutional strength
They have their spring and summer sunshine glare, their wane,
decline and death" This remark is certainly true of the
family whose memoirs are to be unfolded in these pages. Its
ancient lineage, its territorial influence, together with the
brilliant achievements of several of its distinguished members,
placed the family of Granville at one time in the foremost
ranks of the celebrated historical Houses of this country But
that summer sunshine glare which culminated in the reign of
the Stuarts, has long since declined, and in the male line the
old family is no more Yet the name of Granville is still
treasured One family at least represents it in the female line ,
an earldom enshrines its memory, whilst as a Christian name
it has been repeatedly adopted by many a noble and gentle
House, who are proud to trace back a connection by marriage,
or otherwise, with a family which for so many centuries held a
distinguished position in the history of their country

The Granvilles or Grenvilles Greuviles, Grenfells, Greyn-
vills. Graynfelds, Greenfields, Grenefelds. Grauntvilds—for the
name has been variously spelt and corrupted at different times –
claim descent, through the Earls of Corbeil, from Rollo, the son
of Jarl Rögnvald, a Scandinavian chieftain of the highest rank,
who lived in the reign of Harfager, King of Norway

According to various Sagas quoted by Du Chaillu, in "The
Viking Age," Rognvald was the son of Eystein Glumra, son of
Ivar Uppland Jarl, son of Halfdan the Old He assisted King
Harald in the conquest of Norway, and received in return for
his services the two Maers and Raumsdal He married Ragn-

B

hild, daughter of Hrolf Nefja, by whom he had three sons, viz ,
Ivar, who fell in the Hebrides whilst on an expedition with
King Harald   Hrolf or Rollo, as he was afterwards called by
the French, and as he is known to posterity, and Thorir the
Silent who married King Harald's daughter Arbot, by whom he
had a daughter, Bergljot, mother of Hakon Jarl the Great, the
hero of the battle of Gomsviking

   Rollo (nicknamed Gongu, *i e ,* the Ganger because, it is
said, his stature was so gigantic that, when clad in armour, no
horse could support his weight, and he therefore always fought
on foot), was expelled from Norway for an act of depredation
in Viking contrary to the King's commands   Harald desirous
of being included among the civilized sovereigns of Europe, had
strictly forbidden his subjects to exercise their old habits of
piracy on his own coasts, or on those of his allies   Rollo
perhaps considered himself above this new law   His father,
Jarl Rognvald, was the King's chief friend, and presuming on
the favour shown to his family, while returning from an
expedition on the Baltic, he made a descent upon the coast
between Norway and Gothland, and carried off the cattle
wanted by his crew   For this act Rollo was declared an
outlaw   His mother pleaded in vain for him , the King was
inexorable   According to Harald's Saga c 24 the following
was her petition —

> Disgrace not Nefja's namesake,[1]
> Nor drive the wolf from the land ,
> The wise kinsman of Hold [2]
> Why dealest thou thus with him, King ?
> It is bad to worry
> Such a wolf of Ygg's,[3]
> He will not be gentle towards
> The King's herds if he runs into the woods

   Rollo's outlawry led to the establishment of our royal line,
and to that infusion of new spirit into England to which her
greatness appears to be chiefly owing   He first retired with his
fleet among the islands of the Hebrides, whither the flower of
the Norwegian nobility had fled when Harald had become
master of the Kingdom   He was there received with open arms
by those warriors who, eager for conquest and revenge, waited
only for a chief to lead them on   Taking advantage of their
sentiments at such a crisis, he pretended to have had a dream
which promised him a glorious future in France   This served
at least to support the ardour of his followers, but the weakness

H [1]   [2] The higher class of landowners   [3] Ygg (Odin), a wolf of Ygg means a champion.

at that time of the French Government, and the confusion in which it was involved were still more persuasive reasons Setting sail with them, Rollo first plundered and devastated the coast of Flanders, and then turned towards France, where, according to Dudo and other ancient writers, he landed at Rouen in the spring of A D 876 Their arrival caused the greatest dismay to the inhabitants of Rouen, who were scarcely yet recovered from the miseries which had been inflicted upon them by the fierce Danish rover, Hasting Indeed for a long period the coasts of France, like those of England, had been ravaged by the incursions of the Northmen, and for the greater part of a century the monks had made the Neustrian churches re-echo with the dismal chant of the litany " A furore Normannorum libera nos, Domine " The defenceless inhabitants at once determined to capitulate, and Archbishop Franco went forth to meet the Northmen, bearing the keys of the town They offered no violence, and he performed his errand safely The rude generosity of Rollo's character was touched by his fearless conduct, and he readily agreed to spare the lives and property of the citizens on condition that Rouen was surrendered to him without resistance. Entering the town, he established his head quarters there, and so faithfully did the Northmen observe their promise that they were regarded by the Rouennais rather as friends than as conquerors, and Rollo was far more popular than their real sovereign, Charles le Chauve.

Having thus firmly planted themselves at Rouen, successive summers were spent in ravaging the dominions of the French King But a change was gradually coming over Rollo. Insensibly he was becoming softened and civilized by his intercourse with Archbishop Franco, and finding perhaps that it was not quite so easy as he had expected to conquer the whole kingdom of France, he declared himself willing to follow the example which he had once despised, and to become a vassal of the French crown for the Duchy of Neustria Charles le Simple, now King of France, greatly rejoiced to find himself thus able at length to put a stop to the dreadful devastations of the Northmen and readily agreed to the terms proposed by Rollo, (A D 911), and appointed the village of St. Clair sur Epte on the borders of Neustria as the place of meeting for the purpose of receiving his homage and oath of fealty According to Dudo it was necessary to kneel and kiss the King's foot, but this the proud pagan disdained. The prelate who attended the King declared that a gift so magnificent (viz , Neustria and his daughter) deserved his compliance ' I will never ' exclaimed

Rollo, " bend my knees to the knees of any man, nor kiss his foot " 'Ne si by Got " The Frankish nobles solicited him in vain At last as a substitute he ordered one of his knights to do the ceremony for him The knight, revolting like his master at the degradation, murmuringly complied, but instead of kneeling, he seized the royal foot standing upright, and carrying it suddenly to his mouth, threw the King on the floor, a contumelious indignity which on such an occasion a haughty savage only could have offered

The transaction ended, Duke Robert and Archbishop Franco returned to Rouen with Rollo, where, the following year, he was baptized, Duke Robert acting as sponsor The name Robert was given to him on the occasion, but the old name that had honoured him in youth and in age, was alone recognized by the world On leaving the Cathedral, Rollo celebrated his conversion by large grants to the different churches and convents in his new Duchy, making a fresh gift on each of the days during which he wore the white robes of the newly baptized All his warriors, who chose to follow his example and embrace the Christian faith, received from him grants of land to be held on the same terms as those by which he himself held the Duchy from the King, and the country thus peopled by the Northmen gradually assumed the appellation of Normandy. " The thirty wild years as a rover by land and sea, thirty years of rapine and of cruel deeds done to well-nigh defenceless cities, villages and monasteries, would seem a strange preparation for one who was to organize an important nation, who was to weld together men of various races, who was to lay the strong ground stones of a mighty realm, destined in a few short years powerfully to influence the history of the world Yet this is what Rollo the Viking, the wild Northman freebooter, did in Rouen and Bayeux, between A D 911 and A D 927 The first of the seven mighty Dukes of Normandy must have been more than sixty years old when he began his curious, but enduring work For enduring it indeed was What he began his six successors went on with and developed—the strong and firm government, the respect for the Christian faith, law and order, the gradual restoration of the old ruined religious houses and then great educational and other works, the curious welding together of Dane and Frenchman which produced the Norman,—all these changes were the care of the old freebooter Rollo the Viking, his children and children's children for six generations, so that in less than a century and a half after the grim old Dane was laid in his tomb in the Rouen Minster that he had restored, his Norman

land was famous for its new school of architecture, for its lovely
minsters, its vast monasteries, its flourishing cities, was, (still
more remarkable,) famous for its matchless schools, and even for
the wealth and beauty of its "Romance" or French literature
For three generations, that is during the reigns of the first
three Dukes a period of some ninety eventful years, the old
Norsk religion, in which Thor and Odin were worshipped, and
the wild banqueting hall of Valhalla looked to as the glorious
goal of the unconquered fighting hero, struggled with Christianity
in the hearts of the great Norman Dukes and their faithful
companions in arms   Rollo and his two successors were more
than nominal Christians, as we shall see, nay, at times his son
and grandson were even fervent devotees to the Christian faith,
yet ever and anon the spirit of the old loved Paganism of their
fathers influenced them and their followers   This was especially
noticeable in their marriages   The aversion of these brilliant
and successful men to the Christian marriage tie is remarkable,
and the first three Dukes made no concealment of their dislike
to the princesses to whom, mainly for political reasons they
were united by Christian rites.   Their love and affection all
belonged to the partners whom they had chosen for themselves,
and to whom some Pagan rite loosely bound them, and not to
those high-born women, whom, without pretending to love,
they had married with all the ceremony of the Christian
Church "—*The Homes of the Norman Dukes*, by Dean Spence

This was especially the case with Rollo, who as part of the
treaty, had married Gisella the daughter of the French King.
Rollo was an old grizzly warrior, and neither cared for the
other, and when in A D. 919, Gisella died childless, he returned
to his old love Popeé (the Poupeé or Poppet,) daughter of
Beringer, Earl of Bessin and Bayeux, and sister to Bernard de
Senlis Vermandois,[1] whom he had take captive at the capture
of Bayeux A.D 890-1. and married "more Danico."   He now
married her ' more Christiano " and thus rendered legitimate the
two children he had had by her, viz.   William and Gerloc or
Gerletta who received the name of Adela at her baptism, and
afterwards became the wife of William, Duke of Acquitaine and
Poictiers   In A D. 926-7, feeling the cares of government too great
for his advancing years Rollo handed over the reins of government to his son, and dying some five years afterwards, was buried
in the sacristy of the Cathedral at Rouen, but some two hundred
years afterwards his body was removed to the little chapel on

[1] Guillaume Gemmet ex Camdens, Angl. Scripta p 616   Matthew of Westminster p
556 Dudo de St Quentin

the light of the nave, where a sarcophagus, under a plain niche
in the wall, was erected in the days of St Louis bearing his
effigy [1] The figure of Rollo was originally bold and well
executed embodying the notion conveyed by tradition and
history the once mighty man of war thoroughly worn out,
the sunken life, the furrowed brow. " the strength of four score
years come to labour and sorrow." But since Palgrave wrote
his description the effigy has been repaired and renewed so
often that it has probably lost most of its distinguishing
characteristics The tomb bears the following inscription,
though the date of his death is evidently inaccurate, if we are
to believe his history as written by the old historians.

Hic positus est
ROLLO
Normanniæ a se territæ vastatæ
Restitutæ
Primus Dux, conditor, pater
A Francone Archiep Rotom
Baphizatus anno DCCCCXIII
Obit anno DCCCCXVII
Ossa ipsius in veteri sanctuario
Nunc capite navis, primum, condita
Translato altari, hic collocata
Sunt a b Maurilio Archiep Rotum
Anno MLXIII

William, his son and successor, surnamed Longsword, had
been carefully educated by the priests. His height was majestic,
his features beautiful, his complexion pure and delicate as a
maiden's, his strength gigantic, his prowess with all weapons
on foot and on horseback unrivalled, and his wit and capacity
of the brightest and most powerful Born since his father's
conquest of Neustria the tales of Thor and Odin, and the
future Valhalla, were gradually becoming things of the dark
old past to him, and he threw himself, with his whole heart
into the new faith. So intensely devout was he, so fond of
prayer and the rites of the Church, that Rollo had called him
fitter for a cloister than for a dukedom , but the choice was not
open to him, an only son with the welfare of the Normans
dependent on him. He rebuilt the Abbey of Jumièges with
great splendour, and though living in the world amid great
luxury and pomp, he practised in secret the devotions and
asceticism of the cloister to the utmost of his power, longing
earnestly for the time when, like his father, he might lay aside

[1] According to Dudo and others his body was again transferred to the Abbey at
Fecamp.

the weary load of cares of war and government, and retire to
that Abbey as a brother of the Order. On his father's abdication he rendered homage to Charles le Simple, at the Château
d'Eu, but soon after his father's death the lords of Brittany
under the Counts Alain and Berenger endeavoured to recover
their independence. They were however defeated, Berenger
was pardoned, but Count Alain, the prime mover in the
rebellion, was banished

William Longsword's strict keen justice made him greatly
honoured and loved in Normandy, but in France he was hated,
and his transactions were sometimes cunning, sometimes
violent. Though wavering towards France, he remained a
Northman in heart, and vassalage sat lightly upon him. As
an instance of this he called in a Danish colony to occupy his
conquest of the Cotentin, the peninsula which runs out from
St Michael's Mount to the cliffs of Cherbourg and reared his
boy among the Northmen of Bayeux where the Danish tongue
and fashions most stubbornly held their own. With all his
zeal for the new faith, it is clear that he had not entered into
the Church's teaching of the sanctity of marriage, for, like his
father,' he had an half-acknowledged wife, Espriota or Sprota,
the daughter of Herbert, Earl of Senlis, and sister of Bernard
the Dane, who afterwards became the protector and guardian
of the young son he had by her. But though he doted on
Espriota, his love for her could not blind his religious instincts
to the fact that his home-life was not honourable, either morally
or politically. Such sentiments were encouraged by his kinsman, Herbert of Vermandois, who persuaded him to cast off
Espriota, and marry his second daughter, Luitgard, thus
following his father's example in casting off the mother of his
child. There was, however, no issue of this marriage.

In 936, William Longsword accompanied by Hugh the Great,
Herbert, Count of Vermandois, and others, received at Boulogne,
on his landing from England, Louis Outre-mer, the new King
of France, son of Charles le Simple, who received his nickname
from having been educated at the English Court. William
conducted him to Laon and assisted at his coronation. Three
years afterwards, however, he quarrelled with him, and entered
into a formal league against him with Hugh the Great and
Herbert of Vermandois and the remainder of his life was
occupied in invasions and other political disturbances, the last of
which was entered upon for the purpose of forcing Arnouf,
Count of Flanders, to restore to the Count of Ponthou

¹ St Allen   Guillaume de Jumiages

the town of Montreuil which he had unlawfully taken possession of Arnoult, dissembling his resentment, begged of William
to grant him a conference on a small island in the river Somme,
and there having contrived to separate him from his followers,
at a given signal, one of the Flemings struck him down with
an oar and a number of daggers were instantly plunged into
his breast The Flemings made their escape in safety, leaving
the bleeding corpse upon the island and the Normans, who
had seen the murder without being able to prevent or revenge
it, reverently took it up and brought it to Rouen Dudo
narrates that beneath the robes of state they found it dressed
in a hair cloth shirt, and that round his neck was a chain with
a golden key attached to it. which they rightly judged to belong
to the chest where he kept his choicest treasure, but few would
have guessed what the treasure was which was so highly valued
by the knightly Duke of the martial name, and doubtless there
were many looks of wonder among the Norman barons when
the chest was opened, and disclosed, instead of gold and jewels,
the gown and hood, the sandals and rosary of a brother of the
Benedictine Order He fell at the early age of forty-two,
having ruled about twenty years and was buried beside his
father in Rouen Cathedral amid the universal lamentations of
his vassals His body was afterwards moved to a side chapel
on the left hand side of the nave. as his fathers was to one on
the right and the monumental effigy still preserves the tra-
ditional features, bearing date no doubt from a period far more
remote than that of St Louis , and ' as the stranger from
other lands gazes on this remarkable face he feels he is looking
on something not unlike what the mighty Norman was in life
The figure represents a crowned and armoured soldier His
hand formerly rested on the golden hilt of that famous long
sword from which he takes his name but the sword is now
missing. On the still youthful face of the hero Duke is an
expression of intense weariness, worn out with the respon-
sibilities of his busy work-filled life "—*Dean Spence*

The following inscription is on the tomb ·—

Hic positus est
GULIELMUS, dictus LONGA SPATHA
Rolloius filius
Dux Normanniæ
Predatorie occisus DCCCCXXXIV [1]
Ossa ipsius in veteri sanctuario ubi nunc est caput navis primum
condita, translato altari hic collocata sunt ap Mauriho
Archiep Rotum Anno MLXII

[1] The date on the tomb of William Longsword is also incorrect, as well as the date on
Rollo's Anselme, Dudo, Guilli de Jumieges all give 943 Matthew of Westminster 913
as the correct date Probably, therefore, his reign was less than twenty years

Upon William's assassination Bernard the Dane the brother of Espriota, fetched from Bayeux his only child Richard, then barely eight years old, to be solemnly invested with the ducal sword and mantle, and to receive the homage of the Normans Whether his birth was strictly legitimate or not was a matter of very little moment either in Norman or in Frankish eyes If a man was of princely descent and shewed a spirit worthy of his forefathers, few people cared to enquire over minutely into the legal or canonical condition of his mother

"The Norman chieftains gathered round William Long-sword's coffin They included old grey-headed companions of Rollo, with their sons and grandsons men who were the ancestors of the future conquerors of Italy and Sicily , men, whose children's children fought and won on the stricken field of Hastings , men, whose descendants became the foremost Crusaders, the fathers of the proudest Houses of the mighty Anglo-Norman kingdom, and in their midst, standing by his murdered father's coffin, the little fair-haired boy with ruddy cheeks. whom they had fetched from Danish Bayeux One grey-headed chieftain held the ducal coronet on the boy's head, one kissed the little hand, and the others swore eternal allegiance and fidelity to their child Duke Richard, who in sorrow and perplexity stood gazing on his father's coffin It was the last great service Rollo's son could do his people and the land, this welding together by his coffin the varied interests of his mighty chieftains In this solemn moment the Norman Dane and the Norman Frenchman forgot their jealousies. their antipathies, the conflicting interests of the old religion and the new, in their stern resolve to avenge their master's death by raising the throne of their master's son higher than the thrones of any of the Princes of France ".—*Dean Spence*

Having been thus acknowledged by the Norman chiefs as his father's successor, the young Duke found as little difficulty in obtaining a formal investure of the fief from the French King The King came to Rouen, where he was received and entertained with great magnificence, and then Richard rendered his homage Louis grasped at this opportunity for recovering Normandy, and under the pretence of educating the young Duke at his own court, made an overture to the Norman barons that he should return with him to France, assuring them of his care and protection of him This proposal they at first strongly opposed, mistrusting the King, and suspecting the influence of Count Arnoulf, who stood high in his counsels, and who would naturally dread the future retribution of the son for his father's murder Won, however, by the royal promises and seeming attachment to the young Duke, they suffered him to depart, and Louis carried him away to Laon Richard had not been long in the King's power before the fears of the Normans were realized, and Louis, chiefly at the instigation of Count Arnoulf, imprisoned him at Montleon, allowing, however, a Norman esquire, Osmund de Centeville, to accompany him as tutor By Osmund's help he contrived to escape, and sought shelter with his uncle, Bernard the Dane, who had been originally appointed his guardian by Duke William, as well as regent of the Norman territories during his minority A heathen reaction, according to Green, followed the death of Duke William, and the bulk of the Normans with the child Duke Richard fell away for the time from Christianity The young Duke's escape had taken place in A D 945, and Louis, finding himself thus duped, concerted with Hugh the Great and made war against the Normans, entering Normandy by two different roads Bernard the Dane had called to his assistance the King of Denmark, and new pirate fleets again came swarming up the Seine After several engagements Louis was taken prisoner Peace, however, was concluded the following year, when Richard received an augmentation of territory, for which he again paid homage The peace thus concluded was, however, soon destined to be broken It was arranged that Richard, who was then fourteen years of age, should be affianced to Emma, the daughter of Hugh the Great, Count of Paris , but this alliance was so distasteful to both Louis and Count Arnoulf that they concerted with Otho, King of Germany, and war once more broke out However, after ravaging the territory of Hugh the Great and attacking Rouen, they were repulsed by the Normans and Danes under the young Duke, who followed up his success and before long cleared the province of its invaders The courage and ability which he displayed throughout the wars made a great impression on his Danish allies, who were induced in large numbers to adopt the religion of "the Fearless Duke," as they called him, and to live under his government

Louis Outre-mer was succeeded by Lothaire, who inherited all the hatred of his race against the Normans, who were still Pirates to the French around them, then land the Pirates' land, their Duke the Pirates' Duke Lothaire renewed hostilities against Richard, but the struggle only strengthened the power of the Duke Freeman suspects that no homage was ever rendered by Richard to Lothaire, and that it was most probably its refusal which led to the differences between Lothaire and

Richard. Peace was made through the intervention of the Archbishop of Cologne at Amiens, and 'in the end," as Mr Green writes, " the same forces which merged the Dane in the Englishman, told even more powerfully on the Dane in France No race has ever shewn a greater power of absorbing all the nobler characteristics of the peoples with whom they came in contact, or of infusing their own energy into them. During the long reign of Duke Richard the Fearless, the son of William Longsword, a reign which lasted from A D 945 to 996, the heathen Northmen pirates became French Christians and feudal at heart. The old Norse language lived only at Bayeux and in a few local names As the old Northern freedom died silently away the descendants of the pirates became feudal nobles, and " the Pirates land " sank into the most loyal of the fiefs of France "[1] Richard was mainly instrumental in placing on the French throne, after Lothaire's death in A.D 987, Hugh Capet, his brother-in-law and ward Hugh Capet having received the homage of every crown vassal, except Arnoulf of Flanders, proceeded to ravage his country and to seize his towns. Arnoulf, completely reduced, saw no way of escape except in throwing himself on the mercy of Duke Richard, the very man whose father he had murdered, and whom he had pursued with the most unrelenting hatred from his earliest childhood Richard had but to allow royal justice to take its course, and he would have been fully avenged, but he who daily knelt before the altar of the Church of Fécamp, had learnt far other lessons He went to Hugh Capet and so pleaded with him that he not only obtained the pardon of Arnoulf, but the restoration of the whole of his domains and of both his cities Thus, without doubt, would the saintly William Longsword have desired to be avenged by his own son

Duke Richard was a great patron of arts and learning, of agriculture and commerce, and sought in every way to promote the happiness and prosperity of his subjects He not only restored the Abbey of Fécamp with great magnificence, but also enlarged and endowed the Abbeys of St Ouen, Mont St Michel, and St. Wandeille. He also built the Archiepiscopal Church at Rouen. His personal appearance and character are thus described by the old Norman chroniclers, who knew him well in his old age " He was tall and well-proportioned his countenance was noble, his beard was long, and his head covered with white hair. He was a pious benefactor to the monks supplied the wants of the clergy, despised the proud, loved the

[1] Green, V I 1, 1

humble aided the poor, the widow, and the orphan, and
delighted in ransoming prisoners." In his lifetime he caused a
stone coffin to be made for himself, and placed in the Church of
Fécamp, where every Friday he filled it with wheat, which was
afterwards distributed amongst the poor In this Abbey he
died 20th November, 996, aged sixty-three years. William
Gemmelicus describes his last illness and death at length
According to his wish, expressed shortly before he died, he was
buried outside the Church of Fécamp, close by the outer wall,
" where the drops of Heaven falling on him from the sacred
eaves might lave his body from the many sins contracted in
his thoughtless career" In a subsequent generation Henry
Beauclerc caused his remains to be removed from the sarcophagus under the spouting gargoyle, and deposited in the
adjoining Basilica A new tomb was provided for father and
son and Master Wace informs us that, when the translation
took place, he had the opportunity of contemplating both
corpses

As before stated he had married in A D. 956, (or, as some
authors assert, 960), Emma, the second daughter of Hugh the
Great, Duke of France, but he had no issue by her He married
secondly his concubine Gonnor or Gunnora, who is described as
sister to Herfaste, a Dane of noble birth Dudo calls her
" une très belle femme, très adroite et de grand esprit, et une
femme, accomplie, et d'une famille de Dannemark de haute
noblesse" According to Guillaume de Jumièges, Richard first
saw her when hunting in the forest of Arques Night having
come on he slept at the house of (as he is described) a Forester
at Sargeville, whose handsome wife Sainfrie he became
enamoured of, and commanded her to be given up to him.
She, being a clever shrewd woman, substituted her sister
Gunnora in her place, who was a far handsomer woman even
than she herself. Duke Richard, on finding out the deception
next morning, was much pleased with the exchange, and afterwards had several children by her On wishing to make his
second son Robert, Archbishop of Rouen, the appointment was
strongly objected to by the Church on the score of his illegitimacy Richard therefore, his first wife being dead, married
Gunnora and thus legitimated all the children he had had by her,
and created a regular and lawful succession to the Dukedom
Gunnora appears to have lived till the year A D. 1031

Guillaume de Jumièges gives Duke Richard three sons, viz.,
Richard the Good, his successor ; Robert, who became Archbishop of Rouen, Earl of Evreux, and who espoused, *more*

Danico, (for assuredly no priest would give the benediction !) a damsel named Herleva, by whom he had several children ; and Mahger or Mauger, as he is usually called, Earl of Corbeil, the direct ancestor of the Granville family [1] We shall treat of him in the next chapter

Dudo gives Duke Richard five sons, without, however, naming them Possibly these other two were not the children of Gunnora, as Dudo elsewhere mentions two illegitimate sons, viz, Geoffrey, who became the ancestor of the Earls of Clare, and William, the ancestor of the Earls of Eu Guillaume Gemmet and Anselm also mention these illegitimate sons, and two illegitimate daughters. Indeed many of those whose names in after days appeared on the roll of Battle Abbey—the Lindsays, Giffords, Tankervilles, Gournays, Warrenes, Mowbrays, Mortimers,—names written on many a stirring page of English history trace back to sons or nephews or kinsmen of Duke Richard the Fearless

Richard's eldest legitimate daughter was Hawise, the wife of Geoffrey, Earl of Brittany She died, 21st February, 1034, and was buried at Rennes Maud, the second daughter, was married to Endes, Earl of Chartres and Blois, whilst Emma, the youngest "the Flower of Normandy," was twice crowned Queen of England, having married first, in 1002, King Æthelred, (who thus hoped to win the friendship of Normandy, and to close its harbours against the Danish King Swegen, who was at this time attacking England with his pirate bands) ; and secondly, in 1017, her first husband's great enemy, King Canute. By her first husband she became the mother of Edward the Confessor, and by her second of King Hardeanute.

Richard the Good, fourth Duke of Normandy, does not seem to have been in all respects equal to his forefathers, yet chivalry, heraldry, feudality all appear fairly developed in his reign, and the courts of Rouen and Fécamp in the first years of the eleventh century evidently present the first examples of the splendid pageantry, which are one of the great characteristic features of a later age Moreover in the course of this reign the spirit of adventure again seems to have seized the Norman-Frenchman The fair land they had won in France became too strait for some of the restless sons of the Vikings, and we hear of two bold attempts to make settlements in the far south The first of these, to the beautiful peninsula of Spain, seems to have failed, but the other to fair Italy and Sicily was more successful Duke

---

[1] Dudo p 137 Guillaume Gemmet, Hist Angl Scripta, in B Museum, 2070 d p. 455 Speed, p 115

Richard the Good was married three times, having by his first
wife, Judith, daughter of Geoffrey, Earl of Brittany, three sons,
viz , Richard, who succeeded as fifth Duke , Robert le "Diable"
the sixth Duke, who by Ailette his concubine, had William, the
seventh Duke, the Conqueror of England   The third son was
William, a monk at Fécamp   He married secondly, Estute, the
daughter of Suenon, King of Denmark, by whom he had no
issue, and from whom he was divorced   His third wife was
Papia, by whom he had two more sons, of whom Manger, the
eldest, became Archbishop of Rouen, A D 1037, but was deposed
in 1056 by his cousin the seventh Duke   He was drowned in
crossing to Jersey, and left a natural son, Michel "un vaillant
chevalier."   The other son, William of Argues, Earl of Talou,
married a sister of Widon, Earl of Poictiers.

Richard the Good died in 1026

CHAPTER II.

MALIGER or Mauger, the third son of Richard the Fearless, third Duke of Normandy, and direct ancestor of the Granville family, obtained the Earldom of Corbeil by his first marriage in the year 1012, with Germaine de Corbeil, the daughter and heiress of Aubert, second Earl of Corbeil[1] and grand-daughter of Hamon the first Earl, the son of Osmund de Centeville, to whom had been committed the tutorship of Duke Richard during his minority. This title remained for generations in the family, and was revived in the reign of Charles the Second, when Sir John Granville, eldest son of Sir Bevil Grenvile, on being created Earl of Bath was permitted to assume the additional title of Earl of Corbeil[2]

According to Palgrave, Mauger acquired considerable importance in French affairs, having greatly distinguished himself by his policy and valour[3] He took a prominent part in defending Henry, the eldest son of King Robert of France, against his mother, Queen Constance, who, notwithstanding that he had been crowned in his father's lifetime, was desirous of placing her second son Robert on the throne in his stead. As a reward for his services Mauger was invested with the extensive county of Mortaigne as an addition to his patrimonial domains.[4] Mortaigne, however, remained but a short time in the family, for his eldest son William, nicknamed the Wailing, having been detected plotting against the young Duke William, (afterwards known as "The Conqueror,") during his minority, was exiled to Apulia, and Mortaigne was dealt with as an escheat, and conferred upon the Duke's half-brother, Robert de Centeville, the son of Arletta and Herloun

Mauger's second son was Hamon, nicknamed Dentatus, from having been born, it is said, with teeth He is styled Earl of Corbeil, and in several of the old French historians the seigneuries of Thorigny, Granville, Breuilly, Cremilly, Bercy and Maisy are assigned to him Thus St Allais in his work, L'art

[1] Jean de la Barr, Antiquities de Corbeil et St Allais   Anselm
[2] Palgrave III , p 14
Guillaume Jumieges, Antiquities de Corbeil   Anselm
Guillaume Gemmett   Anselm   Palgrave III , p 224

de verifier les dates," writes, "Hamon dit aux Dents, Comte de
Corbeil, Seigneur de Thorigny, Grandville, Breuilly et Creuilly."
Corbeil sur Seine was situated between Paris and Fontainbleau
and contained two Collegiate Churches founded by Hamon the
first Earl In an account of this ancient town we find as follows
"C'est Hamon ou Aimon, Comte de Corbeil qui s etant empare
du Chateau du Comte de Palaiseau vers l'an 912, emporta à
Corbeil les Reliques de S Exupere et de S Loup, Evêques de
Bayeux fit bâtir une Eglise en leur honneur, et qui fonda un
Chapitre. Le tombeau de ce Comte est encore à main gauche
de maitre autel de cette Eglise, qu'on appelle par corruption
Saint Spire " When Dennis Granville, Dean of Durham, went
into exile for his faithful adherence to the cause of his royal
Master, James II, he lived for some time at Corbeil and discovered the tomb of his great ancestor, which he described as
very magnificent, and bearing the same arms as were then borne
by his family. Thorigny was a fortified town upon the borders
of the counties of Bayeux and Coutance Creuilly was near
Caen, and the castle, a construction of different ages, still exists
and is now converted into a dwelling house Maisy is described
as 'le commune littorale du Bessin " Bruilly or Bercy are
unknown, the names not being found in any of the maps of
France or Normandy, whilst the little Norman seaport of Granville is of course still extant and well-known Its situation on
the coast between Avranches and Coutances is singular ; it is
built in steps or terraces under a rocky promontory projecting
into the sea, surmounted by its ancient fort whose presence
restricts many of the buildings from using above one story in
height Previously to the bombardment by the English at the
end of the seventeenth century, the Granville arms existed on
one of the citadel gates, and are thus referred to by George
Granville, the poet, in a poem addressed to his cousin Charles
Granville, Lord Lansdown—

> Those arms, which for nine centuries had braved
> The wrath of time, on antick stone engrav'd,
> Now torn by Mortars, stand yet undefac'd
> On nobler trophies, by thy valour raised

The meaning of the particular bearing which belongs to the
Granville family has always been a matter of uncertainty to
heraldic writers In an old and now scarce work by Gibbons
printed in 1682, and entitled " An Introduction to the Art of
Blason," there are no less than five different characters assigned
to it. Gibbons himself calls it a bracket, according to Leigh it
is a horseman's rest, " a thing whereon to rest the Launce,"

Boswell pronounces it a soufflue from "souffler" to blow—an instrument to carry the wind from the bellows to the pipes of an organ. Gwillim, while suggesting that it may be a rudder, inclines to the opinion that it is a clarion "an instrument used in Battel and Tournaments as we do trumpets " " In many old descriptions of Tilting we find the knights to come in with ' *clarions*" sounding before them ' A writer in the "Gentleman's Magazine," 1845, states that he has very little doubt that it is intended for some sort of musical instrument " probably a kind of hand-organ , for in the wood cut Mrs Jameson gives in her " Legends of the Madonna" p 19 of Piero Lamati's painting of the ' Maria Coronata," the uppermost angel on the left is represented as carrying an instrument exactly similar to this charge as it is usually drawn '

Little or nothing is known of the life of Hamon Dentatus, but the old historians[1] state that he and his brother Guillerin took part in the rebellion of the principal Norman barons against the young Duke William's accession on the ground of his illegitimacy, and that both were slain in the celebrated battle of the Valley of the Dunes. In a note of Robert Wace's quaint poetry, " Le Roman de Rou et des Ducs de Normandie,' it is stated that Hamon fell valiantly attacking the King of France, who had come to the assistance of the young Duke His body was taken to Essay and there interred before the door of the Church He had married Hadwise or Avoye (in some English pedigrees she is called Elizabeth d'Avove) the widow of Hugh the Great, Duke of France, sister to the Emperor Otho, and daughter of Henri l'Oiseleur By her Hamon left three sons, namely, Robert Fitzhamon ; Richard called, as was customary, de Granville, after one of his father's lordships, and Hamon About the identity of the latter there seems some difficulty. He is mentioned in the " Genealogy des Seigneurs de Creuilly " as having been " Grand Maitre d'Hôtel du Roi," and his name appears in 1103 as a witness with his brother, Robert Fitzhamon, to a deed between the Abbot of Fécamp and Philip of Briouse, as well as in a charter of the Conqueror to Saint Denis, existing still at Paris, to which we find as witnesses, "Ego Hamo Regis dapifer" " Ego Robert frater hujus Hamonis ' In the Bayeux Inquest the name " Hugo de Crevecune feodum v mil " occurs,[2] and Hasted says (though his authority may be questioned) that the family name of Hamo Dapifer, or Vice-comes of Domesday,

was Crevequer. Certain it is that Hamon Dapifer was one of
the chief landowners of Eastern England, where the Crevecœur
family lived and, as Barons of Chatham, had great possessions
Hamon Dapifer has an entry to himself in the Domesday Book
for Essex (ii 54 b)   He appears again in 100 b, and in the
town of Colchester (106) he holds " i domum, et i curiam, et i
hidam tenæ et xv burgenses."   A building with some trace of
Romanesque work used to be shown as " Hamo's Saxon hall or
curia "   In Ellis he is made to be the same as " Haimo vice-
comes " who appears in Kent and Surrey (Domesday 1436) and
as Hamo the Sheriff, who was one of the judges of the County
Court when the great cause was tried between Archbishop
Lanfranc and Odo Bishop of Bayeux.[1] To the letter despatched
to recall Anselm by Henry I on his accession are attached the
following names, " Gerard, Bishop of Hereford, William, Bishop
elect of Winchester, William of Warelwast, Henry, Earl of
Warwick, Robert Fitzhamon and his brother Hamon the dapifer
" et aliis tam episcopis quam baronibus meis."   He also witnesses
a letter of Anselm's (Epp iii. 71) to the monks of Canterbury
along with another " Haimo ' filius vitalis ' Wimundus homo
vicecomitis,' and a mysterious " Robertus filius Watsonis "   In
Epp iv. 57 a letter is addressed to him by Abselm, complaining
of damage done by his men to the Archbishop's property at
Canterbury and Sandwich

Hamon was probably too young to join his brothers,
Robert Fitzhamon and Richard de Granville when they came
over to England in the Conqueror's army,[2] where, as his near
relatives, they had naturally a considerable position assigned to
them   Carew indeed states that Robert Fitzhamon was general
of the army on the occasion of the battle of Hastings, but as
none of the old historians mention this fact, and it is well known
that the two brothers were both of youthful age at the time, he
is probably wrong on this point   The mistake may have
arisen from the fact that he was afterwards general of King
Henry the First's army in France

The honour of Gloucester which spread itself into many
counties of England was the possession of the Saxon Brihtric,
surnamed Meaw, or the Golden-haired, the grandson of Leofric,
Earl of Mercia   Brihtric had visited the court of Baldwin V ,
Count of Flanders, as Ambassador from Edward the Confessor,
at which time Baldwin's daughter, Matilda, had cherished a
passion for him, which, however, he did not reciprocate   The

[1] Sir Henry Ellis
[2] Monasticon , Leland

chronicle of Tewkesbury tells us how Matilda, after she had been fourteen years the wife of the Conqueror, and whilst enjoying the greatest happiness as a wife and a mother, had secretly brooded over the bitter memory of her slighted love, and in the very year that her husband ascended the throne of England she obtained from him a grant of nearly, if not quite, all Brihtric's lands and honours, deprived Gloucester of its charter and liberties, and caused the unfortunate Saxon to be seized and conveyed to Winchester, where he shortly afterwards mysteriously died in prison, and was privately buried   Upon the Queen's death her son the Ætheling Henry claimed these lands, but, if he ever came into actual possession, his tenure of them was short, as William Rufus bestowed them upon his two cousins, Robert Fitzhamon and Richard de Granville, the former taking those which lay within the borders of Gloucestershire and Somersetshire, the latter those in North Devon and Cornwall

These possessions were probably bestowed upon the two brothers by William Rufus, not merely on account of the great services they had rendered his father, but also for their allegiance to himself , for upon his accession to the throne a number of the Norman lords raised the standard of revolt in favour of his elder brother, Robert, Duke of Normandy, but Robert Fitzhamon is expressly mentioned, along with Hugh, Earl of Chester, and Robert de Mowbray, Earl of Northumberland, as maintaining his fealty to the King.

In the year 1091, being the fourth year of the reign of William Rufus, Jestin, son of Gwrgan, described as prince of Gwent and Morganwg was attacked by Rhys ap Tewdwr, King of Deheubarth, whose dominions comprised the greater part of South Wales   Jestin turned for aid to Einion, the brother of Cedivor, Prince of Dyfed, and promised him his daughter with an ample estate if he could obtain help from England against Rhys   At Einion's invitation Robert Fitzhamon came into South Wales with an army trained to conquest, his brother Richard de Granville and eleven other knights, selected from the most illustrious names in the kingdom, being his associates in the expedition   In a pitched battle on the borders of Brecheiniog Rhy's army was defeated, and Rhys himself, flying from the field, was taken and beheaded   His kinsmen and followers seem to have been killed or dispersed, and we are told that Robert Fitzhamon and his companions, being well paid for their services by Jestin, went away towards London   When Einion demanded his reward Jestin declined that he would not give either his daughter or his land to a traitor   Then Einion persuaded Robert and his companions to come back and take Jestin's dominions for themselves   Jestin was driven out and his land partitioned.   Robert Fitzhamon and his twelve knights divided the fertile vale of Glamorgan among themselves   Each man established himself in a lordship and castle, and all did homage to Robert as lord of Glamorgan, holding his chief seat in his castle of Cardiff   Freeman supposes that some parts of this story are legendary, for example, the very unlikely story that Robert, or any other Norman, when once standing in arms on British or any other ground, simply marched out again, after receiving a fair day's wages for a fair day's work   That Robert Fitzhamon did conquer Glamorgan and established himself at Cardiff cannot be doubted   The settlement of some of his followers is equally historical, but the list of them as given in the legend is untrustworthy, being largely due to family vanity and contains names of families which did not appear in this district till later

At the consecration of Gloucester Cathedral (to which Robert Fitzhamon had been a bountiful benefactor) a monk from over the sea declared to him his ill-omened dream respecting the king which according to William of Melmesbury Fitzhamon being in his closest confidence, hastened to communicate to William Rufus in Malwood Castle, in the New Forest the evening before the fatal day, when Tyrrel's arrow pierced him to the heart. 1st August. 1100   Fitzhamon was also (according to the legend of Geoffrey Gaimer 1 56) one of the company of barons that gathered round the corpse and bore it covered with his mantle, to the Minster of St Swithins at Winchester

On the accession of Henry I   Robert Fitzhamon was present on the part of the King at the agreement made at Dover on the sixth of March with Robert, Earl of Flanders, whereby the latter bound himself, on certain conditions, to furnish the King with a thousand knights each having three horses ready to be transported into England from Graveling or Widsand, whenever the King should send shipping   For the performance of the conditions on the King's part, Robert Fitzhamon is the first named

Two years afterwards, at the instance of his wife, Sibille, daughter of Roger de Montgomery, Earl of Shrewsbury, and Gerald d'Avranches, Abbot of Cranbourne. Fitzhamon rebuilt the Abbey of Tewkesbury. which had been founded as a priory in A.D. 715   "It cannot be easily conceived," writes William of Malmesbury. "how much Robert Fitzhamon adorned and beautified this monastery where the stateliness of the buildings ravished the eyes, and the pious charity of the monks the affections of all persons." He also transferred the monks of Cranbourne there, and gave considerable portions of land to this and other monasteries

According to Bowyer's Abridgement the castle of Bristol was also built by him, as well as the priory of St James This latter building, however, is generally attributed to his son-in-law, Robert, Earl of Gloucester While at the siege of Falaise, in Normandy, where he was in command of King Henry the First's forces he 'received a dangerous wound with the push of a Pike upon the temples of his head, whereby though by his conduct and personall valour he gott the victory hee had his witts crackt and surviving some time afterwards onely as a man bestraught and madd died March 1107" His body was brought to England, and buried in the Chapter-house at Tewkesbury, but it was afterwards laid to rest in the Church which he had newly built, between two pillars on the south side of the choir Over his tomb, erected many years after his death, viz, in 1397, by Abbot Parker, is the following inscription, now hardly legible —

IN ISTA CAPELLA JACET DOMINUS ROBERTUS FILIUS
HAMONIS, HUJUS LOCI FUNDATOR

In an old deed he is described as " by the grace of God Prince of Glamorganshire, Earl of Corboile, Thorigny, and Granville, Lord of Gloucester, Bristol, and Tewkesbury and Cardiffe, Governor of Wales, near kinsman unto the King and General of all his Highness's army in France "

He left four daughters, but no male issue, and the King being unwilling that his vast estates should be shared among women, married the eldest daughter, Mabel, to his eldest natural son, Robert, surnamed the Consul, by Nesta, daughter of Rhys ap Tewdwr, Prince of South Wales [1]

Robert of Gloucester states in his quaint poetry that when the marriage was first proposed, Mabel refused, saying,

> So van entage as ich habbe, it were ne great shame
> Vor to habbe an louerd bote he had an to name

Or, as it has been translated into somewhat better English.

> It were to me a great shame,
> To have a lord withouten his twa name

[1] From this marriage descended the Earls of Gloucester and Clare, the Spencers, Beauchamps, and Nevilles, and a large portion of Robert Fitzhamou's vast possessions passed at length to Richard III by his marriage, in 1473, with Lady Anne, widow of Edward Prince of Wales, son of King Henry VI and daughter and co heir of Richard Neville, Earl of Warwick

So the King gave to him the name of Fitz Roy, and created him Earl of Gloucester, 1109, and bestowed upon him the whole of the real estates, both Norman and English, which had been enjoyed by Robert Fitzhamon.

Two of the other daughters, Avice and Cicely, professed as nuns, and became respectively the abbesses of Wilton and Shaftesbury, while the youngest daughter married the Earl of Brittany

All Fitzhamon's titles, according to Norman Law, descended to his brother, Richard de Granville, and were borne by him and his posterity till Normandy was lost to the crown of England Richard had received the lordship of Neath as his share of the Welsh conquest, including a large tract of rich fertile land.   In this fruitful place," writes Hals, " that the Priests of the Gospell might eate of the fatt and drink of the sweete, as their predecessors under the lawe had done, the said Richard de Granville, out of piety and devotion towards God, Who had preserved him in all his undertakings, and out of charitie towards poor Christians and schollars, founded and endowed a monastery of Cistercian monks, dedicated to the Blessed Virgin Mary, valued at the suppression, the twenty-sixth of Henry the Eighth, at one hundred and fifty pounds per annum "

Fuller, in his " Worthies," says, ' This Richard in my apprehension appears somewhat like the Patriarch Abraham (Gen. xiv.), for he would have none make him rich but God alone, although in his partage good land at Neath was allotted to him.   Indeed Abraham gave the tenth to God in Melchisedech, and restored the rest to the King of Sodom, the former proprietor thereof. This knight, according to the devotion of those darker days gave all to God, erecting and endowing a monastery at Neath for Cistercian monks, and bestowing all his military acquests on them for their maintenance, so that the convent was valued at one hundred and fifty pounds at the dissolution Thus having finished and settled the foundation, he returned to his own patrimony at Bideford, where he lived in great repute in the reign of King William Rufus, and may seemed to have entailed hereditary valour on his name and still flourishing posterity."

Some Welsh manuscripts in the possession of Lady Llanover (maternally descended from the Granvilles) contain extracts from old records of the history of Glamorgan, which mention that ' Sir Richard Grenvile, brother of Robert Fitzhamon, went to the Holy Land, and on his return had a dream which

NEATH ABBEY.
FOUNDED BY SIR RICHARD DE GRANVILLE, CIRCA, 1129.

impressed him so deeply that he returned to Jerusalem and
there recorded a vow on the Holy Sepulchre to the effect that
he would faithfully perform what he had been told to do in his
dream ; namely, to restore to the Welsh as far as he could
ascertain the rights of owners, all the possessions of which they
had been so cruelly dispossessed by fraud and violence, and which
were in his hands, and to dedicate the remainder to the service
of God only. This he did, and with the remainder built the
magnificent Abbey of Neath, designed by a Saracen architect,
a Christian convert, named Lelys whom he brought back with
him, and who also erected Margam Abbey and several other
ecclesiastical edifices in South Wales "

The Church was distinguished for the beauty of its propor-
tions and general architecture as well as for its spacious
dimensions, which may still be traced   Leland in his
" Itinerary " says ' Neth Abbey of white monks, a mile above
Neth town standing also on the ripe of Neth, it seemed to me
the fairest Abbey in all Wales." Amongst the ruins there have
been discovered some tiles on which the Granville arms are
represented   An account of them has been printed by the
Neath Philosophical and Antiquarian Society, illustrated by
some beautiful drawings from the pencil of Mr Egbert Moxham
The original charters of Neath and its Abbey were also printed,
but not published. by Mr George Grant Francis in 1845, with
rich illustrations   The following is a copy of the original
Foundation Charter of the Abbey .—

Carta fundationis per Ricardum de Granvilla ex Regist de Nethe penes
Edwardum Stradling Equit aur   Circa anno 1129
Notus sit omnibus, tam presentibus, quam futuris, quod Ego Ricardus
de Granvilla et Constantia uxor mea pro salute animæ Roberti Comitis de
Glocestriæ et Mabiliæ uxoris suæ Comitissæ et Wilhelmi filii sui, et pro salute
animarum nostrarum et antecessorum nostrorum, damus Deo et ecclesiæ sanctæ
Trinitatis de Savigneio, totum vastum quod est infra has quatuor aquas
videlicet Neth, Thavy, Cloeld, Poncanum et capellam nostri castelli de Nethe
cum omni decima procurationes nostræ domus in annona et in cæteris rebus,
et cum omni decima hominum nostrorum illius provinciæ, videlicet Francorum
et Anglorum et dimidiam partem totius nostri piscis de Nethe et molendino
de Cloeda et prata omnia quæ sunt a supre dicto molendino usque ad forsatum
de Nethe   et omnia illa quæ habuimus in villa Nassa in feodo quam teneo di
eo in Devensira   quinque denarios , videlicet Bediseg et Crinchentona et viginti
solidos in villa de Lytheham, et terram quam ego teneo de Mauricio   salvo
redditu ipsius Mauritii   id est decem solidos ad festum sancti Michaelis et
molendinum de Pandelia cum multura hominum in illo fædo manentium quem
teneo de Ricardo Sancti Quentini, et domus molendinum cum duabus acres
terræ, et hoc concesserunt   Iaurentius et Richardus inter comitem et comitessam
et ante Wilhelmum filium suum   Hæc omnia damus libere et quiete et absque
ulla seculari exactione et Henrici Regis Anglorum patrociniis   et concessione et
Roberti Consulis Glocestriensis, et Mabila uxoris suæ comitissæ   et Wilhelmi

filu sui voluntate   E tenore quod Abbas Savigneiencis ecclasiæ et conventus ejusdem in eadem elemosina conventum Monachorum per henniter mibi sub Abbate permansurum instituent

Hujus donationis sunt testes   Gardinus, capellanus et Torbertus capellanus et Picotus   Robertus dapifer, Odo filius suus   Robertus filius Bei . Mauritius, Richardus de Sancti Quintini, Robertus de Umfravilla, Paganus de Torbivilla, Wilhelmus pincerna , Robertus filius Ascelinie , Thomas de Estonâ , Rogerus de Newtona   Girolt de Bosco   Herbertus , Robertus de Granavilla , Wilhelmus de Reivilla et ego Robertus Gloucestriæ comes, has omnes res in meo patrocinio custodia et defensione suscipio et Abbas ibidem ce canonice constitutus

The following is Francis's translation of the charter deposited in the Lansdowne Library, British Museum .—

Foundation charter of Neath Abbey by Richard de Granavilla about 1129

Be it known to all, contemporaries as well as posterity, that I, Richard de Granavilla and Constance my wife, for the salvation of the soul of Robert Earl of Gloucester, and Mabel his countess, and William his son, and for the salvation of our own, and our predecessor's souls give to God, and to the church of the Holy Trinity of Savigny,[1] the whole waste land between the four rivers, viz, the Neth (Neath), Tawe (Tawy), Clydach and Pwelleynau (Poman), and the chapel of our castle of Neath with all the tithes of our house in corn and other things, and all the tithes of our people in that province, French (Norman) as well as English, and one half of all the fish from Nethe (Neath) and the mill of Cloada Clydach, and all the meadows from the above mentioned mill as far as the new mill ditch and from the same ditch as far as the river of Nethe, and all that we possess in the state of Naissa (Nash)   In the fief which I hold from him in Devonshire 5d (denarii), viz , Bedeseg (Bedford), near Black Torrington (Devon) and Crincheton, and 20s (solidi) in the estate of Lytleham (Littleham) and the land which I hold from Maurice, save the income of Maurice himself, that is 10s (solidi) at Michaelmas , and the mill of Pandelia (Penyvhn in Glamorganshire) with the miller's toll of the people who live on that fiet, which toll I hold from Richard de St Quentin   and the house of the miller with two acres of land   And these things were granted by Maurice and Richard before the Count and the Countess, and before William then son   All this we give for their free and undisturbed possession, and to be exempt from any secular exaction, and by the patronage and permission of Henry, King of the English, and with the consent of Robert Consulis and Mabel his countess and William his son   Under this tenure, that the Abbot of the church of Savigny and of the convent belonging to it shall on this donation establish a congregation of monks to live there perpetually under them Abbot   Of this donation there are witnesses Gardin, chaplain , Torbet, chaplain , Picot , Robert the Steward Odo, his son , Robert, the son of Bei , Maurice Richard of St Quintin , Robert of Umfravillle , Pagan of Turbiville , William the butler , Robert, the

---

[1] Savigny, to which reference is made, was near Lyons   Bishop Tanner writes, that notwithstanding the original donation to Savigny he cannot find that Neath was ever subject to that foreign Abbey, or accounted as alien   Being an Abbey, it could not have been a cell, but, as Stephen says, was rather a daughter house of Savigny   The common seal of the Abbey represented the Blessed Virgin Mary crowned in a standing position, and holding in her right hand a lily and in her left the Infant Jesus   In base, a shield with the arms of the founder   The legend was "Sigillum comune monaster beatæ Mariæ de Neth "   A very imperfect impression of the seal still exists in the Augmentation Office   A more perfect one was in the possession of Mr. Matthew Gregson

NEATH ABBEY—THE CRYPT.

FOUNDED BY SIR RICHARD DE GRANVILLE, CIRCA, 1129.

son of Acelma, Thomas of Eston, Roger of Newton, Guolt of Boscom, Herbert, Robert of Granavilla, Wilham of Reinville And I, Robert of Gloucester, take all these things under my patronage, guard, and protection, and I desire that an Abbot be instituted there according to the Canon of the Church

Little did either the founders, or the monks who dwelt there, imagine that their fair Abbey would in time be desecrated by the worship of Mammon, and become a smoky ruin, scarcely distinguishable to the passing traveller from the forges, furnaces, chimneys, and squalid outworks of the great manufacturing establishments by which it is now surrounded! The anthems of praise and thanksgiving have been superseded by the clank of the steam engine, and the roar of fires! Strange mutation! Yet the old Abbey is still pleasant to look upon It is a memento amidst the turmoil of life It speaks eloquently of a future It is full of interest to the lovers of antiquity

In a manuscript account of eminent families in Devon and Cornwall, subjoined to a copy of Risdon's Survey, (also in manuscript), the following memorandum and verses were found

' I have lately," says the anonymous writer, under date the 15th of July, 1653, " had communicated to me by Mr John Nichols, of Hartland, a prophesie said to be found in the Abbey of Neath, in Wales, which was kept in a most curious box of jett, written in the year 1400, concerning the founder of that monastery, which is as follows —

Amongst the trayne of valiant knights
That with King William came,
Grenvile is great, a Norman borne,
Renowned by his fame

His helmet ras'd, and first unlac'd
Upon the Cambrian shore
Where he, in honour of his God,
This Abbey did decore

With costly buildings, ornaments,
And gave us spreious lands,
As the first fruits which victory
Did give into his hands

Now let me see what happiness
Shall light upon his line,
Or what endowments shall succeed
To his in future time

They shall in honour long subsist
And fortune still shall smile,
Until at length (ah! woe is me)
When Merlin with a wile

E

> Shall them subdue, and bodily
> In woman's shape appear,
> To show them Mars his shield
> Which they kept full many a year
>
> Within Carnarvon and in brass
> Still seek to have immured,
> But never finding means indeed
> By Mars to be secured,
>
> Because that Vulcan craved a boon
> Of Jupiter the strong,
> That Mars his arms should never free
> A suppliant from wrong
>
> Then shall that famous name decline
> From worldly wealth awhile,
> But then again Charles-Magne's reign
> Shall grace them with a smile

This prophesie was originally written in Latin, and kept there in parchment Anno 1400 "

Having finished and settled the foundation of Neath Abbey, Richard de Granville, who must now have been some fourscore years old, returned to his patrimony at Bideford in North Devon, where he lived in great honour and reputation the remainder of his days, though according to an old pedigree of the family, bearing date 1639, it is stated that in his old age he took upon himself the sign of the Cross, according to the devotion of those times, and went towards Jerusalem, in which journey he died   He was twice married   According to Ordericus Vitalis his first wife was Isabel, the only daughter of Walter Gifford, Earl of Buckingham in England, and of Longueville in Normandy, who was co-heiress with her aunt Rohesia (wife of Richard Fitz Gilbert, Lord of Clare) of the great possessions and lordships pertaining to that family   His second wife, the Constance mentioned in the Neath Abbey Charter, is said to have been the daughter of Caradoc ap Arthur, the lord of Glyn Nedd

By his first wife he had issue five sons   (1) Richard who succeeded him in his honours and estates (of whom presently)

(2) William, who probably is the William de Corbeil who succeeded Ralph d'Escures in 1123 as thirty-sixth Archbishop of Canterbury   This identification is supported not only by the title "de Corbeil,' one of the Norman lordships belonging to the family, but also by the important position which the Granvilles occupied at this time, and their kinsmanship to the royal House   It must be remembered that many of the

Conqueror's relatives held, as was natural, high positions in the Church ; for example, William Warelwast, the King's cousin, held the bishopric of Exeter Moreover, according to Le Neve, who quotes his authorities, William de Corbeil was nominated by the King, and elected to the see of Canterbury, pursuant to the *congé d'elire* of the King, dated Gloucester, February the 4th, 1123 The King certainly appears to have been at Gloucester when the see of Canterbury fell vacant, and re-membering the connection between the lords of that honour and the King, and the consequent influence their relationship must have had, the identity of William, son of Richard de Granville, Earl of Corbeil, with this ecclesiastic seems almost positive

There is a long account of William de Corbeil in Godwin's De Presentibus, p. 97. He says he was first a cleric secular , then a Benedictine monk , afterwards Prior of St. Osyth, a house of canons regular, which Richard de Beamer, Bishop of London, had established at Chich before the year 1118 The priory was erected on the site of a decayed nunnery, originally founded by Osyth, wife of Sighere, King of Essex, in the seventh century. It was situated on the bank of the river Coln, in the hundred at Tendring, in the northern division of the county of Essex. about eleven miles distant from Colchester

The character of William de Corbeil, as given by his contemporaries, is anything but flattering. The author of the Gesta Stephani describes him thus —" He was a man of smooth face and strictly religious manners, but much more ready to amass money than to spend it " Henry of Huntingdon, in his letter to Walter, in which he describes the leading men of the day, thus curtly disposes of him —" The see of Canterbury was filled by William, of whose merits nothing can be said, for he had none " His name was a standing jest , he was called " William de Turbine," or, as it is wittily translated by Arch-deacon Churton, "not William of Corboil but William of Turmoil "

Undoubtedly some allowance, as Dean Hook remarks, must be made for party feeling, which at this time ran high in the Church of England " How differently would the same man be at the present day described by the editors of religious journals representing the opposite factions in the Church , neither party perhaps wilfully perverting the truth, and yet leaving a false impression."

According to Simeon of Durham, William de Corbeil's first appearance in history is as one of the clerks of Ralph Flambard,

Bishop of Durham. To have been a chaplain of the Bishop of Durham is certainly not to his credit. Ralph had been the chancellor and chief adviser of William Rufus, and the ready and efficient instrument of the extortion and tyranny of that monarch. But as a set off against the position of William de Corbeil in the household of this prelate, it is to be mentioned that he was in frequent and familiar intercourse with the saintly Anselm. As Anselm was one of the persons most deeply injured by Ralph Flambard in his worst days, we may infer that their reconciliation took place through the intervention of William de Corbeil who, though himself accused of avarice, was nevertheless always accounted a man of piety.

The evil results of the feudal system upon the Episcopate were never more remarkably seen than at this time. In the long conflict for the crown, the bishops ever came to the front as military leaders, and then spiritual character passes entirely out of view. They affected a royal pomp, built castles and towers and fortified structures, furnished their castles with provisions and weapons, soldiers and bowmen; and while they were supposed to be restraining malefactors and church robbers, were even more cruel and merciless than they in oppressing their neighbours and spoiling their goods.

Foreseeing probably the contest for the throne, which so soon broke out on the accession of Stephen. William de Corbeil obtained of Henry I the custody of the castle of Rochester, which gave him a feudal position of extreme importance, and enabled him to take far too active a part in the struggles which ensued after the King's death.

Pope Honorious II made him his legate over England and Scotland. The bull confirming his appointment is quoted at length by Dean Hook. He has been greatly blamed for accepting this position, but doubtless he thought that by so doing the long standing controversy between the Archbishops of Canterbury and York as to precedence would be settled, and it is clear that he did not imagine that he was conceding the rights of his see from the style which he adopted in convening a council at Westminster, 27th May, 1127. "The canons,' he wrote ' have been prepared by the authority of Peter, the Prince of the Apostles, *and our own*."

Two events principally marked his tenure of the primacy. First, the consecration of the cathedral at Canterbury the 4th May, 1130, after the completion of the work. which had been commenced by Lanfranc and carried on by Anselm. "A dedication so famous." says Gervas, " was never heard of on the earth since the dedication of the Temple of Solomon " Henry, King of England, and David, King of Scotland, with many of the nobles and all the bishops of England, were present The offerings of the King and the Archbishop are recorded The King gave to the Chapter the church of St. Martin's at Dover ; the Archbishop eight pounds a year out of his manor at Reculver The second great event occurred five years afterwards, when William de Corbeil officiated at the coronation of King Stephen This act has also been much criticised, inasmuch as in 1118 he had been the first to make oath that, in the event of Henry's death without male issue, he would acknowledge the Empress Matilda as Queen of England and Duchess of Normandy. But it may be fairly supposed that he did not yield until Hugh Bagot, seneschal of the deceased monarch, declared on his oath that Henry in his last moments had, in his presence, released the chiefs of the realm from the oath of allegiance which they had taken to Matilda

The coronation took place probably on St Stephen's Day, 26th December, 1135 Very soon afterwards the Archbishop's health began to fail, and the partisans of the Empress were not slow in attributing the circumstance to the reproaches of a guilty conscience He was taken seriously ill at Mortlake in 1136, and from thence he was carried in a litter to Canterbury, where he died on All Saints' Day, the 1st November, 1136, having occupied the see for thirteen years. His enemy, the author of " Gesta Stephani,' relates that " at his death the King's officers found immense sums secretly hoarded in his coffers, which, if he had distributed for charitable uses when alive, in imitation of the steward of the gospel, who made friends of the mammon of unrighteousness, and had dispersed abroad and given to the poor, so that his name should be had in everlasting remembrance, he would have better fulfilled the character of a good shepherd."

(3) The third son of Richard de Granville was named Robert He was one of the witnesses to the charter of Neath Abbey, and also to a charter of William de Ligures, lord of the lee of Borestall, in the county of Bucks, three miles from Wootton His marriage is not mentioned, but he had issue two sons, Gerard and Robert, who are both named in the charter of their cousin, Sir Eustace de Grenvile, to William, son of Nigil, of a yard of land in Chilton. Gerard the eldest, married and had issue four sons, but after a few generations his line terminated in coheirs, and his great-grand-daughter Nichola was the wife of Sir Richard Hampden, from whom the

Hampdens of Buckinghamshire claim lineal descent Robert, the youngest son married a certain ' Eineberche," with whose consent, and that of his eldest son Gerard he became a benefactor to the Abbey of Nutley William de Grenvile then second son is frequently mentioned in the register of Nutley Abbey, and attended King John in his expedition to France

(4) A fourth son of Richard de Granville was named Gerard, since he is mentioned as brother to Robert in their nephew, Sir Eustace de Grenvile's deed This Gerard held of Walter Giffard Earl of Buckingham three knights' fees in that county, and is also shown by the Pipe Rolls, 3rd Henry II, to have paid his proportion to an "aid' levied by the Sheriff there in 1156 His son and heir Richard, is the ancestor of the Grenvilles of Buckinghamshire, who have been seated at Wootton under Barnwood in that county from the reign of Henry I, where the family maintained the first rank amongst the neighbouring gentry securing the office of high sheriff, etc The direct descendant of this branch was Richard Grenville, Esq of Wootton, M.P for Andover, and afterwards for the town of Buckingham He married Hester Temple, second daughter of Sir Richard Temple, Bart, of Stowe, in the county of Buckingham, who, on the decease of her brother Richard, Viscount and Baron Cobham, the 13th September, 1749, inherited as Baroness and Viscountess Cobham, and was created Countess of Temple, 18th October, 1749, with the reversionary dignity of Earl Temple to her heirs male Her eldest son, the first Earl Temple, died without issue, and the title devolved on his death (11th September, 1779) upon his nephew George, who was created, 4th December, 1784, Marquess of Buckingham, and whose son Richard was further elevated 4th February 1822, to the Marquessate of Chandos and the Dukedom of Buckingham and Chandos

(5) It remains now to mention a fifth son of Sir Richard de Granville, viz, Ralph, the father of Sir Eustace to whom reference has been already made more than once Ralph appears as a witness to a grant in favour of the Abbey of St Stephen's, Caen, by Roger de Montgomery, Earl of Arundel and Salop, the brother of Sybill the wife of Robert Fitzhamon. Sir Eustace was Constable of the Tower of London, 16 King John and a benefactor to Nutley Abbey.

The eldest son, Richard de Grenville, de Grenvilla, or de Grenvil, (for so the name is variously spelt', married Adelina, daughter of Robert de Bellemont, Earl of Mellent in France and first Earl of Leicester in England by Elizabeth, daughter of Hugh the Great, Earl of Vermandois, son of King Henry of France. She was the widow of Hugh Montfort This Richard, like his father, became a crusader. St Bernard had traversed Europe and awakened the passionate valour of all orders, and the Pope, Eugenius III , had addressed an animated epistle to Western Christendom, promising the same privileges offered by his predecessor Urban, the remission of all sins and the protection of the crusaders' estates and families during their absence in the Holy Land, under the tutelage of the Church. Of all these holy wars none had been announced with greater ostentation ; of none had it been more boldly averred that it was of divine inspiration, the work of God , of none had the hopes, the prophecies of success been more confident , none had been conducted with so much preparation and pomp , none had as yet been headed by kings ; none ended in such total and deplorable disaster. At least thirty thousand lives were sacrificed, and there was not even the consolation of one glorious deed achieved Amongst those that perished was Richard de Granville, 1147.

He was succeeded by his eldest son, Richard, who held the manor of Bideford by half a knight's fee of the honour of Gloucester in the reign of Henry the Second, and in the twelfth year of the same reign he is mentioned in the rolls as holding three knights' fees and a half in Devon and Cornwall In the second year of the reign of King John, 1200, he was knighted, being styled Lord of Bideford and Kilkhampton In the same year his name appears as one of the sureties or manucaptors for Hugh de Stodun and others, and later, according to an ancient deed, he was a witness to the release of Gilbert de Polkwinal to John Kilgarth of all his right in certain lands in Kilgarth and Lanzalewis, in Cornwall In the year 1204 King John (by a charter dated the 14th September), granted and confirmed to him, by the name of Richard, eldest begotten son of Richard de Grenvil, the marriage of the daughter and heir of Thomas de Middleton, with all her inheritance, fees, etc And in case of his demise to the next son, and so from son to son to the youngest And in case of the death of all the sons then that the said heir should be nepoti to the grandson or nephew of Richard de Grenvil, and that he should have the wardship of the said heir till she came of age For this grant he gave the King a palfrey

In Bennett's " History of Tewkesbury," pp 340—344, we find that the living of Bideford had been given in the reign of Henry the First to Tewkesbury Abbey. the patronage being

vested in Mabel, Countess of Gloucester   This Richard de
Grenville had the misfortune to become involved in legal
proceedings with the Abbot of Tewkesbury concerning the
advowson of the Churches of Bideford and Kilkhampton ; and
in the second year of the reign of King John he paid forty
marks and a palfrey to have an assize against that prelate
The lawsuit lasted many years, but at last a compromise was
effected in his grandson's time, and we read in "Nevyll's
Registers," fol. 7, that the advowson of S Mary's Church,
Bideford, was annexed to the manor of Bideford

He married, according to Austin's pedigree, one Gundreda,
by whom he left a young family, all under age at the time of
his death, 1204.   The King gave the land and wardship to
Richard Fleminge, and, in case of his demise, to his sons, one
or more of them, until the children came of age [1]   For this
wardship Fleminge paid the King six hundred marks and six
palfreys   The King's precept to the Sheriff of Devon to deliver
over the possession of the lands in that county to Fleminge, is
dated the 27th April, 1205, and is as follows —

Johannes Dei gratiâ, etc , etc   Sciatis nos concessiste, etc   Ricardo
Fleming custodiam terrarum et hæredum Ricardi de Grenville, etc   6 Regis
Johannis de terris Norman   Ibid Ricardus le Flemmg dat 600 marcos et
sex palfridos pro habendo maritageo custodia terrarum et hæredum Ricardi de
Grenville et maritageo Gundredæ uxoris prædicti Ricardi   Ita quod cum
illos maritare voluent, id Domino Regi seire faciat ut hoc assensu Regis fiat
Et si filius ipsius Ricardi de Grenville infra ætatum decesserit Rex concedit
eidem Ricardo le Flemmg custodiam filiarum prædicti Ricardi de Grenville
cum terris et maritageis earum, eodem modo   Et si Ricus le Flemmg
decesserit infra terminum Rex concedit quod filii sui scilicet Ricardus
Wilhelmus Henricus et Laurentius vel tres vel duo vel unus eorum (si de aliis
humanibus contigent) habeant custodiam prædictam cum prædicto maritageo
eodem modo   (Bowyer's Abridgement, MSS)

His son Richard (the fourth in succession of that name) is
described in the Patent Rolls, 8 John, m 2, as paying five
marks to have the privileges of the inhabitants of Bideford
equalised with those of Exeter   There is also an old charter
(without date) quoted by Watkins in his "History of Bideford,"
which was probably granted by this Richard, who was a contemporary of Sir Richard Coffin, of Alwington, one of the
witnesses of the grant   It is as follows —

*Sciant presentes et futuri quod ego Richardus filius Richardi de Grenvile,
concessi et confirmari et pro me et heredibus meis imperpetuam cartam Richardi
de Grenvile Au mei Burgensibus de Bideford confectam in hæc verba . Sciant
presentes et futuri quod ego Richardus filius Richardi de Grenvile concessi et*

[1] "The King grants to Richard Flaminge the custody of the lands and the wardship and
marriage of the heirs of Richard de Grenville, and the marriage of their mother Gundreda "
—Syll us t Rolls Folers

presenti charta mea confirmavi universis qui burgagium tenent et tenebunt in villa de Bideford, etc., etc. That is, "Let all men that are present and to come, know, that I Richard the son of Richard de Grenvile, have granted and confirmed, for me and my heirs for ever, the writing of Richard de Grenvile, my grandfather, made to the burgesses of Bideford in these words · Let all men that are present and to come, know, that I Richard de Grenvile have granted, and by this my present writing confirmed, to all those who do or shall hold a burgage within the town of Bideford, as well as on the east part of the water of the Torridge, is on the west part, all liberties of Butoha, as far as in my power doth lie, to defend to them and to whomever they shall assign, to be holden and had of me, and of my heirs for ever, that is to say, in such manner, that every one holding one messuage or a garden with six acres of land abroad of my lordship, shall pay for the same on the feast of St Michael, to me or my bailiff, in the town of Bideford, twelve pence , and he that holds one messuage with an orchard only, shall yield to me for the same sixpence the same day, for all services and exactions, excepting only homage And if it happen that any of the aforesaid burgesses shall make default, or offend in any thing in my court, they shall for sixpence be clearly discharged thereof And if they will wage law, they shall do it with their hands. And I have also granted to the said burgesses common of pasture with their beasts throughout, one on the west part of the river Torridge, where, in the time of Richard my father, they were wont to common · And that every one may give or sell his burgage, or otherwise alienate, saving to me and my heirs the rent of assize of every such burgage And that every one for his or their burgage against me and my heirs, shall pay for a release twelve pence and no more And I have also granted to the aforesaid burgesses of Bideford, toward the enlarging of the liberties aforesaid, that they shall do suit to my court from month to month, or for a shorter time, upon reasonable warning, on Tuesday And that the portreeve of the town be at the court to shew forth the attachments and plaints belonging to the lord, as it hath been used and accustomed And I have also granted that all the burgesses of Bideford, and every of them, in fairs and markets throughout all my lands, town, and waters they shall be quiet and free from all toll, custom, censary, or stallage, to be given to me or to any of mine And on the Tuesday next after the feast of St Michael, all the aforesaid burgesses shall come to my aforesaid court (except those of whom it shall be faithfully testified that they are beyond the sea, or on pilgrimage, or in doing their affairs and merchandizing without the country) And then they shall chuse one burgess to be head officer , and the same head officer shall have, throughout the year, toll and censary of the town by land and water, to the year's end for ten shillings to me to be paid, saving to me and my heirs the toll of my market on the Monday And for this my grant and confirmation, the aforesaid burgesses of Bideford have given to me four marks of silver And this my present writing with the impression or print of my own seal I have made effectual for ever, these being witnesses, Sir Richard Coffin, Richard of Spekcot, knights, Peter of Halsberry Richard Snellard, Wellan Dake, Osbert of Bury, Richard of Kokematon, and many others

To this charter is appended a circular seal in green wax, on which is a heater-shaped shield charged with the Granville arms, the inscription surrounding it being "SIGIL RIC DE GRENVILE"

It is also on record that in the 12th and 13th of King John this Richard de Grenvile held three knights' fees and a half in

the counties of Devon and Cornwall of the honour of Gloucester.
He married his father's ward the daughter and heir of Thomas
Fitz Nicholas, of Middleton, and died young about the year
1217. leaving a son, Richard, under age and in ward to the
King, who granted the wardship and custody of his lands to
Ralph Bloet

This fifth Richard de Grenvile it was who in the 22nd Henry
the Third (having before that year been knighted) compromised
the long controversy between his family and Robert, the Abbot
of Tewkesbury, before William of York and his fellow justices
itinerant in Cornwall, at Launceston. The Abbot and monastery
quitted all their claim upon all former controversies of them
and their prececessors to the said Sir Richard, who, on his part,
granted them five marks yearly, as long as he lived, to be
received of Roger de Founteney, and on his decease they should
have his lands in Campden in Gloucestershire. This controversy,
after so many years of lawsuit was thus amicably settled in the
presence of Richard, Earl of Cornwall, the King's brother, and
several others on the 11th June, 1238   ["Annales Monastici'
(Luard) and "Annales de Theokesteria," vol. 1., p 107]

In the "Annales de Theokesteria," p. III his death and
burial are thus recorded —

A D 1240 circa kal Junii obiit Ricardus de Greynvill et sepultus est in
capitulo Sancti Jacobi Bristollis

And in the wall of the south aisle of that church, towards
the east, is a recessed tomb supporting a recumbent figure,
which a modern inscription purports to represent Robert Earl
of Gloucester, the founder of the Priory   But as it is known
that he was buried in the choir, and as the Granville arms are
on a shield, we may conclude that this is the tomb of Sir
Richard   The effigy, that of a young man with beard and
moustache is moreover considered by no less an authority than
Mr Planche to be at least half a century later than the Earl of
Gloucester's demise.   (*Journal* of Archæol Assoc , xxxv , 37)

Sir Richard had married Jane, daughter of William Trewent,
of Blisland, in the hundred of Trigg Minor   There was
formerly a mansion of great antiquity at Blisland, but now
only the large Gothic arch of the principal entrance remains.
After her husband's death she brought forward her writ of
dower to have restored to her the lands in Campden, which had
been granted in compromise to the Abbey of Tewkesbury, and
gained the day   It is a noticeable fact that the Grevilles, Earls
of Warwick, claim Campden as their original home, having
been seated there before 23rd Edward the Third, and moreover,

that then arms are the same as those of the Buckinghamshire Grenvilles, with the tinctures changed and a border added for difference, namely, five torteaux on a cross argent. This certainly seems to point to a common origin

Sir Richard left four sons all under age, viz, Richard, Bartholomew, Robert, and William, who rose to be first Chancellor of England, then Dean of Chichester, and finally Archbishop of York

CHAPTER III

William de Grenvile or Greenfield (as the name appears in the ' Fasti Eboracenses," whence this account of his life is mainly taken), appears as a Student at Oxford, 1269—1270, of which University he became D.C.L. and D.D. He obtained preferment in the Church at an early age, for whilst still at Oxford his kinsman, Archbishop Giffard, collated him to the Stall of Halloughton at Southwell, S Thomas' Day, 1269 This he resigned in the summer of 1272, having been promoted on the 29th of July to a Prebendal Stall in Ripon Cathedral In the month of August, 1287, his name occurs as Canon of Laughton in the Minster of York Between 1291 and 1294 he held the living of Blockley in Worcester, and in the latter year he obtained the Rectory of Stratford-on-Avon, which he held till he became Archbishop. He was also preferred to the Prebendal Stall of Holborn in St Paul's Cathedral as well as to the Deanery of Chichester in 1299 He was, moreover, the temporal Chancellor of the Diocese of Durham But, as was the custom of those times, he combined civil duties with ecclesiastical He was one the clerks of Edward I, probably in connection with the Chancery or Exchequer On the 3rd of February, 1290, he was one of the three persons whom the King sent to Rome about the subsidy for the Crusade The following year he was engaged in treating with the Kings of Arragon, Sicily and France. In 1292 he was with the King at Norham when he was busy with the affairs of Scotland, and he and J de Lascy were appointed to pay the debts which the King had incurred since his coronation In 1295 he received a summons to the Parliament at Westminster, and he was called to the meetings of that body and of the Council in 1297, 1298, 1299, 1301 and 1302 in his capacity as Clerk of the Council. On the 1st of January, 1296, he and others were sent to make a Truce with France[1] and Treaties with Guelders and Flanders On the 25th of April, 1302, he was made one of the King's Proctors to carry on negociations with France, and on the 15th

---

[1] (Year Books of the reign of King Edward the First, Edited and translated by A J Horwood, p xix) "There is among the *Royal and other Letters*, one (No 1367), addressed by Edward I to the King of France (Philip IV) which states that the writer sent the Bishop of London, Roger Brabazon, kt., and William de Grenteud, *Professor of Civil Law*, to settle the terms of a treaty relative to disputes at sea. Very probably the Professor was the William de Greenfield who was afterwards Canon of York, Dean of Chichester, and (A.D. 1302) Chancellor"

of August he was empowered to treat for peace with that country. After serving as a clerk in Chancery, he was advanced to the honourable position of Lord Chancellor of England (30th Sept 1302) as successor to John de Langton The following account of his appointment is taken from "Campbell's Lives of the Lord Chancellors " —

On Sunday, the morrow of St Michaels in the same year in the King's Chapel at St Redegund[1] immediately after mass in the presence of the Lord John de Drakensford and others, Chaplains and Clerks of the said Chapel of the King, Lord Adam de Osgodeby delivered the Great Seal to our Lord the King, who then received it into his own proper hands, and straightway delivered it to Master William de Greneheld Dean of Chichester, whom he had chosen for his Chancellor, to keep, and the said Chancellor delivered the said Seal again to the said Adam to be carried with him the said Chancellor to Dover, and on the same day at Dover the Chancellor received it back from the said Adam, and the next day sealed wills with it in the House of God there

William de Grenvile is described, after having been raised to his new dignity, as "eminent in counsel and very eloquent." He and Edward's other ministers were excessively unpopular, insomuch, that at a Parliament called soon after his appointment, an attempt was made to carry a favourite scheme, which had been several times brought forward in weak reigns about this period of English history, but which we should not have expected to find proposed to him who had conquered Wales, and led his victorious armies to the extremity of Scotland, viz, that the Chancellor, Chief Justice and Treasurer should be chosen or appointed by the community of the kingdom. The King by Grenvile's advice stoutly refused, and his firmness had such an effect that the Barons humbly begged the King's pardon for their presumption

The only other public matter in which Grenvile was concerned during his Chancellorship, was in framing an answer to a letter which the Pope had written to Edward remonstrating with him upon his invasion of Scotland, and claiming that Kingdom as a right belonging to the see of Rome, but his holiness was gravely assured that "ever since the coming of Brute and his Trojans into this island, Scotland had been under feudal subjection to the Kings of England, who had frequently made a gift of it to one of their subjects and resumed the gift at their pleasure."

The Barons of England to the number of one hundred and twelve unanimously concurred in an address to the Pope, 'devoutly kissing his blessed feet," in which they told him

---

[1] (Bradsole Abbey near Dover).

that he had no right to interfere in the affairs of Scotland
which belonged exclusively to the Crown of England. It is
curious that although this address was voted in Parliament
and appears on the Parliament Roll subscribed by all the
Barons, it is not subscribed by the Chancellor or any spiritual peer.

Grenvile had good reason to avoid appearing too openly in
this controversy, yet, in spite of his precautions, the Roman
Pontiff became cognisant of the part he had taken in the
matter, and on his election to the Archbishopric of York
refused to allow his consecration, although he was not liable
to any reasonable objection   Letters and proxies being ineffectual, the Archbishop elect resolved to go in person to Rome,
and in order to show his devotedness to his spiritual duties, he
absolutely resigned the office of Chancellor before his departure.
According to Prynne's Records, iii. 1073, the King himself
sent a certificate and letter to the Pope on Grenvile's behalf,
speaking therein of his merits and services in terms of high
praise [1]   But in spite of this royal intercession his consecration was still delayed, and at last only granted on
the payment of 9,500 marks, " a sum exceeding by 2,000
marks the entire revenues of his cathedral and the dignitaries
places therein, as valued in the King's Books at the time "
The ceremony was performed by Clement V at Lyons, on the
30th of January, 1306, more than a twelve-month after his
election had received the royal assent.[2]   The cost of his

---

[1] Sanctissimo in Christo Patri Domino C divina Providentia Sanctæ *Romanæ* ac Univer-
salis Ecclesiæ Summo Pontifici , *Edwardus* eadem gratiâ Rex *Angliæ*, &c devota pedum
osculà beatorum   Vacante nuper Ecclesia *Eboracensi* aud suæ viduata Pastore, Decanus et
Capitulum ejusdem Ecclesiæ ad electionem de futuro præficiendo Pontifice procedentes,
*inter alios quos ad ejusdem Ecclesiæ regimen utiles fore conspexerunt ad personam dilecti Clerici
et Cancellarii nostri* Magistri *W de Grenefeld* Ecclesiæ prædictæ Canonici suæ considerationis
intuitum direxerunt, & ipsum concorditer eligerunt in ipsius Ecclesiæ Archiepiscopum &
Pastorem , Nos autem ejusdem Electi, cujus altitudo Consilii, assiduis, scientia literalis, &
industria circumspecta ad quælibet agenda salubriter dirigenda, necnon & nobis ac regno
nostro dinoscetur esse perutilis, commodi & honoris desiderantes augmentum, Sanctitati
vestræ omni qua possumus instantia supplicamus, quatinus præmissis clementi meditatione
pensatis, præ, præfatum Electum qui pro confirmationis et consecrationis munere Deo
propitio favorabiliter obtinendo ad præsentiam vestræ dominationis accedit, Apostolici
favoris præsidio dignemini prosequi, et juxta speratam fiduciam celeriter atque fœliciter
expedire   Firmiter enim speratur & creditur, quod per solertem memoratı Electi
industriam & evidentem prærogativam virtutum ipsius, in Spiritualibus & temporalibus
utilia & salubria suscipiat incrementa, quodque per votivam præfectionem illius plus
providebitur eidem Ecclesiæ quam personæ   Conservet vos Altissimus ad regimen Ecclesiæ
suæ Sanctæ per tempora prospera and longiora   Dat. apud *Linc* 31 die *Decembris*, Anno
regni etc 33.
[2] (Hemingburgh ii, p 233) Eodem anno obiit Thomas archiepiscopus Eborum, mense
Septembri scilicet nono kalendas Octobris, et sepultus est apud Sutwell, sexto kalendas
Octobris   Cui successit magister Willelmus de Grenefelde, die Veneris ante festum Sancti
Nicholai electus, et 'Lugduno a papa Clemente XII. confirmatus in sequenti anno

(Murimuth continuatio chronicarum. Ed. E. M. Thompson, p 8)
Hoc anno papa fecit Antonium de Bek, episcopum Dunelmensem, patriarcham Jerosolo-
mitanum, et archiepiscopum Eboracensem W[illelmum] de Grenefeldc confirmavit,

residence at Rome and the enormous sum he had been obliged
to disburse, so effectually drained his resources that he returned
to England literally a beggar. On his arrival the King issued
a writ for the restitution of his temporalities,[1] and on the
30th of May, Grenvile required of the Dean and Chapter
the profits which they had derived from their administration of
the spiritualities of the see during the vacancy. On the 21st of
November, 1306, he wrote to William, Cardinal-priest of St
Potentiana, professing his entire inability to pay the money
which he owed at Rome, and begging the Pope to respite him
till Christmas. He had not, he stated, received any of the
revenues of the Archbishopric for the current year, as they had
been assigned to a certain nobleman [John de Brittania Earl
of Richmond], and he could "neither pay the disme imposed by
the Pope nor the trois disme for the expedition to Wales, to say
nothing of the costly equipment of ten knights which he was
required to provide." On the 15th of February he wrote to
another cardinal to entreat for a little longer time, and pleading
as his excuse the great straits he was in and his poverty. On
the 26th of June, 1307, Francis Rodolossi and the company of
the Bellardi at Lucca, of which he was a member, entered into
an obligation to pay for the Archbishop to the chamberlain of
the Pope and the College of Cardinals the large sum of four
thousand florins. This sum would probably release Grenvile
from his debts at Rome, but the borrowed money was to be
raised and repaid, and to do this he was obliged to throw himself upon the kindness of his friends and to have recourse to
the clergy of his diocese for subsistence, first by way of
"benevolence," and the second time of ' subsidy "—a distinction, it would seem, without a difference.'

York at this time was invested with considerable political
importance. The wars with Scotland had converted it into a
a military position, and it became for a time the capital as it
were, of England. Several Parliaments were held in the city,
and the Courts of Justice were also removed thither from
London, and they did not return for seven years. In 1299 a
large army had assembled at York under the command of John

[1] (Prynne's Records, iii, 1145.) Rex Dilectis et fidelibus suis *Lamberto de Thrikingham
et Johanni de Byron* Custodibus suis Archiepiscopatus *Eborum* sede vacante salutem
Cum Dominus summus Pontifex electionem nuper celebratam in Ecclesia Cathedrali
Eborum de discreto viro Magistro *Willielmo de Grencfeilde* Canonico ejusdem Ecclesiæ in
Archiepiscopum illius loci, *cui prius regium assensum adhibuimus et favorem confirmaverit,*
sunt per literas ipsius summi Pontificis Bullatas nobis inde directas nobis constat, Nos con
firmacionem *illam acceptantes,* cepimus fidelitatem ipsius Archiepiscopi, et temporalia
Archiepiscopatus prædicti prout moris est restituimus eidem. Et ideo vobis mandamus,
quod eidem Archiepiscopo temporalia Archiepiscopatus prædicti liberetis sicut prædictum
est. Teste Rege apud *Wynton,* 31 die *Marcu*

de Warren, Earl of Surrey, for service in Scotland. The position of the Archbishop as a great potentate in the North would necessarily involve him in negociations with Scotland and in the wars that too frequently interrupted them. He was obliged at a great cost to find a contingent for the army. He resided principally at Cawood Castle, the noble old palace-fortress on the banks of the Ouse, whose ruins now look down in melancholy silence on the waters of that turbid river. Here Archbishop Grenvile was frequently called upon to play the part of host to the distinguished men who were passing to and fro from the wars, indeed, during the five years occupied by Edward in subjugating the Scotch, Queen Marguerite herself made it her residence, the King usually joining her there during the winter season. Thus this magnificent pile of feudal grandeur—the Windsor of the north, as it was called—served at this time a double purpose. Within the walls raised by the church for the quiet, secluded home for its prelates and for its own services, the Court was being held—the scene of gaiety and worldly distraction. In the silence of his chapel, which had shortly before Grenvile's time been erected within the walls of the palace, the Archbishop was praying for the safety of his monarch and the success of his arms, and ordering prayers and processions in all the churches of his diocese to be made on behalf of the King, the army in Scotland and those going thither, each time granting indulgences of forty days to the faithful and obedient. In the courtyard of the castle, amidst the constant assembly of armed men we hear the merry laugh of the light-hearted young soldiers as they mount their chargers and ride away to the scenes of death, charmed with the smiles of courtly dames, and impelled by the reputation of "noble names and knightly sires."

> They burned the gilded spurs to claim,
> For well could each a war-horse tame,
> Could draw a bow, the sword could sway,
> And lightly bear the ring away
> Nor less with courteous precepts stored,
> Could dance in hall and carve at board,
> And frame love ditties passing rare,
> And sing them to a lady fair

And thus in intermingling prayers and the clash of arms, those turbulent "times rolled on, changing little either as to hopes or fears"[1]

To Archbishop Grenvile Cawood Castle owed much according to Mountain (though how to reconcile his statement with the

[1] "Old Yorkshire" by W. Smith, F S A S

Archbishop's poverty it is difficult to see), who states that " it was at this prelate's expense, about the year 1306, that the brick work of the Castle was added, or the old stone buildings taken away and new-built with brick "

The Archbishop's advice and assistance were often sought for and required in the Councils of the nation   He was summoned to the Parliament at Westminster in 1306, and on the 2nd of July in that year, he and the Bishop of Lichfield were made the guardians of the Kingdom   In 1307 he was called to Edward's last Parliament at Carlisle, and there he proclaimed the peace between France and England   On the 26th of August, 1307, he was summoned to attend a parliament ' to be held at Northampton, in the quinzaine of Michaelmas, concerning the exequies of the late King and the marriage and coronation of the present King"   On the 18th of January following he was ordered to attend the King's coronation at Westminster   In consequence of the suspension of the Archbishop of Canterbury, the Pope had desired Grenvile to officiate on this occasion, but a reconciliation was subsequently effected between the King and the southern primate, who was thus enabled to maintain and exercise his privilege   The reign of the new King was anything but a happy one   Greatness was always within his reach, for he was by no means destitute of ability, but he forgot it among the fops and fools who surrounded him   York again became the capital of the Kingdom, and Cawood became the royal residence once more, both Edward II and Queen Isabella and their children staying there when the Scottish wars were resumed.   On the 21st of June, 1308, the Archbishop received an order " to be at Carlisle in the octave of the Assumption of St Mary next with all his service, to proceed with the King into Scotland in order to suppress the rebellion of Robert de Brus "   On the 16th of August he was summoned to attend Parliament at Westminster, and again on the 8th of January " to treat with the King and other prelates and magnates concerning the affairs of the Kingdom   He received a similar summons on the 8th of March   On the 11th of June he was summoned " to attend a Council at Stamford, on the Sunday after the Feast of S James the Apostle, to advise concerning the punishment of the Scots who have broken the truce granted to them by the King at the request of the King of France," and in October of that year he was summoned to attend the Parliament to be held at York (afterwards changed to Westminster), on the Sunday next after the Feast of the Purification " to consider the state of Scotland."   In the

D

following June he receives a request that he will "aid the King by way of loan (de prest) with victuals for his Scotch expedition, to wit: of one hundred quarters each of wheat malt beans and pease , two hundred quarters of oats and forty beeves, and one hundred sheep, and that he be ready to deliver the same to the Sheriff of York, at the Gule of August next in order to carry them to Scotland, and if it happen that the Archbishop be unable to furnish each parcel aforesaid, the King desires him to provide it elsewhere, so that the King be aided by him entirely with the same victuals." He is requested to take his request so great and so hastily made, to heart, and to perform it willingly, as he esteems the honour and profit of the King and his realm, and to certify the King without delay by the bearer of these letters of what he has done herein, and of how far the King may be aided by him de prest on this great and hasty business, and the King shall be bound to him in the price of the said victuals to be paid at Candlemas (Chaundel-lour) next out of the moneys to be levied of the tenth or other issues of the realm " This big order is dated Canterbury, 25th June, 1310, and we can only hope that the Archbishop's financial position was sufficiently improved by this time to enable him to meet it. At any rate, in May of the following year (1311) the King made an order to the Treasurer and Barons of the Exchequer to acquit the Archbishop ' of the Scutage that they exact from him for the late King's Welsh armies in the fifth and tenth years of his reign for five knights fees, as the late Archbishop had his service in the said armies, as appears from the rolls of the Marshalsea."

The Archbishop was a great supporter of the Knights Templars, an Order half military, half monastic, which had existed for nearly two hundred years. It was wealthy, powerful and independent But a charge of the commission of the most atrocious crimes against decency and morality, as well as of hideous blasphemy, had been brought against them. When we consider how the Templars had devoted themselves to the service of the Cross, surrendering alike fortune and life for the sacred cause they had adopted, it is incredible that they would belie their glorious traditions, their practice and their vows. Doubtless there were amongst them many Bois Guilberts, half-priests, half-soldiers, with too great a share of the spirit of the latter , but the conduct of the great mass of the Order seems to have been irreproachable. The Society however was doomed to destruction, and the first blow was given in France with frightful vehemence Evidence, which a modern court of justice would reject in derision was listened to against it, and noble gentlemen were led to the stake and to torture, rather than confess themselves guilty of offences which they had never perpetrated Archbishop Grenvile for a long time warded off the attack in England, but at last the power of the Pope prevailed, and though refusing to take any part against the Templars in the province of Canterbury, he consented to preside over a council to be held at York the result of which proved the good sense of the Northern Clergy The punishment of death was not awarded as in other countries, and there was no cruelty nor torturing. The Templars were sent for a year to religious houses to do penance for their errors, and were then released, and a provision made for their wants.

Within a fortnight after the termination of the gathering at York the Archbishop, in accordance with a Royal mandate, took his journey towards the South Clement V. had convened a General Council which was to meet in the month of October, and the king was anxious that he should be present at it as his envoy. The king gave him letters of credence and safe conduct dated the 10th of October, 1311, and he was welcomed by the Pope, who assigned him an honourable position at the Council, placing him next after the Cardinals and the Prince Archbishop of Treves The affairs of the Templars and their offences were fully discussed and the meeting prorogued till the month of April, 1312, when the Order was finally dissolved Evidently the honour paid to the Archbishop of York on this occasion excited the jealousy of the Southern Primate, for the king found it necessary to issue a mandate to him forbidding him "to molest William, Archbishop of York, or his men, on his return from the Council General held in parts beyond the sea, as the king understands that he and his men were attacked in Kent on his way to the Council by the procurement of the said Archbishop." The old feud about bearing the Cross had already broken out on more than one occasion between the two Primates, and when William de Grenvile went to Rome to seek his consecration, the king had written a letter to the Pope begging that he might be allowed to carry his Cross erect on his return, and had ordered the Archbishop of Canterbury to offer no violence to him on his return as had been intended.[1] In the autumn of

---

[1] (Prynne's Records, iii, p. 1112.) Magister *Willielmus de Grenefeld* Decanus Ecclesie Sanctis *Trinitatis Cicestrens, qui de licencia Regis moratur in Curia Romana*, habet litteras Regis de protectione utque ad Festum Natali Domini proximo futurum die datæ al

1314, when the Court was at York, there was a great risk of collision The Archbishop of Canterbury was on his way to the city, and it was not likely that he would cede a single point to his rival in the North On the 31st of August Grenvile ordered his official and the Dean and Chapter of York to resist him if he asserted the offensive privilege, and directed the services to be suspended at every place and church at which he halted, unless it were the Royal chapel. Instructions were also given to the Archdeacon of Nottingham to check the Southern Primate on his entrance into the Diocese. The king, however, intervened and put an end to the danger by ordering Grenvile to allow his brother to carry his Cross erect during his stay in York Grenvile must have submitted most unwillingly, and his Grace of Canterbury was not slow in retaliating, for on the 12th of June in the following year, when there was a chance of Grenvile's going into the Diocese of Worcester, a strict injunction was given to the Bishop by his superior that he should not permit the sacred symbol to be raised

On September 4th, 1312, the King at the request of the Archbishop orders the Sheriff of York to "remove without delay the lay and armed force occupying the Churches, Houses and Manors of the Deanery of S Peter's, York, with the object of disturbing the Archbishop so that he cannot exercise his spiritual office" What this refers to is not known. The following May the Archbishop is summoned to repair at once to the King, "even if he have to be carried in a litter or otherwise" before the Sunday before the Ascension, to have council with the King before the King's journey to France, "whither he is going at the request of the Pope and of Philip, King of France, to attend the ceremony of the knighting of King Philip's eldest son at Whitsuntide," and he received a further summons to attend a Parliament to be held, after the King's

volumus, &c , except de , & except &c , pref. &c , Teste Rege apud *Shene* secundo die *Octob*

(Prynne's Records, iii, p 1116) Rex Omnibus Amicis & Ballivis & fidelibus suis ad quos, &c , salutem Cum Venerabilis Pater *Willielmus de Grenefeild Eboracensis* Archiepiscopus sit ad praesens a *Curia Romana ad nostram praesentiam reversurus,* vos amicos rogamus vobis, ballivis & fidelibus mandantes, quatenus eidem Archiepiscopo aut familiae suae in veniendo ad nos a Curia praedicta non inferatis, seu quantum in vobis est ab aliis inferri permittatis injuriam, molestiam, dampnum, impedimentum aliquod seu gravamen, sed eis potius salvum & securum conductum habere facatis quociens ab ipso super hoc ex parte nostra fueritis requisiti In cujus, &c , utque ad festum nativitatis Sancti *Johannis Baptista* prox futur duratur Teste Rege apud *Caneford*, 10 die *Februarii*

Per Breve de privato Sigillo

Hereupon this Archbishop in his return from the Pope's Court this year, was invited to lodge and feast with the Abbot in the Monastery of St *Augustines* at *Canterbury*, yet with special caution in writing concerning the bearing of his Cross within it, lest it should turn to their future prejudice *Eodem anno Archiepiscopus* Eboracensis *rogatus (est) ab Abbate ad concirandum ser in , facta tamen litera, quod non in praejudicium domus renuit pro Cruce reculvorum, quae talis*

return from France, at Westminster, in the quinzaine of the
Nativity of St John the Baptist

The summer of 1314 witnessed the calamitous defeat at
Bannockburn when the pride of Edward was laid low

> And the best names that England knew,
> Claimed in the death-prayer dismal due

It was with great difficulty that the King made his
escape from the field of battle, and he seems never to
have paused in his flight till he found himself at York
Grenvile, like a loyal patriot, could not fail to be troubled at
the reverse which his country had sustained, and he took an
active part in the attempt to rescue her from her misfortunes
Thus, on the 5th of January 1315, he and the Bishop of
Durham were excused from their attendance at Parliament "as
they were then busily engaged in protecting the Marches of
England against the Scots"

Indeed the Archbishop did not long survive the disgrace,
but died at Cawood on the Festival of St Nicholas (Saturday
Dec 6th), 1315, "leaving behind him," says Carew, "the
reputation of an able statesman and no ill scholar," whilst
Dixon in his "Fasti Eboracenses" speaks highly of his piety
and zeal and says that he was "a most excellent and painstaking
Diocesan A question naturally suggests itself when we see
those who occupied the highest dignities of the Church
employed in secular work of various kinds, presiding over
courts of Justice, acting as Ambassadors or Diplomatists at
some Foreign Court, and even proving their capacity as Military
Leaders in the Field—how fared it with the flock which had
been entrusted to their pastoral care? What oversight did they
exercise over the priests and the people who had been so
solemnly committed to their episcopal charge? Viewing the
matter as we now do, the anomaly was monstrous, but it would
not then be so looked upon. As regarded judicial and diplo-
matic appointments, the clergy were the only class of men
whose education fitted them to fill them, and the vast territorial
possessions of prelates like the Archbishops of York and the
Bishops of Durham, placed them in positions, which involved,
almost of necessity from their proximity to Scotland, no little
attention to the *res militaris*. The routine work of the Diocese,
such as Ordinations, Consecrating of Churches and cemeteries,
and the like, was committed by the Archbishops to the care of
a Suffragan, who was badly paid and too often treated with
scant courtesy by the great Prelate whom he served When
the chair of York was filled by a Primate of great capacity like

Grenville other things were more carefully dealt with than might have been looked for. Considerable light is thrown upon his archiepiscopal career by the study of his Register which proves this commendation to have been deserved. The details of monastic life which his Acts exhibit are most remarkable. He tightened the cords of discipline around his monasteries in a way that none of them would like. He was constantly visiting them and correcting offences even of the most minute kind. He was also very strict with his clergy on the question of non-residence, and he must have been much thwarted and annoyed by the number of foreigners who were sent over to him for some of the best preferments by the Pope. Grenville also was a strict disciplinarian with regard to the sins of the laity, especially with reference to grave offences against decency and morality, and in this he knew no difference between rich and poor, and his register abounds with instances of penances inflicted upon persons of rank and noble birth. Curious illustrations occur here and there in the Register of practices which had crept in, and of the attitude taken by the Archbishop respecting them, *e.g.*, we find a mandate addressed to the Chapter of Ripon forbidding them to hold markets in the Minster. An image of the Blessed Virgin had been set up in the Church of Foston, and crowds had flocked to it in the belief that some peculiar virtues resided in the particular piece of sculpture. The Archbishop prohibits the adoration of the image. It is a remarkable anticipation of the feeling which subsequently assumed so strong a form. He issues a citation to the Vicar-General of Cardinal Gaetano, the Archdeacon of Richmond, concerning the undue burden to which the Clergy of that Archdeaconry were subject, when he was on his visitation. They had been compelled, it seems, to find entertainment for his train of fifteen and sometimes four and twenty horsemen, each of whom had his dog following him, ready for a hunt whenever a stag or a roe-deer might spring from a cover on the road-side.

In 1306 he issued an indulgence for the fabric of York Minster, or rather of the new nave which had been commenced in 1291, and for which indulgences were granted by several successive prelates during the time in which it was advancing to its completion. It was near this new nave, after his eventful life was over, that Archbishop Grenville was laid to rest, in the north transept on the eastern side in the corner adjacent to the choir aisle. The monument which commemorates him, although much mutilated and injured, is a very striking one. The marble

WILLIAM DE GRANVILLE.

CHANCELLOR OF ENGLAND, 1302-5.
DEAN OF CHICHESTER, 1303-4.
ARCHBISHOP OF YORK, 1304-15.

From the Monument in York Minster.

slab that covers his remains was formerly plated with brass, of which nothing remains except a portion of the figure of the Archbishop, which time and neglect have almost entirely obliterated He wears a mitre, and is clad in full canonicals, and his hand is raised in the act of benediction   Above the tomb there towers a lofty over-arching canopy of richly decorated work, surmounted by a statue of the Archbishop This is a valuable memorial of the skill of a recent master mason of the cathedral   Between the tomb and the wall there once stood the altar of S Nicholas, and as the decease of this Archbishop occurred on the Festival of that Saint, this place was most happily and appropriately selected for his interment [1] At the time of Grenvile's death two chantries were in existence at that altar, and on the 28th of April 1346, Richard de Cestria, Canon of York, added a third, at which the souls of the Archbishop, of himself and his parents were commemorated, and it was endowed with a house in Over Ousegate   About the year 1735 the Archbishop's tomb was opened, and a fine gold ring with a ruby was taken from the dead man's finger, and is now deposited among the treasures in the Vestry The lines of Hugo Grotus may well be applied to it—

Annule qui thecam poteras habuisse sepulcham
Hoc natalis erit nunc tibi theca locus

The Archbishop bequeathed another ring, "a pontifical ring, with an emerald in the middle of four rubies and four large pearls" to the Dean and Chapter "to decorate the window of St Wilham." (See Fabric Rolls ed Surtees Society 214) [2]

Goodwin tells us (without, however, stating his authority) that the Archbishop bequeathed his library to the monastery of St. Albans, which at that time was in very high repute His will is not yet discovered. Thomas de St Albans, Canon of Southwell, and William, son of Robert de Grenvile (the testator's brother) were the two executors.   They were released from the responsibility of their charges on the 16th of August, 1322

Robert de Grenvile had died in 1314-5, since on the 20th of February in that year the Archbishop paid to the Friar Preachers and Minors of York 40s. each, and to

---

[1] It was behind Archbishop Grenvile's tomb that the fanatic Jonathan Martin concealed himself when he set fire to the Minster in 1829

[2] This bequest is mentioned in Act Cap T 22 b in the following words "Memorandum quod vij Id Januarii Anno domini M° CCU^mo quintodecimo liberatus fuit annulus, quem dominus Wilhelmus de Grenefeld quondam Archiepiscopus Ebor legavit feretro S Willelmi, Decano et Capitulo" The windows of S William and S Nicholas are close to the monument facing the east

the Augustinians and Carmelites 20s. each, of his alms " to say
a mass for the soul of our brother Robert de Grenefeld, *lately
deceased.*"

The Archbishops eldest brother, Richard, the sixth in
succession of that name, held in the 40th of Henry III. (1256)
" viginti libratas terræ in com Devon," by Knight's service,
and very large possessions elsewhere, and not being at that time
a Knight was summoned to take that degree.   As " Sir
Richard de Granvilla, Knight " he grants Yrania, daughter of
Thomas de Grenvil, and to her heirs and assigns, two burgages
and six acres of land in Bideford, which escheated to him from
Roger de Botelei, of Great Cleve, and " he on the east of
Bideford High Street, the tenement of William Botreaux south,
and that of William Whing north " In 1261 he presented to
the living of Bideford, Henry de Bratton or Bracton, as the
name is usually spelt a celebrated lawyer as well as a divine
Lord Campbell says of him that he was " one of the greatest
jurists who ever lived in any age or in any country " (Lives of
Lord Chief Justices i , 63) , and Sir Travers Twiss says, ' as long
as the law of England lives, the memory of Bracton will never
die " (Bracton's De Legibus Angliæ, Ed. Twiss ii , p lxxx)   In
the last year of Henry III's reign (1272) Sir Richard obtained a
charter for a market for Bideford on Mondays, and a fair at the
Feast of St. Margaret the Virgin   The original charter was
kept in the Record Room under the Vestry of the old Parish
Church at Bideford, but is no longer in existence, though a
copy is preserved in the British Museum, entitled, " Carta
Regis Ricardo de Greynvill pro mercatu per diem lunæ apud
Bideford in com   Devon, et una feria in vigilia et in die S.
Margaritæ Virginis et per tres dies frequentes "

It was found at this time that he held ' antiquas furcas "
and " an assize of bread and water at Bideford, and free warren
on the east side of Toryz (Torridge) water."

He also proved his claim to hold a market by prescription
at Kilkhampton (Plac de Jur et Ass et de Corona 30 Edw. 1.,
p 110 (1302))

From the Register of Bishop Quivil it appears that Sir
Richard was not free from that class of sins, of which his
brother the Archbishop of York, was afterwards so impartial a
vindictator, and the following quotaton is an interesting
instance of that godly discipline, " the restoration of which
(as the Commination Service puts it) is much to be wished. '
Aparently then, as now, the weaker sex was the one to be
punished, whilst the male offender, who was probably the
guiltier of the two, got off scot-free

10th March, 1282-3, at Paignton

Johanna Baschet abjuravit Dominum Richardum de Grevile qui ab eadem prolem susceperat in adulterio, et injunctum fuerat sibi quod stet singulis diebus Dominicis et Festivis extra Ecclesiam, per totam Quadragesimam usque ad diem Jovis proximam ante Pascha, et eciam veniret apud Exoniam reconcilianda cum ceteris Penitentibus, ut est moris super qua Dominus Episcopus scripsit Capellano de Bydeforde, ut compellat eam ad hujusmodi penitenciam peragendam si necesse fuerit

In the 25th of Edward I (1297), Sir Richard was one of the principal persons in Devonshire summoned to be in London on Sunday after the octave of St John the Baptist "to go with the King beyond the seas for their honour and the preservation and profit of the Kingdom," being styled "Dominus Richardus Grenevyle" Four years later (1301) he was summoned to be at Berwick-upon-Tweed with Horse and Arms to march against the Scots (Ryley's "Pleadings in Parliament," p 483)

He married Isabel, daughter of Joscelyn of Monte Tregamion, by whom he had no issue, and dying in 1310, was succeeded in the family honour and estates by his brother Bartholomew, who is styled in his deed, dated Bideford, the Monday after St Augustine's Day, 7th Edward II., "Lord of Bideford " To this deed is appended a fair seal of the arms of Granville, viz., three rests or clarions circumscribed ' Sigill Barth de Grenvile, militis "

In the eleventh year of the same reign (1318) he presents Master Henry Toyt, commonly called Henry de Cornubia, and also Henry de Truru priest to the living of Bideford. (Bp Stapeldon's Register)

In the thirteenth year of the same reign (1320) being again styled "Lord of Bideford " by his deed dated at Bideford, the Monday after S Luke's Day," he grants to Richard de Grenvil his younger son, the Rectory of the Church of Kilkhampton, and to his heirs and assigns his whole land, Hewode, with the appurtenances

In 1325 he died, having been certified the previous year to be of great and almost decrepit age He had married Amy, the daughter of Sir Vyell Vyvyan, Knight of Treviddien, in Cornwall [1] Bishop Stapeldon had granted to " Sir Bartholomew and his wife Amy" a license for the celebration of divine service " in capellâ suâ de Bydeforde " A fine was also levied at Westminster, 10th Edward II, between the said Bartholomew and Amy his wife, Plaintiffs, and Margery, late wife of John de Dynham, Defendant of the manor of Kilkhampton, to the use

[1] By his wife Margaret daughter of Christopher Pol of Kilda

H

of the said Bartholomew and Amy his wife, for life, excepting one messuage, four carucates of land, sixteen acres of meadow, twenty-seven acres of wood, and £60 12s 3d. in the same manor . remainder to Henry, son of the said Bartholomew, and to the heirs of his body

And in 18th Edward II., writing herself Amya, she, " in her pure widowhood, released to David de Truro her right in one acre of land in Carvsdonne and in two acres and a half in Werbyuton. in Bideford manor, which she had of the gift of Sir Bartholomew de Grenvile " This deed is dated at "Byde-forde Tuesday after St. Ambrose's Day," 1325, to which is a fair seal appendant of the arms of Granville impaling the arms of Vyvyan. viz, six mullets, 3, 2, and 1 circumscribed These arms were cut in stone over an old chimney-piece in the village of Morwenstow, having possibly been removed at some time or other from Kilkhampton Church

According to Ped fin Cornw, 10 Ed II, No 1, Sir Bartholomew left two sons and two daughters, Isabel and Johanna The second son, Richard, took Holy Orders. "Master Richard de Greynvyle," sub-deacon, occurs as Rector of Kylkamtone 14 October, 1308 (Bp. Bytton's Register, 35b), and the certificate of his Ordination as sub-deacon by Walter, Bishop of Bath and Wells, in his chapel at Woky (20 May, 1307), under Letters Dimissory granted by Bishop Bytton, is found in Bishop Stapeldon's Register, fol 59b He was ordained Deacon, 19 September, 1310 (Ibid, fol. 226), and Priest the following March (Ibid, fol. 227b) The living was vacant "a die Martis in Vigilia Assumpcionis Beatæ Virginis" (14 August), 1324 He received a dispensation "in forma conciliæ,' 14 October, 1308 and again, 5 October, 1309 (Ibid, fols. 35b, 44) He had a licence for non-residence in order to study in sacred Theology or Canon Law 4 January, 1311-12, and again till the Feast of the Nativity of St John the Baptist, "pro ipsius Ecclesie et suis negociis procurandis" from 3 February, 1320-1, and again to study, etc , in foreign parts or at home, as he might prefer, 21 May, 1624 (Ibid, fols 67, 155, 180)[1] Amongst the Letters Dimissory in Bishop Stapeldon's Register, 130b, one Roger de Grenvyle was ordained sub-deacon on the 26th of September, 1318 Probably he was cousin to the Rector of Kilkhampton.

Henry, the eldest son, survived his father only two years. By inquisition taken after his death at Kilkhampton, 2nd

---

[1] He founded a Chest at Oxford for making loans to poor scholars Five shillings and two pence were paid for his Exequies at Exeter Coll , 1536, (cf Antony à Woods' Colleges and Hall- J Gut he · t l. 1736, pp. 105-110 Boase's Ex Coll , pp 1-34, 189)

Edward III., the jury found that the said Henry, immediately after his father's death, gave a general release to his mother Amy of the £60 12 3 payable to him out of the manor of Kilkhampton for life, reserving to himself £20 annually This inquisition also proves that Dame Amy Grenvile held the manors of Kilkhampton and Bideford for life of the Earl of Gloucester, as of the honour of Winkleigh (Winkleigh being the chief seat of the honour of Gloucester in the county of Devon), forfeited to the King by Hugh le Despencer the younger

In 1324 Henry de Grenvile presented to the Rectory of Kilkhampton Thomas Stapeldon, brother to Bishop Stapeldon, and also Walter de Prodhomme, a nephew of the Bishop's, to the Rectory of Bideford in the same year. The Bishop in his will bequeathed to Walter de Prodhomme a legacy of 40s for the maintenance of Bideford Bridge, as well as 10 marks 'pro defectibus Ecclesiæ de Bidefoide reperandis '

Henry de Grenvile married Ann, daughter and heness of the family of Wortham, near Lifton, in the county of Devon, and was buried at Kilkhampton, where his arms impaled with those of Wortham still exist The exact date of his death is not known, but it was probably before June 1, 1328, as on that day the King, as " custodian of the lands and heirs of Henry de Grenvil tenant in chief,' appointed William de Wellyngoure to the living of Bideford. William de Wellyngoure does not appear in the Bishop's Register as Rector of Bideford, but as we find him[1] presented the same day to ' Lydyford in Dertemore," and as his name appears in the Bishop s Register as Rector of Lydford, he must either have elected to go to the latter parish, or his appointment to Bideford must be regarded as a clerical error Both livings were in the King's gift

---

[1] Calendar of Patent Rolls, Edward III , 37

CHAPTER IV.

HENRY DE GRENVILE left a son and heir, Theobald, who was but four years old at the time of his father's death   During his minority he was ward to Sir John Carew, and on obtaining manhood was knighted   He married Joyce, daughter of Thomas Beaumont, Earl of Mellent

As an instance of the open warfare which was often carried on in the fourteenth century between the secular and ecclesiastical authorities, and of the way in which weapons from the spiritual armoury were brought to bear upon the King's officers, may be mentioned the raid which young Sir Theobald made, as Sheriff of Devonshire, upon the manor of Tawton, near Barnstaple, in the summer of 1347   A suit had arisen upon some disputed presentation, and the court of King's Bench made an order against the Bishop of Exeter for a considerable sum of money   The Sheriff received the King's writ, in which he was directed to enforce execution upon the Bishop's goods and chattels   Accordingly, Sir Theobald, whom Bishop Grandisson designates in his "Register," vol. 1. fol 139, as "juvenis Miles sive Thiro status militaris," on the Saturday after the feast of St. Benedict (July), at the dawn of day, with Thomas de Merton, Richard Tyrel, John de Linscote, John Trenger, and a rabble composed of about five hundred persons, proceeded with arms, offensive and defensive, to the manor of Tawton, and to the glebe and Vicarage house, and forcing premises belonging to the Church, as also houses of free tenants there, "varia bona ecclesiastica sub protectione ecclesiasticâ ibidem existentia, ad valorem ducentarum marcarum et amplius, contra voluntatem dominorum hujusmodi locorum et eorum qui hujusmodi custodiis fuerant deputati, consumere, auferre et contrectare dampnabiliter presumpserunt.'

After severely beating and even murdering some of the tenants and residents of the place, these lawless invaders decamped hooting and shouting, and terrifying all the neighbourhood   In consequence of such notorious outrage, Bishop Grandisson directed the Priors of Pilton and Barnstaple to proceed to the Parish Church, as also to the conventual Church

BIDEFORD BRIDGE.

at Barnstaple, on the Sunday after the receipt of his mandate, and there, at solemn Mass, to publish the sentence of excommunication against the offenders, with bells ringing, the cross erect, candles first lighted and then extinguished, every priest assisting in stole and surplice, and to perform the like ceremonies in the neighbouring churches on Sundays and Feasts, until they received his injunctions to the contrary. The whole of the proceedings was to be explained to the people in the vulgar tongue, and a certified return was to be forwarded to his lordship by the Feast of S. Bartholomew, 24th August. According to "The History of Crime in England" by L. Owen Pike (who gives as his authority the Controlment Roll m. 6 d. Devon), the Bishop and his subordinates were summoned to answer for this act of contempt, and did in the end so far obey the law as to appear by Attorney in the King's Bench. But in the meanwhile, the whole county was thrown into a commotion, greater even than ordinary, by the scandal of open warfare between the secular and ecclesiastical authorities. How the civil power decided the transaction does not appear, but from fol. 144 of the Bishop's Register, it would seem to have determined the case against Sir Theobald. At any rate, on the 14th of the following January he, on his bended knees, made due submission to the Bishop "in aula manerii sui de Chudleigh," in the presence of his sureties, John de Ralegh and John de Dynham, Knights, and of Almaric Fitzwaryn, Sheriff of Devon, and succeeded in obtaining the benefit of absolution.

On the 5th September of the same year he was also guilty of flagrant outbreaks at Kilkhampton, but the determined spirit of the Bishop brought this wrong-headed young knight to his senses.

It was probably during his minority that the famous Long Bridge of Bideford was built. It is the largest in Devonshire, and consists of twenty-four arches of different sizes, the greatest width being the fourth from the west end, which is 26 ft. 8 in. wide, and the narrowest the sixth, which is only 11 ft. wide. The total length of the bridge is 677 ft. It is built of local stone with copings of freestone. The story of its foundation, as given by Prince, is well-known.[1]

---

[1] It must not be supposed that there was no bridge previous to the one built in the time of Sir Theobald de Grenvile and Bishop Grandisson. Prince corrects Fuller for stating that Bishop Quivil (A.D. 1280—1291), was the furtherer of a bridge at Bideford, but probably Fuller was right, inasmuch as in the compotus of the executors of the will of Bishop Stapledon, who died in 1327, that Bishop (as above mentioned), is stated to have left 40s. for the maintenance of Bideford Bridge. There was probably, therefore, an original bridge at this earlier period, which was perhaps destroyed by some flood, and a second and stronger bridge had to be built during the Episcopate of Bishop Grandisson, as recorded by Prince, of which

In 17th Edward III , Sir Theobold recovered in the King's Bench the advowson of Kilkhampton

In 24th Edward III , being styled Theobaldus de Grenvile, miles, lord of Kilkhampton, he gave and granted to Richard de Piggiston and his heirs all his lands and tenements in Stowe in Kilkhampton, together with rents and services of Joane, late wife of Nicholas de Stowe , dated at Stowe the Sunday after the Purification.

In 35th Edward III he is styled lord of Bideford in two grants of lands in his manor of Bideford

In 1st Richard II he conveys to Robert Langdon, Agnes his wife, and John their son, two burgages in Bideford and suit to his Manor Court   This deed has a fair round seal with the three clarions or rests for arms, and another upon a knight's helmet for crest, circumscribed " SIGILLUM THEOB DE GRENVIL MIL "   It is dated Bideford, Tuesday after Michaelmas Day, 1st Ric II

The date of his death is uncertain, but it was probably 1377. He left an only son, named after himself, who survived him only a few years, since John de Grenvile presented Robert Braybroke (who afterwards was consecrated Bishop of London) to the Rectory of Bideford on 26th July, 1381 and Thomas Cary to Kilkhampton on 8th September of the same year, being then described as son and heir of Sir Theobald de Grenvile, deceased   Nothing is known of the life or history of this second Sir Theobald, but there are several grants of land with fair seals of which the last is in the 3rd Richard II , and which must have been very shortly before his death, bearing date at Bideford on Wednesday the Feast of the Conversion of St. Paul, whereby John Stowe, son and heir of Walter de Stowe, grants to the said Sir Theobald and his heirs, two messuages in Stowe in the manor of Kilkhampton and thereto is appended a fair seal of the arms of Granville, quartering a crescent and circumscribed " Sigil Theobaldi de Grenvile, militis "   He married his cousin Margaret, daughter of Sir Hugh Courtenay, of Haccombe and Boconnock, Knight, by his wife, Maud Beaumont.   This Sir Hugh was younger brother to Edward Courtenay, Earl of Devon, commonly called the Blind Earl, and the youngest son of Sir

Sir Theobald was " an especial furtherer and great benefactor "   Doubtless, this new bridge suffered considerably later on, either from neglect or accident, for Bishop Stafford, on the 5th of December, 1396, granted an indulgence to all true penitents who should assist " ad constructionem seu reparacionem longi pontis de Bydeford," and it seems as if an entirely new bridge was erected forty-one years afterwards, since Bishop Lacy promulgated two more indulgences in 1437 and 1444, " ad novam constructionem sustentationem seu reparationem pontis de Bydeford "   The last indulgence connected with the bridge was in the time of Bishop Arundell, 1503, for the necessary repairs of the bridge

Edward Courtenay, fourth son of Sir Hugh Courtenay, Earl of
Devon, and Margaret Bohun, grand-daughter of King Edward
the First

Sir Theobald left issue two sons, John and William

Sir John de Grenvile appears to have resided chiefly at
Stowe Bishop Thomas de Brantyngham licensed a chapel in
that mansion 30th August, 1386, in his favour   This demolishes
the hypothesis of Hals that Sir Thomas Grenvile (temp. Henry
VI.) was the first of the family who resided there   Even in
1350 Sir John's grandfather, in the grant to Richard de Peggiston
had dated from Stowe, and his great grandfather (Henry de
Grenvile) had been buried in Kilkhampton Church (circa 1327)
which certainly points to Stowe having been inhabited even at
that early date

In 19th Richard II , John de Greynevill, by his deed bearing
date at Stowe, Sunday, " the feast of St Peter ad vincula,"
releases and makes free Agnes Choppa, late wife of Roger
Jogaler, with all her children, so that neither he nor his heirs
shall claim anything of them hereafter.   To this deed is
appended a fair seal of the Granville arms, circumscribed
" Sigillum Johannis Greynevill milit "

In 1st Henry IV , being styled Lord of Kilkhampton, he
recites the charter which Richard de Grenvil, his ancestor, made
to Richard de Stanbury and his heirs for his homage and service,
of half a furlong of land in Stanbury, in his manor of Kilkhampton, which he, the said Sir John confirmed to Robert de
Stanbury, his heirs and assigns   This deed is dated at
Kilkhampton the Friday before St Valentine's Day.

In 3rd Henry IV , his brother William styling himself
William Greynvill, son of Sir Theobald, sets forth " that whereas
his brother, Sir John Greynvill, Kt , and Margaret his wife,
held the manor and borough of Bideford in the County of
Devon, with the advowson of the same church, and other lands
and tenements in the parish of Bydeforde, called Fordeland,
Eggeffen, and Thorne, etc . and also held lands in Werdon and
Stowe, in the manor of Kilkhampton, he, the said William
Greynvill, ratifies and confirms them to the said Sir John de
Greynvill."   To this deed is appended a fair seal of arms, viz ,
three clarions or horseman's rests ; and for a crest, a
pelican vulning herself , circumscribed ' Sygillum Willimi
Greynvill "

On the 11th of May, 1402, the King ordered Edward
Bishop of Exeter Sir John Arundell, Sir John Grenevile, Sir
John Heale and seven others to contradict the report that the

King did not intend to keep his promise to observe the laws, and to prevent the circulation of such a report

This Sir John had been knighted by King Richard II, and was High Sheriff for the county of Devon, 15 Richard II being according to Hals, the first of the family who attained to this honour   He was returned as one of the Knights of the Shire in the years 1389, 1394, 1397, and 1402   He died in 1410-11   He married Margaret, daughter and co-heiress of Sir John Burgheish, Kt, by whom he had no issue, and was succeeded in the family honours and estates by his brother William   His widow married John Arundell the younger (Bp Lacy's Register n fol. 27), who presented John Walhopp to Bideford by grant, hâc vice, 11th January, 1420-21

William de Greynvill, being styled Lord of Kilkhampton, surrendered to Ralph de Berncote ' all those messuages in Estrabernecote and Westrabernecote, saving to himself, the said William, the suits in his own courts, and suit to his mill " This deed is dated at Kilkhampton the Monday before St. Margaret's Day, 13th Henry IV

In the 2nd Henry V, writing himself brother and heir to Sir John de Greynvill, Kt, late Lord of Bideford, he confirms the charter which John Arundell, and Margaret his wife, had granted to Richard Godman, alias Pow'll, of all their tithes, etc, etc, dated at Kilkhampton the Monday after the Feast of of the Nativity of St John the Baptist   To this deed is appended a seal of three clarions or Horseman's rests, and for a crest, on a helmet a pelican vulning herself, and circumscribed " Sigillum Willmi de Greynvill armigeri "

It appears from the old records that he was twice married, and that Thomasine, daughter of John Cole was his first wife, as it should seem by indenture made at Bideford the Monday after the Feast of St John ante portam Latinam, 5th Henry VI, between William de Greynvill and Thomasine his wife on the one part. and John Cole on the other part, which witnesseth that the aforesaid Thomasine had certain lands and tenements in Yllecombe and Hodesland, within the manor of Kilkhampton, of Sir John de Greynvill Kt-. deceased brother of the said William, whose heir he is by knight's service, and doing suits to his courts and mill

In 8th Henry VI, being styled Lord of Kilkhampton, he surrendered to William Bond a furlong of land, etc., as also suits to his two courts at Kilkhampton   Dated at Stowe, 30th December, with a seal similar to the above.

In the 24th year of the same reign he is mentioned in a

deed with Philippa, his second wife, a daughter (sister ?) of William, Lord Bonvill of Chuton, dated at Stowe 20th July. Lord Bonvill died possessed of the manors of Week St Mary, Swannacote, and other tenements in the hundred of Stratton, in Cornwall, and the whole of this property came into William de Greynvill's possession by this marriage. Afterwards, in the reign of Queen Elizabeth, Swannacote was one of the principal seats of the Granville family. Norden mentions the place in the reign of James I. as one of the mansions of Bernard Grenvil, by whose son, Sir Bevil, it was sold during the reign of Charles I., in order to raise money for the support of the Royalists.

In the 26th Henry VI., being styed William Graynefild, he grants lands to James (William ?) Chuddeleigh and Hugh Stucles, Esquires. The deed is dated 7th November, and thereto is appended two seals.

He died before 29th Henry VI., for in that year John de Almescombe and Philippa his wife, late the wife of William de Graynvil, had a grant from John de Copleston and others of lands in Wildhays and Guakmore. This John Almescombe and Philippa his wife, Lady of the Manor of Bideford," presented Lewis Pollard to the rectory there, void by the death of John Walhopp, 1427-8 (et Bp. Nevyll's Register fol 6b).

By his first wife, Thomasine Cole he left no issue, but by his second wife, Philippa, he left issue one son Thomas, who succeeded him, and two daughters, viz., Margaret, the wife of John Thorne, of Thorne, and Ellena, who was married (Visit Devon 1620 Harl Soc. Pub p. 322) to William Yeo, of Heanton Satchville, co Devon, the ancestor of the present Lord Clinton and of the Yeo's of Fremington. (See Burke's "Landed Gentry") The arms of William Graynefield, impaled with those of his second wife, were in Kilkhampton Church, on a hatchment of stucco, whilst the arms of Yeo with the Granville quarterings also existed in Petrockstowe Church in one of the windows, prior to the restoration of the Church. These have recently been replaced in the vestry window. There is a bench end in Newton St Petrock Church, near Holsworthy, with the dexter impalement gone, but which may have been Thorne, the sinister are the three clarions or rests (Granville). Thorne bordered on this parish.

According to old deeds and family records, his son Thomas was the first of the family who altogether dropped the pronoun " de " which had hitherto been a prefix to the surname though both the two last representatives of the family had sometimes omitted it.   A

In 27th Henry VI. (1449) he is styled Thomas Greynvile, son and heir to William Greynvile, Esquire, and with Anne his wife grants to Richard Ashrigge a tenement in Bideford, " doing suit to *our* courts," shewing that his father was then still alive   This deed is dated at Bideford the Tuesday after St Bartholomew's Day

This Sir Thomas and his second wife grant to Richard Rede all that his land in Bideford, which John Bishop and others held by grant of William Hankeford, Kt, John Hankeford, Richard Greynvile, William Freye, and Richard Covyan, parson of the church of Lytheham   The deed is dated at Bideford the Sunday before the Conversion of St Paul, 31st Henry VI.

In 20th Edward IV. John Stanbury granted him an annual rent of twenty shillings out the profits of his lands at Stanbury for ten years

In the same year he was high sheriff for the county of Gloucester, and three years afterwards for Cornwall, being at that time a knight

He married first, Anne daughter of Sir Philip Courtenay (the second of that name), of Powderham, Knight, their marriage being celebrated in the Umberleigh Chapel in Atherington parish, by the licence of Edmund Lacy, Bishop of Exeter, 7th September, 1447   By her he had no issue

He married secondly, Elizabeth, sister to Sir Theobald Gorges, Kt, and dying 1st Richard III, left issue. two sons, viz, Thomas, who succeeded him and John a Priest, who was instituted, sede vacante, to the living of Bideford by Archbishop Warham, 21st May 1504, and died in 1509.

Thomas it appears, no sooner succeeded to his patrimony than he became concerned in one of the insurrectionary movements against Richard III   There are no precise particulars as to this occurrence, but there is little doubt of his having been an associate with Sir Edward Courtenay and his brother the Bishop of Exeter, who were his cousins, when they raised a force of Cornishmen to join the Duke of Buckingham in his attempt to dethrone the King   Upon the dissolution of this ill-starred confederacy, Thomas Greynvile in company with Sir Richard Edgcomb, betook themselves for shelter to the best hiding place they could   After a while a pardon came between them and disgrace   In the Statute of Additions he is duly described as "Thomas Greynfield, late of Kilkhampton co. Cornwall, Esquire; alias late of Bydeford in com Devon, Esquire; alias Thomas Greynvild de Kilkhampton and Bydeford, Esquire."

Upon the restoration of the House of Lancaster he was appointed an Esquire of the body of Henry VII and High Sheriff of Cornwall   Three years afterwards the King, reciting that by the advice of his council he intends to send an army to the relief of Brittany, by a commission dated at Maidstone, 23rd December, directs Sir Robert Willoughby de Broke, Kt., Sir Richard Edgcomb, Kt., and Thomas Greynvile, Esquire, to summon and examine what number of archers, armed and arrayed at the King's expense, the county of Cornwall could provide, and to article with them, to review them, and to certify the number of archers that all Earls, Barons, Knights, and others are to find before the quindenes of Hilary next.

In the eighth year of the same reign, by indenture bearing date 11th January, he covenants with Richard Whitleigh, Esquire, for a marriage between Roger Graynfeld, his son and heir apparent, and Margaret, daughter of the aforesaid Richard Whitleigh   This marriage took place, for on the 20th February following he grants to Roger Graynfeld, his son and heir apparent, and Margaret his wife, all those messuages within the manor of Kilkhampton

In the 17th of Henry VII he was installed a Knight of the Bath on the occasion of the marriage of Prince Arthur with Catherine of Spain, and the same year, with John, Bishop of Coventry and Lichfield, Sir Robert Willoughby, Lord Broke, and John Sable, he granted the reversion of certain tenements in Rychason, after the death of Aves, wife of John Keynock, to Richard Greynfield his second son and his heirs for ever, by deed dated the 12th October, 1501   And in the 19th Henry VII, being written Sir Thomas Graynfyld, Kt   he bequeathed to John Arundell and John Basset, Knights, his manor of Wodeford, etc., to the use of Richard Graynfyld his second son and heirs for ever   To this deed John Carew of Haccombe and Roger Graynfyld, son and heir apparent to the said Sir Thomas, are witnesses

In the 20th of the same reign the said Sir Thomas with Roger his son, grants to John Grigge and Joane his wife messuages in Merlona St Peter, co Devon

Sir Thomas married first, Isabella, daughter of Sir Otes Gilbert, of Compton, "a family (writes Prince in his ' Worthies of Devon ') of as ancient standing in the county of Devon as the Conquest, and if we may give credit to an author of our own (Mr. Weste) it was here before, for he asserts that Gilbert possessed lands in Manadon near Dartmore, in Edward the Confessor days. They have matched as they descend as we into honourable houses, and have yielded matches to others, in particular to the noble family of the Grenviles."

By her he had two sons and six daughters. viz , Roger, his eldest, of whom presently. and Richard, High Sheriff for Cornwall, 1st, 10th and 14th Henry VIII., who died without issue

Jane, the eldest daughter married first Sir John Arundell of Trerice, son of Sir Thomas Arundell by his wife Katherine third daughter of Sir John Dinham He was created Knight of the Bath 1494 and Knight-bannaret for valour at the seige of Theroumne and Tournay. His grandson "John for the King" as he was usually called, distinguished himself greatly in the civil wars, and at the Restoration was created Lord Arundell of Trerice. On the death of Sir John Arundell Jane Granville married secondly Sir John Chamond Knight of Launcells, who was High Sheriff of Cornwall 28th Henry VIII , and is mentioned by Carew as having been "very learned in the common laws" By him she had two sons. Two letters addressed to her by her husband are in the possession of Lord Arundell of Wardour The following is a copy of her will which is dated 1st January 1550-1 and was proved at Exeter 9 March 1551-2, her personal property being sworn to the amount of £188 0s 10d.

"In the name of the blessed Trinitie Father Sone and Holy Gost, I, Dame Jane Chamond, widowe, beyng in perfyte mynde and memorie, thankes be gyven to Almyghty God, my Creator and onely Redeemer, perceavyng by Faith and Creation my naturell liffe to be transitorie, holy myndyng Repentaunce, in most humble maner aske Almighty God forgiveness and also of all the world, and here under the protection of God make and declare here my last will and testament in this maner following

First I give and bequeth my soule unto Almyghty God, my bodie to be beried in the Church of St Andrewe of Stratton in the south yeld (aisle) of the Churche theare, in the place betwixt my first husband Sir John Arundell Treirys Knight and Sir John Chamond Knight my second and last husband Also I do give and bequeth to my eldest son Sir John Arundell Treiryse Knight all such somes of money as he oweth me for fyve thousand and haulf poundes of white tynne which he had of me, and also the two cheynes of gold which I have allredye delyvered hym And also all such other somes of money and other thinges that he hath had of myn or owith me—my part in that parte of the premisses that he bestowe to the marriage of his doghters at his pleasure And also besides the premisses I doo give and bequeth to my said sone Sir John Arundell Treirys my basin and ewer of silver Also I give and bequeth to my doghter Dame Juhane Arundell wift to my said sone my best velvet gowne furred and edged with white martens Also I give and bequeth to my doghter Margaret Chamond wifte to my sone Richard Chamond Esquyer my best saten gowne and my best velvet kirtell And as to the rest of my goodes, moveable and unmovable, not gevyn nor bequethed, I doo give and bequeth to my said sone Richard Chamonde partly therewith to mary his children, and hym the same Richard Chamonde I doo make my hole and sole executor to

dispose such part of my said goodes for the wealth of my soul as he shall
think best and pay my debtes and chardgies for my funeral "

Dated and gyven the first day of January in the fourth yeare of the
Reigne of Soveraigne Lord Edward the Sixt by the grace of God etc., which
will and testament was made in the presence of Sir John Chamonde, Richard
Prideauxe, Esquyor, Sir John Lile Clerk, then her Chaplain, Martyn Poyle
gent, John Kympthorne, her servant and desired to be witnes herunto by the
same Jane Chamond "

In Stratton Church there is a monument to a Sir John
Arundell in which his figure is represented in brass lying
between his two wives Gilbert in his ' Survey of Cornwall "
wrongly attributes this to the husband of Jane Granville It
is that of her son who married first, Mary daughter and heir of
John Beville of Gwarnock, and secondly Julyan daughter of
Sir James Erisey of Erisey The male line of the Chamond
family ended in 1624

Mary, the second daughter of Sir Thomas Granville, married
first Richard Blewett of Holcombe Regis near Tiverton, and
secondly Sir Thomas St Aubyn of Clowance, Knight, by whom
she had issue, a son and a daughter In Crowan Church in
Cornwall are many ancient monuments belonging to this family
Formerly there was a table-tomb there ornamented with the
effigies of Sir Thomas and Mary his wife These however
together with the greater part of the inscription have been
taken away, but the arms of St. Aubyn, impaled with those of
Granville, still remain. Amongst the " Lisle Papers " are the
following quaint and amusing letters, written between the
years 1532 and 1540, from Sir Thomas St Aubyn to his wife's
sister Honor Lady Lisle

LISLE PAPERS
(Vol 13, p 96)
THOMAS ST AUBYN TO LADY LISLE

My Mye duptye vnto yoʳ honorabyll gode ladyshypp don' wᵗ moste
hartye & lovelye recōmendacions y recōmende me to yoᵘ & see y wolde y
myght bee to my syngler gode lorde yoᵘ nobyll & moste lovynge bedfelowe
wᵗ all yoᵘʳz & desyrouse the cōtynuance of yoᵘ gode helthys & psperous estate
to the pleasoᵘ of Almyghtie god & to yoᵘ harteʳ desyre Also wᵗ moste hartie
thankeʳ for yoᵘ grete kyndenes & godenes towardeʳ me & myne & yoᵘ bedman
& svantt Trevuna whiche all tymes moste reioysyth & delytyth to speke & to
cōmyn of my seid gode lordships godenes & yoᵘs, & he ys nowe (thankeʳ to
owre lorde & yoᵘ) of a newe flashyon he maye thannke god hylye to haue
the chaunce to bee my lorde svantt & yoᵘʳz, & all hys hole harte & myne ys
to the vttermoste of hys dylygence to doe my lorde & yoᵘ svyce byfore anye
oder & see gode madame y wyll hartlye desyre my lorde & yoᵘ to cōtynewe
yoᵘ godenes towardeʳ hym wherbye (hitt maie see fortune) he maye recōver
suche landeʳ as his flader hathe putt awai for there ys Evydence gode to
nai[1] hym thertoe Moreouᵉ y hartlye thannke yoᵘ gode remembance in

[1] sci.

sendynge of yoᵘ tokyn myne enbracelett whiche y wer accordlynglye as ye
wrote & shall aslonge as hitt endur yth   Also gode madame y thaunke my
lorde & yoᵘ for gullᵉ, y had x, ther was but xxjᵘ in all   my Cosyn Digorye
bad oder x   Thys yer they wer verye ffewe   & the Ravyn hath destroyd the
harnsews[1] thatt none cude be had, hitt hath destroyd above a dosyn sygys,[2]
& bye noe meanvs the Ravyn cannott bee destroyd asyett   & as touchynge
all oder yoᵘ affayrys, hitt shalbe don & koked vnto to the best of my
dylygence as yf hitt wer myne owne & bettᵣ if y can   & anye plesoᵘ &
sᵉvyce thatt y maye doe tor my seid gode lorde & yoᵘ y shall hartlye & gladlye
doe hytt att all tymes   & y am sorye thatt y am nott att the tyme pᵘreyd
of some gode tokyn to send yoᵘ, butt y trust shortlye y shall wᵗ the gᵘce of
almyghtie god whoe euᵉ pᵉsᵉue my gode lorde & yoᵘ wᵗ all yoᵘrz to hys pleasoᵘ
W'ten wᵗ lytill leysoⁿ the morowe aftᵉ Midsomᵉ daye wᵗ the rude hand of me

yoᵘ owne

THOMAS SEYNTAUBYN

yft y maye doe yoᵘ sᵉvauntt Robt Harrys anye gode pleasoᵘ y wyll, for in hys
beinge in Cornwall he was ryght glad to doe asmyche pleasoᵘ to my wyffe & me
as he cude & glad to see & to com to Clewyns att all tymes, & hitt was a gode
syght to see hym & Trevuna togeder & y was right glad when y myght see
them bothe to geder   & gode pᵘise to my gode lorde & yoᵘ, for they bee ij
tall psons, honestlye & clene apoyntyd, & of gode demenoᵘ, & well manered,
wᵗ oder gode qᵘlyties   y see noe suche lyke them yn all thynge yn the west
pties of Cornwall   My bedfelowe hath send yoᵘ ladyshippe half an angell bye
Harrys & Trevuna

[Addressed]   To the rygh' honarabyll & my syngler gode ladye my ladye lysle
delyuᵉ thys,

LISLE PAPERS
(Vol 13, p 97)
Thomas St Aubin to Lady Lisle
[Extracts].

Mye syngler & especyall gode ladye   Carnkye & elswher ben in
gode q'ette & peas, & thoughe yoᵘ casualties & pfytte ther is nott this yer soe
gode as hitt hath ben the yer past, yett notwᵗstondynge ther is nowe (thankᵉ
to almyghtie god) a gode lykelyhod thatt hitt shalbee better this yere
cōmynge   & gode Madame y thaunke yoᵘ tor my fice & y haue as y truste
don the best of my dylygence abowtte yoᵘ Coᵘtys[4] whiche accordynglye as ye
comaundyd hath ben holdyn in all placᵉ   & as touchynge yoᵘ demaunde in
Sowlemoᵘe & elswher Richarde Harrᵉ hath putt hytt in vieᵈ as he can
enforme yoᵘ Hoebehytt Mᵗᵉ Bassett euᵉ allowyd hym therof & of other pcellᵉ
as appeyth by a byll of his owne hand, & for asmyche hitt appeyth in noe
bookᵉ of accompte byfore my tyme noe allowance therof y haue chargyd
hym therwyth as hee hathe ben in yerᵉ byfore, & wylnott allowe hym the
same wᵗowtt yoᵘ ladyshippe geve me in cōmaundementt soe to doe   & as
touchynge the washis y haue ben theratt att all tymes bothe erlye & late flaue
& ffulee to see thatt ye sholde lose noe thynge of yoᵘ pfytt   my wyffe
& y hartlye thaunke yoᵘ for the yeit of the certyne nōb of Conyes thatt ye
gaue vs att Tyhydye whiche dothe me myche pleasoᵘ for myne owne Conyes
att Clewyn bee dekayed   my mynde is to send my lorde & yoᵘ a dyshe of
Puffyns ayenst lent & y maue knowe howe & wher to send hytt   & y wyll
desyre yoᵘ to bee soe gode ladye to Jamys Tyhidye as to geve hym a newe
cote for his olde cote is threde bare   he hath made a flaire newe hall & oder
newe howsyn att hellowe   ffrom Clewyns on halwyn Eve .   .   .

[1] Herons   [2] Cygnets.   [3] Courts.   [4] Use

LISLE PAPERS
(Vol 13, p 98)
Thomas St. Aubin to Lady Lisle

As hartlye as maie bee w^t pen e\p^{e}sse mv dewptie don' y humblye recõmend me to yo^u & soe dothe yo^u gentyll suster my lovinge bedfelowe & y wolde wee myght bee hartlye recõmendyd to my gode lorde yo^u bedfelowe wyth moste lowlye thaunk$\int$ for yo^u gode manyfolde kyndenes & for yo^u venyson a tegge^1 whiche John Davie & pytt$\int$ sentt me from yo^u park att Vmbleye ayenst sentt Crewen is fieste hitt dyd me gode pleso^u also my seid bedfelowe thaunkyth you hartlye for her beed$\int$ hitt is ffaire & godelye & none syche in all Cornwall thatt y knowe Also gode Madame y haue recevyd yo^u lett^e & Cõmission & y shall endever my selff w^t all dilligence to doe in all thing$\int$ coprised in the same accordynglye to yo^u cõmaundementt as y wolde to my selft my bedfelowe & y haue send to my seid gode lorde & yo^u a dosyn of Puftyns whiche Boswarthogga or John Keagwyn of Mount$\int$ baye shall delyu^e yo^u if hitt maie doe yo^u anye pleaso^u y wolde ben glad as owre lorde know^t whoe eu^e p^{e}s^{e}ue yo^u Amen W^{i}ten on Sentt Blasye is daie w^t very lytill leyso^u w^t the rude hand of me yo^u olde kanaffe ^{2}

THOMAS SEYNTAUBYN

[Addressed] To the right honorabyll & his syngler gode ladye my ladye lysle bee this delyu^{e}ed.

LISLE PAPERS
(Vol 13, p 100)
Thomas St Aubin to Lady Lisle
[Extracts].

my very good brood^e & sust^e

My dewptie don [&c] Cõs^{e}nynge the Berton place of Tyhydye ther is none wyllynge to take hytt att v\t^i to my knowlyche as Richard Harr$\int$ they berer can showe yo^u & homyche maie bee had ffor hytt, & whatt ease the heggys & the owtt howsys lyeth in decaye Also for the hegges thatt harry Nanse made hitt is nowe abrode lyke the ffeders of a goose newe pollyd w^t a hungrye ffoxe thes seid berer hath don the vtt^{e}most of yo^u cõmaundementt theryn for the stuffe therof wyll never s^{e}ue for a suche ap^{e}pose agayne & Gode Madame wher ye suppose to haue had yerelye a loste of yo^u Rentt in ffee Marshall ro the value of iij^s vj^d or therabowtt ye haue noe suche lost nor decaie in noe suche thynge^3 oderwyse then hath ben byfore my tyme in M^te Bassett is dues alwaies allowyd as appeyrth by olde p^{e}sydens byfore my tyme & syth ye send me therof y haue syght of suche olde p^{e}sydence thatt p\yth hitt muste bee allowid orels vo^u bavllye ther shulde bee doobyll chargyd

ffurder as cõcernynge of water turnyd from anye of yo^u myllys thes seid berer shall certyfie vo^u the effett therof y had spokyn w^t my Cosyn Iohn Gotholghan therin byfore y had yo^u letter wherbye y suppose hitt was reportyd to yo^u gode ladishippe hitt to haue ben a very grevous offence

As touchynge yo^u right in anye tynworke w^{t}in the samtuarie groũde the custume of stanarie gevyth yo^u nomore then anye man will geve for the seid custume gevyth libertie to anye tynn^e to wurke in all waste grounde w^{t}owtte lycence aswell in the waste of anye santuarie as elswher but wheder hitt bee lafull to anye mcũbentt to lycence anye tynn^e to wurke w^{t}in his closys w^{t}owtte the assentt of his patron or noe y refer thatt pointt to yo^u lernyd councell in bothe lawes

---

^{1} Young deer
^{2} *Sic*
^{3} ldkkvnz ij^d ob of the ordynary Rentt more som tyme iij^s v^s & viij^s to dyscharre Iоаnis therefoore

& heiuppon the settynge of anye man for yo" is forborn tyll my seid lorde ffunder pleso" & yo"z bee knowyn therin   tymnes att Sanit Vnye Sinctuaiye wurkyth nowe aswell w"in 'close as w'out the wunkers w'owtte winkyth by the Custume & w"yn by licence of the pson & els they cowde nott thei winke   Also gode Madame all the workes in Cainkye & Cainbiee ben all in gode pease   y haue don my dylygence abowtte in yo" co"tte & att yo" awdytt & in stede of a better place hitt was keptt att Clewens   & as hitt bee my seid lorde pleso. & yo"z to send me for my ffee y shall bee right well cotenttyd therw' ' & gevynge lowlye thannke for the same & aswell for my seid lorde goodenes & yo"z towarde yo" Chappleyn s" Dnewe for my seid bedfelows sake & myne & y trust he wyll send yo" som ffatt Coingers ayenst lentt for soe he hath pmysed me   Myne owne especiall gode lovynge ladye when ye sett the berton of Tyhydve my gentyll bedfelowe wyll desyie yo" to res"ue som of the Conys thei for her yeilve for all this yet is yett she hath had none   ffrom Clewens   the Sonday byfore Sentt Kat"ines daie

LISLE PAPERS
(Vol 13, p 102)
THOMAS S" AUBIN TO LADY LISLE
[EXTRACTS]

Mve deuptie vnto yo" gode ladishippe   w" moste lovynge thannke for yo" giett iewaide & yfte ye set to yo" nyce my doughters & for yo" Conys Gulle & othei pleso. & for yo" shippe of whete   my Cos"n s" Willim Gotholghan my ladve hys wyffe & the moste paite of all odei Gentylmen & wymen abowtte me w" othei dyn"s substantiall men & manye poure men hath com to haue paite of yo" whete & hath had asmyche as they wolde carye a way & yett noe syne thatt they my had   & wher ye wolde dyn"s tymes my wyffe & y wei itt Calyce (god soe pleasyd) y wolde bee moste ioyfull if hitt soe had ben   my wyffe & y ben right glad of you gode iecoverye & that ye haue yo" helth & thatt also my gode lorde is soe gentyll lovynge & kynde & yo" moste cofoitte att all tymes & moste att yo" vttermost grevance   Wherfor my wyffe & y & also all yo" odei hendy haue cause & ben gietly bounde to p"ie to god for the psvacyon of the cotynewance of my seid god lorde estate & y sperrie for his lovynge kyndenes towarde yo"   . .
W"ten   the laste daye of Ianuarye
Gode Madame y p"ie god to send Trevuna p"ce to doe my gode loide & yo" gode & dilgentt s"uice for he w"tcth to me thatt duiynge his lyffe he is gretlye bounde to p"ie for yo"   yo" olde s"v untt my dought" Phelypp' is deptyd on C"stmas daye almyghtve pdon her soule & my wyffe hath take gnette discofort theibye   but y thannke owie loide she dothe take hitt bett" waye & thannkyth god of his sendynge

Agnes, Sir Thomas' third daughter married John Roscarrock, Commissioner of Subsidies who died 27 October 1537, and was buried at Endelhon

Philipa, the fourth daughter, married first Francis Harris, eldest son of John Harris of Radford, secondly one Stenning and thirdly Humphry Arundell of Newton, co Devon, brother to Sir John Arundell who had married her youngest sister Katherine

¹ Rychard Harrys to pay xxij s^d for his fe.

Honor, the fifth daughter married first Sir John Basset of Umberleigh, Knight, whose first wife had been Ann, daughter of John Denys of Orleigh   The Bassets like the Granvilles, were of Norman extraction, and came over with the Conqueror. They quartered the arms of Plantagenet   The family had long been settled at Tehidy in Cornwall, and had served as sheriffs for that county through many successive reigns   Honor's husband was the first to settle at Umberleigh.   They had three sons and six daughters   Of the latter Katherine (born about 1518) married Sir Henry Ashley of Ashley and Wimborne, an ancestor of the Shaftesbury family.   The eldest son, John was the ancestor of the Devonshire branch of the Basset family, which became extinct in 1796, whilst the Cornish branch was continued by George, the second son, who married Jaquet daughter of John Coffin of Portledge.   The third son, James, was a Privy Councillor to Queen Mary   Sir John Basset died the 31st of January 1529, and his widow afterwards married Arthur Plantaganet Lord Lisle, illegitimate son of Edward IV by Elizabeth Lucy   Whether Elizabeth Lucy was a member of the Charlecote family is not known, but there is no doubt that there was a real marriage contract between her and Edward IV, for more than one chronicler records the anger of Edward's mother, Cicely Duchess of York, when she came to know of his marriage with Elizabeth Woodville, and her passionate upbraidings of him with his cruel falsehood to his troth-plighted wife, Elizabeth Lucy   (Harl MSS 2408 fol 102 Stricklands Queens ii 328)   Her child was born about 1469.   He became a member of Lincoln's Inn February 4th 1487 and was one of the Gentlemen "Spears of Honour" 1513-1514.   Whilst serving as a Captain of a ship of war he was knighted by Henry VIII, October 14 1513, and the following year was appointed Captain to the Vice-Admiral of England   According to Holinshed (in 1532) he was made Constable of Dover Castle and Warden of the Cinque Ports   He was created Viscount Lisle April 25, 1523, and K.G. the following year.   In 1525 he was made Vice-Admiral of all England, and was sent, October 22 1528, as Ambassador Extraordinary (with the Garter) to Paris   At the Dissolution of Monasteries the estate of Frithelstock Priory near Torrington was granted him by Henry VII   On the death of Lord Bernes Lord Lisle was appointed (24 March 1533) as Lord Deputy of the town and marches of Calais, having his wife's nephew, Sir Richard Grenvile, under him as Marshall. The post, however, was a difficult one to fill, his hands being completely tied by the Council, and his administration gave

little satisfaction to the King   Lord Lisle was suspected more
over of favouring the Gospellers who had taken refuge at
Calais and of sheltering them from the persecution which overtook them there   He was especially accused of shielding the
Reverend George Buckler, alias Adam Damplip, whose mar-
tyrdom is recorded in Foxe's Book of Martyrs   According to
Foxe, Lady Honor was of an opposite way of thinking to her
husband, and though devotedly attached to him she secretly
worked against the Gospellers in the hope of screening him from
the royal displeasure   "The Lord Lisly" writes the martyr-
ologist "albeit hee were himselfe of a most gentle nature
beeing fiercelie set on, and incessantlie intised by the wicked
Lady Honor his wife, who was an utter enemie to God's
honour, and in Idolatrie, hypocrisie and pride incomparably
evill, shee beeing dailie and homelie thereunto incited and
prouoked by Sir Thomas Palmer Knight, and John Rookewood
Esquire, too enemies to God's word, beginning nowe to flourish
at Calice ,—these, I say, with certaine other of the Counsell, to
the number of seuen mo besides themselues, seeking occasion or
rather a quarrel, when ro just cause was giuen, began to write
verie heinous letters and greeuous complaintes unto the Lordes
of the Priuie Counsell," against diuers of the towne of Calice,
affirming that they were horriblie infected with heresies and
pernitious opinions" etc.

On the evening of March 3rd 1542 Mr. Secretary Wrio-
thesley was sent to the Tower with the King's signet ring and
a message of hope and pardon   The message did in a few
hours—perhaps in a few moments—what twenty-two months of
solitary agony had failed to do   It killed the prisoner.   He
died at the sudden rapture in the seventy-seventh year of his
age   "Thirty years before that day among the standards borne
in the field by peers and knights had floated that of Sir Arthur
Plantagenet.   The standard was probably granted by the
Crown—semi-royal, lion rampant, fetter lock, and falcon · the

aims of France, England, Ulster and March, debruised by that
baton sinister, which never ought to have touched that shield.
But the device certainly was chosen by the bearer and it was
characteristic of its chooser, "Dieu la volu" Ambition he had
none, had he had it, assuredly he would have been King of
England There were more occasions than one on which that
banner would readily have been made to float above the boar of
Gloucester, and even the dragon of Tudor But no advantage
of these was ever taken Hopes, rights, claims and opportunities alike were buried in the sepulchre over which that
motto was the epitaph, " Dieu l'a voulu."

Lady Honor, who was released with her daughters at the
same time as the pardon reached her husband, lingered on for
some years a broken-hearted and self-accusing widow at the
dower house of Crowe in Cornwall, in very reduced circumstances. There can be but little doubt that she meant well
and loved her husband dearly and thought she was saving him.
She did evil that good might come, and the evil came after all.
A most interesting book respecting the Lisles, entitled " Isoult
Barry of Wynscote," has been written by Mrs Holt from the
Lisle Papers and other unpublished MSS in the British Museum
and State Paper Office.

Katherine, the sixth and youngest daughter of Sir Thomas
Granville, married Sir John Arundell of Lanherne A settlement
was made after marriage bearing date 22 Henry VII (1507).
By a deed dated 8 Feb, 24 Henry VII (1509), Sir John Arundell settled Connerton and other manors on her in lieu of dowry
A third settlement bears date 26 January, 14 Henry VIII ; a
fourth 6 May, 16 Henry VIII., and a fifth 19 October 28 Henry
VIII. Sir John Arundell died at Roscarroc, 8 February, 36
Henry VIII., 1545-6, and was buried at St Columb, where he
is represented on a tomb standing between his two wives (his
first wife was Elizabeth, daughter of Thomas Grey, K G,
Marquis of Dorset, by Cicely Bonville, only daughter and heiress
of William Bonville, by Elizabeth, sister of Richard Neville,
Earl of Warwick, the "King Maker") On the monument are
six shields of armorial bearing, and a broken legend carried
round the edge, of which the following only is still legible :—
' John Arundell, Knight of the Bath, and . . . Greenfelde
Knight, dyed the 8 of February the 36 year of the raigne of
King Henry the Eyght Anno Domini 1546 and the . .
yere of his age" They had issue both sons and daughters, of
the latter, Mary, whose fame is enshrined in the pages of
Ballard's ' Celebrated British Ladies,' was married first to

Thomas Ratcliffe, Earl of Sussex, and secondly to Henry Howard, Earl of Arundell.

Sir Thomas Granville, or (as Dr Oliver, the old Exeter antiquarian called him), "the Venerable Knight,' ventured on second marriage with Jane, daughter of . . Jous and widow of . . . Hills of Taunton, by whom he had issue another son and daughter, viz, John, in holy orders, whom Dr Oliver, Eccl Ant m 41, wrongly states was Rector of Bideford, confusing him with his uncle, whereas he was Rector of Kilkhampton and St Mary Week He died in 1580, and was buried in Kilkhampton Church, his will being proved 7th May, two days after his funeral The daughter, Jane, was married three times The order of her marriage differs in various accounts, but as she was unmarried at the time of her father's will of March 1514, and one of her husbands, Wymond Raleigh, was certainly dead 14th July, 1515, he must clearly have been her first husband. He was the son of Walter Raleigh, of Fardell, and Elizabeth his wife, daughter of Sir Richard Edgecumbe, of Cotehele, and grandfather of the celebrated Sir Walter Raleigh In one of the panels of the pew ends in East Budleigh Church (the first pew at the eastern end of the nave on the north side), there is a shield emblazoned with the Raleigh arms impaling those of the Granville family, viz, Raleigh, Gules five fusils in bend, argent Granville, Gules three clarions or rests, or The Granvilles were known to be related to that of the Raleighs, inasmuch as the great Sir Richard Granville alludes to the great Sir Walter Raleigh as his cousin, e q. "1585 October 29th Sir Richard Greynvill to Sir Francis Walsingham, acquaints him with the success of his voyage . . . The commodities of the country (Virginia), are such as *his cousin* Raleigh advertised of" ("Calendar of State Papers." Domestic Series, 1581-90, p 281)

Jane, having been a wife probably for less than a year, married secondly Humfry Batten, of Dunsland, co Devon, by whom she had a daughter, called after herself And thirdly she is said to have married John Tregagle, of Trevorden, in St. Breock foster-brother to the first Earl of Radnor and his chief steward

Sir Thomas died in 1513, and was buried at Bideford, where a handsome monument (the only one, curiously, in this church to any of the family) was erected The monument is on the south side of the chancel, near the altar. It consists of a free stone table upon which lies the figure of Sir Thomas arrayed in the armour of the time The pauldrons and coudieres

THE TOMB OF SIR THOMAS GRANVILLE IN BIDEFORD CHURCH

are ornamented and the brassarts and vambraces puffed or
ribbed. Taces to which are appended deep lambeaux of over-
lapping plate, a large apron of chain mail, and broad-toed
sabbatons complete his costume, and he is armed with sword
and misericorde. On his breast hangs a double chain. The
head of the effigy is (in accordance with a practice adopted
towards the close of the XV Century with armed figures) bare,
but rests on a tilting helmet, out of which is issuant a small
shield charged with the Granville arms In his hand he holds
his heart, an occurence also frequent with mediæval figures
At his feet is a dog or rather two half-dogs, conjoined so cleverly
that to a casual observer, standing on either side of the monument, there appears only one dog, the two heads being so
carved as to serve equally well for hind-quarters Over the
figure is an arch with screen work, the top of which is
mutilated, and around the arch is the following Latin inscription
in black letter characters :—

> Hic jacet Thomas Graynfyld miles patron isti
> ecclē q obiit xviii die mēsis marcii a d
> MCCCCCXIII cuj aīe fficiet dē Amen

Below the effigy on the tomb, on either side, are shields
displaying the arms of Sir Thomas, as well as his impalement of
Gilbert (on a chevron three roses sculptured in relief) and two
canopied niches for the figures of Saints which are missing

His will, dated 9th March, 1512, was proved P.C.C. 12th
May. It is as follows —

" In the name of God Amen I, Sir Thomas Graynfeld, Knyght, in my
hoole mynde, make my Testament in Maner and Forme followinge First, I
bequeth my soule to Almightie God, and to our blessed Ladie, and to all the
hoole saints in Hevyn My Bodie to be buryed in the Church eithe of Bedyforde, in the south est Part of the Chauncell Dore, where my mynde is y I
lyve to make an Altaric, and a Preste to sing there to pray for mee and myn
auncestors and henes for ever The said Preste and poerc men to bee put in by
discrecion of myn heires and executors Further, I will that my saide Chappell,
whennsoever it bee made, and the Church of Bedyforde in meane season have
my Cope of Tissue and my Vestiment of the same, and a suet of blacke velvett,
to bee made of such velvett gownys as I have, by the discrecion of myn heires
and executors Also, I will that John Greynfelde, yf he bee disposed to be a
Preste, to have the next avoydance of one of the benefices of Bedyforde or of
Kikehamton And yf he will be no Preste, that then my sonne Roger Grayn-
felde and his heires see him have sum resonable living of landes by thence
discreccions Item, I will that my sonne Roger shall marry my daughter Onor,
and I give her in marriage cec markes in money, to bee levyed of my landes
and goodis Item, I will that my daughter Jane, which I had by my last wyff,
to have cec markes in lyke manner to bee leveyed of my goodis and landes
Provided allway that yf the said Onor and Jane fortune to dye or ever they be

marryed, that thenne they to have nothing of the said money   But thenne the saide money whenne it is so levyed to bee disposed for my soule by the discrecion of my sonne Roger   Item, I give to the Church of Bedyforde, and to the Brige of Bydisforde, vi lbs vm s 4d   Item, to the Church of Kikehamton, im lbs

Roger, sonne, I woll desyr you, as my trust in you, to see this my Will performed and fullfilled, and yow I make myn executor "

CHAPTER V.

SIR ROGER GRANVILLE resided chiefly at Stowe, and for his princely liberality was called "The Great Housekeeper." He was thirty-six and more at the time of his father's death, and two years previously had been chosen High Sheriff of Cornwall, an office which he again filled eight years afterwards. In 8th Henry VIII, William Dovell, Abbot of St. Clive, co. Somerset, with the consent of his convent, granted him his heirs and assigns, all their wood and trees growing in Merewood. In 9th Henry VIII. he conveyed to Richard Gilbert, clerk, his cousin, (whom he had presented to the Rectory of Bideford, 3rd April, 1514) his whole manor and borough of Kilkhampton to the use of his last Will. To this deed a round seal is attached, which is somewhat peculiar, since the shield is charged with but one clarion or rest upon it, instead of the three which had been hitherto borne by his ancestors, and which were continued by his successors. Over the arms is the usual helmet, which is surmounted by a griffin's head couped between two wings The seal is circumscribed " SIGILL ROGERI GRAYNFILD AMIGERI."

In 13th Henry VIII, Roger Graynfild and Richard, son and heir of the said Roger, and of Margaret his wife, one of the daughters and heirs of Richard Whitleigh, deceased, grant to Peter Seyntabyn (St Aubyn) the moiety of the manor of Cleghar to the use of Christiana, daughter of the said Roger, in order to a marriage between her and James, son of the said Seyntabyn This marriage, however, probably never took place, as the said Christiana was married to James Ensey.

Sir Roger, as above stated, married Margaret, daughter and co-heiress of Richard Whitleigh, of Efford in Egg Buckland, heir general of Wendon, Waynard and Respryn, by whom he had issue three sons, viz, Richard his heir and successor (of whom presently). John, his second son, of Exeter, and Digory. John, who after taking his B.A degree at Oxford in 1528 and his M.A in 1532, became one of those buccaneers of the day, whose fleets, recruited largely from the harbours of Devon and Cornwall, twenty and thirty sail together, haunted the mouth of the Channel, and

with the connivance of the Government pillaged alike Spanish
gold ships from Panama, French wine ships from Bordeaux, the
rich traders from Antwerp and from their own Thames with
great impartiality, returning if pressed among the dangerous
shoals of Scilly or the distant creeks and coves of the south
coast of Ireland. In 1548 the quarrel with France had extended.
Villegaignon's galleys, after landing Mary Stuart at Brest, had
roamed about the Channel, preying upon English merchant
ships, and, while peace still continued in name, the French
Court professed an insolent confidence that the Protector durst
not resent their violation of it He shrunk, it was true, from
declaring war, but England as well as France could play at the
game of marauding hostility. Convoys of provisions were
passing continually between Brest and Leith, and a French
fishing fleet from Iceland and Newfoundland was looked for in
the fall of the year The Adventurers of the West " were
informed that the channel was very much troubled with pirates
and that they would serve their country by clearing the seas of
them Private hints were added that they might construe their
instructions liberally, but whatever French prizes were brought
in, should be kept for a time undisposed of. till it was ascertained
whether the court of Paris would redress the harms done on
their side. In a letter dated 9 August. 1548, from Lord Seymour
of Sudlye, High Admiral of England, to Sir Peter Carew, Sir
Thomas Denys, and Sir Richard Grenfelde for Devonshire, and
John Grenfelde, Sir Hugh Trevanyon, and Sir William Godolphin
for Cornwall, authority is given to them to commission privateers
to take French ships and goods ; and on the 7th of September
following, John Graynfyld reports from Fowey that he himself
had been on a cruise, and had waylaid, taken, sunk or driven on
shore an indefinite number of French trading vessels; that he
had brought the prizes into Fowey and Plymouth, that he had
obtained information of three hundred sail going to Bordeaux
for wine for the army in Scotland, and " the western men," he
added, " were so expert in their business, that he did not doubt
they would give a good account of the whole of them "

John Graynfyld was Governour of Scilly from 1553 to 1558,
and in the British Museum Additional MSS (25.300) is an
account of the sums raised and disbursed by him for the support
of the garrison there, and amongst the Rawlinson MSS in the
Bodleian Library are two commissions from Queen Elizabeth to
' John Byll, Steward of Cornwall, John Hornyolde, Auditor of
the Exchequer Leonard Loveyour, Receiver-general of Cornwall,
John Grenefyld Esquire and Roger Prydeux " to enquire into

the rents due to the Crown in Cornwall, to survey the castles, peels, manors, etc, also the sites of dissolved monasteries, colleges, etc The commissions bear date 28 June 1561 and 6 April 1562

"John Graynfyld" is named in the Inquisition taken on the death of his father, and also in the Will and Inquisition taken on the death of his brother, Sir Richard, 1550. He died in 1580, and was buried at Kilkhampton He married Lettice, daughter of Thomas Lucas, by whom he had issue two sons, Giles and Gentle, and three daughters, viz, Lettice, named in the will of her brother-in-law, John Buller, Alice, who married Richard Cole of Buckland, second son of Thomas Cole of Slade, and brother to Thomazine Cole who married her cousin Roger Granville, the father of the famous Admiral, Sir Richard Granville, of the "Revenge,' of Visitations of Cornwall 1573, and Anne, who married the above-named John Buller of Exeter, and is mentioned in his will "Jentile Grenfield," the second son, appears as a scholar of Broadgate Hall, Oxford, 21st November 1549

Digery Granville, Sir Roger's third, or as some pedigrees place him, second son, was twice married, his first wife being Philippa, the daughter and heiress of Gough, by whom he had five sons, viz, Richard, Nicholas, Humphry, Roger, and John. By his second wife, Mary, the daughter of Nicholas Cavell and widow of John Reskarrick, he had four more sons, Arthur, Digory, Thomas, and George, and four daughters, Lettice, Honor, Barbara, and Margaret.

By his two marriages, therefore, Digory had nine sons and four daughters, and it is not easy to assign the various descendants their proper places in the family tree. The marriages of four of the nine sons are known, and doubtless many of the Granvilles, Grenfells, Greenfields, and other unattached members, that are scattered throughout England at the present day, may claim descent from some of the numerous offspring of Digory

Richard, his eldest son by his first marriage married Florence, the daughter and co-heiress of John Kelleway of Cullompton, by his wife Joan Tregarthian,[1] and had issue two

---

[1] In Branscombe Church there is a monument to her memory, on which are the small kneeling effigies of herself between her two husbands, John Kelleway and John Wadham, and behind the husbands are the twenty children she bore them, fourteen by her first and six by her second The inscription, now obliterated, is thus given in Prince —

"Here lieth intombed the body of a virtuous and ancient gentlewoman descended of the antient house of the Plantaginets, sometime of Cornwall, namely Joan one of the daighters and heirs unto John Tregarthin in the County of Cornwall Esq She was first married unto John Kelleway Esq, who had by her much issue After his death she was to and t J l u

L

sons, viz George of Penheale, who was Sheriff of Cornwall in 1583-4, and took an active part with his cousin Sir Richard Granville in raising musters for Cornwall, and William, who died without issue There were also three daughters, Mary, Jane and Martha.

George, the eldest son, died 2 September, 1595, having married Julyan, daughter and co-heiress of William Viell, by whom he left three sons, Digory of Penheale, who married Mary Tregarthian , George, who received the honour of Knighthood at Whitehall 23 July 1603, before the coronation of James I , and married Marie, daughter of John Kilhgrew of Arwanick by whom he left an only daughter The following verses on the death of Queen Elizabeth, by " Geo Grenvyll, Cornubiensis Armig " are found in a volume entitled " Oxoniensis Academiæ funebre officium in Memoriam Elizabethæ Anglæ Reginæ '—Oxon 1603-4°.

Non fuit imperiis tua laus inclusa duobus
Sed lapis inclusum corpus, Eliza, tegit
Belgia te luget voce et gens anglica versu
Teq Jovis sobolem vox simul una facit
Obsequioq tuo mea muta aptata, querelas
Tristis ad exequias fundit, Eliza, tuas

O patri claro filia clarior,
O matre pulchra filia pulchrior,
Quam numen ingens inula continet,
Dum terra mater te, dea contegit

The third son of George Granville of Penheale was Richard of Ponghill, who married Gertrude Incledon in 1616, and had issue a son Chamond and two daughters Chamond married Honor, but the surname is unknown, by whom he had four sons and two daughters The eldest of these sons, Richard (born 1657) married in 1684 Mary daughter of the Reverend Joseph Trewinnard, Rector of Mawgan, by whom he left at his death in 1725 two sons and five daughters

A sister of George and Richard Granville, name Ibbot, married 2 April 1612, at Menhemon, Francis Rouse fourth son of Sir Antony Rouse, Knight, of Buxham He was M P. for Truro 1643, Speaker of Barebones Parliament and Provost of Eton where he died 7 January 1658, and was interred in the College Chapel

Nothing is known of Nicholas, the second son of Digory

Wadham of Merybeld in the County of Somerset Esq , & by him had (six) children She lived a virtuous and godly life, and died in an honourable age Sep , in the year of Christ 1581 "

Granville. He is named in the will of his uncle, Sir Richard, and he appears as executor of his brother Roger's will.

Humphry the third son, married Thomazine, the daughter of Richard Michell, of Shebbeare

The will of Roger, the fourth son, bearing date 15 June, 1576, was proved 13 April. 1579 PCC

John, the fifth son, died young

Arthur, the eldest son by the second marriage, is named in his half-brother Roger's will. He was buried at St Tudy in 1613

Digory, the second son, proved Roger's will, the executors first renouncing He married Philippa, daughter of Hugh Prust, and widow of William Leigh, by whom he had a daughter Susan, married to Peter Porter, second son of Walter Porter, of Lancells, by his wife Gertrude, daughter of Richard Chamond

Thomas Granville, of Aldercombe near Stowe, the third son, was buried at Kilkhampton 10 July, 1625 He married at Bideford 28 March 1586, Catherine, daughter of Thomas Spurre, of Trebathe, and widow of one Brownynge, by whom he had issue an only son, Bernard, who died in infancy, 1588, and two daughters, Elizabeth married (21 November, 1615) to James Carey, of Alwington near Bideford, and Bridget married (20 August, 1610), to William Prust, of St Stephen, Launceston

George, the remaining son, is also named in his half-brother Roger's will He married Margery, daughter and co-heiress of Richard Trengrove, of Nance, in Illogan

The names of Digory's four daughters, as above stated, were Lettice, Honor, Barbara, and Margaret Barbara married John Luppingcott, of Webbery, in the parish of Alverdiscott, near Bideford.

Besides these three sons, Sir Roger Granville had six daughters

Agnes, married to John Fitz, of Fitzford, near Tavistock. The first of this family was John Fitz, who, as Dugdale says, "was an eminent lawyer about the year 1428, and had great practice, whereby he acquired a considerable fortune. He settled near Tavistock, at a place called Ford, unto which he gave his additional name, from thence called Fitz Ford unto this day. He left issue Walter, who by Mary his wife, daughter of Sampson, had issue John, who by Agnes his wife, daughter of Sir Roger Graynfild of Stowe had issue John and others."

Jane, the second daughter, was married to Edmund Speccot, Esq., of Speccot, in the parish of Merton, co Devon, the son of Nicholas Speccot

Philippa, the third daughter, married Thomas Tremayne, of Collacombe, near Tavistock   Lysons says 'The most remarkable monument of the Tremayne family, of Collacombe, in the parish of Lamerton, in that church, is that of Thomas Tremayne, Esq, and his wife, Philippa, daughter of Sir Roger Grenville, of Stowe, and their sixteen children, eight sons and eight daughters, with the effigies of five of their sons" Westcote quaintly writes as follows of this union, " Philippa was to him as the Psalmist saith —

> Like the fruitful vine on the house side
> So doth thy wife spring out,
> Thy children stand like olive plants
> Thy table round about

For by her he was the father of eight sons and six daughters, most of which I will silently pass, yea! the fourth which was Richard, only with this remembrance, that he was a doctor of divinity, canon resident and treasurer of the Cathedral Church of St. Peter in Exeter   a very learned and zealous, divine and diligent preacher   The sixth and seventh brothers, Nicholas and Andrew, born at one birth, were so like in all lineaments of body, that I may not forbear in regard it came almost to the height of a wonder to declare unto you, so equal in stature, so coloured in hair   so resembling each the other in face, with such similitude in gesture and sound of words in speech, as they could not be distinguished or known one from the other, no, not by their parents, brothers, or sisters but privately by some secret hidden marks, and outwardly, by wearing some several coloured ribband, or such like thing, which they would also on merriment often change to make trial of their friends' judgment. There was yet somewhat more strange, their minds and affections were but one and the self-same   what the one loved, the other desired, and so on the contrary, what the one loathed, the other hated   yea ' such a combination of the unbred powers in operation of their qualities and sympathy in nature was in them, that if Nicholas were sick or grieved, Andrew felt the like pain and grief   yea ! though they were distant and far removed one from the other, and without any intelligence given   Also it was observed that if Andrew were merry or pleasantly disposed, Nicholas was likewise so affected, though far away separated, which long they could not endure to be, for they still desired to eat, drink, sleep, and wake together ; yea ! so they lived, and so they died for in the year 1564, serving both at Newhaven, the one of them having the leading of a troop of horse was slain ; which the other seeing, stepped instantly into his place and extremity of the danger, notwithstanding would by no persuasions remove, but was there also slain Therefore, of these two gentlemen may truly be said what was but feigned by the poets of Hypocrates, ' Twins, that they were born, eat, slept, and died together ' " This ancient family of Tremayne takes its original upon record from Perys, Lord of Tremain, in Cornwall, whose great grandson, Thomas, married Isabel, daughter and heir of Trenchard, of Collacombe, by which means the family came into Devonshire, " where it has flourished (says Prince) upwards of 300 years "

May, the fourth daughter, was married to John Beauchamp The first mention we find of this family is that John Beauchamp served in Parliament for Launceston in 1328 In the inscription on her monument in Marham Church, in the Hundred of Stratton, which bears the arms of Beauchamp and Granville impaled, it is stated that she died in 1581. The last representative of the Beauchamps died in London, unmarried, in 1817.

Christiana, the fifth daughter, was married to John Ensey, of Ensey, in the parish of Ruan Major, in the Hundred of Kerrier, co. Cornwall The name has been extinct for very many years, but there are several monuments of different members of the family still remaining in the Church.

Amy, the sixth and youngest daughter, was married to John Drake, of Ash, in the parish of Musbury, near Axminster, and died 18th February, 1577, leaving issue Sir Bernard Drake. In the Drake aisle on the south side of the nave in Musbury Church there is a fine series of three pairs of kneeling effigies, the knights in complete armour with gold chains and ruffs, the ladies in black gowns, ruffs, caps, and chains The first pair represent John and Amy, the second Sir Bernard and his lady, and third John, son of Sir Bernard, and his wife. Under the first pair is this inscription —

Here lyeth the body of John Drake of Ashe Esq , and Amy his wife daughter of Sir Roger Graynfield Knight, by whom he had issue six sons, viz , Barnard, Robert & Richard whereof three lived at his death He died 4 Oct 1558 She died 18 Feb 1557

Sir Roger's name is found in connection with an interesting matter of business relating to the Long Bridge of Bideford, the building of which has been already recorded. When that

structure had attained completion, the Image of the Blessed
Virgin Mary was raised at its eastern extremity, holding the
Holy Child in her arms   A Chapel was at the same time
erected on the opposite side of the way, and here from time to
time the charitable were accustomed to present alms, oblations,
and offerings and to bequeath donations for the benefit of the
funds of the Bridge.   "In process of time the amount of these
pious offerings were so considerable as to excite the cupidity of
the then Rector of the parish, the Rev Richard Gilbert   In
the year 1522 differences arose between him and Roger
Graynefelde and the bridgewarden and parishioners respecting
these emoluments   The Rector laid claim to them as belonging
to the chapel, which formed part and parcel of his rectory,
whilst the patron, with the townspeople at his back, insisted
that the votive offerings, being gifts for the maintenance of the
Bridge could not without injustice be applied to any other
purpose   The dispute waxed warm, and was ultimately referred
to the decision of the then recently appointed Diocesan, Bishop
Vevsey, who, after considerable hesitation, with much solemnity,
made and declared his award at the Palace in Exeter, on the
26th of March, 1523 (nostræ consecrationis anno quarto).

‛ The chances are that the Rector got the best of the
contest for in some of the earliest of the old Bridge leases, the
Chapel was let out as a private residence which would scarcely
have been permitted had the golden harvest continued   In
those same leases the spot where the image stood is described
as the Toll House, over which was placed a bell, and the
opposite side of the way is designated ‘ the chapel ’   Both these
remnants of a superstitious age have proved less enduring than
the parchments recording them "—" Memoirs of the Grenvilles
of Stowe," by a Bidefordian

Alas ! since this was written, all the old deeds and papers
relating to the Bridge, town, and church of Bideford have also
perished, having been destroyed some years ago

Sir Roger received the honour of Knighthood only the year
before his death, which event took place at Stowe, 7th July,
1524, and he was succeeded in the family honours and estates by
his eldest son, Richard.

Richard was M P for Cornwall, 21st Henry VIII , Sheriff
of Devon, 24th Henry VIII ; and of Cornwall, 35th Henry
VIII   He had the honour of Knighthood conferred on
him 23rd Henry VIII , as appears from an original deed of
his, dated 20th December in that year, which is sealed with the
single rest used by his father, but quartered with another coat

—a bend charged with three roundles—probably the arms of his mother's family, the Whitleighs

When Henry VIII, in order to acquire popularity with his subjects drifted into wars with Continental nations, Sir Richard accompanied him abroad, and was appointed Marshal of Calais under his uncle, Lord Lisle. According to Pole "he served under th' Erle of Hartford before Hamble Tewe with two hundred soldiers, and at Bolleyne (Boulogne), anno 38 of King Henry VIII" He is described as a man of active and energetic spirit, and devoted to martial pomp, qualifications which ingratiated him with the King. As Carew writes in his "Survey of Cornwall," (pp 111 112), "he was a man who enterlaced his home magistracy with martial employments abroad, whereof King Henry testified his good liking by his great liberality"

Mr Tregellas, in his "Cornish Worthies," (vol II, pp 11, 12), has inserted two poems, written by Sir Richard, which he found amongst the 'Additional MSS" in the British Museum. They are apparently in Sir Richard's own handwriting, and are very indistinct in places. Their queer versification and grammar and odd orthography make them very interesting

"In Praise of Seafaring Men in Hopes of Good Fortune"

Whoe seekes the waie to win Renowne,
  Or flies with wringes of ye Desarte,
Whoe seekes to wear the Lawrell crowen,
  Or hath the minde that would espire,
Tell him his native soyll eschew,
Tell him go rainge and seke Anewe

Eche hawtie harte is well contente
  With euerie chance that shalbe tyde,
No hap can hinder his entente,
  He steadfast standes though fortune slide
The sun, quoth he, doth shine as well
Abrod as earst where I did dwell

In change of streames each fish can live,
  Each soule content with euerie Ayre,
Eche hawtie hart remaineth still,
  And not be Dround in depe Dispaire,
Wherfor I judg all landes a likes,
To hawtie hartes whom fortune seekes

To pass the seaes som thinkes a toille,
  Som thinkes it strange abrod to rome,
Som thinkes it a griefe to leaue then soylle,
  Their parentes, cynfolke, and then whome,
Think soe who list, I like it nott,
I must abrod to trie my lott

Who list at whome at earte to drudge,
  And carke and care for worldly trashe,
With buckled sheues let him go trudge,
  Instead of launce a whip to slashe,
A mynd that basse his hind will show
Of enrome sweet to feed a crowe

If Jasonn of that mynd had bine
  The Gresions when they came to Troye,
Had neuer so the Trogians foyhte,
  Nor neuer put them to such anoye,
Wherfor who lust to liue at whome,
To purchase fame I will go rome

                    Fixis.—Sir Richard Grinfillde's Farewell "

But Sir Richard felt bound to confess that there is quite
another and quite a different aspect of the question, and
accordingly frames the following set off to his former lines

"Another of Sea Fardingers Discribing Evill Fortunes

What pen can well report the plighte
  Of those that travell on the seaes,
To pas the werie winter's nighte,
  With stormie clouds, wisshinge for daie,
With waues that toss them to and fro,
Then pore estate is hard to show

When boistering windes begins to blowe,
  And cruel costes from hauen woe,
The foggie mysts soe dimes the shore,
  The rockes and saudes we maie not see,
Nor haue no Rome on Seaes to trie,
But praie to God and yeld to Die

When shouldes and sandie bankes Apeare
  What pilot can divert his course,
When foming tides draweth us so nere,
  Alas! what fortenn can be worsse
The Anker's hould must bee our staie,
Or ellse we fall into Decaye

We wander still from Lofte to Lie,
  And findes no steadfast wind to blow,
We still remaine in jeopardie,
  Each perelos poynt is hard to showe,
In time we hope to find Redresse,
That long haue lived in Heauines

O pinchinge, werie, lothsome Lyfie,
  That Travell still in far Exsylle,
The dangers great on Sease be ryfe,
  Whose recompense doth yeld but toylle,
O fortune, graunte me mie Desire,
A happe end I do require

When freates and states have had then fill,
    The gentill calm the cost will clere,
The hawtie hartes shall haue then will,
    That longe hast wept with morning chere
And leaue the seaes with them Anoy,
    At whome at Ease to hue in Ioy,
            Finis "

Sir Richard was an early convert to the doctrines of the Reformers, and he managed soon after the dissolution of the monasteries to purchase Buckland Monachorum, near Tavistock, as well as the Rectorial tithes of Morwenstow Church (the next parish to Kilkhampton), which had formerly belonged to the monastery of Bridgewater

The Abbey of Buckland had been founded by Amicia, the mother of Isabella, wife of William de Fortibus, Earl of Albemarle, in 8th Edward I., for monks of the Cistercian Order At the dissolution of the monasteries George Pollard of London, became the first owner of the Abbey, the lands, church, conventual and domestic buildings, which were then intact, being granted to him the year after the surrender, 14th December, 1539, for a term of twenty-one years at a rent of £23 3s. 5d , all great timbers, as well as all trees and wood in and upon the premises, being or growing, being reserved to the King and his successors

Sir Richard was the next possessor, he procuring a royal lease dated 26th May, 1541 For the sum of £233 3s 4d he obtained the reversion of the site of the monastery, houses, buildings, barns, tenements, meadows, pastures, feedings and also the church belfry and burial ground, and in fact everything within the precincts of the late monastery

It is curious to note that a descendant of the Sir Richard de Granville, who in his devotion, in 1184 had founded and erected the Cistercian Monastery of Neath, became a participator in the spoil of another house of the same order The Granvilles, however, did not long continue the owners of Buckland Abbey In 1580 it was sold, under Royal license, for £3,400 to John Hele and Christopher Harris, who nine months later conveyed the property to Sir Francis Drake in whose family it still remains

Sir Richard improved the family estates by his marriage with Matilda, daughter and co-heir of John Bevill, of Gwarnock, the descendant of another old Norman family which had been settled in Cornwall since the Conquest, and with whom the Granvilles intermarried more than once The will of Peter Bevill (the father of John Bevill) was proved in 1515 In it

M

the names of his two granddaughters occur   ' Item do et lego
Marie Arundell et Matilde Greneffelde. fil . Johannis Bevyll
filii mei cuilibet earum £20 '   He also names   Richard and
Roger Greynfelde '

By this marriage he had issue two sons and three daughters
Apparently both sons died in his lifetime   Roger was
Esquire of the Body to Henry VIII, 1545. and was by
him knighted   He was unfortunately drowned in the   Mary
Rose ' on the 19th July, 1545   The " Mary Rose ' was a frigate
of 600 tons, and one of the finest in the navy and was commanded by Sir John Carew   She sank at Spithead with all on
board from an accident similar to that which happened two
hundred years afterwards at the same place, 28th June, 1782,
to the   Royal George '   Being at anchor in calm weather with
all ports open, a sudden breeze caused the vessel to heel over,
when the water rushed in through the lower ports and sank
her   The King himself was an eyewitness of the accident.
The " Mary Rose " had been engaged for several days previously
fighting the French fleet under command of D Annebault, the
French Admiral, off the Isle of Wight, with great success

Sir Roger thus cut off in the prime and pride of youth, left
by his young wife Thomazine, daughter of Thomas Cole, of
Slade, in the parish of Cornwood, near Ivybridge, an only
surviving son Richard, who was afterwards the celebrated hero
of the Revenge   Two other sons had predeceased him, viz .
Charles and John.   The latter apparently died in infancy, but
Charles had died only a year before the untoward accident to
the " Mary Rose," and had been buried at Buckland Monachorum the 28th of August, 1544   Sir Roger's widow was
afterwards married to Thomas Arundel of Clifton, Cornwall
Her brother, Richard Cole as above stated, had married Alice,
daughter of John Granville, of Exeter, the son of the first Sir
Roger Granville.

John, Sir Richard's other son, was also, it would seem,
knighted, since 'Cecille, son of John Grameville Kt ' was buried
at Buckland Monachorum the 19th of September. 1579   As
John Granville does not appear in his father's will (dated 8
March 1545-6). he too must have died young   It is curious
that there is no reference to Cecille in his grandfather's will
Was he an imbecile ?   The purchase of Church property seems
certainly to have brought nothing but ill-luck to the Granvilles
at this time

Jane, the eldest of Sir Richard's daughters, was married to
Robert Whettal Esq . of Calais   Mary, the second was

married to John Giffard, of Brightley, in the parish of Chittle-
hampton, son of Sir Roger Giffard, Knight, whilst Margaret
the third, was married to Sir Richard Lee, Knight

In April, 1548, William Body, one of the royal commissioners for Cornwall for the suppression of Popery was
stabbed to death by one William Kylter, of St Keverne while
inspecting the church at Helston, and demolishing some images
there   Kylter and his comrades were arrested and tried by
special commission at Launceston on the 28th of May Sir
Richard Granville being chief commissioner, and having been
convicted of high treason, were executed   The affair of Kylter
was but a prelude to a general Cornish insurrection   An
organized spirit of disaffection silently spread, and Sir Humfrey
Arundel of St Michael's Mount and Boyer, Mayor of Bodmin,
headed the insurgents   The rebellion broke out at Whitsuntide of 1549, upon the occasion of the English liturgy being
read in all churches for the first time on that Sunday, and soon
the movement spread throughout Cornwall and part of
Devonshire   Lord Russell was chosen by the Privy Council to
head the resistance, but as he was unable to immediately set
out, Sir Peter and Sir Gawen Carew came into the West with
the resolve to promptly and sternly put down the disturbance
The rebels, who had marched ten thousand strong through
Launceston, now held the Castle, and conveyed to it Sir Richard
Granville, whose capture at Trematon Castle is thus quaintly
told by Carew in his ' Survey of Cornwall,' pp 111, 112

At the last Cornish commotion Sir Richard Greynvile the elder with his
Ladie and followers, put themselves into this castle, and there for a while
indured the Rebels' siege, incamped in three places against it, who wanting
great Ordnance, could haue wrought the besieged small scathe, had his friends,
or enemies, kept faith and promise but some of those within, slipping by
night over the walls, with their bodies after their hearts and those without
mingling humble intreatings with rude menaces, he was hereby wonne, to issue
forth at a posterne gate for parley   The while a part of those rakehels, not
knowing what honestie and faire lesse how much the word of a souldier
imported, stepped betweene him and home, laid hold on his aged unweyldie
body and threatened to leaue it hueless, if the inclosed did not leaue then
resistance   So prosecuting their first treacherie against the prince, with
suteable actions towards his subjects, they seized on the Castle and exercised
the uttermost of their barbarous cruelties (death excepted) on the suprised
prisoners   The seely (i e, harmless) gentlewomen, without regard of sexe
or shame, were stripped from their apparrell to their verie smockes, and some
of their fingers broken, to pluck away their rings, and Sir Richard himself
made an exchange from Trematon Castle to that of Launceston, with the
Gaole to boote   After the battle of Sampford Courtenay the insurgents
fled in dismay   " All night,' said the victor in his despatch to the Council,
" we sate on horseback, and in the morning we had word that Arundell was
fled to Launceston who immediately began to practise with the . . . .

keepers of Grenfield and other gentlemen for the murder of them that night The keepers so much abhorred this cruelty as they immediately set the gentlemen at large and gave them then aid with the help of the town for the apprehension of Arundell, whom with four or five ringleaders they have imprisoned "

But although Sir Richard and his companions escaped being deliberately murdered, both he and his wife died a few months afterwards from the hardships they had endured, and were both interred at Kilkhampton, he on the 23rd of March and she on the 25th of April, 1550-1.

Sir Richard's will bears date 8th March 1545-6, after, *i e*, the unfortunate death of his son, Roger, in the ' Mary Rose,' and it was afterwards published at Stowe on his death, 18th March, 1550-1   It begins as follows —

' Perceiving by faith and creacion my naturall lyf to be transitorie, holie mynding repentance in my most humble maner aske of Almightie God forgivenesse, and also of all the world   And under the protection of God make and declare here my last Will and Testament   First, I bequeathe my soule unto Almightie God, my bodie to be buryed in such holie place, where it shall please Almightie God to provide '

He wills to Dame Maud his wife during the term of seventy years, if she so long live, his mansion and lands called Buckland, otherwise Buckland Graynfild, in as ample manner as he had by letters patent, dated 26th May, 1542   And after her decease he leaves them to Richard Graynfeld, son of Roger Graynfeld, his late son and heir apparent, deceased, and his heirs male. Remainder to Degory Graynfeld, his brother   Remainder to John Graynfeld, his other brother

The other mansions, viz, his mansion house in the town of Bideford, and all the residue of his town and borough of Bideford in com Devon , his mansion place of Stowe, together with all gardens orchards and ponds therewith Stowe Park in com Cornwall ; his house and borough of Kilkhampton and his mansion of Woodford in the same county, together with all his other lands in Devon and Cornwall, he leaves to Richard his grandson and his heirs male

Remainder to his brothers John and Digory and their heirs male

Remainder to his right heirs

He bequeaths to his daughter Mary 300 marks for her portion.

To his son-in-law Sir Richard Lee and Margaret his wife 100 marks.

To his son-in-law Robert Whettall Esq , and Jane his wife 100 marks

To his brother-in-law John Drake and Amy his wife 20 marks

The rest of his will shews him to have been a person of sound judgment and a master of economy

His executors were Dame Maud, his wife, his brother-in-law Edmund Speccott, Esquire, John Beauchamp, his brother-in-law, John Killigrew, and John Bevill, Esquires

He made a codicil to his will, dated at Stowe, 3rd January, 1550-1, and another on 10th March, and another on the 15th of March, 1550-1, which was but three days before his death.

CHAPTER VI

THE young grandson who succeeded, and who afterwards proved so celebrated an Elizabethan admiral, was but eight years old at the time of Sir Richard's death   Whether he was brought up at Buckland, or at Stowe or at Clifton under the care of his step-father, is not known, and the story of his boyhood has yet to be discovered.   It was an age of enterprise, restlessness and energy   The sons of English knights and gentlemen, no longer contented with the old routine of duties and a stationary place in the social scale, were early out in search of adventure on the wide world, craving to do some deeds which would bring them name and fame, or at least would better their private fortunes

Thus when barely sixteen years of age Richard Granville. in company with several other chivalrous scions of nobility obtained a license from Queen Elizabeth to enter the service of the Emperor Maximilian against the Turks   In these wars he at once gave such distinguished proofs of his intrepidity and knowledge of the art of war that he obtained the commendation of foreign historians (cf. " Magna Britannia " III Cornwall, p 163, ed. 1814)

He had evidently returned home in 1568 as in that year he grants to John Halse of Efford "all those lands in East Buckland, sometime the property of my grandfather

We next hear of him in Ireland taking part in the reduction of that unhappy country, and suppressing the rebellion of the great chieftain Shan O'Neale, and in this dangerous service young Granville acquitted himself so entirely to the Lord Deputy's satisfaction that he was appointed Sheriff of Cork (1569), an office of great responsibility for one so young   The fall of Shan O Neale was succeeded for awhile by a period of apparent prosperity   A disposition to industry displaced the usual appetite for disorder, and the administration would flatter itself that a new era was commencing   In the harbour towns of Cork, Waterford Youghal, Limerick, and to some extent even in Galway, trade began to revive, and with trade a sense of the value of order and law.

It must have been about this time that Richard Granville found his wife. in Mary the eldest daughter (and ultimately co-heness) of Sir John St Leger of Annery, near Bideford by Katherine, daughter of George Nevil, Lord Abergavenny She had an only brother who died without issue, and three sisters, namely, Frances married to John Studley of Affeton ; Margaret, married to Richard Bellew, Eulalia, married first to Edmund Tremayne of Collacombe, and secondly to Tristram Arscott To the latter her father sold Annery, which he had inherited from his great-grandmother, Anne Hankford, daughter of Sir Richard Hankford of Annery, and wife of Thomas, seventh Earl of Ormonde Sir John St Leger was the son and heir of Sir Richard St Leger and cousin to Sir Warham St Leger, who had also taken an active part in the suppression of the O'Neale rebellion

The marriage between Richard Granville and Mary St. Leger brought in the quarterings of St Leger, Donnet, Butler, Earl of Ormonde, Rochford, Hankford and Stapledon, as given in the shield in the frontispiece, as well as numerous royal descents, both York and Lancaster, besides descents from the great Houses of Neville Percy, Stafford, Beauchamp, Beaufort, Audley, De Burgh, Despencer, Clare, Fitzalan, Knyvett, Montacute, Grandisson, etc (cf Sir John Maclean's History of Trigg, vol 1, p. 683)

The following law case from the Carew MSS at Lambeth Palace (vol. 600, fo 239) is interesting as illustrating the relationship of Mrs Granville with Queen Elizabeth

"MR ST LEGER'S CASE TO HIS TITLE TO THE EARL OF ORMONDE'S LANDS '

' Thomas Butler, Earl of Ormond, took to wife Ann daughter and heyre of Sir Richard Hankeforde, sonne and heire of Sir William Hankeforde, sometyme Cheefe Justice of the Court of the Common Pleas, and they had issue Anne and Margaret

Thomas Earl of Ormond had in his own right divers mannors in fee and divers in tayle, he and his Lady in her right had sundry other mannors in fee and in tayle Anne, the elder daughter, was married to Sir James St Leger and they had issue issue Sir George St Leger and James died Margaret was married to Sir William Bullen, and they had issue Thomas Bullen

Thomas Butler, Earl of Ormond and Ann his wife were bothe dead 7 Henry VIII Anne, the daughter, and Sir George St Leger her sonne, and Margaret and Sir Thomas Bullen her sonne, by indenture, 10 Henry VIII did make partition And parte of the land of the Earl of Ormond was allotted to Margaret and to Thomas her sonne All the rest of the Father's and all the Mother's land was allotted to Anne and Sir George St Leger, her sonne Anne St Leger after died Sir George St Leger had issue Sir John St Leger and died Margaret became Lunatick the same year soone after this partition and died Sir Thomas Bullen had issue Mary Anne ,

and died   May was married to Sir William Cary and Anne to King Henry
VIII   King Henry VIII had issue by Anne Queen Elizabeth of blessed
memory, and Anne died   Mary had issue Henry Cary Lord Hunsdon, and she
and her husband died   Henry Lord Hunsdon did alien that p'te which was
allotted to his ancestors, and had issue Sir George Cary, and died   Sir George
Cary had issue Elizabeth Lady Barkley and died   And Sir John St Leger in
the time of Queen Elizabeth alienated that which by the p'tition was allotted
to his auncestors, and had issue Sir John St Leger that now is   Queen
Elizabeth died without issue "

The case is summed up concisely, and opinion given in these
words, followed by six separate reasons

"I take it that John St Leger had good right to the moietie of the mannors
and hereditaments allotted unto Bullen "

St Leger received with his wife, the heir ess of Ormond, thirty-
six manors in England, which estates were all wasted (see Ped
fin repeatedly temp Eliz), and the descendant John St Leger,
the plaintiff above and brother of Mary Grenvile, died in
reduced circumstances without issue

But to return to Ireland.   A very short time sufficed to
show that the Irish Millenium had not yet arrived, and the
English Government added largely to the difficulties of the
Lord Deputy and other governors by attempting to force the
Reformation upon Ireland, whilst its political and social condition was still unsettled   The peace of the country could not
be preserved without soldiers , the soldiers could not be kept
under discipline without regular wages, and money as usual,
and especially money for Ireland, was a subject on which not
one of her ministers approached Elizabeth without terror,
and with the utmost difficulty sufficient sums were extracted
from time to time to stave off mutiny   Meanwhile the
Queen caused the Earl of Desmond, another dangerous Irish
chieftain, to be arrested and sent as a prisoner to London,
where he was made to purchase his life by a surrender of
everything that he possessed   So enormous were the feudal
superiorities claimed by the Munster Geraldines that half the
province could be construed by complication to have fallen
into the Queen's hands   A case for forfeiture was made out
with no great difficulty against the Irish owners of the
remainder.[1]

In a scheme which was drawn out by Sir Henry Sidney,
the Lord Deputy for the colonizing and military occupation of
this great southern province, the MacCarties, the O'Sullivans,

[1] The area of the land confiscated in Munster at this period was 574,628 acres (see
Leland ii p 302)

and the other chiefs were to have been associated in the
Government in the hope that they would be reclaimed to
civility by the possession of legitimate authority A project,
however, briefer and less expensive, was submitted to the
Queen from another quarter This is Froude's account of it —
" Excited by the difficulties of the Government, or perhaps
directly invited to come forward, a number of gentlemen, chiefly
from Somersetshire and Devonshire—Gilberts, Chichesters,
Carews, Grenvilles Courtenays—twenty-seven in all, volun-
teered to relieve Elizabeth of her trouble with Ireland Some
of them had already tried their fortunes there most of them,
in command of pirates and privateers, had made acquaintance
with the harbours of Cork and Kerry They were prepared to
migrate there altogether on conditions which would open their
way to permanent greatness .   The whole of the
immense territories of the Desmond estates these ambitious
gentlemen undertook, at their own charges, to occupy in the
teeth of their Irish owners, to cultivate the land, to build
towns, forts and castles—to fish the seas and rivers, to make
roads and establish harbours, and to pay a fixed revenue to the
Queen after the third year of their tenure They proposed
to transport from their own neighbourhood a sufficient number
of craftsmen artificers and labourers to enable them to make
good their ground The chiefs they would drive away or
kill , the poor Irish even ' the wildest and idlest,' they
hoped to compel into obedience and civility If the Irish
nature proved incorrigible they would, through idleness, offend
to die ' The scandal and burden of the Southern Provinces
would then be brought to an end Priests would no longer
haunt the churches the countries possessed by rebels would
be inhabited by natural Englishmen , and Kinsale, Valentia,
Dingle, through which the Spaniards and the French supplied
the insurgents with arms, would be closed against them
and their machinations The English settlers would have the
fish, ' wherein those seas were very fortunate,' and ' the
strangers who sold fish to the country people would be driven
to buy for their own markets, to the great enriching of good
subjects ''—*Froude's History of England* chap xxiv)

Such was the project which was submitted to the Queen for
her approval, and though the scheme was not altogether
unfavourably received, the necessary permission was delayed
Meanwhile several of these twenty-seven speculators, whose
ancestors had been forced to leave Ireland during the Civil
War in England in the fifteenth century, and had abandoned

N

their estates to the Geralddines without prospect of recovery, now produced their title-deeds which long had had no value except as historical curiosities. Amongst these Richard Granville, on behalf of his wife (it is supposed,) and her uncle Sir Warham St Leger produced them, and proceeded to look after their so-called properties without waiting for the resolution of the Council Nor were they contented with a mere survey, they carried with them, under the name of servants, considerable numbers of their retainers, believing justly that at such times no title was so good as solid occupation St Leger and Granville took possession of several farms and castles in the neighbourhood of Cork viz Tracton Kerrycurrily and Carigy-legn Castle This occupation of the Desmond estates was stoutly resisted, and an appeal for aid was despatched to the Pope and King of Spain The Lord Deputy was immediately informed of this by Sir Warham St Leger ' The end of that Devilish Prelate " (so St Leger called the Archbishop of Cashel, who had sailed for Rome with the petition) " was to resist the good devices which had been formed for the welfare of Ireland," and he could but hope that the Queen would ' presently with all the speed that might be, send over the well-minded persons who intended to adventure their lives and livings in the conquest "

Finding Elizabeth slower than they wished Sir Warham and Granville hastened back to London to quicken her resolutions, and the moment of their absence was seized upon by the insurgent leaders, Fitzmaurice and the Earl of Clancarty, to call their people under arms A small vessel, which belonged to Sir John Hawkins, was in the harbour of Kinsale with a few pieces of bronze artillery on board, of which Fitzmaurice possessed himself, and with these, in company with the Earl of Clancarty, he came down upon the lands of which they had been dispossessed. Lady St Leger and Mrs Granville who had been left in charge, had just time to escape into Cork, the whole establishment—tenants, servants, farm-labourers—had their throats cut, and ten thousand of their cattle were driven off into the hills. In the Calendar of State Papers (Irish Series vol. xxviii) there are several letters relating to this attack, including one from ' Lady Ursula Sentleger " to the Lord Deputy in which she narrates how, on Wednesday 16th of June, '' the Sheriff ' ' (her husband) ' went for England"; how " next morning James Fitzmaurice with 4000 spoiled Kerrycurrily "; how on Friday they took Tracton and killed John Enchedon and all her men ", how " on Saturday they came to the castle of Cangyleyn , the enemies were informed by the tenants what victuals and provision was in the castle." and she concludes by praying that some order may be taken for her security Fitzmaurice came to Cork with his guns and some thousands of his ragged warriors, and sent a demand to the Mayor "to abolish out of the city all Huguenot heretics," especially Mrs Granville and her family, and to unite with him in purging the churches of all traces of their presence. His letter was as follows —

Mr Mayor,

    I commend me unto you and whereas the Queen's Majesty is not contented to dispose all our worldly goods, our bodies and our lives, as she list, but must also compel us to forego the Catholic faith, by God unto His Church given, and by the See of Rome hitherto prescribed to all Christian men to be observed, and use another newly invented kind of religion, which for my part, rather than I would obey to my everlasting damnation, I had liefer forsake all the world, if it were mine as I wish all others who profess Christ and His true faith to do , therefore this shall be to require you, by the way of charity that ye ought to have towards all them that profess to be Christian men, to abolish out of the city that old heresy newly raised and invented, and all them that be Huguenots, both men and women, and Greynvile's wife and children, and to set up the service after the due form and manner which is used in Rome and throughout all Christendom and as our forefathers have ever used to fore Assuring you that if you follow not this our Catholic and wholesome exhortation, I will not nor may not be your friend, and in like manner I wish and require the Chapter and all the clergy of Cork and of the Bishoprick thereof, to frame themselves to honour God as your ancestors have done, and destroy out of the town all the Huguenots with the first wind

      From Martyrstone this 12th of July, 1569
      Spes nostra Jesu Maria
      Yours, if ye be in good faith,
      James Fitzmaurice of Desmond

How Mrs Granville escaped is not stated, but we next hear of Richard Granville representing Cornwall in Parliament, and on the 18th of April, 1570, he and Robert Hill made a declaration at Bodmin before the Justices of Cornwall of their submission to the Act for Uniformity of Common Prayer and service in the Church But his restless spirit and natural thirst for distinction in the paths of military enterprize induced him to leave England again and participate in the perils and glories of the brilliant engagement at Lepanto (October 1572), when Don John of Austria with the combined fleets of Christendom obtained a complete victory over the Turkish galleys His name next appears in the petition of divers gentlemen of the western parts of England to the Queen, dated 22 March, 1574, soliciting her Majesty to allow an enterprize for the discovery of sundry "ritche and unknowne landes

After this he is next found benefiting the inhabitants of Bideford by obtaining a charter of incorporation for the town   Bideford at this time was emerging from insignificance into importance   A great number of merchants and others, with whom he had been engaged in official business when Sheriff of Cork, followed him it is said, from Ireland, driven away by the disturbances in that unhappy country, and settled in Bideford, and it was then extensive operations in the mercantile world which laid the foundation of the future wealth and prosperity of that port   The Charter of Incorporation received the royal sanction at Westminster the 10th of December, 1574, and Richard Granville was chosen to be one of the first five aldermen, who together with seven capital burgesses elected from their number John Salterne to be their first Mayor

Richard Granville, as already stated, had represented the county of Cornwall in Parliament upon his return from Ireland, and in 1576 he was again elected to the same honour   The following year he was also appointed High Sheriff for Cornwall and received the honour of knighthood from the Queen's hands at Windsor, (cf S Morgan's Sphere of Gentry iii, 90 ed 1661, under Richard Gr(n)field)[1]   Whilst Sheriff of Cornwall it fell to his lot, at the instigation of Dr. William Bradbridge, Bishop of Exeter, who was then on his visitation at Truro, to arrest Francis Tregian, the son-in-law of Sir Thomas Arundell, for harbouring Cuthbert Mayne, a recusant priest, at his house at Golden, near Probus who was discovered concealed under an old tower, having about him copies of the bull of Pope Pius   Tregian, after being bound over to appear at the next Launceston Assizes, was taken to London, there to be examined by the Privy Council, and was sentenced to be imprisoned for twenty years; but Maine was committed on a charge of high treason to the Castle of Launceston, " where, when he came, he was laid in a most loathsome   .   dungeon, scarce able at high noon to see his arms or his legs"   He was tried and condemned to be hanged, drawn, and quartered in the Launceston market place   When the sentence was passed Maine simply murmured " God be thanked," and when the day before his execution he was tempted to recant, he held his ground in disputation from eight in the morning until night,

---

[1] There is a quaint entry amongst the Plymouth Municipal records in the Widey Court Book under date 1577-8 to this effect—

" £86 was spent in entertaining my lord of Bedford and my lord and lady of Bedford on her visits, while sixpence was paid for 'suger' when Sr Richarde Graynevulle did muster upon the hawe
and again
    1s 1d paid for carrying a letter to Sr Richard Grenville

SIR RICHARD GRANVILLE OF THE "REVENGE,"
VICE-ADMIRAL OF ENGLAND.

From an Original Portrait in the Haynes Park Collection.

refusing life and liberty rather than change his religion. After life was extinct he was speedily cut down and as speedily quartered and decapitated, his head being set up on the Castle of Launceston, and his quarters being distributed between Bodmin, Barnstaple, Tregony, and Wadebridge. (cf Morris's "Troubles of our Catholic Forefathers," Dr Oliver's "History of the Catholic Religion in the West of England," and "Memoirs of Missionary Priests," by Challoner)

In 1580 Sir Richard and Lady Mary Granville, after obtaining the royal license to alienate them, sold the Abbey, site, house and lands at Buckland Monachorum to Sir John Hele and Sir Christopher Harris for £3400 and nine months later they conveyed the property to Sir Francis Drake, whose descendants still retain them. The Granvilles had converted the Cistercian Church into the modern house which still exists, and over the chimney-piece is the date MCCCCCLXXVI They also destroyed the greater part of the monastic buildings and laid out the surrounding land in pleasure-grounds and gardens

The coasts of Devon and Cornwall at this time were suffering grievously from the ravages of pirates, and frequent petitions to the Council from ports in the west told the dismal tale of rapine Sir Richard Granville is mentioned, along with other commissioners, as examining John Piers a pirate at Padstow, 25th October, 1581, and in the following May we find him at Penryn enquiring 'as touching the taking away of the Spanish ship out of Falmouth by Sir John Killigrew's servants'

The two following letters, which are amongst the Lansdowne MSS in the British Museum, are addressed by Sir Richard to "the Right Worship" Mr Doctor Julius Cæsar, Highe Judge of the Admyraltye" and have reference to these piracies.

BRIT MUSEUM LANSDOWN MSS 158, Fol 48

Sr Rich Grenvile to Dr Julius Cæsar.

Good Mr Doctor, I do understonde by my servaunt and others howe troublesome some causes wch ptely concerne me haue bene vnto you, and wthall yor good will professed towardes me, for the wch albert hetherto I haue not bene so gratefull vnto you as I sholde, yet in the ende I truste to be founde neither vnmindfull nor vnthankfull to so good a friende There is lately come into thies ptes a factor of one Lemons wth a Comission from yr Courte of thadmiraltie to demannde certeyne gooddes wch he pretendeth to haue made proofe of in vor Courte, but it manifestly apeareth that Lemon intrudeth himselfe as a comon dealer in like causes, vpon some intelligence that he hathe gotten that such a shippe is come into my handes and thereon at happe hazarde hathe made some vniuste proofe of somthinge as by his factors instructions apeareth, for neither knoweth he the iuste quantetie of the gooddes, nor the prises, by wch meanes he is enforced to send to his mr to vnderstoude the same, (as I doubte not but his mr hath sence sent into Hollande to haue the promotion of this cause) But to acquaınte yoᵘ in friendly and iuste sorte wᵗʰ the cause, I can aprove that the gooddes wᶜʰ Lemon wold make claime vnto, were belonginge to Spanıshe fleminges, consigned to Ledgers in Spaine, there residente, & other sent to be Ledger there, wᶜʰ course I thinke the States (relinquishing the governement and their subjection to the K of Spaine) wold never alowe of, Besides this they caried some good proportion of victuall for the Spanish fleete, as butter, bacon, cheese, whereby it maie apeare vnto all men that thies gooddes do rather belouge to such as are wholye Spanishe then ony wares assured to this estate, And that I can make good proofe herof as of other like couloıed dealinge of thies men to this estate, and then states there, in the processe of this cause it shall furder apeare, yet notwᵗʰstoudınge on my Lo Admiralles favorable ᵗ˙ies in their cause whose ho shall comaunde bothe my liefe and all that I possesse in [his] service, I can be contente to deale well wᵗʰ Lemon in such soıte as I may , for this shıppe being taken bv some of my company, that acounte hath never come to mi sıghte wᶜʰ Lemon demaundeth , And that wᶜʰ hath come hath bene so spoiled wᵗ˙ wette and other sea accidentᵉ, as it amounteth not by farre to that qualıtie and quantitie, that is Imagined, & yoᵘ knowe how hardly such a company as men in like actions must vse at sea wilbe kept from spoile of such thinge as come to then fingers, And my selfe hath bene offeıed the one halfe for the other even bv Douchmen , wherfore seing thies spanishe fleminge haue so vnequall a cause as in pleading for my selfe I muste and will make it apeare I hartely praie you in my iuste cause to geve me that favoᵣ that a trewe Inglıshe Subiecte to her Matie and his countrey shall deserve of the wᶜʰ as from yoᵣ owne inclinacõn I doubt not, So shall yoᵘ goveıne and comaunde me in ony thinge as yoᵣ poore fiende This having laid open the estate of this cause vnto yoᵘ as to him who I am ᵖswaded is my very good fiende in ony my iuste a˛cous assuringe yoᵘ that I will not be vnmındfull of yoᵗ courtezies towarde me, wᵗʰ my very hartie Comendacõns I praing yoᵘ to pdon my boldnes wᵗʰ yoᵘ, I comitte yoᵘ to the protection of the almightie Bedyforde this 27 of februaıy 1586

Yoᵣ assured loving fiend

R᷑ GREYNVILL

[*Addressed*]　To the worshipplˡ my very Lovinge fiende Mᴵ Doctoı Cæsaı Iudge of the Admiraltie geve thies

[*Endorsed*]　27° februarij 1586 S˙ Richard Grenefield about an hulk of Amsterdam

BRIT MUSEUM LANSDOWN MSS 143, Foı 264

S˙ RICHARD GRENVILE TO Dᴿ IULIUS CÆSAR

Good Mᴿ Doctoı I muste nowe crave vow to staude fiendlve for my kynesmā, that made the seasıre on the shippe and wynes at Padstowe for that theeıe are others wᶜʰ ptend Rıghte vnto it, yett I thinke and hope, that the fiıste seasuıe by a Comission of Reprısıll is good If that hee so then this otheı auethoıytie commethe to late as is to bee Iustified bv these newe dealinge Garıat Mellines is also putt out of possession his Baıgaıne wᵗʰ mee for the wynes hathe caused mee to brınge downe a couple of marchauntᵉ to theıre great chaıge and hvnderaunce wᶜʰ if his clayme to the goodᵉ bee vntrew, I thinke he oughte to Recompence them, whereme as also that my kynesmā mave haue youıe favouıe to Imove the seasuıe that hathe bvne made I shall moste hartelye desıre yoᵗ favouıe And that this honest marchaunte Mr Gynms whoe hathe taken great paynes in this cause on Mellynes worde maye haue faruourable accesse vnto yow in tollowinge this cause I haue written to my Lo Admyrall therine as Mr Gynms can advertise yow I haue taken order wth Mr Gynms to paye the Douche m$\bar{a}$ the 120^{li} for the oyles and figges vpon the makinge of suche [grauate] and dischaige for the same as yow shall allowe of ffor the other causes accordinge to my speeche wth yow the nexte wicke (god willinge) I shalbe able to advertise yow to the pformance thereof, whereby yow shall alwayes fynde me Juste to the moste of my power And so I beseeche god euer to prosper yow At my howse in Bedifond this 19th of Maye 1589

Youre assured poore frend

R GREYNVILE

[*Addressed*] To the Righte Worship^{ll} Mr Doctor Julius Cæsar Highe Judge of the Admyraltye

[*Endorsed*] Sr Richard Grenvill touching the ship and wynes arrested by a kinseman of his at Padstowe 19° May 1589

On the 27th of December, 1583, Sir Richard writes from Redford as to the custody of the castle and island of Tintagel ' The isle, as it is now left, is a dangerous receptacle for an evil-affected person, and is kept by one John Hendey, who is thought to be evil-affected in religion," and he recommends his cousin Mr. George Granville, " now sheriff of the county,' to be appointed to take charge of it, and the same year the confession of Alexander Baray is taken before Sir Richard and Barnard Drake touching a Popish book and Catechism, set forth by one named Lawrence Vaux, belonging to William Edmonds, servant of Mr Chapell, and used by him in the church of Great Torrington

Among the Plymouth municipal records in the " Black Book," under date 1584, is the following entry

" Sir R Grendefelde, Knighte, departed from Plymouth with vi shippes and barkes for Wingane Dehoy wher he caried vi hundred men o^f therabowts "

This entry is interesting, as it is generally supposed that Sir Richard's first voyage to America did not take place till the following year. 1585

In the Calendar of State Papers belonging to the year 1585 there is a letter from Sir Richard to Sir Francis Walsingham, in which he " denies the truth of the reports raised against him of having committed unlawful violence in the Parsonage house of Kilkhampton to the terror and danger of Mrs Pagett, who kept possession of the house " He encloses " a true declaration of his dealings with Mistress Pagett in obtaining possession of the Parsonage house of Kilkhampton, of which benefice her husband, Mr Pagett, had been legally deprived "

The following year we find him acting as one of the Commissioners for Dover Haven and proposing the erection of a mole at Folkestone. He sends Sir Francis Walsingham an account of the charges of re-edifying the quay and pier at Botreaux Castle in Cornwall in four months ending 6th August, 1584, with a note of the mode of executing the work, which might serve for a model for Dover or Folkestone. Later on he suggests that the pier of Dover should be made of stone and chalk combined, and encloses a well-executed drawing of the masonry

He again represented Cornwall in Parliament in 1584 and writing from Penheale (the seat of George Granville), August 6th, says he has been so busily engaged in the musters that he could not make collections for Namptwich, which had been destroyed by fire, but on the 17th of October he sends from " my poor house of Stow" a further sum of £20 for this purpose

Queen Elizabeth, at this time, though successful in all her foreign undertakings was kept in a state of perpetual uneasiness at home by reason of conspiracies which followed one upon another with increasing rapidity in the effort to place Mary Queen of Scots on the throne. The feverish apprehensions of the Protestants took shape in the famous bond of association or organisation of loyal subjects into an universal committee for the protection of the sovereign and the Empire Sir Richard Granville's name is amongst the signatures to the bond of union, and it appears from the following authority from Sir Francis Walsingham, the Queen's Secretary, to the Ordnance officers, that he was appointed to the command of the trained bands in Cornwall at this time

BRITISH MUSEUM ADD MSS 5752, Fol. 288

Sr Fra Walsingham to Mr Paynter, etc

"After my hasty commendacons   Whereas Sr Richard Grenfeld hath ben appointed by the rest of the Comissions for musters in the County of Cornewall to make prouision here of armor and municon for the furnishing of the numbers appointed to be mustered and trayned in the said County, and for that he hath nowe a shippe readye to take in the lading of the said armor and municon wch is to depte out of hand   Theis are therefore to desier you to make deliuye vnto him out of yor office of the peells contaynid in the inclosid scedule for the wch I will not faile to procure you further warraunt

from my Lts of the Counsell when then Hps shall meete next here   And so
I bid you fare well

' At the Co^rte the xxvij^th of Maye 1584

"Yo^r loving friend

" FRA WALSYNGHAM

" To my loving frende
Mr Paynter, Mr Bouland
and the rest of the Inferio^r officers of thordinñce "

What was the result of the petition of divers gentlemen of
the western parts of England to the Queen, in 1574, for
permission to explore " sundry ritche and unknownen lands " is
not known, but about this time Sir Richard turned his thoughts
more directly to foreign colonization and associated himself
with his kinsman, Sir Walter Raleigh, in an undertaking that
would give scope to their adventurous spirits The result of
their co-operation was the discovery of Virginia and Carolina,
in the year 1584, by two ships belonging to Sir Walter
Raleigh and his company, commanded by Captain Philip
Amidas and Captain Arthur Barlow The magnitude and
eligibility of the territory acquired by the Crown was on
everyone's lips ; and the accounts of those who had been
eye-witnesses of the country, its productions and inhabitants,
hastened on Raleigh's preparations for taking possession of his
newly-found dominions As soon as the good news spread
among the country people of the west, hundreds of hardy
adventurers offered themselves as the willing pioneers of
colonization in that quarter A fleet of seven ships, of which
Sir Richard took the command, was got ready with every
possible despatch ; and when the anchors were weighed at
Plymouth, on the 9th of April, 1585, there were none among
the thousands there assembled but shared the belief that their
relations and friends were departing for a land flowing with
milk and honey The following is the account of the voyage
taken from ' Holinshed's Chronicles " .—

' In this 1585 year even in April at the pleasant prime, Sir Walter Raleigh
Knight, being encouraged by the reports of his men of the goodness of the
soil and the fertility of the country which they had discovered the year last
past, and now by her Majesty called Virginia, with Knightly courage counter-
vailable to his double desire of honour by undertaking hard adventures
furnished, to his great charges, eight sails of all sorts, and immediately set
them to sea, ordering Sir Richard Grenfield, his kinsman, a gentleman of very
good estimation, both for his parentage and sundry good virtues (who, for love
he bore unto Sir Walter Raleigh, together with a disposition that he had to
attempt honourable actions worthy of honour was willing to hazard himself
in this vo— his h ur in   c j nei.. 'in ntl r ;   n l

O

leave some gentleman of good worth with a competent number of soldiers in the country of Virginia to begin an English Colony there. Who, with the ships aforesaid, having in his company Sir John Arundell, Thomas Cavendish, Ralph Lane, Edward Georges, John Stukley, Edward Stafford, Philip Amidas, Arthur Barlow, Thomas Heriot and divers other gentlemen with a competent number of soldiers, departed from London,[1] in April aforesaid. But after they had sailed a certain number of leagues at sea, by force and violence of the foul weather they were separated one from another, so that Sir Richard Greenfield, being singled from his fleet, all alone arrived at the island of Hispaniola in the West Indies about the middle of June following,[2] where he determined resolutely to remain until he had built a boat, for he had lost his own boat in the tempest aforesaid. Whereupon immediately after his landing finding a place to his liking he esconsed himself in despite of the Spaniards, who by all possible means did their best endeavour, by proferring of sundry skirmishes, to enforce him to retire to his ship. But he, nothing appalled by their brags, kept his ground. Twelve days after his arrival there Thomas Ca(ve)ndish arrived at the same place where Sir Richard Greenfield was esconsing himself, to the great rejoicing both of themselves and of their companies. The Spaniards finding it too hard for them (notwithstanding their multitude) to remove these few resolute Englishmen by violence, came to a parley, and in the same concluded an amity that one nation might with safety traffick with the other. Now when Sir Richard Greenfield had tarried in that island almost a month and had built his boat, having re-victualled himself and laded his ships with horses, mares, kine, sheep, swine, etc, to transport with him to Virginia, because these sorts of cattle heretofore were not to be found in that country, he departed thence; on his way he made discovery of many islands and havens upon the continent adjoining, and arrived safely in the new discovered country, where he met with the rest of his fleet, that attended his coming thether, about the middle of July next ensuing, not without great danger of shipwreck for at the very entrance into the harbour his ship strake on the ground, and did beat so many strokes upon the sands that, if God had not miraculously delivered him, there had been no way to avoid present death. In this danger his ship was so bruised that the saltwater came so abundantly into her that the most part of his corn, salt meat, rice, biscuits and other provisions, that he should have left with them that remained behind him in the country, was spoiled. After he had remained there certain days, according to his commission from Sir Walter Raleigh, he began to establish a colony, appointing Master Ralph Lane, a gentleman of good account, general of those English which were to remain there, being in all to the number of 107 persons, amongst whom divers gentlemen remained, namely, Philip Amidas, Edward Stafford, Mervin Kendall, Prideaux, Acton, Heriot and others. When he had taken sufficient order for the establishing of Master Lane and his company aforesaid, leaving with them as much of all provisions as his plenty would give him leave, he weighed anchor for England. But in his return not having sailed many leagues from the cost of Virginia, he descried a tall ship of

---

[1] This should be Plymouth.

[2] The following is Captain John Smith's account of the voyage. "The 14. day we fell with the Canaries, and the 7 of May with Dominico in the West Indies. we landed at Portorico after with much a doe at Izabella on the north of Hispaniola, passing by many Isles. Vpon the 20, we fell with the mayne of Florida, and were put in great danger vpon Cape Fear. The 26 we Anchored at Wocoken, where the admiral had like to beene cast away. presently we sent to Wingina to Roanoak, and Master Aruudell went to the mayne with Manteo a saluage, and that day to Crooton. The 11 The General, victualled for 8 days, with a select company went to the mayne and discovered the Townes of Pomeiok Aquascogoe Secotan and the great Lake called Paquipe. At Aquascogoe the Indians stole a silver Cup, wherefore we burnt the towne, and spoyled their corne, so returned to our fleete at Tocokon"

100 tons or thereabouts, making the same course as he did, unto whom he gave chase and in a few hours by goodness of sail overtook, and by violence won, richly laden with sugar, hides, spices and some quantity of gold, silver and pearls. She was the Vice-Admiral of the fleet of Sancto Domingo that year for Spain. After this good fortune, having a merry gale, not many days after, he arrived at Plymouth in October next ensuing,[1] when Sir Walter Raleigh meeting with him did presently resolve upon another voyage to supply Ralph Lane and his companions that were left with him in Virginia, the next spring following, which accordingly was performed with all expedition "

The Spanish ship which Sir Richard succeeded in capturing was almost as richly laden as the treasure ship the "Cacafuego" which had enriched Sir Francis Drake and his crew, for in this vessel, which Sir Richard towed into Plymouth harbour, was stowed away a cargo worth £50,000 sterling. According to Hakluyt ("English Voyages" p 736, ed. 1589), Sir Richard had "boarded her with a boate made of boards of chests, which fell asunder and sunke at the shipe's side assoone as ever he and his men were out of it "[2]

On the 29th of October Sir Richard writes from Plymouth to Sir Francis Walsingham, the Queen's Secretary, and acquaints him with the success of the voyage, that he has preformed the action directed him, and discovered, taken possession of and peopled a new country (Virginia) and stored it with cattle, fruits and plants "The commodities of the country are such as his cousin Raleigh advertized him of "

But Lane apparently had quarrelled with Sir Richard, as we find him writing to Walsingham, on the 12th of August, from " Port Ferdinando, Virginia," and again on the 8th of September from the "New Fort in Virginia," saying that " he had thought it good to advertise him concerning Sir R. Greenefielde's complaints against Mr Candyshe, their High Marshall Edward Gorges, Francis Brooke their Treasurer and Captain Clerk." He certifies to their faithfulness and industry, and to the tyrannical conduct of Sir Richard from first to last, through whose great default the action had been made most painful and perilous. He refers him to an ample discourse of the whole voyage in the hands of the bearer, their Treasurer, directed to Sir Walter Raleigh, wherein Sir Richard's intolerable pride, insatiable ambition and proceedings towards them all, and to Lane in particular, are set forth. He says he has had "as much experience of Greenefielde as to desire to be freed from the place where he is to carry any authority in chief "

[1] Captain John Smith gives the date the 18th of September 1587
[2] ... Punch ... Programme ...

Upon Sir Richard's retirement from Virginia, the colonists, instead of applying their minds to agriculture, were attracted by the cunningly devised tales of the natives about the pearl fisheries and inexhaustible gold and silver mines of the country. Lane and his associates felt their mouths water with the prospect of the golden rule of Pizarro and the Spaniards, which had so often proved the subject of their day dreams, and now stood before them as though about to be realized   The valuable time, therefore, which should have been devoted to agriculture, was squandered in researches after a visionary substance, and, exasperated at the deceptions practiced upon them by the natives, the colonists visited their wrath upon them and severely punished them.   Their utmost labours now barely sufficed to keep body and soul together.   The long looked-for reinforcements of men and stores, which Sir Walter Raleigh's crippled finances had prevented him from obtaining at the proper season, failed them at their utmost need.   Every source of subsistence was dried up.   The extremities of hunger were dispersing them over every part of the island, each to find food as best he could, when, as if sent by a merciful Providence to those who had no other trust, Sir Francis Drake, on his return from a successful raid against the Spaniards, appeared in sight with his fleet.   He gladly assisted them with food for their immediate wants, and promised them a good supply of stores and necessaries out of his fleet, but unfortunately the vessel he had set aside for their service was dashed to pieces by a sudden storm, and his inability to provide another frustrated his good intentions.   Accordingly, the island being no longer tenable, and worn out by famine and disappointment, the colonists petitioned for leave to accompany him back to England, and they were landed at Plymouth the 27th of July, 1586

The fleet, however, had no sooner left Virginia than the ship which Sir Walter had despatched with stores and provisions approached the island of Roanoak, but finding it abandoned, returned homewards   A fortnight afterwards Sir Richard Granville himself with three ships, hove in sight, having been delayed, it is said, by his vessel being beneaped on Bideford bar   Ignorant of what had happened, he landed with the confident hope of adding vigour and strength to the infant colony, but finding no traces of his colonists, he, too, returned home, leaving however, fifteen of his crew ashore, " plentifully furnished with all manner of provisions for two years," for the purpose of retaining possession   This handful of men soon became involved in hostilities with the natives, and were by them destroyed to the last man

On his return voyage Sir Richard landed on some of the islands of the Azores, and spoiled the towns of such things as were worth carriage, and captured several Spaniards

It was probably on this voyage that he brought back with him the Indian, whose baptism in Bideford Church took place on the 27th of March, 1588, and who received the name of Raleigh The English climate soon killed him as his burial in Bideford Churchyard is recorded as having taken place on the 7th of April in the year following. He is entered in the Parish Register Book as a native of Wyngandıtoıa

However disheartening this unlooked for succession of disasters might have proved to men of ordinary stamp, they only incited Raleigh and Granville to more vigorous operations Early therefore in the following year 1587, they fitted out three more ships, which were entrusted to the command of Captain John White, a native of Devonshire, a man well-versed in all the difficulties and trials attending enterprises of this nature With a hundred and fifty men White landed at Hatorask, and proposed to found a town, to be called Raleigh, in the new country. Every species of disaster attended this third colony The continuous mass of forest and the endless savannahs of the country seemed only fit for the abode of savages, and these new colonists, with one accord, solicited White to return to England and bring fresh supplies, that their uncomfortable position might at least be made tolerable. White arrived in England, in the midst of the excitement caused the following year by the preparations for the great Armada, and the expedition, which Sir Richard had fitted out to relieve the colonists, and which was only waiting for a fair wind to put to sea, was stopped by Government at Bideford, and being joined by a contingent from Barnstaple, the little North Devon fleet, consisting, some say of five, others of seven vessels, sailed over the bar to join Sir Francis Drake at Plymouth. The names of some of the vessels composing this fleet have been preserved, and the galleon "Dudley," 'The Virgin, God Save Her," and the "Tyger,' are believed to have formed Sir Richard's contingent from Bideford, which joined the Barnstaple ships, towards the defence of England against the Invincible Armada The former of these, a vessel of 200 tons was commanded (Lediard's Naval History, 1735, p. 238) by Captain James Erisey, a second cousin to Sir Richard He belonged to the ancient family of Erisey of Grade, co Cornwall, and is described as "a Sea Captayne" in the pedigree of the family in Vivian's Visitations of Cornwall and was thirty com years of age in 1588[1] ' The Virgin, God Save Her' was commanded by Sir Richard's second son, Captain John Granville, who was afterwards slain in the Indies whilst serving under Drake in the unsuccessful expedition of 1595, and the "Tyger," 140 tons, was the ship in which Sir Richard had returned from his first expedition to Virginia, when he captured the Spanish plate ship.[2]

Thus it came to pass that the unfortunate colony in Virginia obtained no assistance, and the painful fact must be recorded that our first settlers there were suffered to perish miserably by famine, or to fall ignominiously from the savage hatred of the tribes that surrounded them.

Thomas Hariot, who has been mentioned as forming one of the earlier colonists, was a mathematician of first-rate eminence in his day He afterwards wrote " A Brief and True Report " of the voyage and colonization of Roanoke in Virginia, which was published in 1588. We have also another account of the colony entitled, " Admiranda narratio fida tamen de commodis et incolarum ritibus Virginiæ nuper admodum ab Anglis, qui a Domino Richardo Grenvile equestris ordinis viro eo incoloniam A.D 1585, deducti sunt inventa," etc. There was formerly in the Duke of Buckingham's Library at Stowe a perfect copy entitled " A briefe and true report of the newe founde lande of Virginia, discovered by Sir Richard Grenvile, Knight, in 1585 ' Sir Walter Raleigh undertook its publication and it was printed in folio by De Bry at Frankfort in the year 1590.

---

[1] Mr Cotton suggests that this ship was Sir Richard's Spanish prize, re named after Dudley Earl of Leicester, and he mentions that she appears once again in history Job Hortop, whose remarkable sufferings as a galley-slave in Spain are narrated in Hakluyt, escaped from San Lucar is a Flemish vessel, which was captured at sea by the *Galeon Dudley* and carried into Southampton This happened two years afterwards

[2] She is associated with an early *shark* story, related in the Hawkins' Voyages (H S , 1878, p 151) " A sharke cut off the legge of one of the companie sitting in the chaines and washing himselfe.''

CHAPTER VII

THE news of the preparations of the Spanish Armada reached England early in 1588 Alarmed Elizabeth and her subjects might well be, for the English as a people were now unused to the art of war, and the navy consisted of only thirty-four ships bearing the Queen's commission, with such vessels as the maritime towns and trading companies saw fit to supply.

Sir Richard Granville was selected by the Queen as one of the nine members who formed the famous Council of War, summoned in March, "to consider the meanes fittest to be obteyned for the deffence of the Realme in order to w'thstand any Invation" (Capt. Digby's MS). Such a direction would, under ordinary circumstances and in the first and foremost place, include general instructions as to the disposal of the navy as well as that of the general army, but this they were not required to do. The navy is scarcely mentioned, and the army only in the possibility of a landing being effected in Scotland. Its action was apparently limited to the military forces on the coast, so as either to prevent the invaders from landing, or, if the latter were successful, to hinder their onward march Sir Richard accordingly was given not a naval but a land appointment, being entrusted with the superintendence of the defence of the western parts,[1] and the Council wrote to the Lord-Lieutenants of Devon and Cornwall to inform them that he had received this appointment and was returning to the West in order "to survey the maritime defences and review the trained bands, and bidding them give instructions for the furtherance of this service" Sir Richard's measures proved him to be fully equal to the emergency. Every weak point on the seaboard was converted into a barrier of defence against the invading foe A compact force of 7,760 able-bodied men, sailors and soldiers, was raised, and Sir Richard himself at his own cost, provided "303 men armed with 129 shott, 69 corsletts, and 179 bows" (cf Harl MS 4228 f 70)

The story of the defeat of the Armada need not here be told, since Sir Richard was not called upon to take part in any

<hr/>

[1] Hakluyt expressely states that he was "personally commanded not to depart out of Cornewall."

of the engagements at sea, but when the remainder of that mighty fleet had been driven "to sundry parts on the west coast of Ireland," he received the following royal command, dated September 14th, 1588, for the stay of all shipping upon the north coast of Devon and Cornwall, and to await further directions from Sir Walter Raleigh

Queen Elizabeth to Sir R Greenville

Whereas We have some occasion offered to Us by reason of certain ships of the Spanish Armada that came about Scotland and are driven to sundry parts in the west of Ireland, to put in readiness some forces to be sent into Ireland as further occasion shall be given Us, which We mean to be shipped in the river of Severn to pass from thence to Waterford or Cork, We have thought meet to make choice of you for this service following   We require you that upon the north coasts of Devon and Cornwall towards Severn you make stay of all shipping meet to transport soldiers to Waterford and to give charge that the same ships be made ready with masters, mariners and other maritime provisions needful, so as upon the next warning given from Us or from Our Council, they may be ready to receive Our said soldiers, which shall be 300 out of Cornwall and Devon, and 400 out of Gloucestershire and Somersetshire   We have also some other further intention to use your service in Ireland with these ships aforesaid, whereof Sir Walter Rawley, Knight, whom We have acquainted withal, shall inform you, who also hath a disposition for Our service to pass into Ireland either with these forces or before they shall depart

And from this date until the time when, as Vice-Admiral, Sir Richard sailed from England in the "Revenge," to meet his glorious death, he seems to have resided chiefly in Ireland.

The administration of that unhappy country during the preceding eighteen years had presented a series of recurring features—severity ineffectually sustained and attempts at conciliation, which were only a fresh temptation to rebellion ; but the destruction of the Geraldines and the crushing of the rebellion in the Pale had been followed by a mutinous calm The single element which promised better things lay in the English settlements that were beginning to take root in Munster   The first commencement of colonization, ten years before, had, as we have already seen, called the entire south into rebellion ; but the chiefs who then rose in defence of their land were all dead, their children were in exile or were hiding in the cabins among the mountains   The Geraldines were gone, the properties of three-quarters of the clans had been confiscated, and with some pretence of justice, where insurrection had been tried and failed, the conquerers entered into possession   Cork, Kerry and Limerick were mapped out and divided on paper into blocks of 12,000 acres each, to be held on quit-rents under the Crown.   Each undertaker of such lands was by his letters patent bound to import English colonists into his seigneuries before Michaelmas, 1594 Beautiful pictures were drawn, which remain among the curiosities of the Record Office, of model Irish properties, great squares with a church in the centre of each, at one angle the Lord's demesne, a thousand acres of park, with a handsome Elizabethan manor house, over against it "her Majesty's portion" four hundred acres, set apart to maintain a police station In a third angle stands the school, and the rest is divided into smiling farms with solid barns and cattle sheds So excellent and inviting was the conception that, desolate as the country was now represented to be, many an English adventurer was found willing to turn his hand to convert it into reality Walter Raleigh took a grant, and Chidley and Champernowne and cadets of half the families in Somerset and Devon Stowells, Chichesters, Pophams, Coles. Carews, Bullers, Harringtons, Waries Hippesleys, and scores besides them (cf "Frondes History of England," ch. xxxiii.)

Sir Richard Granville and Sir Warham St Leger, undeterred by their former experiences had also accepted large grants of land They appear as "undertakers" of the country of Kerry-whirrie, Kyrricurrihie, and seven ploughlands in Ballyngarrie in Kynnole in the county of Cork, having as their dwelling house the castle of Cangroghan. Sir Richard also purchased the moiety of Kinalmeke of Hugh Worth, "who could not endure the sickness of the country," on behalf of his brothers-in-law Richard Bellew and Alexander Arundell, an estate of 24,000 acres In January, 1588-9, Sir Warham St Leger sends a letter by Sir Richard to Lord Burleigh as to the best means of preventing foreign invasion and writes at the same time to Walsingham to inform him that Sir Richard Grenevyle departs hence to the Court" A little later the Privy Council inform the Lord Deputy that "Sir Walter Rawley, with the help of Sir Richard Grenvile, has undertaken to raise 200 men of the 600 appointed to be levied in Ireland" Evidently Waterford was one of the ports to be especially strengthened, as on the 21st of February, Sir Thomas Norreys and Edmund Yorke write to the Privy Council to tell them that "Sir Richard Greenvile and Sir Warham Sent Leger were hindered from meeting them at Waterford, and that Waterford will find 150 labourers a day at their own charges so long as the fortifications continue, and the country 60 more."

The following October, writing from Stowe in Cornwall,

P

Sir Richard addresses himself to Walsingham on the subject of the occupation of these Irish estates :—

Being newly arrived out of Ireland he wishes to make known the state of the undertakers in the county of Cork The instructions given to Sir E Waterhouse and the other Commissioners appointed with him were—

(1) To decide the title between Her Majesty and the freeholders for the chargeable lands

(2) To alter the cesses of the soldiers on the lords and captains of countries into a certain revenue as in Connaught

(3) To see what Englishmen each undertaker had bought over and planted

When Her Highness had Justice Anderson and Mr Attorney before Her at the Court, they delivered their opinion that in respect of the charge which was found by office that the traitor Earl (of Desmond) had on the land, Her Majesty might justly take three parts of four parts of the land into Her own hands for the undertakers, according to which rate the Lord Barry, the Lord Roche, with the captains of the other countries in Cork, do at this present deal with their freeholders Yet Her Majesty's pleasure was that some sorts of the freeholders should have a third part The manner of the Commissioners dealing therein was by calling the freeholders before them and demanding of them what they would willingly yield unto Her Majesty in respect of the charge formed on their land (as due to the Earl of Desmond) They gave two days respite of answer, at which time they, having agreed together, said they would yield to no composition It was well known that of themselves they will never yield to better conformity Wherefore, except Her Majesty please to direct a certain course by the advice of Her learned council who have heard all their titles according to that which by law she may do, Her Majesty shall greatly prejudice Herself and hinder Her purpose in planting that country with Englishmen As for my own part, I mustered before them 100 Englishmen that I brought over with me to plant there, yet have I not five ploughlands to place them in I was very earnest with the Commissioners to procure them to set down order according as I had heard the Judge and Mr Attorney yield their opinions, but nothing was done, which hath been to my great harm And albeit that those freebooters of themselves will not yield, yet in my own knowledge I am sure they expect to have but after the rate of the other lord's freebooters, which is a fourth part For one of them, before the Commissioners came, sold me his fourth part of one ploughland in my seignory, he claiming no more thereof And since the Commissioners departed another freeholder came unto me and yielded a ploughland into my hand, and prayed me to give him the fourth part of that I made of it All the forwardest of them can say against her Majesty is that the Earl laid this charge upon them by extortion Many ways appear to prove their error in that, for as there are divers sorts of charges on the land, so are there divers sorts of freeholders likewise that yield only a small rent and suit of court to all, which sorts the Earl and his officers ever held one course, never taking more of any freeholders that owed only rent and suit but that And yet there is a third part of that my uncle Sentleger and I hold that was held by rent and suit And of the other lands that are found to owe this charge he often made leases to the strangers when the freeholders would not inhabit the same, to answer him his three parts, leaving to the freeholders his fourth part And when my uncle Sentleger and I first planted there, being more than twenty years past, we being then tenants to the Earl, all those who now seek to keep the whole of the chargeable lands yielded then to give us as much rent for every of those ploughlands as any lord or captain of the Tribe do make of their own private land at this day. If the Earl had therein dealt as a tyrant by extortion he would have done it generally, the which he did not do, but took a noble of some, ten shillings of others, and of some, but only suit of court, and so held an equal course with everyone according to his tenure. And when it is known that this Earl and divers other lords of countries had in times past many thousand pounds of certain rents which could not be raised but on these lands which are now chargeable; and if this chargeable land be held as the freeholders now seek the same I do protest unto your honour I would not exchange the poor portion I have in England for the greatest lord's living in Munster. Unless some speedy settlement be made of this question the project of peopling Ireland will be greatly hindered and the Queen prejudiced.

Concerning the altering the cess of the soldiers, the Commissioners called the lords and captains of counties together and declared Her Majesty's instructions, which lords and captains seemed unwilling to yield a certain revenue out of their livings for that might somewhat touch themselves, where now though the cess be very grievous, yet it never hurteth them. For that the whole burden thereof lighteth on the freeholders and inhabitants, who nevertheless yield unto their lords their whole demands. But a great number of the freeholders and their followers were very willing to agree to it. Inconveniences grow by the uncertain course that the lords and captains hold in settling their lands to their tenants, who hold the same not above four years, and so wander from one place to another, which course being redressed, and they commanded to set their lands as the undertakers must do would do much good to breed civility generally in the country; for whereas now the poor man is never certain to enjoy the fruits of his own labour and knoweth not in certainty what his lord would have of him. For fear he must depend on him and follow all his actions, be they good or bad; whereas, otherwise, if the poor tenant held his land by lease for his life or for twenty-one years at a certain rent, then were he sure of his charge, and that the overplus were his own, so would he depend on Her Majesty and Her laws to be defended against the oppressions which now too commonly every lord useth. The question of the chargeable lands must be quickly settled. Next Michaelmas the half rent must be paid to Her Majesty and Sir Richard has not as yet as much land as he is allowed for his own private demesnes, so he cannot place any tenants or raise any rents. Sir Richard is for some years to make his abode in Munster so for his credit's sake amongst his neighbours in Cornwall he wishes for permission to transfer the charge of such private bands of men as he has to his son and also that his son may supply a place with the rest in justice.

The following March Sir Richard petitions for a fee farm of the abbey of Fermoy, and on the 24th of October the Queen herself writes to Sir W. Fitzwilliam, the Lord Deputy, on his behalf, that he may have the grants of the Abbey of Fermoy and Gilley Abbey passed to him, as signified by former letters dated 22nd April, 1589; and it would seem that some little dispute had arisen between Sir Richard and Sir Warham St. Leger, inasmuch as the Lord Deputy had passed on the grant of Gilley Abbey to Sir Warham and the Queen bids him to order that Sir Richard is not to be disturbed in the quiet possession thereof, and St Leger is to have "some other thing there."

The same day, October 24th, Sir Richard receives a Royal Letter commanding him to repair to Her Majesty for some causes of service which he shall understand, and to make the Lord Deputy acquainted with this Her pleasure.

What this special service for his Queen and country was, we can only guess,[1] but probably it was that last great one he achieved, and in the discharge of which he so nobly sacrificed his life.

In 1590 the King of Spain was busy with his new Armada. The first had failed wofully, it is true ; but it had failed, so the Spaniards plumed themselves, by no inferiority of ships or men. The winds and waves had destroyed it, not English valour or seamanship.   The Pope and his priests would no doubt arrange matters better with Heaven next time   Still it behoved him on his part to neglect no precaution , and one of these was to stop the plate fleet for that year   One, and an unusually rich one, was lying at Havannah ready for the homeward voyage, but the risk of losing so much material at such a time was too great.   For somehow or other, despite the high words, Philip could not altogether blink the sad fact that when English and Spanish sailors met on the high seas, it was not as a rule the former who got the worst of it.   So the plate fleet was ordered to winter at Havannah, and even not to sail next year till much later than usual, the chances of bad weather being preferred to the English guns   Elizabeth had been advised of this, and accordingly, as we may suppose, sent for Sir Richard from Ireland, and having appointed him Vice-Admiral of England under Sir Thomas Howard, despatched them to spoil Philip's game by intercepting the Spanish fleet at the Western Islands. A fresh fleet under Lord Cumberland was also sent to the Spanish coasts, in case the prize should slip through Howards hands   But Philip knew what was going on as well as Elizabeth, and in August about the time when the Havannah fleet might be looked for at the Azores, he despatched a part of his Armada down to those islands   On the last day of the month the two fleets came in sight of each other off Flores, the westernmost island of the group

[1] A commission was issued in 1590 to Richard Grenvile, Piers Edgcumbe, Arthur Basset, John Fitz, Edmund Tremayne, W Humphreys Alexander Arundel, Thomas Higges, Mortimer Dare, Dominick Chester and others to fit out and equip a fleet for the discovery of land in the Antartic Sea, the special object of their search being an approach to the dominions of the ' Great Cam of Cathaia "

Howard had six men-of-war with him, and nine or ten smaller vessels carrying few or no guns, victuallers as they were called, and pinnaces His fighting ships were the " Defiance," carrying the Admiral's flag, the " Bonaventure," the " Lion," the " Foresight," the " Crane,' and the " Revenge," flying Sir Richard's flag as Vice-Admiral   Of these, the " Foresight," and the " Crane" were of small size and light armament   The " Bonaventure " was of six hundred tons, an old ship, but a good one   She had been with Drake in the West Indies, and had carried his flag in the memorable raid on Cadiz in 1587   Though she had now seen thirty-one years hard service, the sailors vowed there was not a stronger ship in the world

The " Revenge" had been built in 1579 at Chatham by Sir John Hawkins, and was the crack ship of her class in the Elizabethan navy, in which she ranked as what would now be called a second-rater   She was of 500 tons burthen, with a picked crew of 250 men, and carried from 30 to 40 guns Sir Francis Drake, whose skill in seamanship was probably unsurpassed, had chosen her to fight his fight as Vice-Admiral against the Spanish Armada in 1588, and when commanding her in that memorable series of engagements, captured the galleon " La Señora de Rosario," of 1,050 tons and her captain, Don Pedro de Valdez.   The " Revenge," however, in spite of her fighting qualities, was notoriously an unlucky ship, and Sir Richard Hawkins gives the following account of her mishaps (1622 Observations).   " As was plainly seene in the ' Revenge,' which was ever the unfortunatest ship the late Queene's Majestie had during her raigne, for comming out of Ireland with Sir John Parrot, she was like to bee cast away upon the Kentish coast   After, in the voyage of Sir John Hawkins, my father, anno 1586, shee strucke aground comming into Plimothe before her going to sea.   Upon the coast of Spaine she left her fleete, readie to sinke withe a great leake   At her returne into the harbour of Plimothe, shee beate upon Winter-stone , and after, in the same Voyage, going out to Portsmouth Haven, she ranne twice aground, and in the latter of them lay twentie-two houres beating upon the shore, and, at lengthe, with eight foote of water in her hold, she was forced off, and presently ran upon the Ooze, and was cause that she remained there (with three other ships of her Majestie's) six months, till the springe of the yeare   When comming about to be docked, entering the river Thames, her old leake breaking upon her had like to have drowned all those that were on her.   In anno 1591, with a storme of wind and weather, riding at her moorings in the river at Rochester, nothing but her bare mast overhead, she was turned topsie-turvie, her kele upper-most "

A chapter of accidents surely ' and it is a singular testimony to her excellent qualities that, despite all her ill-luck, her model should have been selected, after the experience gained in the great conflict with the Spaniards of 1588, by the first seaman of the time, as the best type for future ships, for in the state papers of Elizabeth is this entry —"1588 November 20th   Device by Lord Admiral Howard, Sir Francis Drake, Sir William Wynter, Sir John Hawkins, Captain William Brough, and others, for the construction of four new ships, to be built on the model of the 'Revenge,' but exceeding her in burthen ; the dimensions to be 100 feet by the keel, 35 feet in breadth, and 15 feet depth in the hold."

When the Spanish fleet hove in sight many of the English crews were ill on shore, while others were filling the ships with ballast or collecting water   Imperfectly manned and ballasted as they were there was nothing for it—at least so Sir Thomas Howard appears to have thought—in the face of so enormously preponderating a force as they found at hand, but to weigh anchor and escape as best they could, and so it became a complete *sauve qui peut*.   Eleven out of the twelve English vessels got away to the windward of the enemy—but Sir Richard was in no haste to fly.   He first saw all his sick safely brought on board and stowed away on the ballast, and then, with no more than a hundred men left to fight and work the ship, he deliberately weighed, uncertain, as it seemed at first, what he intended to do   He was by this time hemmed in between the Spanish fleet and the shore, and could not gain the wind.   In this situation he was recommended to cut his main-sail and cast about, and trust to the superior sailing of the ship to get away   But this he utterly refused to do, saying he would rather die than leave such a mark of dishonour upon himself, his country and his Queen   He told his men that he would pass through the two Spanish squadrons in spite of them and compel the Seville ships to give him way   This indeed he performed upon several of the foremost who sprang their luff and fell under the lee of the " Revenge " but the wind was light and the " San Philip,' a hugh high-cargoed ship of 1,500 tons, came up to windward of her, and becalmed her sails in such sort as the " Revenge ' could neither make way nor feel the helm ; and then—

Sir Richard spoke and he laughed, and we roared a hurrah, and so
The little "Revenge" ran on sheer into the heart of the foe,
With her hundred fighters on deck, and her ninety sick below ,
For half of their fleet to the right, and half to the left were seen,
And the little "Revenge" ran on thro' the long sea lane between

What end could there be, but one, to courage so chivalric, so desperate, and so devoted as this ? "After the 'Revenge' was entangled with this 'Philip,'" says Raleigh, four others boarded her, two on her larboard, and two on her starboard The fight thus beginning at three o'clock in the afternoon, continued very terrible all that evening But the great 'San Philip' having received the lower tier of the 'Revenge,' discharged with cross-bar shot, shifted herself with all diligence from her sides, utterly mislaking her first entertainment Some say the ship foundered, but we cannot report for truth, unless we are assured The Spanish ships were filled with companies of soldiers, in some two hundred, besides the mariners, in some five, in others eight, hundred. In ours there were none at all, besides the mariners, but the servants of the commanders, and some few voluntary gentlemen only After many interchanged volleys of great ordnance and small shot, the Spaniards deliberated to enter the 'Revenge,' and made divers attempts, hoping to force her, by the multitudes of their armed soldiers and musketeers, but were still repulsed again and again, and at all times beaten back into their own ships or into the seas "

And the rest they came aboard us, and they fought us hand to hand ,
For a dozen times they came with their pikes and musqueteers,
And a dozen times we shook them off, as a dog that shakes his ears
When he leaps from the water to the land

"In the beginning of the fight," Sir Walter Raleigh continues, "the 'George Noble,' of London, having received some shot through her, by the Armadas, fell under the lee of the 'Revenge' and asked Sir Richard what he would command him, being but one of the victuallers, and of small force , Sir Richard bade him save himself and leave him to his fortune [1] After the fight had thus, without intermission, continued while the day lasted, and some hours of the night, many of our men were slain and hurt, and one of the galleons of the Armada and the admiral of the hulks both sunk, and in many other of the Spanish ships great slaughter was made "

[1] The 'onesight' had kept near the Revenge as well until entangled, etc

The great marvel is how a fragment of the brave little craft was still afloat, for

Ship after ship, the whole night long, then high-built galleons came,
Ship after ship, the whole night long, with their battle-thunder and flame,
Ship after ship, the whole night long, drew back with her dead and her shame,
For some were sunk, and some were shattered, and some could fight us no more ,
God of battles ! was ever a battle like this in this world before ?

"Some write," says Raleigh, that " Sir Richard was very dangerously hurt almost in the beginning of the fight, and lay speechless for some time before he recovered, but two of the 'Revenge's' own company brought home in a ship of Lime (Lyme Regis) from the islands, examined by some of the lords and others, affirm that he was never so wounded as that he forsook the upper deck, till an hour before midnight , and then being shot into the body with a musket as he was dressing, was again shot into the head, and withal his chirurgion wounded to death.   This agreeth also with an examination taken by Sir Francis Godolphin, of four other marines of the same ship being returned, which examination the said Sir Francis sent unto Master William Killigrue, one of Her Majesty's Privy Chamber"

But to return to the fight.   'The Spanish ships which attempted to board the 'Revenge' as they were wounded and beaten off, so always others came in their place, she having never less than two mighty galleons by her sides, and aboard her , so that ere the morning, from three of the clock of the day before, there had been fifteen several Armadas assailed her ; and all so ill-approved their entertainment, as they were led by break of day far more willing to a composition than hastily to make any more assaults or entries   But as the day increased, so our men decreased , and as the light grew more and more, by so much more grew our discomforts , for none appeared in sight but enemies, saving one small ship called the 'Pilgrim,' commanded by Jacob Whiddon, who hovered all night to see the success , but in the morning bearing with the 'Revenge,' was hunted like a hare amongst many ravenous hounds, but escaped

All the powder in the 'Revenge was to the last barrel exhausted, all her pikes were broken, forty of her best men killed   .   the masts all beaten overboard all her tackle cut asunder, her upper work altogether razed, and in effect evened she was with the water, but the very foundation of a ship, nothing being left overhead either for fight or defence."

Mr. O. W. Brierly's recent engraved picture of this stage of the fight, showing the little " Revenge," with her mainsail down and lying over her " like a pall," surrounded by her overtowering enemies, still afraid to approach the dangerous little bark, gives a vivid and probably accurate idea of the tremendous odds against which the devoted Englishmen had to contend

Sir Richard, finding himself in this distress, and unable any longer to make resistance, having endured in this fifteen hours' fight the assault of fifteen different Armadas, all by turns aboard him, and by estimation eight hundred shot of great artillery, besides many assaults and entries, and that the ship and himself must needs be possessed of the enemy, who were now all cast in a ring about him, now gave the order to destroy his gallant craft

> We have fought such a fight for a day and a night
> As may never be fought again,
> We have won great glory, my men,
> And a day less or more
> At sea or ashore,
> We die, does it matter when ?
> Sink me the ship, Master Gunner—sink her—split her in twain,
> Fall into the hands of God ! not into the hands of Spain '

To this the master-gunner readily assented, but according to Raleigh's account the captain and master pointed out that the Spaniards would doubtless give them good terms, and that there were still some valiant men left on board their little ship whose lives might hereafter be of service to England   Sir Richard was probably by this time too weak and wounded to contest the matter further, the counsels of the captain and master prevailed, and the master actually succeeded in obtaining for conditions that all their lives should be saved, the crew sent to England, and the officers ransomed   In vain did the master-gunner protest and even attempt to commit suicide Tennyson has summed up the story in one sad line —

> And the lion lay there dying, and they yielded to the foe

The 'Revenge' being filled with the bodies of the dead and dying, and resembling a slaughter-house, the Spanish sent to have Sir Richard removed out of her.   Sir Richard answered " that he might do with his body what he liked, for he cared not ; " and as he was carried out of the ship he swooned, but reviving again, desired the company to pray for him

Sir Richard was taken on board the ship called the " Sant Paule,' wherein was the Admiral of the fleet   Don Alonso d

Baisan, there his wounds were dressed by the Spanish surgeons, but Don Alonso himself would neither see him, nor speak with him All the rest of the captains and gentlemen went to visit him, and to comfort him in his hard fortune, wondering at his courage and stout heart, for he showed not any signs of faintness nor changing of colour

But no fair words nor surgery could save Sir Richard He died on the second or third day after his removal, and all the Spanish gentlemen mourned for him as though he had been of their own blood. His last words were in Spanish, and therefore addressed to the Spanish officers.

" Here die I, Richard Grenvile, with a joyful and quiet mind ; for I have ended my life as a true soldier ought to do, fighting for his country, Queen, religion, and honour , whereby my soul most joyfully departeth out of this body, and shall leave behind it an everlasting fame of a valiant and true soldier that hath done his duty as he was bound to do "

When he had finished these or such other like words he gave up the ghost, with great and stout courage, and no man could perceive any true sign of heaviness in him

The dying words of Wolfe on the heights of Abraham, Moore on the hill over Corunna, or Nelson on the " Victory " at Trafalgar, do not surpass those of this fine old seaman warrior, who spoke his own epitaph when he lay on board the Spanish ship, his life-blood ebbing away.

Whatever Don Alonso's motive may have been for not seeing Sir Richard (whether anger at his severe loss of two ships and 400 men, or gentlemanly feeling in refusing to gloat his eyes on his dying foe), he appears to have behaved more kindly to the English prisoners than Spanish commanders in those days were wont to do Linschoten met the English captain of the soldiers of the " Revenge ' at dinner at Captain Bartandono's—one of the Spanish captains who had commanded the Biscayans in the Armada Bartandono " seeing us, called us up into the gallery, where with great courtesy he received us , being then set at dinner with the English captain that sat by him and had on a suit of black velvet , but he could not tell us anything, for he could speak no other language but English and Latin, which Bartandono could also speak a little " " The English captain (who had commanded under Sir Richard) was permitted by the Governor to land with his weapon by his side," so the Spaniards even strained courtesy so far as to allow their prisoner to retain his sword. He was in his own lodging " The Governor of

Tercera bade him to dinner, and shewed him great courtesy The master likewise, with licence of Bartandono, came on shore and was in our lodging He had at least twelve wounds as well in his head as on his body" The English captain was sent to Lisbon and was received with courtesy and sent to England The master died of his wounds

But the 'Revenge," like Sir Richard, had fought her last fight. The Spaniards patched her up as well as they could, and put a crew of their own on board. But a few days after the fight a great storm arose, and the "Revenge" went down off St Michael with two hundred Spaniards on board, and fourteen of the galleons went down with her to give her honourable burial Several more were lost among the other islands, and of the great plate-fleet itself. "the cause of all this woe, what with this storm and the English cruisers, among whom the brave little "Pilgrim" figures again, less than one-third ever came safe into Spain ·Thus (wrote Raleigh) it hath pleased God to fight for us"

This last fight of the "Revenge" has well been called "England's naval Thermopylæ" It was, from the first, as hopeless a battle as that of the Spartans under the brave Leonidas, and its moral effects at the time were hardly less than that of Thermopylæ. "By many men's judgments" the ruin of the great Spanish fleet in the fight, and in the storm afterwards in the Azores, "was esteemed to be much more than was felt by their army (Armada) that came for England (in 1588), and it may be well thought and presumed that it was no other than a just plague purposely sent by God upon the Spaniards, and that it might truly be said the taking of the 'Revenge' was justly revenged upon them, and that not by the might or force of man, but by the power of God" Spain disheartened by the Armada, lost all prestige by the Thermopylæ of the sea, and has never regained it

The death of Sir Richard made a deep impression on his countrymen; there is but one historian that speaks in a slighting manner of his conduct and death, and that one is Sir William Monson, a cold, unfeeling and heartless censurer of most other men's actions He calls Sir Richard a "stubborn man, so head-strong and rash that he offered resistance to those who advised him to cut his cable and follow his Admiral," that his wilful rashness made the Spaniards triumph as much as if they had obtained a naval victory," etc

Other feelings prompted greater men to view Sir Richard's conduct in a different light 'The fight of the 'Revenge'" says Lord Bacon, "was memorable even beyond credit, and to the height of some heroical fable for though it were a defeat, yet it exceeded a victory, being like the act of Samson, that killed more men at his death than he had done in the time of all his life This ship," he adds, "for fifteen hours sat like a stag among hounds at bay" This was that enthusiasm or rather madness of courage which some will have to be the highest perfection in a sea-officer It was a maxim of Admiral Howard, who lived in the reign of Henry VIII, that a degree of frenzy was necessary to qualify a man for that station" Granger's ' Biographical History "

' It is true that valour alone, without discretion, is not unlikely to lead to discomfiture, but it has been owing to such stuff as Greenvil was made of, that the navy of Great Britain has acquired that high prominence, which, since his time, it has never ceased to hold, that, in short, produced a Nelson, who, in like circumstances with Greenvil, would have fought like Greenvil" Barrow's "Naval Worthies of Queen Elizabeth's Reign."

In 1595, Gervase Markham wrote a poem, entitled, "The most Honorable Tragedie of Sir Richard Grinvile. Knight Bramo assai, poco spero nulla chieggio ," a very rare book, only two copies of it being known, but it has been reprinted by Arber It is a lengthy and somewhat fantastic production ; we may however well quote the following lines from it —

> Rest then, dear soul, in thine all-resting peace,
> And take my tears for trophies to thy tomb,
> Let thy lost blood thy unlost fame increase,
> Make kingly ears thy praises' second womb,
> That when all tongues to all reports surcease,
> Yet shall thy deeds outlive the day of doom
> For even Angels in the Heavens shall sing,
> Grinvile unconquered died, still conquering

The December following Sir Richard's death an enquiry was held, with Sir R Bevill as chief commissioner, into the circumstances of it, and it was doubtless in order to justify the memory of his friend against the aspersions of such men as Sir William Monson that Sir Walter Raleigh wrote his "Report of the Truth of the Fight about the Iles of the Acores this last Summer betwixt the ' Revenge' and an Armada of the King of Spaine "

The conduct of Lord Thomas Howard in not coming to the rescue of the ' Revenge' has been questioned In Linschoten's version of the story, Sir Richard s dying speech is said to have ended thus "But the others of my company have done as traitors and dogs, for which they shall be reproached all their lives and have a shameful name for ever." Thomas Phillippes in a letter to Thomas Barnes, says, "they condemn the Lord Thomas for a coward, and some say he is for the King of Spain." He supposes his friend Barnes "has heard of the quarrel and offer of combat between the Lord Admiral and Sir Walter Raleigh.' To talk of men like Howard and Fenner as cowards is ridiculous. But it is clear from the trouble Raleigh takes to excuse both parties that there was some disputing afterwards, when it was seen what this one ship had done, as to what might have been the issue had the whole squadron given battle. Yet Raleigh himself allows that "if all the rest had entered, all had been lost." Therefore the shade of Sir Thomas may fairly be suffered to rest in peace, and Sir Richard's well-known temper and his disappointment at seeing so great a fight fought in vain, may no less fairly excuse his hasty words against his comrades—*if he ever uttered them.*

Five years afterwards, when England determined to attack Cadiz, and to strike a blow in Spanish waters from which Spain would never recover, Sir Walter Raleigh, leading the van of the English squadron in the 'War Sprite" avenged his cousin's death. On the 21st June, 1596, at break of day, he sailed into Cadiz Bay. In front of them, ranged under the wall of Cadiz, were seventeen galleys lying with their prows to flank the English entrance as Raleigh ploughed on towards the galleons. The fortress of St Philip and other forts along the wall began to scour the Channel, and, with the galleys, concentrated their fire upon the "War Sprite." But Raleigh disdained to do more than salute one and then the other with a contemptuous blare of trumpets. "The 'St Philip,'" he says 'the great and famous Admiral of Spain, was the mark I shot at, esteeming those galleys but as wasps in respect of the powerfulness of the others." The "St Philip' had a special attraction for him. It was five years since his dear friend and cousin, Sir Richard Granville, under the lee of the Azores, with one little ship the "Revenge," had been hemmed in and crushed by the vast fleet of Spain, and it was the St. Philip " and the "St Andrew" that had been foremost in that act of murder. Now, before Raleigh, there rose the same lumbering monsters of the deep, that very "St Philip and "St Andrew' which had looked down and watched Sir Richard Granville die as a true soldier ought to do, fighting for his country, queen, religion and honour.' It seems almost fabulous that the hour of pure poetical justice should strike so soon, and that Raleigh, of all living Englishmen, should thus come face to face with those of all the Spanish tyrants of the deep As he swung forward into the harbour and saw them there before him, the death of his kinsman in the Azores was solemnly present to his memory, "and being resolved to be revenged for the 'Revenge,' or to second her with his own life," as he says, he came to anchor close to the galleons and for three hours the battle with them proceeded "English Worthies—Raleigh, by E Gosse

In the end the greater part of the Spanish ships of war were obliged to cut and make their escape; two, the "St. Matthew" and "St Andrew," were boarded and taken , whilst two others the "St Philip" and "St Thomas" were set fire to, and burnt down to the water's edge The Spaniards themselves set on fire and destroyed all the small shipping, to prevent its falling into the hands of the English The loss said to be sustained by Spain was equal in value to more than twenty millions of ducats, not to mention the indignity which that proud and ambitious people suffered from the sacking of one of their chief cities, and destruction in their own harbour of a fleet of such force and value

There is a portrait of Sir Richard in the possession of the Thynne family at Haynes, near Bedford, painted in the year 1571 when he was twenty-nine years old. This picture, as Charles Kingsley describes it, represents him with the most keen and determined expression imaginable. "The forehead and the whole brain are of extraordinary loftiness, and perfectly upright , the nose long, aquiline, and delicately pointed . the mouth fringed with a soft silky beard, small and ripe, yet firm as granite, with just pout enough of the lower lip to give hint of that capacity of noble indignation which lay hid under its usual courtly calm and sweetness If there be a defect in the face, it is that the eyes are somewhat small and close together, and the eyebrows, though delicately arched and without a trace of peevishness, too closely pressed down upon them The complexion is dark, the figure tall and graceful , altogether the likeness of a wise and gallant gentleman, lovely to all good men, awful to all bad men ; in whose presence none dare say or do a mean or ribald thing , whom brave men left feeling themselves nerved to do their duty better, while cowards slipped away, as bats and owls before the sun So he lived and moved , whether in the court of Elizabeth, giving his counsel among the wisest; or in the streets of Bideford capped alike by squire and

merchant, shopkeeper and sailor, or riding along the moorland
roads between his house of Stowe and Bideford, while every
woman ran out to her door to look at the great Sir Richard,
the pride of North Devon, or sitting in the low mullioned
window at Burrough, with his cup of malmsey before him,
and the lute, to which he had just been singing, laid across
his knees, while the red western sun streamed in upon his
high bland forehead and soft curling locks, ever the same
stedfast, God-fearing, chivalrous man; conscious (as far as
soul so healthy could be conscious), of the pride of beauty
and strength and valour and wisdom, and a race and a name
that claimed direct descent from the grandfather of the
Conqueror, and was tracked down the centuries by valiant
deeds and noble benefits to his native shire, himself the
noblest of the race. Men said that he was proud, but he
could not look around him without having something to be
proud of, that he was stern and harsh to his sailors, but
it was only when he saw in them any taint of cowardice or
falsehood, that he was subject at moments to such fearful
fits of rage that he had been seen to snatch the glasses
from the table, grind them to pieces in his teeth, and swallow
them, but that was only when his indignation had been
aroused by some tale of cruelty and oppression, and above
all by those West Indian deviltries of the Spaniards, whom
he regarded (and in those days rightly enough) as the
enemies of God and man."

The following review of the influence which Sir Richard
and men of his ilk had upon England's maritime and industrial
greatness shall conclude this chapter:—

Extraordinary as the man was, it is impossible to consider Sir Richard
Grenville altogether apart from the famous band of Devon and Cornish sailors
of whom he was one. Yet history has scarcely ever produced a group of men,
having one chief object in common, whose individual personalities have
remained so distinct. It may be difficult to follow Mr Froude's eloquent
advocacy of all their actions, or to admit that, because they were true, fearless
Englishmen, with "royal hearts," they were therefore inherently superior to
the law of nations as recognised even in their time. Still less, on the other
hand, does it seem possible to speak of them with Professor Seeley as in many
respects little better than buccaneers. Modern Englishmen, for the most
part, are content to accept them in relation to the great national work they
performed, and to cherish their memories in the character denied to them by
no one, as the founders of England's maritime and industrial greatness. Two
new and dominant forces had just sprung into existence in their day—the
Reformation and the discovery of the New World. It was the sailors as much
as the statesmen of England who aided Elizabeth to use these forces to the
lasting good and greatness of the country. England, it has been well said,
entered on an entirely new period at the time of the Spanish Armada. Before

she turned away from the Continent and began to look towards the ocean and the New World

That she looked with such good effect, and with the eventual result of making two small islands the nucleus of the greatest Empire in the World, was due, in the first place, to the splendid conduct of the Elizabethan sailors, and to the lasting effects on the national mind of the traditions of daring and seamanship handed down to succeeding generations. As we have said, it required much more than a mechanical group united by their buccaneering qualities to accomplish this, and a short study of Grenville and his companions will show that they were not unworthy of the confidence shown them by Elizabeth, or less bulwarks of her great reign than the Cecils, Walsinghams, Bacons, and Philip Sydneys who formed her Court. Drake, for instance, when "he climbed the tree in Panama, and saw both oceans, and vowed to sail a ship in the Pacific," or again, "when he crawled out upon the cliffs of Terra del Fuego and leaned his head over the southernmost angle of the world, may fairly be said to have represented the spirit of enterprise at its highest. Sir Humphrey Gilbert, in the "Golden Hinde,' stands forth as the exponent of all that was best in the chivalry and natural piety of the age. Raleigh remains the great link which united the men of action to the culture and statesmanship of Elizabeth's court. A little apart from all these, Sir Richard Grenville is the final representative of the indomitable force and fierceness by which the rivalry of England and Spain, whether in the New World or the Old, whether on behalf of the Reformation or against it, was marked throughout the reign of Elizabeth

CHAPTER VIII.

SIR RICHARD as above stated, had married Mary, the eldest daughter and coheiress of Sir John St Leger of Annery, near Bideford. Lady Granville survived her heroic husband thirty-two years, and was buried in Bideford Church. The following is a copy of the entry of her burial in the Parish Register —

The Ladie Mary Grenvile, daughter unto the right worthie Sr John St Leger, Knight, deceased, and wife to that famous warior Sr Richard Greavile, Knight, also deceased, beinge in his life time the Spanniards terror. She was buried in the Grenviles Ile in the Church of Bediford, the ffifth daie of November Anno dni 1623

By her will, dated 11 November 1618, she left forty shillings to the poor of the several parishes of Bideford, Winkleigh, Broadwoodkelly and Monkokehampton. By this marriage Sir Richard had issue three sons and five daughters, viz —

1. Bernard, who succeded him
2. John, who commanded " the Virgin, GOD save Her,' one of the three ships which formed Sir Richard's contingent from Bideford that took part in defeating the Invincible Armada. He appears to have succeeded to his father's Irish estates, but having been put out of possession of some parcels of land in Munster by the Bishop of Cork, the Queen wrote to the Lord Deputy and Council to take care of his interest, as he had been appointed to a certain service on the seas,[1] and in compensation for the temporary loss of his estate he was to be forborne certain arrears of rent for the Abbey of Fermoy. The Royal Letter bears date the 15th of March 1591-2. Evidently, however, the estate was not restored, for on the 16th of the following December Sir Warham St Leger and John Granville address the following petition to Lord Burleigh —

In most humble wise beseeching your Honour. That whereas there were very late 'petycionit' letters sent unto you and the rest of the Privy Council from Sir Warham Sentleger, Knight, in most humble sort to crave your favour towards himself and one of Sir Richard Greynvile's sons,

[1] He was in command of the ' Margaret and John," under Sir Martin Frobisher, watching the Spanish coast to capture the great curracl

R

for suffering them to enjoy the benefit of Her Majesty's most gracious letters, (extant to be shewn), written on the behalf of Sir Warham to the Lord Deputy and Council of Ireland, for permitting him to enjoy the seignory of Kerrywhirry, which was mortgaged unto them by the Earl of Desmond with a statute of £7000 for performance of the same, and, in consideration he was willing to surrender his said mortgage unto Her Majesty, he should hold it at half the rent that other undertakers of that county did pay, and not in any sort to be disturbed by Mr Cowper, or any other that might pretend interest thereunto as undertakers   And Mr Cowper intimating that the said mortgage was redeemed, the contrary is manifestly to be proved that both mortgage and statute remains yet of force in Sir Warham's hands ready to be shewn unto you   Since which former petitionate letters there hath been delivered by their agents unto you and the rest of the Privy Council a most humble petition, declaring the whole estate of their distressed cause, which doubting not, if it were read, would move you to have commiseration of them   And seeing that of so great a seignory, which contains 56 plough lands, there remains only 15½ to your poor petitioner Sir Warham Sentleger and to Sir Richard Greynvile's youngest son, whose father Sir Warham conjoined with him as a partner in that seignory, but now a poor partner in the least part thereof, it is most humbly and incessantly desired of you that Sir Warham and Sir Richard's son may enjoy this least part, according to Her Majesty's letters written in that behalf for the whole , if not in regard of the mortgage, yet in respect of the charge in general they both have been at in peopling of that county, which was waste to the expense between Sir Warham and Sir Richard at least of £8000 within these six years, besides many losses and spoils they have many years past sustained in that country   If neither in respect of that, yet in regard that many poor people have been trained over and settled in that country by them, having sold by their persuasion all their goods and livings in England only to plant themselves there, and being supplanted are utterly undone   If these causes and reasons can not prevail, yet lastly it is most humbly and petitionately desired that you will consider of the grievous and distressed time of Sir Warham's old age, and his long time spent in the dutiful service of Her Majesty , and then to think on the sudden death of Sir Richard in Her Majesty's service, whereby his youngest son your poor supplicant, hath not left any other portion but this poor Irish patrimony to live on, being also at the time of his death in Her Majesty's service in the Low Countries, where he performed, to the testimony of many, the part of a faithful and valiant soldier Neither hath he any other means to relieve himself if this be taken from him

Wherefore it is eftsoons most humbly desired that you will vouchsafe to write letters to the Lord Deputy of Ireland, that, notwithstanding your former letters written on behalf of Mr Cowper, a patent may be passed unto your poor and humble supplicants of that mean proportion which is left unto Her Majesty of that seignory of Kerrywhirry   So shall they be bound always to pray for the prosperous estate of your Honour, and your poor supplicant, Sir Richard Greynvile's son, will be ever ready to serve Her Majesty in all Her Highnesse's services as a faithful and loyal soldier

I most humbly beseech you to consider of the estate of your poor supplicant, Sir Richard Greynvile's son, whose father even to the end carried a true testimony of his loyal mind towards his prince and country, as the world generally doth witness, which together with his services is hoped to be by your Honour so regarded as that of two sons leaving the youngest (by reason of his unexpected death) altogether unprovided for of any living, saving this poor Irish portion, and your poor supplicant carrying the like mind of his father, ready to serve Her Majesty, and to that purpose exercising himself in the Low

Countries in martial affairs, you will vouchsafe to have that remorse of him as that he may be the better encouraged to good actions, and be able to relieve himself as the son of him, who lived and died Her Majesty's most loyal and vowed soldier and servant, or otherwise he shall be driven to wander as a distressed soul to seek his relief, which were a case most lamentable

Three years afterwards, whilst serving under Drake in the unsuccessful expedition of 1595, John Granville was killed Carew wrongly states, that he "followed Raleigh and was drowned in the ocean which thus became his beddle of honour" He was never married

3   Sir Richard's third son, Roger, had died young, and was buried at Kilkhampton, 10th December, 1565

Of the five daughters, the eldest was —

1   Bridget, who was married first to Sir Christopher Harris of Radford, co Devon, the close friend and executor of the will of Sir Francis Drake, who on one occasion lodged part of his captured treasure at Radford. Harris and Serjeant John Hele, as already stated, acquired Buckland Abbey in 1580 from Sir Richard Granville for the sum of £3,400 for Drake, and assisted him to make a munificent gift of water to Plymouth, when Harris was chosen M P to secure the passing of the Act

Bridget Granville married secondly the Rev John Weeks, Rector of Sherwell and Prebendary of Bristol, and was buried in Bristol Cathedral, 14th of February, 1627, where a monumental tablet, now nearly defaced, contains the following epitaph —

To the memory of Mrs Bridget Weekes, descended from the noble families of the Grenvils in Cornwall and the St Legers in Devon, wife unto Mr John Weekes, Rector of Sherwell and Prebend of this Cathedral

> By birth a Grenvill, and that name
> Was enough epitaph and fame
> To make her lasting, but the stone
> Would have this little more be known ,
> She was, whilst she did live, a wife
> The glorie of her husband's life,
> Her sex's credit and the sphere
> Wherein the virtues all move here
> And 'tis no doubt but grief had made
> The husband, as the wife, a shade,
> But that his death heaven did defer
> Awhile to stay and weep for her

Nine years afterwards, however, he consoled himself with a second wife, Grace, the fourth daughter of William Cary, of Clovelly, and sister of Sir Robert Cary, and of George Cary, Dean of Exeter from whose house she was married in the

Cathedral, 1st August, 1636   He became Vicar of Banwell,
Bristol, Dean of Bunyan, and Chaplain to Archbishop Laud
He was B D of Cambridge University and D D of Oxford

2   Catherine, who was married in Hartland Church,
1st June, 1589, to Justinian Abbot, second son of William
Abbot, of Hartland Abbey   Hartland Abbey was granted to
the Abbot family at the dissolution of the monasteries   One of
the co-heiresses afterwards brought the estate to the Luttrells
and a co-heiress of the Luttrells to the Orchards and a
co-heiress of the Orchards to the Stucleys, the present owners
Justinian Abbot was buried at Bideford, 6th February, 1602

3   Ursula, who died unmarried and was buried at Bideford
10th March, 1643

4   Rebecca, who also died unmarried and was buried at
Bideford 9th June, 1589

5   Mary, married at Kilkhampton, 11th June, 1586, to
Arthur Tremayne of Collacombe, this being the second
marriage between the two families, Thomas Tremayne of
Collacombe having married Phillipa, daughter of Sir Roger
Granville   Both these unions of Tremaynes with Granvilles
were productive of large families, and curiously enough of the
same number of children in each case, namely sixteen   The
first alliance it will be remembered produced eight sons and
eight daughters, this second alliance seven sons and nine
daughters   The eldest son of Arthur and Mary Tremayne was
true to the king during the troublesome times "and was several
hundred pounds deep in their books at Haberdashers' Hall for
his loyalty "   He is also stated to have repaid a considerable
portion of the money borrowed for the necessities of the Queen
during her sojourn at Exeter at the time of the birth of Princess
Henrietta, and to have never had it refunded   He became a
victim to sequestration and imprisonment at the hands of the
Parliamentarians

The following deed was made and executed by Sir Richard
in the year 1586 —

This indenture, made the syxtenthe daye of March, in the seven and
twentith yere of the Ragne of o[r] Sov'aigne Ladie Elizabeth, by the grace of
God, of England, ffrance, and Irland, Queene, defend[r] of the Faithe, etc
Between S[r] Richard Greynvill, of Stowe, in the countie of Cornwall, Knight,
of the one p[r]te, and S[t] Walter Rawley, S[t] Arthur Basset, S[r] Francis Godolphin,
Knights, Henry Killigrew, Richard Bellew, John Heale, and Christopher
Harrys, Esquires   Thom's Dorton and John ffacie, Gents, of the other p[r]te
Witnesseth that the said S[r] Richard Greynvill for div'se good causes and con-
sidera'ions now especiallie moving   Hath given, graunted, and enfeoffed and
by these p[r]nts for hym and hens, do give, graunt, and enfeoffe unto the saide
S[r] Walter Rawley, etc, and their heires   All that his man'con howse and

demayne landes of Stowe, lyeing and beinge with'n the p'she of Kilkehampton, in the countie aforesaide And all that the Manor of Kilkehampton, togeather wth all his landes, ten^ts, hereditaments, rents rever'cons, and seisms, lynge or beynge wi^th'in the p'she of Kilkehampton aforesaid Together with all his landes, ten^ts, and hereditaments, rents, rever'cons, and service, lynge or beynge in the p'she of Stratton, in the countie aforesaide Together with one tenement called Berrage, and all other his landes, tenem^ts, and hereditaments, rents, rever'cons, and service, lynge or beine wi^th'n the p'she of Morewenstowe, in the county aforesaide

And all those his two manners of Woolston and Wydermouth in the countie aforesaid Togeather with all his landes, ten^ts, and here^dts, rents, rever'cons, and service, lyeinge or beynge wi^th'in the p'she of Gwynape, in the countie aforesaid

And all that his mann^r of Swan'cott and Wykeborough Togeather with all his landes, tene^ts, and here'dits, lynge or beynge wi^th'in in the p'she of Sainte Marie Weke, or ellswhere wi^th'in the county aforesaide

And all that his mannor of Bediforde, and all his landes, ten^ts, and here'dits, rents, etc, in the countie of Devon And all that his man^r of Lytelham togeather with all his landes, ten^ts, etc, lynge or beynge wi^th'in the p'she of Lytelham, in the countie of Devon aforesaide

And all that his manor of Lancras al's Lanclras, or ellswhere, wi^th'in the countie of Devon aforesaide

And also all that his mannor, territorie or iland, commonlie called or knowen by the name of the ile of Lundye, w'in the p'cincte or libertie of the countie of Devon aforesaide, and all other his landes, ten^ts, and here^ds wi^thin the Realme of England

To have and to hold, all and sing'lar, the said manors, landes, ten^ts, and here^ds, and all other the p'misses, with the app'tenances unto the said Sr Walter Rawley, Sr Arthur Basset, etc etc, and their heires to the onlie use and behoof of the said Sir Walter Rawley, etc, and of their heires, and of the surviv^rs of them for and during the term of the naturall life of the saide Sr Richard Greynvile And that after the death of the saide Sr Richard Greynvile, the saide Sr Walter Rawley, etc shall stande and bee seased of the saide Man'con Howse and demesne landes of Stowe, in the countie of Cornwall, and alsoe of the saide all mannors of Kilkehampton, Woolston Wydmouth, and all landes and lyeing or beying in the sev'rall p'shes of Kilkehampton and Poundstock, wth all and singler the app'tenances in the saide countie of Cornwall, to the use and behoof of Dame Marie Greynevile, now wife of the said Sr Richard, for and during the term of her naturall life, if she shall soe longe live, sole and unmarried, in full recompence of the joynter or dower that the saide Dame Marie shall or mue anye w'ye clanne or demande, after the death of the saide Sr Richard, of anye landes, ten^ts, here^ts, whereof the said Sr Richard is, hath been, or shall be, seased of anye estate of inheritance whereof the saide Dame Marie is or may be dowable

And that after her decease, or if she happen to marie, then the saide Sr Walter Rawley, etc, and the surviv^r or surviv^rs of them and their heires, and anie of them, shall stande and be seised for and duringe the terme of twentie years, to be accompt'ed from the tyme of the death of the saide Sr Richard Greynevile, of all and singler the foresaide p'misses wth the app'tences, whereof the use is before lymyted to the saide Dame Marie to the use and intente of for the paymente of the detts, marriage of the daughters, and p'formans of the will of the said Sr Richard Grenevile, accordynge to the last will and testament of the saide Sr Richard, and after that to the use and behoofe of Bernarde Greynevile, sonne and heire apparente of the saide Sr Richard, and of the heires males of the body of the said Bernarde lawfullie begotten.

And in defaulte of such issue to the use of John Greynevile, second son of the saide S[r] Richard, and of the heires males of his bodie lawfullie begotten

And in defaulte of such issue to the use of Nicholas Greynevile and of the heires males of his bodie lawfullie begotten

And in defaulte of such issue to the use of Hu'frie Greynevile, brother of the saide Nicholas, and of the heires males of his bodie lawfullie begotten

And for defaulte of such issue to the use of Arthur Greynevile, and other brothers of the said Nicholas, and of the heires males etc

And for defaulte of such issue to the use of Thomas Greynevile, one other brother of the said Nicholas, and of the heirs males, etc

And for defaulte etc, to the use of Digorie Greynevile, one other brother, etc

And for defaulte of such issue, etc, to the use of the ryght heires of the saide John Greynevile, second son of the saide S[r] Richard, etc

And after the death of the saide S[r] Richard Greynevile, the saide S[r] Walter Rawley, etc, and then heires, shall stande and be seized of the foresaide mannor of Lanchas al'as Lanchias, in the county of Devon, and of all the landes, ten[ts], and hered[ts], rents, rev'cons, and service, lynge and beyinge in p'she of Lanchias aforesaide

And all those landes, etc, etc, knowen by the name of Upcote, lyinge or beyinge w'in the p'sh of Byddeford aforesaid   And also of the saide mannor, territorys, or Iland of Londye aforesaide, wth all and singler the app'tences for and during the term of twentie yeares, to the use and intente of, and for the payment of the detts, marriage of the daughters, and p'form'ce of the will of the saide S[r] Richard Greynevile

And after that to the use of the saide John Greynevile, second sonne of the saide S[r] Richard, and of the heires, males, etc

And for defaulte, etc, to the use of the same Bernard Greynevile, eldest sonne of the saide S[r] Richard, and heires, males, etc

The remaynder to the use of heires males of the bodie of the saide S[r] Richard, lawfullie begotten

And for defaulte, etc, to the use and behoof of George Greynevile, etc, of the heires males, and for defaulte to the use of the saide Hu'frie, and of the heires   And for defaulte, etc, to the other brothers   And for defaulte, etc, to the use of the ryght heires of John Greynevile for ever

And of all the residues of the forsaide mann[rs], lordships, lande, ten[ts], heredit's, rents, rever'cons, and s'ces, and all other the p'misses w[th] app'tences, lyeing or beyuig w[i]n the said ccuntie of Cornwall, wherof there is no use lymited to the same Dame Marie

And alsoe the saide mann[r] of Bediforde and Littleham, and all other p'misses before specyfied, with the app'tences, lyeing or beyinge w[th]in the Realmes of England whereof there is use intaile before lymited, the saide S[r] Walter Rawley, S[r] Arthur Basset, etc, for and during the terme twentie yeares next after the death of the saide S[r] Richard Greynevile, accordynge to the last will and testament of the saide S[r] Richard

And after that to the use and behoof of the saide Bernarde Greynevile, and of the heires males, etc

And for defaulte to the use of the saide John Greynevile, seconde sonne of the saide S[r] Richard, and of the heires males, etc

And in defaulte to the use of the heires males of the bodie of the said S[r] Richard

And for defaulte to the use of the saide George Greynevile, of Penheale, and of the heires, etc

And for defaulte to the use of William Greynevile, heires, etc

Then to the saide Nicholas Greynevile, heires, etc.   And for defaulte to

the saide H'ine and heires, etc   And for defaulte to the saide Arthur and
heires, etc   And for default to the said George, brother of the saide Nicholas,
and heires, etc   And for detaulte to Tho'ms, and heires, etc   And for
defaulte to the said Digorie and heires, etc   And for defaulte to the ryght
heires males of John Greyneville for ever

Provided, neverthelesse, that if it shall hap that the saide S'r Richard do
die, leveng the saide Dame Marie, and she do take or marrie a seconde
husband, by reason wherof her estate, use, interest, to her lymitted in the
pr'misses aforesaide shall cesse and determine   That then the intente and full
meanyng of the saide S'r Richard, and of all the parties to these p'ts, is that
the saide S'r Walter Rawley, etc, shall stand and be seised of all and sing'ler
the foresaide p'misses, w'th the app'tences, to the use and intente, that the
saide Dame Marie shall have and pay out of the said p'misses q'r'ie duringe
her life, the some of two hundred pounds of lawful Inglyshe monye, from the
tyme of her marriage so accomplished, to be paide at the fioure most usual
daies of feasts in the yere, by geven por'cons in lew and recom'pens of her
joynter and dower as aforesaide

Provided alwayes, and itt is covented, graunted, condescended, and fullye
ag'yed, by and betweene all the saide p'tes, that if the saide S'r Richard at
anie tyme or tymes duringe his naturall life by himselfe or in his own p'per
pp'onne, or by anie other p'sonne by him speciallye warranted by writinge
under his hand and seale of armes, at or in the saide p'she church of
Kilkehampton aforesaide, require or demande or the saide S'r Walter Rawley,
etc, etc, the some of flyftie thousand pounds of lawful Inglyshe monye
The .   shall not be to him then and there fullie satisfyed, contented, and
paide accordinge to his demande on that behalfe to be made as aforesaide
That then and from thenceforth all and sing'ler estates, condi'cons lymyta'cons,
and other things before in these p'ts declared or expressed, shall cease and be
utterlie voyde, and from thenceforth the saide S'r Walter Rawley, etc, etc,
shall stande and be seised of all and sing'ler the foresaide pr'ses w'th the
app'tences to the onlie use and behoof of the saide S'r Richard Greyneville, his
heires and assigns for ever

And to no other use, intente or pp'ie, anye thinge in these p'nts,
contayned to the contrarie, in anyewise not w'th standinge

In witness wheroff both the p'ties to the . .   indenture have enter-
chang   sett their seales   Given the daye and yere firste above
written

eyneville   (Seal wanting)

Indorsed

sealed and d by de'd the daye and yere w'th'in, and wryten in the p'sence of
those whose names are subscribed

Tho Roscarrock	Degorie Tremayne
Phyllph Cole	Degorie Ned .
A Arundell	Josh Deg Greynvill
Thom C	Geo Greynevill

Bernard Granville, Sir Richard's eldest son entered
University College, Oxford in 1574, being then fifteen years of
age. From old letters and documents he appears to have been
a person of some literary attainments, and an antiquarian and
genealogist   He compiled the pedigree of his family, which has
been published by the Harleian Society   In the Heralds'
Office is also to be seen a fine drawing of his coat of arms

displaying the armorial bearings of the different intermarriages from the earliest dates   He was, as Dr Oliver expresses it, "most fortunate" in his marriage with Elizabeth, daughter and sole heiress of Philip Bevill of Brinn, in the Parish of Withiel, Cornwall, third son of John Bevill of Killigarth, in the Parish of Talland, of which places he became eventually possessor in right of his wife   She was also heiress of her uncle, Sir William Bevill.   The Bevill family was one of earliest and most honourable in the annals of Cornwall, being descended from De Beville, a Norman knight, who accompanied the Conqueror in his expedition to England, and was placed at Truro as Commander-in-Chief of the Western District   There had already been an intermarriage between the two families, Bernard's great-grandmother, Matilda, the wife of Sir Richard Granville, the Marshall of Calais, being the younger daughter of John Bevill, High Sheriff for Cornwall in 1557

Bernard married Elizabeth Bevill on the 10th of July, 1592 in Withiel Church, about ten months after the glorious death of his father   Stowe, where doubtless he brought his bride, must probably have been at this time, as Kingsley has described it, "a huge rambling building, half castle, half dwelling house   On three sides, to the north, west, and south, the lofty walls of old ballium still stood with their machicolated turrets, loopholes, and dark downward crannies for dropping stones and fire on the besiegers, but the southern court of the ballium had become a flower garden with quaint terraces, statues, knots of flowers, clipped yews and hollies, and all the pedantries of the topiarian art   And towards the east, where the vista of the valley opened, the old walls were gone, and the frowning Norman keep, ruined in the wars of the Roses, had been replaced by the rich and stately architecture of the Tudors   Altogether the house, like the time, was in a transitionary state, and represented faithfully enough the passage of the old Middle Age into the new life which had just burst into blossom throughout Europe—never, let us pray, to see its autumn and winter   From the house, on three sides, the hills sloped steeply down, and from the garden there was a truly English prospect   At one turn they could catch over the western walls a glimpse of the blue ocean, flecked with passing sails , and at the next, spread far below, range on range of fertile park, stately avenue, yellow autumn woodland, and purple heather moors, lapping over and over each other up the valley to the old British earthwork, which stood bleak and furze grown on its conical peak   And standing out against the sky on the highest

SIR BERNARD GRANVILLE.

From an Original Portrait, by Zucchero, in the Haynes Park Collection.

bank which closed the valley to the east, the lofty tower of Kilkhampton, rich with the monuments and offerings of five centuries of Grenvilles."

Here lived Bernard Granville then, "treading" (as Carew says) "in a kind magnanimity the honourable steps of his ancestors.' He was appointed High Sheriff of Cornwall, 38 Eliz 1596, and served in Parliament for the borough of Bodmin the following year. In 1599 we find him at the head of a determined body of volunteers, ready at his call to earn distinction in arms, when the fears of another Spanish Armada, threatening to invade our shores, were uppermost in the minds of the British people. There was no standing army at that period. The only constitutional force was the militia, which was raised by the Lord Lieutenants of the counties, and all able-bodied men were liable to be impressed and enrolled by the constables of the several hundreds for training and service. But besides those pressed for the militia, many served as volunteers, and the ardent spirit of loyalty evoked by the news of a second Armada, resulted in the enrolment of more than six thousand sturdy volunteers in different parts of the West, burning to do battle with the menacing Dons. Of these, no less than one thousand rallied round Bernard Granville at Stowe.

A meeting of the deputy-lieutenants of Cornwall, Sir William Bevill, Sir Nicholas Parker, Bernard Granville and Richard Carew, was held at Pendennis Castle on the 13th of August in this same year, when orders were agreed upon, touching the distribution of the militia forces (which were also a thousand strong) and as to the particulars of their places of rendezvous, etc, and four days afterwards they addressed a letter to the Bishop of Exeter, in which they wrote as follows —

It is required in these dangerous expectations that we endeavour on all sides to further Her Majesty's service and the defence of our Prince and Country, and this country has been raised throughout to a greater provision of arms both of horse and foot. The clergy, whose charge is referred to your Lordship, are yet at their former rates, which is very inconvenient by reason of the ill-suiting of them, so that they are now fain to fetch arms out of divers parts of the shire for the furnishing of one man, and generally the whole clergy are charged at a far less rate than the laity. We therefore ask that some one or more nominated may with uprightness make a new rate of arms to be furnished by the clergy according to their ability throughout the country.

The following letter to Bernard Granville, written just one month after the death of Queen Elizabeth is from Eliza, Countess of Bath, whose husband, William Bourchier the third

Earl, was afterwards in 16'3, Lord Lieutenant of Devon. Tawstock, the ancient seat of the Bouchier family stands on the left bank of the river Taw, about two miles above Barnstaple, in a hollow lying between two gently swelling hills, facing the east The old house built in the reign of Elizabeth was burnt down in the year 1786, all but the gate-house which still stands and bears the date 1574 In front of the house, which with its range of gables, faced the river and the open downs of Coddon Hill on the opposite side of the valley there were by successive gradations a terrace walk, a bowling green, and a pleasance bordered by trimly-clipped hedges and formal alleys On the slope which fell away gradually to the river, midway—emboweled in trees, stood the parish church of Tawstock, now well-known for its picturesque interior and sumptuous monuments of the Bouchier family

The contemplated journey referred to in this letter was possibly to be taken in order to be present at the entry of James the First into London, which took place the 7th of May, 1603

THE COUNTESS OF BATH TO BERNARD GRANVILLE

Good Mr Grenvile

Whatsoever your fore passed thoughtes by heare say hath byn, yet I hope you are longe agone satisfied of me as a La that hath never wronged you And therefore, as out of a sincere conscience I think I may be thus bold w'th you as at this time to intreate your kinde favor in this little request, wch is to lett me exchaunge wth you for your sorrell geldinge wch I heare you hav For my happ is suche as I had thought I had byn well fitted for twoe Geldings for my Coache But one I had from Mr Stukley that will by no meanes serve, and our tyme in stay is shorte to enquire further of Therefore I am bold wth you to make tryall if yours will serve, and offer you no ill one, for this is wthout faulte, and, if he be not to yor hkinge, yet I will contente ame thinge you finde defective, by supplyinge some money over and besides the exchaunge, if your Gelding will serve my Coache And in this doinge I shall thinke my selfe beholdinge to you, and rest in all good wishes to you and yor wife

As yor frend if you so accept

ELIZA BATH

Tawstock 24 April 1603

When Sir Arthur Chichester was appointed Lord-Deputy of Ireland, Bernard Granville served under him, and took part in those wise measures of administration which tended so forcibly to the diminution of crime, that in a very short time, "there were were not found in all the Irish counties so many capital offenders as in the six shires of the western circuit in England" In consideration of his services, Bernard Granville, who had succeeded to the Irish property on the death of his brother

John in 1595, received fresh grants of land in Ireland, and was knighted at Christ Church, the 5th of November, 1608. In 1618 (May 15) he ordered a court leet and a court baron to be holden at Fermoy, co Cork, and another for the Seignory of Kynalmeaky, and in 1624 a grant was made ' to Sir George Horsey on the petition of Sir Bernard Grenville of the reversion of the sites of the monastery of Fermoy and Gilley, etc , whereof Sir Bernard was seized in entail." On the 25th August, 1641, a petition was lodged by Richard Earl of Cork respecting this Irish property of which the following is a copy taken from the appendix of the fourth report of the Historical MSS Commission, p 93

PETITION OF RICHARD EARL OF CORKE

Twenty years ago petitioner agreed to purchase from Sir Barnard Greenvile the seignory of Kynalneaky, containing one moiety of the cantred or barony of Kynalmeaky and the monestery, abbey, or religious house of Fermoy, and of the reversion of the monastery, abbey, or religious house of Antro Sacri Finbarry [St Finbar], alias Gill-Abbey, with all lands, tenements, &c thereunto belonging, in the county of Cork, for 3,500*l*, but when petitioner had actually brought the money to Bristol ready to perform the agreement, the Earl of Middlesex, then Lord High Treasurer, induced Sir Barnard Greenville to refuse completion of the purchase, and to sell the lands to him for the same sum The Earl of Middlesex having thus got possession of the lands, told Sir George Horsey that he was ready to sell them again Petitioner hearing this employed Sir George to buy them, but was forced to pay 4 500*l*, the Earl of Middlesex promising to procure a grant of the reversion of Gill-Abbey from the King, but when applied to by Sir George Horsey to do this he replied that he was in disfavour with His Majesty and had more suits of his own than he had friends in Court, and advised Sir George to employ some other means, promising himself to pay the cost Accordingly Mr Smithsby, a servant of his then Majesty, was employed to beg the reversion of Gill-Abbey, and received 150*l* for his recompense, but petitioner has never been able to obtain either this sum or the 1,000*l* extorted as above mentioned, the Earl of Middlesex constantly putting him off with evasive promises, saying that his agent in Ireland should pay the money, and then sending no directions to that effect Prays for redress

L J iv 376

In 1610 Sir Bernard was instrumental in procuring from the Crown a new charter for Bideford, the former one, procured by his father, not being sufficiently explicit in some particulars, and the town standing in need of a greater extension of its privileges, especially in the matter of making bye-laws for the good government of the borough The commerce of Bideford was rapidly extending at this period The merchants of the port were quick to grasp the advantage of the traffic with America and Newfoundland, and this trade continued to extend until the commencement of the last century when the export shipping trade to Newfoundland was exceeded by only two other ports in the Kingdom—London and Topsham , and the import trade by London only   Great was the harvest reaped in these days by the French and Spanish privateers, who preyed upon the ships of Bideford and Barnstaple to such an extent that the offing of the Taw and Torridge was named by them "the Golden Bay"

Sir Bernard evidently took a warm interest in the welfare of the town, and we find him serving in 1620 as an alderman of the borough   There was also among the municipal archives (no, longer, alas! extant) an agreement concluded by his commissioners (John Harris of Lanrest, Bevill Granville, his son, William Carnseige, Raphe Byrd and Mr Nicholas Rowe) with Mr Antony Arundell, Mayor of Bideford, and the Aldermen and Burgesses of the borough in the year 1619, whereby the commissioners, on the part of Sir Bernard, agreed to confirm to the Mayor and Corporation the new quay then lately built by them, and another quay then in contemplation, for which they were to pay Sir Bernard and his heirs "the somme of twelve pence yearly at the Feaste of St Michael the Archangel"   Sir Bernard was likewise to receive the "full moyetie and halfendall of the profits arising from the said Kays in the same manner as his predecessors had done"   At a later period these preliminary proceedings were ratified by a most solemn engagement, and a deed under seal was executed between Sir Bernard, of the one part, and the Mayor and Corporation of the borough, of the other part, whereby he granted to them for twenty-one years a moiety of the dues for holding markets and fairs, and the right to exercise divers privileges which had been conferred on former lords of the mannor by royal charter

The Rector of Bideford at this time was William Easte, who had been appointed by Sir Richard in the last year of his life He was the author of many religious pamphlets and sermons, many of which are dedicated "To the Right Worshipfull Sr Barnard Graynuile, Knight, my singular Patron"   After Easte's death in 1625, an Inventory of his possessions was taken by his executors and *inter alia* is curiously this item, "An Advowson of the Rectory of Byddeford and all the rest of the chattells etc £100"   Certain it is that "by grant of Sir Bernard Grenville, Knight, his successor Philip Isaaks was appointed by Thomas Cholwill and Charles Yeo," but how the advowson could be considered part of Easte's personal estate is not clear.

Sir Bernard is mentioned in 1626, as one of the most active of King Charles the First's Commissioners against Sir John

Eliot and the other prominent champions of constitutional right in Cornwall, his own son Bevill Granville, as we shall see in the next chapter, being one of them. Sir James Bagg writes to inform the Duke of Buckingham that

none had been so forward to express their loyalty as Mohun and Barnard Grenvile." "I know" he adds "they will put down their lives and fortunes to your feet

As a reward for his faithful services, Sir Bernard was appointed in 1628, a gentleman of the privy chamber to the King. He also took a leading part in securing a free election for Knights of the shire at the election of Charles the First's third Parliament, when Eliot's supporters, (Arundel, Trevanion, and Bevill Granville) " came to the election with five hundred men at each of their heels." Sir Bernard and the other commissioners, on the strength of being deputy-lieutenants and justices of the peace, had taken upon them, in virtue of what they termed an ancient custom, to name and elect beforehand, Mr John Mohun and Sir Richard Edgecumbe and had branded Sir John Eliot and Mr Coryton who stood for election as representatives of the constitutional party, as " unquiet spirits having perverse ends, being in His Majesty's ill-opinion, and aiming at objects respecting not the common good, but such as might breed mischief to the State." When Parliament met, the constitutional party being in a majority, Sir Bernard and his fellow commissioners were immediately sent for, and a serjeant despatched to arrest them. Sir James Bagg wrote to the Duke of Buckingham in great alarm from Plymouth on the 29th of March

My Most Gracious Lord,
   I understand the honest western gentle men who for their duty to His Majesty on service to their country, desired Eliot and Coryton not to stand for knights, are by the Lower House sent for ' I cannot at this instant think other but that act of theirs to be grounded upon the information of others I sorrow that they have so resolved ' That those gentlemen truest and best affecting His Majesty's honour and service, should be so troubled ! God give this parliament a happy end and me the honour to the end to continue
                              Your grace, his most humble slave,
                                             JAMES BAGG

But Buckingham had not waited for Bagg's hint. Upon the first move of the Committee, the most strenuous resistance to it had been determined on, and received the sanction of the King. Word was sent down to Cornwall to assure the persons under question of the countenance under which they were to rely, and for a time it was believed that the Commons would be balked of their prey It proved, however, a miscalculation of forces The message was despatched to its destination, doubtless through Bagg, and reached Cornwall before the Commons' messenger Four of the magistrates with the Mohuns were engaged in sessions business, but Trevanion Granville and Edgecombe, happily for themselves, were absent, the first have been taken "sixty miles away" by domestic affairs. Time being thus afforded them, they had the sense to profit by it On the part of Sir Bernard and Trevanion, explanations were subsequently offered, such as the House could only have rejected by direct collision with the King, which at the moment they had special reasons for avoiding ; and Edgecombe, a few weeks later, presented himself voluntarily before the Committee with a personal submission, which was at once accepted (Foster's "Life of Sir John Eliot," ii, 123-124)

The compulsory loans which Charles I endeavoured to raise throughout the country were nowhere more strongly resisted than in Cornwall To Sir Bernard, as one of the King's Commissioners, the task of levying them was entrusted, but the attempt proved a complete failure.

Writing from Tremeer the 19th of July, 1629, "to my honourable friend, Sir James Bagg, Knight, at Captain Buckton's house, near St Martin's Church in the Strand, London." Sir Bernard describes the failure of his efforts and attributes it to "the malevolent faction of Eliot " Everything, he complains, was out of order, and all the Deputy Lieutenants were either fearful or unwilling to do the duties commanded them by the Council, and he himself was weary of his Lieutenancy 'seeing I see it so much undervalued."

The Lieutenancy is grown into such contempt since the Parliament began as there be that dare to countermand what they have on the Lord's command willed to be done They have certified many but it is observed that nothing is done in it, therefore they put on greater liberty

Eight days afterwards, Sir Bernard again writes to Bagg to say, that at the recent muster at Bodmin (where there had been frequent musters in past times), when the parish wherein Tristram Arscott dwells was called, he presented a petition, as he said, at the request of all the country, although got up only by his earnest labour Sir Bernard told him he would consider of his petition Presently after he came with a throng of people and demanded an answer Fearing a mild cold answer might embolden his accomplices and "our busy-headed Parliament men, with whom Arscott is a great sider," Sir Bernard answered roughly that His Majesty should see his petition and he would then receive his answer Arscott at once rode to London to anticipate Sir Bernard's complaint, depending on his cousin Meanty's and his master the Earl of Bedford Sir Bernard concludes his letter by saying, that although he has been a Deputy Lieutenant two or three and thirty years he has never met so ill affections as at the present time and begs Sir James Bagg to oppose this foul demeanour or else to free him from the Lieutenancy

And, again, on the 16th of the following October, Sir Bernard writes to Ralph Byrd and complains of the conduct of his co-deputy-lieutenants of the county of Cornwall and begs him to speak to his (Sir Bernard's) father-in-law, Endymion Porter, to get him exempted, or to procure a reformation by the King's command 'All these disorders have sprung from the humerous actions of the two late Parliaments" and there is another letter dated, Tremeer, March 16th, 1629-30, from Sir Bernard to his father-in-law, Endymion Porter, in which, after expressing his ' strong filial regard to him and his honourable mother with affection to his pretty brothers" he solicits his favour to a work "in which honest Ralph will beg his assistance '

Ralph Byrd was probably the Vicar of Tremeer He belonged to a Sussex family and was a Doctor of Divinity. He married Rebecca, daughter of Henry Blaxton, of Blaxton Hall. The Byrds are referred to in several other letters, and they were present at Sir Bernard's death and nursed him through his last illness

The exact relationship between Endymion Porter and Sir Bernard is not known It was doubtless through the Bevills He married Olive, daughter of Lord Boteler, who bore him several children. The two eldest sons, George and Charles, the "pretty brothers" referred to in the last letter both became soldiers and had commands in the Civil War. In the Domestic State Papers (James I) are several very affectionate letters between Endymion Porter and his wife. He was one of the Grooms of the Bedchamber to James I and also to Charles I whom he attended, when Prince of Wales, into Spain Charles I employed him in several negotiations abroad (cf Granger's "Biog. Hist. of England," vol iii p 110), and he was very active in secret service for the King in the Civil War, and was no less dexterous in conveying his intelligence So obnoxious was he to the Parliament that he was one of those who were always excepted from indemnity. He died abroad in the Court of Charles II

Sir Bernard's last letter extant has reference to Lundy Island, which was originally the property of the Earls of Ormonde, but which had descended from them to the St Legers and from the St Legers to the Granvilles   On this Island had recently expired Sir Lewis Stukeley, by whose scoundrelly manœuvring his own kinsman, brave Sir Walter Raleigh, had perished on the scaffold.   Detecting the Stukeley hand in this judicial murder many gentlemen deliberately avoided Sir Lewis's society   In bitter chagrin he complained to his Sovereign, but with characteristic ingratitude James scoffed at the victim of such richly-deserved unpopularity and refused all assistance   Sir Lewis, within a brief interval, was caught tampering with the King's coin, and he fled to Lundy to Marisco's Castle where he miserably expired   For many years continual complaints had been made by ship-owners and local authorities to Government of the piracies in the Bristol Channel, and in 1608 a commission had been issued to the Earl of Bath, who sat at Barnstaple, and took the depositions of three persons there to the effect that the merchants were daily robbed at sea by pirates who took refuge at Lundy   In 1625 three Turkish pirates had surprised and taken the Island with its habitants and had threatened to burn Ilfracombe, and in 1628 it was the' headquarters of some French pirates   In 1630 Captain Plumleigh, who was in command of a ship-of-war, wrote to the Lord Treasurer, "Egypt was never more infested with caterpillars than the Channel with Biscayers   On the 23rd instant there came out of St Sebastian twenty sail of sloops ; some attempted to land on Lundy but were repulsed by the inhabitants" From this time to 1634 the Island was a perpetual source of trouble to the Government, the reports and communications with the various authorities, civil and naval, as also with the Lord Deputy of Ireland being frequent and all much to the same effect—the Lundy pirates and the means of suppressing them Sir Bernard's letter is on the same subject   It is addressed to the Secretary of State (30th June, 1633), and reports that—

A great outrage had been committed by a Spanish man-of-war, who, on the 16th instant, landed eighty men at the Island of Lundy, when after some small resistance, they killed one man called Mark Pollard and bound the rest, and surprised and took the Island, which they rifled, and took thence all the best provisions they found worth carrying away and so departed to sea again.

This was verified by depositions from a number of sailors and fishermen of Clovelly, one of them (George Rendle) who happened to be at Lundy with his pinnace, had all his money and provisions taken.

After this the Government took more decisive and energetic measures, and they ultimately commissioned Sir John Pennington to put down the piracies, and he appears to have proclaimed martial law there

It difficult to avoid the inference that the relations between Sir Bernard and his son Bevill must have been far from cordial in consequence of the very contradictory character of their political feelings ; undoubtedly Sir Bernard's latter years were much embittered by this opposition to his views and actions on the part of his own flesh and blood. It is therefore pleasing to know from the following letter written by Bevill to Mr Byrd on hearing of his father's death, that whatever estrangement their difference in politics had caused, a reconciliation had taken place some little time previously to Sir Bernard's death, and that they had 'lived comfortably togeather."

BEVILL GRANVILLE TO THE REV MR BYRD

Worthy S^r

I do wth a much grieved heart receave y^r sadd newes, and shall endeavour myself to retume you as good an aunswer as the distemper of my passion will p'mitt, w^{ch}, if it be imperfect, I shall intreate you to impute it to the overflowing of my griefe, w^{ch} (as I hope for heaven) I vow doth exceed all ordinary bounds My hope and desire was great that we might have lived longer comfortablie togeather, and I have taken more comfort in his late loving expressions to me then ever I did in any thing in my life but I have learn'd long agoe to submitt my selfe to the will of God, and though the familiar acquaintance wch I have had w^{tb} misfortune and unhappie accidents had so prepar'd me against all chances, as I did thinke myself prectily fortifyed against all accidents, yet I must confesse this touches me neer But God's will be done to Whom as I heartely prayed for his health and recovery, so I shall no lesse petition Him to send us a joyfull meeting in another world His body I shall desire (as I have already acquainted you) may rest here among his Auncestors such as the war hath spared, wher I hope myself wth others of his Posterity may lve by him if it so please God It was reputed an honour in the oulde world for those ancient Saints of God wch then lived, to be gathered after their deaths to their fathers, and I conceave it to be the last honor I can do unto my good father to gather him again to the poore remainder of his owne family This is my last request unto you for him I shall also beseech you to acquaint Mr Davies that I desire him to use the meanes of his Art for the preservation of his corpse till I may prepare myself with most decency to fetch it away This is as much as the time wth mine owne sorrow will p'mitt Lett my best service and my wife's be presented to good M^{rs} B wth my unspeakable thanks for all y^{or} loving care and good respects to my deire father both in his life and death, for wch I beseech God to reward you all and I shall ever rest

Y^{or} faithfull fr to ser · you

Bevill Grenvile

Sir Bernard died the 16th of June, 1636, probably at Tremeer, where he seems latterly to have resided, and was

T

buried at Kilkhampton ten days afterwards as the Parish Register bears witness.

"Sir Bernard Grenvile, Knight, buried 26 June 1636"

The portraits of Sir Bernard and his wife (who evidently predeceased her husband, though the date of her death is unknown), painted by Zucchero, were formerly in the possession of the Duke of Buckingham and were sold at the great sale at Stowe in 1848, and purchased by the Duke of Sutherland and added to the collection of family portraits at Trentham. Another portrait of Sir Bernard is in the possession of Mr Thynne, at Haynes Park, Bedford whilst a miniature portrait is in the possession of the Granvilles of Wellesbourne.

Bernard Granville had issue a numerous family —

(1) Bevil (of whom presently)

(2) Bernard. In all the pedigrees no mention is made of this son, yet it appears from the "Alumni Oxonienses" that there was a "Bernard Grenvile" who took his B A. at Exeter College 16 Feb 161$\frac{4}{5}$ and his M A 24 July 1619 and in the "Theni Exoniensium in obitum D Johannis Petrei Baronis de Writtle, Oxon 161$\frac{8}{9}$" are some verses signed "Barn: Grenvile Coll. Exon Armig fil" which seems conclusive There are also verses in "Justa Bodlei, Oxon 161$\frac{3}{4}$" and in "Epithalmia in nuptias Frederici Comitis Palatini, Oxon 161$\frac{3}{4}$" also signed with his name.[1]

---

[1] [From "Justa funebria Ptolemæi Oxoniensis Thomæ Bodlei." Oxon 1613, 4º]

1 A Ccipe BODLEIO cur æquiparatur Apollo,
　　Effe pro ut poterint virq , Planeta pares,
2 Letificat Phœbus difperlo lumine terras,
　　Bello illa illius numine leta fuit
3 Sol inter reliquos eft dignior orbe planetas ,
　　BODLEIO nullus dignior altei erat
4 Vt fol Mutarum patei eft fub nomine Phœbi,
　　Thefpiadum turbæ fic patei ille fuit
5 Sol tenebras noctis lucenti diffipat ortu,
　　Lucem Pieriis fic tulit ille choris
6 Phœbus ad occatum directo tramite vergit,
　　Ft fubit Hefperias illius axis aquas
　　Ille suæ vitæ finito in funere curfu
　　Mœftificæ mortis trifte fubivit onus
7 Vt nullo turpi maculatui crimine Phœbus,
　　PODLEII curfus fic fine labe fuit
8 Vt folem in cœlo femper celer evehit axis ,
　　Axis BODLEII fama corufca fuit
9 BODLEIUS Phœbufq Academia Cynthia, luce hinc
　　Sumfit Sol cœli gloria, & ille foli
10 Deniq , vt occiduis fol eft reditutus ab undi
　　Redderet vt folutum lumen in arce pol
　　Sic ille occiduus lethi redituius ab vmbris,
　　funlem miu in luce reiuiset vui

Probably he died young as there is no reference to him in any of the letters extant, or he may possibly have been the son of Sir George Greynvil, though his christian name suggests otherwise.

(3) Richard (of whom presently)

(4) John, baptized the 29th of September, 1601, at Kilkhampton, and living 18 July 1641 as his letter (given in the next chapter) shows

(5) Roger, baptised the 17th of April, 1603 at Bideford, and drowned in the service of Charles the First He was unmarried

(6) A nameless son, buried at Kilkhampton, 12th of September, 1605

There were also two daughters, viz. —

(1) Elizabeth, buried at Kilkhampton the 12th September, 1605

(2) Gertrude ; baptized at Kilkhampton, the 8th of May 1597 She married first, Christopher Harris of Lanrest, co

Interea Mutæ lugent Academia mæret
BODLEII tumus flens 'fue fine tui
Salicet occubuit BODLEIVS noster Apollo,
Quid facerent mufæ cum pater ipfe perit ?
BARN GREYNVILE Col, Exon

[From 'Threni Exoniensium in obitum D Johannis Petri Baronis de Writtle] Oxon 1613, 4

Ad illuft Baronem Guli Petreum
C O i mces aquile non generant aeq,
Spina ex Palladia provenit arbore
Nec clarus genuit te Pater vince
Gnatum dissimilem fui
Sic tu femper avo iis fimilis Patri
In te nec titul
Qui mites fuerint reinider, & Domus
Fulgens Exoniæ decus
Sic vltra asinteros fama feret polos,
Sic tecum mentis Exoniæ pieces
Duces, & decus, & præmia gloriæ
Virtus contribuet tui

Ad Illust Cath innam Baronis Petri exorem d Comitis Wigorniensis filiam
Anna, Maria dux Charles, & facra fuere
Sydera in Exi mo femper habenda polo
Tu Catharina Annam, Catharina, imitare Mariam,
Periectus Charitum fluit ex ista chorus
Dum nos foverunt jamam genuere perennem,
Fama tua vt vivat, nos Catharina tove
BARN GREYNVILE Coll Econ Armig fil

[From ' Epithalmia   in nuptias Frederici Comitis Palatini Oxon 1613, 4]
Q Vam pia, quam prudens, tanto qui cojuge digna est,
Pulchra probat species, nomen (Elisa) probat
Quam pius & prudens, tanta quam conjuge dignus,
Testantur, cælum, fydera, terra, tretum
His cælum benedixit eis pia fydera lucent
Mite tretum reditu, terra benigna manet
Anglia dudum nunc his conceflit moris
Cætera pars CAROLO debita tota minet
BARNARD GREYNVILE Coll E   Co

Devon. M.P. for West Looe, a great-nephew and heir
of the Sir Christopher Harris, who had married her
aunt Bridget ; and secondly, by license dated, Exeter,
the 28th of June, 1624, Antony Dennis of Orleigh
near Bideford, and of Lesnewth, Cornwall, who died
June, 1641, (will dated 30th April, with codicil 15th
May, 1641, proved 4th July following, P C C. 88,
Evelyn).   There were six children the issue of this
marriage, viz : Richard, who died in infancy , Mary,
who became the wife of Sir Thomas Hampson, Baronet
of Taplow, near Maidenhead ; Elizabeth, who wedded
Sir John Hein , Gertrude, who married Nicholas Glynn,
of Glynn , and two other daughters who died young
In the partition of the Dennis estates, Orleigh fell to
Nicholas Glynn, who sold it to John Davies a Bideford
merchant   The Cornish estates passed to the Hampsons.
Sir Thomas Hampson died the 22nd of March, 1670,
and his widow in the following year, suffered a fine
in the manor and advowson and bailliwick of the
Hundred of Lesnewth, probably for purposes of settlement, ' to Thomas Turner and Philip Vennyng
gentlemen "   Lady Hampson died in 1694, and by
her will, dated 4th March, 1678, devised her Cornish
estates to her second son Henry Hampson, who died
without issue in 1719, and his elder brother dying
also in the same year, the property devolved upon
William Glynn, grandson of Nicholas and Gertrude
Glynn, in whose family it remained till purchased by
Lord Churston (then Sir John Yarde Buller), in 1828.

Mrs Gertrude Dennis ended her days with her daughter,
Lady Hampson, and was buried at Taplow in 1682, in the
86th year of her age.

SIR BEVILL GRANVILLE.

SLAIN AT LANSDOWNE.

From an Original Portrait, by Vandyck, in the Wellesbourne Collection.

CHAPTER IX.

BEVILL GRANVILLE Sir Bernard's eldest son, was born on the 23rd of March, 1595-6 at Birin, probably Great Birin, the seat of the Bevills—but not a stone of the old mansion is now standing—in the little Cornish parish of Withiel, and was baptized two days afterwards, on the Feast of the Annunciation in Withiel Parish Church

His boyhood was spent at Stowe, where he doubtless became familiar with those martial exercises in which he was afterwards destined to excel, his father being at the head of a large body of soldiers, both militiamen and volunteers The first event recorded in his life must have occurred when he was quite a boy, and is in connection with another lad, who in after life exercised great influence upon him in the world of politics, namely John Eliot Eliot, ardent and impetuous, and but little restrained by an indulgent father, had fallen under ill report from jealous neighbours, and one of them, a Mr, Moyle,[1] took upon himself to warn the father that such was his son's repute. He might have done so much without offence, but unfortunately he seized the opportunity to reveal some money extravagance, of which he had obtained the knowledge unfairly, and this being repeated with aggravation, young Eliot, who was then barely fifteen, went in hot chase and passion to Moyle's house What words ensued, or whether any further provocation was given is not known, but the quick-tempered lad drew his sword and wounded Mr Moyle in the side For this an "Apologie" was afterwards sent, signed by Eliot and witnessed by William Coryton and Bevill Granville

The apology is impressed in every word by the generous heart eager to atone for unpremeditated wrong. It was thus— "Mr. Moyle —I do acknowledge I have done you a great injury, which I wish I had never done. and do desire you to remit, and I desire that all unkindness may be forgiven and forgotten betwixt us, and henceforth I shall desire and deserve your love in all friendly offices as I hope you will mine."

---

[1] Afterwards Sheriff of Cornwall (1624) and one of the sequestrators, 1648 He died at St. German 9 October, 1661

From Stowe, Bevill went to Oxford, and matriculated the
14th day of July, 1611, at the famous old west country college,
"Exeter," where he was placed under the care of Dr. Prideaux,
the Rector. He seems to have distinguished himself at the
University in various ways, *e.g*, by giving a silver cup to the
College, by contributing poetry to an "In Memoriam" upon
a deceased friend[2], and by taking his B A degree before he
was eighteen, *viz*, on the 17th of February, 1613-14

His University career being over he entered the world of
London—a world in which Lord Bacon, Sir Walter Raleigh,
(his kinsman) and Arabella Stuart, Car, Earl of Somerset and
his notorious wife, and Villiers, afterwards Duke of Buckingham,
were living actors Here, to judge from the kindly responses
from his father, the young man's affections seem soon to have
been engaged —

SIR BERNARD GRANVILLE TO BEVILL

Bevill, you write to me to understand my liking of your affection to
IX daughter She is of greate bearthe that I mutch aproone her person
I see & must like wᵗʰ your eyes & Judgement a wise Jenerall in yᵉ warrs will
not put on upon any service but yᵗ he will first be sure to speed or to cū off
wᵗʰ honoure do yᵒ Imitate that provident care & goe forwarde wᵗʰ yᵒʳ
resolution, but if you firste attempte before yᵒ haue hope of prenayling & in
yᵉ end be bittne wᵗʰ an honorable frowne it will bee a Corasive though it cū
from greatness you have chofue well to worke by yᵗ wise knights aduise who
& IX have longe before this nighteberhood been very intimat friendes he
hath greate reason to love yᵗ offspringe of Sʳ R G & sure I thinke hee doth
confeue wᵗʰ him or aney other yᵗ yᵒ know can worke powerfullyest with JX
or his Lay & if by these or by your owne merritt in yᵉ eyes of yᵉ yeounge
Ladey yᵒʳ hopes do geive yᵒ an incouragement to proceed promiss aney thing
of myne estate yᵗ shall stand wᵗʰ yᵒʳ owne good & yᵒʳ possteriteys & it shall be
made good you write to have my Cosen W C sente up to you I will do my
best to sende him but first let mee understande by yᵒʳ lers whether yᵒʳ hopes
will make his trauayle to aney purpose, if it will I know his loue is such to us
all yᵗ dowbteless he will shunne no trauayle to do us good offices espesially in
this keinde, but I wowld bee loth to send him in a frutcless errand. I have
hende yᵗ JX hath sayed he had rather many his daughter to a Jentleman of a
good famyley yᵗ hath a comptente estate to mayntayne him then to a greate
Lorde this geiveth mee hope though sū ot yᵒʳ frendes feare that greateness
will be yᵒʳ opposate put on for it I like well yᵒʳ choyse a meaner hearth then

[2] [From "Threni Exoniensium "]
Displicent Parcis (quid enim non displicet illis ?)
Mata:um domui, te superesse Petram,
Ergo *Petrie* secant tua candida pensa, putantes
Si Petra tanta ruat, corruet ipsa Domus
Has tamen falli video tecando
Penfa *Petrey* ruitura non eft
Sacra Mataum Domus, alter istam
Sustinet Atlas
BEVILL GRENVILE, *Equitis*
filius ingenutus

yours hath obtayned greater honor asure yourselie ther shall bee nothing omitted of my part y^t will farder it my chafest desire is to see your prosperytey in all goodness I pray God to blesse you &

So I rest your louing father

BN GRENUILE.

at Keligarth y 6th of August
1614

you vse a thing y^t I cannot tell how to blame you for, because it is to ottne a fawlte in myself y^or lef̃s beare no date wch maketth us not to know hew long they ar in cumming to us

To my beloved sonne Benill Grennile
at Vieines howse on ye backside of St
Clementes Churtch in Strand neue London

Two other letters from his father written to him in London during the next three years are extant —

SIR BERNARD GRANVILLE TO BEVILI.

I am caled on by a sodden knowledge of owld Rasheys riding for London to morrow morning to scribble hastely because I will nott skippe anev I can leaue to write by y^m sodden going & my not knowing of it made mee for gette to talk wth y^o of Captayn Henry Skipwell & my vnkle s^t legers busines & now I have not time to write scars sins but if y^o may htly speake w^t my vnkle let y^or hast & my not knowing it excus my not writing to him by the next I will I pray deliuer this box & letter to Mr Pollard safely I also for gatt to mynde y^u to leine how I might bee serued wth thos peeses of armors y^t ye cuntry wante as Powldrons, tassis gorgetts & scherrions as well as ye whole armours let mee know by your next I heere nothing of Mr Connoe since y^or departure I am merinlowse woe for his sickeness you must now leaine to stande by your selfe & negotiat y^t business alone w^t Mr Pollards aduice I know not vnless Cootly bee fitt whom to send w^h it vnless Mt Carnsew who is wise will take a Journey who y^u thinke best I will send if you will haue aney S^r L Stukeley follows hotly for S^r R Bassatt Sir F G for his brother lein wch is the hopefullest I mutch feare B for his sister . . . tax him mutch they say he doth loose (?) mutch Patrimony & I woulde be loth to put so tender a hart to sorrow seing the best may bring enongh I pray send mee down by the first 3 or 4 cockes to bee sett on them beckes pipes to lett water owt of the hedde they must be stautch & no greate wous Mr Pollard can aduise y^u wch I showlde write of more but time will not permitte me I being now caled to an ende & my remembrance bad I pray God to bless you & prosper all y^or good actions in hande I wch I must leaue to his good guidance & so I rest

Yo^r louing father
BAR GRENVILE

ye hist of
May 1615
wen ye Docter cam
backe to Colocombe hee
fownd ther S Weekes & his neney
Ackland ther hee thinkes all is
doon.

To my beloued sonne
BEVILL GRENVILE

this

SIR BERNARD GRANVILLE TO BEVILL

I reseiued y^or By y^or m̃a & sent ye enclosed to Mr Byrd I am glad y^o resolue to make but small stay in London I pray God y^o howld your resolution Keligarth will bee more safe & more quiett if ye Lady howld her strickte peruerce humor I may well suppose it is to make a breatch I wish shee might know tho y^t thei ai as maney women as men in England how so euer it stand I will euei honowi y^t Noble Lord & exceedingly loue his vertuowse weife while I liue if y^o leaue it throwgh then inforcement forenot but wee shall bee able & willing to pay debtts w^h owt their portion D Tremayn¹ cums eeuen now fr̃o Bedford whei Beuill Prideaux² arriued w^t a barke of Corne fr̃o Ierland or

¹ Richard Tremayne, 6th son of Arthur Tremayne, who married Mary, daughter of Sir Richard Granville

² Bevill Prideaux, eldest son of Humphry Prideaux of Westwood, Crediton, who married Johanna, daughter of John Bevill of Kelligarth

wals & hath mad greate bost to my cozen M Weekes & others y^t he will haue Beuills lande fr̃o us being next ayie unto it by an espessiall intayle I cannot but smyle to see how y^c foole feedes him fatt   Commend mee to C Skipwill I pray tell him I shall bee glad if he can gett mee good place for youi Brother Rg y^t he c̃a gett mee aquayntance w^t s̃u honest maitchant y will supply him w^t moneys theare & bee payed heei by mee on Dicks acknowledgement of ye reserte looke heedely to yowi self & I pray God to bleese you.

Y^or louing father
BAR GRENVILE
To my beloued son
Beuill Grenvile
this w^t speed

21 Martij
1617

Evidently the lady, whom we may suppose was JX's daughter did " howld her strickte perverse humor " " The breatch " widened and the engagement ended, for in December of the same year Sir Bernard writes to his aunt Lady Grace Smith, consenting to a marriage between his son Bevill and Grace her only child, by hei second mairiage with Sir George Smith of Madford, Heavitree, near Exeter   Lady Grace Smith was the daughter and co-heiress of William Vyell, Esquire of Trevorden, and had married as hei first husband Peter, the second son of Petei Bevill of Gwainick, and uncle of Elizabeth Bevill, Sir Bernard's wife. He therefore calls her aunt.

SIR BERNARD GRANVILLE TO LADY GRACE SMITH

My Honble
     Ladey the Idolitiy of Aron in the 32 of Exodus in setting up a gooldne Calfe foi ye Israelites to worship cannot dehoit my minde from y^r La^p ow̃i Byrd did singe youi affection to us so sweetly at his retuine from yow as it hath aimed me to slight all opposition & to signifie unto yow y^t my desire is so aiemouable to make y^i daughtei myne & my soun youis as aneys dishonest practises cannot alter owie honest thowghtes fiom so good a resolution takine I hope in a happey hower I beseitch you bee asureed of my Constansey & know y^t ye Ladey Smithes vertues have more powie to bynde me then the

stormes of a whole winter have to remove me mutch lesse power have y⁰ mid winter gustes I am dowtefull of trowbling y" to longue & therfore will ende with recommending my faithfull service to yow & my hartey Love to my prettey Cozen your daughter & I will ever bee

Your faythfull neuey

BAR GRENVILE

31ᴰᵉ· 1618 at Keligarth

To my mutch honowred awnte y⁰
Ladey Grace Smith at Maydeworthey mie Exon

Sir George Smith was one of the leading merchants and citizens of Exeter He had great possessions at Filford, in the parish of Norherbury, Dorset, at West Knighton, Staffordshire, besides at Madford, Kingskerswell, Cadhay, Dolton, Harford, Whimple, Lympstone, Parkham, Dawlish, Iveden, and Exeter, in Devonshire He was Sheriff of Exeter in 1583, and Mayor in 1586, 1597, and 1607, and Sheriff of Devon 1615 He had been knighted 2nd June, 1604 By his first wife he had had a daughter, Elizabeth, married to Sir Thomas Monk, of Potheridge, a gentleman of noble birth, but poor means Sir Thomas had succeeded to a heavily encumbered estate and an increasing family had added to his difficulties and sorrows His second son, George, afterwards the celebrated Duke of Albemarle, had been born December 8th, 1608, and grew up a fearless high-spirited boy and Sir George Smith had taken such a fancy to this grandson that he had undertaken to educate him, provided he might live half the year at Madford. Poor embarrassed Sir Thomas could only consent, and hence the Granvilles and young Monk were thrown together more intimately than might otherwise perhaps have been the case, and this early connection throws no little light upon those subsequent events in connection with the Restoration of Charles II, in which both families took so prominent a part

The following year Grace Smith became the wife of Bevill Granville, and their marriage was a singularly happy one, as their affectionate letters fully prove The following letter was probably written towards the end of the year 1619, and the postcript contains congratulations on the betrothal The writer, it is supposed, was Thomas Drake, the eldest son of William Drake of Wiscomb, and a cousin of Bevill Granville's. The relationship between the Drakes and the Granvilles arose four generations previously, when John Drake, of Ash, married Amy, daughter of Sir Roger Granville.—

THOMAS DRAKE TO BEVILL GRANVILLE

My worthyest Cousin Condemne me not if the desire I had, to heare from you hath inforsed me to be the more earneste wᵗʰ you flor indeed I have beene so jealous of thy health is I desire nothinge more then its contineuances And by what meanes should I more truly be ascertained of it, then by your

ι

self, who can best wittnesse it ·/   Besides, It much troubled me; heretofore
you havinge pleased to grace me, wth the frequent enterchaunge of your letters,
that of Late I soe seldome heard from you   It made me some-what suspitious
your occasions had caused you to neglect y^r ffreind   And blame me not
(myne owne soule) If I have to severly taxed thee, whose love I preferr above
all things hvinge; ffor should I loose that comfort of y^r affections (wherin I
am only happy and in nothing els) It weare but the meanes to shorten my
days wch I desire only to enjoy, to the end I may acknowledge my devoute
thankefullnesse in my services vnto you   I write not this as if words weare a
sufficiente harvest for your ffavours, but you shall fynde me, (when so ever
you shall please to imploy me) most redy to serve you even to the hazard of
my life   But lett it suffice (sweet S^r) that your absence ffrom London,
debarr'd me of the happynesse I might have sustayned in yor letters   Your
two last (my welcomeste guests) have redeeme your longe sylence /   S^r you
have highly pleasured me, in Boughtons businesse   It is but a farther
engadgment wch should move me the more sincearly to observe you   I cannot
better my affections your deserts do chalenge a perpetuall Love & service ffrom
me, wch I heare presente you wth all and wth it my self, whom you shall ever
freely comaunde, and who desires ever unfaynedly to serve you

Your Thom Drake

S^r the latter end of your letter acquaynts me wth your happy proceedinges
in y^r greatest affaires   I cann but rejoyce wth you, & wish you may flynde as
much worth in her, as y^r good choise hath approved buety   I beseech you to
remember my services to my M^{ris} and Mr Hunt   It God of his goodnesse
enable me wth health I shall not be longe from you & them   I must ffarther
desire you to remember my affectioned service to good Mr Mohun and
Captayne Lower if he be wth you—

All Tho Drake Thyne
perpetually
To my ever honored
ffreind Bevill Grenvile
Esq give these /

In the first year or two of their married life the young
couple seem to have lived at Tremeer in the parish of Lanteglos,
two miles west from Fowey, and the following letter was
probably written at this time by Bevill during some temporary
absence from his wife —

BEVILL GRANVILLE TO HIS WIFE

Dearest of all my misfortunes this is my greatest that now encountreth me
to have you sicke & in my absence when I nether can be present to do
you service my selfe, nor am in place to send for Phisicions that might do what
were fitting   my broken lines expres the fracture that these tidings do make
in my heart & sinews   yett they have not so tame deprived me, but I can
resolve this, y^t if you canot send me better news by this bearer (whom I have
expresly will'd to be wth me before too morow noone) then I will be wth you
by god's helpe before I sleepe, though I leave all the rest of the busines undon
& for god's sake make not the matter better than it is—yis

B Grey

hast   Tuesday night
Superscription)
To my best frend
Mrs Grace Grenvile
at Tremere
Speed   d d.

At Tremeer their eldest son, Richard, was born the 19th of March 1620-1 and was baptized, as Bevill himself had been, on the 25th, the Feast of the Annunciation, by Nicholas Hatch, Vicar   Subsequently they resided at Stowe, which Sir Bernard probably gave up to them, while he himself resided either at Bideford or Kilgarth, and in a letter which he addresses to Stowe he gives Bevill directions about some live carp he was sending him from his ponds at Bideford with which to stock the fish ponds at Stowe, with instructions where to stop and give them fresh water on the journey

At Stowe " Bevill's principal care was to maintain his own credit and the dignity of his family, not by an ostentatious magnificence, but by a prudent management of his estate, a kind of paternal tenderness for his servants, and a most courteous and respectful behaviour to all the gentlemen around him   To these engaging qualities he added a strict attention to whatever regarded the public service, and by a number of experiments showed that it was both practicable and profitable to use coal instead of wood in melting of tin, and he likewise contrived several methods to hinder the wasting of the metal in the blast, which, having brought to perfection at his own private expense, he, from a principle of public spirit, communicated to his countrymen for their common advantage "

But it was not in mechanical matters only that Bevill Granville interested himself, but also in politics, and his political views, as already hinted at, appear to have been greatly moulded by him, whose apology for a boyish escapade he had witnessed many years before, viz, Sir John Eliot, ' the most illustrious confessor in the cause of liberty whom that time produced," as Hallam calls him   Eliot, who was three years older than Granville, was returned to Parliament for St Germains six years before his friend found a seat for the county of Cornwall   The Parliament of 1614, to which Eliot belonged, lasted only four months, that of 1620, in which Granville first sat, was dissolved after it had sat seven months, and there is reason to believe that just as Eliot in the one was on the side of the opposition in refusing to grant supplies until certain grievances had been redressed, so in the other Granville was in the opposition, in entering upon the journals of the House a formal protestation to the effect that ' the liberties, franchises, privileges and jurisdiction of Parliament are the ancient and undoubted birthright and inheritance of the subjects of England "

It was on his return home after the adjournment in June

of the Parliament made memorable by the impeachment of
Lord Bacon, that the following letter from his brother John
was written   It is dated from Lincoln's Inn, where he was
evidently studying law, like other young men of those times,
not necessarily with any view to practice as a barrister, but to
obtain such a knowledge of the law as would be helpful to him
as a magistrate

Nothing more is known of this John Granville, but he
probably died before May 1626. as in one of his letters to his
wife written in that month before the birth of his second son,
Bevill writes, "If God send us a boye I have a goode minde
to have him caled John *for my poor brother John's sake*"

JOHN GRANVILLE TO HIS BROTHER BEVILL

Deare brother   Mr Bonde makinge me acquainted wth his returne I could
not but lett you understande of Wells the Barbers honest delinge wth you   the
matter is this, a fewe dayes before Mr Byrds departure he came unto him, and
demands of him whether Mr Byrde had any directions by Doge from you to be
payde of his moneye, Mr Byrd tolde him how he had none whereupon he swore
you had delte scornelye with him and sayde ere long you should heare of it
and againe saide hee was basely abused by you, and since he was thus serued
hee would lett the towne knowe of your dealings, and did you all the dishonor
he could amongst the cheifest friends you had in London ney farther he sayde
since you had God plighted him in this he could forgett you as well in greater
matters   Deare brother I must needs confess I harkened to his talk with
exceedinge greate impatience, when he had ended I tolde him these speeches
became him not, and what dealings there is between my brother & you I know
not, if he haue (as you saye) iniured you, I make noe questione but he will
shortly giue you satissfactione , but if you goe about to scandalize him wth
such assersions as you say yo^u will, I can assure you (I tolde him) you will
purchase y^r Railinges dearly, presently he would awaye and gaue mee noe
answere and if I had knowne that he could haue done you noe displeasure in
y^r business I vowe before God he should haue had cause to speake those
words, or if I might but understand howe you take it he shall soone perceive
his speeches cannot be soe soone forgotten   My lor of Oxford is sente to the
Tower for a peremptorye answere he gave the kinge upon a late examinatione
before the councell, my Lor of Essex went latly to the Lowcuntries, and is
sente for backe againe, as it is reported   The Kynge begins his progress this
day, so entreatinge you to remember my best love to my sisters in hast
I remayne

                    Yo^r assur'd faithfull brother
                             Jo GRENVILE //

Lincolns Inne July the 18th
                1621
                    To the worth my dearest
                    brother Bevill Grenvile
                    Efq in Cornwell these

As knight of the shire for Cornwall from 1621-1625,
Bevill Granville would of course reside in London during the
sitting of Parliament. where his wife seems occasionally to have

been with him, and there in all probability Elizabeth, their second child was born in 1621-2, but as a rule Mrs Granville stayed behind at Stowe, and perhaps the following undated letter may be assigned to the earlier part of this period before the birth of their daughter —

BEVILL GRANVILLE TO HIS WIFE

My dearest, I am exceeding glad to heare from you, but doe desire you, not to be so passionat for my absence, I vowe you canot more desire, to have me at home, then I do desire to be there, & assoone as I can dispatch my busines, I will instantly come away. I am yett so new in the towne, as I have beene able to do nothing. I hope you will not have child so soone as you feare I will, as fast as I can, send downe those provisions. I have left no order wth any boddy, for the Moorestone windores but Pomeroy, I would have him to gett them to be well wrought up, against my comming downe, & then I will take course for the fetching of them. you shall do well to send to yr mother for that money, assoone as you can, for feare you want, & if you have need of more you may entreat Nat Gist, to lende you some of my rent before hand. I would have the masons, to goe on as fast as they can, about the stable, that if it be possible, the walls may be up & finished against my comming downe. I am afraid, as Allen is, that the Ploughs will not be reddy soone enough to bring home the Timber, tell him make what shift he can wth that at home, but be sure he cutt none elsewhere but out of that Plott I appointed. they may take all that is there but spare the rest bid him be sure to putt in none, but strong & sufficient stuffe. have a care that the People want no provision & lett my co Tremayne take up Oxen & sheepe enough, to serve all the yeare & make his Bargain so as I may pay for it after my comming home, which shall carefully be performd. I would have some of my co Tho Arundell or both sorts, & allow for it in his Xpeas Paymt, but the 100ll now at whitsontide I depend on, & he must not faile me of. I would have Mr Billing to take some course to returne it speedely to me, but if it so fall out that he canot so early, as he may be sure it will be wth me before whitsontide, then do you reserve it safe for me in yr owne handes, because I will come away before whitsontide if I can so god keepe you & yrs you shall heare from me as often as I can, but I confesse I find it much more difficult to send to you now then when you were at Madford

Yrs faithfully
BEVILL GRENVILE

Make all the haste you can to thresh out your corne for feare it be spoild & observe how many bushells it is

lett Charles the joyner make a board for the Parler assoone as you can, as plain & cheape as possible he can make, only 2-or-3-deale boards joynd togather & tressells to stand on, & so long as to reach from the bay windore to the little dore, but not to hinder the going in & out

(Superscription)
To my best Frend
Mrs Grace Grenvile
at Stowe these d d
d

The following Indenture for the sale of lands that came to Mrs Granville after the death of her father, Sir George Smith, is extant among the "Additional Charters" in the British Museum (7058).—

This Indenture Tripartite Made the second daye of Maye in the yeare of the Raigne of o' Soûaigne Lorde James by the grace of God Kynge of England ffraunce and Ireland Defender of the faithe &c the twentith and of Scotland the fiue and fiftith   **Betweene** Bevill Grenvile Esquier sonne and heire apparent of Sr Barnard Grenvile of Stowe in the County of Cornwall Knight and Grace the wif of the saide Beavile Grenvile of the first pt, John Arundell of Tierise in the saide County Esquier and John Prideaux of Treforder in the saide Countie Esquier ot the second pt, And John Code of Pelynt and George Giste of Kilkhampton in the foresaide Countie gent of the third pt   **Witnesseth** that the saide Bevil Grenvile and Grace his wif for and in Consideraçon of the som' of one hundred poundes of good Money to them in hand paide by the saide John Arundell and John Prideaux Whereof the saide Bevill and Grace acknowledge themselues fully satisfyed and paide, and thereof doe by theise pnte acquite and discharge the saide John Arundell and John Prideaux theire heires Executors and admin^rs And to the intent that the Mano^rs landes Tenem^ts and hereditam^ts hereafter in theise pnte Mencyoned shall and May be conveyed and estated vnto and vpon the saide John Arundell and John Prideaux, whereby to make them pfect Tenante of the freehold thereof, that therevpon a good and pfect recouy or seuall recoues thereof May be had against the saide John Arundell and John Prideaux to such vses as are hereafter in these pnts lymitted expssed and declared, And for other good and reasonable causes and consideraçons especially Moveinge doe by theise pnte bargaine and sell giue and graunt vnto the saide John Arundell and John Prideaux and theire heires, All that the Capitall Messuage or Mansion howse Barton and demeasne Landes called or knowen by the Name of Maydeworthy als Madford wth thappu'tenance scituat lyinge and beinge w^thin the pishe of Heavitree in the County of Devon, And all gardens landes Orcharde Meadowes pastures and hereditam^ts to the saide Messuage or Tenem^t belonging or appertayninge or togeather wth the same vsed occupied or emoyed or as pt pcell or Member thereof being or comonly reputed or taken to be, And also all those the Mano^rs of Trethewell & Tregerean als Tregereanstean in the Countie of Cornwall wth there and euy of there Righte Members and appu'tenance, And also all those Messuages, landes Tenem^ts Meadowes pastures Woodes vnderwoodes rentte reûcons service and hereditam^ts whatsoeu, scituat lyinge or being w^thin the Townes Boroughes pishes Hamlette Villages or feildes of Trethewell Tregerean als Tregereanstean St Mawgan in Pider St Viall als St Ewall St Firyn St Merryn Padstow als Padistow, Litle Petrock St Isye St Breage, St Dennys, Roche, Bodmyn Lansallos St Peran in the sand, Kenwen, St Key, Tiurow St Kevern als St Keryon Mawgan in Meaneage, Gwendron Helston and Madelyne in the saide County of Cornwall or w^thin any of them, wch at ame tyme were the landes Tenem^ts hereditam^ts or Inheritance of Sr George Smyth Knight deceased father to the saide Grace wth all and singuler there and euy of there righte Members and appu'tenance (Exceptinge only those Messuages landes and Tenem^ts w^thin the foresaide pishe of St Isye wch the saide Sr George Smith did purchase of one Richard Tregolles and Nicholas Tregolls or one of them) **To** haue and to houlde all and singuler the pmisses wth the appu'tenance vnto the saide John Arundell and John Prideaux and to theire heires to the intent and purpose that a good and pfect recouy or recoues May be thereof had against them to the aboue named John Code and George Giste to such vses intente and purposes as are in theise pnte hereafter lymitted expssed and declared   **And** the saide Bevill Grenvile and Grace his wif doe by theise pnte farther covenant conclude and agree to and wth the saide John Arundell and John Prideaux and there heires, That they the saide Bevill Grenvile and Grace his wif shall and will before the laste daie of ffebruarie Next ensewing the date hereof leauye one or More fyne or fynes wth proclamation, vnto the saide John Arrundell and John Prideaux and to the heires of them or one of them or vnto the survivo^r of them and his heires of all and singuler the p̃misses for the More p̃tect and assured setlynge of the freehold of the p̃misses vpon the saide John Arundell and John Prideaux and there heires or the heires of one of them for th'intent and purpose afore saide vntill the saide recouy and recouyes be had and p̃fected as aforesaide, And it is further covenanted concluded & agreed by and betweene all and euy the pties to theise p̃ntẽ, and the trew intent and Meaninge of them and euy of them and of theise p̃ntẽ is that aswell the saide recouy and recouies as also the saide ffyne and ffynes from and after the p̃fectinge of the saide recouies, And also all and euy other fyne and fynes recouy and recouies conveiance and assurance to be hereafter leavyed passed suffered Made or executed of the p̃misses any or pt thereof by or betweene the saide pties to theise p̃ntẽ or any of them shalbe and shalbe taken expounded and admdged to be to such vses intentẽ lymitacõns and purposes as are in theise p̃ntẽ lymitted expressed & declared, and to none other, That is to saie first to the vse and behoof of the saide Bevill Grenvile and Grace his wif for and during the term of their Naturall lives, and the lif of the longest liver of them. dispunishable and w^thout Impeachm^t of or for any Maner of Waste whatsoeu, And after to the vse of the eldest issue Male of the bodies of the saide Bevill and Grace betweene them begotten wch shalbe livinge or in venter sa mere at the tyme of the deathe of such of them the saide Bevill and Grace as shall first happen to dye, and of the heires of the bodye of such eldest issue Male lawfully begotten or to be begotten The remaynder of all and singuler the p̃misses wth the appu'tenancẽ to the vse of the second issue Male of the bodies of the saide Bevill and Grace wch shalbe livinge or in venter sa mere at the tyme of the death of such of them the saide Bevill & Grace as shall first happen to dye and of the heires of the bodye of such second issue Male lawfully begotten and to be begotten The Remaunder of all and singuler the p̃misses wth the appu'tenancẽ to the vse of the third issue Male of the bodies of the saide Bevill and Grace wch shall be livinge or in venter sa mere at the tyme of the death of such of them the said Bevill and Grace as shall first happen to dye, and of the heires of the bodie of such third issue Male lawfully begotten and to be begotten, The remainder of all and singuler the p̃misses wth the appu'tenancẽ to the vse of the fowerth Issue Male of the bodies of the saide Bevill and Grace wch shalbe livinge or in venter sa mere at the tyme of the death of such of them the saide Bevill and Grace, as shall first happen to dye and of the heires of the bodie of such fowerth issue Male lawfully begotten and to be begotten, The remainder of all and singuler the p̃misses wth the appu'tenancẽ to the vse of the fifth issue Male of the the bodies of the saide Bevill and Grace wch shalbe lyvinge or in venter sa mere at the tyme of the death of such of them the saide Bevill and Grace as shall first happen to dye, and of the heires of the bodye of such fifth issue Male lawfully begotten and to be begotten, The Remainder of all and singuler the p̃misses wth the appu'tenancẽ to the vse of the issue and issues female of the bodies of the saide Bevill and Grace betweene them begotten wch shalbe livinge or in venter sa mere at the tyme of the death of such of them the saide Bevill and Grace as shall firste happen to dye, and of the heires of the bodye and bodyes of such issue and issues female lawfully begotten or to be begotten, The Remainder of all and singuler the p̃misses wth the appu'tenancẽ to the vse of the saide Bevill Grenvile and Grace his wif and of the heires of there two bodies lawfully begotten and to be begotten The Remainder thereof to the vse of the right heires of the saide Bevill and Grace his wif for eu'more provided alwaies Neu'theles and the trew intent and Meaninge of all and eu'ry the pties to theise p̃ntẽ is, That it shall and May be lawfull to and for the saide Bevill Grenvile and Grace his wif at one tyme or tymes during the

coverture betweene them by there deede or deedes Indented vnder bothe
there handes and seales and after the death of any one of them then to and
for ye survivor of them, at anie time or times during his or her Natuall lif by
his or her deede or deedes Indented vnder his or her hand and seale to sell
lett demise graunt or appointe any pt or pt^e of the p̃misses to any pson or
psons, for term of one two or three lives in possession or for anie Number of
yeares in possession, determynable vpon the death of one two or three pson or
psons, or for the term of two Lives or any Number of yeares determynable
vpon two lives in reu'c̃on or remaynder of one lif or in reu'c̃on or remaynder
or any Number of yeares determynable vpon one lif or for term of one lif or
for anie Number of yeares determynable vpon one lif in reu'c̃on or remaynder
of two lives, or of anie Number of yeares determynable vpon two lives or for
term of one and twenty yeares in possession So as by and vpon eu'y such lease
and demise, deede and deedes there be reserved yearely during the continuance
of the saide termes and estates so Much or more yearely rentte and service as
hath bene respectively reserved yearly, paiable for ye same for the Most pt of
Twenty yeares Next before the Makeinge thereof   And the trew intent and
Meaninge of theise p̃ntte and of all and eu'y the pties to the same is, That
vpon all and eu'y such lease demise graunt or lymitac̃on to be had or Made of
any the p̃misses as aforesaide the saide ffyne and ffynes Recou'y and Recou'ies
and all and eu'y other Conveyance and assurance aforesaide to be had and
executed of the p̃misses or anie pt thereof by or betweene the saide pties to
theise p̃ntte or any of them for and Concerninge such pt and pt^e of the p̃misses
as shalbe so leased demised or graunted as aforesaide shalbe and be taken
expounded and adiudged to be and the Recognisees and Recou'ors and there
heires and the Survivor of them and his heires and all and eu'v other pson
and psons wch shalbe seised of anie the p̃misses so to be leased demised or
graunted as aforesaide shall stand and be thereof seised to the vse of all and
eu'y such pson and psons respectively to whome the same shalbe so seased
demised or graunted as aforesaide for and during such estate and estates, and
and in such Man'q and form and wth and according to such lymitac̃ons Condic̃ons
Covenantte Reservac̃ons and agreem^ts as shalbe contayned and specifyed in the
saide Indenture and Indentures of demise and graunt to be Made as aforesaide
respectively, And of the reu'c̃on and reu'c̃ons thereof wth the rentte and
service to be reserved as aforesaide for and during the continuance of the saide
leases demises and grauntte And as the saide leases demises and grauntte shall
seu'ally and respectively end or determyne, then of the saide Landes Tenem^ts
and p̃misses to be demised leased or graunted, to the vse of such pson & psons
and in such Man'q and sorte as the same is herein before lymitted expressed
and declared any thinge in theise presentte contayned to the Contrary thereof
in any wise Not^with^standinge   En wittnes whereof the pties aforesaide to
theise present Indentures Triptite have Interchangeably put there seales even
the daye and yeare first above written   1622

JOHN ARUNDELL   JOHN PRIDEAUX
   of Treuse
JOHN COOPE   GEORGE GISTE   [*Endorsed*]

Signed sealed & deliuered in the presence of those whose names are
heerevnder written

[REGINALD MOHUN]   BAR GRENVILE

[J]o GRENVILE
                                 RAPH BIRD
p ANTHON' PYE [Jun]   THO [BURGER]
   JOHN GEALARD   REGINOLD BILLINGE
   THOMAS ANNESLEY
   GEORGE COOKE

Sealed and delivered by the w^{th}in named John Arundell & George Gist the 20th day of May 1622 in presence of

GEO BERE   ROBERT WILSON

2^d May 20 Ja^s 1623 [sic]
Grenville &c Deed to make a
Jen^t [sic] to precipe for suffering Recovery
of Premi^ses in Devon

The following letter from Grace Granville to her husband is also extant, though so much damaged by age as to be scarcely decipherable —

MRS GRANVILLE TO HER HUSBAND

My ever dearest.—I received   from you yesterday by a foo glad you continue so res   purpose to have me with   ning my sister Harris I w .   your directions y^t it was never pose to part from my lady Elis .   if she will goe too, then of my . accord I shall be willing to see my   sister Hen, but I thinke my mother will scarce like it, and therefore I am in the more doubt what were best to doe. If you have not already retayned Sr Henry Yelverton my mother doth now intreate you to forbeare to doe it until you heare more from her My mother will'd me to remember her to you, and to tell you y^t she is much against my going to London, and y^t is very true, for you can not imagine how vehement she is against it I doe every day wish y^t coach were come, that I might sooner be wth you, and   of hearing the perswasions that are us'd against it Dick hath been very well ever since you went till . he hath now gotten a colde, yet I assure you he hathe never   his cloth with his neck with .   out to see the lambs, and the weather hath been very sharpe   jocund and so busy as tis 2 or 3 peoples work to play with him, and Bessy grows a lusty girle and I thinkes eats more meate than I, for I have gotten a colde as well as Dick, and can neither taste nor smell with it, and before you went you know my hearing was somewhat detective, so you may well imagine you have a very   wife, but yet pray send for her, for if I were once with you I thinke to be sooner cured .   only by that then by taking any Phisicke, for had I not hoped to have come to you I had been dead by this time So Dearest, farewell, and God give me life no longer than I am

                 Yours in all constancy,

March 13, 1623   GRACE GRENVILE."
To my best Friend Mr Bevill Grenvile
at ye signe of the Raynbow
beteen ye two Temple Gates
         these wth speed

In the Parliament of 1623, Granville and his great friend Sir John Eliot both sat for the first time together, Granville being again elected for the County, and Eliot finding a seat for the now disfranchised Newport. a portion of the late Parliamentary Borough of Launceston In this Parliament, Eliot was to the front, making the first speech of the session, in which he demanded a consideration of the liberties and privileges

V

of the House, and of the way to maintain them in time to come ; and from what is known of the friendship which had all along existed between the two men, and of that which will be seen to have existed in later years between them, there is no room to doubt that Granville was in Eliot's company at such time as the opposition led the House to a division   When this Parliament was dissolved, as it was by the death of James the First in 1625, the relations between Eliot and Granville became even closer, for at the next election, while the former was re-elected for Newport, the latter was for the first time returned for Launceston, the two boroughs forming practically one and the same town

" The Members chosen " said Eliot in a letter written at this period, " forthwith repaired to London, to make their attendance at the time , no man would be wanting , love and ambition gave them wings , he that was first seemed happiest ; zeal and affection did so work, as even the circumstance of being first was thought an advantage in the duty "

Parliament was opened on July 18th, and it was while in London that Bevill received the following letter, written by his wife from her old home at Madford

MRS GRANVILLE TO HER HUSBAND

Dearest, as yet I have not yr later boxe of Glasses, the reason why they are not deliver'd you may perceave by my hē written last saturday by the Car   I heartily wish you home both for my own content and yt you might take yr part of a Syde of Red Deare that my Cosen Ed Tremayn sent me this day , if you be not guilty of Sr Jo   Eliots sinne last yeare you may have a share, for I vowe to keep one Pye till yr coming, but if it offend yr nose, the faulte be yr   Yr servant Will   Way is gone and is now servant to my cosen Dick Tremayne out of a desire to goe in this fleet, my mo   servants are so few & myne none, now he is gone I cannot send a message to Towne   Freeston is still very sick and keepes his bed altogether, I thinke you must not depend too much on him, his weaknes is such   My sicknes hath made me a poor woman in body and purse, and yet I have been a borrower since yr going   my mo   comends her to you and the little crew are well   and I am better then I have been   God keepe you

Yrs ever

GR GRENVILE /.

Madford July 4 1625
To my best Friend Mr Bevill Grenvile
at ye Rainbow in in Fleet Street
beteen yr two Temple Gates these
                dd /

The fleet alluded to in this letter was the great expedition by which Charles the First and Buckingham meant to revenge themselves upon the Spaniards for the ignomious failure of their escapade to Madrid   The fleet was choking Plymouth harbour with disorder and confusion at the time Mrs Granville wrote, and the supply of money for its equipment was one of the chief causes of contention in this Parliament

In conquence of the plague which was now raging in many parts of England, but especially in London, Parliament was adjourned on 11th July, and Bevill may have returned to Stowe unexpectedly At any rate the following letter from his wife, written also from Madford, supports such an idea It bears no date beyond " Sunday evening "

MRS GRANVILLE TO HER HUSBAND

Dearest,

I do very much long to be at home wth you, and am sorry that it was not my happ[ne] to have been home before you, but indeed it was not my desire y[t] kept me backe, but wante of health I give you many thanks for y[t] care and sending to me, and if I had know'd how, you should have heard from me, but I was loath to send away Stanbury or Joseph, because I intended, as soone as my strength would give leave, to be at home The Plaisters you sent me, I trust in God, hath done me much good They came in a happie time, I hope, for I was then extraordinarily ill, and had they not come at the instant, I had been in ill case, but I heartily thanke God and you for them My lady will bring me home, and to-morrow night we intend to be at Trebersy and r[e] next day with you, if it please God You may assure y[r] selfe y[t] I am very ill if you see me not on Tuesday night then I hope you will come to me I am sorry Bessie mends no faster, I long to see you and our Boys God keepe you all well and I am, whatever happens,

y[rs] immoveably

Sunday evening

GR GRENVILE

I pray charge Grace Winslade to fitt things as handsome as she can My ladye desires to come Efford way, because she would call there with my cosen if she be there, and if your leasure serve I should be glad to meet you there "
To my best Friend Mr Bevill Grenvile
at Stow —these

dd /

The Parliament re-assembled at Oxford early in August, whither, however, the plague followed them, and the wife's fears for her husband's safety are tenderly expressed in the following letter

MRS GRANVILLE TO HER HUSBAND

Dearest I have received y[t] h[re] by Dowrish am glad to heare you are well but I am in much feare & griefe to heare y[t] the plague is in Oxford, would God but grant you were home, till which my heart will never be quiett, O pray as you love y[r] self, y[t] children, & me be carefull of y[t] health, otherwise we are all lost The sicknesse encreases heer apace & is much dispers'd abroad in the Citty, & where it comes it goes through the house, & ends all wherfore I beseech you, be not displeas'd with what I have done, you will'd me to send the linen in y[t] absence to Stow, but not to stirre my selfe till you came, but seeing that the poor people would not be kept away, & y[t] the servants went

still into Town, & Exeter people come to us dayly, so as we are in as much
danger as those of y᷎ Citty, wherfore I have adventur'd to remove thither also
with y᷎ children w᷎ᶜʰ I fear will not well like you, & w᷎ᶜʰ hath much troubled
me & still doth my dearnes & care of the children hath made me adventure,
& I hope y᷎ tendernesse will be my best frend, to perswade you not to dislike
it, my Cosen D Tremayn & Jo are heer, & have brought horses for me, for
myselfe my sister Deñis hath lent me her mare & to morrow, we begin our
journey G Winslade came last week, to Stow & there upon this necessity will
made a bad shift, till you come w᷎ᶜʰ pray let it be, as soon as you can y᷎ᷥ bedds
are brought to Stow, but your linnen you left w᷎ᵗʰ Geo Membry my fa sent
for & had it away, before they came Jo Gea brought back the money from
Bydeford, for my aunt Ab & my aunt Brid held it untill that my aunt
Ursula should give that security unto w᷎ᶜʰ they themselves putt their hands
& seals, & drew a perticular one, for my aunt Ur to seale, w᷎ᶜʰ she did, &
sent both acquittances, also w᷎ᵗʰ a bond given by y᷎ʳ father for securing the
Annuity, which if she shoud seale would be y᷎ʳ security, upon this necessity I
have presum'd to take-11ᶫᵇ-14ˢ-out of y᷎ʳ fourscore, & I have left y᷎ᵉ keys of the
Trunck & Cabinett, with the key of y᷎ᵉ Roome but nothing else I open'd
Fursmãs hē, & M᷎ʳ Fawcetts but my cosen Trefrys was as it is now, the other
things, are in the Presse, & the rest in y᷎ᵉ Trunck, & in y᷎ᵉ new cabinett are
things belongᵉ te my cosen Jo Herris pray be not displeased for taking the
money, for I will assure you it was for nothing but necessary ends, & in a
strange place & to keep house, I must needs say I dishked to borrow, &
w᷎ᵗʰ w᷎ᵗ you left I have payd all reckonings God be prays'd we are all in health
yet you may the better excuse my removing, because so many others do it,
M᷎ʳˢ Bampfilde is gone & her children, & M᷎ʳˢ Isack with sons dughters &
children are gone from Portlow, & all the Citizens y᷎ᵗ can possible gett horses
doe remove but my mo will by no means stir w᷎ᶜʰ I am very sorry for she
hath given me a good bedd & Bolster 3-paire of Pillows-2-or-3-paire of blanketts
& Coverletts some w᷎ᶜʰ she had of you & she will speedely, send another Bed
after me, I cannot gett the Bedsteed Chaire, & Stooles from Plimouth by no
means y᷎ʳ case of Pictures was loose & almost open, before I had it, & y᷎ᵉ Kg᷎ˢ
& S᷎ʳ Jo E hath received some hurt in carriage but none since it came
hither I pray you make haste & come home, so God keep you well, & be not
angry w᷎ᵗʰ me however I am & still will be

y᷎ʳˢ ever & only
GRACE GRENVILE /.

Madi August y᷎ᵉ 10-1625
I pray you let y᷎ᷥ Coate w᷎ᶜʰ coms from
Fawcetts be well ayrd & lye abroad
a while before you weare it
　　　　To my dearest & best Frend
　　　　M᷎ʳ Bevill Grenvile these dd /

　　Two days after this letter was written Parliament was
dissolved It was perhaps well that Grace braved her husband's
displeasure and removed to Stowe, for the plague increased
with great virulence in Exeter in the autumn, so much so that,
to the bitter disappointment of the inhabitants, the young King
was unable to visit it, when in the middle of September he went
down in person to Plymouth to hasten the departure of the
fleet

Much as this expedition occupied the thoughts of most Englishmen, it must have had a special interest to the Granvilles, as no less than three of their family sided with it, namely, Richard Granville, Bevill's brother, Dick Tremayne, his cousin, (already referred to in Mrs. Granville's letter of July 4th) and, on the eve of its departure, young George Monk, who was smuggled off to escaped the clutches of the law. The story of his escapade is as follows 'When the King passed through Devonshire on his way to Plymouth, great preparations had naturally been made to receive him at all the principal points of his route, and it was impossible that a man of such a position in the county as Sir Thomas Monk should not go and pay him his respects, but unfortunately there was an annoying difficulty in the way. He was by this time hopelessly in debt, and so many judgments were out against him that he was little better than a prisoner at Potheridge. To appear in public meant certain arrest. There was but one escape from the dilemma, namely, to bribe the under sheriff. George was selected for this delicate mission, which he successfully carried out, and Sir Thomas rode out to meet his Sovereign with all the best blood in Devon. But before the royal party came in sight the proceedings were interrupted by a painful incident. Either the under sheriff had blabbed, or George had been indiscreetly boasting of his diplomacy. At all events the rascally attorney had received a bigger bribe from the other side, and now at this solemn moment and in the face of the whole county, the villain came forward and arrested Sir Thomas. George, who was then barely sixteen years of age, was not a boy to sit down quietly under such an indignity. Without saying a word to any one, he took the first opportunity of slipping off into Exeter, regardless of the plague and went straight to the perfidious attorney, and having told him in the plainest words what he thought of him, then and there proceeded to administer such a severe chastisement that he was with difficulty dragged off his victim. To cudgell an under sheriff was an outrage of which the law was likely to take a very serious view, and the bruised lawyer threatened merciless proceedings. It was clear that the boy must be concealed till the storm blew over. There was only one way of doing it. The fleet was lying in Plymouth Sound nearly ready to sail. Once there he would be safe; so George, to his intense delight, as we may be sure, was smuggled off and hurriedly engaged as a volunteer under his kinsman, Richard Granville. The baffled attorney had consequently to hang up his unserved writ upon the office files, and George Monk, by the

straitened circumstances of the family, found himself prematurely
a soldier, with the burden of an imperfect education to carry
through life."

Richard Granville, under whose care young Monk thus
started in life, was a typical Low Country soldier   After
leaving Oxford he had entered the army, first serving in France
and then in Holland   He was afterwards engaged in the
Palatine war in Germany, where he took part in several
services, as well as in the Netherlands, where he served under
the first captain of his kind, Prince Maurice, in the regiment of
that pattern soldier, Lord Vere, the General of all the English
troops   In that service he earned the reputation of being a
man of courage and a diligent officer in the quality of a captain,
to which rank he attained after a few years service.   He was
now twenty-five years of age, and was in command of a
company in the regiment of Sir John Burgh, chief of the staff

It is unnecessary to follow closely this disastrous expedition
to Cadiz   Ill-planed, ill-disciplined, ill-officered, and ill-
supplied, it was doomed from the first to failure, and
returned in a short time to Portsmouth covered with disgrace.
While the whole nation rang with complaints, and cast the
blame of the defeat rather on the King than on his general,
Charles, though disappointed of the plunder on which he had
counted, was far from putting an end to a contest, from which
it was now evident to all others that he could derive nothing
but an increase of difficulties, and proceeded to summon his
second Parliament, which assembled early in February, 1626,
and gave immediate proof that it was actuated by the same
disposition which had swayed its predecessor   Bevill Granville
sat in this new Parliament for Launceston, but was probably
absent from London at the commencement, as five weeks after
the opening, he writes the following letter from Stowe to his
cousin Rous —

BEVILL GRANVILLE TO MR ROUS

S^r y^r motion wth the considerations that accompany it (which I acknowledge to be wise & reasonable) shall be as fair accorded unto, as there is power
left in me to doe   but this Tye lves on me, above half a yeare since, I did
engage my self by my word, (wch I value above all worldly wealth & will not
breake it for an Empire)   I did I say promise to be order'd by a frend, in this
very point wth you now move me & since that time I heare he hath us'd his
power, & disposed of the Iland   but the certainty I yett know not, speedely I
shall   if I am at libertie y^t self (for any frend of v^{rs}) shall as farr dispose of
me as any man in England, & however it be when I know the Certainty you
shall be speedily inform'd how the case stands   this is all I can say for the

present thereunto, but I shall never cease to wish, that it were in my power to do you service, or expresse my affection to you, wherin I shall not be slack if opportunity be offer'd, but manifest my self to be

Y[r] very affectionate Kinsman

& servant

B. Gr

Stow Mar-20
    1625
S[r] my La S & my wife, wth thankes
for y[r] loving remembrance do as heartely
resalute you

But whatever cause had detained Bevill Granville in the West at the commencement of the session, the following letter to his wife shows that he had started for London about the middle of April, breaking his journey apparently at Madford

BEVILL GRANVILLE TO HIS WIFE

My Dearest I have rested all this thursday heere, & doe intend too morrow, to goe onwards in my journey y[r] sister Smith hath you heartely remembred & saithe shee will see you, when you lye in, therefore I wish you to make as good provision as you can, & pray doe not neglect to make speed in preparing a midwife, be careful of my businesses at home I have desir'd your mother, to make w[t] shee can of the oxen & to send you the money it were good you did quicken her a little w[th] y[r] l[r]s for it, for feare it were I doubt you will have need of it, if you see my co Th Arundell, urge him to make w[t] hast he can in paying the other—100[li] to R. Filling, that he may returne it to me I have will'd juell to call att A[r] De?o Cottons for a couple of cheeses that he gave me, if he bring them home lett them be kept safe for me & if he bring home also my civell Picture, I would have the same care had of it likewise tell Pomeroy I would by any means have my moorestone windor's bespoken speedely & in the same Forme we agreed of, but lett him gett a good workman to so them, w[t] shift soever he make I feare I have forgotten to take wth me the Acquittances w[ch] Ja Walker is to have from my father, if I have pray send them after me if you can they be in some of the black Boxes in my study windore or llord, they are 3 in all, send all if you can, but be careful to hurt no writing or seall in ye boxes & to putt every thing just as you finde it there is one round Boxe on the edge of the Bord, wherin are the writings of Treley, wth that you need not meddle, for I am sure they are not there be sure to send them by a trusty messenger as my brother Denis if you can & for god's sake be carefull to disorder none of the writings the acquittances are, one for 500[li], another for 1000[li] & the other for 1500[li] yis

B Grenvile

Aprill 20 1626
To my best Friend
Mrs Grace Grenvile
at Stowe these dd /

The next letter is from London and shows Bevill busy in making household purchases for Stowe

BEVILL GRANVILLE TO HIS WIFE

My Dearest   I have receav'd yrs by Mr Browning and Dicks   I cañot expresse my joye for all your healths, but shall pray for the continuance Yr Bedds are a making, and some Turkey worke for stools and chaires I have seene, but not yet bargain'd for , it is verrie deare, but if money hould out I will have them   I have lighted upon a prety commodetie of Damaske and and Diaper and am told it is so cheape as I shall not meet wth it soe ordinarily, therfore I ventur'd a little money in it   There is of brode table cloth Damask 12-yards, 3 quartrs in one peece, and of Narrow Napkin Damaske suteable 40-yards & halfe in another peece there is 8 yards halfe of Diaper in one peece for bord cloth and 2 peeces of 12 yards in a peece for napkīs, tell it when it comes home to see whether it be right   I do now send it to the carriers wth this lrē, but forbeare cutting of it till I come Downe yt wee may consider togeather   I hope it is verrie good. Yr shooes & the Childrens are a making   I wold gladly understand how my worke goes onward, how farre they have brought the walls to the height, and how many beames be in ect I hope my co   Tremayne hath long before this sould my Topps and rindes at Lancells out of wch money I would have him to be paid   that rootes them up tell my co   Trē   he must make the fellowe to fill the holes after the trees be up   My cosen Porter is to pay 5li for the rindes he sould send for it,   I have paied him his full money for the timber alreddy, 30li send me if it be possible my co   Th   Ar —100li I shall have great need of it   I shall not possibly com away before whitsontide but will assoone as I can   I have bespoken 4 plumes of Feathers for yr bedd   you must be carefull to make reddy the bedstead   so I comēnd you & yrs to God   resting yrs ever

BEVILL GRENVILE

Charge Postlett & Hooper that they keepe out the Piggs & all other things out of my new nurcery & the other orchard too   lett them use any meanes to keepe them safe, for my trees will be all spoild, if they com in wch I would not for a world

London   May 6-1626
To my best Friend Mrs
Grace Grenville at
Stowe   these dd /

The two next letters show that Bevill Granville was certainly in his place in Parliament when Sir John Eliot denounced the Duke of Buckingham with such effect that, together with a personal friend, Sir Dudley Digges, he was called out from his place in Parliament, arrested at the door of the House and sent to the Tower   The first letter has reference to god-parents for the child, of which Mrs Granville was soon expecting to be confined, and Bevill tells her of his " hope that Sir John Eliot shall be there too, if it be a boy, though the King hath lately sent him to the Tower for some words spoken in Parliament, but we are all resolved to have him out again or will proceed in no business." In the second letter, written two days afterwards, he wrote again " We have Sir John Eliot at liberty again   The house was never quiet till the King released him "

THE FONT IN KILKHAMPTON CHURCH

BEVILL GRANVILLE TO HIS WIFE

My Dearest, Since mvne by Stanburie, I have receav'd y[s] by my co Trevilhans man, wherin you say you have not heard from me, w[ch] I wonder at, for surely I have written often unto you, both by way of Exeter, & otherwise But you doe much amate me to tell me you are so[e] much distress'd for want of a midwife for gods sake, be sure to have one under hand whatever it cost, and you canot excuse y[r] fault, in neglecting it soe long Howsoever have myne (Aunt) Abbott by, if all else faille, shee I hope will do her best, & I assure my selfe can do well enough There is little hope of having my of the Plate home is yett, but all that can be don shall be I am glad you have fetch'd some of the Timber, to keepe Allen aworke, for I desire the worke should goe on wth all possible speed If my co Arundell be at Efford when you have child, it will be very fitting shee should be a Godmother too, therfore though it be a boy, entreat both her & my sister too, it is noe more, then we have don formerly My bro Den is the man, whether it be boy or Gurle, & I hope S[t] Jo Eliot shall be there too if it be a boy, though the King hath lately sent him to the tower, for some words spoken in the Parlm[t] but we are all resolv'd to have him out againe, or will proceed in noe busniesse & if y[e] child chance to be borne before my coming downe stay the Christning till we can heare from one another I will write shortly to you againe, in the meane time doe rest

Y[r] owne
BEVILL GRENVILE

Remēber my duty to y[r] Mother
& forgett me not to my sister
May 18 1626
To My best Frend
M[rs] Grace Grenvile
at Stowe
these dd

BEVILL GRANVILLE TO HIS WIFE

My Dearest, how all the things, that at severall times, I have, & shall send to you from hence, will nowe come unto you, I know not, because they are to passe thorough so many hands, but I will hope the best I have this weeke sent you a boxe of Dried sweet meats, ass many sortes, & the best I can gett, saving only apricots, whereof there are but one pound, & those not verrie good, though the best that can be gotten too there were fewe or none don the last yeare, because of the sicknes, & that makes the scarsety. The note of perticulars is heerein closed, wanting only one boxe of the Quidmock, w[ch] I have eaten I hope my lady be nowe wth you, therefore remēber my duty to her We have S[r] Jo Eliot at liberty againe, the House was never quiet, till the King releas'd him If God send us a boye, I have a good minde to have him caled John, for my poore brother Johns sake, if it be a Gurle, Grace but I would faine perswade my selfe, that I could be there at it, though I am now in some doubt & therefore will heartely pray for you if I cānot be present Keepe my Aunts and my sister by any meanes wth you, & remember me to them So I hastely comend you to God resting   Y[rs] ever

BEVILL GRENVILL

London May 20 1626.
To my best frend
M[rs] Grace Grenvile
at Stowe dd

    X

A week afterwards comes this third letter " concerning the Gossips " and other homely matters

BEVILL GRANVILLE TO HIS WIFE

My dearest I wrote (hastely) by my brother Dennis concerning the Gossips, as for the name, if it be a boy, lett it be John, if a mayd Grace & I will not trouble S' Jo Eliot, unlesse it be a boye, but if my co Arundell be not in the Cuntrie, to be S' Jo Eliot's Depnty, then make use of y' sonne Richard for that office I would not have any boddre, but my cossen Arundell or Dick to be S' Johns Deputies I have receaved y' l'rs by Trungoe whereby I am much joyed to find you so well, but am some my lady is not yet w'th you remember my humble Dutie to her & tell her I had written once or twice more to her if I had not thought shee had been gonne from Madford I do humbly thanke her for her great token of Salmon & Lamprey Pyes you say you have receav'd but-2-l'rs from me I have written many more I pray God my ladyes saddle fitt her, it is the best I could get for money I am verry glad some of the healing stones are home, & no losse, for my two mares good encrease but if they be not putt to the black horse before this comes to y' hands, give strickt charge that they come not neere him or any horse till my coming down for they & all the mares I have shall have the Stalhon w'ch I bring downe, w'ch is a goodly horse & as handsom an one as any is in Englåd for gods sake be carefull heerof, but if they have had the horse already then there is no remeddie I know not what newes to write to you & you know I do not much love to trouble myselfe w'th writing of newes remember me most heartely to my Aunts & my sister, & I doe much rejoyce to heare that they are w'th you & do hope you are provided of a midwife long before this & so god keepe you & send you a good tune yis immovãbly

BEVILL GRENVILE.

May 26 1626
    I have sent home by this footpost French 6 paire of bootes & 3 paire of shoes lett Stanbury put them up safe for me
To my best frend
M'is Grace Grenvile
at Stowe these
        dd /

The Parliament, which Bevill was attending, was dissolved on the 15th of June 1626, a week before the birth of his second son, who after all was named after himself and not after his brother John As it was a boy and not a girl, Sir John Eliot was probably present at the christening to stand as god-father The child only lived nine years,

In the height of his disappointment the King had assured the Commons that if they still persisted in refusing the supplies, of which he stood so much in need, it would become his duty as sovereign of the realm to ' follow new councils.' Of what nature these new counsils were he immediately proceeded to give proof The sheriffs were directed to procure from the freeholders in their different counties a voluntary levy of what the House intended to have granted. Something had been said in the late

session of a vote of four subsidies, which the Commons held out
as a bait to tempt the Court into concessions This was the
money which Charles now gave orders should be extracted under
the denomination of a loan Nothing could have been more
unwise than this proceeding, which was carried forward, moreover, with such harshness, that the whole extent of the Kingdom
presented one wide scene of arbitrary exactions on the part of
the government, and of bitter complaints on the part of the
people. In Cornwall Bevill Granville's two friends, Sir John
Eliot and Coryton, are mentioned by name in the letters of
Sir James Bagg to Buckingham, as having used their utmost
exertions to induce the freeholders of Cornwall to refuse a loan
to the King unless a Parliament was called, whilst Sir Bernard
Granville is one of those who are specially mentioned as being
"well affected to my lord," and as being "as forward in the
business as any friend my lord hath." Eliot was ousted from
his office of Vice-Admiral of Devon, Coryton was deprived of the
Vice-Wardenship of the Stannaries, and Ambrose Manaton (who,
like Coryton, was subsequently to become Bevill Granville's
colleague in Parliament,) was threatened with the loss of his
justiceship of the peace Sir Bernard, on the other hand, was
appointed a commissioner to raise the forced loan, and on Eliot
and Coryton refusing to contribute, they were imprisoned,
June, 1627. Early in August, the month in which the next
letter was written, eight others had been sent for from Cornwall
to answer before the Council for their refusal to lend It is by the
light of these facts that the allusions in the latter part of the
following letter must be read, from which it may be inferred that
it was written by Bevill Granville to one of his imprisoned
friends, and he seems to express surprise at not sharing the
same fate himself.

"S^r, I have a long time been y^r debtor in this kinde, but it hath been
the crime of my fortune in wanting conveniency of sending and not of my
affection, wch would not have slipp'd any opportunity. Concerning the youth,
my ward, in whose cause you used y^r pen, I am in myne owne disposition so
faire enclined to w^t may be for his good, as no friend he has shall therein be
more forward then myself, and y^r selfe shall be the lawe-giver unto me in all
concerning him I took him not for to make a prey of him, but to use the
helpe of my title to save him from being Preyed on by others Y^r directions
have been dewly observed whereof as also of my respects ũto you, in
y^t perticular y^r worthy nephew can give you an exact accompt I am struckt
in point of Title for the preservation of my inheritance, but that being don,
y^r selfe shall have full power in this as in all things else to comand and
dispose of me But leaving this, I cañot but out of the fullness of my griefe
be verrie Passionate at y^r long suffering, from wch there hath not wanted the
prayers of many good men to redeeme you, but whence it growes y^t I am thus

long left at home, when now of late also more of the honest knot are fetch'd away, drives me into wonder and amazem^t, no man hath wth more bouldness declar'd his resolution in this perticular then my selfe, wch nor me nor torture can divert me from, while in myn owne heart I am satisfied y^t it belonges unto the duty of an honest Englishman so to do I have much to say but I know not how safely this may com to y^r hands, wherefore abruptly I present my service to you and my co Trefusis, and my prayers to God for yee all

ever resting
y^r faithful lo and ser ,

Stow-Aug-23-1627   B G

     Pray remember my service and lo to my co Nicoll "

That the loving wife feared the same fate for her husband is cleat from the following letter, in which she expresses "the much feare" in which she has stood of the arrival of a "Pursuivant" or messenger from the Privy Council.

MRS GRANVILLE TO HER HUSBAND

Sweet Mr Grenvile, these h5 I have receiv'd in y^r absence, & did make bolde to open Mr Billings because I imagined I might find some news of the Pursivant of whose coming heer I stood in much feare of, but I hope now we shall hear no more of this businesse , and y^t I shall be so happie as to have your company heer at home, though it be much against y^r will the Soape Boyler came this day, because I know not whether you would be home tc-morrow or not he would needs goe to you / I heartily wish you home, for I have scarse slept since I saw you, so desiring to be remembered to all my friends wth you, & beseeching God to encline y^r heart to love her who will in spite of the divill ever be

y^s immoveably

GRACE GRENVILE

Stowe Fryday night
my mother comends her to you &
I have given a shilling to Mr Billings man

It might have been thought that the king, thus embroiled both at home and abroad, had at least as much upon his hands as he could manage, and that he would have been careful not to provoke the hostility of a new enemy till he had delivered himself from the presence of the old Buckingham, however, who never forgave the treatment of the French court, had long laboured to effect a breach between Charles and his brother-in-law, and now, under the pretext of supporting the Hugenots, who were again preparing to rebel, he succeeded in accomplishing his design Orders were issued for the equipment of a fleet and army, of which the destination was kept a profound secret till, under the command of Buckingham, who desired eagerly to distinguish himself in the field, it appeared suddenly before Rochelle

In this expedition, which proved as disastrous as the first, Bevill's brother, Richard Granville, served in Sir John Burgh's regiment as major (or sergeant-major as the rank was then called), a post involving all the duties which are now performed by adjutants as well as the command of a company. Before leaving Portsmouth he and three others, viz Fryer, Cunningham, and Tolcann received the honour of knighthood, the 20th of June, 1627

The Rochellois, being unprepared for this mission from England, refused, though bigoted Hugenots, to admit the allies within the walls, and Buckingham in consequence landed his troops on the island of Rhé, on Wednesday, the 11th of July, and laid siege to St Martin, the citadel of this island Its capture proved a more difficult task than he had anticipated. Already nearly a fortnight had been expended in fruitless attempts when the Duke's anxieties were further increased by the unwelcome news that a large combined naval and military force was being prepared in France to relieve the island. This news was brought from the King by none other than young George Monk, who at the risk of his life had made his way from England through France, passing the army which lay before Rochelle. For this daring service, the risks of which it is difficult to exaggerate, Sir John Burgh gave him a commission as ensign in his own regiment under Sir Richard Granville, and it was most probably his kinsman's colours that he carried, and this is why he always regarded him as his father-in-arms The issue of this expedition was disastrous in the extreme. The English army was repulsed at every point, and obliged to make a speedy retreat. They were furiously attacked in the rear and thrown into irrecoverable confusion The English cavalry came up, and " to save themselves, which they could not do," broke in and trampled down their own infantry, and rendered vain all further resistance. No word of command was heard. Each man shifted for himself Buckingham kept in the rear, the post of danger in retreat, but courage was the only quality he showed His troops were pushed by hundreds into the marshes and salt pits. Without help of an enemy, says Clarendon, noble and ignoble were drowned or crushed to death. No man. said one of the sergeant-majors to Denzil Holles, could tell what was done, nor give account how any other man was lost, not the lieutenant-colonel how his colonel, or the lieutenant how his captain, no man knew how any other fell. This only, Denzil adds, "every man knows, that since England was England it received not so dishonourable a blow Four colonels slain and besides the colours lost, thirty-two taken by the enemy   Two thousand of our side killed, and I think not one of theirs "   Not more than half the English force were able to reach their ships, and the wreck of the expedition returned to England, where matters were beginning every day to wear an aspect less and less encouraging

Sir Richard Granville's diary, containing a full account of this disastrous expedition, as well as of the previous expedition to Cadiz in 1625, was published by his great-nephew, George Granville, Lord Lansdowne, in 1732

It was while smarting under this national disgrace that the following letter was written by Bevill Granville to Mr Oldisworth, secretary to the Earl of Pembroke, the lord chamberlain.

BEVILL GRANVILE TO MR OLDISWORTH

S[r]

In a season of so much infelicity when the sence of both Publick & private misfortunes hath almost broken my spiritts, I have not foüd any other so great or reviving consolation as this, that so noble a fiend as y[r] selfe doth suffer me to live in y[s] memorie and think me worthy of a salutation from you   I confesse that my ambition (being strongly wrought on by the apprehension that you were turn'd Courtier & I Clowne) did not soare so high a Pitch, as to hope for such an honor, but since y[r] virtu is so great (in despite of the custom & iniquitie of the times, & the pride of the place you live in) as to thinke of an ould fiend y[s] hath nothing to make him worthy but y[r] love , I cañot but be affected wth great wonder to see so much vertue remaining in our age, acknowledging mine owne infinite obligation for y[s] favours to exceed all possibilitie of requitall   & yett you shall never find me unfurnished of a heart y[t] will faithfully love and readily serve you on all occasions wishing y[t] it were possible for me (in my meane Orbe) to have opportunity to expresse it then should my Zeale appeare greater then my words   but least I trespass against y[r] many better occasions I will forbeare much of what I would willingly say   beseeching you to rest assured y[t] I am & will be ever
Stowe Jan 18   y[r] unfeigned lover & faithfull servant
1627 (Mr Oldisworth)   B G

To prepare for service the fleet and army, which thus miserably failed in their application, Charles had expended all, and more than all, the proceeds of his late exactions.   He could not venture again to have recourse to such measures ; for the prisons were already full, and men's minds appeared wound up to a pitch of determination, against which it would be useless to contend except with force   Under such circumstances a Privy Council was held, and a resolution passed, that it had become absolutely indispensable to call another Parliament.   Writs were issued accordingly, and on the 17th

of March, 1628, a Parliament met, to which the people of
England stand more indebted than to any other which has ever
assembled under royal authority, since the Commons forced
the King to assent to the famous Petition of Right, which,
when passed into law, because next to the Magna Charta, the
great palladium of an Englishman's liberty.

That he might meet his commons with a better grace,
Charles had set at liberty almost all persons who had been
guilty of no other offence than resistance to the demands of
his revenue officers   A large proportion of these obtained
seats in the new Parliament   They had but to offer themselves
in order to secure election, in spite of the utmost efforts of the
Court party.

We read in a contemporary letter addressed to the Duke of
Buckingham by Sir James Bagg, that Bevill Granville was one
of the foremost in assisting to secure the success of the anti-
loan candidates, and Sir James expresses the desire to have
Eliot, Granville, and John Arundell (another Cornish member)
"outlawed and put out of the House," for "here," he continues,
"we had Beville Grenville, John Arundell, and Charles
Trevanion coming to the election with five hundred men at
each of their heels"   Bevill himself was again returned for
Launceston   Mr. Forster, describing the main lines in the
composition of the House, remarks that the Court could not
have observed without alarm the presence of a large number of
men marked for their attachment to Eliot's principles, among
them he instances four of those known in after years and to all
time as ' The Five Members," and third on his list, immediately
succeeding Pym and Hampden, and before Strode and Holles,
he places Bevill Granville.

It was at this time that Bevill received the following letter
from his wife, who was staying with his sister, Mrs. Dennis at
Orleigh Court, near Bideford

MRS GRANVILLE TO HER HUSBAND

Deare M͏ʳ Grenvile   I thanke God I am come back well hither   & doe
long to heare of yͬ health, in London, wᶜʰ pray let me knowe of, so soon as
you can   I heare yͭ our young Cine at Stowe are well, I came from Madford,
on Tuesday last, where I would willingly have stayd longer, had it not been
to have been with my sister, at her lying downe   I can gett no hope from my
mother, to see her at Stowe till Whitsontide be past, & were it not to see
my Children, & yͭ yͬ occasions are such as will of necessity, call me thither   I
should not for some reasons much desyre to see Stowe, till yͭ returne for the
Place hath not been so fortunate to me, as to drawe my love much to it   I
have received of my bro Deñs—29ᶫᵇ·10ˢ—wᶜʰ he sayes is all yͭ is due from
him to you, & from my Co Osmond I knowe not whither I shall have any of

no for he sayes, you appointed him to pay a 100ˡ & to returne you yʳ other, & that he heard not of any I should have   I am sorry you did not please to remember me for I knowe not what to doe in this case   I have entreated earnestly for 60ˡ wᶜʰ must be payd away as soone as I have it, there was above 80ˡ due before yʳ going & I have payd 20ˡ and better, & I shall dayly have use for money to keepe the house besides what is to be payed   I beseech you consider of this, & let me knowe yⁱ minde in it   My sister yet holdes out & heartily com̃ends her to you, & so I rest

Yʳˢ ever & only

GRACE GRENVILE

Orley Aprill 4
　1628

　　　　　To my best Friend Mʳ
　　　　　Bevill Grenvile at yᵉ
　　　　　signe of yᶜ Rambowe
　　　　　in Fleet street between
　　　　　yᵉ two Temple gates
　　　　　London　　　　dd /

The two following letters are Bevill's answer to the above and Mrs Granville's reply—

BEVILL GRANVILLE TO HIS WIFE

My Dearest, the sadde aspect of yʳ lre, purporting nothing but yʳ griefe & sicknesse, fills me wᵗʰ infinite sorrow & anguish yea more then all other worldly crosses whatsoever, could occasion   I beseech you disquiett not yʳ minde & use wᵗ means you can to preserve & continew yʳ health   I am sorry to heare you did remove so soone from Madford, where you might best have settled that, but if you have need, gett Mr Flay unto you wᵗʰ his Phisick & give him content w'ever it cost   I hope you will gett in yʳ money & follow my directions in my last lre concerning yt   I desire to have all things paied at home if it be possible & when Vanston hath finish'd the house, lett him make out the wall at ether end, for to keepe the garden more privat, but lett him be careful to carry it just as I directed him before Chibbett, & toot it wᵗʰ stone just as he doth the house, the rest Cobbe   You must make a new bargain wᵗʰ him for the wall, wherein take some advice, if he doe not perfectly remẽber my directions for the carrying of it then let him forbeare it, for I would not for a world have it don otherwise then I intend, but if they be sure not to mistake me, I wish it were don wᵗʰ all possible speed   if you be at Orley pray remẽber me heartily to the masʳ & mʳˢ there and to my Aunts   I hope my sister is pass'd her Plundge if shee be not I do heartily pray to god for her   I thanke god I have had my health reasonable well since I parted from you & so I conclude as I begun, beseeching you to be comforted in minde & carefull of yʳ bodie, as you love me, or will have me live a happier hower in this world so I rest yʳ owne

BEVILL GRENVILE

London Aprill—8—1628

MRS GRANVILLE TO HER HUSBAND

Sweet Mʳ Grenvile

I have receav'd two lrs from you since yʳ going & did according to yʳ directions sende the inclosed heer I returne you the answer as it was sent me   I have written to Mr Osmond to pay yʳ Fathers Rent to Mr Billing & 10ˡⁱ to Mʳˢ Brooking if she deliver yʳ bond but how much is due to

M⁺ Billing y⁺ lre doth not expresse & for y⁺ home occasions y⁺ require money I did aquaint you in my last & I have already received 10ᴸ of my co Osmond & doe desire to have 50ᴸ more or else I knowe not what to doe, perhance you will blame me & thinke I take too much but y⁺ Scores were so high before y⁺ going as all this if I have it will but cleare them & not leave me 10ᴸ for all weekely expences in y⁺ house and workmens wages I am yet heer for my Sister hath not childe, but she desires to be remembered to you and so doth my Brother & my Aunt Abbott my Aunt Badgett is at Sherwell, & I am in no better health of minde or body then when we parted but God keepe you well however I am y⁺ will never be other then

Y⁺ faithfull wife

GRACE GRENVILE

Orley—April—11 –
    1628

> If you please to bestowe
> a plaine black Gownd of
> any cheape Stufe on me I will
> thanke you & some black Shooes
> I much need My Aunt Abbott
> prayes you to deliver the
> inclosed to my co Weekes

CHAPTER X

Parliament was prorogued at the end of June and the next
letter was written by Bevill to his wife during the recess in the
autumn of 1628   He was staying with Eliot (whose wife had
died in the preceding June. " a loss never before equalled ') at
Cuddenbeck, the family jointure seat, on his way to Mr Trevanion at Carhayes, where the four friends who had taken so
active a share in the elections of the previous Spring were to
meet

BEVILL GRANVILLE TO HIS WIFE

Sweet hart, Pray watch dilligently for my co   An' coming to Efford or
     this week & let him have this lie   wth speed, because it
concernes his meeting of S^r Jo Eliot & me on tuesday next at Carihaies,
wherfor wth y^r uttmost speed lett him have the lie, we are making a visitt to
Mr Trev   wth wille keepe me a little the longer from you you must gett
in a little money, & send me now, or I am spoiled, for God's sake do what you
can in it gett it ether of Browning or Na   Gist or how you can, & send it
sealed in a paper not letting the boye knowe what he carries if you can chuse
in both these pray do what you can, & remember my duty to my lady, & lett
the boy be with me either to merrow night here or on Munday at Foy
                                        I rest Yo^r owne
                                             BEV   GRENV

Cuttenbick
        Nov 29 1628
S^r J   El rem
him to you
                    To my best fiend
                    Mrs Grace Grenvile
                    at Stow   dd /

It cannot be doubted that the conversation of the four
friends at Carhayes would turn on the recent events of the late
Parliament, the fall of Rochelle, the assassination of the Duke
of Buckingham and especially the prospects of the coming
session   When, however, Parliament re-assembled two months
later in January 1628-9 Bevill Granville was absent, detained
in Cornwall by a lawsuit, and among the Port Eliot MSS is the
following letter from him to Sir John Eliot apologising for his
absence and neglect of duty --

BEVILL GRANVILLE TO SIR JOHN ELIOT

Sⁱ,

I hope in the mercifull Court of yᵗ judgment I shall not undergoe a harder censure for my so longe constrained absence and neglect of duty in my attendance at yᵉ Parliament, then In mine owne thoughts I doe inflict on my selfe None can acknowledge his faulte more, nor shall blame me so much for it as I doe my self This is enough to so noble a freind and my occasions have not been ordinary I shall humbly beseeche you to procure the Speaker's lrē for me to yᵉ Judges of our circuit for to stoppe a Tryall yᵗ concernes some land of mine for this Assisses, because I cañott attend itt, and deliver it to Kitt Osmond, who will attend you for it I thinke this is an ordinary courtesy for to be graunted to a member of yᵉ house by the Speaker, but if you please to procure it you shall much oblige him yᵗ hath vowed himself to be

Yʳ faithfull servant

Stow, Feb 14, 1628

BEVILL GRENVILE

Eliot's reply bears date on the 25th Feb, when the sitting had been suddenly broken up by a message from the King, but beyond special expressions of anxiety and personal unhappiness at having missed Granville's service, on which he lays much stress, he says nothing of the crisis in which they stood It would not have been safe

SIR JOHN ELIOT TO BEVILL GRANVILLE

Sʳ,

had not the daile expectation of yᵗ coming up prevented mee, I had long ere this given yoᵘ some sence of the unhappines I conceave in that distance nowe betweene vs, for as yoᵗ assistance in the phamᵗ is some cause whie I desire yᵒʳ presence for particuler reasons, doe inforce it as the objecte of my affeccon In yᵒʳ busines I knowe not what answeare to retorne to geve yoᵗ satisfaccon yᵗ instructions are soe shorte, thoughe they geve mee the hope of yoᵗ requeste for the stoppinge of a tryall yet they have noe mention of the parties in whose names it is to be, nor of the Countie where the sceane is laid, soe as I muste confesse thoughe I p̃sum'd to move it in the generall, and had it ordered by the house a mandate should be graunted, it exceeded both my knowledge and experience and all the abilties of the Speaker howe it mighte be drawne Mʳ Osmond was gone before I red the lrē and I can by no diligence inquire by whome to be inform'd, soe as I muste on this occasion render yoᵘ onlie my good meaning for a service yet thus muche by another waie to satisfie yoᵗ if yᵘ please by your owne Letter at the Assises or by a mocõn of yᵗ Coũn sell to intimate yoᵗ p̃viledg of parliament, it will have the same operation wᵗʰ thother and no Judge will once denye it I receaved this date A lrē from Mʳ Treffry importuning his old suite, wᶜʰ yet I have not had opportunitie to move nor soe much time (thoughe mine owne hct were in the ballance) to sollicitt it When yoᵘ send to him I praie geve him this excuse wᵗʰ the remembrannce of my service and geve him this assurance that what his owne Judgement would allowe him were hee serving in my place, the same respects by mee shalbe geven to this case And when I maie effecte anie thing worthie his expectation hee shall have a juste accompte And soe craving yoᵗ p̃don in other things wᵗʰ the representation of my service to my sister, kissing yoᵗ handes, I rest

Yoᵗ affectionate Servante,

Westminster 25 ffebⁱ, 1628

J E

We know no more than Eliot what the trial may have concerned, but whatever it was, Granville could not, when it came on, plead for any indulgence because of being a Member of Parliament Eliot's answer had probably not reached him when a scene, unprecedented and never since equalled, was enacted within the walls of the House of Commons, in which two of Granville's personal friends and several political acquaintances took prominent parts, and which precipitated a dissolution Parliament resumed on March 2nd, after its enforced adjournment and as soon as prayers were said and Eliot had risen to make a declaration regarding "the miserable condition we are in, both in matters of religion and policy," the Speaker stated that he had the King's command to again adjourn, and this time for eight days The House refused to adjourn, Eliot continued to speak, and upon the Speaker attempting to leave he was held in the chair by some of the Members, the mace was removed, the doors locked and the keys kept till Eliot had concluded his remarks. Then and not till then, were admitted the King's messengers, and thus closed what, in the words of an eye-witness was "for England, the most gloomy, sad, and dismal day that had happened in five hundred years" The next day a proclamation of dissolution was signed Eliot and Coryton the two Cornish Members who had taken a prominent part in the proceedings, were committed to the Tower, and for eleven years the voice of a Parliament was not heard in the land

No sooner did Bevill Granville hear of his friend's imprisonment, (which only ended in his death) than he made the long journey from the West to see him, but was forbidden an interview Sir Allen Apsley, Lieutenant of the Tower was particularly careful in preventing Western men from seeing him, ' giving them their weary journey in vain " The business in which Granville was engaged in London, when his wife wrote the following letter in the autumn of this year, was possibly connected with Eliot's trial, which took place about that time

MRS GRANVILLE TO HER HUSBAND

"Sweet Mr Grenvile,
 I cañott lett Mr Oliver passe without a line though it be only to give you thanks for yrs, wch I have receaved, and will in all things observe yr directions as neer as I can, and, because I have not time to say much now, I will write again to-morrow by the carrvr, and therin you shall receive advertizment concerning as much as you desyre I can not say I am well, neither have I bin so since I sawe you, but however, I will pray for yr health and

good successe in all businesses, and pray be but so kind as to love her who takes no comfort in any thing but you, and will remayne

Y^{rs} ever and only,

Fryday night, No 13 1629   GRACE GRENVILE

    To my ever dearest and best friend, Mr Beville Grenvile, at the Rainbow in Fleet St   dd

After being nearly seven months in the Tower, Eliot and two of his fellow prisoners were removed to the Marshalsea "To Eliot's friends outside," says Mr Foster, "the change seemed at first to promise some chance of speedier liberation" Bevill Granville wrote eagerly to him on hearing it

BEVILL GRANVILLE TO SIR JOHN ELIOT

" Dearest S^r,

    While I am deprived of my great happines, the seeing you, it will be my next to heare from you y^t you ar well, wch I covetously desire and shall ever pray for as a Publick good I know the unfittness of the time for my Copiousnes to passe between vs, and therefore will use none, only I begg to know (as my greatest Cordiall) whither there be yett any more hope of so great a blessing is the seeing you shortly in the west It is not fitt to say more, as I canot be quiet w^{thout} saying something Farewell and love him that will live and dye

Y^r faithfullest friend and servant,

Cheeswike, Novemb 26, 1629   BEVILL GRENVILE

    My best service, I pray, remeber to y^r two noble consorts, whose well being I shall no lesse pray for then y^{is}

    The Noble Master of this house kisses y^r hands, then whom you have not an honester nor truer Feind "

One of the consorts (Holles) had submitted to the Court, as Coryton also had already done, and had been released Only one consort therefore, now remained, yet in his reply Eliot is magnanimously silent on such forsaking

SIR JOHN ELIOT TO BEVILL GRANVILLE

" S^r,

    if I could make an agreem^t and reconciliation betweene my power and will, I should instead of these restore my selfe for answeare My readinesse to serve yo^u I p^rsume cannott be in question, and my affection to be wth yo^u carries too much reason to be doubted The times onelie are malevolent, and because I am not worthie will not admitt mee to that happines My desires and wishes shall attend yo^u in yor journey (as the like services yo^u have from my consorte in captivitie) while yo^u remaine wth yor noble frind, whose yo^u nowe are, my better part waites on yo^u, when you are travelling my affection muste still followe yo^u, when that trouble is at end and yo^u arrive at the p^rsence of yor La (that centre both of yor felicitie and rest) there shall I likewise meete yo^u intentionalhe, making an acknowledgem^t of that debte to wch so manie favors have oblig'd mee, and noe libertie is graunted for satisfaccon but my thancks, too slighte a retribution for soe much excellence of meritt I have noe other paym^t but the rep^rsentation of my service,

for that noe argument can assure mee of acceptance but yor charitie, yet experience makes mee confident, as I have found yo^t manie demonstrations to
Yo^r Servante,
Novemb 26, 1629   J E"

Three years longer Eliot lived, still a close prisoner in the Tower, during which time correspondence with his friends outside was carried on with great difficulty

The following letters have been preserved at Port Eliot, and help to throw some light on a period in Bevill's life which otherwise would have been unknown as no letters seem to have been preserved except these

SIR JOHN ELIOT TO BEVILL GRANVILLE

' S^r

haveinge wth much affection receaved yor letter and yor token, it is now tyme to give you some returne at least in an acknowledgm^t of yor favor and my thankes, and to make a Confession of my debt beinge not in power for satisfaction, but first take my apologie for the delaie that has been past, least y^t circumstance accuse me that I be not thought faultie in these minutes wch have any relation to y^r service but may trulie be discern'd in the cleernesse of that readmesse wch is owinge to y^r meritt   I have been all this terme kept by your Countriman Arrundell, in hope and expectation of yor comminge vp, and vppon that defer'd my writeing, but now being freed from that and haveing a safe conduct p^rmissed me, I cannot but tell you how much I toye in y^r absence from this towne, though I grieve for the want of yor p sence to my self ther is nothing heer to please yo^u, nothing worthie of yor view (re Court beinge not w^thin the Compasse of yor spheare) imprisonm^t is a favour secluding the corruption of the tyme, wch is so epidemicale and common that it leaves almost noe man vninfected nor a safe retreat for libertie or virtue but the countrie   This is enough to commend the happines of Devonshire, wch is fortunatelie dissituate, but haveing more excellence by yor beinge, nothing can be added but the envy of yor enemies, wch wilbe held in Counterpoise by the prayers and wishes of y^r friends, in wch numbers are included the devotions of
Y^r servant and Brother
Tower, Junij. 1620   J E '

The next letter is interesting in its reference to Lundy Island, which, as the letter shows, Sir Henry Boucher was anxious to purchase from Bevill Granville

SIR JOHN ELIOT TO BEVILL GRANVILLE

' S^r,

the consent between my condition and the tyme, is a full excuse for my seldome writeinge, ther beinge not (as I dare not be a relater if ther were) anything that's newes, such matter being to me as fire was to the Satire, more dangerous than pleasant   I have only my owld affection still to serve yo^u, wch I hope needes not these expressions, that assurance being given yo^u in such characters as cannot be obliterat, the p^rsent occasion y^t commandes me is for the satisfaccon of Sr Henrye Bourchen, who has much importun'd me to know whether yo^u would be p^le s'd to depart again with Lo ndy either in fee or lease. He seemes to have a great desire of it, and if you intend that ware I beleeve he wilbe drawne to a faire price. What answear yo" direct me I shall give him, and if thei may arise from thence any advantage vnto yo" I shalbe readie to improue it wth the best endeavours of

Y^r frinde and brother,

J. E.

Prsent my service to y^r good Lady, and tell her though the pversuesse of my ffortune will not suffer me to kisse hir handes at Stowe, yet I hope hir sweetnes does deserue so kinde a husband as will sometymes shew hir London, and then I may craue the happines to see hir

Tower, 17° August, 1630."

Granville's answer to this letter is lost, and the following letter from Sir John has no reference to the sale of the islland.

SIR JOHN ELIOT TO BEVILL GRANVILLE

"S^r,

the opportunitie of this messenger being so faire an invitaçon I cannott but desire to kisse y^r handes, though it may seem a rudenes in a prsoner to presse vppon y^r libertie wch has better entertainm^t than weake mentions (of) the profession of a friend's induiance, who maie have an affecçon to y^r service but nott more, beinge prcluded of all vse. If yo" consider how longe it is since I had the happines to see yo" and that in all this tyme noe paper intelligence came from yo", yo" may pardon it v^thout wonder that I prsume thus now wch is but a formall way of begginge a petition for that favour wch you weer wont to graunte me, and by Custome though not right I may Challenge at y^r handes. I hope I lessen not in y^r Charitie and esteem sure I am I doe not in the admiraçon of y^r worth, wch has the full command of my affecçons as of my indeavours, might they be vsefull to y^r service to wch I am devoted in all the faculties of

J. E."

Tower, 28° ffebr., 1630.

From the following letter it is clear that the proposal to sell Lundy Island did not meet with Granville's approbation. He was attached to the "desolat Iland," and moreover, as we shall soon see from other letters, that his "designe upon it," alluded to in this, was to fortify it against the frequent attacks of pirates.

SIR JOHN ELIOT TO BEVILL GRANVILLE

"S^r,

the desire I made beinge satisfied, I must now returne yo" an acknowledgment for that favour, wch was doubled in the second letter that yo" sent me cominge to my handes as I was readinge of the former. Y^r affecçon therein mention'd to that Iland yo" call desolat I cannot but commend, soe farr am I from the prudice thereof, and I confess the overture I made yo" at the request of others had in my intention but that end, by their estimation to endear it. But y^r designe vppon it I know not how to censure, there beinge many consideracions in that worke wch must be first resolv'd on. Y^r owne wisedome I prsume in a thinge of this importance suffers yo" not hastilie to doe any thinge and weighs iswell the Councells that are given yo" as they must weigh the action. Noe man comp'hends all knowledg in himselfe. All men are subiect to error by their confidence, and the judgment is not greater that makes a p'fect act then that discerns of Councells successes beinge not more doubtfull vnto actions then Councels are to men   My manner is not to obiect much where I cannot giue my reasons therefore in generall I shall rest with this caution, and aduise as Strato in Herodotus look't for the sunn risenge in the west   Lett yᵉ eye in this intentioñ seeke for the conclusion in the east Reflect vppon the constellations of this place, and obserue the aspect they carrie, wᶜʰ haue a large power and influence, and if you find them ommous or averse, lett not youe cost purchase yᵗ repentance   Pardon this freedome in yᵗ freind, that would say more if he were p'sent wᵗʰ voᵘ nŧt to disaffect but to prepare voᵘ for the worke, that the foundation be not sandie, but worthie the super-structure of yᵗ vertues, wᶜʰ haue noe seruant more honouringe and admiringe then

                                                                                                                        J E '

Tower, 5th May 1631

The following undated letters probably belong to this period of Bevill's life   The first, addressed to Sir William Waller, was very likely written previously to 1633, as the wife mentioned in it was probably his first, Jane, daughter of Sir Richard Reynell, and who died in that year

BEVILL GRANVILLE TO SIR WILLIAM WALLER

Most honᵈ Sᵗ,
        I made all the haste I could to fulfill yᵗ comand and though I could not performe it wᵗʰ in the precise time of yᵗ appointed 10 days, yet on the eleventh the nagg was at Exeter but found you gone, and so he was brought me back againe, but I still attended to receaue yᵗ order for the deliuery of him   I haue now sent him to you by yᵗ seruant   I am sorry he is not better, but on my word he is the best I can get in all this Country   He is but 3 yeare olde, and if you please to giue him but a yeares rest, till he haue attaynd his strength and stature, you shall find his shape and seruice much the better to satisfie you, and I know his race to be perfectly good   I beseech you name not money betweene you and me it is a thing so much beneath my thoughts, and under the respect I owe you, my noblest friend, as it is not considerable wᵗʰ me   If it please you to Vouchsafe the acceptance of him I am more than satisfyed   It is my grief that I cañot serue you more fully to my desires, but sure I am, if any thing wᵗʰin the utmost extent of my life or fortune can be of use to you, it is as absolutely yᵗˢ as my owne, and so Sᵗ, with tender of my most humble seruice to your dearest selfe and yᵗ most noble lady, I rest
                                                        Yᵗ truest honoᵗ and faithfullest seruant.

                                                                                B GR

I wrote you an answer to yᵗ former lᵗ before my last wᶜʰ came wᵗʰ the nag to Ex two in all before this, but I cañot hear whither you haue ree the first My wife craues leaue humbly to kisse yᵗ handes and yᵗ ladies,

This letter affords a melancholy illustration of the sad result of the civil war that was soon to follow, in that two friends, betweeen whom so much cordiality had existed, should have taken up arms on opposite sides, and in the action in which Bevill was afterwards killed, Sir William Waller, his former friend, commanded the opposing army

There is an interesting letter quoted by Dr Gardiner in his
' History of the Great Civil War," (1 196), which bears upon
this After the fight at Chewton Mendip, June 12th, 1643, and
just three weeks before Bevill's death, Sir Ralph Hopton wrote
to Waller proposing a private interview

"Certainly,' replied Waller, ' my affections to you are so unchangeable,
that hostility itself cannot violate my friendship to your person But I must
be true to the cause wherein I serve The old limitation, *usque ad aras*, holds
still, and where my conscience is interested all other obligations are swallowed
up I should most gladly wait upon you, according to your desire, but that I
look upon you as engaged in that party beyond a possibility of a retreat and
consequently uncapable of being wrought upon by any persuasions And I
know the conscience could never be so close between us but that it would take
wind and receive a construction to my dishonour That great God, Who is
the searcher of my heart knows with what a sad sense I go upon this service,
and with what a perfect hatred I detest this war without any enemy, but I
look upon it as sent from God, and that is enough to silence all passion in
me The God of Heaven in His good time send us the blessing of peace, and
in the meantime fit us to receive it ' We are both upon the stage, and must
act such parts as are assigned to us in this tragedy Let us do it in a way of
honour and without personal animosities " (Clarendon St P n 155
Polwhele's ' History of Cornwall " 1 98)

BEVILL GRANVILLE TO MY CO PORTER '

S¹

I have ever wished you well, and shall still doe so, unlesse I finde
great cause to the Contrary I am informed of base and lying Speeches
delivered of me wch I cañot endure but will acquitt my self of the injury or die
in the cause, and tho I can be kinde yett I will not be trampled on I am
engaged the beginning of the next weeke to ride from home againe, but after my
returne I shall take time to talke wth you, resting now hastely

Y^e well wishing kinsman

B G "

BEVILL GRANVILLE TO Mr POLLARD

Dearest, S^r,

If I were to erect the Frame of a new friendship, I wond lay some
fairer colours upon my weak worth, and search for some good words to set forth
my affection, but when I consider that there is so faire a building already raised
between us I hold that is not only uselesse but may be prejudiciall in drawing
that integritie under the censure and dispute of words, wch is in itself
unquestionable and beyond utterance Be pleas'd therefore (in briefe) to take
me in my native and pure simplicity, wch is unsophisticate and and shall ever
be untainted towards you, and truly glory in nothing more then I am y^rs
nor will be my owne longer then I am at y^r comand S^r, you will make me
very unhappie if you do not bestowe some of y^r leasure time on me I infinitely
long to see you and shall complaine on the Tiranny of y^r business if it deprive
me of so deare a hope We meet seldome, wch is my misery, but when we are
so near, as at this time, let me be made so happie as to see you if possible,
yet when I consider how y^r occasions may otherwise dispose of you, (I confesse)
I check myself for my importunity, and shall alwaies submitt my desires to y^r
conveniency and yet pray come if you can and bring my deare Co Gif w^th

you, for unlesse it be by yⁱ meanes I shall never see him here   I know not
what more to say, but must live in hopes, and will ever rest
                              Yⁱ faithfullest fie   and humblest ser

Sⁱ I must not breathe longer then I will ⎫
be a devoted ser   to yⁱ excellent father and ⎬
mo   whose hands I humbly kisse   ⎭

I had almost forgotten to chalenge you of great unkindnesse, you promis'd
me another visit when you were last in the Country and brake   Pray make
me amends now for that, even for yⁱ promise sake, tho not for myne owne
worth w⁰ʰ can chalenge nothing

BEVILL GRANVILLE TO Mʳ WEBBER

My dear Homer,
    Yⁱ Noble Muse hath enriched me with a great treasure, and I am sorrie
my dull braynes cañot so answear you in the like Heroick Strayne, as might
invite you to the farther exercise of yⁱ Pen wᶜʰ were pitty it should rust
I do admire thy ingenious raptures   I do hope by what I now see that
the spiritt of Poesie hath not forsaken our nation, nor is extinct, though
he hath lately had some Shrewd trances   But I joy to see him so well reviv'd
in thee   I do wish I knew how to add any few ell to thy sacred fire   I have
nothing left unto my dulnesse but admiration and affection aᶜʰ for want
of better faculties I hope shall pt se.   Proceed, (dear friend), and strike up
such a heat in these times as n w outgoe the Ancient flame, and fire the
hearts of all posterity to emulate, though not to equall, thee, and I (that can
do nothing else) will not faile to love thee so is thou and all posterity shall
owne me for

                              thy faithfullest fr   and ser

BEVILL GRANVILLE TO   MY CO   HARRIS OF HAINE,'

Sⁱ, yʳ noblenesse doth multiply favours on me, and those do embolden me
to crave the extension of yⁱ love a little farther in a businesse of such
consequence is this is   I beseeche you meet me at Pol   a thursday morning
I cañot doubt but more gooduesse will flowe hoᵐ the noblenesse of my
loˢ owne   but then can froᵐ any secondary or mercinary instruᵐⁱˢ, well
knowing yᵗ by such and the inconsideration   and therfore the
young man (whom my lo cañot except at) shall make his addresse only to his
loᵖˢ favour, and I will accompiny him being loth to see so much virtue (as I am
a witnesse of in him) to suffer   I have had cause in myself (from my lords
honᵇˡᵉ respect) to conceave yᵗ I stand in no very remote degree of his loᵖˢ
favour, nor am I conscious of any occasion why it should be declined or
alter'd   I cañot therefore but presume I may obtaine something, and must in
this businesse put it to the Test whither my lo will make me a perpetuall
Bondman or stranger unto him   I shall not use many words to yʳ deare selfe,
knowing yⁱ wisdom can by a few conceave me   Lett me finde yʳ love and
ready inclination in this basines, and make me to my last gaspe
                              Yⁱ most faithfull ser

In the next letter Bevill Granville is evidently acting the
part of peacemaker in some quarrel

BEVILL GRANVILLE TO Mᵖ RAISHLEIGH

Sⁱ,
    It may please you to remember that out of the peaceableness of my
disposition, I made bolde to move you at our last meeting that those unhappie

disputes wch were between you and y^r Neighbours might be composed w^{th}out the extremity of lawe and I do wth thankfulnes acknowledge that I found you not intractable to my propositions, but so inclined as became a wise and temperate gent   I am still confident of the like disposition in you, neither can I wth the little sence I have, conjecture but that some meete freinds between you may do you as much right as the lawe, at a much cheaper rate, and an accord so made will bring love wth it (wch all good men will wish) wheras, if the lawe proceed whatever the end be it will leave a harshnes behind   You conceav'd that when I made you the proposition the time was not fitt for it, because the proofs were not published, but after publication you said you would heare reason wch makes me trouble you so far as to be a suitor unto you that so good a worke as such a treaty may goe on   I am confident that it will be for y^r much ease and profitt, by the saving (besides losse of time) a greate deale of expence, wch would be bestow'd upon such as will give you no thanks for it   I hope you canot misconceave of me for my good intentions, who have no perticuler ends but the generall good of yee all, and am so far from being sett on to this by the other party, as I have little acquaintance wth any and none at all with som of them, nor ever had any conference about it, this you may undoubtedly beleve, from him that wishes you much happines, and who will ever rest

Y^r faithfull kinsman,

B G

Let (I pray) my best service be presented to my noble Co y^r worthy consort '

We return now to the correspondence between Granville and Sir John Eliot, and find the latter asking his freind to do him a favour in connection with a case to be tried at the Launceston Assizes, just as Granville had asked a favour of Eliot regarding a case of his own, at probably the same Assizes, a year or two before

SIR JOHN ELIOT TO BEVILL GRANVILLE

S^r,

I have a suite in lawe wth Sr Richard Edgcombe of some value wch comes to triall at Launceston this assises wherin it is in y^r opportunitie to doe me favor, wch for y^r owne worth and goodness, though seconded by noe desert in me, I shall now presume to crave   Yo^u know the disadvantages I have, if it depend upon the judges, and what uncertainties if not more, are implyed in common juries, the presence and practise of my adversarie wth his sollicitous adherents and the reputations of their Justiceships compar'd wth my nothing, and that absent, it is not w^{th}out reason that I seeke the assistance of y^r arme to add some weight unto that number wch must take the decision of our cause   Ther are neer yo^u some of discretion and sufficiencie return'd vpon the jurie, whose integrities may counterpoise those dangers My desire is that yo^u will (though they attend not vsually in such services) ingage them to appeer, and what shalbe the resolution of their judgments vpon the hearing of the cause shall be a satisfaction vnto me, who covett nothing (though in want of all things) but what shalbe duhe thought myne owne, (if I may yet claim propriety), and that but by y^r consent and furtherance, and to y^r service being in all things devoted

Y^r most faithfull frind and brother,

Tower, x^{mo} July 1631   J E"

The next letter from Su John is a long one and contains
his opinion respecting fortifying Lundy Island

SIR JOHN ELIOT TO BEVILL GRANVILLE

S⁰,

haveinge receaved y⁺ papers and letter sent me by M⁺ Ascott, inclosed in
another of his, out of Oxfordshire, I have wth that litle judgment that is
myne pervsed them to the utmost, and followed them wth such considerations
as a businesse of that nature doth require First, I have weighed y^r reasons
and desires, then I have studied what in this tyme I might to know the
former vse therein whence yo^u may see what latitude is before yo^u and then
be directed by y^rself To build there is a free liberty to all men, but not to
fortifie w^thout leave The proportion is not stinted either by reason or
example, but they may enlarge themselves at pleasure vpon then owne
interest and proprieties Keyes are vsuall and vnquestioned, made for honor
or advantage, either a publicke good or a private benefit therein has sufficient
warrant for such workes, and if the word offend, though then capacitie be
large, they may beare the name of harbors, but no color of fortification is
allowable The Duke of Gloucester, building at Greenwich in the tyme of
H 6, was faine to have licence 'muros illos battellare' wch could not be
authenticke but by patent or by parliament, and therefore his grant was
turnd into an act Such is the right in all tymes, the caution more in some
whose jelousies interpret that all longe eares are hornes The Importance of
y⁺ Iland was thought much in elder tymes and ther was a Constable and
other officers to gard it It seemes to have beene much peopled and
inhabited, and a care had of them As for the preservation of the place, in
the days of H 3, I finde by the records of that tyme, much trouble was vpon
it One Maiisers a Baron of that tyme, made an attempte and tooke it, vpon
wch afterwards two severall writts were granted, the one for the strengthening
of the fort the other for ye reinforcinge of the guards These were 26⁰ and
27⁰ of y⁺ raigne, of wch for yor better satisfaction I send yo^u heer the Copies.
By this yo^u may see there was a great consideracon of the place, and while it
was fortified by whom it was commanded, wch likewise at Arwarncke is made
plaine, w^ch, if the land-right carried it, should be in Killigrewe's Command, but
wher princes fortifie their owne men doe manage it, and seldome or never was
it p'mitted vnto subjects, yet it is lawfull to defend that wch is ones owne
Though he doe not fortifie he may keep it, wth what strength I may gard
me in my howse I may secure me in an Iland All resistance to any enemy
is safe wher ther is a cleer openesse to the State Leaveing those words then
of fortification and inhabitoringe, I see not but yo^u may p'fect the worke yo^u
have begunn for the generall good and benefitt To make a suite in that is
but to se[cure] a trouble A licence w^thout patent is but voluntary, and
stands but at the pleasure of the granter It imports noe warrant for the
future, and the reason of Comon benefit has as much, wch for ought I see is
w^thout exception in y⁺ purpose, and thereon I should rest, wch is to make what
I might safely keep w^thout the help of a standing fortificacōn Yet remember
that the cares were once made homes, and therefore lett not y^r disbu(r)sments
be too much, but wth the publicke good preserue y⁺ owne interests and
faculties You see what power yo^u have to draw this weaknes from me Let
it make yo^u confident in the rest that if further yo^u conceaue any thinge
necessary or expedient wherein I may assist yo^u, yo^u have a full power and
interest to command

                                                        J E

The following is Bevill Granville's reply, thanking Eliot for his advice, informing him respecting his recent trial, and concluding with a reference to some stable troubles

BEVILL GRANVILLE TO SIR JOHN ELIOT

S^r,

I am infinitly bound unto you for many noble favours, and not least for y^r last, wherin you have dealt so ingenuously with me concerning my late undertaking at Lundey, wch I confesse hath open'd mine eyes and given settlement to my resolutions, and I hope I shall walke wth y^r caution in this affaire, as you shall not have cause to repent y^r advice, wherin I will say no more till I may have the happinesse to see you   I thinke I never gave you any accompt of the service you commanded me at Lanceston, since I receav'd that he, but I presume y^r servant hath given you notice of what pass'd, and of my readinesse to serve you, wch I shall ever retaine   My neighbors I sent all foorth, wch did not deceave y^r trust, nor faile my expectation, and if I had been (or may be heerafter) of counsell with y^r agents in the first nominations of y^r Jurers, I should have found enough in mine owne quarter to have made up y^r number of such as for their honesties could not have been excepted at and for my sake would not have been terrified or beaten from a good cause And now S^r I shall conclude with the lamenting of my unfortunatenesse in many things, but lately (to omit others) in the mortallity of my horses, which have diverse of them runne madd and beaten themselves to death, no prevention being able to remedy it   Amongst wch y^r faire Mare made one, whose losse more grieves me then all the rest, but she hath left behinde her a brace of lovely stone Colts, wch I hope will live to do your service, and thus S^r, for want of better businesse I make bolde to trouble you with such poore relations, my poverty can but wish it could do you service, and that it doth unfeignedly, but instead of power, you shall be ever sure of the praiers of
Y^r faithfull frend and servant,

Stow, 9^{ber} 4° 1631   BEVILL GRENVILE

Soon after this Sir John Eliot was placed under a closer restraint by warrant from the King, for a supposed abuse of liberty in admitting a free resort of visitants, and under that colour holding consultations with his friends   " My lodgings are removed," he writes to Hampden, 26th December, 1631,   and I am now where candle-light may be suffered, but scarce fire   I hope you will think that this exchange of places makes not a change in mind   The same protection is still with me and and the same confidence, and these things can have end by Him that gives them being   None but my servants hardly my sons, may have admittance to me   My friends I must desire, for your own sakes, to forbear coming to the Tower

Under these circumstances it is not surprising to find that letters from his friends often failed to reach him   Granville, however, writing from " Bydeford, was more fortunate in his messenger

BEVILL GRANVILLE TO SIR JOHN ELIOT

"S",

I am now way by whom I write, because I have heard that a little more straitnesse and restraint was lately laved on you, and therfore chose this worthy bearer, my especiall good friend and neighbour of Barnstable Mr Newton, one that is an Officer in the Admiralty, but one of the most Gentile and honest Gentlemen y^t ever I knew live in that Towne, and had not my assurance of the man been such as it is, I would have forborne to trouble you with my lies Sr, I receav'd y^{rs} by Mr Penman, and that you may ever see you cañott speake to me without effect. I graunted y^t desires and all his for y^t sake at full, though there were not a thing in the world that you could have more tryed my love in, for the man had in his former Sheriffwick express'd such a particular malice unto me, as I did suffer in the valew of neer 500^{lb} by it The particulars are too tedious to relate but what I say is true I had therfore to requite him, taken such course with my cosen Prideaux as he gave me his faith that Penman should never be his officer, and when Penman came unto him he gave him the repulse unlesse he could gett me to release him of his promise All wch upon the receipt of y^t he I did, and to second it made a journey purposely to my kinsman to further his suit, which unlesse I had done I daresay he had failed and yett I lett him knowe that it was not for his owne sake He was desirous to give me any security y^t I should receave no prejudice by him this yeare beinge (as I must confesse) not yet altogether out of then danger, I answer'd him that I scorned to take any assurance from him but I had y^r word and theron would relye, and if that were not sufficient safety for me lett me suffer, and I would much more willingly doe it then be beholden to him This was that passage Since that time there have been rumors very rife in these parts of a Parliament If it be so I wish you would lett me have some timely notice, that I may doe you service, wch I more desire than any earthly thing besides, and I presume I have some interest in the affections of the people, but though you thinke me not worth the sending to, yet I have taken such course as you shall be sure the first knights place whensoever it happen, but I assure you you shall not have y^r olde partner, whosoever be the other I cease to trouble you farther, but with my service to you and prayers for you I rest

Y^r unfeignedly to serve you,

Bydeford Jan 30, 1631   BEVILL GRENVILE '

"The olde partner" Bevill here refers to was Coryton, who had fallen away from his great colleague, and whose defection had been a bitter source of regret to Eliot and Granville

Eliot's answer to the above letter bears date the 17th February, and it is the last letter which he was allowed to address to his old Cornish neighbour

SIR JOHN ELIOT TO BEVILL GRANVILLE

"S^t,

the restraint and watch uppon me barrs much of my entercourse wth my friends whose then presence is denied me, and letters are soe dangerous and suspected as it is litle that way we exchange, soe as if circumstance shall condemne me I must stand guiltie in their judgm^{ts} yett y^{rs} though wth some difficultie I have receaved, and manie times when it was knockinge at my dores, because their convoy could not enter they did retire againe wherin I must commend the caution of your messenger, but at length it found a safe passage by my servants and made me happie in y^r favour, for wch this comes as a retribution and acknowledgment Y^r concession to John Penman adds much to the reckoninge of my dept, though the obligation be the same y^r interest in me tormenhe was such as it had noe limitt but my ail, and I cannot give yo^u more, wch if I could this reason does deserve it, that you have lett down soe much of y^r selfe for him that is soe unworthy, who must confesse the greatnes of that Countesie, and I doe hope the other will strive to meritt it ffor those rumors wch you meet that are but artificiall or by chance it must be y^r wisedome not to creditt them Manie such false fiers are flynge daihe in the ear when there shalbe occasion expect that intelligence from friends, for wch in the meane tyme yo^u doe well to be provided, though I shall crave, when that dispute falls properhe and for reasons not deniable, a change of y^r intention in perticuler as it concernes my selfe In the rest I shall concurr wth all readines to serve yo^u and in all you shall command me who am nothing but is y^{rs} Represent my humble service to y^r Ladie and tell her that yett I doubt not one day to kisse her hands Make much of my Godsonne— men may become pretious in his tyme To whom, wth all y^r sweet others and y^r selfe I wish all happines, and felicitie, and rest

Y^r most faithful frind and brother '

Iower, 17° ffeb, 1631

A little more than nine months later during eight of which he was allowed no communication with the outer world, Eliot died of consumption Bevill had made one more effort to write to him, endeavouring to induce him to make such concessions on the point of good behaviour as might open some way to release, but apparently his letter never reached him, as it was not found amongst Eliot's papers after his death A copy of it is amongst the Coham MSS, but bears no date

BEVILL GRANVILLE TO SIR JOHN ELIOT

"O my Deare S^r, such and so great is my agony and distraction at the reports wh fly e abroad and strik mine eares as I cañot expresse it, nor will tell what I would say, but sure I am it putts me out of my little witts and much beside myself one while you are voiced for dead, another while sick, another while well, but all thats sertaine author for other being but cômon fame, which I have ever found uncertain and lying I dare not give creditt unto any part of it I must confesse (that in the distemperature of my passions) I do feare the two first, for feare cañot beleeve ye last, and yet I must also confesse that the passion of feare hath seldom had power over me and never any for my selfe, but this hath putt me beyond resolution, beyond constancy and wholly from my selfe For God's sake be so pittifull to me as to give me the certainty how you are and wth speed too, or you cañot imagin what I shall give my selfe over unto, nor how I shall be abandoned It is lately reported that y^r Phisitions say ye cuntry air would be a great preserver of you, and it hath long been reported y^t you may have y^r liberty, if you will but ask it wch if it be so, I humbly beseech you, (for y^r cuntries sake, y^r childrens sake, y^r friends sake, wch respects the excellency of y^r wisdom and courage hath chosen to prefer above y'self, as the constancy of y^r sufferings doth declare,) I say, I beseech you be not nice, but pursue y^r libertie if it may be had on honorable termes I will not desire you to abandon a good cause, but if a little bending may prevent a breaking yeald a little unto it it may render you the stronger to serve y͏e cuntry hereafter. I do w͏th great Agony deliver these words while y͏e life is caled in question, but I beseech you think on it. You shall not perish alone. Pray afford me instantly some comfort or make accompt that you shall not long find

Y͏e truthfullest frend and servant,

B

You will perchance condemn my folly in   but you cañot do it w͏thout acknowledging   it repents me not.'

Bevill Granville was appointed one of Eliot's executors under his will, and was bequeathed a gold ring of the value of forty shillings, bearing the motto " Amore et confidentiâ '

The date of the following letter can be ascertained from the reference in it to Mrs Dennis, of Orleigh, having recently buried her only son, at a time when she was near her confinement. The Burial Register of Bideford Church records that "Richard, sonne of Wm Antony Dennis, Esqre was buried the 4th November, 1631, aged two years and four months," whilst the Baptismal Register records a month later that "Grace, daughter of Mr Dennis, of Orleigh was baptized the 4th December, 1631. The letter is addressed—' To my Co Arundell " This was probably John Arundell, of Trerice. The and Arundells frequently intermarried. The father of Granvilles John Arundell, Sir John Arundell, had been buried in Stratton Church, near Stowe, probably either from his connection with the Granvilles, or else perhaps on account of his family having resided at Ebbingford, (Efford), near Bude Haven, hard by Indeed one Raynulfe Arundell was lord of Albamınster and Stratton so early as the days of Henry III. Bevill's correspondent was known as " John for the King ", he afterwards valiantly held Pendennis Castle for the King. His mother was Gertrude Dennys, of Holcombe who had married Lord Morley as her second husband, Richard Carew, the historian of Cornwall, married his half-sister Julian

BEVILL GRANVILLE TO "MY CO ARUNDELL"

S͏r, As no man can love you better than I do, so none hath a greater share in any of your griefs than I have. You are, I know in your owne wisedom better able to speak unto y͏e selfe on such an occasion then mother can, and therefore it would become me to be silent but in my affection I cannot but say somwhat, because I hear you do a little too much punish y͏r selfe w͏th sorrowing. I must joyne w͏te you in acknowledging you have lost a noble and a loving mother, but w͏th all it must be confess'd Shee hath lived a fair time with you and dyed full of age and honor, so as you are bound (as a well resolved Christian) to be thankfull unto God that He hath lent her unto you so long, and not to repine at His good pleasure in takeing her so soon, besides (in the place and stead of her person) she hath left the memory of her vertues (whereof she hath been a great example in y' family) to be ever fresh in y' minde, as the knowldge of it is also sweet and delightfull to me and all such as love y' house. Be therefore y' selfe and not dejected, neither lett God bestow so much reason on you in vain. While we live in this world we must expect to be daily encountred wth such unwelcom accidents, and therfore we must rather howerly looke for them then wonder at them when they com. So I cease to trouble you farther on this unpleasant subject, wherein I have been too bould. I know you will pardon it because it proceeds out of my love in the carefullnesse wherof I could not but say somewhat to a friend whose welfare I wish so much. S', I am blameworthy (but by my misfortune, not my will) in that I waited not on you at this solemnity, being the last duety I could performe ūto that hon^{ble} friend wch is gon to God and a respect I owed unto y' selfe. Sure I am I never intended any more fully then to have waited on you this whole weeke, but in the unhappie instant that I was setting forth I was diverted another way by the like unpleasant news, which called me to comfort my sister, who had then lost her only sone, as hopefull and preety a boy as ever I sawe, and shee herselfe, being then great wth child, did by her inconsiderat passion neerly adventure the losse of her selfe likewise, but when I had left her preetily settled, and was againe addressing my selfe towards you, I rec a message from my father that he would be wth me the middle of this weeke, wherin neverthelesse he hath failed, by som occasions but by another message he hath promised not to faile being wth me the next weeke. If these just excuses cañot free me from a censure in y' judgment for so unwilling an offence, then impose what you please on me and I shall willingly undergoe it, though I find it a great punishm^{t} unto me to be so long kept from seeing you and my worthy cosen y' wife, wth my sweet young cosens wch are lately returned unto you, and whose happy growth both in minde and body I am more than I can expresse joyed to heare of, so kissing all y' hands I rest

                Y' true lo and fa ser

                                    B G

It is to the marriage of one of the "sweet young cosens" just mentioned that the next letter to Mrs. Arundell, of Trerice, a daughter of George Cary, of Clovelly, has reference. Goviley, the estate mentioned in the letter, belonged to the Arundells of Trerice. The proposed marriage to Mr Trevanion took place in 1634, for among the Bishop of Exeter's Transcripts there is the record of the marriage of John Trevanion, Esquire, and Mrs Ann Arundell, at Newlyn, 8th December, 1634. John Trevanion being the eldest son of Charles Trevanion, of Carhayes, and Ann Arundell, the daughter of John Arundell, of Trerice. The married life of this young couple was short, Col. John Trevanion being killed in the lifetime of his father, at the head of his regiment at the seige of Bristol, where Sir Nicholas Slanning also fell, the 16th July, 1643. It is of them

                                                 2 A

and of Bevill Granville who had fallen at Lansdowne eleven
days previously, that this oft quoted couplet was written —
" The four wheels of Charles' wain,
Grenvile, Godolphin, Trevanion, Slanning, slain "

MRS GRANVILLE TO MRS ARUNDELL

" My dearest, noblest Cosen,
I do acknowledge the favor to be greate that you do both Mr Gren
and me in thinking us worthy to impart such a secreat to us, but I doe wthall
knowe that we are very unworthy to give advise to frends so every way more
able and discerning then ourselves It is by M^r G's direction what I write
now, as I confesse it was what I said last in my lie, though we could not fully
conceave y^r meaninge then, yett we ghest it did point some thing towards such
a businesse and though we are not worthy to advize, yett our loves must ever
be so free as to ad our opinion, when it concerns the weale of so dear frends
To be briefe therefore We cannott thinke that the west of England can
affoorde you a better or more convenient motion then this of Mr Tre The
family is noble, the estate greate, the young gent of good disposition, and that
wch in my opinion is not least considerable, is the neerclesse of his habitation,
wherbye you shall still have at hand the Comfort of so deserving a child as
your worthy daughter We can not thinke of any thing that is fitt to give
impediment to so good a proposition As for the slight objection of my co
Ar^{lls} being in debt and therefore cannott spare such a portion, it is not worth
the thinking of in this businesse, for we well know that if you will put y^r
minde to itt, you can, without hurt to y^r estate, raise greater sums then will
defraye y^r debts and paye portions likewise, and I must be playne in the love
I beare y^r house I cannot butt say that being so well able I thinke itt a
crime that you do neglect to itt In the name of God lett the mar of Govrley
assure the portion You may free itt againe, if you putt but y^r minde to it,
and if you do yett itt is not ill bestowed upon so deserving a childe unlesse it
be much more worth than we take itt to be, and we know y^r estate can well
beare itt Itt may be we are too bould in delivering so free an opinion, but I
canot doubt of pardon from so noble frends
We have no greater wish nor desire then the honor and happie subsistence
of ye noble house and every branche therof and for the procuring of it, I am
sure you shall never want the heartie prayers of Mr Gren and me, that am
Y^r truest lo and faithfull
GRACE GRENVILE
We desire our best services may be presented to my co Ar y^r self, and
all my sweet cosens "

Here is another letter of congratulation upon a cousin's
marriage

BEVILL GRANVILLE TO ' MY CO RI PRIDEAUX AFTER HIS MAR '

My dear Sonne,
Did I not much prefer my fiend's content before mine owne, I should
extremely bewaile my infelicitie in being made a greater stranger to you then
in former times It was ye lov'd company made me love this country It doth
abundantly recompence all the wants of my desire, while I see you travaile in
the way of honor, proffitt, and content Go on therfore, (deare fiend), Pursue
y^r hopes, and follow the ible advices of y^r owne brain till a full measure of

happiness from heaven and earth be showred down upon you, to Crowne y^r noble meritts   Rest securely in the bosom of that excellent Consort of y^{rs} that Center of y^r felicity and Rest, and let no storme ever awake you, but such sweet Calmes as may be still an invitation to the enlargement and increase of more and more happines   This hath been, is, and shall be the prayer of your truest lover, which is a title I claim as my propri inheritance, but because coarse sallads may somtimes refresh a Stomack cloy'd with dainties, reflect a little upon our barren North, wch hath in former times pleas'd you, and w^h you can be best spared then afford a little time to make these parts happie.   Let my humble thanks and best service be presented to the noble La Car and y^r good la with the like to No Sr Thos Har and Mr Godol whose many, many favours have render'd me his bondman, and I must confesse unto you I do scarse sleepe quietly, because so great an obligation lyes on me wch I cañot yet repay unto him   But I accompt y^r happines in nothing greater then the felicity of y^r situation, who can inhabit under a roofe with a Gent of his noble parts and rare accomplishments, whereof I protesse my self to be a great admirer, but I cease to trouble you and will ever rest

Y^r faithfull fr and ser

Stow, Feb 8, 1634   B G'

The following letter from Bevill's sister, Mrs Dennis, to Mrs Granville shows that sickness had again visited Orleigh, and nearly claimed another of her children   The illness was of an infectious character and the little sister of the invalid was meanwhile sent to Stowe to be taken care of.   The child recovered, and was afterwards (21st June, 1664) married at Littleham to Nicholas Glynn of Glynn, in the county of Cornwall.

MRS DENNIS TO MRS GRANVILLE

Dearest Sister,

I thanke God we are nowe all well againe, wch makes me presume to write to you   I durst not when Gartye was sicke for fear of hurting you   I did mutch feare she would have dyed   But I prayse God she is now very well again, but most extreamly altered wth it yett, but I am glad she is alive   Mr Dennis wth my self do most infinitlye thanke my good brother and you for your love and great care of our poore girle ther wth you   Y^e Lord reward it a thousand fold into your owne harts   I beseech you both she may stay a while longer wth you, for I would not yett have her home for ye world   I am sure shee is mutch better wth you then with me   Y^e sight of her sister's face now would frighte her but I hope it will be mutch better in time   My prayers shall never cease for you all, and I beseech God to preserve my brother and you wth all yours in perfect health and happye prosperitye, this wth my best service and respects to you both in hast I remayne

Yours untaignedly,

GARTRED DENNIS

Sweet sister, be not afrayed of what I send to ye girle or any of yours, for I am very carefull that none here y^t comes neere sicke persons it ever touches it   God knowes I ever pray for all your healths more then mine owne

To my Dearest and most Honnered Sister, Mrs Grace Grenvill, thers dd "

The Granvilles themselves at this time had five sons and three daughters, they had buried two infants, a boy and a girl,

in 1632 Richard, then eldest, was now fourteen years of age,
and Elizabeth twelve and a half   Bevill Grenville (as Lord
Lansdowne tells us) turned Stowe into a kind of academy for
all the young men of family in the county   He provided the
best masters for all kinds of education, and the children of his
neighbours shared the advantage with his own   'Thus in a
manner he became the father of his county, and not only
engaged the affection of the present generation, but laid a
foundation of friendship for posterity which has not worn out
to this day "

It is evident that he was fond of field-sports and that he
kept a pack of hounds, witness the following letters addressed
to his first cousin, Edmund Tremayne, of Collacombe

BEVILL GRANVILLE TO EDMUND TREMAYNE

Dear Cosen,

You did infinitely mistake me if you did conceave that I would desire the
abridgement of my Unckle's pleasures in any kind, neither could my words, I
thinke, bear any such construction, for I would perish myselfe and wish all
the other friends I have without the content wch they most desire, rather then
any way diminish my good Unckle's delight   I did but desire one hound, if
you could conveniently spare him, without hurting y^r sport, and would in no
sort have him if it might be any prejudice there unto   but my hope was y^t
you had been better stored because you have been breeding so long, and I am
sorry you sent this, seeing y^r store is no greater   But being come Sir
Robert's man liked him so well as I could not keepe the dogg from him, and
the rather gave way unto it because it is a whelpe and not for the present use,
and you have more of the same age coming on   I hope my Uncle is not
displeased with my bouldnesse, for I would rather dye than give him any
cause of distaste, so I beseeche you lett him knowe from him that presents his
best service to him, y^r selfe, y^r wife, and will ever reste

                                         Y^r faithfull friend and servant,

Stow, Decem 21, 1634   BEVILL GRENVILE

My noble cosen,

I cannott thinke upon the death of your excellent Father but with an
infinite sad heart, for as I lov'd and honor'd him and his virtues while he lived
above all men, so I cañott chose but be sensible what a masse of goodnesse is
buryed wth him, and am resolved in my selfe that I shall never see such a
man againe   But it is weak and womanish to complaine of that wch is
remedilesse, and no lesse sinfull to repine at the will of God   I am therefore
silent, as it becomes those to be who are indued wth reason   As for the
attending of his noble corpse to its last mansion, no man living should have
been forwarder to have done duty to it then my selfe, if I had knowne the
tyme, or found that you had thought it convenient to have made a publick
businesse of it   But I guessed by y^r silence that you thought this way more
convenient, and I allowe of y^r reasons, being my selfe very well satisfyed, if
you be, but as well assured how ready I would have been to have served
either you or him   As for those trifles called Herriotts, they are things I
cannott thinke of with such a friend as you are   Doe wth me as you please.
I expect nothing of you, nor ever will crave or chuse, but if there be any

thing due upon the land which was S¹ Geo Smyths, it belongs not to me during my sister Smyths life, wheras you speake of some trust reposed in me I hope I shall never deceave of you or any other friend that thinkes me worthy to be trusted, but I cannott yet assigne a tyme when I shall be able to wayte on you, by reason of some important occasions that now lie on me, but hereof I will write unto you againe as soon as I can I present my best service with my wifes to you and my good cosen

Y^{rs} and so I rest

Y^r faithfull frend and servant

Stow, Feb 9.   BEVILL GRENVILE

It may be you are not so affectionate to greate hounds as y^r father was, wch if it be soe, you may doe me a greate kindnesse, if you spare me a couple of good ones, with very deep mouthes.

Edmund Tremayne was certainly not willing to spare any hounds His want of generosity receives a somewhat sharp rebuke in the following letter

Certainly S¹

I shall be ever even and quitt wth you in my good wishes to you and y^r family, and to manifest that was the cause that I lately us'd my pen, because I desyred you should see how much more power you had wth me then I had founde my self to have wth you   But to cleare some points wch are disputable in y^r former l^{re} I am bould to trouble you once againe   You may remember I sent you two l^{res} to one effect, and if I had been worthy of an answear to the first I had not troubled you with a second aboute so poore a businesse as a dogg.   When I had y^r answear I was satisfyed, though I must avowe it was much short of the power and interest wch you should have founde y^r self to have had wth me upon the like, or any other occasion, and though my motion were for   . conditionall, yet my request did disc . . . .
that I could not thinke so weakly of y^r store as that it would utterly impoverishe y^r kennel, neither can you thinke, without doing me   . . .
that I would abridge you of any of y^r delights   But if you had pleas'd to use my service in the like or any other kinde, I should more have endeavou'd myselfe to have serv'd you then I did this gentleman, though he be my very noble and especiall friend

But, I thanke God, I found other friends that did not faile me, in whom I promis'd myselfe lesse interest then I did in you   And nothing but my too much confidence made me erre, wherunto I was the rather incouraged because I was conscious to my selfe you might have commanded me in a thousand tymes greater matter   And so S¹, God keepe you with all y^{rs}, and send you a plentifull increase of all the pleasures and content that y^r owne heart can wish and I shall rest

Y^r affectionate Cosen and Servant,

Stow, June 6, 1635   BEVILL GRENVILE

Pray turne over leafe

S^r as for Herriotts I have received them, seeing it is your pleasure to send them, otherwise I should not have troubled you with demanding them, much lesse wth making choice   My affection to all y^r family is many degrees above such poore considerations, and therfore I am sorry you mention such other petty conditions as the lease speakes of, and for mine owne parte I could willingly have remitted the whole, if you would have accepted it, for sure I never should have demanded any of you   Y^r other lease for yeares I am not

in case to buy, but I thanke you for yʳ kinde offer   I shall wish you a good
chapman and no way hinder yʳ markett, but if you please to lett me knowe
when you goe aboute the disposing of it, I will give notice to one or two that
are willing to deale   who I know will be as free offerers as .   . .
all the service I can do you in this particular .   My service with my
wife's be prsented to my honor'd Cosen, yʳ wife "

The following anecdote, recorded by Prince in his " Worthies
of Devon" in his character of Dennis Rolle Esquire, of Bicton,
is equally to the honour of Granville and Rolle—

" The famous Sir Bevill Grenvill, in his generous way of living, having
some more than ordinary occasion at that time for a considerable sum of
money to the value of several hundred pounds, took it up from Mr Rolle on
his own bond   But it happened shortly after, as they were both together in
company, that Mr Rolle sent for the Bond and cancelled it before Sir Bevills'
face, saving that the bare word of so honourable a person was to him sufficient
security for that and a greater sum, and withal threw the Bond into the fire
Sir Bevill, being thus greatly obliged by the noble favour of his friend, as soon
as he returned home made a mortgage to the use of Mr Rolle, unknown to
him, of his manor of Bideford and left it in some trusty hand that, if it should
please God to take him off by death e'er the debt was paid, Mr Rolle might
not lose his money "

The said mortgage was for one thousand pounds and is still
extant   It is dated August 1635, evidently therefore prior to
his mortgaging his estates for supplying re-inforcements for the
Royal Cause

The next letter is interesting from its domestic character.

BEVILL GRANVILLE TO HIS WIFE

My Deare,
      I have only putt aboard the barke—3—tunns of white and clarrett,
wᶜʰ according to the direction, you will cause to be safely fetchd home and
placed   I will furnish my selfe with Sack otherwise   I have also sent
you—3—sides of roofe beef, wᶜʰ keepe by itselfe that I may know it from
the rest /   Pray cause Jo Skin to close up all the meddowes safe, except
Hovcham, but there the two weaned Colts shall goe awhile   I do much
desire, that you would not let the boyes loose time from their scooling, let me
hear a Saturday night whither the Picture came home safe, and did scape the
wett   I rest

                                                    Yʳ owne

                                                                    B G

I have sent my hogshead of Vinegar also, but
wᵗʰ age it is somthing weaken'd lett one of yʳ Vinegar
barrells be sent notwᵗʰstanding   One of the lesser sort
because the *horse may not be too much loaden*   Postlett needs not
goe wᵗʰ so many plowghs as was appointed, for I have not sent
by a Tun so much as I thought by reason of the Sack
To my best Friend
Mrs Grace Grenvile
at Stow dd /
Byd —Mar 29—1636

The next letter is from Bevill to his father and must have been written within a day or so of the foregoing one to his wife. The date is ascertained by the reference in it to the new Lord Treasurer, Bishop Juxon, who was appointed the 6th of March, 1635-6, and to the separation of Lord Essex from his second wife, which also took place that month. In this letter mention is made of Sir James Bagg who has already been alluded to in reference to the forced loan, pp. 133-135. He had been appointed to succeed Sir John Eliot as Vice-Admiral of Devon, and from that time onward had gained for himself a prominent position in the West. Eliot and his party had had no more bitter opponent, and it is difficult to fathom the motives which brought together two men of such opposite motives and opinions as Bevill Granville and Bagg.

The two son-in-laws of Sir James Bagg mentioned in the letter were Sir Nicholas Slanning, who had married his daughter Gertrude; and Mr. (afterwards Sir) Henry Cary of Cockington, the husband of his daughter Amy. Sir James Bagg had married Grace, daughter of John Fortescue of Filleigh, Esq., about the year 1612.

BEVILL GRANVILLE TO SIR BERNARD GRANVILLE.

"S^r,

I humbly thanke you for y^r kinde lie by Mr Trott, wch came in my absence, so I sawe him not, but mett it after my returne. S^r, there necessity of my sending him to London that I did, it was not only a money businesse (though I sent a greate sum) but some other affaires that he was proper for, and acquainted wth wch I sent, otherwise I should not have been unwilling to have made use of Mr Trott, whom I shall use in what I find him fitt, and have already some courtesie to for y^t sake, and so shall still. I did not send Jo Gel up purposely about my busenes, but he, haveing some of his owne that carried him up, I sent a dispatch by him to my other servant that was there before. It is true I find him too much given to drinke and cañot for my life reforme him, though I have endevor'd it, and it doth much displease me, and were it not for his wife's sake, whom I desire to do good unto, I should not indure it. But I must also say that though he be too faulty therein both to God and himself, yet I never found him false in what I have trusted him. I met at Exeter the news of the new lo. Tre. and of my lo. of Essex his parting wth his lady, but she deserv'd to be cast of if the report be true, and I am sorry for his unfortunatenes in wedlock, for I honor the man. The Prince delamor is not a bar but only a kt., as I hear by some of his familiar friends. My journey to Ex. was to meet Sr Jas. Bag. as he appointed me by his lre., and there I found both his sonnes in Lawe and diverse others expecting him, but he came not, neither have I heard of him since. I pray for his happines, and with my service to M^r and Mrs B. I crave y^r blessing, resting

Y^r mo. ob. so.

B. G."

Ten weeks later Sir Bernard was dead, attended to the last by his faithful friends, Mr and Mrs. Byrd, whose names occur several times in these letters (Cf. pp 135 and 137).

Undoubtedly "the request of a dying father" referred to in the following letters, to retain the command of his regiment and his Deputy-lieutenancy, had no a little influence in winning Bevill over to that side on which he afterwards laid down his life It is not known for certain who the person is to whom the next letter is addressed. but it is supposed to be either Sir James Bagg or Mr Richard Escott

"Sr,

It hath pleas d Go l (to my greate griefe) to take my good father out of this world by a short and painfull sicknesse, but God's mercie, to the comfort of all his frends, did abundantly appeare towards him, for his Christian resolution, his pious expressions, and the wonderful continuance of his excellent sence and memory even to perfection, in despite of all anguish and torment unto his last gaspe do declare he was not meanely supplied with heavenly grace I do confesse it was my earnest desire and zelous prayer that it would please God to have given us some longer time to have lived comfortable togeather, but since it pleaseth the Divine Wisdome otherwise to dispose of us, I submitt unto it and have learn'd long ago to applie myself wᵗʰ patience to the will of God I expected no worldly goods from him and therein I am not deceav'd, for neither to my self nor any child he had hath he given the value of a penny, wᶜʰ (for myne owne pᵗ) I am rather glad for then sorry that my love may appeare to him for his owne and not for any worldly sake, and my minde hath ever dispis'd all muddy and mercenary considerations, but in the loving and kinde expressions he now at last made unto me, wᵗʰ the heartie bequeathing of his blessing and good wishes, I take more comfort then in all the wealth of the world But leaving this subject (wᶜʰ I cañot touch wᵗʰout passion) I shall make bould to trouble you wᵗʰ a word or two in another businesse It pleas'd my father when he found his disease and danger to grow uppon him, to send hastily for me and I posted to him all night He made many requests unto me concerning severall persons, wᶜʰ I granted all, and at last concerning my selfe he tould me he had one earnest request unto me, wᶜʰ I durst not deny him I answer d him he should never speake to me in vaine, neither would I deny him any thing He then tould me it was concerning his Regimt and Depu Lieu that I would accept of it and execute it, wᶜʰ I had often before refusd but he hoped that now I would not deny the request of a Dying father He added for reason likewise, that seeing those places had ever been in the hands of my Ancestors ever since the first institution of them, and that the Regt lyes about my habitation, and in the heart of my estate, it were unfitt for me to suffer a stranger to come in I confesse I could not answear his reasons nor deny his request, and yet I remonstrated myne owne unfittnesse wᵗʰ my resolution not to intermeddle wᵗʰ the affairs of the comñonwealth, and the disproportion between my disposion and the comse of the time, but neverthelesse he persisted and I promised In conformity wherunto I make bould to address my selt unto you, beseeching you to acquaint my Noble and ancient frend Mr Oldsworth, that if I may be thought worthy to succeed my father therein I will thankefully accept it, but I will not write to him before hand, because, (though I will accept it, yet) I will not sue for it. This is all I will trouble you wᵗʰ at this time, but I will ever rest

Yᵗ faᵗ fr and ser

If my Capᵗ Joᵗ Est be in towne, pray send him away speedely "

The allusion in this letter to Bevill's "resolution not to intermeddle wth the affairs of the comonwealth," points perhaps to the fact that, though still disapproving of much of the King's policy, he foresaw with true clear-sightedness the dangers that were besetting the State by the extreme measures of his late party. He had determined, therefore, to remain neutral, and the acceptance of those offices, which tended to break that neutrality, was only undertaken at the urgent request of a dying father. That the change was believed, even during the heat of the time, to have been a conscientious one, is certain from the fact that while Coryton was denounced as a traitor to the popular cause, and while a main factor in the hatred felt for Strafford was that he turned his back upon the principles he in early days had professed, Bevill Granville was always mentioned with respect even by his enemies, and by his friends was looked upon with something akin to veneration.

Dr Gardiner, in his "History of the Great Civil War," vol i pp 4-6, quotes two letters, which evince the same spirit of loyalty to the King, in spite of disapproval of his practices and principles, as existed in Sir Bevill One is from Sir Edmund Verney, a pure minded and thoroughly religious man, whose dislike of the Laudian practices had led both him and his eldest son, Sir Ralph, to vote steadily as members of the House of Commons in opposition to Charles' wishes Yet he could not endure to desert his master in his hour of peril, and he thus explains to Hyde the motives by which he had been influenced "You," he said, "have satisfaction in your conscience that you are in the right, that the King ought not to grant what is required of him, ... but, for my part, I no not like the quarrel. and do heartily wish that the King would yield and consent to what they desire, so that my conscience is only concerned in honour and in gratitude to follow my master I have eaten his bread and served him near thirty years, and will not do so base a thing as to forsake him, and choose rather to lose my life—which I am sure to do—to preserve and defend those things which are against my conscience to preserve and defend, for I will deal freely with you. I have no reverence for bishops, for whom this quarrel subsists"

Sir Ralph Verney, his son, however, would not join the King's party, and his younger brother, Edmund, wrote thus to him

"Brother, what I feared is proved too true, which is your being against the King Give me leave to tell you in mine opinion 'tis most unhandsomely done, and it grieves my heart to think that my father already, and I, who s^

dearly love and esteem you, should be bound in consequence—because in duty to our King—to be your enemy I hear it is a great grief to my father I beseech you consider that Majesty is sacred God saith, "Touch not mine anointed" It troubled David that he cut but off the lap of Saul's garment I believe ye will all say ye intend not to hurt the King, but can any of ye warrant any one shot to say it shall not endanger his very person I am so much troubled to think of your being of the side you are, that I can write no more, only I shall pray for peace with all my heart, but if God grant not that, yet that he will be pleased to turn your heart, that you may so express your duty to your King that your father may still have cause to rejoice in you" (Verney MSS)

We in these days, unhappily, have but little idea of the sacredness with which the King's person and throne were in those days regarded, and it must be remembered that Bevill sprang from a family full of gallant services to their sovereigns Within less than a century one Sir Richard Granville had succumbed in Launceston Castle to hardships inflicted by rebels he could not subdue , and the great Sir Richard had ended his life " as a true soldier ought to do, fighting for his Country, Queen Religion, and Honour "; whilst Sir Bernard, though not filling such a glorious page in the history of loyalty, had nevertheless shown his devotion to King Charles by taking part with him in the Cornish troubles, in the matter of the forced loan, at the very time when his more illustrious son was using his utmost endeavour, together with Eliot and Coryton. to rouse the country against it

The following letter to Sir William Wray has also reference, it will be seen, to his fathers' funeral.

BEVILL GRANVILLE TO SIR WILLIAM WRAY

" Noble S^r,
It was my very greate griefe that I was prevented of y^r loved company at the sad Exequies of my deare father, but my hope was, when I fetch'd away his corps, that I should have been able to have kept it diverse daies, and so have had time enough of the side sent to you, but I found after my coming to Stow that the negligence of the Embalmer had been so great, as I could not delay the interment a jott, but was forced to dispatch the funerall the next morning wth greate haste and much inconveniance, and therfore I hope you will pardon me for that wch I could not prevent, and no man in the world should have been gladder of y^r company then myselfe, neither is there any place where you can have better welcom then to my house, wherof I hope you do not doubt I wish I might be so happie as to enjoy y^r company at my musters, and so wth the presentm^t of my best service to you and y^r noble lady I rest
Y faith kin . and ser "

The following two letters relate to a visit of Mr. Oldisworth[1] to the West of England.

---

[1] Mr Oldisworth was Secretary to the Earl of Pembroke the Lord Chamberlain A previous letter is given on page 166.

BEVILL GRANVILLE TO MR OLDISWORTH

" Most Deare and noble S^r,

From how greate a joye I am fallen in being prevented of a happines that I thought so neare and certaine, I cañot expresse I did sollace my self wth the hope of reviving our ancient Fiendship, which those distances and mists that have been between us (I fear'd) might a little obscure I do pretend beyond my neighbours unto y^r Friendship, and favour antiquity and (with that) as much faith and Zeale as can be in the heart of man Yet I only must be depriv'd of you, and I do not wonder to be unhappie, for all mine age hath been nothing else but a sceane of misfortune I am conscious to myself of many unworthinesses, that may discourage you from honoring me, or the poor place that I am buried in, wth y^r presence , and besides, I dare not use an invitation, while I am sure y^r paines and peñance must be great, and the recompence can be nothing but the exercise of y^r owne virtue in trying y^r pacience I would faine hope well of y^r conditional promise for Munday, and do exceedingly grieve at y^r indisposition of health, but if I cañot be so happie as to see you under my poor roofe, I will strive to finde you somewhere else as soon as I can, and had now done it instead of these hastie lines but for the Civill respect that I owe unto some frends wch are now wth me, who came to kisse y^r hands, as I do also, who will ever remayne

Y^r faith fo and h^{m}ble Ser^t,

B G "

BEVILL GRANVILLE TO MR. CORITON

S^r,

I never thought to have had so just a cause of exception to you in my life as now I have, considering the affectionat pasages wch have been between us I can pretend as good a Title to the friendship of my no fi . Mr Oldis as any man in these parts, if antiquity of acquaintance, mutuall entercourse of friendly expressions, and faithfull performances wthout interruption for many years, be Pleas of any Vallue , yet you engrosse his most lov'd Company so wholy as you will not give me a Share, and therat I cañot but complaine The last time that he was in these parts I subscrib'd unto y^r greater meritt, and wthout repining I gave way to y^r enjoying him fist, but I hop'd you would not so wholy exclude me from my most coveted happinesse at this his second coming I have no suite or ends upon him, but only a Zealous desire to observe the lawes of friendship and to acquit myself of those things wch in honor do lye upon me, and therfore I cañot chuse but (in the liberty of a friend) tell you I take it a little unkindly, yet will rest

Y^r faithful kins and ser

B G "

On April 20th, 1637, Bevill is found with John Trefusis reporting to the Council that they had endeavoured to settle a municipal dispute at Bodmin, but in vain (Domestic State Papers, 1637-38, p. 9)

The first part of the next letter (belonging to the Coham MSS.) is much torn. It refers to some dispute about a lease.

BEVILL GRANVILLE TO MR EDMONDS

woman is so foolish and unreasonable in her I will have no dealing with her at any hand It is not . nor suitable wth my disposition to think .   .   other peoples means, neither should I have in any way made an offer for this land had she not intreated me to buy it, therby to prevent the danger that shee was in, but seeing she understands no better, lett her take what follows   I will pursue my first purpose and see what the lawe will allow me, notwthstanding the good advice wch she saies she hath taken   I will not do her nor anybody wrong, but it is lawfull, I hope, to do my selfe right according to condition of the lease   You have offer'd her a high and full value, all things considered, and more than I would have given unlesse it had been for y^r sake, but since she hath not the witt to consider of it, she shall never have the like offer of me again, so lett her stand to her hazard   I have done wth that busines till she hears from me in another kinde. S^r, it is true what I wrote concerning Eyre, and Mr Waler was moved out of view of their dissembled feares but did not write anything on his own knowledge of their estate, nor doth know the people so well as I do The others were all the kindred of Eyre, and made up to serve his turne Howsoever, you have not done amisse   like it only my sorrow is for that you should   .   anything, and for the other field I will do you what service I can in it   You shall not be a loser by it   I present my best respects and will ever rest

Yours unfeignedly,

B G "

This next letter from " y^r assured B G. to my much honor'd friend, Bevill Greenvile, E^sq^{re}," is also among the Coham MSS.

"S^r,

I was willing to have dd these lies to you wth mine owne hand, and that made me detaine them so long, but seeing you canot conveniently com for them, I have sent them to you just as I rec them, having opened none but my owne wch I send you likewise, the contents whereof doth not over much please me   If there be any lis in y^r packett for me I would gladly have them, for I wonder I can see   no answear from Mr Imperiall, but I shall forbear to say much till I speak wth you, wch I desire may be as soon as you can, but I would not have you to neglect y^r wife by any meanes, so I rest

Y^r assured,

B G "

The following letter, addressed by Bevill Granville to the wife of the Chancellor of the Diocese, shows that he was not unmindful of the spiritual needs of his friends and neighbours. The Vicar of Fowey referred to in it ceased to sign the register about the time this complaint was made against him ; we may therefore conclude that he was deprived of his living in consequence of Bevill's letter.

BEVILL GRANVILLE TO THE WIFE OF THE CHANCELLOR OF THE DIOCESE.

"Good Madam,

Coming to the Towne of Fowy about a little busines of myne owne, I find the inhabitants therof, (some of wch are worthy gent and my good friends,) addressing themselves to exhibitt a generall complaint unto y^r Noble husband, the worthie Mr Chancelor, against a verrie worthlesse Vicar, that they are now and have long been much Plagued wth. I have in former times lived near that place, wherby I had occasion and opportunity to take good notice of the man and his course of life   I do not know it to be all true that they charge him w[th], and yet he is a person so void of Edifiable parts as, for ought I can perceive, I think him utterly unable to contribute helpe unto, or any way further, the work of salvation, but is wholy possessed wth the spiritts of obstinacy and ignorance, unable in himselfe to do his duty, in w[ch] respect the towne, out of a pious disposition, doth but desire leave from M[r] Chancellor to have a lecturer at their owne charge   They desire not to do their owne minister any wrong, nor will take a penny of his means from him, but because of his unworthines they desyre to have a worthyer to do som part of his duty, w[th]out cost to him at all   The man they have chosen is M[r] F G   But now, because I may not presume to trouble M[r] Chan   w[th] my l[rs], having not yet had the honor ever to be made known to him, there is another business w[ch] this bearer, M[r] Hatch, hath the solliciting of, w[ch] concerns a title of my bro R tho' he be out of the kingdom I am confident the caus is good   I do but humbly desire that in his absence it may have a faire bearing, whereof I make no doubt from so noble a judge as M[r] Chan   and presenting my best wishes to you both, wth my hearty prayers for the recovery of y[r] health w[ch] I am sorry you have of late wanted, I humbly kisse y[r] hands and rest

Y[r] true honorer and faithfull servant,

B G "

There are also extracts extant from another letter of Bevill's addressed to the Chancellor himself, in which he requests him to oblige the minister of Sutcombe, near Holsworthy, to allow the parish to appoint a lecturer "as he is scarce able to read, utterly unable to preach, and what he speaks in the church can hardly be understood."

The business "which concerns a tittle of my brother R tho' he be out of the Kingdom" and for which Bevill solicited the Chancellor's help was probably respecting the leasing of the tithes of Tywardreth, a Benedictine Priory half way between Lostwithiel and Fowey   After the dissolution of the monasteries the small tithes had been granted to the Curzons from whom it passed by purchase to the Bevills, and so by marriage to the Granvilles   It is with reference to the deeds connected with them the next two letters refer.   His deeds would doubtless have been in Sir Bernard's possession during his life time. and evidently had but recently passed into Bevill's custody, and were still unexamined   Roger Granville, who is referred to in the first letter, was baptized in Bideford Church 17 April 1603, and was afterwards drowned in the service of Charles the first

BEVILL GRANVILLE TO HIS BROTHER SIR RICHARD GRANVILLE

" Good Brother,

I shall not need now to tell you how forward and inclinable I am and still have been to serve your occasions   I doubt not but you have had so

good experience of it in all times hertofore, as I assure my self you will
acknowlidge it so freely as I need not to mention it, only I did hope that
those former acts of myne might have wrought so good effects that you
should not have been brought again to these extremities, as if you had
husbanded them well this needed not to have been   For my part tho' I liked
not your leasing of the tyethes and advised the contrary, out of my fears only
that hereby you would afterwards want meanes, wch I now see proves too true
yett when nothing else would satisfie you, I gave way unto your will, and if
you feele the want of it heerafter you cañot blame me   Now also out of my
love to you I finde my self tyed in conscience to deliver my opinion and advise
when it may be for y^r good, and then you may do w^t you please, y^t if the
event prove ill you may blame none but y^r self   First I thinke the same
spoken of no valuable consideration for the enheritages of it, next, when it is
morgaged, I know you nor will, nor can, ever redeeme it again, and one half
of the money, must goe away for the buying in of the lease, so a very small
matter will come into y^r purse, and lastly (wch is the greatest reason of all)
how will you do afterward for means when this is gon, I know how small y^r
estate will be then, and how greate y^r mind and expences are I would I could
not have heard soe much of and for farther helpe from me heerafter you must
not expect it for how willing so ever I am, I know I shall be utterly unable to
doe any thing more for you, for so great is the burthen lying on me, as I pray
God I may be able to find my self and young family bread, heerafter   Now
for the Purchase deed from Colthurst, I never sawe it nor know not where it
is, all the writings that my grandfather had concerning Tiverdieth I have and
will search at any time for y^r satisfaction, I am sure nothing that concern'd
Truard ever came neere any of my fathers writings for I had them all
imediately from my grandfather B   and therfore you need not trouble your
self to seek among my fathers for I know it could not come there, but if I can
find it you shall have it   And wheras you desire me to joyne wth you in the
sale I must desire you to excuse me, for I thinke my joyning needs not, and
besides in truth I am bound by promise unto S^t W^m C   and S^r H   S . not to
joyne wth you or Rog   in the disposing of any thing till you have satisfied
them the debt you owe them, wch promise I may not breake and you cañot
but remember how many times I have holpe you to mony for to pay y^r debts
and yett nothing is don   I will trouble you no farther at this time but w^th
the remembrance of my best love wch you shall be ever sure of I rest
          Y^r unfeigned lo   bro
                              B : G

      G   B   I am sorrie you do not thinke y^r owne Power wth me is as
much as Mr Billings, though I love him well, yett if you had understood me
rightly you would have knowne that no man could have prevailed more w^th
me then y^r self & therf^e you needed not to have used any others mediation,
for w^t I should not have don for y^r owne sake I shall not do for any others
but for myne owne honesty I shall do more then for all the worlds sake
wherfore I never intended to keep any of these writings from you but said in
my h̃e I would search for them & as soon as I could finde them you should
have all I had, but for that deed I never sawe it yet I hope it is among
my Grans writings & if I have it you shall be sure of it   I have not rested a
day since I received y^t h̃e but have searched for the writings that concerne
Truard   to give you satisfaction   diverse I have found but not yett that,
how be it I hope I shall, but when I do I will delivei it to no hand but y^r
owne & till you come will not leave my search unlesse I find it, for tho I am
not so much in your favour, as that you will once in 3 quarters of a yeare see
me for love, yett (whither you will or noe) I will see you for y^r owne busines

sake or it shall not be dispatched though I cañot but take notice how much
lesse I am beholden to you in that kind then others yᵗ have not deserved so
well of you as I have & to make you the more beholden to me I will leave no
paines untaken for to find out this deed, wᶜʰ is not easie to be don my things
lying so confusedly, and this being a deed I never sawe nor heard of but
now after all this kindnes I must come to your unkindnes You say my
reason is unreasonable in that I cañot joyne wᵗʰ you because of my word
& solemn promise to Sʳ H S to the contrarie I am sorrie you value those
things so slightly as to thinke there is no reason for the keeping of them
for myne owne pte I see so much reason in it as for all the wealth of the
world I will not breake one if yⁿ be able to dispose of it yʳ selfe wᵗ needs my
joyning & if I be no ptie in it I do breake no promise and there do desire you
should do it by yʳ selfe but whereas you talke of paying 20ˡˢ more then you
owe & that you owe not the whole money, you must learne by my woefull
experience that what you becom bound for you must accompt to be vᵗ owne
debt for whither you will or no you cañot avoid paing of it you should have
done wisely to have disputed before you had given bond but having done it,
it is to late to plead conscience, thus wᵗʰ the best reason I have, I have
hastely answar'd, & will accordingly performe the deliverie of all the writings
when you will come to fetch them, in the meane time how unreasonable
soever you deeme me yett I know I have shewen my self

yʳ ve: lo b

The reference in Bevill Granville's letter to the wife of the
Chancellor to the Diocese to the absence of his brother Richard
from the kingdom probably fixes the date. Sir Richard had
married, in 1628, Mary, the widow of Sir Charles Howard,
fourth son of Thomas, first Earl of Suffolk, afterwards Lord
High Treasurer of England. She was the daughter of Sir John
Fitz, of Fitzford, near Tavistock, where the family had been
established for generations, and her mother was Bridget, sixth
daughter of Sir William Courtenay Sir John Fitz was a
dissolute character, and in a drunken brawl had treacherously
stabbed Nicholas Slanning, and six years afterwards, while
evidently suffering from delirium tremens, had killed himself.
Mary, his only child, then became the ward of the Earl of
Northumberland, and when but twelve years old was married
to Sir Allen Percy, brother to the Earl They however never
co-habited, and Sir Allen died three years afterwards Lady
Mary, who was now fifteen years old, was very beautiful,
having inherited her dissolute father's handsome looks
Moreover, she had a clear rental of £700 a year in land, besides
much property in houses, flocks, herds, etc The little
Devonshire heiress was accordingly much sought after, and
many offers were made for her hand, but she choose her second
husband for herself by eloping one evening with "my lord
Darcye's eldest son," a youth of the same age as herself!
Young Darcy, however, only survived his matrimony a few
months, and Lady Mary who was still a ward, was now

married a third time to Sir Charles Howard, as above stated,
by whom she had two daughters, but no male issue   By this
marriage she had, in addition to her own private fortune, a
jointure of £600 a year   Sir Charles Howard died in 1622, and
six years afterwards, chiefly, it is said, by the countenance and
solicitations of his friend and patron, the Duke of Buckingham,
she became the wife of Sir Richard Granville, who was just
returned from the expedition to the Isle of Rhee, in which he
had greatly distinguished himself.   He was four years Lady
Howard's junior   The marriage settlements, which were signed
the 22nd November, 1628, show very plainly that Lady Mary
did not trust her fourth husband "all in all," for, without
consulting him, she by it conveyed all her land to "Walter
Hele, of Spriddleston, in the county of Devon, Esquire, Antony
Shorte, of Tenton Drew, Doctor of Divinity, and William Grills,
of Tavistocke, Gent, in trust to permit the said Dame Mary,
during her life, *whether sole or married*, and such persons as
she should appoint, to receive the rents, etc, and to dispose
thereof at her will and pleasure, etc., etc   Reserving to her a
general power of appointment over the premises, and limiting
the premises, in default of appointment, to the lady's heirs
Subject to a proviso for making void said Indenture upon said
Dame Mary .   or her heirs .   tendering to said Trustees,
or their heirs, the sum of 12^d, and signifying and declaring their
intention to revoke and make void the same, etc."   The
witnesses are George Radford, who "attorned" to the deed,
John Maynard (probably the famous Sir John), George
Cutterforde (at whose instigation possibly the deed was drawn),
and Thomas Cruse.   All Tavistock names; but the marriage
did not take place at Tavistock Church   It was perhaps
celebrated in town, but the happy pair soon took up their
residence at Fitzford, with Mary Howard, the lady's younger
daughter.   Elizabeth, the elder, probably died before this date,
as we hear no more of her.   Sir Richard, to judge from
subsequent events, made himself thoroughly acquainted with
all his wife's possessions, and saw that as much money as
possible was squeezed out of the tenants   Here, in May, 1630,
their first child was born, and christened Richard after his
father   The entry in the Tavistock register is " Maye 16,
(1630), Richard, the sonne of Richard Greenfield, Knight*
baptized."   Up to this child's birth things appear to have gone

---

* According to some authorities Sir Richard had been created a Baronet
on the 9th of April, 1630

pretty smoothly, though, no doubt, to a high-spirited woman, who for more than seven years had managed her own affairs, Sir Richard's imperious temper and military notions of obedience without question, must have been galling

But when Sir Richard discovered how his wife's property had been tied up, so that he had no control over it, then indeed his rage must have been terrible, and he commenced a series of insults and threats by way of revenge. He confined her to a corner of her own house, Fitzford, and "excluded her from governing the house and affaires within dore, and one M[rs] Katheryn Abbott, Sir Richard's kinswoman (his Aunt), ordered and ruled all things."

This was bad enough, but there was worse to come, his violence and bad language towards her were so great that she was forced to appeal to the justices of the peace, who ordered him to allow her forty shillings a week. This after a time he refused to pay, unless she would grant him an acquittance. All this is afterwards stated in the Lady's plea in the High commission Court, 9th February, 1631-2, for a divorce (*a mensa et thoro*) He called her bad names before the justices, " she being a vertuous and a chaste lady " " He gave directions to one of his servantes to burn horse-haire, wooll, feathers, and paringes of horse-hoofes, and to cause the smoke to goe into the ladye's chamber, through a hole made in the plaisteting out of the kitchen " Apparently an attempt to murder her by suffocation " He broke up her chamber doore, and came into her chamber at night with a sword drawn That for the key of his closett which she had taken away and denyed to give him, he tooke holde of her petty coate and tore it, and threw her on the ground, being with childe, and, as one witness deposed, made her eye blacke and blewe That the lady being with childe, he did threaten her that she should not have her own midwife, but one of his own providing

Sir Richard endeavoured to make his defence thus " That they had lived quietly together by the space of two years, and till they came to this Court . . . That she hath often carried herself unseemly both in wordes and deedes, and sunge unseemly songs to his face to provoke him, and bid him goe to such a woman, and such a woman, and called him poore rogue and preety fellow, and said he was not worth ten groates when she married him, that she would make him creepe to her, that she had good friends in London would beare her out in it That she swore the peace against him without cause, and then asked him 'Art thou not a preety fellow to be bound to the good behaviour?' That she say'd he was an ugly fellow, and when he was once gone from home she said 'The devill and sixpence goe with him, and soe shall he lack neither money nor company' That she voluntarily refused to have servants to goe with her abroad That she said such a one was a honester man than her husband, and loved Cuttofer (George Cutteford, of Waheddon, her steward) better than him. That he was content she should have what midwife she would, and soe she had That there were holes made in the kitchen wall by the lady or her daughter, that he gave direction that they should be stopped up, that she may not harken what the servants said in the kitchen That she had ten roomes at pleasure, and had whatsoever in the house she would desire That she locked him into his closet, and tooke away the key, and it is true he endeavoured to take away the key from her, and hurt his thumb and rent her pocket That he earnestly desired to dwell with her, etc

After hearing arguments from counsel "the court was of opinion that there was such breach made that it was not likely they could forgett it easily, and not fitt to compell her to live with him, and therefore to have one halfe of her meanes, being 700^h per annum, that is 350^h per annum,

Sir Richard before this had sued his wife's brother-in-law, the Earl of Suffolk, in chancery about some of his wife's money due to her as the widow of Sir Charles Howard The case came before Lord Coventry, and according to Lord Clarendon's account, judgment was given in favour of the Earl, but according to "The Vindication," which was afterwards written by his great-nephew, George Granville, Lord Lansdowne, Sir Richard won his case, and obtained a decree for payment of the debt The Earl, however, stood out all Process of Law, in contempt of the chancery, for which a Commission of Rebelhon was issued against him. But he delayed the execution of it by bringing a counter-charge of rebelhon against Sir Richard, and accusing him of designs against the State Sir Richard was cited to appear at an appointed day to answer to the charge and was rudely brought up to London from Fitzford, a prisoner in charge of a pursuivant

"After a long and expensive attendance nothing appears nor is alledged, only in the Interim of his confinement, Overtures are made to come to some Composition, which he

utterly refusing, is dismissed for the present and returns back
to the Country "

There the above-narrated appeal by his wife to the justices
of the peace takes place, and upon winning her case she must
have doubtless communicated with the Earl of Suffolk who
despatches a second pursuivant, more powerfully armed than
the first, with a warrant of the Court of High Commissioners,
to take Lady Granville to London as his prisoner, where she
was delivered to his care and lived for some time in his house,
and where doubtless, since no record of her birth can be found
in Devonshire, her second child by Sir Richard, Elizabeth was
born ' It is very possible," admits Lord Lansdowne, " upon
such strong provocacions Sir Richard might fly out to use some
expressions offensive to the Earl, a man of a more humble
Temper could hardly have forborn Be that as it will—the
Pretence is taken. He is cited to the Star-Chamber, and
condemned to a Fine of no less than eight thousand Pounds,
one half to the Earl, the other to the King, upon the bare oath
and single testimony of one of the Earl's own servants, that he
heard Sir Richard say his Master was a base Lord, tho four
Persons present at their Discourse deposed the contrary "

This exorbitant sentence was put in execution with the
utmost rigour, and Sir Richard, being unable to pay the fine,
was committed close prisoner to the Fleet, and there remained
for the space of sixteen months without being able to find, by
all the endeavours he could use, either justice, redress or
mitigation."

Meanwhile the Earl of Suffolk advised and directed his wife
to bring the suit for divorce against him , a commission was
moreover sent to search the house, as he was suspected of
clipping, if not of counterfeiting, the King's coinage. Sir F
Drake and William Strode visited the house, but notice of their
coming had in some way been given They thoroughly searched
" tronkes, chests, and cabinetts," examined servants and Mrs
Katherine Abbott, Sir Richard's aunt, " who had the rule of
the house " Pincers, holdfasts, files, " smoothe and ruffe," one
of which had been much used for yellow metal, were found,
and the servants admitted that they had melted silver
lace, etc All this, though suspicious, was not considered
conclusive, for nothing was done against Sir Richard on this
charge

In November (10th) Lady Granville petitioned the King,

"she being a ward, and under the protection of the Court of Wards, when Sir Richard married her."

In Chancery also, on March 22nd. 1632-3, this pre-nuptial settlement was declared good against Sir Richard "in a vacation" (writes Sir Richard) "out of term beyond president it was contrived with Pye, Attorney of the Court of Wards, that my wife's estate was wholly ordered away out of my power by authority of a Lease made unto the Earls of Pembroke and Dorset, to the King's use for eight years, on pretence that she was then a ward to the King, as not having sued forth her Livery, which being done, nothing was found prevalent to revoke or remedy that act" Sir Richard was also "compelled by many processes at Law to pay many great debts of my wife's, which were owing to her before ever I saw her, and notwithstanding I could not receive one penny of her estate for any occasion whatever."

By means of these "injustices and pressures" he was compelled to sell away his own private estate and to "impawn his goods, which by it were quite lost"

"Thus finding neither justice nor law in England for me, but on the contrary that all pass'd for justice against me. on the 17th October, 1633, I gave myself liberty, and conveyed myself from England into the Swede's service in Germany"

Nothing is again heard of Sir Richard until 1639, when the troubles broke out in Scotland. and then, nothwithstanding all the provocations he had received, and the oppressions he had endured, he returned to lay his life and fortune at the King's feet

During these seven years his emancipated wife lived in various places—for the first four or five years with the Earl of Suffolk, and afterwards at her own house in London   She resumed the name of Howard, by which she was always known, and is described in legal documents as "Howard als Grenvil' Her children were probably with her, and to their number must be added one George Howard, whose existence, it is to be feared, cannot be regarded otherwise than as a blot on his mother's fair fame. and who was probably born after the divorce, during Sir Richard's absence from England.

CHAPTER XI

It was probably after Easter, 1637, that Bevill Granville sent his eldest son, Richard, to Gloucester Hall, Oxford, where Mr Wheare, a West countryman of great celebrity, was Principal The two next letters to Mr Wheare are interesting, as showing the arrangements made for, and the expenses of a young man at the University in those days, as well as the extreme care of the father for his son's education and welfare

BEVILL GRANVILLE TO THE PRINCIPAL OF GLOUCESTER HALL, OXFORD.

"Mos hon Sᵣ,

I should sooner have given you notice of my intentions, but some accidents have hindered it, and I heare you have been inform'd thereof by my frends   It is my purpose to cōmitt my eldest Son wholy to yʳ trust   I intend he shall depart hence the next weeke after Easter   I will say nothing to yʳ better judgmᵗ by way of direction, but cōmitt him wholy to yʳ care, only beseeching you to conceave (as I do) that it is a greater trust then if I cōmitted my whole estate into yʳ hands   I only will acquaint you with my desire, but the way and manner I leave absolutely to yourself   I desire to have him a good scoller, and kept strictly to those courses that may conduce to that end   I have been as carefull to have him well grounded as I cān, that he may be the fitter to be wrought upon   I will allow him a competency to maintain him like a Gent · but not to invite him to excesse or prodigallitie I am not unwilling he should use decent and gentile recreations, as well for exercize and health as for gracefulness, as fencing, dancing, etc , but I would have them used as recreations and not hinderances to his study   You now see my desire, and the benefit wᶜʰ you may confer will be of a large extent , you shall oblige more then him and me, and for mine owne part you shall ever find a gratefull minde in me, and I hope in the rest   I shall wish more particularly by him , in the meane time I thought fitt to trouble you thus farr and will ever remaine

Yʳ most oblig · frend and ser

My wife joynes wᵗʰ me in the presentmᵗ of her serv   to the good gent   yʳ wife "

"Sᵣ,

If you have rec   my former le you partly know my minde, and I shall now but only coment on the same text   I have at length sent you my Son, humbly beseeching you to goe on wᵗʰ the worke I have begun, in making him a scoller.   Let no indulgence nor Connivance hinder it   I am serious in this purpose, so farr as I shall thinke myself injured by you (whom I trust above

all the world and with more then all the world else is to me) if you faile of y^r endevours, and he for his part looses all the interest of a Childe in me   It is a strong vowe I have made   I am unalterable in it   I do with griefe finde mine owne defects, and feel an infinite mayme by the want of h$\bar{e}$s   I am desirous therefore to have it supplyed in him   He is (unless I am abused by those I trust) conveniently prepared for a Country Scoller   I have been strict in bringing him to it   I kept him longer to Schoole then most of my friends were willing, because I would take off all objection that a Tutor might make, now at his coming up, so as if I faile in my expectation, the fault must be so greate either in his Tutor or himselfe, as it will be unexcuseable, and for the boy he is irrecoverably lost and must never see my face again   It is but the spending of three yeares that I desire, not for mine own good but his, and for it I will be but his drudge in the meane time, and give him all that I have in end   I confesse I have been severne to him, but it hath been only to this end, and I sawe his nature needed it, or he would not have gone the way I wished I am willing to have the same course continued, and yet not his spirits suppress'd or kill d   I debarr him not from Gentile recreations or fitt exersize I know these necessary   But I would not have him to make studies of them Lett him use them as whetstones to encrease an appetite to his studys, and so he shall find benefitt and I comfort   But, I beseech you, wthdrawe him (as much as you can) from the infection of that generall contagion wch hath spread itself not only over the university but the whole kingdom, and wch I can wth sad experience say was the ruin of divers hopefull gent^s there in my time You may guesse what I ayme at   I will not name   There was a nation of ancient seniors (and I doubt not but there is a succession of them unto these days) who, having gotten a convenient stock of lear in their youth to make them good company, did employ their parts to nothing but the encrease of good fellowship, and changed from the better study to the worse   They were my destruction and many others in my time   I am willing to prevent a mischiefe and yet I am far from being Stoicall or Rigedly severe   I debar no fitt or sober liberty, only I would prevent the abuse, and have him study this short space that he may therby know how to govern him well and to use pleasures aright, and then he shall do what he will   My Zeal to a good worke and my confidence in y^r worth makes me bouldly tedious, but I hope you will pardon it, knowing whence it springs   He hath some imperfection in speach and a body nothing strong   I know that industry may somewhat amend both I desire that he should attaine to a fluent latine tongue and not loose his Greeke   I will say no more, and when I have all sayd I comitte the whole worke to y^{or} trust and better judgm^t I will allow him 80^l a yeare, whereof I would have him to bestow 10^l a yeare upon his servant and to be at no farther charge with him   The other 70^{ls} I desire you would take into your custody, and order in such sort as it may serve his turne to live in as good quality as he can wth it, but by no means to exceed that proportion, for more he cañot have, and I beseech you to direct his habitt and garm^{ts} in such sort as you think fitt I have now sent wth him 50^{ls} wch I would have thus disposed, 5^{ls} of it I have given him to putt in his purse, 10^{ls} I would have bestowd in a faire piece of plate for y^r Hall   The rest all (except what must defray their expences up) I have entreated Mr Sharsell to dd unto you, and I beseech you order it as you think best for him, and so the rest of his exhibition wch I will send quarterly unto you, for he will not be yet fitt to governe money   More I cañot say   I comend this my most important (and all) busines unto you and will ever rest
                                       Your very gratefull fr to ser you

    I expect that the 70's should defray his dyet, his Cham rent, his clothes his Tutor, and all other charges whatsoever, for more he cañot have."

The following letters from Bevill to his son at college are full of fatherly counsel and advice, and show the deep anxiety he felt for his welfare, an anxiety which after events proved to have been well founded

BEVILL GRANVILLE TO HIS SON RICHARD

" Dick,

The time is come wherein you are visitted by my first lines   I expect a very exact and punctuall observation of my directions   You know both y^r reward or punishment, neither is contemptible   I will not despaire, though you have given me some disheart'nings, but hope that, if to my honest desires you add carefull endevours, God will give an happie event, y^{rs} will be the benefitt, mine my comfort   I have been so affectionately large in my discourse unto you at your departure, as I shall say little thereof, affecting not repetitions and affying in y^r memory, but in the generall I say that you know the end you are sent for   It is not for pleasure but profitt, howbeitt that profitt drawes wth it the truest and most essentiall pleasure in the world, as if you be wise you will quickly understand   It is no long time that I confine you to, wch spend to my satisfaction and my whole study shall be to give you pleasure and content afterward   The taske is not greate, the time not long, the benefitt infinite   I am so overwhelm'd wth the multiplicity of cogitations as it doth confuse me and prevent much of what I would say ; so greate are my desires, cares, and doubts, now you are sent abroad into the Forrest of the world, where so many wilde beasts wayte for the devouring of all youths, I meane ye depraving of their maners, as renders my passion not improper or unreasonable   But I shall leave much to y^r owne judgm^t, wch I would fain hope might conceave me by few words   You know what I have adviz'd you to, warn'd you from   I ct not the restraint seeme hard   If you have witt it will not, weighing the reasons and valuing the benefitts, Neither let the view of other youths' liberty or mispending their time disquiett or ensnare you   You shall hereafter finde the advantage you shall have over them by making use of these wholesom counsells and by well spending of this short but most precious time now assign'd you, wch if you loose it can never be recover'd againe, nor any opportunity had afterward   It is sayd by some wise writers in the Art Militaiy, that a genera'l in the war can err but once for if he comitt any one error in the rules and discipline of their art, his watchfull enemy (if he be a prudent leader) will take advantage of it to the others ruine, whereupon hath followed the destruction of many a goodly Army and glorious enterprize   I now say unto you on a different subject (and I speake it Prophettically as what shall more undoubtedly come to passe) that in the maine and principles of my directions you shall err but once, for y^t error shall be y^r ruine, and never shall you have another opportunity   I am heerin serious and unalterable and God is witnesse to my vowe   I will say no more, you may conceave me by what is say'd   I will hope the best and I beseech God to blesse the event   I shall not hence forward be hastely angry with you, but my next will be the laste and everlasting   If I have been quick in times past it was for y^r good and because I found y^r nature needed it, being not so tractable as I wish'd   Somthing I dislike since y^r departure, but it shall not mount unto an anger   I was not pleas'd wth some passages at Ex   I know no need you had to make alteration in y^r Clothes there, wch I am sure were well enough fitted before y^r departure, neither needed you to bestow such a price in a new saddle, for that wch you had was not olde nor much worne, but sufficiently able to have done service, and of stuff and trimming of the richest sorte   Besides, in Ox   you are not to make use of Saddles   I say this to lett you see y^r vanity & weaknes, wch I wish you to reforme   Be wise & conforme y'selfe to the quallity of my enfeebled fortune   I doe (to show my affection) strayne myselfe beyond my power in the proportion I have allotted to you   You must not exceede it   If you doe, you are undone   But if you carefully apply y'selfe to follow my advice you shall finde me ever

Y^r very loving father
BEVILL GRENVILE

Stow—April 30
1638—

And after you came to Oxford, though it were long before you would dispatch my servant, yet when you wrote, it was in such haste as it wer nothing like y^r hand & in some places faulty in orthography.   I would have you continue the fairnesse of y^r writing and be carefull to write advisedly,   At leisure times practize after the Copies you have, for much hasty and ill writing will spoile the hand   I like y^r lre well enouge to my cosen Prideaux, but on the superscription you putt only two lrs (Ri) for his name, wch is not fitt upon a lre—for directions on a lre   must be at large

I know not y^r Tutor and therefore cañott
well tell how to write to him   be carefull
to follow all exercises of learning, make
large and exact note bookes and forgett not
y^r Greeke, but better it that you can

(Superscription)

To my loving sonne Richard
Grenvile at Gloucester Hall
in Oxford these.   dd.

Dick

My cosen Prideaux hath again saluted you by this lre cõming herewith I would have you answer him respectfully, as his love doth well deserve   I have sett downe some briefe notes, wch may serve as heads for the drawing up of y^r lre to him they are heer inclosed, but reforme, and amend them as you think fitt   From my selfe I have no more to say, I have said enough if you make good use of it, pray be carefull of the spending of y^r time, wch once lost cañott be recover'd it is not long y^r I shall continue you where you are, but I would not have this short space lost, you will finde the happines of it through y^r whole life, and pray begin in time to fall upon some considerations of providence and thrift, it will be very necessary after such wastfull predecessors as we have succeeded, and if you neglect it, the poor remainder of a fortune y^r is left for us, will hold but a little while   You may daily observe, that small stocke being providently and discreetly order'd, in short space grow to greate estates whereas the greatest estates are by improvidence ruin'd in a much shorter space, if you run into debt or exceed y^r allowance, you must suffer for it, for I protest from me you shall not have a peñy   My means can hardly pforme my limited pportion wch I send for you and if you cañot live wth this I will allow no more, and shall have no hope of any good husbandry in you   I beseech God you may have the grace to guide y'self aright   I'm tould you take too much time in pleasures, if it be so you are a lost man, you have better things to fixe upon   I require you to avoid those nocent things wch will be hindrances into the good work wch I have designed you for, and so God blesse you

Y^t lo. fa   B G

P S —You give me no information whither you make any benefit out of y^r Heb Lee or whither you yet begin to relish it, the hearing of y^r pficiency in any good litterature, would be the best news to me I hope you will not deceave my hopes, & be sure to inform me of no untruths think what it is to breake that faith & those promises wch you have given me, if you breake a part you faile in the whole I do not yet tell you what I begin to suspect wch will make a great breach, but when matters are ripe for my discovring my selfe I shall give but one judgm^t more I hope you will in time thinke of it, tis not yet too late

Dick

This is my third he since y^r departure one by my Co Ch Mo & another by my Tenāt jo Wh besides this, it will be convenient for you to give me notice what h$\tilde{s}$ you receave, that I may know wch do miscarry I have rec from you one by Flint, & another now lately by my Co Por I shall lett slip few opportunities of writing when my leasure will give leave & so I wish you to do also I have been ample in my advices & direction heretofore, I will not farther enlarge thereon but expect a conformity in y^r obedience to my desires, & then you may undoubtedly expect all the blessings that I can power on you, & I am willing now to intreat you rather wth familliarity then Authority, that you be carefull not to swerve from those profittable rules that I have prescrib'd unto you, do not think you can delude me wth faire shewes unlesse y^r heart be right, truth will not long be hid, nor can my jealous eye be blinded, wch is watchfull over y^r welfare, as my heart is wholy intentive upon the pious worke of establishing you in the perfection of learning & good manners let me not loose my hopes, & I will be no other but a Drudge for you some things in the carriage of y^r boddy, as well as in the composition of y^r minde do need reformation, but y^t care & industry may supply those defects, there is nothing so difficult but these may overcome You cañot have better directions then the Excel Pr^{ll} will continually give you, & in the way of learning, I doubt not but y^r Tutor will do his part besides you know I have taken that course wth Mr Shar to assist y^r studies, as it must be infinitly y^r fault if I faile of my expectations I have already cause to object some things unto you, but it shall yet be wth mildness it troubles me not a little that I find you have so sodainly cast of all care of continuing the famnes of writing, truly those l$\overline{rs}$ wch I have rec from you, are in a worse hand then you wrote seven years agoe so as I perceive all the labour & expence I have bestow'd on you since is lost, what hopes can I have of satisfaction from you in other matters, so easy to be perform'd by you, but I will avoid all bitternes & not close wth despaire in any thing, besides you write in greater haste then becomes you to a parent these things are easily reformed, & I am not Angry it is no difficult thing for you to allott some few spare minutes in the exersise of y^r hand, & not to loose all the pains wch have been bestow'd therein already, I do not recommend this to you as an essentiall part of y^r study, this is enough & too much in so small a matter wch though I cañot but for many reasons recomend unto, yet I mean subordinatly wth greater respect to the other more imposing affaires, y^t stile & Phrase I do not dishke, but do allow to be passable for y^r age & experience, but I wish you to plie y^r self wth care to the Attayning as good a forme of uttering y^r minde as you can it will be of singuler use and ornament & nothing will conduce more to the affecting of such a thing than the proposing to y^r selfe someone person for a Pattern to imitate who is of choise elloquence, & truly you cañot follow a better precedent then y^r worthy Pr^{ll} I wish you would contract y^r sentences into a little shorter forme methinks the short

D 2

sentences (if they expiess the full sence) are ever the most ellegant, but wch this caution, that in laboming to be short you do not fall into obscurity, noi yet foi want of words to faile of expressing the sence the meane is excellent & iaie, wheiunto few haie attayn'd   I will hold you no longei now, present my sei vice to y^r Pii^ll y^r Tutoi & Mr Shei & so I beseech God to blesse you & indue you wth wisdome

            & I shall evei be y^r ver lo fa

Shun drinking houses & drunken companions as poyson, if you do not you aie utteily lost in my opinion for evei, & be carefull to keep w^{th}in tLe compasse of y^r exhibition, foi moie you cañot haie

Between the last letter and the next Dick had evidently ieceived a visit from his father, who was greatly vexed to find that he was not giving himself to his studies as assiduously as he had exhorted him to

Dick

    I do believe you have bestowed y^r time bettei since I parted from you then heietofoie, & I iejoice at it, yett am I not satisfied at full, for I peiceaie by y^r Tutoi that you do not betake y^rselfe chiefly to the same studies wch I specially wish, & wch I know would be most phtable for you, it is true some benefitt you may ieape out of all Authois, but not out of all alike, & the uniiersity is specially appointed, foi the teaching of those hardei & moie difficult Aites wch aie not to be had elswhere, but pleasing and familher knowledges they aie to be had eveiywheie so as if you implore not y^r time while you aie theie in Attayniug the more Accademicall Aites, you will haie no advantage at all ovei those wch nevei went faithei then then owne home I theiefoie (wholy intending y^r own ppei good,) do eainestly desire, that foi my satisfaction you awhile suspend the fiequenting of Human Authois, & seiiously fixe upon Log Phil till you have attayn'd some perfection therin, you will then fiude how infinite easily all other knowlidges will come on, & be a iecieation to you   my meaning is you should bestow y^r time moie on Aiist & men of that ianke, then on Vug Hom or any Histo as yet wch tho they aie excellent, yet aie they not piopei for y^r present time, & if you once fixe upon the sweetnesse of them, you will abandon all the haisher studies wch would be most phtable foi you   but I pray satisfie me heerin a little, & you shall haie time enough to satisfie y^rself abundantly heerafter wth any Authois you please, when you shall well please me in doing whatever you like if you will but satisfiy me foi a few months, tis no gieat mattei that I ciaie, but of infinite consequence, & y^r selfe will find ieason in it quickhe   I am veiy seiious in this point, & shall take it veiy ill if you do it not   I do moieovei know that you haie an infinite advantage by the helpes you may have of Mr Shai & whose collections, confeiences, & expeiiences, may supphe you wth y^t in an instant wch you cañot otheiwise by y^r own laboui in many yeaics attaine, & I know him ieady to do it, but in nothing haie you offended me moie, then in that you haie not made moie use of him in that kinde, I wish you would iefoime this, foi I have w^{tn} giiefe observ'd it, & you know it was as stiict a charge as any wch I gave you   piomise a carefull obseivance of my diiections, I expect to find it in these peiticuleis wch I have now touch'd, I will not longei hould you from y^r studies, think not lightly of what I say but use youi endeavoui while I piay God to blesse you in it, & I will be—y^r ev lo fa

                               B

I wish you would not altogeather leave of y^r friendly comerse wth my co Pri & I should be glad if you did take a little more paines in y^r h̄ you do rather decline in y^r stile then amend, wheras I would have it you amend still besides in those verses wch you sent to y^r sist tho they have som passable young conceipt in them, yet som words are wanting here & there wch makes the sence imperfect & verse false it is only for want of care for if you had advizedly read them you would have found it y^r selfe

You are I pceave in nothing more defective then in this even in the very termes & notions of Lo neither may you think them below you till you have the perfection of them you thinke them Niceties & fetters & suppose it sufficient to have things in grosse, wch will bring you to confusion if you do not speedely reforme that opinion, proceed methodically herein, etc

In the next letter we find Mrs Granville urging Dick to obey his father's directions, and to give him the satisfaction he demanded

MRS GRANVILLE TO HER SON RICHARD

Dick,

It seems by y^r last that you hope to give y^r father better content heerafter then you have for the time past wch will comfort us & proffitt you many waies, & my dayly praiers are and shall be for y^r good proceedings if you serve God as you ought, & follow y^r fathers precepts, you cañot do amisse you may perceave how zealous & carefull he is for you in all perticulers, & therfore it will behoove you to answear it with an observant duty & obedience I am not willing to doubt it, it would so much distract me, but I live in hope you will be a man of y^r word It is impossible you can any way deceave y^r father, though at such a distance, but that you will in short space be discover'd therefore I hope y^r discretion will advise you to walk circumspectly / you need not make it a request to be advertiz'd if I know y^r father at any time displeas'd with you, I shall do it of my owne accord I have not time to say more now, but I beseech God to give you his grace & so I hastily rest

Y^r intirely affectionate mother

GRACE GRENVILE /

Stow Feb—10—1638

I receav'd the books & doe thanke you for them /
To my loving Sonne Richard Grenvile
at Glocester Hall in Oxford these dd /

The following letter is from Bevill to his mother-in-law, Lady Smyth, to acquaint her with her daughter's illness, and to ask her to come to Stowe. The prunelloes which Mrs. Granville fancied were a species of dried plum imported from France The child referred to in the letter was born the 24th of June, and christened by the name of Mary, but she died the following year

BEVILL GRANVILLE TO LADY SMYTH.

Good Madam,

My wife hath many times been my Secretary, I am now hers She hath stay'd the messenger some daies thinking to write her selfe, but some fitts of

sicknesse have, (to my great griefe) hinder'd her   Wherfore she entreats me
to certifie y^r la^p both of it and that you shall not faile of Horses on saturday
Her sicknesse is a greate paine of spleene, wch is accompanied wth greate
vomiting so as scarce any meate will stay wth her & makes her very faint, but
I hope there is no danger of the childe, and I trust she will overcome it also
quickly   We both thought good to acquaint you wth it and do thinke y^r
company would do her much good   My wife saies also that you need not to
remove any thing, if you so please, but may consider therof at leasure   Shee
desires if there be any Prunelloes that you would get her som and send them
by the first messenger, and I will entreate you that one of y^r servants may
bespeake some Lamprey Pyes for me against I send, and so wth the presentm^t
of both our humble dueties to you I rest

Y^r obedient sonne
BEVILL GRENVILE

Stow—May 13—1638

Superscription
To my Honble   good Lady &
Mother the lady Smyth
of Madford present these

Early in the spring of 1638-9, a summons was received by
all who held lands of the Crown to furnish the King with men
at arms and join the royal standard at York   Unwisely
attempting to force upon the Scotch Presbyterians the liturgy
of the English Church, Charles found himself opposed in the
most determined manner, and both sides resolved on war   A
declaration was circulated containing the King's reasons for this
expedition, in which he set forth the insolent treatment he had
received from the Covenanters, and his own readiness to heal
the disorders of the State   Looked upon almost in the light of
a religious war, the English gentry in general showed great
alacrity in joining, and many contributed the greater part of
their fortunes for the King's service

Sir Richard Granville, on hearing of the troubles in Scotland,
and ascertaining that the decrees made by the Court of Star
Chamber were repealed, and the persons grieved absolved from
those penalties, returned from his seven years' exile abroad, to
lay his life and fortune at the King's feet; whom he joined
" at the head of a troop composed of the principal gentlemen of
Cornwall and Devon, every one with an equipage suitable to
his quality," and Bevill Granville likewise raised a troop of
horse and hastened to join the King on his northern march,
taking with him young Dick from Oxford.

It has generally been supposed that the following sweet and
gallant letter, addressed to Sir John Trelawny, the first baronet
of that name —evidently in reply to a communication urging

LADY GRACE GRANVILLE.

WIFE OF SIR BEVILL GRANVILLE.

From an Original Portrait, by Vandyck, in the Wellesbourne Collection.

Bevill not to embark in some perilous enterprise—was written at the opening of the great Civil War in 1642, but some of the expressions lead to the conclusion that it is to this Scotch expedition that it refers For example, "my journey it is fixt." For fully eight months after the Civil War had broken out, the operations of the Royalists in Devon and Cornwall never took Bevill Granville more than fifty miles from Stowe This could scarcely be called a "journey" Again, the expression, "If they be not prevented and mastered near their own homes they will be troublesome guests in y^{rs} and in the remotest places ere long," implies that the homes of the enemy were at some distance rather than at the door of the writer, and so commingled that half the neighbours were friends and half foes, as was the case in the Great Rebellion

BEVILL GRANVILLE TO SIR JOHN TRELAWNY

Mo hon S^r /

I have in many kinds had trial of your noblenes, but in none more then in this singular expression of y^r kinde care & love I give you also & y^r excell Lady humble thanks for y^r respect unto my poor Woman, who hath been long a faithful and much obliged Servant of y^r Ladies but S^r for my journey it is fixt I cañot contain myself wthin my doors when the K^g of En^{ds} Standard waves in the field upon so just occasion, the cause being such as must make all those that dye in it little inferiour to Martyrs And for myne owne p^t I desire to acquire an honest name or an hon^{ble} grave I never loved my life or ease so much as to shunn such an occasion wch if I should I were unworthy of the profession I have held, or to succeede those Ances of mine, who have so many of them in several ages sacrificed their lives for their Country S^r the barborous & implacable Enemy (notwthstanding his Maties gracious proceeding wth them) do continue their insolencies & rebellion in the highest degree & are united in a body of greate strength, so as you must expect if they be not prevented & mastered neer their own homes they will be troublesome guests in y^{rs} & in the remotest pts ere long I am not without the consideration (as you lovingly advize) of my wife and family, & as for her I must acknowledge She hath ever drawne so evenly in her Yoke with me, as She hath never prest before or hung b^k & hindd me, nor ever oppos'd or resisted my will, & yet truly I have not in this or any thing else endevor d to walke in the way of power with her, but of reason, & though her love will submitt to either yet truly my respect will not suffer me to urge her wth power unless I can convince by reason So much for that, whereof I am willing to be accomptable unto so good a friend I have no suite unto you in mine own behalf, but for y^r prayers & good wishes, & that if I live to come home again you would please to continue me in the number of y^r servants I shall give a true relation unto my very nob fr M^r Mo of y^r & his Aunts loving respects to him wch he hath great reason to be thankful for So I beseech God to send you & y^r no family all health and happines, and while I live I am

S^r/ y^r unfay lo & fa Ser

B G

Though history has shewn it to have been a bloodless campaign, an expectation to meet a well-drilled Scotch army of 22,000 men must have made it appear a formidable enterprise, and Bevill, fully realizing the possibility of his falling in the coming war, before his departure made every preparation for the settlement of his worldly affairs, signing his will the 10th April, 1639   The following is a copy —

In the name of God—Amen   The tenth day of Aprill, in the ffifteenth yeare of the raign of our Soveraigne Lord Charles, by the grace of God, King of England, Scotland, ffrance, and Ireland, Defender of the faith, etc

I, Bevill Grenvile of Stowe, in the countie of Cornwall, Esquire, being in good health of body and of sound and perfect mynde and memory, (for which I heartilie thank Almightie God), Doe make and ordaine this my last Will and Testament in writinge

And ffirst I commend my soule into the hands of Almightie God, my Maker and Redcemer, in full assurance that all my sinnes are washed away by the precious blood of Jesus Christ my Saviour, Who is the Lambe of God that taketh away the sinnes of the world, and that at the last day I shall be presented to him without spot, and received into his kingdom of Glorye, there to live evermore.   My body I comend to the earth from whence it came, to be decently interred

And wheras I have by Deed indented bearing date the nynth day of Aprill, in the ffifteenth yeare of the raigne of our Soveraigne Lord, King Charles, conveyed and assured the Burrough and Mannor of Bideford, in the Countye of Devon, with the Rights, members, and app'ten'ces therof, and the right of patronage of the Parishe Churche of Bydeford

And the Burrough and Mannor of Kilkhampton, in the Countie of Cornwall, with the Rights, members, and app'tenn'ces therof, and the right of patronage of the Parishe Churche of Kilkhampton, and the capitall messuage, Bartons, and Demesnes of Stowe and Dinsmouth, wth the app'tenn'ces, in Kilkhampton aforesaide   And the mannor, capitall messuage, Barton, and demesnes of Wolfston, and the Mannors of Wydmouth and Woodford, in the saide countie of Cornwall, wth members and app'tenn'ces therof

And the mannor, capitall messuage, Barton, and Demesnes of Northleigh, in the Parishes of Kilkhampton and Moorwinstowe, with the rights, members, and app'ten'ces therof

And all those messuages, land, tenements, and hereditaments in the Parishes of Kilkhampton, Moorwinstowe, and Stratton, in the saide countie of Cornwall, which I purchased of Nicholas Smyth, Esquire, deceased, and were sometime parcel of the Mannor of Michell Morton, in the said countie of Cornwall

And the advowson or patronage of the Rectory and Parish Church of St Mary Weeke, in Cornwall aforesaid, Unto my loving friends, John Arundell of Trerice, Esquire, John Acland of Colum, Esquire, Arthur Bassett of Heanton Punchardon, Esquire, Antony Denys of Orleigh, Esquire, Richard Prideaux of Thuckborough, Esquire, and William Morrice of Churston, Esquire, to have to them and their heirs and to the use of them and their heirs for ever

Nevertheless, to the intent and purpose, and upon condition that they and the surviv^{rs} and the surviv^r of them and his and their heirs should devise, lease, graunt, convey, assure, or otherwise dispose of the same and such and soe many of them, and such partes and parcells of them or any of them in such manner and for such uses, intents and purposes, as I by my last Will and

Testament in writing should lymitt, appointe, and declaie, as by the same deed whereunto for more certentie therein I referre myselfe

And foreasmuch as Grace my wife hath alwaise been a most loving and virtuous wife unto me, her deserts fair exceedinge any re-quital wch my fortune can afford, I do lymitt, appoint and declaie that my saide wife shall and may during her life quietly have and enjoy such and soe much of the said mannors, messuages, land, tenements, and hereditaments before mentioned as are by any Deede or assurance lymited to her for her jointure, and that my saide ffeoffees John Arundell, John Acland, Arthur Bassett, Antony Denys, Richard Prideaux and William Morrice, Esquires, and the survivors and survivor of them and his and their heires, shall upon request after my death sufficiently assure unto the saide Grace, my beloved wife, all those messuages, mylles, lands, tenements, and hereditam^{ts}, called or known by the name of Stowe saide, and the rever con therof And also all those severall grounds and parcells of land called or known by the severall names of Cleve and Colworthy, all which I have late annexed to my Burton and demesnes to be therewith all used and enjoyed To have to her the said Grace for and during the term of her naturall life in augmentation of her jointure, and as a remembrance of my love to her, and my desire to my saide ffeoffees is that my saide wife may not be troubled or molested in the quiet enjoyment of her saide jointure and lands aforesaide, but may be by them ayded and assisted as much as they may

And I do hereby further declare, lymitte, and appointe, and my will and meaning is that my said ffeoffees, John Arundell, John Acland, etc, etc, and the survivors and survivor of them and their and his heires out of the Rentes issues, and profitts of my saide Mannors, Messuages, lands, tenements, and hereditaments, or by demysemge or leaseing all or any parte or partes thereof in possession, rever'con, remainder, or expectancye, att theire willes and pleasures, and by such some or somes of money as shall be raysed and had by the graunting and selling of the inheritance in Fee simple of any parte or partes therof shall satistye, pay, and dischaige all the just and true debts and somes of money I doe owe or am indebted to any p'son or p'sons for myne owne proper debt And alsoe the annutyes and yearelye somes, legacys guifts, por'cons, some or somes of money given, lymitted, or appointed to any person by this my last Will and Testament

And for the particular accidents wch may happen to my saide Mannors, lands, and premisses in the values thereof, I do therefore lymitt, appointe and declare, and my will and meaninge is that my said fleoffees and the survivors and survivor of them, their, and his heires shall and may from tyme to tyme, and att all tymes demise and lease, or graunt, convey, and sell the inheritance of the saide mannors, messuages, lands, and pr'misses, or such or soe much of them or any of them, and such partes and tenements parcels of them, for such uses, intents, and purposes as are in this my Will and Testament lymited, appointed, or declared, and the performance and execu'con of the trust in them reposed, as they and the survivrs and survivr cf them, then, and his heires shall in their wisdom think fitt and convenient for the same

And I do lymitt and appointe and my will is that during the tyme of payment of my saide debts and Legacies, and untill the same be fully paide and discharged, that my saide fleoffees, and the survivr and survivr of them, then, and his heires shall pay and satisfye unto my son and heir apparent, Richard Grenvile, one annuity or yearlye rent of one hundred pounds yearely, to be issueing and going out of such of the pm'isses as my said ffeoffees and the survivrs and survivr of them their heires shall lymitt and appointe to be yearely payable at the ffeasts of St John Baptist, St Michaell Th' Archangle, The Birth of our Lord God, and the Annunciation of our blessed Lady St Mary the Virgin, by equall por'cons

And I do heiebye give and appointe the saide annuitye unto my saide sonne Richaid, to be received in manner aforesaide

Item I do give, lymitt, and appoint to each of my younger sonnes (viz[t], John Grenvile, Barnaid Grenvile, George Grenvile, and Denys Grenvile), one annuitye or yearely some of twentie pounds yearely apiece, to be paide to each of them at the ffower ffeasts aforesaide, untill each of them respectivelye shall attaine to his severall age of seaventeene yeares, and as each of them shall attaine to his severall age of seaventeene yeares, then the payment of their saide annuitye of Twentie pounds yearely of him so attaining to his age of seaventeene yeares to cease and determine

And I do fuither lymitt, appointe, and declare, and my will is that within some short time after each of my saide younger sonnes shall severally attaine to his saide age of seaventeene yeaies, that one annuitye and yearely rent of ffiftie pounds be giaunted and assured to each of my saide younger sonnes, John, Barnaid, George, and Denys respectively, to be issueing out of some parte of the mannois, messuages, lands, and premises, to bee paide yearely at the ffeasts aforesaid, and to continue to each of them during his natuiall life, iespectively with clauses of distresses, the same to be done in such manner as counsel learned in the lawe shall reasonablye devise, by the appoyntment of my saide ffeoffees and the survivr[rs] oi survivr of them, their, and his heires Then I doe give, lymitt, appoynte, and declare to my eldest daughter, Elizabeth Grenvile, the some of one thousand and five hundred pounds of lawful money of England por'con And to each of my other daughters, viz · Bridget Grenvile, Joane Grenvile, and Mary Grenvile, the some of one thousand pounds of lawfull money of England apiece to be iaised out of the rents, issues, and profits of the said mannors, messuages, lands, and piemisses, oi by demiseing and leaseing, oi by sale of the inheritance of some parte theieof, as my said ffeoffees shall think fitt and convenient, the saide sev'rall poi'cons to be paide unto my saide daughters iespectively as they shall accomplishe their severall ages of twentie yeaies, oi sooner if conveniently the same may be iaised

And untill then saide severall poi'cons shall be fully paide unto them, I doe give, lymitt, and appointe to each of them the some of ffoity marks yearely to be paide to them iespectively tor their　　　　　maintenance and lyvelyhood out of the rents, issues, and profitts of the saide mannors, messuages, lands, tenem[ts], and hereditam[ts] aforesaide

Provided allwaies and I do heieby lymitt, appointe, and declare that if Giace my saide wife and Richaid my sonne, oi such othei of my saide sonnes as shall be my right heire at the tyme, oi one of them shall with[n] one yeaie next after the death of Dame Giace Smyth, widdow, by sufficient assuiance in law, convey etc, all the mannois, messuages, lands, tenem[ts], and hereditam[ts], with the app'tenances, in the saide Countie of Cornwall, wh the saide Dame Smyth now holdeth and enjoyeth, by conveyance and assuiance fiom Sii Geoige Smyth, Kt, deceased, hei late husband, and also the Mansion Howse and lands　　　　　all used and enjoyed, called oi known by the name of Maydwoith, situate and being in the Parish of Heavitiee, in the Countie of Devon, unto my saide ffeoffees, John Aiundell, John Acland, etc, etc, and to the survivrs and survivr of them, then, and his heires, and such othei othei person oi persons as shall be in that behalfe appointed to be sold oi disposed of by them oi any of them foi and towards the paym[t] of my debts and legacies aforesaide, and performance of the tiust and uses in this my last will men'coned, that then the saide ffeoffees shall and may at the same tyme, well and sufficiently as counsell in the lawe shall reasonable advise, convey, and assuie unto my saide sonne, Richard Grenvile, and h s

heires, or unto such other of my sonnes as shall be my heire   If my saide
sonne Richard bee dead and to his heires such and so much of the saide
mannois, messuages, lands, tenem^ts, and hereditam^ts, to them by me issued as
aforesaide, as shall amount to the full and cleere yearely value of the saide
mann^rs, messuages, lands, tenements, and hereditaments of the saide Dame
Smyth as both parties shall

And I doe hereby further   and declare that with^n some
convenient tyme after my saide debts and legacies before men'coned bee
satisfyed and paide as aforesaide, that they, my saide ffeoffees, shall by good
assurances in the lawe att the charge of my heire, convey and assure unto my
saide sonne, Richard Grenvile, or his heires, or unto such of my sonnes as
shall be my heire, all such and soe many of the saide mannois, messauges,
hereditaments, and premises by me conveyed and assured as aforesaide as
shall then remaine unsold and not disposed of, charged nevertheless wth the
sev'all annuities to my saide younger sonnes during the continuance thereof
respectively

And I doe will, give, and appoynte that all my Plate, Linen, and other
utensils of howshold and howshold stuffe, and the furniture of my house at
Stowe aforesaide, be remaine and continue in my saide howse, and come to
my sonne and heire which shall be owner of my saide howse

Nevertheless I doe will and appoynte that Grace, my beloved wife, shall
have the use and occupa'con thereof during her life   And her, the saide
Grace, my wife, I doe herebye make and ordaynee to be   and sole
executrix of this my last Will and Testament   And I doe   my
saide ffeoffees to pay such debts and somes and money for which I have
mortgaged any of my mannois, lands, or prem^s, or any part thereof, and
redeem the saide mortgage, if they shall think it fitt

In witness whereof I, the saide Bavill Grenvile, to this my last Will and
Testament have hereunto sett my hand and seale, given the day and yeare
first above written Anno Dmi

BEVILL GRENVILE

Sealed and published in the presence of Robert Cary, Thomas Priest,
Richard Pomeroy, And Cory, William Maisters, F Cottle, and T Venynge

The royal army assembled at York on the 1st of April,
and from thence Bevill wrote to his much honor'd kinsman,
"William Morice, Esq," giving him ' an account of such
collections as he could gather there," but that letter has
been unfortunately lost   He then moved on with part of
the army to Newcastle, and the following letter to Mr Morice
was in the possession of Hugh Gregor, Esq , and is published
in the *Thurloe State Papers*, 1742 (vol i, pp 2-3) —

BEVILL GRANVILLE TO WILLIAM MORICE ESQ.

My dear and noble friend,

I DO with a sad heart salute you from hence, because I have neer heard
of your sicknes   I hope the heavens have not design'd such a punishment for this age, (otherwise sufficiently visited) as to add your sickness to
the former evills ; and though for my private cause I have enough to complain,
yet the publick interest is such in you, as you must be look'd after with a
general care   But of this theame I have not time to be copious   My dearest

r'

worke is to powei out my orisons for your health, my next is to assure you, that in all foitunes, and howevei God may dispose of me, I will live and dye youi faithful fiend and servant   I have made a collection of the truest newes that is heci stirring among us, and have sent you a copy of it, which tho' it be not veiy note-woithy, yet because it carnes the badge of trueth with it, and may contradict the false iumois that run about the country, I piesent it to you, and foi expedition (in the copie) I am foic'd to use the helpe of anothei hand   God keepe you, youi woithy mother, wife and family, and for my part I goe with joy and comfoit to ventuic a hfe in as good a cause, and with as good company, as evei Englishman did, and I do take God to witnes, if I weie to chuse a death, it should be no other but this But I cannot be laigei at this time   Expect to heaie from me againe after some memoiable action, if I survive it, who am

Newcastle, May 15,   Youi most affectionate kinsman
        1639   and faithful servant,

                                        BEVILL GRENVILE

To my much honoi'd kinsman *William Mo-*
rice Esq at *Cheiston* present these

My laste shooke hands with you at Yoike, and gave you an account of such collections as I could gathei theie, in which couise I shall proceede iathei to correct the various and unceitaine iepoits, which you dayiy meete in the countiey, then to give you any notable newes from hence, where hitheito nothing more than ordinaiy is to be obseived   The nynth daye after my ainival at Yoike, the kinge iemoved with the iegiment of his house hold in two dayes to Duraam, the iest of the troope to Newcastle in Northum-beiland, being twelve myles faithei, and the weeke followinge his majestie removed thithei also, where we aie all yet, the town full with as many as it can hold, the rest billetted in the country about   I cannot yet give you a ceitain list of the aimy, foi besides the iegiments alieady hcre diveis otheis are sent foi, and no doubt but theie will be need of them, foi our army is not yet veiy stionge, not such as will become the majestie of soe great a monaich to maich with into a countiy, where he is suie to meete blowes   It hath byn thought impossible that the Scottes could be so impious as to lift their hands against him, but it is now taken foi granted, that nothinge but force can ieduce them to obedience, for they are guilty of this aggravation to then offences   the Kinge sent a pioclamation lately into Scotland to pardon all offences past, if they would yet submitt, but they have slighted it, and not a man comes in, but iathei aie confirmed in then insolence by his gra-tiousnes, and continually some fall off fiom the kinge to them, as of late some great ones near his Peison   The marques of Hamilton was sent with a good fleete of the King's shippes and some five thousand land souldiers to lye about the coast of Scotland, and being lately desirous to iefresh some of his sicke men on the shore, he was foibidden by them, and had the cannon threatened to him, if he did attempt to land, soe he must endure the sea till we meete   Oui aimy is goveined by two seveial and distinct policys, having diveis geneials without being subject each to othei   My loid of Aiundel is geneialissimo, and comandes the greatei pait of the aimy   But the King's houshold with all his seivants both in ordinaiy and extraordinaiy are of a body apait, and designed foi the guard of the Kinges person, which aie all undei my loid chambeilaines command, who is oui absolute generall without subjection to any but his majesty himself, and we consist of diveis tioopes of hoise, but the most glorious in the woild, whethei we consider the quality of the persons, oi the biavery of armes, appaicll, hoises, and furnituie   Theie is a regiment of foote also appointed for the guard of the King's person, in which Sir Nicholas Slanning hath a company, and is sergeant major of the regiment The marques of Huntley, who was reported at Yorke to be absolutely revolted, is said not to be so nowe, but though he gave way to some things, yet he opposed them in others, and is imprisoned by the covenanters Thus you see we have uncertain reports here as well as you in the country We are not certain of our abode heere in this place, but as soon as thinges can be ready, we shall march to Barwick, where we are threatened with bad entertainment in a very barren countrey, and the last newes is that Lesley is marching with a goodly army to welcome us upon the frontiers as soon as we shall appear there, and that they have three armyes in areadiness consisting of threescore thousand men in all Thus you see I am forced to pick upp petty matters for want of better newes, which, when it happens, you shall have your share of

BEVILL GRENVILE

From Newcastle the 15th
of May 1639

Mrs. Granville's anxiety for the safety of her husband and son must have been greatly increased by hearing that they had both fallen sick after their arrival in the North, Dick's illness being "foolishly gotten" To add to her anxiety, the following letter discloses sad money worries and the threat of a writ Perhaps the Mrs Herewyn, at whose instance the Writ had been issued is the "woman" who had been "so foolish and unreasonable" in her demands, and who is referred to in a former letter of Bevill's, see page 195

MRS GRANVILLE TO HER HUSBAND

O my Dearest

I have receavd yrs dated the -15- of May from Newcastle, bringing me the glad tidings of yr recovery before I heard of yr sicknes, wch I praise GOD for & shall long to heare the same of Dick, whose sicknes being so foolishly gotten, I feare may prove dangerous, & must confesse till I heare againe shall remayne in much doubt I am both sorry & ashamed he should err so much to his own prejudice, having had so many warnings, but I shall & doe beseech GOD to restore him & blesse him wth judgment & grace to serve GOD truly & obey your precepts I must beseech you though at this distance, that you will pardon ordinary errors in him, hoping that by degrees they will be reform'd though not so instantly as our desires are I am glad to find you have receavd one Packett from me & I hope before this can come to you that -3- severall Packetts more have found you out, the one bearing date the -9- of May & another the -15- of sent by the Post, & another since of the -18- of May by Mr Pollarde, in both wch I acquainted you as occasion then requir'd I thanke you for accepting my care, wch shall not be wanting to the uttmost of my poore abillity & however the successe be of my cares, sure I am my intentions are right Since I wrote last, Mr Prickman was heer, who shewd me a writt & tolde me it was to be delivverd the Sherriff to extend both yr lands & goods for Mrs Here-wyns money, wch he saies is -500l- that is behinde, of the statute, I entreated him to consider how impossible any thing was to be done, to give them satisfaction now in yr absence, desiring they would forbeare any extremity of lawe, and I well knew you would performe justly on y^r side, wherupon he promisd me, that there should be nothing done in it, for the present, or by him att all in y^r absence, and that he would use his best endevour to pacifie Mrs Herwyn & her Agents, though he pretends they are already jealous of him on y^r behalfe & that now his forbearance would make them much to differ in a verie unkinde way, he saies he cañott undertake for Mrs Herw , though he will doe his best, and he knows it will be but for some short space that she will forbeare and then may imploy some stranger tht will beare no respect unto you	he heares, that you have putt away some part of Straton Man^or & he wishes & beleeves she would willngly take land on indifferent terms but withall he sayes he beleeves you are willing to heepe ye Statute a foote, for other reasons, but certain he is som thing must be done, for twill not be longe forborne	he wishes the Statute might be layd on Killgarth and that some fiend of y^rs paying Mrs Herwyn her money might have the Statute assigned him & beleeves you by such a way may redeeme Killgarth for the same price you sold it	he hath written to this effect and desires to know y^r minde at full	& he also tells me of Millards Debt which is likewise in his hand against you—600^ℓ at least he saies it is	for Christ sake duely consider what is to be done & both write to him about these severall perticulers and also direct me what is to be dcne if 1 should be vext with these lawe extremities	God knowes they are busineses as farr beyond my capacity, as power to compose, & though now to my infinite sorrow & misfortune, we ar so farre devided yet consider my condition with pitty I beseech you, for I labour under an insupportable Burthen of cares and feares, were not Gods mercies great unto me in the middst of my affliction, for the cares though they are many I value not but the hazardous way you are in is my dayly tormentor	I will when I speak with Mt Mylton consider with him, how y^r money may be safely returnd but as yet, I have not receavd it & I shall also desire a more full direction from you, concerning it.	Capt Hills Arreares shall be allowed & I will strichtly charge Jo Gealard to be carefull in the dates of the acquittances	I am willing to give you a full accompt of all things I can remember	y^r corne prospers well & y^r young trees.& y^r stable affaires proceed according to y^r order	y^r Coults thrive very well also	since y^r going M Welsh hath buryed his only sonne & now hath only one daughter between - 12 - or - 14 yeare olde & I am tolde, that they wish a match between you & them if you should incline thereto	though at such a time it may be unseasonable, yet I cañott but acquaint you with what I heare that if I should heare any more of it I might the better know what to say or thinke of it	the Parents conditions doth not take much with me, but the Estate is good	pray let me know y^i inclination hoerin, if Dick be well but many times I am in doubt that his sicknes was more than y^r life expressed, & that you might by degrees prepare me for worse news	God grant my feares be vaine & deare Mr Grenvile pardon my infirmity in doubting the worst if there be no cause	My mother is now returnd and I praise God we are in the state of health though very unhappie in y^r absence	Besse besought me to present her humble duty to you when I wrote	She is now at Orley with y^r sister all the rest according to their knowledge both often enquire for you & finde you wanting	Byddie complaines you have stayd very long already, & Jone & Deñis are allwaies prattling of you these are my poore companions wch doe passe the tedious howers away	I sent y^r lrs and papers of news to y^r frends as you directed & I have sent you now a lre from my cosen Morice—Mr. Prust desires to know whither you please the Leases should be sent you to be seald that he hath agreed for & then about 200^li will be ready at y^r appointm^t	he thinkes the Leases may have safe conveyance by the Poste I had allmost forgott to tell you that I paid M͏ͬ Prickman 20ˡⁱ due to him from you as appeares by a Bill under yͬ hand, wᶜʰ I have taken up though I was so much out of money, then as I was faine to borrow it yet I would not refuse to doe it doubting a greater shrewd turne if he were putt off but he makes as large protestations now as ever of his greate respects and service to you and I hope it doth not displease you that I payd him I will trouble you now no longer but doe continually pray for you and will ever remayne

Yͬˢ faithfully

Stow—May—30   GRACE GRENVILE
      1639

My mother bidds me give
you her hearty remembrance
who praies for yͬ safety

Superscription
To my best Frend M͏ͬ Bevill
Grenvile these   dd

It was not till the 28th May that the English army arrived at Berwick-on-Tweed. Here the King found the Scotch army so formidable that his threats at once broke down   He was conscious too of his own weakness, for although he had a somewhat stronger force than Leslie, his men had no will to fight, and he was forced to evade a battle by consenting to the gathering of a free Assembly and of a Scotch Parliament. During the time the negotiations which followed were pending, Bevill Granville received the honour of Knighthood from the hand of the King on the 20th June. The circumstances attending it are conveyed in the following letter (the beginning of which is unfortunately much torn) to his wife, who must have been first made aware of the honour conferred upon her husband by the novel address which greeted her eyes on receiving the missive —

To my best Friend *the Lady Grace Grenvile,*
  at Stow these dd /

  . .   .   .
of seeing Lincolnshire & Cambridgͬᵉ as I returne when I have not been I came upwards through the middle of Eng̃ I have this morning sent Dick away to Ox in the conduct of my bro & some servants   The King hath been gratious to me both in words & Actions, yet one thing I wish had been forborne, but it cañot now be holpᵈ   I see it was a plot between my lo Genˡˡᵉ & my lo Chañ before I thought on't   As I was on Saturday last in the Privie Chamber among diverse others, upon a sodaine my lo Generall (being wᵗʰin in a inner roome wᵗʰ the Kᵍ) came to the doore and call'd for me by name.   I went to him & he took me by the hand before all that were present, and ledd me in wher the Kᵍ was, and he, after gratious

words, upon a sodaine drew my lo Gen^{lls} sword and gave me a dubbing   I value all his favors very pretiously, otherwise I should have wished this forborne, but it cañot now be holp'd   My lo Chamb· hath made me promise to spend a week or two wth him at his residence of Wilton as I returne, so I reste
.					Y^{rs} in all faithfulness
						B^y GRENVILE

Berwick June 25th 1639

Those the K^g hath honored wth this favour in this journey are S^r Jo Hele & S^r Ja Thin, the eldest son of Sr Thomas, besides my selfe

The following letter from Sir Richard Granville to George Monk's eldest brother also contains the news. It was written the following day from Durham, as he was on his way south with young Dick —

SIR RICHARD GRANVILLE TO MR MONK

Deare Cosen

I can send no newes to you but y^t o^r Army is cassier'd & a peace concluded betwixt o^r King & ye Scots, during wch imploym^t y^r broth^r George was Sergeant maior unto my lord of Newports Regem^t   At ye dissolution of o^r Army ye King made but 3 Knights, viz Sr Bevill Grenvile Sr John Heale & St James Thin   S^r whereas you received 30^{lb} of my brother (by my appointm^t) to y^r broth^r George his use, y^r broth^r George hath imformed me y^t he stands now disingag^d of y^r debt & y^t you should repay unto me ye said 30^{lb} when ever I would so require it   wherefore I now pray you to cause so much money to be paid to me at London with all convenient speede & to direct me by y^r letter of whom I shall receive it   Let yor letter be directed to me at London, inclosed in a paper directed un'o Mr Mich Oldsworth (Secretary to ye Earle of Pembrooke) at White Halle & so in hast I conclude my selfe
					Y^r faithfull kinsman & servant
						RY. GRENVILE

Durham June 26
1639/
			(Superscription)
				To my Deare Cosen
					Mr Thomas Moncke
						present these
					with speede At Puderidge
						in Devon

After fulfilling his promise to stay with the Lord Chamberlain at Wilton House, Sir Bevill returned home, and the two following letters to his "most honor'd Cosen Edmund Tremayne Esqr at Collacombe" show him once more taking an interest in his stables .—

SIR BEVILL GRANVILLE TO MR EDWARD TREMAYNE

My noble Cosen

I was lately made very joyfull to hear of my cosen Edgcombes well affecting his busines I should be glad to know the particulars & whether I did him any service   Sure I am I wish'd him well however it spead

I hear you are willing to accept my Barbary horse which I am very glad of, and you shall doe me a kindnesse in it, for he is not for the saddle, butt as handsome & good for a Stalhon as can be   But I have no inclosed ground to turn him loose in & it is to no purpose to keep him in the stable being lame And I have already bred upon him 3 years, which is as much as I desire of any horse.   Yet I think he is as good for that purpose as ever, & he is as yett but younge.   When you please to send for him he is at y^r service and soe am I S^r to my last gaspe

BEVILL GRENVILE.

Stowe Oct 2 1639.

My dearest Cosen
    I am so joyn'd to you in all my Affections as I cañot be disjoin'd from any of y^r joyes & griefs, & therefore I must have a greate sense of this unjust trouble that is put upon you & I sorrow much for that gentleman who by endangeringe you will more dishonour himselfe then he can doe by any other thing in the world I wish I knew how to doe you service in it wch I would do if I could
    S^r I hope you shall not repent the having of this horse, for I know none in England better for y^r purpose, & I will be beholden unto you for to have 2 or 3 mares run with him for a month next spring   And now I must tell you it do the much displeasure me that you would not lett my man pay for the fish he had   I would not have had sent for them but with the intente to pay, wherof since I am prevented I will send no more   I present my best service to you my noble cosen y^r wife & my godson, so doth my wife & I am ever S^r

Y^r faithfull kinsman & servant
BEVILL GRENVILE.

Nov 1 1639

After taking part in the expedition to Scotland, Dick appears to 'have returned to Oxford with numerous ' excellent directions " from his father as to his behaviour, as the following letters show .—

SIR BEVILL GRANVILLE TO HIS SON RICHARD.

Dick
    You perswade me that you have constantly bestow'd the forenoone since we parted in Logick & Philosophy , I am glad of it if it be so, & would not wish more, for so many howers of a day spent therein, would very sufficiently effect what I desire   but take heed doe not abuse me, whereof I doubt , for if you say true, neither could you be so defective therein, nor y^r Tutor have cause to complaine   I am very serious in this desire of mine, because I know how much y^r wellfare depends on it, wherfore pray deceave me not in it I doe no way dislike those other Authors you name (whither Poetts or Historians), but admire them, the one sort for their witt & learned Allegories, the other [*for their*] Elloquence & glorious examples of Courage, magn[*animity &*] all other virtues wch may stirr up an ingenious & active (*spirit*)tt to imitation   but these are so facile & pleasing studies, as [if] you fasten once upon them you will never touch with the other more, & so loose the staff wch would best support you heerafter   but if you will use those humane Authors only for a recreation & refreshm^t till you have attayn'd perfection in the others, you are then in the right, & shall please me & proffitt y^r selfe infinitly

I will say no more of it having said enough heertofore, & me thinkes y^r owne discretion should suggest no lesse unto you then I have often inculcated. I am my selfe in this very point a wofull example , I pray God you be not such too   I was left to my owne little discretion when I was a youth in Oxford, & so fell upon the sweete delights of reading Poetry & History, in such sort as I troubled no other bookes, & doe finde my selfe so infinitly defective by it, when I come to manage any occasions of waight, as I would give a limbe it were otherwise   This is enough heerof, & you have had enough of me also in other points   I beseech God to open y^r Eyes & guide y^r heart aright, then shall you with comfort enjoy what I with care & paines have preserv'd for you, when it was upon the brinke of a Gulph to have been overwhelm'd everlastingly , wherin my toile hath not been small   There rests farther of y^r part nothing to be more seriously thought of then thrift   You are to succeed so many wastfull predecessors, as if y^r discretion guide you not to hould a little, we are gone in an instant, & you will see in your daies the woefull end of a family, wch hath (without dishonor) endur'd the heats & coulds of many 100 years   I am contented to try you, & therfore have given way y^t Mr Principall should entrust the managem^t of some part of y^r Exhibition in y^r owne hands   I have also now, for an encouragm^t while you doe well, sent you a supply larger then is due or you can expect, & you shall not want what I can helpe you, if you make good use of y^r time   But above all things be sure to keepe out of debt, nor will I ever trust you more, if you run into it   You may believe this, for it is resolutely vow'd by

Y^r very , .   father

B[EVILL GR]ENVILE

Stow Jan 12
   1639
    [40]

Dick
    Those Historicall & Poeticall Authors wch you name, will doe you much more good, if you use them in their Originall languages rather than in the Translations which though it be a felicity I could never arrive at, yett I conceave the benefitt of it   I doe not precisely limitt you in the point of time for the writing to Dick Prideaux, but only that I would have you doe it sometimes, & be carefull to doe it well when you doe write   Y^r stile is much fal'ne in y^r hs to me, whereas I did hope it would have rather better'd still   I wish you to take a little more paines in y^r hs , they are things gracefull, & will gaine a man good opinion among wise men, if well done.   I have seen some of y^{rs} that have been tolerable, but not of late, wch shews y^r care is lesse   Tell Mr Sharshell I have not now time to write to him, but comend me to him, & doe you make use of his frendly helpes, if you respect me.
(Superscription)
To my loving Sonne Richard
Grenvile   these dd

His mother writes by the same messenger to urge him to follow his father's commands strictly and to " expresse how evenly her desires walke hand in hande with his father's for his good proceedings."

LADY GRACE GRANVILLE TO HER SON RICHARD

Dick

Since I last wrote I have receav'd 2 from you in both wch you professe good resolutions to follow strricktly y^r fathers com̄ands, and my hopes and prayers are for y^r good performance then wch nothing will more profitt you or please me You have now began a new yeare, wch I wish with many yeares more may prove prosperous to you in all things, and though as long as you have such excellent directions from y^r father I need sett down no rules to you, yet my affectionate care will not lett me rest but tht I must expresse how evenly my desires walke hand in hand with your fathers for y^r good proceedings He moreover sayes that he is not well pleas'd you doe so long neglect my cosen Prideaux he hath severall times adviz'd you to it, and y^r selfe promis'd it this last returne, but you forgett y^r promises to him He saies allso tht he hath written to you concerning y^r cosens in Ex Col but you never returnd him one word in Answer He would have you more punctuall in answearing each perticular of his lre. You need not make it a serious request to me to give you notice of such things as I finde y^r father dislikes for I shall doe that of my owne accord and doe wish you to make the right use of it so shall you well please me who will never cease to pray you may be allwaies Gods servant and then I can never be other than y^r

Y^r most affectionate Mother
GRACE GRENVILE

I thank you for y^r token
Stow Jan—12—1639
(Superscription)
To my belov'd sonne Richard
Grenvile these dd

But in spite of all the excellent directions and commands of his parents, Dick appears to have again fallen under Sir Bevill's severe displeasure, and the mother had evidently had to intercede for the wayward son. The following is Sir Bevill's answer to her pleadings

SIR BEVILL GRANVILLE TO HIS WIFE

Deare love

In y^r last hs you do farther use that power wch I will not resist You will not have me take exceptions to y^r son for smale matters, but as I have forgiven what is past, so I should not be over sensible for the time to come You shall prevaile in all, I will use few words to him in any kinde, I pray god to guide & blesse him. He shall stand or fall by his owne judgm^t for mine is dispis'd by him The way I propos'd, was a path would assuredly leade to wealth and honor but he likes it not, and calls my advice the severest rigour I tooke it not to be so when I gave it, but I thought seeing I was prevented of leaving him a great estate, I should have done as well in putting him into a way to have gain'd one If he otherwise conceave I cannot helpe it, I shall be sorry to see him live in want, but I hope some of his brothers will finde the way to raise their fortunes by this course wch he dispises So I leave all to God, resolving to trouble my selfe as little as I can heerafter Pray lett him spend his time as well as he may while he is in the Countrey, & assoon as I can I will call him thence The directions he hath from me for the countrey will do him no hurt to follow them, what course soever he take

1 -

Young Mr Chichester doth somtimes aske kindly for him, & wish for his
company   pray bid Dick to write a handsom complement to him, taking
notice from me that I have lett him know, how kindly that gent remembred
him, & therfore he could do no lesse then present his humble service to him
by his pen , wth what other expressions his witt can fall upon   You say the
hopyard will not hould all the trees   I know you are misinform'd, for there is
ground enough for many more trees, if they sett them where I us'd to till
beanes as I would have them to do, & pray lett all be remov'd if possible this
yeare, that we may the sooner have good of them   I am willing some of y^r
syder should be kept for me, especially that wch had baggs putt into it, & if
you have vsd any of it I desire to know how it proves   You have sent me a
good note of ye mares , I pray god so many of them hould, & let none of them
be us'd or putt to labor heeraftei, for I would not have them miscarry for a
world , lett great care be had heerof   Lett the gates wth gapps of y^e
Orchards be made so strong as nothing breake in to hurt the trees   I am
sorry I heare no good news of my Barb . mares but lett them be well usd,
notw^thstanding   I sent some direction to you concerning my Span Ducks,
wherof I have heard nothing   Let not the Tenants of Madf feare to use
their ground , I will warrant them from harme   I have conferr'd wth Taylor
about it & I presume he will not so injure me againe   Present my duety to
y^r mother , I pray for her health & would gladly heare of it   I am laboring
what I can in her busines, & do hope to give her some accompt of it ere long
So I end, resting ever

Y^rs faithfully
BEVILL GRENVILE.

Lond Feb 16 1640.
[Addressed]

To my best Frend the Lady Grace Grenvile
at Stowe   present these

I desire M Newman of Exeter to convey this safely

It is impossible to read the following lines of passionate
pleading for pardon from Dick himself without feeling their
sincerity, and trusting that the short remainder of his young
life merited his fathers approval —

RICHARD GRANVILLE TO HIS FATHER

I was doubtfull w^t to say y^t I blotted a quire of paper to write one lfe
and so crossed it y^t it look'd like an old mercers Booke and yet I am so far
from knowing w^t to write as I was in ye beginning.   w^t can I possibly say
S^r to regain y^r lost favour wch you are possest y^t it is an indifferent thing to
me whither I enjoy it or not & y^t all my unhappy errors proceeded fro^m a
heart to disoblige you   unless you pleasd S^r to change that opinion I cannot
hope to give you ye least contentment in the world   could you see my heart
you would find there ingraved in a plain character all filiall duty   I shall
therfore beg a General Pardon for all my offences, my good intentions wch are
best known to my selfe embolden me thus once more to aske forgivenesse
pray pardon the phrensy of him who is distracted y^t he cannot appear to be.

To my honoured   Y^r most obedient and most humbly
Father Sr Bevill Grenvile   affectionate Sone
        K^nt   R^d Grenvile.

CHAPTER XII.

FOR eleven years England had been without a Parliament, but, all resources being exhausted, and a treasonable correspondence between the Scots and the French Court having been discovered, which could not be overlooked, no way appeared open to the King except to summon another   Sir Bevill was returned for Launceston, his colleague in his old constituency being Ambrose Manaton, who had been a co-protestor with him against the forced loan of 1627, and who was now to prove himself with Granville a staunch Royalist in the King's hour of need   The new Parliament met on the 13th of April, 1640, but the King failed to obtain from it the subsidy he had hoped for. " Statesmen like Hampden and Pym, were not fools enough to aid the great enemy of English freedom, against men who had risen for freedom across the Tweed.   Every member of the Commons knew that Scotland was fighting the battle of English liberty.   All hope of bringing them to any attack upon the Scots proved fruitless   The intercepted letters to the French Court were quickly set aside, and the Commons declared, as of old, that redress of grievances must precede any grant of supplies.   No subsidy could be granted till security was had for religion, for property, and for the liberties of Parliament   An offer to relinquish ship-money proved fruitless   and after three weeks' sitting the ' Short Parliament' was dissolved " (Green's *History of the English People*)

The Scots, thus encouraged, again took up arms, and marched a body of 23,000 foot and 3,000 horse across the Tweed   and, meeting but little opposition, soon overran Northumberland, Durham and a large portion of Yorkshire.   In spite of not being able to obtain the necessary supplies from Parliament, the King, at the instigation of Strafford, undertook a second expedition against the Scots, and issued his Proclamation on the 20th of August   It is probably to this Proclamation that reference is made in the following letter :—

SIR EDWARD SEYMOUR TO SIR BEVILL GRANVILLE

My deare Honor'd Brother
   The Comfort I lost when I left you, cannot be repayrd, but by you   I am now extremely sensible of my vnworthines in leauing Stow, for Stratton

I would redeeme that erro' with any ransom   It hath sate athwart me ever
since, and I beleeue I shall disgest all the meat I shall eate this tweluemonth,
before that   Dear Brother forgiue and thinke on any occassion to summon me
thither to serue you   It not I come very shortly, ffor I cannot long liue
with out yor society, in wch ther is soe much cheerfullness as it sweetens all
misfortunes, and makes them none wher you ar.   I make no question but you
haue heard of the Proclamation wch hath struck wth such amazement all our
Gentlemen heere in Wilts, w^{·h} hold in Capite   What effect it workes in other
Countryes I know not   My L^d of Harnatt receaud a lett^r from his Matie very
lately to repayre to him with all the forces of the Coūty of Wilts, as well
Traine as other able men   What euent this generall distraction will produce
is yet vncertaine   I only know this, noething in the world shall alter this
resolution that I am

Dear brother & euer will be
Yo^r vowed ffriend faythfully to
serue you

Ew. SEYMOUR.

Bradly 2^d of
September

My wife & selfe tender our most
deuoted respects & seruise to my
Lady & yor noble sweet ffamily
(Superscription)
ffor my most Honord Deare
ffriend Sr Beuill Greenveile
at his Stowe
psent these in
Cornewall.

In answer to this Proclamation a number of the Lords began
to rally round the King, who raised from the most devoted of
his adherents a slender pecuniary supply, and again set out at
the head of 20,000 men to meet the invaders · but after being
obliged to make humiliating terms with his rebellious subjects,
Charles only returned to London in time for the meeting of
Parliament on November 3rd.

In this second expedition Sir Bevill was unable to take any
share, in consequence of the pecuniary straits in which he found
himself at this time.   His own " wasteful predecessors," as he
calls them, the expenses he had incurred in raising and
equipping a troop for the first Scotch campaign, as well as the
needs of his own large family, had all contributed to this
embarrassment, and just before the election for the " Short
Parliament," he was anxious to mortgage some of his wife's
property, and the only embittered feeling to be found in all the
correspondence that is extant between husband and wife, reveals
itself over this matter.

SIR BEVILL GRANVILLE TO HIS WIFE

Dearest

My many contentmᵗˢ in yᵉ company makes me somtime forget my most necessary business, as now for instance   you know what I am going about & how it concerns me, I know not what kinde of security he will pitch upon   I will tender him what he please of mine owne estate or jⁱⁿ, but if he accept jⁱˢ then he cañot be well satisfyed wᵗʰ out view of yᵉ Deed, wᶜʰ whither yᵉ mother will venture out of her hand or no, I know not   I leave it to yᵉ wisdom to consider what is fitt to be done in this case   if the Deed be sent me I will bring him safe again, and he shall never be out of my hand   I leave it also to yᵉ selfe, whither you will acquaint yᵉ moᵉ wᵗʰ the reason ci no, but if you send the deed be sure to pack him safe wᵗʰ wooll & paper & seale the boxe, & take care to prevent the wett   he must be wᵗʰ me heer too morrow night if at all

I am ever—yᵉ owne   B G

Hayne—Mai—15—1639

I have no news of the footman, if he be come home he may be fitted to be trusted wᵗʰ the deed—

You are heartely remebred heer

To my best friend the Lady
Grace Grenvile at Stow

dd /

Dear Grace/

I have wᵗʰ sadnesse rec   yᵉ two last lrs because wᵗʰ so much passion & sharpness you do fall upon me, while I conceave I did not deserve it   tis true I expiest in my former hē grief that you should distiust me, & that you should think I would so endanger you as to leave a necessity upon you that should force you to sell yᵉ land   truly love I have no such designe, I have had some confeiences wᵗʰ you to contrive what may be best for our estate, & som resolutions we have fallen upon, wᶜʰ seeing you dislike I will never piesse more   you need not exeisize yᵉ pen so much to satisfie me, I am no way displeas'd, nor can be wᵗʰ you   I have nothing in the world pleasing delightfull or contenting to me but yᵉ selfe, in you my love did begin & must end whei with I end, leaving the rest to our conference & iesting

entirely yᵉˢ
B G

Bodmin - Mar - 25 1640

I will stay the Election heie, so it may be late eie I come home.

To my best fiiend The lady Grace Grenvile
dd /

Indeed in most of his letters at this period there is an allusion to money worries

SIR BEVILL GRANVILLE TO MR. ACLAND

Dearest Sᵉ/

I still finde the continuance of yᵉ singulai favoui & affection, I have not a greatei ambition than to make my self worthy of it   but we must lay aside all un necessaiy piotestations for a while, wᶜʰ tho true, yet must give place to more necessary business. I find an unconscionable conspiiacy among all

moneyd men to ruine those that must make use of them   they know my
necessity, & the danger my best Ma^r stands in, & therfore by a generall
consent & agrem^t among themselves will not offer by - 2000^{ls} as much as the
land wch I tender to sell is worth   I would therfore take a little more time if
I might, wch may well be done if Mª Crew will spare y^t money.   Pray know
what security will content him, for he shall have satisfaction   I will engage
By   or what he will wth will be disengaged by the helpe of his money   M^r L
hath been wth me to treat for St   but sticks just on the rate of other men
Yet hath promis'd to send speedely to his bro   Cr   & father in lawe to farther
the other busines   I will be bound to give 2000^{ls} more for Stratton 7 - year
hence then I will now take for it   I doubt not but by some meanes that
I may use I shall be enabled to it—I will say no more   I beseech
you continue y^r noble goodnes & helpe to me in this my dangerous distresse, I
must else loose one of the finest man^{rs} that this pt of the kingdom hath, &
as I shall be more oblig'd to you then to all the world, so I vow I am a divell
or worse, if I am not ppetually—

y^r absolute & intire serv^t

Pos Sc   /

I am tould casually by som y^t seeme to know that M^r C ^{s} money is all in
his fa   in laws hands, & not in his power to dispose that ther is much doubt
he may faile me, I beseech you consider what a rock I may be cast against

SIR BEVILL GRANVILLE TO MR ROE

Worthy co   matters do fall out somthing unfortunately, I am to receave
a good sum of money on the 28th of novemb^r but yor day of pay^t is on the
2^d—I shall therefore earnestly desire to know whither you may be pleased to
do me much favour as to stay for y^{rs} untill my receipt, if you can it will be
an exceeding great courtesy unto me, but if you canot I shall desire to understand wth some speed, for I will make any shift rather than disappoint or
displease you   I made accompt some other moneys would have come in unto
me before that time, but I am sure of none before the 28th—therefore I shall
earnestly beseech such a small favor of you if it may be wch if you can do I
desire you would take bond for y^r money before the day, & give me y^r acquittance.   I desire but a months forbearance, & will willingly allow interest for it
S^t I am many waies bound unto you & will ever rest/

y^r thankfull kinsman & servant
B G ·

The following letter to Sir Ralph Sydenham also concerns a
loan of money, but it is unfortunately much torn and dilapidated.
Sir Ralph was chief agent to the Earl of Bath at Tawstock
He lived at his Manor House of Youlston, and afterwards, when
the Civil War broke out, raised a troop of 500 horse   " In the
north of Devon there is not any which stands for the Earle
of Bath but Sir Bevill Grenevile and Sir Ralph Sidenham "
(King's Pamphlets, otherwise Thomason collections, British
Museum, vol iii)   Lord Ar and Surr, referred to in the letter,
was Thomas, Earl of Arundel and Surrey, afterwards created Earl
of Norfolk, 6 June. 1644   He married Lady Alathea Talbot,

daughter, and eventually sole heir, ot Gilbert, 7th Earl ot Shrewsbury, by whom he had three sons, the eldest of whom Lord Ma(ltravers) is also referred to in this letter. Sir James Ba is Sir James Bagg

SIR BEVILL GRANVILLE TO SIR RALPH SYDENHAM

Sʳ

I hv'd in hope to have seen you and yʳ noble lady in this poore place ere now I had made bould to have wayted on you in person wᵗʰ my pen long ere this but I see it is impossible for . . happiness though I have been . . . of it by yʳ Chaplain & now that tempests have so sodainely drawn winter . altogether in despaire of it However I cañot be more yʳ servant then I am, nor will I be lesse then the poore powers I have can stretch unto, & so I hope you (and yʳ owne native noblenesse) will conceave me better then I can expresse, or else you shall not do me right

And now Sʳ I shall trouble you wᵗʰ a word or two about our old business concerning the money wᶜʰ you may expect from me at this time. I have been delay'd by my lo of Ar for that great sum wᶜʰ is between us, ever since his departure & cañot be satisfied till his returne. But I was lately so staggered by a leᵗᵗ which Sʳ lames Ba brought me signed wᵗᵒ his name of Ar & Surr. & of my lo Ma his son, & dated in the end of July, that I verily beleved he had been returned, for the leᵗ did imply no lesse & declared that in the begiñing of Mich terme all things should be ended between us Whereupon I was confident that he was return'd, but finding it contradicted by everyone I was some thing troubled at it & sent to Sʳ James Ba to understand this Riddle to me, who returned me word that . his lady was not yet returned but the leᵗ from him . . . you see upon 't . . & have expected . . . . . . to use other means in confidence of know not how therfore to pay in . than you should suffer I will sell anything in the world & what interest is due so lett me know , it shall be speedely sent But if it may be forborne till that business be dispatched . . . . great courtesy equall wᵗʰ any of those noble ones I stand formerly obliged unto you . you too much I conclude resting

                            . . . .
                     & faithfull . .

I beseech you lett my humble service & my wifes be presented to yʳ no la I have sent you my lo of Ar h with Sir James also, as they came to me, for yʳ better satisfaction, but I understand by another h given from Sʳ Ja that it was my ladies' subscribing & that she & her son will performe the business whither my lo returne or no I shall entreate you to returne me those two lrs again seal'd up, when you have perus d them.

SIR BEVILL GRANVILLE TO THE RIGHT HONᵇˡᵉ LORD ROBARTES

My very good Lord

I am contrary to my purpose prevented of wayting on yʳ Loᵖ in person, by reason of some unexpected occasions, in this short time of my abode in the

countrey   I am very sensible of y^r Lo^{ᴘˢ} good disposition in Generall, and of
y^r favour to my selfe in particular, and as I cañott but admire the one, so will
I study to be gratefull for the other   I know not what the Sum is that y^r Lo^ᴘ
may expect from me, but I have sent by my servant enough I hope to satisfie
it casting my selfe at y^r Lo^{ᴘˢ} feete to be order'd as you please and resolving
that y^r favours shall not be sowen in barren ground   I would heer end unlesse
it be necessary to add a word, conceining the late action I was engag'd in   It
was my griefe to appeare in any kinde y^r opposite, my heart is inclin'd to
observe and obay you in any thing, but I was indispensably engag'd to my
deare fiend and near Kinsman, before I knew any purpose of y^r Lo^{ᴘˢ}, and I
know you will allowe the preserving of faith inviolate, but I hope I bare my
selfe with modest civility, as I shall strive to do in all things and likewise to
manifest my selfe to be ever

(My Lord)
y^r gratefull & most humble
servant
BEVILL GRENVILE

Stow—March 31
    1640
    (Superscription)
To the Right Honb^{le} my very
good Lord the Lo   Roberts
    Humbly present these

In the Long Parliament, which assembled on the 3rd of
November, Sir Bevill was elected Knight of the Shire, leaving
his place at Launceston to be filled, though for a very short
space, by his old fellow-patriot and now fellow-Royalist,
William Coryton, who was Mayor of Bossiney, a village close
to Tintagel or Trevena, as it is called in the following letter.
These two villages, Bossiney and Tintagel, each returned a
member of Parliament up to the time of the Reform Bill, the
Wortleys, belonging to Lord Wharncliffe's family, having
Bossiney as their pocket-borough   Acting as mayor of Bossiney,
Coryton had unduly interfered with the return of members,
and the Long Parliament had not been in session many days
betore the vengeance of those who had not forgotten or forgiven
his defection from Eliot, began to be visited upon him.   The
matter came before the Committee of Privileges the Commons
instructing that inquiry should be made, not only into the
election at Bossiney, but also into " the undue proceedings of
the said Mr. Coryton as Vice-Warden of the Stannaries, contrary
to the Petition of Right "   In the next month it was ordered
" that the Committee for Mr Coryton's Business shall consider
also the Misdemeanous committed by Mr Coryton as Steward
of the Duchy and Deputy-Lieutenant of the County " and,
after a long inquiry, it was resolved on August 18, 1641, ' that
Mr Coryton shall not be admitted to sit as a Member in this
Parliament," and a new writ was issued " for electing of

another Burgess to serve for the Town of Dunnevett instead of
Mr Coryton "

The following letters have reference to this election —

SIR BEVILL GRANVILLE TO MR CORYTON

S^r

When I last sawe you I thought not of this business, since wch time I am
become by purchase a freehoulder wthin that burgh of Treveña I therfore
have some reason not to suffer it to be abus'd by any undue course Moreover
most of the inhabitants & other gentle neighbors which have free hould there
do complain of the wrong & desired my assistance to redress it, wch I will
endevor to do You know as well as I what the opinion of the Law hath ever
been in the point of E'ection You will find that all wch pay scott & lott &
which are suitors to the towne court have voice in all elections So I have
known it adjudged many times & I will try it heer I oppose not my lo , I
oppose a wrongful course and unjust oppression (wch hath been long us'd there)
for the comon welth sake Many points of this passage are unjustifiable I
was willing to joyn wth you as I signified by my lett^s & by my serv^t that spake
wth you before the Election, whereby my lo might have been sure to have one,
wch you refused, wherby he may misse both, wch I am sorry for. There was
election made of 2 other more besides those you recomended at the same
time   as will stand, when a Clandestine   .
not hould. I will trouble you .   .   .   speak reason & be willing to
                                        Y^r affec   .

                                                                    .   .

I am enforced to take a sodaine journey to Ex wch makes me think I
shall not meet you at Tre I therfore am bould to trouble you wth these lines,
but I shall be willing to waite on you at Bod to do my lo whatever ser I can.

SIR BEVILL GRANVILLE TO "MY CO. W. DRAKE"

Dear Cos

I thanke y^r care I find my go fr inclin'd not to serve in this Par:
wch I am sorry for I will persuade him what I can to it, but if he will not,
yet lett me not loose the disposing of it Pray take care of this & entreat my
son to do the like, to whom I have written to that effect. I have entreated y^r
mayor to defer the Elec for a few daies, because I am sodainely call'd to
Ex upon an important occasion, but he shall heare from me before this week
passe
        I hastely rest
                                        Y^r serv :

SIR BEVILL GRANVILLE TO SIR RALPH SYDENHAM

Mo ho S^r,

That I am willing to serve you I hope I need not now to tell you as the
following discourse shall be an argum^t of it yet at best I can but imbark you
in a biabling title truly S^r if all the power I had in the world could have
served you better it should, but by this you may perceave how difficult a thing

                                                                    C.²

it is to effect such a busineſs. I attempted many places for to procure burg^hs but found no hope but in a poor burgh in the par^sh of Tint & you must understand that in all my estate there is not one in that place I found the inhabitants grieved at a course that was held wherin 9 or 10 did take upon them to be the only chusers of the burg^rs wheras they conceiv'd that the rest had as much right to do it as they & I well know that the opinion of the Par^mt house hath ever been that all inhabitants, being free men, have voice & so I have known it often adjudged whereupon I urg'd them to give me their voices for you & I would try the title to put them in a right way Mr Cor 's power is great there he continues himself mayor divers years & supports the former custom of chusing by a few because they are mostly at his command I gave him to understand that I was willing to joyne wth him if he pleased wherby my lo . Chamb should be sure of one if he would lett me have the other but he was absolute & would have all or none, wherby I believe he will loose all . . Rob is powerfull there & his . . . took the course of . . have cary'd both against Mr Cor if I had not interposed—nevertheless he in a private & unlawfull way having gotten the writt into his hands went to the election calling none but those which were at his disposion but the others learning of it went in & declared for whom they were so there are two elections made one by Mr Cor 's men & another by all the freemen who are we hear 3 to one against him & they have chosen you & another cal'd S^r Jo Clot · on my lo Ro recommendation You shall haue the mañer more pt : culaily certified you & if it be follow'd I am confident y^r election must stand. Now S^t one taske I must impose upon you to prevent my lo Chamb from having a misconceit of me he is my good co & I haue special relations to him I believe he will be inform'd tht I oppose him wch truly is not so for I offer'd to joyn wth m^r Cor wch he refused & if I had not interpos'd my lo Ro agents would haue carry'd both by that way of election I shall not be up at first sitting Pray hasten in y^r petition as soon as you can that you may be first heard advise with some of experience & take y^r no co M^r Ed Sydenham's helpe to keepe in right wth my lo . Chamb

               & I am Dear S^r
                 Y^r fa ser

                     B G

Sir John Clot above referred to is Sir John Clotworthy, a gentleman of Ireland, and utterly unknown in England, who was by the contrivance and recommendation of some powerful persons returned to serve for a borough in Devonshire " against Lord Strafford See Clarendon's *History of the Rebellion,* Bk iii , p 172.

The next letter is to Sir Edward Seymour, and is also concerned with the election to this " Long Parliament." Sir Edward was the son of Lord Edward Seymour, and grandson of the Protector, Duke of Somerset He built within the walls of the ancient castle of Berry Pomeroy a stately home, which was destroyed, it is said, by fire about a century later, and has never been rebuilt

SIR BEVILL GRANVILLE TO SIR EDWARD SEYMOUR

Mo . ho S^r

Glad I am to hearc from you again & shall ever accompt it among my greatest happinesses that afforde me y^r company, & next to it y^r lines I had all y^r newes before I rec y^r lr̃e, but truly it never made any impression in me, untill it sounded wth the harmony of y^r pen wch makes a musick when it strikes next to that of the spheres, & has no lesse enchanting power over me. But these expressions are needless where my heart is known & y^t my affection cañot containe it selfe upon the sight of y^f Bajazet w^{th}out some ejaculation S^r I am wretched for I fear I shall not be able to serve you as you desire for by God I am not sure of a Bur^{gh} in all the Coun they are so taken up by lo ᵗ lr̃es before I knew of the Par & such base meanes hath been us'd by some ill m^{ebrs} in the country as all places were forestalled before I knew of it A towne or two hath sent to me that they will chuse me if I will serve my selfe, but will not give me leave to putt in another, & on my faith there is not one Bur^{gh} in all my owne land but they abound in the poor [?] townes of the Stannery, where I have nothing to do I will not injure our friendship so much as to make protestation, but let me not enjoy heaven if I would not serve you to the utmost extent of my life .   .   .   for Gods sake make y^r selfe sure (?) I feare how it will go wth S^r T H I will do all I can however, & lett us meet if it be possible that I may still tell you how much I am

                                        Y^r humble ser   " B G "

Tho my power in bur^{ghs} faile yet I doubt not but to make whom I please K^{ts} of ye Sh

During the early days of the Long Parliament, Sir Bevill took no forward part in the angry disputes which marked its progress. " He saw sooner than most the bad designs that were forming, and apprehended very clearly the pernicious consequences which must follow from them. In this situation he conducted himself with equal steadiness and prudence. He adhered to what he took to be his duty to his King and country, but he would not plunge himself into the depths of party " It was at this time that Sir William Waller, smarting under the unjust sentence of the Star Chamber, first threw in his lot with the Presbyterians, a defection for which Sir Bevill expresses so much concern in the following letter —

SIR BEVILL GRANVILLE TO SIR WILLIAM WALLER.

Mo ho S^r/

The fullnes of my griefe for the irreperable losse, wch both I & our country doth sustaine by being deprived of you, I cañot expresse but it is no new thing wth me to loose my joyes, or to be frustrated of my hopes I have been inured to it long, & so well exercis'd in misery as the frequencies of it hath so fortified me against all the chances of this world, as nothing should shake me, and yet my frailty hath been touch'd to the quick of late by the death of an excellent friend but I have learnt long ago to submit myself to the will of God S^r tho I may not say much at such a distance, yet I cañot but open soo far to you as to say, that I wonder nothing at what the Divine justice doth threaten the iniquity of the present times w^th, but I rather wonder (all things consider'd) that it hath not sooner happen'd   lett others looke upon secondary causes, I contemplate the originalls & do beleeve the evills are deserv'd but perchance silence is best   I will conclude wth a motion wch let it not offend you because what ever y^r resolution be, it shall not displease me the losse of my late noble fr   hath drawne on me a sodainer trouble than I expected & tho I might safely have been at his mercie, yet I doubt I may not at others that ai left behinde   some convenient waies of accomodation were privatley thought on between him & me, wch would have been convenient for both   but the Divine Wisdome hath otherwise determined the busines & taught me that I ought to have recourse to Himself & not affied too much in an aime of flesh   I have design'd & publish'd the sale of so much land as is worth ten thousand le^ls & will w^h all the speed I can dispose of it, but whither by the time (wch is our la   day) I shall be able to effect it wholy or gott in enough to make up my full paym^t of 6 000^li I am doubtful to be therfore certain, & to prevent the danger wch may fall upon my ma^n of Bid wch l hope is worth 3 times the money, I am willing to try all waies, tho it strain my modesty somthing to do it.   I desire to know whther I may be beholden to y^r power, (for y^r creditt l will not presume to trouble) but I say y^r power to produce me a brace of m^hbs upon the security of my estate or any pt of it   peichance it will not need, but if it do, l only desire to know whither such a thing may be possible by y^r favour, & that you would pardon the presumption of y^r antiently obliged, & still—

mo   devoted ser^t
B G^r

S^r you were pleasd to extend y^r lo
& court to my Son in Ox wherby as
you much honord him so you no less
obl. me for wch my than is too poor a requitall.

In the Long Parliament Sir Bevill soon found opportunity of showing that he was now as strongly Royalist as once he had been strongly Parliamentarian. The Commons determined to impeach Strafford, and the trial commenced the 22nd March, 1641, and continued until the 10th of April. Stafford's defence proved so eloquent, so touching, and so manly, that his judges exhibited manifest symptoms of an intention to acquit him The Commons withdrew to their own house ; the proceeding by impeachment was abandoned, and a Bill of Attainder brought in and read with closed doors. Sir Bevill strongly opposed the passing of the Bill of Attainder, and wrote to his colleague in the representation of Cornwall, Sir Alexander Carew, " Pray, S^r, when it comes to be put to the vote, let it never be said that any member of our country [*i e* , county] should have a hand in this fatal business, and therfore pray give y^r vote against the Bill." But Sir Alexander did not share his colleague s views, and immediately replied, " If I were sure to be the next man that should suffer upon the same scaffold with the same axe, I would give my consent to the passing of it."

The Bill was carried through both Houses of Parliament, and after much hesitation the King (and only after receiving from Strafford himself a letter, couched in the most chivalrous and romantic terms, in which he besought his master to accept the blood of a devoted servant, as a voluntary offering for the peace of the nation) gave the royal assent to the fatal Bill, and on the 12th of May, 1641, this high-minded nobleman was beheaded on Tower Hill, amid the shouts and yells of a bloodthirsty mob

One outcome of the popular movement had been a Pro-testation, declaring attachment to the Reformed religion and to the rights and liberties of the subject   Hundreds of members signed on May 3rd, the day on which it was first laid on the table of the House, Sir Alexander Carew being amongst the first.   For more than a fortnight signatures of laggard Members were added almost daily, but Sir Bevill. though not ranked by the populace as a Straffordian, did not sign at all.

Instead thereof, he ' left London as soon as he could do it with safety, and retiring into his own country, employed him-self in opening the eyes of other honest gentlemen to see that their welfare and happiness depended on the preservation of the Constitution in Church and State , for the support of which, therefore, he advised them, whenever it should become necessary, to venture their lives and fortunes as they could have no security for either if the Constitution was destroyed "

It must have been about this time that Dick died, probably at Oxford, and the sorrow that his death caused his parents may be gathered from the following letters   The first is addressed to " Sir Nicholas Slanning, Governoor of Pendennis Castle, Falmouth," and the allusion in the postscript to " my ancient, most dear and noble friend of Tref ' doubtless refers to Mr Trefusis of Trefusis, whose house stood at the head of Falmouth harbour.

SIR BEVILL GRANVILLE TO SIR NICHOLAS SLANNING

Mo ho Sr/

    I am many waies dejected, & it adds to my sadnes, that I cañot now be reviv'd by seeing you wth these my freuds that will kisse yr hands   I am not yet fitt after so late & heavy a losse (being the greatest that could have befalne me) to looke upon so good company, & truly I doubt whether I may be worthy of so much mercy from you, as to be thought admittable to yr friendship, whom the heavens have so heavily sensured, I wish you muth &

comfort, & will as soon as I am capable of any come to receave some from y^r excellent favor & goodness   May you long live S^r wth y^r rich Stock of worth to maintaine ye world in credditt, wch otherwise by such losses as we have lately had must needs grow bankrupt, & may you be so pittiffittful (these are my prayers) as for charity sake to love

Y^r thrice humble & most affec   ser

B G

You are (S^r) envirom d wth many rare felicities,
& I wish them Centupled, but I only grutch you
one wch is neighborhood to my Ancient, most dear
& nob fr of Tref   because I cañt share it with you

FROM LADY GRACE GRANVILLE TO HER HUSBAND

Dear Love

You are (I hope) confident of my readiness to observe all y^r directions to the uttmost I can, both what you tolde me & since wrote of from Holsworthy Brute hath sett all y^r Acornes & Sycamore seeds and Ching is about the Barly Ground according to y^r order   I hope to receave som money from [you?] by Cottle & then will pay it according to y^r order & putt off such servants as are faulty & reforme all disorders what I can   I still labour with the same desires of being proffitable to you, though my misfortunes doe every day more and more disable me   It was impossible for me to part wth you & continue well (truly Love)   The next day after we parted, I was most extreame sick with violent headache, fainting and severall vomitting fitts, so I doubted I should have fayld my gossip at Stratton, but I ventured next day, finding myselfe some-what better & mett my cosen Arundell there & Mrs Vigures in my cos Bassett's room who came not by reason Sr Rob Bassett was sodainly taken so ill as they thinke he is now bidding farwell to this world   Deare Love, I must not omitt to thanke you for y^r kinde care & wishing me to be comforted & tis my endevor to submitt to the will of God, desiring his mercy still, wch I humbly acknowledge hath allwaies been plentifully miv'd with his corrections, & tis & shall ever be my praier, that I may make the right use of both   I confesse my late sorrow hath created so many new feares in me, as I hate my selfe to thinke how contemptible a creature it may make me in time, if it con-tinue so burthensome on me wch made me expresse my unwillingnes so sodainly to adventure Jack especially this winter, doubting he is but crazy & not of so strong a constitution as perchance you imagine   Wherfore for God's sake excuse me & consider of these perticulers in season, that we may not seeme by our earnest covetting his Learning to pluck on new sorrows by hazarding Death without which he canott learne at all.   Lett not I pray my tendernes cause a misconstruction for God knows I desire heartily he may be a schollar and can be well contented with his absence so he be safe, but the sad remembrance of my late losse & the doubt of the sicknes being so dis-persd abroad doth fill me with feares which I canott conceale, though tis with much unwillingnes I fall on anything contrary to y^r opinion   I pray for y^r health & his wch is all I can doe & that I will not faile to performe beseeching you to shun danger & be carefull in all points of y^r owne health as well as his. Pardon my distracted lines & love ever

Y^r faithfull & affectionat

GRACE GRENVILE

My Mother prayes for y^r
wellfare & enjoynes me to intreate
you, to confer with Hutchings & to use what meanes
you can to gaine her the Possession

I earnestly entreate you to gett me & send it as speedely as you can, a Bottle of perfectly good Blew Syrup of Violetts, a pound of the Syrup I desire, it cost 6ˢ a pound the last, it came safe and was excellent good I canott want it for my owne use & oftentimes for the children also therfore pray hasten it to me A dozen of white Gloves I desire & 2-paire of thicker Gloves

LADY GRACE GRANVILLE TO HER HUSBAND.

My ever dearest,

I have receaved y{rs} from Salisbury, & am glad to heare you came so far well with poore Jack ye shall be sure of my praiers wch is the best service I can doe you I cannot perceave whither you had receaved mine by Pom or no, but I believe by this time you have mett that & another since by the Post truly I have been out of frame ever since you went, not with a cough but in another kinde much indisposed However I have striven with it, and was at church last Sunday but not the former I have been vex'd with divers demands more of money then I could satisfie, but I instantly paid what you sent, & have intreated Mr Rous his patience a while longer as you directed It grieves me to thinke how chargeable yr Family is, considering yr occasions, it hath this many years troubled me to thinke to what passe it must come at last, if it run on after this course how many times what hath appeard hopefull, & yet proved contrary in the conclusion, hath belaine us, I am loth to urge, because tis farr from my desire to disturbe yr thoughts but this sore is not to be cured with silence or patience either, & while you are loth to discourse or thinke of that you can take little comfort, to see how bad it is, & I as unwilling to strike on that sting wch sounds harsh in yr eare (& the matter still grows worse) though I can never putt it out of my thoughts, & that makes me oftentimes seeme dreaming to you, when you expect I should sometimes observe more complem{t} with my friends or be more active in matters of curiosity in our House wch doubtlesse you would have been better pleased with, had I been capable to have performd it and I believe though I had a naturall dullness in me, it would never so much have appeard to my prejudice, but twas increased by a continuance of sundry disasters wch I still mett with, yet never till this yeare, but I had some strength to encounter them, but truly, now I am soe cleane o'recome as tis in vain to deny a truth It seems to me now tis high time to be sensible that God is displeased, having had many sad remembrances in our estate & children of late, yet God spared us in our children long & when I strive to follow yr advice in moderating my grief (wch I praise God) I have thus farr been able to doe as not to repine at Gods will, though I have a tender sence of grief wch hangs on me still, & I think it as dangerous, & improper, to forgett it, for I canott but think it was hand & correction sent from God to check me. for my many neglects of my duty to GOD it was the tenth & last Plague GOD smote the Egiptians with, the death of their first borne before he utterly destroyed them, they persisting in their disobedience notwithstanding all their former puñishm{ts} this apprehension makes me both tremble & humbly to beseech him to withdraw his punishments from us & to give us grace to know, & amend whatever is amisse. Now I have pour'd out my sad thoughts, wch in yr absence doth most oppresse me, tis my weaknes hardly to be able to say thus much unto you, how brimfull soever my heart be, though often times, I heartily wish, I could open my heart freely unto you, when tis over charged but the least thought it may not be pleasing to you will at all times restrain me, consider me rightly I beseech you & excuse I pray the liberty I take with my pen in this kinde. & now at last I must thanke you for wishing me to lay aside all feare, & depend on the Almighty who can only helpe us   for his mercy I dayly pray, and y' wellfare & our poore boyes so I conclude & am ever

                •   Y^{rs} faithfully & only
Stowe Nov 23—   GRACE GRENVILE /
  —1641—

I sent by yⁿ to Mr Prust but this
from him came after mine was gone
last weeke   Ching is gone to Cheddor
I looke for Bawdon still but as
Yett is not come   Sr Rob Bassett is dead /

     I heard from my Cosen Grace Weekes who writes that Mr Luttrell says if you & he could meete, & liking between the young people, he will not stand for money you shall finde   Parson Weekes wishes you could call with him, & y^t he might entice you to take the castle in y^r way downe, she says they enquire in the most courteous maner y^t can be imagined   Deare Love thinke how to farther this what you can

               For my best Frend S^r
                  BEVILL GRENVILE /.

LADY GRACE GRANVILLE TO HER HUSBAND.

Deare Love,

     I shall now returne you a few hasty lines only to thank you, for y^r affectionate wishing me health   Since I wrote last I have been very ill, & kept my Bed most part of the time, but now I praise God, I am much better , but dare not stirr out of my Chamber, and I doubt this new sicknes will make me capable of a relapce into my old distempers especially this dead season of the yeare   I canott so well inform you, by lffe, in what kind I have been ill, but it hath weakned me as much as any Childbed   I refer myselfe to Gods good pleasure, but if he please to restore me to a more healthfull condition I humbly desire it, for others sakes more then my owne ·/ what passionate lines soever you receave from me, I hope you will consider my many imperfections, & not suffer any misconceipt to creep into y^r breast, for they proceed from a faithfull heart, though at times so much oppress'd as it forces me to write in a strame I afterwards fear'd did distaste you   I am glad you & Jack be well, I long to heare of y^r coming downe & few things desired in my lies I need much   Pray try it Mr Manaton be in London whither he will match on reasonable terms   You know whom I meane & for y^r friendship . if he be not engag'd I hope he would the sooner hearken to it

               Y^{rs} only & ever
                   G G
             Stow—Dec—1—
                1641

     To my best Frend Sr Bevill Grenvile,
at the Hatchett behind St Clements Church in London these /
Entreate Mr Newman to convey this /

"Jack," the third son of Sir Bevill and Lady Grace, was now the heir to the property; his two elder brothers, Richard and Bevill, having both died. He was thirteen years of age, and had accompanied his father to London, whence he writes to his Grandmother as follows :—

JOHN GRANVILLE TO LADY SMYTH.

Madam

The consideration of y^r benefitts hath emboldened the inability of my pen & compelled me to resolve rather to shew my ignorance by speacking then to be wilfully guilty of a neglect by silence & not acknowledging the multiplicity of y^r benefits in not presenting you with my humble thancks   But I am sufficiently confident y^r goodnesse is soe great that it will accept of this although not as a reall satisfaction yet as a true testimony of my gratitude for y^r undeserved favours   Thus hoping you will excuse both my presumption and ignorance in writing I humbly crave your pardon and rest

Y^r observant and obedient
Sonne

London December 22
   1641

JOHN GRENVILE

      (Superscription)
      To his most honored Grand-mother
      the Lady Grace Smyth at
      Stow thesse
         humbly present

SIR BEVILL GRANVILLE TO HIS WIFE

Deare Love

I perceave you rec my lře but not the other things, wch I did hope should have been wth you as soone as the lřo, but I hope they are before this & I wish they may fitt & please you   I will bring Hatts for the boyes & am glad you say they learne well,   I thank god I have attayn'd my health pretty well, though not fully my strength, but I resolve to come away this weeke.   I am very glad to hear my sister is well & wth you   I beseech god to keepe her and hers so still   I will bring y^r Phisick wth me also.   Write no more hither   Present my duty to my la Sm wth my service to my sister, my coz   Frank & my neipces & I shall ever rest

Y^{rs} constantly

London Mar 8
   1641.

BEVILL GRENVILE

Pray send away these lřs speedely & make for me against my comeing y^r Purging ale that you were wont, be sure to putt in all the ingredients and lett it be well done, it will be wholesome this spring time—turn over leafe

(over leaf)

Bid Symon Cottle give speedy notice to my Cos Wm Rolle that I will houlde the Sheafe no longer because I loose by it every yeat   I have said it to Sr Sam Rolle heer & he saies I must do the like to his Uncle   I heare not whither there be any provision of wine made for me as I appointed   We are

H^2

undone if there be not & it must be had home speedely Pray provide store
of good Sallad hearbes & increase the Rampions I wish Ned Flint & Ching
to looke carefully whither my young horse Coults do beate about the mares &
to sever them if they do till I come down to take other course Make it
knowne to all my neighbours and Tenants of the west side of our Parrish that
I shall take it ill if they grind not at my mill, and lett the Tenants of
Noithlegh know that if they do it not, as they are bound, I will put them in
suite.

Seale Mr Braddon's lre & pray farther that busines

(Superscription)
To my best Frend the
Lady Grace Grenvile at
Stowe   these   dd
I desire Mr Newman of
Exeter to convey this

SIR BEVILL GRANVILLE TO HIS WIFE.

My Dearest
    I am infinitly perplex'd in minde wth doubt of y^r health I do feare
you do not tell me the worst & my griefe is not small that I cañot yet come
to you I give you thankes for expressing so good care of my health, I am as
wary as I can be of avoiding all infected places There is but little apparence
of the Plague, but the Smale Pox is very coñíon and more mortall then usuall
Fewe or none do escape Since Mr Wise his death, another good member of
our house, called Sr Hen Rainsford, is also dead thereof and at least a dozen
more of the house since our first meeting are dead of several diseases I am
not wth out carefull and passionat thoughtes for those considerations wch you
touch both of our Children & estate I would to God I could settle all
things, but I will be tractable to any course & at our meeting conferr with
you heerof Let Ned make use of the Elder great Bay Horse for my mares ,
not the Darke bay wch I rode in the north, but the other I would not have
him mistake and lett him be doing wth the mares as fast as he can, beginning
with ould Barbary, but the two Poulet mares and my brothers Grey keepe
from the horse I will send them to another—herein mistake not. I hope
the horse Coults are gelt Lett Mr Prust and M^r W^{ms} use all the wayes they
can for money and so wth my praires for y^r health I rest

Y^{rs} constantly
BEVILL GRENVILE

Lon Ap —14—1641

(Superscription)
To my best Frend
the Lady Grace
Grenvile at Stow
these

Meanwhile State matters had been rapidly proceeding from
bad to worse in England, and within twelve months of the
execution of Strafford civil war was clearly inevitable. The
early months of 1642 were occupied in preparation by the rival
parties Both King and Parliament strove their utmost to
secure the various fortresses scattered throughout the country.

The Commons, by passing the Ordnance of Militia, had assumed the control of the whole auxiliary forces of the Kingdom. To meet this the King issued "a Commission of Array," which was to all intents and purposes the same thing under another name and authority There were thus in every county recruiting centres. Cornwall was naturally disposed towards the Royal cause The tenantry entertained an hereditary attachment to their landlords, the reputation of ancient families, who had little degenerated from the lustre, honour, and virtues of each other by intermarriages, perpetuated the most hospitable intercourse To dissolve such family compacts, the Covenanters had multiplied their emissaries and had introduced considerable armed reinforcements into the county. But Sir Bevill was determined that now, as in the old days, Cornwall should side with him, and joining his forces to those of Sir Ralph Hopton, whom the King had sent into the western parts of England to form an army, and who had gained possession of Pendennis Castle, Falmouth, he organized the Royalists in the West, making Truro their headquarters, the Parliamentarians, on the other hand, held the eastern part of the county, with Sir Alexander Carew and Sir Richard Buller at their head, and Launceston as their rallying point. Fancying themselves powerful because they were unmolested, they prepared to indict the leading Royalists as disturbers of the peace, and to question their authority to raise troops, and at the Launceston summer assizes of 1642 (and not at the quarter sessions, as Lord Clarendon states ; those being held at Truro, which was then occupied by the Royalists,) they made a presentment "against divers men unknown, who were lately come armed into the county against the peace of the King" The Royalists' answer was effective Sir Ralph Hopton and seven other leading Royalists, including Sir Bevill, went to Launceston market-place with the Sheriff, and read the King's Proclamation, at which they declared the people to have been well pleased while the others threatened These "others" had reason to threaten, for things went badly with them within the Court as well as in the market-place. Sir Ralph Hopton appeared to dispute the presentment. He handed in the commission by which the King had appointed the Marquess of Hertford to be General of the West, as well as the commission by which the Marquess had appointed him Lieutenant-General of the Horse, and the jury, after what Lord Clarendon calls "a full and solemn debate," acquitted Hopton and all his companions of any breach of the peace, and, moreover, declared the gentlemen at Launceston guilty of promoting a riotous assembly, and authorized the Sheriff to call out the forces of the county against them   Thus the Royalists completely turned the tables on their adversaries.

Meanwhile Sir Bevill had applied for the King's warrant not to leave the county except by his Majesty's express command   This warrant was granted and the need for it soon appeared, for no sooner did the Parliament receive intelligence from its Committee as to how badly it had fared at the Launceston assizes, than the Lords agreed with the Commons in directing Sir Bevill, not like two of his companions in the market-place, to be "sent for as a delinquent," but simply to be summoned to attend the service of the House   Five weeks later his reply was read in the Commons to the effect that he had "received the King's special command to continue in his county to preserve the peace thereof"   A resolution was hereupon immediately passed (Sept 21st) disabling him from continuing a member.

While this was going on, Sir Ralph Hopton had gathered about 3,000 Foot of the trained Militia, and accompanied by his small body of Somersetshire Cavalry, had advanced towards Launceston, which the Committee had partially fortified and "thence had sent messages of great contempt."   From the following letter from Sir Bevill to his wife, it appears that a conference was arranged to see if they could compose matters; whether it was held or not does not appear, but on hearing of the advance of the Royalists, Sir Richard Buller and his confederates, not daring to abide the storm, quitted Launceston by night in great disorder, and drew into Devonshire, and so towards Plymouth, so that Hopton found the gates open and entered without resistance

SIR BEVILL GRANVILLE TO HIS WIFE

Deare love

I will detaine Sym Cottle no longer, nor can he bring you much more newes then I sent you yesterday We found men enough at the place appointed well arm'd, & for my part I am impatient (as all my honest friends else are) that we did not march presently to fetch those traitors out of then neast at Lanceston. or fire them in it, but som of our faynter bretheren have prevaild so farr wth the Sherriff, as there is a conference agreed on this day between 6 of a side, to see if they can compose matters but we will march on neverthelesse, to be [before]hand if they agree not. My neigh[bors] did ill that they came not out, [& a]re punishable by the lawe in a high degree, & though I will do the best I can to save some of the honester sort, yett others shall smart They were not in this to have commands from me, it is a legall course wch the Sherriff is directed to by the Statute, & he is the comander in the busines, & not the Collonells, but he may take to his assistance whom he ple[ase   M]y neighbors did perchance looke to hear from me, & if we proceed I shall expect they should yet come forth, or they shall suffer, & they shall have farther direction from me   The Gallant Prince Rupert goes on gloriously in his Uncles service, he hath given another blow to the enimy greater then the former, & hath well nye cut off all their Cavallry wth his, so as the great cuckhold is forc'd to shutt himselfe up wth his foote w^{th}in the walls of Worcester, not being able to keepe the field, whitherward the King is moving wth his Army to give the last blow, being able to barr him from all reliefe, & his army is mightily encreas'd.   Cottle hath a note; Publish it to y^r frends, I have sent it already to my Co\~s Cary I hope we shall shortly see good daies againe   My Noble frend the brave Wilmott had a shrewd wound, & the Prince himselfe slightly hurt, but they killed 2000 of the [enim]y wth little losse

Y^1

[B G]RENVILE

Bodmyn
  Octob 12 164½
[Addressed]

To my best Frend the
Lady Grace Grenvile

The Simon Cottell referred to in the above letter was afterwards Treasurer to the army in Cornwall, 1644, *cf* R. Symonds' Diary of the Royal Army, p 77.[1]   A copy of a letter from Sir Richard Granville (30 March, 1645) to "Captayne Symon Cottell" is preserved amongst the Mount Edgcumbe MSS   Sir Bevill's threat that those who came not to his help should "smart" was probably fulfilled.   In a contemporary letter printed in the *Retrospective Review*, xii. 189, we read, "Sir Bevill Grenville hath been a tyrant, especially to his tenants, threatening to thrust them out of house and home, if they will not assist him and his confederates"   As the above letter is dated from Bodmin, it would seem that Sir Bevill was left in charge of Cornwall when Sir Ralph Hopton, following up his success at Launceston, moved towards Saltash, which was held by Colonel William Ruthven, a Scotch soldier of fortune, and about 200 Scots, who had put in from stress of weather when on their way from Ireland to France for the service of the French King.   On the approach of the Royalists the Scots "as kindly quitted Saltash as the others had Launceston before." The Parliamentarians were thus entirely driven out of Cornwall, and as the Cornish-trained bands refused to cross the Tamar (a determination which afterwards proved the ruin of the King's cause in the West), they were disbanded "till a new provocation from the enemy should put fresh vigour into that

---

[1] He belonged to Morwen-stow

county." The deep indentations of the western coast especially
hindered the growth of common patriotism, and as in Wales
and Lancashire, so too in Cornwall, the inhabitants were not
united in feeling, as were the.inhabitants of Kent and Sussex
with those of Suffolk or Northamptonshire   "Cornishmen,"
said they, "summoned by the Sheriff were bound to keep the
peace of Cornwall; they were not bound to leave the county
to interfere in what was, in that secluded district, considered
to be almost a foreign country "

Having dismissed the trained bands with a good grace, Sir
Ralph Hopton called upon Sir Bevill and others to raise a small
force for permanent service by voluntary enlistment   This
they at once did, and soon an entirely volunteer force,
numbering nearly 1500 foot, was in the field, ready to follow
their leaders wherever they chose to lead them   In order to
supply money for his troops Sir Bevill mortgaged his estates
and even sold his plate and other valuables for the King's cause,
and his example was followed by several others of his
neighbours, *e g.*, Sir Nicholas Slanning of Marystow , Mr.
Arundell of Trerice and Mr Trevanion of Carhayes

Early in November the Royalists passed into Devonshire
with the purpose either of marching to join the King's army,
then lying about Reading, or of forming a junction with such
Devonshire Royalists as could be got together, and making a
dash upon Exeter   If we may credit a tract printed in
December, 1642, the former project was the one more in favour
with the loyal but truculent Cornishmen. "They cry all is
their owne swearing and daming, blaspheming and cursing that
they will up to the King in spite of opposition · and for the
city of London they intend there for to keepe then Christmas,
and make the citizens wayte upon their trenchers, but for the
Roundheads, as they so terme them, they will send them pell-
mell to then father the devil." (A true Relation of the present
estate of Cornwall   King's pamphlet, B.M. small 4to vol. lxxxv.)

Exeter, however proved to be the first object of attack.
On the 18th of November the Royalists approached the city
"flinging up their caps," so runs a Parliamentary account,
' and giving many shouts of joy that they were arrived so
neare the Centre of their ungracious wishes .   . . . but they
reckoned without their host " Propositions were sent in to the
Mayor and Aldermen, "requesting them in friendly sort, in his
Majesty's name, to render possession of their city to Sir Ralph
Hopton " The Mayor, in reply, "desired Sir Ralph that he
would with his cavaliers depart from before their walls other-

wise they should quickly receive such a greeting from thence as should be smally to their contents."

Entrenchments were then made by the Cornish on the west side of the city, and an artillery fire was opened upon it, which the citizens briskly answered from the ramparts. These details have been taken from a rare contemporary tract, entitled, " True and joyfull Newes from Exeter Shewing how Sir Ralph Hopton, Sir Bevill Greenvill with divers of the Cornish Malignants made their approaches thither with five thousand Horse and Foot, intending to plunder that great and rich City ; and how they were manfully repulst by the Valour of the Citizens with the losse of fifteen hundred of their men on Munday last being the one and twentieth of November London Nov. 25th."

Notwithstanding its voluminous title, from which all experience teaches a moderate expectation of what is to follow, this tract gives a really spirited description of a night-sally led by the Mayor himself from the east gate of the city upon the rear of the beseigers' works. The citizens surprised the drunken sentinels, and got into the centre of the enemies quarters like ' hungry lyons ' bearing down their prey with halberts, poleaxes, and butts of their muskets Dutch engineers threw hand-grenades among them Many of the Cornishmen were drowned in the river Sir Ralph and Sir Bevill, with their officers, stood together opposing to then uttermost until day-light appeared, when the townsmen issuing from the city on all sides, completed the business, and the army of the besiegers was routed and temporarily dispersed Shortly afterwards however, they occupied Tavistock and proceeded to threaten Plymouth (*cf.* perfect Diurnal E 242. 35) and by the middle of December were able to hold the open country up to the very walls of Exeter According to journals favourable to the Parliament (Special Passages, pp 142—144) the Cornish Cavaliers, " like brethren in iniquity," were suffered to do as they like, plundering the residences of their enemies. They were also reported to be in much distress, " having so lamentably plundered the country that it is unable any longer to sustain them " (*cf Diurnall*, Occurances Truly Relating the Most Remarkable Passages which have hapned in both Houses of Parliament, and other parts of this Kingdome and elsewhere, for the week from Nov. 28 to Dec. 5, 1642, p. 40) It was also rumoured that " Sir Ralph Hopton is either dead or dangerously sicke, and that Sir Bevill Greenvill and the rest of the Malignants in Cornwall are determined to break up their army, being no longer able to continue them together for want of money and provisions."

These rumours, however, were false ; but when the Royalists heard, in the last days of December, of the approach of the Earl of Stamford with a large force from Somersetshire, they retreated by way of Torrington and Okehampton to Launceston. (*cf.* Mercurius Aulicus a Diurnall communicating the intelligence and affaires of the Court to the rest of the Kingdome. No. 2, from Jan 8 to Jan. 14, 1643.)

The following letter to Lady Grace from Sir Bevill has reference to the billetting of the soldiers in the parishes round Stowe .—

SIR BEVILL GRANVILLE TO HIS WIFE

Deare Love

I shall be willing that Jack may repose himself awhile at home, seeing our actions abroade are not more worthy of his bestowing his time in   There comes wth him a rare man, one Mr Coxe, a Divine, though for some imploym^{ts} wch he hath it is not amiss to have him somtimes in a grey coate   His learning, his parts, his conversation are excellent   I hope he will retire himselfe awhile at Stow, and thereby imprint some formes in the boy, w^{ch} (if he hath the witt to make use of) may season him while he lives   Pray afford him the best usage and respect you can both in Dyet lodging and attendance, Lodge him in the Redd Chamber and because y^r chamberlain is sick let some trusty body see his bed well furnished wth neat linnen and all things appertayning sweet and cleane, wth good fyr^{es} beneath and above , all which I leave to y^r discreation and my^{self} for ever to remain

Y^r owne

B Gren

Lances. Jan 6 1642

I am of the mind to billett some companies in the Parrishes about you as namely 5 compa   in 5 Par   one in a Parrish for the defence [of the] country against Plunderers   Wherefore   Mr Rowse to prepare the inhabitants of Kilkham . Morwingt · Stratton, Pughill and Lansells to dyett a 100 men a peace in several howses   They shall be allow'd for each man two shillings by the weeke, wch is enough for a poore soldier , and, to be briefe, it they will not do it willingly, they shall do it whither they will or no   and in this I expect a speedy answer

Since the writing of this . . . .
Mr Coxe cañot come

To my best friend the
Lady Grace Grenvile
these/

The trained bands, which had refused to march into Devonshire, now rallied round Hopton as soon as he touched Cornish soil. There was no such subordination on the other side as to render the Earl's army really formidable. Colonel Ruthven, who commanded the garrison at Plymouth, with something perhaps of the contempt of the professional soldier for the titled commander to whom his obedience was due, pushed on hurriedly to attack the Royalists without waiting for Stamford. On January 13th New Bridge was taken after a smart engagement, and the Royalists retreated from Launceston to Bodmin The Parliamentarians followed them in the direction of Liskeard, and on the 19th battle was joined at Bradock Down, and Ruthven was signally defeated. The details of the fight can have no better chronicler than Sir Bevill himself, who writes thus to his wife .—

SIR BEVILL GRANVILLE TO HIS WIFE

My deare Love.

It hath pleas'd God to give us a happie victory this present Thursday being ye 19th of Jan^y, for which pray joine wth me in giving God thanks We advanced yesterday from Bodmin to find ye enemy w^h we heard was abroad, or if we miss'd him in the field we were resolved to unhouse them in Liskeard, or leave our boddies in the highway. We were not above 3 miles from Bodmyn when we had view of two troops of their Horse to whom we sent some of ours, wch chased them out of the field, while our foot march'd after our Horse, but night coming on we could march no farther than Boconnocke Parke where (upon my lo Mohun's kind motion) we quartered all our Army by good fires under the hedge The next morning, being this day, we march'd forth and ab^t noone came in full view of the enemies whole army upon a fair heath between Boconnocke and Braddocke Church They were in horse much stronger than we, but in foot we were superior as I thinke They were possest of a pretty rising ground, wch was in the way towards Liskeard and we planted ourselves upon such another against them w^{thn} muskett shott, and we saluted each other wth bulletts about two hours or more, each side being willing to keep their ground of advantage and to have the other come over to his prejudice But after so long delay, they standing still firm and being obstinate to houlde their advantage, Sir Ra Hopton resolved to march over to them and to leave all to the mercy of God and valour of our side I had the van, so after solemne prayers at the head of every division, I led my part away, who follow'd me wth so good courage both downe one hill and up the other as it strooke a terror in them, while the seconds came gallantly after me, and the wings of horse charged on both sides But their courage soon fail'd them as they stood not our first charge of the foot, but fled in great disorder, and we chast them diverse miles Many were not slain because of their quick disordering, but we have taken above 600 prisoners, among which Sr Shilston Calmady is one, and more are still brought in by the soldiers Much armes they have lost and Colours we have won and 4 pieces of Ordnance f^{rm} them, and without rest we march'd to Liskeard and tooke it wthout delay, all their men flying fr^m it before we came, and so I hope we are now again in the ye way to settle the Country in peace. All our Cornish Grandies were present at the battell wth the Scotch Generall Ruthven, the Somersett Collonells and the Horse Captains Pim and Tomson, and but for their horses speed had been all in our hands, Let my Sister and

1^2

my Coseus of Clovelly wth y^r othe1 frends understand of God's mercy to us
And we lost not a man, so I rest

Y1^s ever,

BEVILL GRENVILE

Liskerd Jan 19 1642

For the Lady Grace Grenvile
at Stow d d

The messenger is paide, yet give
him a shilling more

This interesting letter is sealed ; a horseman's rest upon a
cap of maintenance   The reference in it to the "solemn
prayers at the head of every division" before the commencement of the battle, proves the fact (afterwards confirmed by
similar devotions after the battle of Stratton), which is sometimes apt to be overlooked, that reliance on "the God of
Battles" was not confined to the Puritan side in the Civil Wars
Lord Clarendon, too, tells us that when the Rebels observed
prayers being said by the Royalists they mocked and told their
fellows "they were at mass," in order to stir up their courage
in the cause of religion

Ruthven fled to Saltash, which he thought to fortify, and
by the neighbourhood of Plymouth and assistance of the
shipping, to defend, and thereby still to have an influence upon
a good part of Cornwall   The Earl of Stamford, who had
meanwhile occupied Launceston, receiving quick advertisement
of this defeat, retired in great disorder to Tavistock to preserve
the utmost parts of Devon from incursion

The Royalists, after a solemn thanksgiving to Almighty
God for this great victory, and a little refreshing their men at
Liskeard, divided themselves , Sir John Berkley and Colonel
Ashburnham, with Sir Bevill's, Sir Nicholas Slannings, and
Col Trevanion's Volunteers, and such a party of Horse and
Dragoons as could be spared, advanced to Tavistock ; whilst
Lord Mohun and Sir Ralph Hopton with Lord Mohun's and
Colonel Godolphin's Volunteers, and some of the Trained
Bands marched towards Saltash to dislodge Ruthven, who,
within the three days that had elapsed since his defeat at
Bradock Down, had cast up such works, and planted such store
of cannon upon the narrow avenues that he thought himself
able (with a goodly ship of 400 tons, in which were 16 pieces
of cannon, which he had brought up the river to the very side
of the town) to defend that place against any strength that
was likely to be brought against him   But he quickly found
that the same spirit possessed his enemies that drove him from

Liskeard, and the same that possessed his own men when they fled from thence, for as soon as the Cornishmen came up they fell upon his works, and in a short time beat him, first out of them and then out of the town, with a good execution upon them, many being killed in the fight and more drowned, Ruthven himself hardly getting into a boat, by which he got into Plymouth, leaving all his Ordnance behind him, which, together with the ship and seven-score prisoners, and all their Colours, which had been saved at Liskeard, were taken by the Conquerors, who who were now once more entire masters of Cornwall

The Earl of Stamford had not the same patience to abide the other party at Tavistock, but before their approach quitted the town, some of his forces making haste into Plymouth, and the rest retiring into Exeter. (Clarendon, vi pp 134, 135)

SIR BEVILL GRANVILLE TO HIS WIFE

Deare love

I will write a hasty line by my Cos Porter We marched wth some foot and horse from Plimpton to prevent the enimy from gathering power at Tavistock, wher he forbare to come for feare of us We then marcht to Okehampton to finde him, we being sure they were there wth 5000 men, but they ran away before we came there were sent some horse & Dragoones to Chagford to pursue them in the night, but for want of good foote, & the approch to the towne being very hard, our men were forst to retire againe after they were in & one losse we have sustaind that is unvalluable, towitt, Sydney Godolphin is slaine in the attempt, who was as gallant a gent as the world had I have time for no more

Y^{rs} ever

B Grenvile

Oke Feb 9 1642

[3]

[Addressed]

For the Lady Grenvile
at Stowe
these

Early in February the miscellaneous and irregular forces, which made up the Parliamentarian Army of Devonshire, met at Totnes, and, being raw and undisciplined, a few days were spent in drilling and organizing them. On Monday, February 20th, the whole force moved to Kingsbridge, where a council of war was held, and a party was detailed " to march to a place called Huttonbridge to make good a passage " This bridge, which is probably identical with the bridge at Aveton Giffard, was distant about three miles from Kingsbridge, and nearly

half-way on the direct road to Modbury. To secure this, which
was the only practicable passage, was a matter of strategic
importance. It was here the Royalists had at first intended
to dispute the advance of their opponents Mr. William Lane,
Rector of Aveton Giffard, Mr. Champernowne, and other
Royalist gentlemen had begun to build a fort on a hill, part of
the glebe of Aveton, commanding the bridge, but there had
been no time to finish it. The disposition of the Royalist forces
about Plymouth at this time is learnt from the following
highly interesting letter written from Plympton by Sir Bevill
to his wife on the 20th of February, the same day on which
the Parliamentarians seized the bridge at Aveton Giffard .—

SIR BEVILL GRANVILLE TO HIS WIFE

My Deare Love
Y^r great care & good affection, as they are very remarkable, so they
deserve my best thankes, & I could wish that the subject wch you bestowe
them upon, could better requite you I shall returne y^r messenger wth but
little certainty concerning our present condition Our Army lies still in
severall quarters S^r Ra Hopton wth my lo Mohun, is upon the north side
of Plimouth wth two Regim^{ts} Collo Asbourn S^r Jo Berk . & I, are on the
east side wth two Regim^{ts} & S^r Ni Slan . wth Jack Trevan & then two
Regim^{ts} were sent the last weeke to Modbury to possesse that quarter before
the enimy came, being the richest part of this countrey, whence most of our
provision & victualls does come, & if it were taken from us we might be
starv'd in our quarters Modbery lyes 6 miles to the Eastward of us, & now
the Enimy wth all the power y^t they can gather, of those that we disperst at
Okeham & Chag & other ayd advanc'd wthin two mile of at
Modbu they are many thousand as the report goes, & we are like to have
speedy worke We have sent more ayde to them both of horse and foote :
god speed us well Plimouth is still supplied wth men & all sorts of provision
by sea, wch we canot hinder, & therfore for my part I see no hope of taking
it So now the most danger that hangs over the K'gs side is in these parts,
for he hath had great successe in those parts where he is Cissister w^{ch}
prince Rupert tooke, hath drawne in all Glocestershire The Citties of
Glocester & Bristoll do offer to render themselves wthout Force, & they are
places of great importance The Earle of Newcastle hath given the Parl^{ts} power
a great defeate in Yorkshire The Queene is coming wth good Ayde to the
K'g The Parl did attempt to force severall Quarters where the K'gs Army
lay, & were beaten off wth great losse to themselves in all places We
have advertizm' that some ayde is cominge from his Matie to us, but it is so
slowe as we shall need it before we see it but gods will be done , I am
satisfied I canot expire in a better cause I have given some directions to
Jack for his study, pray cause him to putt them in execution, & to make some
exercize in verse or prose every day Intreat my Co . Bar Geal
to take a little paines [wth] him I have releas'd the Prisoners that Bar
Geal wrote for Lett Cap · Stanb know it is all one to me whither he
goe by Byd or Pads so he make haste
& now to conclude I beseech you take care of y^r health , I have nothing
so much in my prayers Y^r Phisition Jennings is turnd a Traytor wth the

rest, wherby he hath lost my love, & I am doubtfull to trust you wth him Present my humble duety & thanks to y^r Moth^r, & I beseech god to blesse ye young People   I rest

                                    Y^r owne ever

Plimp · Feb 20 1642   BEVILL GRENVILE
            [3]
     My new cap is a little to straight
I know not what forme of a Certificate
it is that Jo Geal desires, but if he will
send it to me drawne, I will gett it sign'd
[Addressed]   To my best Frend
            the Lady Grace Grenvile.   these

The plan of the Parliamentary leaders was to attack the Royalists occupying Modbury by a force sallying out of Plymouth at the same time that the main body, advancing from Kingsbridge, assailed them on the other side   But the Plymouth contingent were slow in advancing, and the two thousand Royalists—the victors of Bradock Down—held the strong defensive position on Stolhford Hill against the eight thousand Devonshire Parliamentarians (half of whom were, however, a rudely armed[1] and undisciplined mob) for some hours   Driven at last from this position, and attacked at the same time by the fresh arrivals from Plymouth on their flank, the Royalists seem to have retreated fighting, field by field and through the streets of Modbury, to the Court House of the Champernowne's, which had been fortified   This they defended during part of the night until compelled to evacuate it.

We find Sir Bevill writing four days afterwards from Tavistock, and saying that they had been "forc'd to retire to Plimpton for want of Amunition, having spent all their stock," and also that they had raised their siege of Plymouth, which he, for his part, had never expected could have been successful, "yet in submission to better judgm^{ts} I gave way." "Your neighbour of Souldon," who was reported killed, was Humphry Prideaux, of Soldon, in Holsworthy parish, who married Honor, daughter of Edmund Fortescue of Fallapitt

SIR BEVILL GRANVILLE TO HIS WIFE.

Deare love

There have been some changes since I wrote last. We have raisd our siege of Plimouth, wch for my part I never expected could have been succesfull, yet in submission to better judgm^{ts} I gave way , & we are now at

---

[1] " Some had sad heavy clubs, some thick quarter staves with iron and steel pikes at the end, others with a pike and a cicle, others with gardeners' rakes with iron teeth, some with very long helved pick-axes, some with hammers, some with sawes instead of swords, and divers other such kind of weapons "

Tavistock, united againe in one boddy The Party of ours wch was at Modbury indur'd a cruell assault for 12 howers against many thousand men, & killd many of them, wth the losse of fewe, & some hurt , but ours at last were forc'd to reture to Plimpton for want of Amunition, having spent all their stock [1] We are still threatned, but I hope gods favour will not forsake us. Y^r Neighbour of Souldon I heare is one of the dead at Modbury, & will not now Plunder y^r countrey if it be true If my soldier Hugh Ching continue sick, pray lett there be care had of him, & lett him not want what you can helpe him Bidd Tom Ansley have speciall care of the busines I have now writt to him Give my duety to y^r Mother , & I beseech god to keepe & blesse you all, & if it be his will to send us a happie meeting,

So prayeth
Y^r faithfull

BEVILL GRENVILE

Tavistock
Feb 25, 1642

[3]

I have sent home some peare grafts, lett them be carefully grafted, some by Brute, & some by Io Skiner I beseech you make Jack to pursue the directions I have given him.

[Outside]

[Addressed]

I did send home some Peare graffs
from Trurroe about Michellmas ,
lett them be carefully graffed also,
& note wch is one & wch the other.
To my best Frend the
Lady Grace Grenvile at
Stow.

The Parliamentarians admitted the loss of only seven men killed and a few prisoners, whilst the Royalists were reported to have left behind them five pieces of artillery, besides about a thousand muskets which they threw away in their flight Their loss is further vaguely stated to have been one hundred killed and twice as many wounded, and more than a hundred prisoners (*Perfect Diurnall*, Feb. 20-27, and Feb 27—March 6, 1642-3 , *King's Pamphlets*, B M. small fo's, vol vii). One of the accounts satirically states that " fifteen hundred fled, many of them being Cornish hullers (wrestlers) and nimble of foot." Luckily we have Sir Bevill's own contradiction of these figures, contained in another letter to his wife.

SIR BEVILL GRANVILLE TO HIS WIFE

Dearest

I shall write to you without delay having a little Alarme at this instant, and so we had last night wch kept me up late Our losse at Mod was little , the enemie's great We had not 10 men slaine , the enemies about 300 , some say 500, and they retreated safe to us in despite of them. I know not what course we shall hould herafter but you shall heare as soon as I can Tell my cos Geo Cary I give him great thanks for his favor to Jack wch I

---

[1] This want was partly replenished, according to the *Mercurius Aulicus*, by the seizure of a ship at Falmouth laden with powder, bullets, and all sorts of ammunition

entreate him to continue The boy doth amend his hand a little, let him continue to do so and he shall be the better for it There is yet no ayde coming to us, but I hope there will be, tho' I feare too late

Yis intirely
B G

Feb 26 1642

To my best Frend

the Lady Grace Grenvill /

these.

As Sir Bevill has told us in his letter to Lady Grace of February 25, while the fight at Modbury was going on, the garrison at Plymouth had made a vigorous sortie with horse and foot, and fallen upon the works of the besiegers, forcing the Royalists to retire out of them, and the siege of Plymouth was consequently raised. The Earl of Stamford then combined his forces and followed Hopton to Tavistock, where a parley took place, and a treaty or arrangement was made between the gentlemen of Devon and Cornwall that for twenty days (until midnight of the 22nd of April) no actual warfare should occur in the two counties [1] It was hoped that in the interim general terms of peace between the King and the Parliament might be settled, for negotiations were being opened with Charles at Oxford at this very time It is clear, however, that neither party had much confidence in such a result, and each side made preparation accordingly Sir Bevill, writing from Launceston the 9th of March, alludes both to the treaty and to the suspicions he had of its durability

SIR BEVILL GRANVILLE TO HIS WIFE

Dearest

If you accompt yrselfe fallen from any happiness by the want of me, I have a thousand time more reason to be miserable when I am devided from you Pray be of comfort however things goe, and I beseech God to enable me to deserve yr love For newes, there is a cessation agreed on for 20 daies, from whence for my part I looke but for knavery We heare that the Queene is landed in the north, for whose guard the King hath sent those forces wch should have come to us, whereby we are prevented awhile longer, so one thing or other hinders us still, but I hope God will not forsake us The force wch was at Tavistock is all disbanded Enquire whither my Regmt maye be billetted in good houses of the hundred of Stratt during this cessation, and then I will be nearer home Pray kepe me some Pearmains

Yis

B   .. ...

Lanc· Mar 9   For the Lady Greville
1642.   these /

---

[1] To make this truce binding "nine of the principall gentlemen of each county not onely took their corporall oathes, but received the sacrament" (*Mercurius Aulicus* 13 March, 1643)

Queen Henrietta Maria had been in Holland throwing herself with characteristic ardour into the task of raising money with which to purchase arms and of inducing officers and soldiers of English birth to forsake the Dutch service for that of their native Prince. She had also pawned the Crown jewels. She landed at Bridlington Quay on the 22nd of February, and was conducted by Lord Newcastle to York, where she awaited an opportunity of rejoining the King with safety. The "Pear-mains" which Sir Bevill was anxious should be kept for him were a particular sort of apple.

While Sir Bevill's troops lay at Launceston the church was apparently used as barracks, and several entries of payments for firewood and candles for use in these unusual quarters occur in the accounts of the borough, *e.g.*, Kingdon, the Constable, records that on the 28th of February " in came Sr Bevell Grinfild and that night they had for the gard 3 seame wood and 2 li candells." March 1st the Mayor "p^d for cairing a warrant to Lawhitton at 8 of the clocke at night for raising the 'posse cometates'" March 5th, "Being commanded to send away a warrent of the 'posse commitatis' at midnight," he was allowed 6d for his service. March 6th, Mr Kingdon states "when Sr Bevell came backe from Stratton they had that night by reason of the great company 4 seam wood and 2½ li candells for the gard." March 8th, he "sent Sr Bevell Grinfild p^r Mr. Mayor's order, a pottell sacke 2^s 4^d " and " p^d for a lanteron for the gard 2^s," etc., etc.

Whether truly or not, the Royalists were accused of treacherously breaking the treaty by plotting to seize and fire the town of Bideford, with the object of opening a way for some supplies expected from Wales. The following are some particulars of the story as told in one of the weekly news-sheets :—

" From Excester in Devonshire they write, that the Treaty betweene the gentry of Cornewall and Devon is continued for ten days longer from Tuesday last untill Friday next, and in the mean while the Toune of Beddiford in the North part of the County of Devon should have been betrayed and delivered up to Sir Ralph Hopton in this manner. Sir Bevil Greenvill sent some of his soldiers into the toune like countrimen, one after one, who confederated themselves with some of the malevolent Townsmen, to surprise the Watch of the Towne and to cut their throates in a certaine night, and then an Alarm sho^d have been given by them as a call to the rest of Sir B. G's Regiment, which sh^d have attended neere to the Toune to have come in to their aide

and finished the exploit · but it pleased God in his mercifull
providence to discover the Treachery thus; One of the Conspirators being a Tounsman hapned to be drunke the afternoon
before that dismall night, and in his drunkenesse openly babbled
out what feates he and the rest of his Complices meant to
performe the night following, which being taken hold of and
thoroughly examined, the Conspiracie was discovered and all
the Conspirators were instantly apprehended together with all
Sir B G's souldiers that were then in the Toune, and their
persons secured and committed to safe custody to receive con-
dign punishment according to their demerits" ("Certain
Information," etc, April 10-17, 1643 "King's Pamphlets,"
B.M., small 4tos., vol. cii.)

The plot, as Mr Cotton observes, was probably only one of
the numerous scares of the period But whatever may have
been the truth about it, some alarm was very likely to have
arisen from the incident which was thus reported—"that a
small bark was taken coming from Wales to assist Hopton in
the West Countries, set out by the Earl of Worcester, laden
with store of money and plate, and five or six hundred arms
covered three feet deep with coals . . that the bark was
brought into Barnstaple, and that three companies were sent
from Exeter thither to unlade the same and bring the arms
and money to Exeter" (Certain Speciall and Remarkable
Passages, etc, April 20-27, 1643, King's Pamphlets B M,
vol civ.)

The Treaty and Cessation of Arms expired on Saturday,
April 22nd, and "now they prepare for the warre on both sides,
for which purpose the Inhabitants of Barnestable and Beddiford
had sent 5,000 Foote and 9 Troopes of Horse to Holsworthy   .
to fall into Cornwall, which forces were remanded from thence
again with much discontent" (Certaine Information etc,
April 24-May 1, 1643, ibid vol. cv)

On the eve of the expiration of the Treaty, the Earl of
Stamford being laid up with the gout at Exeter, Sergeant-Major-
General Chudleigh (a younger son of Sir George Chudleigh,
Bart of Ashton and grandson of John Chudleigh the navigator.)
took the command and occupied an entrenched position at
Okehampton, with the purpose it may be assumed, of preventing
the advance of the Cornish army, which was then quartered at
Launceston. On the 22nd he occupied Lifton, and on the
morning of Sunday the 23rd, the Parliamentarians, being in
number about 1700 Horse and Foot, and having with them a
few pieces of Artillery, advanced to Polston Bridge, which

h²

crosses the Tamar about two miles from Launceston. Captain Drake's troop drove in an outpost of the Royalists which held the bridge, and the Parliamentarians, preceded by their pioneers, made their way through the fields towards the town, beating out "like sheep" it is stated, the Royalist musketeers who lined the hedges. The Cornish headquarters had received an "alarum" in the night, but the Royalist troops were scattered and evidently unprepared for this prompt resumption of hostilities Sir Ralph Hopton had constructed a "kind of fort" on Windmill Hill, and old beacon station which flanked the eastern front of the town of Launceston. The fight, which began about ten o'clock, lasted the greater part of the day, Chudleigh meeting with a more vigorous resistance than he expected, and at last his Foot were forced to give ground, he having no oppurtunity of bringing on his Horse to assist them by reason of the many hedges. Sir Ralph's forces, seeing them shrink, stoutly pushed on their success and sent a Regiment of Foot and three Troops of Horse, to wheel about and fall on their rear and re-take Polston Bridge behind them But this was prevented by the coming in of some broken companies of Colonel Meyrick's Regiment from Plymouth under the command of Lieutenant-Colonel Calmady, and 100 of Colonel Northcote's Regiment under the command of Sergeant-Major Fitch, who secured the bridge, so that Chudleigh was able to effect his retreat, and to bring off his ordnance, ammunition and carriages without any extraordinary loss (*cf* Rushworth's "Historical Collections," pt III., vol ii, pp 267,8). That night Chudleigh lay at Lifton, and the next day marched to Okehampton, "where they lay as in Garison"

On the morning of the 25th, Chudleigh pushed forward a party of horse to Bridestowe, a village six miles distant on the Launceston road, to watch the enemy's movements They returned with the intelligence that the whole body of the enemy was advancing The disorganization of Chudleigh's force had meanwhile begun Many men had already "gone away disheartened," and others had gone on the well-understood errand of bringing the deserters back His transport service had also broken down; carriages had been dismissed as not able to serve longer, and no new supply of horses and "plowes" (teams of oxen) had come in His artillery was consequently immovable. His force within his entrenchment was reduced to about one thousand foot and sixty horse To retreat or to stand still seemed equally disastrous, and to involve the loss of "their artillery, ammunition, themselves, and by probable consequence, the whole county " (*Cf.* " Exploits Discovered," etc , " King's Pamphlets," B M , small 4tos , vol cv.) The Royalists, on the other hand, were reported to be drawn out on Sourton Down to the estimated number of 500 horse and dragoons, and between 400 and 500 Foot

The road from Launceston, almost immediately after leaving Bridestowe, was for two miles an open trackway over Sourton Down, a strip of outlying moorland on the flank of Dartmoor, from which it is separated only by the wild and picturesque valley of the West Okement river   Here, according to the contemporary tracts and news-sheets of the day, Major-General Chudleigh and Captain Thomas Drake (the second son of Sir Francis Drake, the first Baronet of Buckland Abbey, and a grand-nephew of the great Admiral) made a brilliant charge with their sixty horse, and completely routed the Royalist troops, who were seized with a sudden panic, and drove them from the bleak heights of Sourton Down.   A violent thunderstorm with vivid lightning occurred during the battle, and the Puritans reported that " the Lord sent Fire from heaven so that the Cavaliers powder in their bandaliers, flasks and muskets, took fire, by which means they hurt and slew each other to the wonder and amazement of the Parliament's Forces," and it is added that this mystic fire " so lamentably scorched and burnt many of their bodies that they sent for 12 chysurgions from Launceston to cure them " (*cf.* "Joyful Newes from Plimouth," published in London 18 May 1643, and " Rushworth,' iii , vol. ii., p. 268) The fight is described in the news-sheets as a " most miraculous and happy victory," " a great Deliverance and a wonderful victory," " such as hath not hap'ned since this warr began, nor may be paralleled by the stories of many ages past , the memory whereof most worthily deserves to be engraven on a memorable pillar or high towring Pyramides."

The Royalist song-writers were not slow to satirize this gust of Puritan triumph.   The following are the first two verses of a ballad entitled, " A Western Wonder," and attributed to Sir John Denham · - ·

> " Do you not know, not a fortnight ago
>   How they bragged of a Western Wonder ?
> When a hundred and ten slew five thousand men
>   With the help of lightning and thunder
>
> There Hopton was slain, again and again,
>   Or else my author did lie ,
> With a new thanksgiving for the dead who are living
>   To God and his servant Chidleigh."

Hopton was erroneously reported, and not for the first time, to have been killed.

The moral effect of this defeat on the Cornish army was not less remarkable than the physical   Lord Clarendon, who passes over the action itself with the briefest possible notice, admits, however, that it " struck a great terror into " the Royalists, and " disordered them more than they were at any time "

Encouraged by Chudleigh's success on Sourton Down, the Earl of Stamford, having recovered from his gout, placed himself at the head of an army, and on the 11th of May set out from Exeter for the rendezvous of the Parliamentary army of Devonshire at Okehampton.   When brought together these undoubtedly heterogenous forces, (according to credible information, derived, it is said, from its own officers) consisted of 1,400 horse and dragoons and 5,400 foot " by the poll "   These were mostly the militia levies which the Parliamentary Committee, during the preceding months, had been actively organizing.   A train of artillery, consisting of thirteen brass guns and a mortar-piece, was attached to the force

The Royalists, on the other hand, had less than half the number, and so destitute were they of provisions, that the best officers had but a biscuit a day, and with only a handful of powder for the whole force   They, nevertheless, marched out of Launceston "with a resolution," as Lord Clarendon says, " to fight with the enemy upon every disadvantage of place or number'

The Parliamentary troops divided.   Sir George Chudleigh (father of the Major-General) was detached with 1,200 of the Horse to march to Bodmin by a route not mentioned, but evidently by the Tavistock road, which had been practically cleared of the enemy by James Chudleigh's victory   The meaning of this movement or diversion, if it may be so called, is not obvious ; and we learn only through Royalist sources, that its object was to overawe the Sheriff of Cornwall, and prevent further Royalist levies from being made, and also to cut off the anticipated retreat of Hopton's army.   The destination of the remainder of the Parliamentary forces, was Stratton , where they eventually took up a strong position on a hill within a mile of that town.   The horse, not exceeding by all accounts two hundred, appears to have already reached Stratton on the 12th of May (*cf* " Perfect Diurnall," etc , 15-22 May, 1643. " King's Pamphlets," vol. ix), and the foot probably followed on the 13th and 14th.   The Royalists approached Stratton on the

morning of the 16th   They had the advantage of having
amongst them one to whom every inch of ground must have
been perfectly familiar   But a few miles to the north, on the
bleak hill-side above the waves of the Atlantic, lay Stowe, and
it would have been strange if, on this day of peril, the ordering
of the fight had not fallen into Sir Bevill's Granville's hands
" The number of foot was about two thousand four hundred,
which they divided into four parts, and agreed on their several
provinces   The first was commanded by the Lord Mohun and
Sir Ralph Hopton, who undertook to assault the camp on the
south side   Next to them, on the left hand, Sir John Berkeley
and Sir Bevill Granville were to force their way.   Sir Nicholas
Slanning and Colonel Trevenion were to assault the north side ;
and on the (their ?) left hand Colonel Thomas Basset, who was
Major-General of their foot, and Colonel William Godolphin
were to advance with their party ; each party having two pieces
of cannon to dispose as they found necessary , Colonel John
Digby, commanding the horse and dragoons, being about five
hundred, stood upon a sandy common which had a way to the
camp, to take any advantage he could on the enemy, if they
charged ; otherwise to be firm as a reserve." (Clarendon,
p 424 a.)

For some hours (from 5 a m to 3 p m) every effort was in
vain against superiority of numbers and superiority of position
At three in the afternoon word was brought to the commanders
that their scanty stock of powder was almost exhausted   A
retreat under such circumstances would have been fatal, and the
word was given that a supreme effort must be made   Trusting
to pike and sword alone, the lithe Cornishmen pressed onwards
and upwards   Their silent march seems to have struck their
opponents with a sense of power   The defence grew feeble, and
on the easier western slope, where Granville fought, and on the
northern, on which Sir John Berkeley led the attack, the outer
edge of the plateau was first gained   Immediately the handful
of horse, which had remained with Stamford, turned and fled.
In vain Chudleigh, now second in command, rallied the foot for
a desperate charge. For a moment he seemed to make an
impression on the approaching foe, but he incautiously pressed
too far in advance and was surrounded and captured   His men,
left without a commander, at once gave way and retreated to
the further end of the plateau   By this time the other two
Royalist detachments, finding resistance slackening, had made
their way up, and the victorious commanders embraced one
another on the hard-won hill-top, thanking God for a success,

for which at one time they had hardly ventured to hope. It was no time to prolong their rejoicings, as the enemy, demoralized, as they were still clung to their heights Seizing the cannon which had been abandoned in the earth-works, the Royalist commanders turned them upon Stamford's cowed followers. The frightened men threw down their arms and fled, Stamford himself, if rumour did not speak falsely, having already set the example From that day the spot, on which the wealthy Earl demonstrated his signal incompetence as a leader of men, has been known as " Stamford Hill "

Such is Gardiner's account of the battle written after personal observation of the ground. There are two graphic historical accounts of it which have come down to us, one by Lord Clarendon and the other by Dr. Thomas Fuller, the quaint and facetious author of the "Worthies of England." Both accounts, from certain internal resemblances which they bear to each other, appear to have been derived from the same source ; and Fuller, who was afterwards chaplain to Sir Ralph Hopton, states that he obtained his information from a paper revised by Hopton himself We may be sure, therefore, that the Royalist commander was the common authority of both writers

At one period of the battle Chudleigh, with a body of pikemen, charged Sir Bevill's regiment and threw it into disorder, Sir Bevill being " in person overthrown," and, as he tells his wife, " bruised " The disaster was retrieved by Sir John Berkeley leading the musketeers, who flanked Sir Bevill's pikemen on each side.

The Royalists admitted the loss of but very few men and of no considerable officer According to the same authority about three hundred of the Parliamentarians were killed on the field, seventeen hundred were taken prisoners,[1] and all their cannon, seventy barrels of gunpowder, and a large magazine of biscuit and other provisions fell into the hands of the captors, " which was as seasonable a blessing as the victory to those who for three or four days before had suffered great want of food as well as sleep, and were equally tired with duty and hunger "

To the Rev Henry Wilson, Rector of Buckland Filleigh, who attended as chaplain of the army and waited on Sir Bevill to congratulate him after the victory, the soldier piously and politely replied that it was more owing to the parson's good prayers than to anything else. (*cf* Walker's " Sufferings of the Clergy," pt ii, p. 392).

Sir Bevill's local celebrity and the fame of his chivalric

---

[1] Including Chudleigh and thirty other officers

bravery earned him a prominent place in connection with this victory. It has not been given to every military hero to fight a pitched battle in the parish next to his own ; still, we are not, as Dr Gardiner observes, to attribute the prominence given him in the inscription on a tablet—which formerly marked the battle field, but is now affixed to the wall of the Tree Inn at Stratton—as entirely due to local or family feeling.—

IN THIS PLACE
Y^E ARMY OF Y^E REBELLS VNDER Y^E COMMAND
OF Y^E EARL OF STAMFORD RECEIVED A SIGNAL OVER
THROW BY Y^E VALOVR OF SIR BEVILL GRENVILLE AND
Y^E CORNISH ARMY ON TUESDAY Y^E 16th of MAY 1643

One man connected with this battle, whose name must not be omitted, was Antony Payne, Sir Bevill's henchman He was a remarkable man in many ways Born in the Granville Manor House at Stratton, he is said to have measured seven feet without his shoes, when, at the age of twenty-one, he was taken into the establishment at Stowe. He afterwards added two more inches to his height After the battle of Stamford Hill Sir Bevill returned for the night to Stowe, but his gaint remained with some other soldiers to bury the dead. He had caused trenches to be dug to hold ten bodies side by side, and in these trenches he and his followers deposited the slain On one occasion they had lain nine corpses in their places, and Payne was bringing another tucked under his arm, when all at once (so the story goes) the supposed dead man began to kick and plead for life. " Surely you won't bury me, Mr. Payne, before I am dead ? " " I tell thee, man,' was the grim reply, " our trench was dug for ten and there's nine in it already, thou must take thy place " " But I be'ant dead, I say I have'nt done living yet—be massyful, Mr. Payne—don't ye hurry a poor fellow into the earth before his time " " I won't hurry thee, thou can'st die at thy leisure," was the reply. Payne's purpose was, however, kinder than his speech. He carried the suppliant to his own cottage, and left him to the charge of his wife. The man lived, and his descendants are among the principal inhabitants of Stratton at this day." (Hawker's " Footprints of Former Men in Cornwall ")

Another story told of him is that one Christmas Eve the fire languished in the hall at Stowe A boy with an ass had been sent to the woods for logs, but had loitered on his way. Lady Grace lost patience. Then Antony started in quest of the dilatory lad, and re-entered the hall shortly after, bearing the

loaded animal on his back.   He threw down his burden at the
hearth-side shouting, "Ass and fardel, ass and fardel, for my
lady's yule."   On another occasion he rode into Stratton with
Sir Bevill   An uproar proceeded from the little inn-yard.   Sir
Bevill bade the giant find out what was the cause of the
disturbance   Antony speedily returned with a man under each
arm, whom he had arrested in the act of fighting   "Here are
the kittens," said the giant, and he held them under his arm
while his master chastised them with his riding whip   At the
Tree Inn, Stratton (which is said to have been the headquarters
of the Royalists on the night preceding the battle), the hole in
the ceiling is still shown, through which years afterwards the
corpse of poor Antony was removed from the room in which he
died, his coffin being too large to be taken out of the window or
down the stairs in the usual way [1]   At the Restoration of
Charles II, Antony was made Halberdier of the Guns at
Plymouth Citadel, and Sir Godfrey Kneller was commissioned
by the King to paint his portrait   It was engraved as a frontis
piece to the first volume of Gilbert's "History of Cornwall,"
and the picture itself was afterwards sold for £800

> His sword was made to match his size
> As Roundheads did remember,
> And when it swung 'twas like the whirl
> Of windmills in September —*Stokes*

The King was not unmindful of the gallant Sir Bevill's
share in the fight, as will be seen from "His Majestie's Letter
to Sir Bevill Granvill after the great victory obtained over the
Rebells at the Battle of Stratton "—

To our Right Trusty and Well-beloved Sir Bevill Granvill at
  our Army in Cornwall
    Charles R

Right Trusty and Well-beloved   Wee greet you well   Wee have seen your
Letter to Endymion Porter Our Servant   But your whole conduct of Our
Affairs in the West doth speak your Zeal to Our Service and the Public Good
in so full a Measure as Wee rest abundantly satisfy'd with the Testimony
thereof   Your labours and your Expenses Wee are graciously Sensible of, and
Our Royall Care hath been to ease you in all that Wee could   What hath
fallen short of our Princely Purposes and your Expections Wee know you will
attribute to the great malignity of the Rebellion   Wee had and have here to
wrestle withall   And Wee know well how effectually a diversion of that
mischievous strength you have made from Us at your own hazzards   Wee
assure you Wee have all tender sense of the hardness you have endured and
the state wherein you stand   Wee shall not fail to procure you what speedy
relief may be   In the mean space Wee send you Our most hearty thanks for

---

[1] The Stratton Register records his burial as having taken place on 13th July, 1691

some encouragement and assurances on the word of a Gracious Prince that (God enabling us) Wee shall so reflect upon your faithfull Services as you and yours shall have cause to acknowledge Our Bounty and Favours And so Wee bid you heartily farewell

Given at Our Court at Oxford the 24th May 164¾

The following letter from Sir Bevill to Lady Grace was written about a week after the battle, and refers to his "bruise" Lady Granville and the children had evidently gone to stay with the Arundells of Trerice, their cousins, when the opposing armies were reported to be advancing towards Stowe —

SIR BEVILL GRANVILLE TO HIS WIFE

Deare Love

I have rec severall lrs from you since I wrote last, & in all do see yr excellent affection & mine owne obligation   god reward you if I cañot   you are doubtfull lest my bruise stick by me, I thanke you, but I hope it is preetily over, though I am something sore & did spitt bloud two daies, & bledd at nose much   I had no Slatt, neither I do now need it I think, but I did wish I had had some at that tune   you may safely returne to Stow, & I am perswaded you would have had no hurt if you had staid   our Army is at Okeham & what farther will become of us I know not, we are sure of yr good prayers as you are of myne who will ever remaine

Yrs constantly

Okehampton   BEVILL GRENVILE.
May-24-1643

Present my ducty to yr mother & my best service to my noble cosens of Trerise

(Superscription)
To my best frend the
Lady Grace Grenvile
these

By this decisive victory not only was Cornwall cleared of the enemy and secured for the King, but the whole of Devon also, with the exception of Bideford and Barnstaple in the north, and Plymouth, Dartmouth, and Exeter in the south, fell into the hands of the Royalists. The "fitters of that broken army," to borrow the language of Bruno Ryves in his *Mercurius Rusticus*, streamed back over Devonshire   Most of the militiamen probably found shelter in the above-named garrison towns, others returned to their homes ; but they were never again organized as a field force. The Earl of Stamford retreated by Barnstaple to Exeter, attended, it may be presumed, by the remnant of his body guard. Sir William Waller, Sir Bevill's former friend, with a force of two thousand horse and dragoons detached from the Parliamentary army, was ordered by the Earl of Essex to proceed at once from Bristol " with all haste to

L²

Devonshire" to suppress the Royalists, who, on the other hand, were advised by an express from Oxford of the advance of Prince Maurice and the Marquess of Hertford into Somersetshire and directed to co-operate with them

Leaving a small detachment in the neighbourhood of Plymouth for the protection of Cornwall, Sir Ralph Hopton reached Chard about the middle of June with about 3,000 foot, 500 horse, 300 dragoons and four or five field pieces, and met Prince Maurice, whose forces were somewhat less in number But " how small so ever the Marquess's party was in numbers, it was supplied with all the General Officers of a Royal Army ; viz , a General, a Lieutenant General, General of the Horse, General of the Ordnance, Major General of Horse, another of foot, without keeping suitable command for those who had done all that was passed, and were to be principally relied on for what was to come so that the chief officers of the Cornish army, by joining with a much less party than themselves, were at best in the condition of Private Colonels Yet the same public thoughts still so absolutely prevailed with them that they quieted all murmurings and emulations among inferior officers and common soldiers, and were with equal candour and estimation valued by the Prince and Marquess, who bethought themselves of all expedients which might prevent future misunderstanding." (Lord Clarendon). Clarendon also praises the Cornish contingent for their discipline and conduct " The chief commanders of the Cornish army," he says, " had restrained their soldiers from all manner of licence, obliging them to frequent acts of devotion , insomuch that the fame of their religion and discipline was no less than of their courage "

The combined troops then advanced from Chard through Taunton and Bridgwater to Wells, where they fell upon the advanced guard of Waller's forces, which they routed and drove back upon Bath. A junction with the King s troops at Oxford had been the intention of the Royalists, but by taking post on Lansdowne Hill, outside Bath, Sir William Waller sought to prevent it. When the morning of the 5th of July dawned the Royalists perceived that Waller still blocked the way The road by which Hopton hoped to pass was for some three miles the main road from Chippenham to Bristol. At Tog Hill another road branches off to the left, dips steeply down into a valley, and then ascends with a winding course on the opposite side till it reaches the north-western end of Lansdowne The height once gained a level road runs along the ridge till the ground falls sharply down to Bath. If the Royalist army could gain possession of this ridge all else would be comparatively easy. Essex was lying in hopeless inactivity at Aylesbury, and from him Waller had no aid to expect   As the Royalists pushed on through Cold Ashton to Tog Hill they could see that Waller intended to contest any attempt to scale the heights of Lans-downe   His cannon were planted behind a breastwork, and horse and foot were ranged so as to command every available approach   As he remained immovable, when Hertford and Hopton drew up their forces at Tog Hill, the order to retreat was given.   The sight of the retiring enemy was too much for Waller to endure   Leaving his infantry at their posts, he sent his horse and dragoons in pursuit   Amongst them was a newly-formed regiment of London cavalry, under Sir Arthur Hazle-rigg, known popularly as "the Lobsters,' from the complete armour in which they were encased on back and breast   At Cold Ashton they found the enemy halted.   The charge of "the Lobsters" was successful for a time, but in the end superior numbers told, and the Parliamentary horse was driven back to its old position on the edge of Lansdowne   The victors followed as far as Tog Hill, and drew up to examine the position once more.   To descend into the valley and to climb the guarded heights was a formidable task, but the sight of the enemy posted in apparent security only exasperated the Cornish-men   "Let us fetch off those cannons," they cried to their officers.   The officers assented, and the nimble feet which had stormed the heights of Stratton were once more in motion, working their way upwards through woods on either side, in which the enemy had placed musketeers to hold the ground   The horse advancing along the road was less fortunate.   It was charged and driven back   Then Sir Bevill, who was stationed with his regiment at Tog Hill, gave the word to advance and descended into the valley.   Placing the pikemen in the centre, his horse in the open ground to the right, and his musketeers on the left, he steadily pushed on.   It is possible that Sir Bevill was protected by the very steepness of the ascent, and that Waller's cannon could not be sufficiently depressed to strike the ascending force.   The bend of the road to the right was un-doubtedly in his favour, as it gave him the shelter of a stone wall running almost at right angles to the enemies fire   It was only on approaching the top that the road sweeping round once more made straight for Waller's position.   Then came the real struggle of the day.   Five times did the Parliamentary cavalry charge with all the advantage of the slope, and five times it charged in vain   At last the whole Royalist force surged over

Waller's breastworks   The moment of victory was also the moment of sorrow   Of the 2,000 horsemen which had marched out of their quarters in the morning, 600 only were still in the saddle when the day was gained.   The Cornishmen were saddened by the fall of their beloved leader, Sir Bevill Granville, struck down in the thick of the fight

The account of his death is given more in detail in Gilbert's "History of Cornwall"   It appears that "after gaining the brow of the hill in the third charge, while Sir Bevill was rallying his horse, he received, among other wounds, a blow on the head with a pole-axe, which put a glorious end to his career of honour"   He did not, however, die on the field of battle, but was removed to Cold Ashton Parsonage, some four or five miles to the north where he expired the following day (6th of July, 1643)   Sir John Hinton, M D , in his memorial to Charles II , writes thus —

' The bloody and tedious battle of Lansdowne lasted from break of day till very late at night, when Sir Bevill Grenvile (father to the now Earle of Bathe), bravely behaving himself, was killed at the head of his stand of Pikes, and in his extremity I was the last man that had him by the hand before he dyed "

The following touching letter from Antony Payne, Sir Bevill's henchman, conveying the sad news of his master's death to Lady Grace, is said to have been found in an old chest in the farmhouse at Stowe —

ANTONY PAYNE TO LADY GRACE GRANVILLE

Honored Madam,

Ill news flieth apace   The heavy tidings no doubt have already travelled to Stow that we have lost our blessed Master by the enemy's advantage   You must not, dear Lady, grieve too much for your noble spouse   You know, as we all believe, that his soul was in heaven before his bones were cold   He fell, as he did often tell us he wished to die, in the great Stewart cause, for his country and his King.   He delivered to me his last commands and with such tender words for you and for his children as are not to be set down with my poor pen, but must come to your ears upon my hearts best breath   Master John, when I mounted him upon his fathers horse, rode him into the war like a young prince as he is , and our men followed him with then swords drawn and with tears in then eyes   They did say they would kill a rebel for every hair of Sir Bevills beard   But I bade them remember then good master's word when he wiped his sword after Stamford's fight . how he said, when then cry was "Stab and slay," "Halt men, God will avenge "—I am coming down with the mournfullest load than ever a poor servant did bear to bring the great heart that is cold to Kilkhampton vault   O ! my lady how shall I ever brook your weeping face ?   But I will be trothful to the living and to the Dead

These—honoured Madam
from thy saddest truest servant
ANTONY PAYNE

Never was man more universally or deservedly beloved than Sir Bevil, and though, during those times of civil fury and discord, each party seemed willing to confine all merit to themselves, yet complete justice was done to his memory, even by Parliamentary writers, and it is said that his untimely death was as bitterly lamented by the Parliamentary troops as it was by his own followers.

The following beautifully-expressed letter from Sir John Trelawney to poor Lady Grace on the death of Sir Bevill has been preserved amongst the Halswell MSS It will be remembered that Sir John had written to Sir Bevill before the first Scotch expedition, urging him, for the sake of his wife and children, not to embark in so perilous an enterprise (see page 212).

SIR JOHN TRELAWNY BARONET TO LADY GRACE GRANVILLE

Honourable Lady,

How cann I containe my selfe? or longer conceale my sorrow for ye Death of yt Excellent man yt most deare Husband, & my noble Friende? Bee pleased wth yr wisedome to consider of the Events of Warr, which is seldome or neuer constant, but as full of Mutability, as hazard And seeing it hath pleased God to take him from yr La{pp} yet this may something appease yr greate fluxe of Teares, That hee died an Honorable Death, wch all Enemies will Envy, fighting with Invincible Valour & Loyalty, ye Battle ouercome his God, his King & Country A greater Honour then this, noe man liuing cann enjoy But God hath cal'd him vnto himselfe, to Crowne him (I doubt not) with Immortall Glory for his noble Constancye in this Blessed Cause. It is to true (most noble lady) tht God hath made you drincke of a bitter Cupp, yet if you please to submitt vnto his Deuine Will & Pleasure by kissing his Rodd Patiently, God (noe doubt) hath a staff of Consolation for to comfort you in this greate Affliction & Tryall Hee will wipe yt Eies, drie up the flowing springe of yr Teares, & make yr Bedd easye, And by yr Patience ouercome Gods Justice, by his retourning Mercie Maddam, hee is gonne his Journey but a little before vs, we must March after when it shall please God, for your La{pp} knowes yt none fall without his Prouidence wch is as greate in the thickest showre of Bulletts, as in ye Bedd I beseeche you (deare Lady) to pardon this my Trouble, & Boldnes, And ye God of Heauen bless you, & comfort you, & all my Noble Coseus in this yr greate visitation which shalbee the vnfayned Prayers of Him that is

Most noble Lady
Your Ladishipps Honorer, & humble Servant
JOHN TRELAWNY.

Trelawne 20 July. 1643

(Superscription)
To my Honorable Lady the
Lady Grenvile att Stow these
humbly present

To the King Sir Bevill's death was a cause of deep grief, and he had designed to confer upon him the dignity of an Earl, the

patent for which, together with the letter which the King had
written him after the battle of Stratton, was found in his pocket
after his death   The King's letter, written on white
sarcenet, was naturally prized highly by Sir Bevill since he
had endorsed it with the words ' keep this safe."   It was handed
down as an heirloom, and George Granville Lord Lansdowne gave
it to Sir William Wyndham, Baronet on the 26th of April, 1764,
with the injunction that he should preserve it "in honour of your
and my Grandfather," Sir William Wyndham being the grandson of the Lady Jane Granville, daughter of John, 1st Earl of
Bath, Sir Bevill's eldest son

Sir Bevill's body was brought back to Cornwall, and having
rested one night at Launceston Castle was conveyed the next
day to Kilkhampton, and buried in the church with all honours
the 26th of July, 1643.   He was forty-eight years of age.   His
grandson above-mentioned, George Granville Lord Lansdowne,
erected the fine monument to his memory that still exists in
Kilkhampton Church.   The epitaph runs as follows —

Here lyes all that was mortall of the most noble and truly valiant Sir
Bevill Granville of Stowe in the County of Cornwall, Earl of Carbile, and Lord
of Thorigny and Granville in France and Normandy, descended in a direct line
from Robert[1] second son of ye warlike Rollo, first Duke of Normandy, who after
having obtained divers signall victorys over the Rebells in ye west, was at
length slain with many wounds at the battle of Lansdowne July ye 5th 1643

He was born ye 25th of March 1595 and was deposited with his noble and
heroic ancestors in this Church ye 26th day of July 1643   He married ye
most virtuous Lady, Grace daughter of Sr George Smith of Exeter of ye county
of Devon, by whom he had many sons, eminent for their loyalty, and firm
adherence to ye crown and church, and severall daughters, remarkable examples
of true piety

He was indeed an excellent person, whose activity, interest, and reputation
were ye foundation of what had been done in Cornwall, & his temper & affections so publick, that no accident which happened could make any impression
on him & his example kept others from taking anything ill, or at least seeming
to do so   In a word, a brighter courage & a gentler disposition were never
marryed together to make ye most cheerfull and innocent conversation.

Vid Earl of Clarendon's History of ye Rebellion

[1] 'Robert, second son of ye warlike Rollo, first Duke of Normandy " This is an evident
mistake, which has found its way into several genealogies of the family, e g , when Moreri
published in Paris his " Dictionnaire Historique," Ld Lansdowne led him into the same
blunder by sending him this incorrect statement to insert   Burke, who no doubt copied
from old Peerages. falls into the same error   In an old Peerage date 1714, contemporary with
Lord Lansdowne, the pedigree is thus written —
   " Rollo the first Duke of Normandy had two sons by Gillette daughter of Charles the
Simple, King of France, viz , William the elder, called Longue Epée, and Robert, his second
son, who was the first Earl of Corboil "   This statement is clearly wrong in three respects
First, Rollo never had any children by Gillette   Secondly, Rollo had only one son by
Popeia, viz   William Longue Epee, and one daughter, Gerloc (see page 5)   Thirdly, the
first Earl of Corboil was Hamon (not Robert) son of Osmond, the Dane, whose grand daughter
Germaine, married Manger, the 3rd son of Richard Sans Peur the ancestor of the Granville's,
who became 3rd Earl of Corboil in right of his wife ' (see page 15 .

To the immortall memory of his renowned Grandfather, this monument was erected by ye Right hon^{ble} George Lord Lansdowne, treasurer of ye Household to Queen Ann and one of Her Majesty's most honourable Privy Council &c in the year of our Lord 1714

> " Thus slain thy valiant ancestor did lye,
> When his one Bark a navy did defy,
> When now encompassed round the Victor stood,
> And bathed his Pinnace in his conquering blood,
> Till, all his purple current dried and spent,
> He fell, and made the waves his monument.
> Where shall your next famed Granville's ashes stand ?
> Thy Grandsire's fill the seas, and thou the Land "

This verse is taken from an Elegy " On the death of the Right Valiant Sir Bevyle Grenvyle, Knight, who was slain by the Rebels on Lansdown Hill, near Bath, July 5th, 1643,' by Dr Llewellyn, the Principal of St Mary's Hall, Oxford, which was the tribute of honour with which that University graced his memory Many others sang his praises, including Sir Francis Wortley, Robert Heath, and William Cartwright Of recent years his noble death has thus been recorded by the graceful pen of the late Rev. R S Hawker, Vicar of Morwenstow —

SIR BEVILL—THE GATE SONG OF STOWE.

Arise and away ! for the King and the land,
　Farewell to the couch and the pillow
With spear in the rest, and with rein in the hand,
　Let us rush on the foe like a billow.

Call the hind from the plough and the herd from the fold,
　Bid the wassailer cease from his revel,
And ride for Old Stowe, where the banner's unrolled
　For the cause of King Charles and Sir Bevill

Trevanion is up, and Godolphin is nigh,
　And Harris of Hayne's o'er the river,
From Lundy to Looe " One and All" is the cry,
　And " the King and Sir Bevill for ever '

Ay ! by Tre, Pol and Pen, ye may know Cornishmen
　Mid the names and the nobles of Devon,
But if truth to the King be a signal, why then
　Ye can find out the Granville in heaven

Ride ! ride with red spur ! there is death in delay,
　Tis a race for dear life with the devil,
If dark Cromwell prevail and the King must give way,
　This earth is no place for Sir Bevill

So at Stamford he fought and at Lansdowne he fell,
　But vain were the visions he cherished,
For the brave Cornish heart that the King loved so well
　In the heart of the Granville is perished

A monument was erected in 1723 by George Lord Lansdowne, his grandson, upon the spot where Sir Bevill fell   It is a stately stone pillar with four tablets, and on the top a griffin passant, the crest of the Granvilles
The tablet on the north side has the following inscription —

> " When now the incens'd rebel proudly came
> Down like a torrent without bank or dam,
> When undeserved success urg'd on their force
> That thunder must come down to stop their course,
> Or Granville must step in   There Granville stood,
> And with himself oppos'd and checkt the flood
> Conquest or Death was all his thought—so fire
> Either o'ercomes or doth itself expire
> His courage work't like Flames, cast heat about
> Here, there, on this, on that side , none gave out
> Not any Pike in that Renowned Stand,
> But took new force from his inspired hand ,
> Souldier encouraged souldier, man urg'd man,
> And he urg'd all   So much example can.
> Hurt upon Hurt, Wound upon Wound did call
> He was the But, the Mark, the Aim of all
> His soul, this while retir'd from cell to cell,
> At last flew up from all, and then he fell
> But the devoted Stand, enragèd more
> From that his Fate, ply'd hotter than before,
> And proud to fall with Him, sworn not to yield,
> Each sought an Honour'd grave, and gained the Field ,
> Thus he being fall'n, his Action fought anew
> And the Dead conquer'd whilst the Living flew "

To the immortal memory of his renowned and his valiant Cornish friends who conquered dying in the Royal Cause 5 July 1643   This column was dedicated by the Honourable George Granville Lord Lansdowne 1723
Dulce est pro Patriâ mori

On the south tablet are inscribed Lord Clarendon's words .—

" In this battle, on the Kings part were more Officers and Gentlemen of Quality slain than private men , but that which would have clouded any victory was the death of Sir Bevill Granville   He was indeed an excellent person, whose activity interest and reputation were the foundation of what had been done in Cornwall , his temper and affections so public, that no accident which happened would make any impression on him, and his example kept others from taking any thing ill or at least seeming so to do   In a word, a brighter courage and gentler disposition were never married together to make the most innocent and cheerful conversation "

On the east side are the Royal Arms of England resting on the joint arms of George Monk, Duke of Albemarle and of John Granville, Earl of Bath (Sir Bevill's son) with military ornaments beneath, emblematic of the Restoration of King Charles II by the efforts of those two noblemen.

On the west side of the column are trophies of war emblematic of the actions of Charles Lord Lansdowne (afterwards 2nd Earl of Bath) in Hungary The Granville arms borne on the Roman Eagle with inscription, and the date September 12th, 1683, being significant of Lord Lansdowne's creation as a Count of the Roman Empire on that day.

This pillar was restored by Court Granville, Esq , of Calwich Abbey in 1827, and has since been repaired more than once, but it has somewhat fallen into decay owing to its exposed position.

Mrs. Bray writing of a visit to Kilkhampton church in 1845, says—

We observed on the walls above the arches in the nave and on the southern side the arms and quarterings of the Granvilles, also what I suppose to have been the helmet of Sir Bevill himself, as it has his crest on the top   I have no doubt the helmet was borne with its gauntlets on his coffin into the church at his funeral, and there left as a memorial of his prowess   Part of the helmet by modern barbarism had been painted white as well as the crest, the steel bars of the vizor, however, were left untouched   There was another helmet of a much earlier date opposite , probably, as they were a valiant family, of some former Granville eminent in battle   The iron gauntlets of Sir Bevill remained one lying on either side of the rails of the altar, and one of them was placed on the alms' box   No doubt these were the very gauntlets that were on his hands when he was killed at Lansdown fight, and were brought hither on his coffin   They were well made and of the time of Charles the First, the fingers jointed like a lobster's back, the whole lined with stout leather in parts decayed   I put on one with great reverence   The backs of the seats near the altar in Kilkhampton church were on the North side composed of pieces of old carvings nailed together, that had, I conclude, been found in the church, but one long piece fixed and running along the top of the same must either have been taken from the altar or from Sir Bevill's house at Stow   It is of oak and forms one of the most exquisitely bold and raised pieces of carving that I have ever seen. I could put my fingers between and take hold of some of the stems and stalks of the flowers, and the wood is as hard as if but just cut [1]   I asked a very poor woman, who showed us the church, in what part of it was the vault of the Granvilles   She pointed out the spot at the south of the chancel, and said it had been opened and examined about fifteen years ago, that it was formed of arches below the pavement, the steps to descend into it still remained   There were six coffins in it all of the Granville family and Sir Bevill's among them   The cause of its being opened was that the church had sunk in that part and it was supposed to arise from some defect in the vault beneath

There are many portraits of Sir Bevill   One is the well-known engraving by Fairthorne in Prince's " Worthies of Devon "   Another in Lloyd's Worthies, and one by Dobson is in the fine collection at Petworth Park, where there is also a group described as " Sir Bevill Grenvile, Anne (Mary ?) St.

[1] The carvings were doubtless by Michael Chuke who decorated Stow House   He was accounted equal to Grinling Gibbons

M²

Leger (his grandmother), and John, Earl of Bath, his son, after Vandyck." The portraits of Sir Bevill and Lady Grace also hang at Haynes Park, Bedford, and at Wellesbourne Hall, Warwick. The Rev. W. W. Martyn, of Lifton, near Launceston, has also another of Sir Bevill, as well as an original picture of the second Stowe (built by Sir Bevill's son) and a sea piece with a large vessel in full sail, which is said to have come from Stowe. A miniature of Sir Bevill in a gold enamelled case, richly studded over with diamonds, emeralds, opals and rubies, and worn as a locket. is in the possession of the Chichesters, of Hall, near Barnstaple, into whose family it descended from Sir Bevill s daughter Elizabeth (the wife of Sir Peter Prideaux) as an heirloom.

All these portraits represent him in armour, the complexion delicately fair—the hair, auburn and flowing, is separated over the forehead—the eyes are uncommonly piercing. He wears moustaches, and appears to be about forty years of age. They are evidently striking likenesses.

SIR RICHARD GRANVILLE.
"THE KING'S GENERAL IN THE WEST."

From an Original Portrait, by Cavaliero Moro, in the Wellesbourne Collection.

CHAPTER XIII

WE must now for a while follow the fortunes of Sir Bevill's brother Sir Richard Granville

After the conclusion of the Scottish expedition he had petitioned to have his case about his wife's property re-heard, vowing never to leave off petitioning till he had gained his will. Several of his petitions are preserved in the State Papers (Domestic).

On Tuesday, 26th March, 1639, his wife, writing from London to her agent, says she ' is glad to hear our business goes on so well in Devonshire, but here has been a huge stir about Sir R The king had spoken to the Earl of Arundle to make Sir Richard a cornen " (colonel); the Earl told His Majesty " it could not be done with honour, Sir Richard having run out of his kingdom," and then put the king in mind of the Star Chamber decree " to which the king answered he had forgotten," so he was put by, but he is said to have gotten some one to make an offer to the king, that if he would assist him in un-doing the divorce, and getting back his wife's estate, then the Star Chamber fine should be raised on that estate. This she hears through Maine, her lawyer, and Porter (Endymion Porter ?), to whom Sir Richard had written to be his friend, but Porter sends word to Lady Mary that " since he knew it would displease her, he would be hanged at Court Gate before he would do her any injury."

The king seems to have had some regard for Sir Richard, probably because he was a brave soldier and good officer, and such qualities were then especially valuable to him

Sir Richard had petitioned the king on the 28th October , this had been answered by two petitions, one from the Earl of Suffolk on the 4th November, the other from Lady Mary, probably in the same month, in which she prays that she " may not be disturbed in her life and fortune so legally settled (by the High Commission Court), and alludes to Sir Richard's *most false* petition."

He carried his case before the king's council, setting forth all his grievances in a long brief, in which he makes out that the Earl of Suffolk owed him £12,656 to the 28th of November, 1639 (of State papers (Domestic) Vol 443-80).

A committee was appointed to hear Sir Richard's, among other causes, in December, 1640, and so hopeful was he of success that he went down to Fitzford, turned out the caretakers, and installed his aunt, Mrs Abbot, in the house, whereupon Lady Mary writes to her agent " in a very great distraction " on hearing of these proceedings

Sir Richard borrowed (8 Jan , 1640-41) £20 from Sir William Uvedale " being like to give his lady a great overthrow in Parliament "

But before his case was brought to a conclusion the Irish rebellion broke out and he was given a command   The insurrection spread like a deluge over the whole country in such an inhuman, merciless manner, that forty or fifty thousand English protestants were massacred without distinction of age, sex, or quality before they suspected any danger, or could provide for their defence in towns or elsewhere

The cruelties and barbarities were innumerable and incredible, and such as might melt the most obdurate hearts in the world, and never again, perhaps, till the story of the Cawnpore massacre set the nation's teeth, did such frenzy of revenge take possession of the English people.

More and more troops were voted every week   Every tale, no matter how hideous or improbable, was greedily believed · It was necessary that something should be done at once.   Lord Leicester was ordered to raise two regiments of foot and one of horse by voluntary enlistment , and that the Parliament might keep a firm hand on the reins, it was further resolved that he should submit the list of officers he proposed to commission for the approval of the House

George Monk was named for lieutenant-colonel, and Henry Warren for major of Leicester's own regiment of foot, whilst Lords Lisle and Algernon Sydney (Lord Leicester's two sons) were nominated for the other, and Sir Richard Granville was given the command of the horse   These nominations were at once approved, and on 21st February, 1642, the troops landed in Dublin.

From Carte's " Life and Letters of the Duke of Ormonde " Sir Richard appears at first to have gained the good opinion of the Lord-Lieutenant and to have behaved with great bravery Thus on one occasion he was appointed with 900 foot and 200 horse to convoy provisions from Dublin to Athlone.   In his march he was encountered by the rebels but forced his way through all opposition to Mullingar, where he arrived 29 January 1643, and advanced the next day to Athlone where he delivered the provisions under his care to the Lord President. Having rested two or three days at Athlone, he set out with his army about the 5th of February and having passed Mullingar was met on the 7th of that month by a body of the enemy at Rathconnel, in a place of great disadvantage to him The rebels were 3,400 foot and six troops of horse but were defeated with the loss of 250 of their number killed and Colonel Anthony Preston, the General's eldest son with some others taken prisoners

Nor did his bravery escape the notice of the King, for in his answer to a petition, asking him to relieve the distresses of the Irish Army, the King writes expressing " the most touching grief at the distresses of such a body of noble eminent, and well-deserving persons and for his own inability to give them present relief " He was persuaded most (if not all) of them knew wherein the obstruction to their relief came, and how much he was himself distressed by his rebellious subjects in England. Yet he would not omit any opportunity wherein he might either relieve his distressed Kingdom of Ireland and encourage and recompense such there as had deserved so eminently of him ; desiring the Marquis of Ormonde to return his thanks in particular to the Earl of Kildare, Sir Fulk Huncks, Colonel Gibson and Sir R. Grenville for their respective great services and singular respect to him and his government, and to assure them of his Royal favour and regard in whatsoever might tend to their advantage "

Unfortunately there was a difference of opinion as to the manner in which the rebels should be dealt with

Some were for pursuing all advantages against them in the field , others for gaining them over by treaties and accommodations.

Lord Leicester was said to encourage the first, Lord Ormonde, the Lord-Lieutenant and Commander-in Chief, the latter.

Sir Richard and Colonel Monk, as his rank now was, were devoted to the Earl of Leicester (indeed Monk was some relation of his), and both had served under his command in the Low Countries. They felt it was one of those cases in which severity becomes necessary justice

Sir Richard has been accused by Archdeacon Echard, in his " History of the Rebellion," of great cruelty in his conduct of putting down the insurrection, *e g.*, ' hanging men who were bed-rid because they would not discover where their money was that he believed they had, and old women, some of quality, after he had plundered them and found less than he expected."

Innumerable inventions of English and Irish barbarities were published on both sides, too outrageous to be implicitly believed.

The extravagant exaggerations of parties exasperated against one another, especially where religion is concerned, are never to be literally credited.

But beyond all doubt in fire and blood the wretched Irish had to do penance for their outburst of savagery, to which they had been goaded by Strafford's imperious rule

Sir Richard and Monk took no pains to conceal their feelings against the policy of the Duke of Ormonde, and expressed themselves so strongly, that their words were reported by the Duke to the King, who ordered their immediate return.

On landing at Liverpool Monk went straight to the King and threw himself at his feet and was immediately restored to a regiment, but Sir Richard, to whom great arrears were due for his services in Ireland, reflecting that the King was somewhat short of money, whilst the Parliament had plenty, and that he had received his commission from Parliament, rode straight to London, and demanded his arrears from the House of Commons He was graciously welcomed, and received the thanks of Parliament by the mouth of the Speaker for his services, and no temptation was omitted that they might engage him in their service   His reputation as an officer, and the credit of his name and family in the West, made it worth their while

He took the hint, and dexterously flattered their hopes till he had obtained all he could desire to enable him to execute his secret design

"He openly before the House of Commons, as a further testimony of his real affection to the Parliament, made a serious protest, how that he would never take up arms against, but for the Parliament, and die in the defence of them with his last drop of blood " (A Perfect Diurnal, Sep 28th, Oct. 2nd 1643. King's Pamphlets B M large 4to vol. X.) His arrears were paid, they gave him a commission of Major-General of their Horse, and a regiment, with power to name his own officers, whom he did not fail to choose out of the most trusty of his friends and dependants

"O credulous Parliament ! If Sir Richard Granville was indeed a Red Fox, what were the sagacious ones who harkened to him ?" (Lilly's Almanack 1645. Mercurius Britt No. 42, 1644.) Sir William Waller communicated to him all his designs, as to an entire friend, and an officer of that eminence, by whose advice he meant to govern his own conduct.

His first and principal design was to surprise Basing House, the seat of the Marquess of Winchester, with the connivance of Lord Charles Paulet, the Marquess's brother, who had the custody of the place, and for the better execution of this, Sir Richard was to be sent before with his Horse, that all things might be well disposed and prepared against the time when Waller himself should come to him. Having received from Parliament a considerable sum of money for his equipage, "in which," says Lord Clarendon, "he always affected more than ordinary lustre," he set out from London on March 2nd with his regiment, himself travelling in a coach drawn by six horses accompanied by other stately appointments, amidst the plaudits and blessings of the citizens

His banner was carried in front, a map of England and Wales on a crimson ground, with "England bleeding," in great gold letters across the top

(Sloane MSS 5247 fo. 72, B.M.)

At Bagshot a halt was called Sir Richard harangued his officers and men, setting forth the sinfulness of fighting against their anointed King, and concluded by inviting them to follow him to Oxford, to fight *for* the King instead of *against* him

All the officers cheerfully assented, and, followed by most of his soldiers, Sir Richard went straight to Oxford, and presented himself to the King with a well-equipped troop and with news of the intended treachery at Basing House, which, thanks to his timely warning, was saved

The duped and deceived Parliament hurled thunders at the deceiver's head Proclamation was made declaring him "a Turke, Infidell or Imme of the Devill" "traytor, rogue, villain and skellum"

This latter word, according to "Bibliotheca Devoniensis," p 76, was derived from the German 'Schelme,' and means a scoundrel Burns has the term in his Tam O'Shanter. "She tauld thee weel thou wast a skellum." According to Rider Haggard, who uses the word in his novel "Jess," it is still in vogue in Dutch South Africa, and means a *vicious beast.*

The epithet was deemed so suitable, that Sir Richard was ever afterwards known as "Skellum Grenville."

He was hung in effigy in the Palace Yard, Westminster, and "over against" the old Exchange (Mercurius Britt, No. 45) and it is to his treachery that William Lilly the astrologer, refers when he says "Have we another Red Fox like Sir R. G acting

his close devotions to do our army mischief?   Let's be wary!"
(Almanack of 1645.)

There was a good deal of changing sides during the war, but
there had been nothing as yet parallel to this, except the
desertion of Sir Faithful Fortescue, who had gone over with his
troops from the Parliamentary to the Royalist army in the
midst of the battle of Edgehill

The same excuse has been made for both, that they were
Royalists at heart, but having been employed by Parliament
before any disruption was thought of, only awaited the best
opportunity for their own personal interests of declaring their
real sentiments

Yet this scarcely justifies Sir Richard's gross deception, nor
even does his vindicator, Lord Lansdowne, attempt to do so,
but remarks, " all that can be said for it is that it was putting
the old soldier upon a pack of knaves, and biting the biter"
The king received him with some favour, though he did not
immediately give him a command in his army.   But he gave
what Sir Richard desired much more, namely, all his wife's
estates in Devonshire, on the ground that her continued
residence in London made her a rebel

Not much time was lost by Sir Richard on his journey westward.   Exactly a fortnight after he left London with his
parliamentary troops he arrived at Tavistock with powers from
the King to take possession of all his wife's estates

His first action was to revenge himself on Cutteford, her
agent, for his continued opposition to his " felonious little
plans"   A Royalist army, under Prince Maurice, was at this
time quartered at Tavistock   From him Sir Richard obtained a
warrant addressed to

" The Provost Marshall Generall, his Deputy or Deputys,
together with any of his Majestyes officers or loving subjects.
For as much as George Cutteford of Walraddon in the
county of Devon, gent, hath received great somes of money of
Sir Richard Grenevyle's tenants without giveinge any account to
Sir Richard Grenevyle for the same   These are to authorize
and require you to remit to safe custodye the person of the said
George Cutteford untill he shall satisfye Sir Richard Grenevyle's
just demands. hereof you are not to fail at your perill   Given at
Tavistocke under my hand and seale at Armes this XVIth of
March 1643

MAURICE—"

Armed with this warrant Sir Richard delivered poor
" Honest Guts " (as Lady Mary was wont familiarly to call him)

to the custody of the Provost Marshal General, entered Walreddon, Cutteford's house, took and detained the corn, cattle,
sheep, and household goods to the value of £500, caused his
wife to be imprisoned, and would have imprisoned his son
George also, but that he could not find him (*cf.* Cutteford's
statement at the trial at the Chapter House at Exeter, 7 Nov
1644).

After being six months in prison Cutteford petitioned the
King for a hearing, and expressly begged that Sir Richard
might be ordered to "prosecute noe further" against his son,
against whom the only thing Sir Richard could object was
"that he lived in the house with his mother while Essex's
forces were in these parts, which allegation is most untrue or if
it had been true, your petitioner hopeth it doth not deserve
imprisonment" He specially begged that his son might be left
in peace "that he, the petitioner, might be the better inabled
to provide himself for a hearing by getting his writings and
evidences, which none but your petitioner and his son can
produce, they being hidden away for feare of the Parliament's
forces"

This latter sentence is particularly interesting, inasmuch as
a small secret chamber has recently been discovered at Walreddon, containing chicken bones, etc, probably the very place
where young George was hidden away with the precious
papers.

The siege of Plymouth by the Royalists under Lord Digby
had commenced the previous autumn, not without great
difficulties in the way of the besiegers, one of which is shewn
in the record that the cavaliers threatened to hang all those
who would not join their forces. Sir Richard at once volun-
teered his assistance. Lord Clarendon here relates what he
considers an act of unnecessary cruelty on Sir Richard's
part.

"One day he made a visit from his house (Fitzford) which
he called his own, to the Colonel and dined with him, and the
Colonel civilly sent half a dozen troopers to wait on him home,
lest any of the garrison in their usual excursions might meet
with him. On his return home he saw four or five fellows
coming out of a neighbour's wood with burthens of wood upon
their backs which they had stolen. He bid the troopers fetch
these fellows to him, and finding that they were soldiers of the
garrison, he made one of them hang all the rest, which to save
his life he was contented to do · so strong his appetite was to
those executions he had been accustomed to in Ireland, without

N²

any kind of commission or pretence of authority" And in " A continuation of the True Narrative of the Most Observable Passages in and about Plymouth from January 26th 1643," is the following · "We have omitted one barbarous act of Sir Richard Greenvill (that Runnagado) committed the week before Who having taken two of our souldiers going out into the country, inforced one to hang the other presently at the next tree they came to, the cavaliers dispatching the survivor, Skellum Greenvill sitting on his horse beholding the spectacle."

But an incident had occurred during the blockade of Plymouth which may somewhat account for this severe treatment of his prisoners.

The governor of Plymouth was Lord Roberts, whom Lord Clarendon describes as of a sour, surly nature It happened in some skirmish, where prisoners were taken on both sides, that a young gentleman about sixteen years of age, near kinsman to Sir Richard and of his own name,[1] fell into the enemy's hands Sir Richard by a civil message claimed him as his kinsman, offering any terms by ransom or exchange. Lord Roberts ordered the poor boy to be hanged up at the gate of the town, in sight of the messenger, without any other reply "After an execution so cruel," (adds Lord Lansdowne, who quotes the story in his "Vindication of Sir Richard") "so inhuman and of so exasperating a nature, what could follow but the utmost returns of vengeance"

Shortly after, upon a sally made with horse and foot from the town Lord Digby was severely wounded with a rapier in the eye, and Sir Richard was placed in command by Prince Maurice, at the earnest request of Sir John Berkeley

It was before this same Sir John Berkeley and four other judges that the unfortunate George Cutteford succeeded on November 7th in getting his case heard.

Sir Richard was too occupied to attend, he probably felt safe in the judges' hands. After reading Sir Richard's letter in which he accused Cutteford of "having sent moneys to London to the Lady Grenville, who had ayded and assisted the Rebels there" and hearing Cutteford's answer

"The commissioners doe conceive that the said Mr. Cutteford should give satisfaction to Sir Richard Grenville for all his cattell taken away by Cutteford, his wife or children, also that he should account for the rent of Walriddon since September

---

[1] Probably a descendant of Digory Granville, of Penheale, *cf* p 73 Others suppose this was an illegitimate son of Sir Richard, and the Puritan newspapers of the day euphuistically describe him as 'a whelp" or "spawn of Skellum Greenvils "

1641 after the rate of 30ʰ per annum · for Prince Hall at 40s per annum ; for the tenement of Whitchurch at 16s and for a tenement in Meldon at 34s since the death of the widow Radford unto this daye, and all rents etc received of any of the tenants of the said Sir Richard Grenville since November 1641 deducting all such high rents, weekly rents and other payments as hee hath bonâ fide payed to the Lady Grenville betweene November 1641 and the King's Proclamation, being about November 1642, and all interest for debts incurred for Lady Grenville before November 1641." Sir Richard to restore to Mr Cutteford possession of Walreddon, on Cutteford's giving Sir Richard "a true copy of the lease thereof; the Cattell, corn, horses, household stuff, etc to be restored to Cutteford He to be sett at liberty, and with his wife and children to continue so." Because there were cross claims and witnesses "John Short of Ashwater, the elder, Gent, and John Edgcombe of Tavistocke, Gent. were appointed to hear witnesses, etc."

The petitions of Mr. George Howard and Mrs Mary Howard had been sent by the King to the said Commissioners, who hearing from Cutteford that "it was true as alledged in their petitions that Mr. George Howard received 40 *li*, and Mistress Mary 60 *l* from their mother for their maintenance," upon consideration of the distracted times, whereby the revenues of the said estates are much lessened, they the said Commissioners doe thinke fitt and desire Sir Richard Grenvile to allow unto the said Mr. George Howard 26 *l* per annum, and unto the said Mistress Mary Howard 40 *l*, the first payment thereof to beginne from our Lady-Day last "

Another instance of Sir Richards vindictive character is given by Lord Clarendon "Shortly after Sir Richard had assumed the command of the blockade of Plymouth upon the wound of Lord Digby, one Braband an attorney-at-law, who had heretofore solicited the great suit against Sir Richard in the Star Chamber, on the behalf of his wife and the Earl of Suffolk, living in those parts, and having always very honestly behaved himself towards the King's estate and service, knowing it seems, the nature of Sir Richard, resolved not to venture himself within the precints where he commanded, and therefore intended to go to some more secure quarter, but was taken in his journey, having a mountero on his head. Sir Richard had laid wait to apprehend him. He had likewise concealed his name, but being now brought before Sir Richard was immediately by Sir Richard's own direction and without any council of war, because he said, he was disguised, hanged as a spy, which seemed so strange and incredible, that one of the council asked whether it was true, and he answered very unconcernedly, Yes, he had hanged him for he was a traitor and against the King; and he said he knew the country talked that he hanged him for revenge, because he had solicited a cause against him, but that was not the cause, though having played the knave with him, he said smiling, he was consent to find a just occasion to punish him "

On the 16th of April, the Royalist forces under Sir Richard Granville, numbering near 500, appeared before Plymouth, but were signally defeated by Colonel Martin, Governor of the town, in an engagement at St Budeaux. Three days later they again returned to the attack, but met with no better success, and two days afterwards they " fled like hares " before a sally and lost sixteen foot, arms, one drum, five hogs, and five cows According to " A Narrative of the Siege," bearing date May 10 1644, among the pieces of intelligence that reached the besieged were the following respecting Sir Richard's doings :—" First, we are informed that Skellum Grenville builds very much on Fitzford ; (I hope castles in the air, or houses without foundation) and boasts of having Plymouth speedily, but garrison and Plymouth will not believe him."

" Second ; that the said renegade Grenville hath seized on the Lord Bedford's estate, and Master Courtenay's estate, and sent him prisoner to Exon, making havoc of his goods and corn."

Failing to carry the siege Sir Richard wrote the following letter to Colonel Gold the Governor of Plymouth "together with the officers and souldiers now at the Fort and Towne of Plimouth, these "—

Gentlemen

That it may not seem strange unto you, to understand of my being ingaged in his Majestie's service to come against Plimouth as an enemy, I shall let you truely know the occasion thereof It is very true that I came from Ireland with a desire and intention to look after my own particular fortune in England, and not to ingage myself in any kind in the unhappy difference betwixt the King and the pretended Parliament now at London. But chancing to land at Liverpool, the Parliaments forces there brought me to London where I must confesse I received from both the pretended houses of Parliament great tokens of favour and also importunate motions to ingage me to serve them, which I civilly refused Afterwards divers honourable persons of the pretended Parliament importuned me to undertake their service for the Government and Defence of Plimouth, unto which my answer was that it was fit (before I ingaged my selfe) I should understand what meanes they could and would allow and provide for the effectuall performance of that service Upon that a Committee appointed for the West, thought fit with all speede to send a present reliefe of men and munition to Plimouth which wth very great difficulty was brought thither, being the last you had Afterwards there were many meetings more of that Committee to provide the meanes that should give Plimouth reliefe and enable it to defend itself, and notwithstanding the earnest desires and endeavours of that Committee accordingly, I protest before God, after six months' expectation and attendance on that Committee by me, I found no hopes or likelyhood of but reasonable means for the reliefe and defence of Plimouth which made me account a lost Town and the rather because I, being by Commission Lieut-Generall to Sir William Waller, had an ordnance of the Parliament for the raising of 500 horse for my Regiment at the charges of Kent Surry Sussex and Hampshire who in 3 mouths time had not raised 4 Troopes, and my own Troope, when I left them, having 2 moneth's pay due to them, could get but one month, for which extraordinary means was used, being a favour none else could attain, it being very true that the Parliament's forces have all been unpaid for many moneths in such sort that they are grown weak both in men and monies and by only good words kept their forces from disbanding   The processe of so long time spent at London made me and many others plainly see the iniquity of their Policy, for I found Religion was the cloake for Rebellion, and it seemed not strange to me, when I found the Protestant Religion was infected with so many independants and sectaries of infinite kinds, which would not heare of a peace but such as would be in some kind as pernicious as was the warre   The Priviledges of this Parliament I found was not to be bound by any of the former, but to lay them aside and alter them as they advantaged their party.   This seemed so odious to me that I resolved to lay my selfe, as I have done, at his Majy feete from whence and his most just cause no fortune, terrour, or cruelty shall make me swerve in any kind   And to let you see also what hath formerly past I have sent you these inclosed   Now for a farwell   I must wish and advise you out of the true and faithfull love and affection I am bound to beare toward mine own country that you speedily consider your great charges, losses and future dangers by making and holding yourselves enemies to his Majesty who doth more tru'y desire your welfare and safety then it seems you doe your selves, wherefore, (as yet my friends), I desire you to resolve speedily of your Propositions for peace, by which you may soone injoy your liberties contents and estates, but on the contiary, the contrary which with a sad heart I speake, you will very soon see the effect of   Thus my affection urgeth me to impart unto you out of the great desire I have, rather to regaine my lost old friends by love than by force to subject them to ruine and in that consideration I must thus conclude

Your loving friend

Fitzford 18
Rich Grenvile.
Martu 1643

The enclosure in Sir Richard's letter was a book entitled "The Iniquity of the Covenant," which was burnt, by order of the Council of War, by the common hangman, and the following is the contemptuous answer sent by the Commanders of the Garrison to his letter:—

Sir,

Though your letter meretting the highest contempt and scorn, which once we thought fit by our silence (judging it unworthy of our answer) to have testified, yet considering that yourself intend to make it publick, we offer you these lines that the world may see what esteem we have of the man, notorious for apostacy and treachery, and that we are ready to dispute the justice and equity of our cause in any lawful way, whereto the enemy shall at any time challenge us You might well have spared the giving us an account of your dissimulation with the Parliament, we were soon satisfied, and our wonder is not so great that you are now gone from us, as at first when we understood of your engagements to us, and to tell you truth, it pleased us not so well to hear you were named to be governor of this place, as it now doth to hear you are in arms against us, accounting ourselves safer to have you an enemy abroad, than a pretended friend at home, being persuaded that your principels could not afford cordial endeavours for an honest cause

You tell us of the pretended Houses of Parliament in London—a threadbare scandal suck't from Aulicus, whose reward a bp blessing you may chance to be honoured with for your court service, and how they make religion the cloak of rebellion, a garment which we are confident your rebellion will never be clad with , you advise us to consider the great charges we have been at, and the future charges we run ourselves into by make ourselves enemies to his majesty who more desires our good than we ourselves, and thence would have us propose conditions for peace.

That we have been at great charges already we are sufficiently sensible, and yet resolve that it shall not in any way lessen our affections to that cause, with which God has honoured us, by making us instruments to plead it against the nation's adversaries

If the King be our enemy, yet Oxford cannot prove that we have made him so That His Majesty desires our welfare, we can easily admit, as well as that his mischievous counsellors so near him, who render him so cruel to his most faithful subjects, and as for proposing conditions for peace, we shall more gladly do it, when it may advance the public service, but to do it to the enemies of peace, though we have been thereto formally invited, yet hath it pleased the Disposer of all things to preserve us from the necessity of it, and to support us against the fury of the enraged enemy

The same God is still our rock and refuge under whose wings we doubt not of protection and safety, when the seducers of the King shall die like a candle, and that the name, which by such courses is sought to be perpetual in honour shall end in ignominy For the want of money to pay the Parliament Soldiers, though it would not be such as you would persuade us, yet certain we are, then treasury had now been greater, and honest men better satisfied, but that as some unfaithful as yourself have gone before you in betraying them both of their trust and riches where-as you remind us of the lost condition of our own town, sure it cannot be you should be so truly persuaded of it, as they are of your personal, who subscribe themselves and so remain

FRIENDS TO THE FAITHFUL

In July the Royalists again marched on Plymouth and were again repulsed, and soon after Prince Maurice made another attempt, but meeting with no better success left Sir Richard to continue the blockade, which he did till the approach of Lord Essex with a large army compelled him, in order to avoid being between two fires, to retreat into Cornwall with his troops

Essex took up his quarters at Tavistock, and from thence, with his own regiment and another, marched against " Skellum Greenvile's " house at Tavistock—(*The Scottish Dove*, No. 42,

26th of July to 2nd of August) They were resisted on the
way by some forces that lined the hedges, "which after some
dispute they passed" (*John Near's Magnalia Dei Anglicana*
iii. 297) and after the salute of some great shot on the house on
Tuesday 23rd of July they desired parley, and on Wednesday
morning hung out their white flag ; but the soldiers had not
patience to treat, but got over the walls and entered the house.

The souldiers within called for quarter, but they would not
promise it to them, so the enemy threw down their arms, and
committed themselves to the Lord Generall's mercy.

His souldiers told them "if they were all English they
should have mercy, but not if there were any Irish "

There was about six score in the house, three score have
taken the covenant ; the rest not so willing, and are still
prisoners. "There was in the house very good pillage,"
"excellent pillage for the souldiers," says Vicars, "even at least
3,000 pound in money and plate, and other provisions in great
quantity. . Two Canon, and there was a roome full of excellent
new muskets and many pair of Pistolls, as good as can be bought
for money." The newspapers were full of the capture of
Fitzford They rang changes in Essex's valour, and the
discomfiture of the ' State Apostate," the "most impious
and impudent rotten-hearted Apostate Skellum Greenvile
'the Runagado'" who "flies from Westminster as from the
gallowes." Essex himself writes to the Council from Tavistock
on the 26th of July.—(*Mercurius Britannicus*, Vicars, p. 96.
Scottish Dove, No 42. S P Dom, vol lii)

While this was going on Sir Richard abandoned his works
before Plymouth. and passed into Cornwall by Saltash. The
Earl of Essex continued his march on the 26th, advancing to
the Tamar at two points, viz , Newbridge and Horsebridge At
the former place Sir Richard Granville's force, consisting of
three regiments of Foot—Colonel Acland's, Colonel Fortescue's,
and Colonel Carew's—was in position to dispute the passage

A "hot encounter" ensued in which the Parliamentarians
lost about fifty men, but they finally carried the bridge, and
entering Cornwall seized Launceston, the shire town, where they
took divers barrels of powder."--(*c f. Rushworth's Collections*,
v. 691, *Whitelock's Memorials*, ed 1682, p. 92)

Sir Richard fell back upon Truro, and in a letter to his
nephew, John Granville, dated Truro 29 July, he writes, "We
have here made a stand with our forces and the garrisons of
Saltash and Milbroke and others considerable have come up and
added to our former, and we hope well."

His Horse was also augmented by an additional hundred, under the command of Captain Edward Brett, being the Queen's escort which were left behind when her Majesty embarked from Pendennis Castle for France, so that he was now 8,000 strong

Essex had been assured by the Western men that he should want no victuals in Cornwall and that a great part of the country stood well affected.

This he soon found to be an utter delusion The county had almost unanimously risen for the King, who was already in pursuit, and had reached the Devonshire side of the Tamar.

On the 31st of July the King received a message from Sir Richard urging his Majesty to hasten towards the West The King dismissed the messenger with the reply that he was "coming with all possible speed, with an army of 10,000 Foot and 5,000 Horse and 28 pieces of cannon"—and the next day crossed Polson Bridge, and passing through Launceston, which Essex had vacated five days previously, came to Liskeard and Lostwithiel, and took up his head-quarters at Boconnoc, Lord Mohun's house, where he awaited the arrival of Sir Richard, to whom orders had been sent to occupy Grampound, in order that the Parliamentary army might be cut off between the two forces from all chance of living upon the country

Sir Richard in his march from Truro fell upon a party of Lord Essex's Horse near Bodmin, and killed many and took many others prisoners, and was able to join the King Sunday 11th August, and to give his Majesty a good account of his proceedings, and in particular of his forces, although Lord Clarendon, with his usual spleen against Sir Richard, endeavours to underrate them

Essex, fearing to be assailed at a distance from the sea, marched from Bodmin to Lostwithiel, where he called lustily upon Parliament for provisions for his hungry soldiers, and above all insisted that Waller should be despatched to effect a diversion in his favour by attacking the King's army in the rear. (The Kingdom's *Weekly Intelligencer*, E 4 20 Essex to the Com of B K , Aug 4th, Com letter book *Walker's Hist Discourses*, 51.)

"At Lostwithiel " (as Lord Clarendon quaintly puts it) " he had the good town of Fowey and the sea to friend, by which he might reasonably assure himself of a great store of provision, the Parliament ships having all the jurisdiction there " and where, if he preserved his post, which was so situated that he could not be compelled to fight without giving him great advantage, he might well conclude that " Waller, or some other force sent from the Parliament would be shortly upon the King's back, as His Majesty was upon his"

In this hope he refused all overtures to treat, saying he had no authority from the Houses to do so; and the month of August was occupied for the most part with skirmishing

But at length it was resolved by the Royalists to make his quarters still straiter, and to cut off his provisions by sea, or at least a good part of them

Accordingly Sir Richard drew his men from Bodmin, and occupied Lanhydrock, Lord Robert's fortified mansion, two miles west of Boconnoc, and finding Respryn Bridge over the Fowey river unguarded, seized it, so that there was now free communication for the Royalists across the Fowey river from east to west, and at the same time Sir Jacob Astley, with a good party of Horse and Foot, made himself master of Hall, another house belonging to Lord Mohun, and of Polman Fort, a mile below it, at the mouth of the Haven, so that it would be difficult, if not impossible, for vessels with supplies to enter Essex was therefore obliged to content himself with such provisions for his men as had already been landed, and to support his horses for a time on the scanty forage which was still to be found in the fields round the head of Tywardreath Bay, with the addition of a few boatloads of necessaries that might be landed on the open beach. For a week or ten days no action beyond certain skirmishes was taken, but at last Lord Essex, finding his provisions failing, and despairing of help from the Parliament, determined to break through with his whole body of Horse and to save the best he could

Although the Royalists had secret information of his intention, Lord Essex, under the cover of a dark and misty night, managed to effect his purpose, and the Horse escaped to Plymouth with very trifling loss.

The next day withdrawing his infantry from Lostwithiel, Essex fell back upon Fowey, where he hoped to await the arrival of the expected transports.

A smart engagement took place at Broadoak Down, near Boconnoc, in which he was defeated, and the following day being Sunday, the first of September, he sent to the King desiring a parley, but himself escaped " with Lord Roberts and such other officers as he had most kindness for" and, embarking in a small vessel at Fowey, sailed for Plymouth.

Major-General Skippon was left behind to make the best conditions he could

O²

A cessation was accordingly concluded, and hostages inter-changeably delivered.

Skippon " delivered up 38 pieces of cannon, 100 barrels of powder, with match and bullets proportionable, and about 6,000 armes." The officers were to have liberty "to wear their swords, and to pass out with their own money and proper goods, and, in order to secure them from plunder, they were to have a convoy to Poole or Southampton ; all their sick might stay in Fowey till they were recovered, and then have passes to Plymouth "

Sir Richard had meanwhile been sent with the Cornish Horse and Foot towards Plymouth, in order to join Lord Goring in pursuit of the Horse which had escaped, and " which " writes Lord Clarendon, " by passing over the bridge near Saltash they might easily have done, but Sir Richard slackened his march that he might possess Saltash, which the enemy had quitted, and left them eleven pieces of cannon with some armes and ammunition which together with the town, was not worth his unwarrantable stay."

This kept him from joining with Goring, who thereby, and for want of the Foot, excused his not fighting the Horse

The King now commissioned Sir Richard to command all the forces of Cornwall and Devon He became (as he was proud of calling himself) " The King's General in the West," a title which was engraved on his tombstone at Ghent years afterwards, and he received his Majesty's orders to blockade Plymouth, and to resist and suppress all rebellious persons in the two counties The King left him only 300 Foot and no Horse with which to blockade Plymouth, which had then in it about 5000 Foot and Horse. On "Thursday, September 5th, he sent, by the King's appointment, a trumpet in his Majesty's name to Plymouth, to render the town."

" Friday 6th. The trumpeter returned with this answer (but first abused and imprisoned) that they would send an answer by one of their drummers."

" Satterday 15th Between 6 and 7 of the morning His Majesties army, etc , with drums beating and colors flying, marched off, leaving the siege (of Plymouth were they had arrived on the 10th). But Sir Richard Grenville with 30 or 40 Cornish, is appointed to lye at Plymtou and make workes to stopp them from foraging into the country." (Symond's Diary, pp. 78-82.)

The following letter was written by Sir Richard to Mr. Edward Waller, Secretary of the Council of War to His Majesty, from Plympton, on the 19th. (Brit. Museum, Add MS. 15750 fol. 20.)

SIR RICHARD GRENVILE TO EDWARD WALKER

S[r]

Haveing pass'd these two days in debate with the Cōmiss[rs] of Cornewall for the raysing of a guard for His Ma[ties] Person, and for the recruiting of o[r] Regiments, The Country brings in unto vs theyr just request that wee would recōmend theyr sad complaints unto His Ma[tie] That theyr Oxen and horses haue beene Impress'd for his Ma[ties] service for ye draught of the Artillery, and noe Assurance has been given them of the returne of their stuff againe.

S[r] I therefore in the country's behalfe desire to certify you, y[t] vnless these Cattle bee sent backe without impane, many of theyr Owners (whose whole estates depend uppon theyr Ploughs) will suffer in an utter undoeing and most of o[r] countrymen will be at least discouraged, yf not disabled for any future assistance to his Ma[ties] service in y[t] kind, And (which will tend much to the disadvantage of y[e] service wherein His Ma[tie] hath entrusted mee) I shall hardly hereafter bee furnished with a Plough for y[e] draught of o[r] Amunition, or provision, uppon any necessity w[t]soeuer

S[r], my request therefore is, that you would giue knowledge to his Ma[tie] of this o[r] countrymen's just and humble suit, That theyr Ploughs may bee seasonably and safely sent backe, and that the country through which his Ma[tie] dos march, is faire better furnished with Ploughs and Carts than these Westerne parts, and y[t] by Impressing of fresh cattle and horses (those of o[r] countrymen haueing been much tyred out by the Employm[ts] of soe many Army's in ye West) his Ma[ties] March will by faire more speed and convenience bee advanced

S[r], I shall request you to cause an Order to Ishue forth to this effect, that all such cattle and carriages may bee sent backe, and in soe doeing you will much oblige

Y[r] Humble Servant

R[y] GRENVILE

Plympton this
19th of Septem[br]
1644
(addressed)

To my Honoured ffreind
M[r] Ed Walker Secret[ry]
of the Councell of Warre
to His Ma[tie]
p̃sent   these

(endorsed)

S[r] Rich Green[vhle]
Ser

Sir Richard was richly rewarded by the King for the skill and valour he had displayed in this short campaign

We may dismiss as incorrect Whitelock's assertion that he was created Baron Lostwithiel, but it is probably true that (as Lord Clarendon states) he was granted the sequestration of all the Duke of Bedford's estates, as well as those of Sir Francis Drake at Werrington and Buckland Monachorum, at which latter place he chiefly resided and conducted from thence the siege of Plymouth.

Buckland Abbey, it will be remembered, had been the property of his illustrious grandsire, the great Sir Richard of the " Revenge," who sold it to the Drakes in 1580

Sir Richard fortified the Abbey, and held it until after the capture of Dartmouth, when his garrison quitted it, and Sir Francis Drake recovered possession

Sir Richard had also Lord Roberts' estate in Cornwall assigned to him.   All these properties, together with his wife's, he enjoyed by the sequestration granted from the King, and ' of which," writes Lord Clarendon with his usual acerbity, " he made a greater revenue than ever the owners did in time of peace , for that besides he suffered no part of these estates to pay contribution (whereby the tenants very willingly paid their full rents) he kept very much ground about the houses in his own hands which he stocked with such cattle as he took from delinquents "

" For though he suffered not his soldiers to plunder, yet he was in truth the greatest plunderer of this war, so that he had a greater stock of cattle of all sorts upon his grounds than any person in the West of England   Besides this, the ordering of delinquents' estates in those parts being before that time not so well looked into, by virtue of these sequestrations, he seized upon all the stock upon the grounds, upon all the furniture in the several houses, and compelled the tenants to pay him all the rents due from the beginning of the rebellion   By these means he had not only a vast stock, but he received great sums of money, and had such great stores of good household stuff as would furnish well all those houses he looked upon as his own "

As an instance of his high-handed proceeding, the following, taken from Mr. Cotton's " Barnstaple during the Civil War " may be quoted :— ' A rumour having been set afoot that the Earl of Bath had come in to his Excellence the Earl of Essex, Sir Richard, on the mere suspicion of the Earl's insincerity, and although the Bouchier and Granville families had been on terms of the greatest intimacy, at once sent Captain Edward Roscorrock to Tawstock House with a warrant, which alleging that divers officers of His Majesty's army had lost their horses by hard duty , that the Earl of Bath had forty or fifty horses and men , that neither he nor any of them had appeared at the Posse , that he had not given any advice or encouragement by letter or otherwise , and, worst of all that as he (Sir R Granville) was informed he had protection from the Earl of Essex, authorised him, the said Roscorrock to search for and take six of the Earl of Bath's horses, whereof a grey horse called 'York' is especially named"

The morose Earl was no soldier, which may account for these shortcomings, if true, but he was not the one to submit tamely to the indignity, he therefore complained directly to the King. Sir Richard, called upon to explain, excused himself, and submitted whether it was not with sufficient reason he had acted ? Nothing could have been more graceful than the soothing letter which thereupon Lord Digby, on the part of the King, wrote to the incensed Earl.

" The King would be very sensible of any disrespect offered to one of his (the Earl of Bath's) quality, and asks him not to press the matter, and not take too much to heart the roughness of a soldier "

The sequel is not revealed, but it may probably be inferred that the much-coveted " York " was returned to his stable at Tawstock.

Sir Richard in addition to his other honours was made Sheriff of Devon this year, a position which he apparently utilized to the utmost in order to prosecute his exactions

All this time the blockade of Plymouth continued. Sir Richard had in a short time increased his small army of 300 Foot which the King had left him to above 5,000 Foot and 1,000 Horse by means of the *Posse Comitatus* which as Sheriff he was empowered to raise, and (according to his own account in his " Narrative of the Proceedings of his Majesty's affaires in the West of England since the defeat of the Earl of Essex at Lostwithiel in Cornwall A D 1645," published amongst the Duke of Ormonde's Papers in Cartes' Letters 196) " did so necessitate the Plymouth forces by a strict blockeeing that the enemies horse were almost all starved and lost, and their foot grown almost to desperation in such sort that if the said Army had then been suffered to remain but two months longer before that town, very probably Plymouth had been thereby reduced into obedience to his Majesty "

But Sir Richard's commission was evidently a source of envy to Sir John Berkeley and others in command of the Royalists troops at Exeter. In February, Sir Richard had received information that they were doing their utmost to procure his removal from before Plymouth to some pretended greater employment elsewhere

At the end of March Sir William Waller was in the West The Prince and Lord Goring were endeavouring to reduce Taunton, but within three or four days before the design was ready for execution, it was reported that Waller was advancing with a strong force to its relief   Thereupon the attempt was stopped until more troops arrived, and Sir John Berkeley was summarily called on by Goring to send him in as many men as he could spare, and Sir Richard Granville was ordered to come in person, with the bulk of the Forces with which he was then besieging Plymouth   leaving only sufficient men before the town to block it up

The orders may have been good in themselves, but Goring had no commission empowering him to give them, and he had no idea of condescending to entreat a favour where he had no right to command

Berkeley, an honorable and loyal soldier, did as he was told, but Granville, at least for a time, hung back, and when Prince Maurice repeated his commands positively to him to " advance towards the Lord Goring and to obey all such orders as he should receive from his Lordship " Sir Richard as positively sent his Highness word that " his men would not stir a foot, and that he had promised the commissioners of Devon and Cornwall, that he would not advance beyond Taunton till Taunton was reduced, but that he made no question, if he were not disturbed, speedily to give a good account of that place," *i e*, Plymouth

In the meantime Lord Goring, although he had fallen successfully upon Sir William Waller's quarters twice by night, and killed so good a number that it was generally believed that Sir William Waller was lessened near a thousand men by those encounters, refused to follow up his success upon the main body of the rebels without the addition of Granville's foot, but professing that if he had an addition of 600 men he would be in the Town within six days."

At length however, Sir Richard arrived, (possibly having heard that Lord Goring had gone to Bath on account of his health, and brought up his forces, consisting of 800 Horse, and 2200 Foot) within musket-shot of Taunton

But the very day he arrived, in attempting to take Wellington House, he received a wound in his thigh of so serious a nature that at the time it was considered likely to prove mortal

About this time the Prince of Wales, a lad not yet fifteen years of age, was sent into the West as of greater security than Oxford, and with him came a Council composed of some of the King's most trusted personal advisers, viz, Lords Capel and Colepepper and Sir Edward Hyde, afterwards Lord Clarendon,

It was hoped that the Prince's presence and authority would have composed the factions and animosities in the West " which miserably infested the King's Service." In order that the Prince might have the requisite authority for the arrangement of these differences and the restoration of order, he had received from the King a Commission making him Generalissimo of the whole of the Royalist armies. Remembering his age this position is somewhat startling, but it was of course only nominal. The same remark applies to the Prince's ostensible political precocity. Lord Clarendon, who never allows us to forget that the real oracle was the Prince's Council, invariably attributes its resolution, with courtly obsequiousness, to the inspiration and sagacity of the Prince

Lords Capel and Colepepper (as members of the Prince's Council) visited Sir Richard as soon as he was placed in the litter to be carried to Exeter, and informed him that they had selected Sir John Berkeley to take over his command, ' the which he seeming very well to approve, they desired him to call his officers (most of the principal being there) and to command them to proceed in the work in hand cheerfully under the command of Sir John Berkeley ; the which he promised to do, and immediately said something to his officers at the side of his litter, which the Lords conceived to be what he had promised , but it appeared after that it was not so, and very probably was the contrary, for neither officer nor soldier did his duty after he was gone during the time Sir John Berkeley commanded in that action."

While Sir Richard lay at Exeter recovering from his wounds the Commissioners of Devon presented a complaint against him to Prince Maurice

That complaint was as follows :—

" That upon his first entering upon the work of Plymouth, and his assurance under his hand that he would take the town before Christmas Day, and that he would forthwith raise, arme, and pay twelve hundred Horse and six thousand Foot, they had assigned him above one half of their whole contribution, amount-ing to above eleven hundred pounds a week, and for providing armes and ammunition, had assigned him the arrears of the contribution due from those hundreds allotted to him, which amounted to near 6,000*li*., he having likewise the whole con-tribution of Cornwall, being above seven hundred pounds weekly, and had received most part of the letter and subscrip-tion money of that County towards the same service ; that he had from his first entering upon the charges quietly enjoyed those contributions in Devon which were duly paid, and had received the greatest part of the arrears assigned to him for the provision of armes and ammunition.

'Notwithstanding all which, he had never bought above twenty barrels of powder or any Armes, but had received both the one and the other from them, out of their Magazines, and had never maintained or raised near half the number of men to which he was obliged, till the week before he was required to march to Taunton, when he had called the *Posse Comitatus,* and out of them forced almost the whole number of Foot, which marched with him thither bringing them with him as far as Exeter unarmed; and there compelled the Commissioners to supply him with armes and Ammunition—that having left scarce two thousand Foot and four hundred Horse before Plymouth, he continued still to receive the whole contribution formerly assign'd, when he was to have twelve hundred Horse and six thousand Foot, and would not part with any of it So that he received more out of Devonshire for the blocking up of Plymouth, (having all Cornwall to himself likewise) than was left for the garrisons of Exeter, Dartmouth Barnstaple and Tiverton, and for the finishing those fortifications, victualling the garrisons, providing armes and Ammunition, with which they had before not only supplied themselves, but had sent great quantities to the King's Army, to the Lord Goring, and to the siege of Taunton,—that he would not suffer them to send any warrants to collect the letter and subscription money, to settle the Excise, or meddle with Delinquents' estates in the hundreds assigned to him for contribution, and that he had those continual contests with Sir John Berkeley, being Colonel-General of the County, and the other Governors of garrisons, pretending that he had power to command them, that there was such an animosity grown between them, that they very much apprehended the danger of those divisions, there having been some bloodshed, and men killed upon their private contests.

"They therefore besought his Highness, by his Authority, to settle the limits of their several jurisdictions in order to the Martial Affairs, and likewise to order Sir Richard Greenvil to receive no more contributions than would suffice for the maintenance of those men who continued before Plymouth, whereby they could only be enabled to perform their parts of the Association"

This was pressed with so much earnestness and reason, that it was thought very advisable for the Prince himself to go to Exeter, where both the Commissioners and Sir Richard were—

and there, upon the hearing of all that could be said, to settle the dispute

The King, however, expressly inhibited his going farther Westward, and Lords Capel and Colepepper and the Chancellor of the Exchequer, Hyde, accordingly went by themselves, with instructions to examine all the complaints and allegations of the Commissioners, and to settle the business of the Contribution, and "upon view of the several Commissions of Sir John Berkeley and Sir Richard Greenvil, so to agree the matter of jurisdiction, that the publick service might not be obstructed"

As soon as the Lords reached Exeter, they went to visit Sir Richard, who was still bed-rid of his hurt They intended it only as a visit, and so would not reply at that time to many very sharp and bitter complaints and invectives he made against Sir John Berkeley, who was then at the Leaguer before Taunton, but told him "they would come to him again the next day, and consider all businesses." Accordingly they came, when with great bitterness he again complained of the Governor and some disrespects from his Lieutenant-General, but when he was pressed to particulars, he mentioned principally some high and disdainful speeches (the most of which were denied by the others) and the withholding some prisoners from him, which he had sent his Marshall for near Taunton

On the other hand, Sir John Berkeley complained by his letters, that the soldiers who had been brought to Taunton by Granville every day mouldered away, and he had reason to believe it was by his direction ; whilst those who stayed, and the officers, were very backward in performing their duties, and that they had burned Wellington House contrary to his commands

Sir Richard denied that he had used his influence in the ways suggested, though it appeared that all such soldiers as left their colours and came to him, were kindly used and had money given to them—and that Lieutenant-Colonel Robinson, after he had received order from Sir John Berkeley not to destroy Wellington House, rode to Exeter to Sir Richard Granville, and and immediately upon his return from him caused it to be burnt.

Sir Richard also maintained that he levied no monies, nor issued out any warrants but what he had authority to do by his Commission

In the end, the Lords of the Council showed him their instructions from the Prince, thoroughly to examine all differences between them, and to fix the limits of their respective Commissions

P²

Thereupon, Sir Richard showed them his commission under His Majesty's sign manual, by which he was authorized to command the forces before Plymouth, " and in order thereunto, with such clauses of latitude and power, as he might both raise the Posse, and command the trained bands, and indeed the whole forces of both Counties   He was to receive orders from his Majesty and his Lieutenant-General ; and, moreover he was at the time High Sheriff of Devon."

Sir John Berkeley's Commission was precedent and more formal, being under the great Seal of England, of Colonel-General of the Counties of Devon and Cornwall, and to command the whole forces of both Counties, as well trained bands as others.

It is clear that these Commissions over-lapped each other, and it was little wonder that a plentiful crop of discussions and jealousies had sprung up between the two Commanders, who were each pushing their own schemes.

After the perusal of his Commission, the Lords inquired " what forces were necessary in Sir Richard's opinion for the Blockade of Plymouth ? " and he informed them that the forces then there were sufficient and proposed an allowance little enough for the service.

He then said that it " troubled him to be confined to such an employment as the blocking up of a place, whilst there was like to be so much action in the field, and he therefore hoped His Highness would give him leave to wait on him in the Army, where he thought he might do him much better service "

They told him they had " Authority from the Prince, if they found his health able to bear it, to let him know that his Highness would be glad of his service in the moulding that army which was then raising, and in which he had designed him the second place of command."

Sir Richard cheerfully received the proposition for himself in the Army ; " and for Plymouth (he said,) no man was fit to undertake the work there but Sir John Berkeley, who had the Command of both Counties."

All things being thus agreed upon, the Lords resolved to return to the Prince, to obtain his sanction, whilst Hyde was left behind at Exeter to agree with the Commissioners upon the settlement of the Contributions, and to settle some other particulars which they had resolved upon.

The Council having promised to send him his new commission within a few day, Sir Richard agreed to resign his commission as General in charge of the blockade of Plymouth

to Sir John Berkeley   But this new commission was never sent,
"which" (adds Sir Richard in his Narrative), "was none of the
weakest reasons why that associated army was not raised"

"Being almost cured of his wounds and desirous to advance
his Majesty's service all he could, Sir Richard sent forth his
orders into certain parts of Devon and Cornwall for the taking
up and bringing together his runaway soldiers and also to levy
others.   But Sir John Berkeley wrote to the Cornish Commissioners a letter, dated May 26ᵗʰ, declaring his own power over them
and the County as Colonel-General, and commanding them not
to obey any of Sir Richard's orders   The like did Sir John
Berkeley to those in Devon and before Plymouth, which was
brought to Sir Richard under Sir John Berkeley's own hand"

Sir Richard accordingly determined to lay his case before
the Prince and his Council, who were now in Barnstaple,
whither they had retired to escape the plague which had broken
out with great virulence in Bristol   Accordingly in June he
"made his first journey to present his duty to the Prince with
his humble desires to the Lords that he might be reinstated in
the command of those men he had formerly levied"

Whatever these high-mettled Cavaliers might have done if
left to themselves to settle their punctilios as to precedence, it
is tolerably certain that the Council, though acting in the
Prince's name, could do but little to smooth matters.   This
conflict of authority was already breaking up the strength of
the King's party in the West

One only of the military competitors was pure and dis-
interested; while others were standing each upon his dignity,
Lord Hopton was declaring that, for his part, he was ready to
sacrifice his own honour in the service of the Prince

The Prince's Council finally decided to give Sir Richard
altogether a separate command, and entrusted him with the
blockade of Lyme, for which purpose men were to be drawn
from the garrisons of Dartmouth, Exeter, and Barnstaple, in
addition to certain troops that were to be given him from Lord
Goring's force

The rendezvous was to be Tiverton, and those from Exeter,
according to order, appeared at the time appointed, but those
from Barnstaple and Dartmouth marched a day's journey and
more towards Tiverton, and then were recalled by the Prince to
Barnstaple to defend that town, as rumours of an advance of
the enemy under Fairfax was bruited abroad.

Sir Richard was naturally greatly incensed at this treatment, and in a cover directed to Mr Fanshaw, the Secretary

for the Council, returned the Commission of Field-Marshal
which the Prince had given him, and within two or three days
afterwards, on the 5th of July, he sent a very insolent letter to
the Lords of the Council, complaining of the many undeserved
abuses offered him, and expressing his intention of serving in
future as a volunteer, until such time as he "might have
opportunity to acquaint His Majesty with his sufferings"

At about the same time in which Sir Richard Granville was
bringing his complaints to the Prince's court at Barnstaple, but
whether immediately before or after is uncertain, he was using
his position and authority as Sheriff of Devon, to raise the
county forces with the object of putting himself at their head.

The design is candidly avowed in the "Narrative" above
alluded to, but it was frustrated it seems by the Commissioners

The following is his own account, although written in the
third person :—

"Sir R G was desired by many of the gentry of Devon, as
Sheriff, to command a general meeting of all the inhabitants of
Devon, at Crediton—i e, 4 or 5 of the chief of every parish to
advise of speedy means to raise a powerful army in the County,
for the defence and security of the same against the enemy"
The Prince's Council, receiving information of this, commanded
Sir Richard by an order in writing "that he failed not at his
peril speedily on sight thereof to attend his Highness's pleasure
in Cornwall" Sir Richard obeyed, having first desired some of
the Commissioners of Devon "to favour so much their own
welfare as to meet the inhabitants of Devon at Crediton," which
was then to be the next day following

Some of the Commissioners met at Crediton accordingly, and
"found there present above 5,000 of the chief inhabitants of the
county, whose propositions were, that if they might have Sir
R Grenville for their Commander, and that none of their arms
should be taken again from them, nor they carried out of their
county without their own consents, that they would generally
provide themselves of arms and munitions upon their own
charges towards the defence of the County against the enemy,
and that such as would not join with them in the same courses,
should be taken and dealt with as enemies

" But the Commissioners, denying them leave to choose their
own commander and by words giving the country great distaste, made them depart very much discontented, and the
hopeful meeting to raise a great army became desperately lost,
which hastened the ruin of the west."

The proceeding which seems to have been of the nature

stated in the *Narrative*, was considered a highly reprehensible contempt of the Prince's authority, and gave great umbrage to the Council.

It is scarcely necessary to remark that the description of the assemblage at Crediton was a mere gasconade—even four or five persons from every parish in Devonshire would not have produced half the number, and if the agricultural parishes only were meant, as is more probable, the absurdity of the estimate becomes more glaring ; if there was no intentional exaggeration the subtraction of one or even two final numerals from the 5,000 of the text may be the more correct reading

After this Sir Richard established himself with his own horse and foot at Ottery St. Mary, and, without any commission, indulged in the most arbitrary excesses, raising what money he would and imprisoning what persons he pleased

It was here that his quarrel with Sir John Berkeley took its acutest form

He adopted a highly original method of offence by ordering a "warrant" to be read in the churches of the district over which he had assumed control

" That all persons should bring him an account of what moneys or goods had been plundered from them by Sir John Berkeley or any under him.'

Such were the relations existing at that time between the Royalist commanders in the West, whilst the enemy was preparing for a vigorous march upon them.

The tradition which is said to exist, that children were hushed by their mothers with the threat of "Grenville's coming!" is probably fabulous, but it is one of the accretions which show how real was the wide-spread terror in common life, for which the excesses and cruelties of this unprincipled cavalier were responsible.

Sir Richard's conduct naturally begot great resentments, and the Commissioners of Devon sent an express to the Prince, who was then in Cornwall, beseeching him "to call Sir Richard Greenvill from thence, and to take some order for the suppressing of the furious inclinations of both sides, or else they apprehended the enemy would quickly take an advantage of those dissentions and invade the county before they otherwise intended."

The Prince therefore sent for Sir Richard to Liskeard and told him—

" The sense he had of his disrespect towards him in the sending back his commission in that manner, and of his carriage after, and asked him what authority he now had either to command men or to publish such warrants "

" He answered that he was High Sheriff of Devon, and by virtue of that office he might suppress any force, or inquire into any grievance his County suffered, and as far as in him lay give them remedy "

He was told that " as Sheriff he had no power to raise or head men otherwise than by the *Posse Comitatus,* which he could not neither upon his own head raise, without warrant from the Justices of Peace that in times of War he was to receive orders upon occasions from the Commander-in-Chief of the King's Forces, who had authority to command him by his Commission

" He was asked what he himself would have done, if, when he commanded before Plymouth the High Sheriff of Cornwall should have caused such a warrant concerning him to be read in Churches ? "

He answered little to the questions, but sullenly extolled his services and enlarged his sufferings.

Afterwards being reprehended with more sharpness than ever before, and being told that " whatever discourses he made of spending his estate, it was well understood he had no estate by any other title than the meer bounty of the King that he had been courted by the Prince more than he had reason to expect, and that he had not made those returns on his part which became him.

" In short, if he had inclination to serve his Highness he should do it in the manner he should be directed ; if not he should not, under title of being Sheriff, satisfy his own pride and passion "

" Sir Richard," becoming much gentler (Lord Clarendon adds), " upon this reprehension than upon all the gracious addresses that had been made to him," answered he would serve the Prince in such manner, and was accordingly discharged, and returned to his house at Werrington, where he lived privately for the space of a fortnight or thereabouts, without interposing in the public business.

In July Lord Goring and Sir Richard privately entered into a correspondence, and a letter, dated August 1st, was written to the Chancellor by Lord Goring, in which he said several propositions had been framed upon conference with Sir Richard, which he desired might be presented to the Prince, and if consented to, confirmed by His Highness. He said he would engage to have in a short time an army of ten or twelve thousand men, that should march wherever commanded Concluding in these words, " I see some light now of having a brave army very speedily on foot, and I will be content to lose my life and honour if we do not perform our parts, if these demands be granted." The letter was graciously received by the Prince, and the particulars proposed were signed by him, he expressing a further resolution " to add whatever should be proposed to him within his power to grant, so that there was once more a hope of looking the enemy in the face, and having a fair day for the West "

The next day Sir Richard himself waited upon the Prince at Launceston, and it was decided that he should receive a certain portion of the contributions of Cornwall, and £5,000 of the arrears   Sir Richard promised to gather together all the stragglers, who, he said, would amount to 3,000 foot, and to raise 300 more in Devonshire, and at once sent out his warrants levying men and money.

But before the end of August the friendship between Goring and Granville grew colder.   Sir Richard observing a better correspondence between Lord Goring and Sir John Berkeley than he hoped would have been, and hearing that Goring used to speak slightingly of him (which was true) he wrote a very sharp letter to him, in which he said he would have no more to do with him

However, Sir Richard continued as active as before, being now in Devon and then in Cornwall, where he commanded absolutely without any commission, and very seasonably suppressed an insurrection near St. Ives " which might else have grown to a head, and hanged two or three fellows, who I believe were guilty enough, by his own order, without any Council of War, and raised what money he pleased, and then returned to his house at Werrington "

About this time the popular feeling with regard to Goring and Granville found vent in a curious tract, of which the following is the title

" A true and strange Relative of a Boy who was entertained by the Devill to be servant to him, with the consent of his Father about Crediton in the West

" And how the Devill carried him up in the aire, and showed him the torments of Hell and some of the Cavaliers there, and what preparation there was made for Goring and Granville against they come.

" Also how the Cavaliers went to Robbe a Carrier, and how the Carrier and his Horses turned themselves into flames of fire, etc "   London, printed by G H 1645.

After the loss of Bristol, and the motion of the enemy inclined westward, it was thought fit to draw all the trained bands of Cornwall to Launceston under the command of Sir Richard Granville, and to these were added his own three regiments of old soldiers which he had formerly carried to Taunton, but which had refused to serve under Goring, and had therefore been disbanded

They were only now got together again upon the assurance that they should be commanded by Sir Richard. Besides, his experience and activity were then thought most necessary to the marching army.

The trained bands met, and marched from Launceston to Okehampton (the pass being of great importance to hinder the enemy's communication with Plymouth), which he barricaded; but at the end of the month for which they had been engaged (November) they returned to their homes.

On the 4th October Lord Goring writes to Lord Colepepper " Sir Richard Greenvile distracts us extreamly, but when the Prince will be pleased to enable me, I hope eyther to bring him into better order, or keepe him from doeing any hurt."

And a few days after, the Prince, in writing to Lord Goring, says, with reference to the usual dispute about precedence, " that he has sent direction to Sir Richard Grenville to receive orders from his Lordship, and desires that there be good intelligence and correspondence preserved between them."

Towards the end of November Sir Richard suddenly withdrew his forces from Okehampton, in defiance of orders to the contrary from Lord Goring, and occupied Launceston, which he fortified , and, according to Lysons, " caused proclamation to be made in all the churches in Cornwall that if any of Lord Goring's forces should come into the County the bells should ring, and the people rise to drive them out."

Very shortly after this, Lord Goring suddenly, on the pretence that both armies were going into winter quarters, and that his health required attention, abandoned his command and embarked at Dartmouth for France. The truth seems to have been that jealousy of his rivals, intolerance of the authority of the Prince's Council, and disappointed ambition, overpowered his loyalty, if that, indeed, was not open to suspicion He left the country amid the execrations of the people, whom he had harassed and pillaged.

His defection was undoubtedly a relief to the Prince's Council, but, unfortunately, did not rectify matters.

According to Sir Richard's " Narrative," the Prince's Council, then at Truro, importuned him on the 26th of November to propound unto them some speedy course for the preservation of the Prince's person, and so much of the country as was then in his possession ; which he did the next day, directing it by way of letter to Mr Fanshawe, the Prince's secretary at war This letter, Sir Richard tells us, " occasioned a strange rumour in the world, as if he went about to sett up the Prince against the King " He accordingly inserts it faithfully verbatim in his " Narrative "

Sir,

     Upon conference with the Lords of his Highness's Council last night their Lordships were pleased to lay their command upon me that (in this time of extremity) I should propose what course I conceived might best be taken for the advancement of his Majesty's service, the safety of his Highness's person, the preservation of this county and the maintenance and augmentation of the Western forces Sir, the thought of this hath much perplexed me , many things have offered themselves to my imagination which further consideration rejected

     It is to be considered that the enemy is in all parts of the Kingdom very prevalent, and his Majesty's forces as much lessened and disheartened , our late losses have brought us nigh despair, and we may too truly say his Majesty hath no entire county in obedience but poor little Cornwall and that too in a sad condition by the miserable accidents of war under which it hath long groaned The country is impoverished by the obstruction of all trade, and in my opinion it is not to be hoped that Cornwall, with our ruined county of Devon, can long time subsist and maintain the vast number of men that are requisite to oppose the enemie's army in case they advance upon us Sir, what we wish is not in our power to act It rests then that we lay hold on the occasions that offer the fairest face And who knows but some overture well managed may by God's blessing in a short time produce a longed-for peace to this languishing Kingdom To effect which I shall make it the offer of my sense that his Highness by the advice of the Lords in Council may send propositions to the two Houses of Parliament in London to have a treaty, wherein articles, proposed by their Lordships, tending to some such effect as these following, may be discussed , viz —

     i   That his Highness hath not been at all reflected on in the proceedings of Parliament nor ever had an hand in the bloodshed of this war

     ii   That a great part of his Highness's present maintenance is his Dutchy of Cornwall, where he now remains

     iii   That his Highness may assure the Parliament not to advance with an army further eastward than the towns and places of Devon now within his power.

     iv   That the Parliament give the like assurance to his Highness not to molest or disturb the country now within his Highness's power with incursions of armies or otherwise

     v   That the parts and places now within his Highness's power be permitted to enjoy a free trade unto and from the parts beyond the seas without disturbance at sea of any shipping within the power of the Parliament

     vi   That the shipping under his Highness's power do permit the parts and places now in the power of the Parliament to enjoy a like free trade and traffic without their molestation at sea

Q²

vii. That such part of the profits of his Highness's estate as lies in Wales or elsewhere be paid unto him as the same shall from time to time become due

viii That upon breach of any article made by any particular person, that party injured is to appeal for relief which either parties are to give without molestation of the articles

Sir,—These particulars are such as the shortness of my time hath given me leave to think on, and I shall desire you they may be presented to the Lords of his Highness's Council to be suppressed or altered as to their Lordships shall seem fit and most likely to conduce to the honour of his Majesty, the safety of His Highness's person and the preservation of the country from absolute destruction And I must advertise you, Sir, and desire you to inform their Lordships that in my opinion such a treaty will much tend to the speedy putting of an end to the wasting divisions of this kingdom And for the present, if these or the like articles be agreed on, his Highness's person will be secured, his revenues twice trebled, trade revived and the country enriched Besides, in such a vacancy of troubles here, it may please God to open a way for restoring his Majesty to his rights and we shall be enabled to fortify our frontiers, ports and towns, and to provide necessaries to defend ourselves against the worst of fortune

And if his Highness will be pleased to commit the managing of his forces and all things thereunto appertaining, unto the care of some fitting man with a competent power, his army of foot within a short time may well be raised to the number of 10,000 and maintained without the country's ruin and both them and the horse brought into due obedience, which want of government hath made them almost unserviceable, and in case the proposed way of treating produce not its desired success, yet the whole county, seeing his Highness's sincere endeavour and desires for peace, and that his Highness's labour tends only to the preservation of these parts from utter ruin and destruction, I am most confident that after a General Meeting of the chief Gentry of this county (which I desire you to beseech his Highness may be speedily appointed), the whole body of this country then finding how far the preservation of their persons and estates are concerned, will unanimously join in the defence thereof, and (with God's blessing on our endeavours therein) I doubt not but we shall be able to defend this county against the greatest force our enemies can pour against us To conclude, I will make it my suit unto you that you will become my advocate humbly to entreate his Highness and the Lords that what I have written may receive no misconstruction, and that my meaning which is to advance the honour and service of his Majesty, and his Highness, and the preservation of the country may not be perverted but be plainly interpreted as it is honestly intended by

Sir
Y^r affectionate Servant
R Grenvile

Truro
Nov. 29th 1645

Not long after this, the enemy, being possessed of the greatest part of Devonshire and likely to advance westward of Exeter, Sir Richard further "proposed and desired that the Lords would be pleased to have the affairs so ordered for the apparent security of so much of the western parts as then remained" in the possession of the Royalists. He urged that these particular

places in Devon should be speedily occupied with troops, viz,
Newton-Bushel, Okehampton and Chimley (Chulmleigh?), and
these quarters to be fortified and a line of communication made,
extending from the one place to the other. It was probably
also at this time that he propounded the notable scheme of
cutting a deep trench from Barnstaple to the South Sea for the
space of nearly forty miles, by which he said he would defend
all Cornwall and so much of Devon against the world. Lord
Clarendon ridicules the scheme, but Lord Lansdowne, in his
"Vindication of Sir Richard," writes "Is there anything new
or strange in defending a country by entrenchments? Is not
the practice as old as Julius Cæsar, and mentioned by himself
in his commentaries of the war with the ancient Gauls? Was
it not thus that the modern Gauls in our own times defended
the French Flanders?" The forcing of those Lines will stand
for ever upon record among the first of the late Duke of
Marlborough's military glories. What was there then so
ridiculous, so mad, or so extravagant in this proposal as to
be thus singly pick'd out to be quoted as a proof of the
man's being out of his wits? It were to be wished we had
been told the rest of this General's schemes; perhaps among
military judges they would not have been thought so wild
and impracticable as they might appear to persons of another
calling, tho' never so able and learned in their respective
professions."

CHAPTER XIV.

THERE is very little personal record of the four unquiet years of Lady Grace's widowhood. The only gleams of happiness apparently were the marriages, first of her second daughter, Grace to Robert Fortescue of Filleigh, and secondly of her eldest daughter, Elizabeth,—"Besse," as she was familiarly called, to Peter Prideaux, eldest son of Sir Peter Prideaux, Baronet, of Netherton and Farway, co Devon.

The following letter from Lady Grace to Hugh Fortescue, Esq, the father of Grace s future husband, has been discovered among the old deeds at Castle Hill —

LADY GRACE GRANVILLE TO HUGH FORTESCUE, ESQ

Noble Sir

I returne you thankes that in some measure you expresse a willingnes on my proposall to performe parte, & were it in my choice to accomplish it so easy, as I wish, I should not urge it farther   But when your owne wisdome shall duely consider the safety & conveniency it may procure I hope you will not stick to advance the full 500, for I well know having made some attempt to farther the business already, that much more is expected, and doubtlesse will be so farr prest as you will very hardly avoyde it, wch made me wish you to fall on so noble & free a way to tender such a sum, (wd though the times are difficult enough to rayse money) yet in such a case as this, I hope not altogeather impossible by you to be performed   Sir I confesse if the match proceed between us, I shall much desire, both your Honor & profitt, & a Person of your Fortune & quallity will not easily shipp nice observation, in these doubtfull times, therfore it will behoove you, to settle a faire opinion in his Matie of yr readines to assist him, as well as a willingnes to receave Pardon from him, for Sir, what hath endangerd you, but an assisting the contrary Power, & nothing can secure you, but a cleare testimony of your Loyall affection to the King wth promises honor & prosperity to yr Family, wch is heartely wishd by me who am farr from any Pollitick end, or practise, but must needs acquaint you, with so greate a trueth, as to lett you know that what I have proposed is the easiest way I can devize to attayne your desires, & I despaire of being able to accomplish anything of my owne Power without you Performing this full sum, it being the lowest that your Quallity can tender   To perswade you I can doe it and faile you at last, suits not my disposition, but if you will adventure one 500 this way, I will use all the meanes I can to accomplish it & that with speede.   the sooner I know your full resolution heerin, the better, not knowing how soone I may be incapable of business   so with my best service to you & yr Family, I rest

Yr well-wishing kinswoman
GRACE GRENVILE

Stow Nov 22 1643

My mother salutes you heartely, & I doubt not her approbation if that is convenient be afforded

(Superscription)

To my Honord Kinsman
Hugh Fortescew Esqr
present these

The Fortescues of Wear Giffard took the Parliamentary side. They were not however active partisans, although they contributed money largely to the cause They appear to have been successful in assuming an outward attitude of neutrality, as on the King's coming into Devonshire in 1644, a letter of protection under the King's hand was obtained, which is still preserved at Castle Hill

But before the wedding could take place Lady Smith was taken ill and died at Stowe, and was buried at Kilkhampton on the 16th of February, 1643-4, and the marriage was postponed in consequence

There is a local tradition that the Queen, in her flight from Exeter to Falmouth, honoured old Stowe with a visit. The Queen had been delivered of a princess (afterwards Duchess of Orleans) on Sunday, June 16, 1644, at Exeter, and hearing that Lord Essex was marching into Devonshire with a large army, and that the Parliament wished to capture her and commit her to the Tower, and moreover that the fleet at Torbay was watching the mouth of the Exe in order to cut off her retreat by sea, she felt there was no road left open to her but the west, and with the hope of finding the means of escape in Falmouth, she left Exeter by night, within a week of her confinement, in a litter with a small party of attendants, and made for Okehampton Here, so the traditions runs, Antony Payne met them and guided them to Stowe by a series of by-tracks and lanes, in order to secure greater secresy From Stowe she is said to have gone to Lanherne and from thence to Falmouth In confirmation of this theory, a letter is said to have been seen from Lady Grace, in which she mentions the fact of the Queen having slept at Stowe and departing to Lanherne, but, unfortunately, this letter cannot now be traced, and although it would be pleasing to accept the tradition, and to picture Lady Grace lovingly comforting and entertaining her loyal mistress at Stowe, it seems impossible not to accept the evidence adduced by Mr Paul L Karkeek in a very interesting paper on the subject of the Queen's Flight, printed in the "Transactions of the Devonshire Association," vol. viii pp 467-479, that from Okehampton the Queen went to Launceston, (the most direct route,) under the escort of Prince Maurice, and from Launceston to Truro, and so to Falmouth and Pendennis Castle, whence she escaped, hotly pursued by three Parliamentary ships, who came close up to them, and "bestowed a hundred cannon-shot upon them," and landed near Brest on July 15th a month save a day after her confinement.

Pendennis Castle was a place of considerable importance as a fortress at this time, (though it could have afforded but scanty accommodation to the Queen and her suite,) and was commanded by John Arundell of Trerice, a cousin of Sir Bevill's. He had married a daughter of George Cary of Clovelly It was to this fortress, as to a place of greater security than Stowe, that Lady Grace sent her chests of valuables, when Lord Essex's army entered Devonshire ; for the home of such noted Royalists was scarcely likely to escape the plunderers, and armies must have passed and repassed at no great distance from Stowe for many months to come. Lady Grace and her children must have had a terribly anxious time, and lived in constant expectation of being attacked.

The following letter, written just a fortnight after the Queen's escape from Pendennis Castle, was written by Mrs Arundell to Lady Grace to acknowledge the arrival of the valuables —

MRS ARUNDELL TO LADY GRANVILLE.

Honord La

I have reseved 9 chestes and do promies to keepe them as safe as any of my one, for the shall on stand by the other (that God that hath hetherto defended vs and fought the kings battelles will louke on vs in marsey) I can not dispare tho wee are shrodly thretened every day Madam to you and yours I wish as much happiness as to our one famely and shall ever remeane

Your La affecttionat
Cousen and humbell
sarvant
MARY ARUNDELL

Pendence the
   30 of July
I can not present
Mr Arundells sarves to your
La for hee is now at Paris, but I know
hee owes you as much as any freud
you have in the world.
   (Superscription)

To my honored
freud and deere cosen
the La Grase Grenvell
thes present.

John Granville, " Jack " as he was familiarly called, the eldest surviving son was not yet fifteen when Sir Bevill was killed He had been a gentleman commoner at Gloucester Hall, Oxford, but if we are to accept Antony Payne's letter as authentic, he was with Sir Bevill when he fell, and there and then took command of the troops in his place. " Master John, when I mounted him upon his father's horse rode him into the war, like a young prince as he is, and our men followed him with their swords drawn and with tears in their eyes" Certainly a year previously the University and several Colleges had sent money and plate to the King, and on the 13th of August an order had been given for view of arms Graduates and undergraduates had eagerly responded to the appeal Books were flung away, and day after day some three or four hundred members of the University had diligently practised their drill (*cf.* Gardiner's "History of the Civil War," I , 33) Very probably therefore Jack had joined his father, and was with him at the battle of Lansdowne At any rate he was in command of his father's troop afterwards, and took part in several of the engagements, and particularly in Cornwall at the defeat of the Earl of Essex. At the second battle of Newbury he narrowly escaped meeting his father's fate. Being in the thickest of the fight, and having received several wounds in various parts of his body, he was at last felled to the ground with a most dangerous blow on the head from a halberd, and he lay there for some time in an unconscious state until a body of the King's Horse, charging the enemy afresh, beat them off the ground, where he was discovered afterwards amongst the dead, covered with blood and dust Upon being recognized, he was carried into that part of the field where the King and the Prince of Wales were, who sent him to Donnington Castle hard by, to be treated for his wounds But it must have been long before tidings of hope could reach the anxious mother, for no sooner were the armies drawn off from the Field of Newbury than Donnington Castle itself was besieged by the Roundheads, and their bullets, it is said, constantly whistled through the room where he lay during the twelve days which elapsed before the defenders were relieved by the King at the third battle of Newbury. But the warrior-boy came round at last safely, and the following letter, preserved in the collection of MSS , formerly called "the Rupert Correspondence," contains his grateful thanks to Prince Maurice for his attention to him.

JOHN GRANVILLE TO H.R.H PRINCE MAURICE

May it please y^r highnes

The great favour y^r highnes has donne mee, in sparing y^r surgeon, has already almost recovered mee of my wounds and for my health (the Phisitians tell mee) wth some repose in ye country will be in a condition good enough, soe y^t (I hope) I shall be able to doe y^r highnes service againe, wch is my chiefest ambition It lies now in y^r highnes power greatly to obleige mee & enable mee for ye future to serve y^r highnes wth a good recruite of souldiers

Barnestable, who can never keepe their fingers out of a rebellion, haue beene
of late highly guilty in y^t kind, wch haue made our wise comissioners of Devon
to thincke of placing a garrison in y^t towne   In a busines of this nature I
knew unto none I ought more fitly to addresse myselfe then unto y^r highnes,
and if y^r highnes thincke me worthy ye goverm^t of this towne, I doubt not
but be very serviceable unto y^r highnes in this commaund   I have some
interest in y^t part of ye county, in regard ye toune lies soe neare my estate,
and I know I can be noe where in a better capacity of doing ye King service,
then in this toune, because it stands in ye midst of my tenants and acquain
tance, and I'me confident (if y^r highnes vouchsafe's me this government and
ye contribution of ye north part of Devon for ye maintenance of my men)
I will bring into ye feild to march unto y^r highnes next sumer a thousand men,
and leave a good garrison behind in ye towne, all wch souldiers I will be
obleiged to pay during ye war   Thus much uppon these conditions I will
engadge myselfe to do uppon mine honour, but I wholely submitt myselfe
unto y^r highnes and shall attend y^r highnes answer unto

Y^r highnes most obedient servant
JOHN GRENVILE

Bristol Decem 23
(Superscription) 1644
        For his highnes Prince Maurice
                These

The wish of the youthful cavalier was not, however, to be
gratified in that way at any rate   The time was indeed ripe, or
considered to be so, for the formal imposition of a garrison upon
the refractory town of Barnstaple referred to in young
Granville's letter, but Sir John Berkeley appointed his own
lieutenant, Sir Allen Apsley, to the command.

Jack came back to Stowe to recover of his wounds, and his
sister Grace's wedding was arranged to take place at once
The following letter from the bride-elect was written to her
lover a month previously   It is a charming example of
maidenly diffidence and affection, which will not, however,
appeal very strongly to the nineteenth century young woman

GRACE GRANVILLE TO ROBERT FORTESCUE, ESQ

Noble S^r

I am very sorry that sicknesse of all other reasons should prevent your
visiting this place, and tho your presence be an honer which I much desire yett
I cañott but lett you know I hope the respect you bear your owne health will
keepe you from venturing sooner a broade than you may doe it with safety,
which I heartily pray may be spedily   I must confesse your affectionate
respects do more and more every day teach me a new study which formerly I
have not bin acquainted withall, it will therfore be much against my will to
be guilty of soe greate a crime as ingratitude, to prevent which I beseech you
receive my most humble thankes both for your curteous lre and token, with

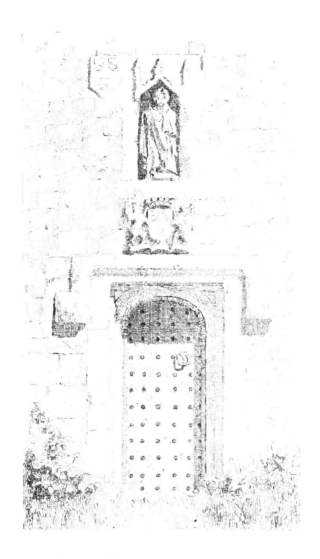

THE ENTRANCE TO THE GRANVILLE AISLE IN
KILKHAMPTON CHURCH.

this assurance that ther is not any one doth more really wish your happinesse and desire to heare of your recovery then

S^r

Y^r most affectionate Cousen
and humble servant
GRACE GRENVILE.

Stow Janury^e
  12 1645

It will be a favor if you please to present my humble service to your Noble Father and Mother

(Superscription)

For my Noble ffreind & Kinsman
Mr Robert Fortescue
present
these

The marriage took place from Stowe on the 20th of February, 1644-5, and the two following letters from Lady Grace to Mrs. Fortescue may as well be inserted here, although not strictly in chronological order as regards other events to be recorded in this chapter —

LADY GRACE GRANVILLE TO MRS ROBERT FORTESCUE

Deare Grace

I was much joy'd to heare y^r Husband and selfe, with the rest had a pleasant jorney, & that yee mett such affectionat wellcome I have often wished myself with you, but doe finde had I adventurd, twould have proved a trouble to my frends to have had a sick Guest, for truly I have been much vexd with such sick fitts, as you know I am subject to, & the colde weather begins roughly with me Prithee be carefull to present my best Respects & service to my Brother & sister Fortescue & all my noble Cosens let me know when I shall see you againe, & pray fayle not to consider all things, may be most contenting to those friends, whom it will become you carefully to observe I expedited y^r brothers home before now they must loose no longer time, so beseeching God to blesse you & my son Fortescue & y^r Brothers & graunt us happie meeting

Y^r tenderly affectionat mother
GRACE GRENVILE.

Stow Oct 16
  1645

(Superscription)

For my dear Daughter
Grace Fortescue at
Weare these dd

Wear Gifford, where Grace was staying, is an ancient seat of the Fortescue family, four miles south of Bideford, in the valley of the Torridge, nearly opposite Annery, the home of the St. Legers. Wear Gifford Hall, picturesquely set in beautiful grounds and covered with climbing plants, contains some of the finest carved panelling in the country, and the oaken roof of the hall has for

R²

its richness been compared to that of Henry VII.'s Chapel at
Westminster, though the device is altogether different. The
old house suffered a good deal at the hands of the Roundheads
only a few weeks after the next letter was written, the courtyard wall being destroyed amongst other things. It is this
approaching danger that is referred to in the letter probably.

LADY GRACE GRANVILLE TO MRS ROBERT FORTESCUE

Deare Grace

Had I not expected to have heard from you by Mr Gealad, who promisd
when he went hence a speedy returne, I should have sent ere now to be more
certainly assurd where and how you are, for you may be sure though our
Persons are separated yet my affection and Care still follows you it disquietts
my minde much to consider you are in so unprovided a condition to begin
housekeeping, fearing you have not so much patient resolution to undergoe it
as I had wch begun on such terms   Glad I should be to heare you meet some
courteous helpe to comfort you in the beginning   however prithee have a
good heart & doe not distrust the Divine providence I long to heare some
certainty of y^r being with childe, I am resolv'd y^r sister shall lay down her
Belly heere, for I can with no conveniency be with her upon all occasions
elsewhere   I should be glad to do the like for you assoone as her Pull is past
if it please God you be in the same case, which I heartily pray for.   I have
had my health reasonable well (I praise God) since my coming hither, & doe
live very privatly heer, having seen very few strangers since my coming
hither & as yet have been no where abroad but at Church   Orchard is not
yet come out of the west which hinders my buying anything, for without
ready money heir's no buying any thing   I sent to enquire of the Torrington
Caryer for you but heard nothing, however I meant to have written but he
was gone before I knew it   I hope you are not yet removed from Ware, be
not too hasty in doing it unlesse there be just reason for it   I hope my Son is
well whom I affectionatly salute, praying to God to bless you both and I am
undoubtedly

Y^r affectionat mother
GRACE GRENVILE

I am providing a Bed
Furniture & some Pewter
for you

Madford Jan. 20 1616
Y^r sister Prideaux salutes you & my son Fortescue

Grace Fortescue was delivered of a daughter that year, who
also was named Grace. She afterwards married Sir Halswell
Tynte, first Baronet of Halswell, Somerset, the ancestor of the
present Mr Halswell Melbourne Kemeys-Tynte, by whose kind
permission several of the Granville letters in his possession have
been printed in these memoirs. This was the only offspring of
this marriage, and the mother soon afterwards died, and her
husband married as his second wife Susannah, daughter of Sir
John Northcote, first Baronet of Hayne, Devon, by Grace his
wife, daughter and co-heiress of Hugh Halswell, of Wells,
Somerset

Lady Grace's other daughter, referred to in the above letter, was Elizabeth Prideaux, who had been married on the 17th of November, from Stowe The husband succeeded his father as third Baronet, and Lady Prideaux died in 1692, and was burried at Farway, near Honiton, leaving a numerous issue.

In the beginning of January, 1646, the relative positions of the two armies were broadly these ·—The main body of Fairfax's forces were at Tiverton, with detached garrisons holding posts on both sides of the Exe. The Royalist army was now grouped in two divisions, separated by Dartmoor , the one, principally of Horse, occupying the country between the Dart and the Teign; the other, consisting of both Horse and Foot, lying partly at and about Okehampton, and partly at Tavistock, where Prince Charles himself was collecting all the loose contributions of men, money and supplies which could be obtained from the country in his rear.

He calculated that when every available man had been brought into line, he would have 6,000 Foot and 5,000 Horse at his disposal Unfortunately for him his body was formidable in numbers only. The brutalities of Sir Richard Granville in Cornwall, and the ravages committed in Devonshire by the Cavalry which had been deserted by Goring, had exasperated even the most loyal subject who had anything to lose The army itself was little better than a mob, scarcely an officer of rank would take orders from his superior, and the men, stinted of every kind of supply, were scattered in small groups from the neighbourhood of Exeter almost to Land's End.

Fairfax's new army was indeed somewhat weakened by the necessity of despatching Fleetwood and Whalley to watch the motions of the King's Cavalry at Oxford, but it was still strong enough to continue the blockade of Exeter, and to deal with the approaching enemy in his existing state of disorganization.

On January 8th orders were given to advance, and part of his army pushed on to Bow, to distract the enemies attention : another part surprised the Royalist Horse, under Lord Went-worth, at Bovey Tracey, by a night attack, and captured four hundred of them.

Insubordinate and tyrannical as Sir Richard Granville was, he was at heart a soldier, and his first impulse on hearing of Wentworth's mishap, was to write a letter to the Prince, in which he represented the impossibility of keeping the army together, or fighting with it in the condition it was then in

He informed him that he had the night before sent directions to Major-General Harris (who commanded the Foot that came

from Plymouth) to guard a certain bridge but that he returned
him word that he would receive orders from none but General
Digby; that General Digby said he would receive orders from
none but his Highness; that a party of Lord Wentworth's
Horse had the same night come into his quarters, where his
troops of guard and his fire-locks were, that neither submitted
to the command of the other, they had fallen foul and two or
three men had been killed, that they continued still in the
same place, drawn up one against the other, and therefore he
urged the Prince to appoint a Commander-in-Chief, from whom
all independent officers might receive orders

He therefore desired his Highness to constitute the Earl of
Brentford or Lord Hopton to such a post

Therefore the Prince made an order, on the 15th January,
commissioning Lord Hopton to take the sole charge of the army
upon him, and appointing Lord Wentworth to command all the
Horse, and Sir Richard Granville the Foot.

The Prince sent Sir Richard a letter of thanks for this
advice, and which he had said he had followed

But Sir Richard evidently expected to receive the supreme
command himself, and not the inferior one which the Prince
had assigned to him, and he absolutely refused to act in a
subordinate position to anyone

To the Prince he wrote desiring to be excused on account of
his indisposition of health, and at the same time expressing his
belief that he could do the Prince better service by collecting
the soldiers who straggled in the country, and in suppressing
the malignants, and guarding the passes of Cornwall

But to Lord Colepepper he made no disguise, stating openly
that he could not consent to be commanded by Lord Hopton.

The Prince sent for him and told him "the extreme ill
consequence that would attend the public service, if he should
there, and in such a manner, quit the charge his Highness had
committed to him—that more should not be expected from him
than was agreeable to his health, and that if he took the
command upon him, he should take what adjutants he pleased
to assist him."

But notwithstanding all that the Prince could say to him,
or such of his friends who thought they had interest in him, he
continued obstinate, and positively refused to take the charge,
or to receive orders from Lord Hopton.

Such insubordination was unpardonable, and the Prince
therefore caused him to be arrested, and committed him as
a prisoner to the Governor of Launceston Castle on the 19th

day of January, 1646, and the following day he was cashiered
from the various regiments he had commanded without any
court-martial having been held

Sir Richard's arrest caused great distractions; the whole
county took offence, even the very persons who had complained
of his tyrannous conduct, as much as any, expressed great
trouble, and the soldiers, who were sincerely attached to him in
spite of his overbearing manner, refused " to be commanded
either by Gorrans or Hoptonians " (' The Moderate Messenger,
No. 2, from Feb 3 to Feb 10, 1646, p 11 ")

" Whoever had observed the temper of that County towards
Sir Richard Grenvil," (writes Lord Clarendon) or the clamours
of the common people against his oppression and tyranny,
would not have believed that such a necessary proceeding
against him, at that time, could have been any unpopular act .
there being scarce a day in which some petition was not
presented against him.   As the Prince passed through Bodmin,
he received Petitions from the wives of many substantial and
honest men, amongst the rest of the Mayor of Listithiel, who
was very eminently well affected and useful to the King's
Service, all whom Grenvil had committed to the Common
Goal for presuming to fish in that River, the Royalty of which
he pretended belonged to him by virtue of the Sequestration
granted him by the King of the Lord Roberts' estate at
Lanhetherick . whereas they who were committed pretended
to a Title and had always used the liberty of fishing in those
waters as Tenants to the Prince of his Highness' Manor of
Listithiel, there having been long suits between the Lord
Roberts and the Tennants of that Manor for that Royalty
And when his Highness came to Tavistock he was again
Petitioned by many women for the liberty of their husbands,
whom Sir Richard had committed to Prison for refusing to
Grind at his Mill, which, he said, they were bound by custom
to do. So by his Martial Power he had asserted whatever
Civil Interest he thought fit to lay claim to, and never
discharged any man out of Prison till he absolutely submitted
to his pleasure . .   . . Yet, notwithstanding all this, Sir
Richard was not sooner committed by the Prince, than even
those who had complained of him as much as any. expressed
great trouble, and many Officers of those Forces which he had
Commanded in a Tumultuous manner, Petitioned for his release,
and others took great pains to have the indisposition of the
people and the ill accidents that followed imputed to that
proceeding against Sir Richard Greenvil, in which none were

more forward than some of the Prince's own Household
Servants, who were so tender of him, that they forgot their
duty to their Master"

Even his imprisonment did not check his tyranny. Lord
Clarendon states that there were in the gaol at Launceston, at
this time, where he himself was committed, at least thirty
persons, Constables and other men, whom he had committed
and imposed fines upon some of them four and five hundred
pounds, upon pretence of delinquency (of which he was in
no case a proper judge) for the payment whereof they were
detained in prison

Amongst the rest was the Mayor of St Ives, one Hammond,
who had there the reputation of an honest man, and was
certified to be such by Colonel Robinson the Governor and by
all the neighbouring gentlemen.

After the late insurrection there he had given his bond
to Sir Richard Greenvil of five hundred pounds to produce
a young man who was then absent, and accused to be a
favourer of that Mutiny, within so many days.

The time expired before the man could be found, but
within three days after the expiration of the time, the Mayor
sent the fellow to Sir Richard Greenvil.

That would not satisfy, but he sent his Marshall to the
Mayor himself and required fifty pounds of him for having
forfeited his bond, and upon his refusal to pay it forthwith,
committed him to the gaol at Launceston.

The son of the Mayor presented a Petition to the Prince at
Truro for his father's liberty, setting forth the matter of fact
as it was, and annexing a very ample testimony of the good
affection of the man. The petition was referred to Sir Richard
Greenvil, with direction " that if the case were in truth such,
he should discharge him." As soon as the son brought this
petition to him, he put it in his pocket, told him " the Prince
understood not the business, and committed the son to gaol,
and caused irons to be put on him for his presumption."

Upon a second petition to the Prince at Launceston, after
the time that Sir Richard himself was committed, he directed
the Lord Hopton "upon examination of the truth of it to
discharge the man ; of which when Sir Richard heard, he sent
to the gaoler ' to forbid him at his peril to discharge Hammond,
threatening him to make him pay the money,' and after that
caused an action to be entered in the Town Court at Launceston
upon the forfeiture of the bond "

Sir Richard's imprisonment, and the dissentions that arose

in consequence, gave the finishing stroke to the war in the West ; the service everywhere languished, the soldiers gradually deserted, and Lord Hopton was compelled, after some faint resistance, to disband, and accept of such conditions as the enemy would give.

Lord Clarendon writing in his retirement at Jersey to Sir Edward Nicholas a few months afterwards, commented on the incident of Sir Richard's arrest as follows —

> In the imprysoning of Sir Richard Grenvile (who is most unworthy of ye reputacion he had) we were absolutely necessitated to it . . We had no reason to believe his interest in ye country soe great , neither in truth was it, but ye genal indisposicon wch at ye time possessed men was very apparent, when those very men who complayned against him, and seemed to despise him, took occasion to grumble at his removal (Clarendon MSS. Printed in Lister's "Life of Clarendon," iii , 38)

After Sir Richard's committal, the officers and soldiers of the Army to the number of 4,000 presented a petition to the Prince that he might be speedily brought to his trial before a Court of War, there to receive the justice that belongs to a soldier, or else he restored to his former commands ; and Sir Richard himself petitioned the Prince that he might speedily account for any crime he had been guilty of, or else have leave to depart the kingdom for his own safety and preservation. But both petitions were rejected, and the Prince's Council returned answer that Sir Richard's " crime was against the King and his service, and therefore his Majesty should be first acquainted therewith and then Sir Richard should know his answer."

So marked was the feeling of indignation amongst the soldiers against Sir Richard's imprisonment, that it was deemed expedient to remove him from Launceston, and a warrant was signed for consigning him as a prisoner to Barnstaple. (*cf.* Sir Richard Granville's Narrative of the Proceedings of His Majesty's affairs in the West of England, &c. Carte's letters I. 96)

But as the course of events rendered this impracticable, his destination was altered to St Michael's Mount in Cornwall, whither he was conveyed under the care of a corporal and ten troopers.

Whilst Sir Richard was a prisoner in the Mount he employed certain of his servants to remove such goods as he had then in Cornwall into some place of safety. " Some of which goods being nigh Penryn were on their removal made stay of, his truncks broke open and searched, where finding nothing questionable they were afterwards dismissed The other part

of his goods being embarked at Padstow had a more severe
fortune, for General Hopton, without any order from his
Highness, sent an officer of his to survey the goods, and he
compelled all to be again brought on land, and then he with his
associates broke open every trunck, chest, pack, and box locked,
forcing the servants away from the sight of their actions   And
then every man took to himself what he found pleasing, and
also invited others of the army to share of what was left ; and
shortly afterwards the enemy drove them thence and took all
the remainder of the goods of any great value."

On the 2nd of March, when news came that the Royalist
army was retiring from Bodmin and that the enemy, in the
words of Lord Clarendon, were "marching furiously after"
there was reasonable apprehension of the Prince's safety in the
minds of his Council, and that same night he embarked from
the secret water-port of Pendennis Castle, and, on the 4th
landed at one of the Isles of Scilly.   Amongst those in attendance upon him was young "Jack" Granville, who had been
promoted on his recovery from his wound to the rank of a
Brigadier of Foot, and the following year had been appointed
a Gentleman of the Bedchamber to the Prince of Wales (*cf.*
Lady Fanshawe's Memoirs, 1829, p 56).   The Prince, it appears,
had formed a strong attachment for him, he being much about
the same age as himself, and he obtained the King's consent
thus to have him near his person   There was a remarkable
letter upon his appointment found amongst the Queen's letters,
(ungenciously printed by Order of Parliament to expose her
influence in the war), wherein it appears that she was offended
at young Granville's promotion, as done without her partici-
pation   The King excuses himself on the ground of the lad's
promising merit, the signal services of his father, the interest
of his family and the earnest request of the young Prince
himself.   This letter is still extant in the εἰκὼν βασιλική.

After a stay of nearly six weeks at S. Mary's, where
they were much straitened for want of necessary provisions,
the Prince and his Council transferred themselves to Jersey
There he was gladly entertained by Sir George Carteret in
Elizabeth Castle, where, though he was barely sixteen years old,
he held levies and dined in state, proving himself already a
proficient in the art of obtaining popularity, for says the old
Jersey Chronicler, "C'est un prince grandement benin"   Sir
George Carteret got him a pleasure boat from St Malo, and the
Prince, with John Granville, doubtless, as his attendant, spent
hours in steering about the island-bays, though never venturing

beyond range of the castle guns. He stayed more than two months in Elizabeth Castle, and then left to join the Queen in Paris

Upon the advance of the enemy into the heart of Cornwall, Sir Richard had sent another petition to the Prince "for leave to depart the Kingdom. and that his services might find some other reward than the delivering him up into the hands of that enemy from whence he had no reason to expect the least degree of mercy" Accordingly the Prince, before he escaped himself from Pendennis Castle, left orders behind that Sir Richard should be allowed to escape also, to prevent his falling into the hands of the army, and the day following the Prince's escape (March 3rd) Sir Richard took boat and sailed for Brest where he arrived on the 14th, and journeyed thence to Nantes Here, after some delay, he was joined by his son Richard and his tutor, Mr. Herbert Ashley, who had been living at Rouen since January, 1843-4

The following letter from Sir Richard to Mr. Ashley was written when young Richard was first sent out of danger's way. It is amongst the Tanner MSS. in the Bodleian.—

SIR RICHARD GRANVILLE TO MR HERBERT ASHLEY

S^r

I have rec'd y^r of the 6th of this, and ame very glad of y^r safe arrivell at St Mallowes, if yo^u may finde Cane fitter than Rohan for y^r residence and my sonnes education I shall leave it to y^r choice —Cane being a more pleasant and healthy place and lesse inhabited by English, in which respect I conceive it fitter, then Roan, yet I leave it to y^r choice and earnestly desire yo^u that my sonne may converse with soe few Englishe as may be, nor presume to doo any thinge wthout your knowledge and leave For his education I desire he may constantly and dilligently be kept to the learneing of the French tongue, readinge, writinge, and arithmetick—Also rydeinge, fenceinge and daunceinge, this is all I shall expect of him which if he follow accordinge to my desire for his owne good, he shall not want any thinge But if I understand that he neglects in any kind, what I have herein commanded him to doe, truely I will neither allow him a penny to mayntaine him, nor looke on him againe as my sonne—And that you may the more fully execute and performe the trust which I have imposse on yo^u concerning his welfare, I have sent heerwith vnto yo^u a warrant of authority for the same I have latly in the night attempted to force Plymouth workes, and tooke one of them, nighe the Maudlin worke, and had my seconds perform'd their parts, Plymouth (by all probability) had been now certainly ours but all proceeds with us successfully and hopefull

The Scots have certainely lost two great Battels, and by it, many of their best Townes are now possest by the Kings M^{tye} whereupon Generall Leisley is gown out of England with most of his forces to releeve his Scotish friends

Just now credible newes is brought me that by fowle weather and a leake, a great London Shipp come from the Straights was glad to save herselfe by

S^4

thrustinge into Dartmouth, whither she is secured and is conceived to be worth above an hundred thousand pounds, besides forty thousand pounds in silver, which she hath brought with her   You shall speedily receive from me a bill of exchange for twenty pounds and I must desire you to be soe p'vident as conveniently you may, because monyes with me is very hardly to be gotten, and soe God blese you all

Buckland Monachorum y^e
     17th January 1664

Y^r affectionate friend
Ry Grenvile

The next letters are also from Sir Richard to Mr. Ashley, and are written after his arrival in France, urging him to bring his son as quickly as possible to Nantes —

S^r

I am now travailing towards Nants, and intend to stay there till I heare from you and so do now write again to ye same effect, wch is, to desire y^t you come with my sonne to me at Nants with all convenient speede   and y^t you bring with you all ye remainder of y^t mony made of ye sarges I sent over longe since, and an accompt of ye same   Mr Geo Potter, merchant, is now at St. Maloes, and will assist you for y^r iourney in any thing needful

Brest   Y^r friend
24th March   Ry Grenvile
New Stile

S^r

By my two former letters I advertised you y^t I landed at Brest in Brittany on ye 14th of March   and by both those 2 letters I desired y^t you and my sonne should come to me so soone as you could, and to bring with you all ye remainder of ye monies made, or to be made of ye sarges I last sent over for y^r maintenance   but because I have heard nothing of you since my landing, I now therefore againe desire you, together with my sonne to travaile to Nantes, where Mr John Hole merchant will advise and assist you in what I desire you should followe

I pray take notis y^t Mr George Potter merch^t is one y^t will take sufficient order for y^r comeing to me if you meete with him, he is now at St Maloes and will be (as I am informed) speedily at Roan   If you come to St Maloes and finde there a ship bound for Nantes, it may chance to be y^r speediest passage by sea   but if you come by land, your best meanes wilbe to agree with ye usuall messenger y^t comes weekely to Nantes   I desire y^r coming to me should be so private as may be, and as speedy

Nantes   Y^t faithfull friend
3rd Aprill 1646   Ry Grenvile

Nants 18th Aprill 1646

S^r

Yo^rs of y^t 31th of March, came to my handes ye 16th of this   I have not received a word from or of you else, since I came into France, though I have sent 5 severall letters to you, wch imported (as doth this) y^r speedy comīg to me, now at Nants where with trouble I stay expecting you   I conceived ye sarges would well have yeilded monies to supply y^r necessary occasions, but being not sold as by y^t letter I have taken order, y^t Mr George Potter (an English merch^t at St. Maloes) should order his correspondant at Rouen to

pay you 300ᵗʰ or 400ᵗʰ Livers bournois, if you needed it, and to advise you to
come to me with my sonne yᵉ shortest or nighest way, if yᵗ stay be longe,
you will misse me, for I am speedily for Italie   I pray send to Mr George
Potter merchᵗ at St Maloes a copy of yᵉ note of yᵉ severall pieces of sarges,
wᶜʰ I sent you from England, or else as they now remaine, that he may know
how to dispose of them yᵗ are not yet sold   Let yᵉ iorney be so private as
it may

yo   affectionate friende
Ry Grenvile

Richard and his tutor must have joined Sir Richard soon
after this letter was written, as they all left Nantes that month
and proceeded to Italy, "for the war against the Turk, not
much unlike the unhappy war of England"   There they stayed
about a year, visiting Naples and other cities

But before leaving Nantes, Sir Richard wrote the following
amusing letter to "an Honorable person in the City of
London concerning the affairs of the west" which he caused to
be published   It is a Parthian shot against his old enemy
Lord Colepepper, one of the members of the Prince's Council,
who, (with Hyde, afterwards Lord Clarendon,) had taken the
initiative in having him deposed from his command and
incarcerated in Launceston Castle —

Right Honorable

Former obligations have moved me to represent unto you my affectionate
service   I am now at Nantes in France and about to depart hence towards
Italy for the war against the Turk (not much unlike the unhappy war of
England)   My Lord, I truly value you in the number of my best and
honorable Friends, and therefore have presumed to send you herewith a
narrative truth concerning the former proceedings of the affairs of the West
of England, though not so particular as the evil managing thereof deserved,
since which an unhappy feast chanced at Penrin (a town nigh Pendennis
Castle in Cornwal) for Hopton with his new forces (lately before) taking a
strange affright at a party of the Parliament's forces at Torrington in Devon,
and flying into Cornwal with his men dispersed several ways, like a wilde-goose
chace, the sad Newes thereof made the Prince command the Earl of Brandford
and Lord Culpepper with all speed to meet the Lord Hopton and Lord Capel
at Wadebridge nigh the heart of Cornwal, to advise on affairs for the safety of
the West, (I think, to shut the stable door when the horse was gone), but
Culpepper in his haste and way finding some gentlemen merry and drinking
in Penrin town, he would needs make one amongst them and so did till night
came, and then Bacchus prevailing, Culpepper's eloquence displeased Mr
Slingsby by which grew a quarrel betwixt them two onely, and at bare
fistycuffs they were a good space till the company parted them, and
then Culpepper and Slingsby in the Moonshine got them into the
garden, and like two cocks at the end of a Battel not able to stand wel,
offer'd and peck'd at one another till the weight of Slingsbie's head drew him
to the ground, which advantage Culpepper took hold of and by it got
Slingsbie's sword, and then like St George made much more triumphant
flourishes over Slingsby then a German Fencer at the beginning of a Prize,

but by good fortune the rest of the associates came in and easily persuaded
the Duellists to end the quarrel by the cup again, which service continued till
the next day with divers and various bouts at fisty cuffs   the next day (about
ten of the clock) they having red Herrings and mustard for Breakfast,
Culpepper again gave Slingsby distaste, whereon he threw a dish of mustard in
Culpepper's face (taking his nose for a red Herring) which procured another
grievous incounter in such sort that the Market people (to part the fray)
thronged the house full, whereby that also was taken up, and the saucy Lord
fain to get his mustard-Face Eyes Beard Band and Coat wash'd , and about
four of the next evening Culpepper rid on in his hasty journey to overtake
the Lord of Branford, who rid chafing and staying for him above twenty four
hours in his way   Such a Privie-Councellor will soon finish his Master's
businesse one way, prefering his own delights before the important businesse
that concerns the safety of the Prince etc   This story is indeed very true in
every particular, and so I leave it with you and depart

Your Lordship s humble servant,
R GRENVILE

Nantes in France
  9 April 1646
  New Stile

Whilst Sir Richard was in Italy, and young "Jack" in
attendance upon the Prince in Paris, Lady Grace, broken-
hearted and sorrowful at the total overthrow of the Royal
cause in the West, to which so much life and treasure had been
sacrificed, sickened and died, and was laid to rest by the side
of her brave husband in Kilkhampton Church on the 8th of
June, 1647   Few as are the fragments handed down to us
after the lapse of nigh three centuries, every letter written by
Lady Grace serves to enshrine some characteristic of a sweet
and noble woman   Each presents to us a vivid picture of
successive stages of her history , from the letters of her earlier
married years, when her life was rich in happiness, to those of
later days when, overwhelmed with sorrow, she penned words
which must find an answering echo in the hearts of all
Compared with that of her heroic husband, her character must
needs seem drawn with softer outlines, yet, gentle as she was,
she bravely bore her part in the troubles of the time, and
endured her crowning sorrow with a patient courage, which
makes us glad that such as she have lived and left so sweet a
record of their lives

Besides Jack and her two married daughters she left four
younger children, namely Bridget, who was now sixteen, Bernard,
who was fourteen, Joana, ten, and Dennis a year younger
Probably is was to comfort Jack and his young brothers and
sisters in their bereavement, and to superintend the management of the estate, that Sir Richard was induced to take a very
venturesome journey to England at this time   He knew well

the estimation in which he was held, and how odious he was to
Parliament; so odious that, in the following year, he was
expressly named in the Treaty of Newport as one of the
seven to be excluded from pardon, and again afterwards under
the Protectorate, in a secret article of a Treaty with France, he
was one of the twenty obnoxious persons to be excluded from
from either country   But venturesome as the journey was he
undertook it, his son having already preceded him.

He disguised himself, cutting off his hair and wearing " a
very large perewigg hanging on his shoulders," and keeping his
beard, which was doubtless auburn like his brother Bevill's,
(hence his nickname "Red Fox"), black, "with a blacklede
combe," so that "none would know him but by his voyse"
(*cf* Examination of William Matthew "Comander of ye good
shipe the Expedicon of Plym° taken before Ch Ceely, Mayor of
Plymouth and Barth. Nicholls, Justice of Peace, 5 July, 1647).

How long Sir Richard stayed in England is not known, or
whether he was recognized. Records of all kinds are very
scanty for the year 1647   It is certain, however, that he
escaped with his life, and returned to Holland, where he was
soon after this date living with his daughter, but of his son we
hear no more   It is probable that he met his death by treachery,
as Lord Lansdowne particularly mentions that the son fell into
the enemy's hands and was hanged, whilst Hals gives the
incredible story in his MSS. that he was executed at Tyburn,
"for robbinge Passengers on the highway to releive his
necessity"

Towards the end of the year 1648 the Scilly Islands revolted
from the Parliament and became the last rallying point of the
Royalists   On the 8th of December in that year John
Granville was Knighted and appointed Governor of these Islands
to hold them for the King (Ormond's Letters 1 , 377), but he
had been there barely three weeks when tidings reached him of
the execution of the King   With passionate indignation he
immediately proclaimed King Charles the Second, and could
find no words hard enough for Cromwell and the regicides   He
wrote violently from Scilly —

"The extraordinary ill newes I have heard since my being
here concerning the horrible murder and treason committed on
the Person of his Most Sacred Majesty has transported me
with grief . ..   .. . I hope God will avenge it on the
heads of the damned authors and contrivers of it ... .
As soon as I was assured of this sad truth and had solemnly
paid here our abundant griefs in infinite tears, having

commanded throughout these islands a day of mourning and humiliation for our most fatal and incomparable loss, I thought it my particular duty to proclaim His Majesty, that now is, King" Brit Mus , Egerton MSS 2533. fo 474

But the war between the two parties was not ended by the King's death. Defeated by land the Royalists once more acquired a considerable strength by sea

In Jersey Sir George Carteret collected a squadron. built on the model of the privateers of St Malo, for sailing in the narrow seas, and was victorious far and wide ; Prince Rupert made Kinsale his head quarters, whilst Sir John Granville fortified the Scilly Islands already strong from their natural position and the works erected there by former Kings   From these three points this robber warfare was opened against the trade of the English Republic   Whatever sailed to and from England, or lay off its coasts, was declared fair spoil, let the owners be who they might   The communication between Ireland and England was rendered insecure, and sometimes completely interrupted, by royalist privateers. For such a power as England, devoted to the sea by nature, this was an intolerable state of affairs.

The Parliament accordingly fitted out a powerful fleet under Admirals Blake and Sir George Ayscue to recover the Scilly Islands   Sir John had been joined by his young brother Bernard, who was then barely eighteen years of age, and who had made his escape from his tutors   Young Bernard managed to carry considerable reinforcements to his brother, by the help of Mr Rasleigh, at whose seat at Menabilly, near Fowey, he lay concealed for the purpose

In the interim of the siege Van Tromp, the Dutch Admiral, appeared before Scilly with a powerful fleet, and tempted Sir John Granville with the offer of no less a sum than one hundred thousand pounds to cede the islands to the States-General   But the noble Cavalier stood there to contend against treason, not to imitate it ; and he refused to yield up an inch of British soil to a stranger   He thought it, however, his duty to acquaint with the King with the offer, but His Majesty, notwithstanding his great necessities, rejected the bribe also, and chose rather to direct a surrender to the Parliament than to dismember any part of his dominions, indigent as he was and hopeless at that time to recover the possession to himself, " such tenderness had that Prince, whom it is become the fashion to load so heavily, for his country, even when he was under the greatest distress " (Pamphlet by George, Lord Lansdowne)

Accordingly, Sir John and his brother were at last compelled to surrender the Islands, June, 1651, yet on terms so favourable, that the Parliament refused to ratify the conditions ; but Blake, who was a man of honour, insisting on making good what he had signed or threatening to throw up his commission, the Parliament acquiesced By these Articles it was provided that Sir John himself and all others, of whose names he gave a list, should be at liberty to return home and be restored to their estates. Under these conditions Sir John Granville resided in England, and was employed by commission from the King to manage the royal interests at home, being a leading member of " the Sealed Knot," and took part in all the eight several attempts that were made between 1652 and 1659 for the restoration of the Monarchy

The following account of the next few years of Sir Richard's life is taken from the " Vindication " ·—

· In February, 1650, I received in Holland His Majesty's gracious commands by Letter from Jersey, imparting his Pleasure to me that for some special occasions towards his service, he would have me return speedily to a Place convenient in France nigh him, to be resident to attend to his services. Accordingly I obeyed, and found His Majesty at Beauvais in France, in his way for Holland I continued at hand, attending his Pleasure, till to my great grief, he departed for Scotland."

The following is a copy of the " Safe conduct of Louis XIV for Sir Richard from Holland into France to join the King" But Museum, Add MSS 15856, fol 63, v.

SAFE CONDUCT OF LOUIS XIV FOR SIR RIC. GRENVILE

Sr Rich
Grenvilles
Passe to goe
from Holland
into France

A tous &c t supra que vous ayez a laisser seurement et librement passer par tous les endroicts de vos pouvoirs jurisdictions et destroicts le Sr Richard Grenville, Chevalier Anglais, venant d Hollande en ce Royaume passant par la Flandres avec dix Anglais de sa suite pour le service de nre trescher et tresamé bon Frere et cousin le Roy de la grande Bretagne sans luy donner ny a ceux de sa suite aucun arrest treuble ou empeschement, mais au contraire toute ayde faveur et assistance car tel est nre plaisir Donne a Dijon le 28e jours de mars mil six cens cinquante.

Louis

Par le Roy la Regne
Regente sa Mere prete
 Delomme

After the King's departure to Scotland Sir Richard lived for a time in Brittany, and the following letter was addressed by him to his Royal Highness the Duke of York, who was then in great distress in the Island of Jersey

SIR RICHARD GRANVILLE TO HIS HIGHNESS THE DUKE OF YORK

May it please your Royal Highness

Hearing your Highness is under some straits at Jersey, since his Majesty left you there, I have presumed out of my great zeal for your Highness's Service, by the assistance of an honest loyal Merchant here in St Malo's, Mr John Richards, to make your Highness a present of Six Hundred Pounds, which I humbly present by the Bearer, Major Madien, a Cornish gentleman who was Major to my regiment when I had the honour to be His Majesty's General in the West

He will further acquaint your Highness, that I have likewise out of my small Stock sent Relief of Clothes for the soldiers and Provisions to Colonel Hodge Burges at Guernsey Castle, which will enable him to defend that place the longer against the Rebels in the Island

These voluntary services I hope will preserve me in your Highness's good opinion, notwithstanding I have so powerful an enemy as Sir Edward Hyde to misrepresent my Actions and Loyalty to the King, to whose service and to your Royal Highness's I shall be always devoted with great sincerity

Presuming therefore upon my Duty to your Highness, I must beseech you to admit me to make an humble Petition, on behalf of a nephew, my godson now with me, second son to my brother Sir Bevil Grenvile who was slain at Lansdowne That your Highness would be pleased to receive him with your Family and Service near your Person His education has been, since he left his brother in Scilly, at an academy in Angers, and I find his inclinations lead him to venture his life and run his fortune in the immediate service of your Highness Wherefore I will be answerable for him and support him if your Highness will please to accept of his service, beseeching your Highness to believe me with the utmost Submission and Duty

May it please your Royal Highness

your Royal Highness's most obedient

and most dutiful servant

RICHARD GRENVILE

From S Malo's
    1650

The following is the Duke's answer from Jersey —

Sir Richard Grenville

I have received from the hands of Major Madren the Six Hundred Pounds you have most seasonably supply'd me with in this Place, the want of money having detained me here ever since the King went to Breda, but now with this Help I will suddenly remove, and wheresoever I am retain a memory of this your particular service to myself What you have desired of me concerning your nephew, now with you, when I am in a position to increase my Family I will take into my Service upon your Recommendation, but for the present my condition will allow me no more near my Person but Harry Jermyn and Charles Bucley When I leave this Place you shall know where to address to

Your affectionate Friend

JAMES

After this Sir Richard followed the Court into Holland, where he seems to have attempted reprisals upon the Earl of Suffolk, for we find that one of Milton's Latin "State Letters" is addressed to the Archduke Leopold of Austria, Governor of the Spanish Netherlands (undated), to the effect that Sir Charles Harbord, an Englishman, has had certain goods and household stuff violently seized at Bruges by Sir Richard Granville.

The goods had originally been sent from England to Holland in 1652 by the then Earl of Suffolk, in pledge for a debt owing to Harbord, and Granville's pretext was, that he also was a creditor of the Earl, and had obtained a decree of the English Chancery in his favour.

Now, by the English law, neither was the present Earl of Suffolk bound by that decree, nor could the goods be distrained under it. The decision of the Court to that effect was transmitted, and His Serenity was requested to cause Granville to restore the goods, inasmuch as it was against the community of nations that anyone should be allowed an action in foreign jurisdiction, which he would not be allowed in the country where the cause of the action first arose. Nevertheless, in spite of much litigation and this State Letter, Sir Richard continued to retain these goods, worth, is is said, £27,000 until his death, when they we given up, without compensation, by his daughter Elizabeth.

In October, 1652 Sir John Granville married Jane, the only surviving daughter of Sir Peter Wych, Knight (who had been Ambassador at Constantinople for twelve years, and was afterwards Comptroller of the Household to King Charles I) by his wife Jane, daughter of Sir William Meredith, of Wrexham, in the county of Denbigh, Knight, paymaster of the army in the reigns of Elizabeth and James I. Lady Meredith was the daughter of Sir Thomas Palmer, of Wingham, Baronet, who was Knighted by the Earl of Essex for his valour at the taking of Cadiz, and afterwards advanced to the dignity of a Baronet.

Sir John's first child, a daughter, was born in August, 1653, and baptized at Kilkhampton on the 23rd of that month, being named Jane after her mother. The following August a second daughter was born, and was named Grace after poor Lady Grace. The baptism took place at St Giles in the Fields on the 3rd of September, 1654, and the following letters to Sir John from his young wife were written shortly before her second confinement —

JANE LADY GRANVILLE TO HER HUSBAND.

June the 14

My Deare Heart,

I reseued thy letter of the 7 from Stowe, I am sory to see that insted of comming hether thou art gone backe againe. I deliuered my brother the

T²

lettai thou senst him, and perceue by that, that thou wouldst have him come
doune to thee, which I could skears have beleud, had not I seen it oundar
thine one hand, hauing not wiot on woord to mee of it, I am now without
anny man in the house, my father being gone, and Jacke is drounk all day,
and leyes out of nights, and if I do but tell him of it, hee will be gone
piesantly, tharfore for God sake make hast up, for I am so parpetualy ell that
I am not fit to be anny longgar left in this condission, my poore motther hath
now so much bisnese, that I do not know how long she will be abble to tarry
with me, and if that should happen which God forbeed it should, at anny
time, much moie now, what dost you thinke I should do, I want the things
thou prommysed to send me, very much, which being so long to put in a
lettar, I ha.e giuen my biother a not of, my deare considar how nere I am
my time, and many women comming this yeare before thar time, on o' our
nabours heeie is come in the 7 month which I now am in, the child being
bourne without etther haie or nalles thay aie both yet alive but dangarusly
ell, thou may st now thinke how impasiont, I am tell I see thee agane, thinking
eveiy day a huudared yeaie, my aftecksion being so gret that I wounder how
I haue stayd tell the outmoust time, I will saye no more now, hopping to see
thee every day but that I am evei will bee

thy most affectionate and fathfull wife
and saivant

Thy babe bages thy bles-ing   JANE GRENUILE.
(Supeiscription)   For thy deare selfe.

FROM THE SAME TO THE SAME

July the 4 1654

Deare Hearte
I have ieseued thine of the 30 June, pardon my not answeiing thine of
the 15, foi ieally I was very besse a getting up my clouts I hope that will
pled my excuse, but that of the 22 I did awnsar which I hope ere this is come
safe to thy hands and likewise gave thee an iceount of the mis cariy of thy
wiitting, which I can heere nothing of as yet on the day apointed for the
deleuing of it in which was thuisday last My lady my Mother and I
wayted in the Cou t aboue 4 houres wheie att last with much adoo and
shewing my lettar and   to the loids commesseuai, got 3 weekes longer
time, and if it be not found and delleveied by that time, the commitment to
stand good, and I beleue they wil follo it hard, foi Mr Chute and Mr prideex
both speke veiy ougiely I am glad to see thy lettar datted from that good
house of Cadleigh, hopping that then thou waiste comeing up, but finding
thy ietourn agane into Coinwall doth make mee very mellancolly, but I hope
all thy bisnese is done u this, and that thy ietourning letter is butt to send
me up that lettel plate which hath been so long a comming I hope that and
thee will come now veiy speddely for thou hast been so long goue now that
thou hast foigott to wiit thy selfe housband, but setting that quarrell aside
thy geail bages thy blessuig She hath now 4 teese and can almost goo alone.
I thank God she longs to se thee too, foi she doth nothing but call, dad, dad,
littel Jack is veiy well, hee longs to see thee to, that nevei long'd for nothing
My lady my mothei sends thee hir blising and wishes all helth and piosperity
She wiit unto thee by the last post, which I hope eie this is come safe to thy
hands I shall say no more att piesant butt that I am and foi ever and ever
shal be

thy most affectionate and most
faithfull wife and sarvant

(Supeiscription)
     Foi Sr John Greniule
          these

Cadleigh mentioned in the above letter was the home of Bridget, Sir John's sister, who had married Simon Leach, grandson of Sir Simon Leach, of Cadeleigh. He died the 25th of June, 1660, leaving two children.

Whilst he was in Paris, in April and May, 1653, Sir Richard Granville heard, on what he says he believed to be reliable information, that Sir Edward Hyde, (his old enemy, who had been one of the Prince's Council and had caused him to be imprisoned at Launceston,) was holding private communications with Cromwell with a view to betray the King

He weighed the evidence carefully and secured his vouchers under hand and seal, and then, feeling that concealment was high treason, he considered it his duty to communicate the information he had received in a private letter to the King (August 12th)

The Marquess of Ormond, on the 19th of September, wrote saying the King required to know Sir Richard s grounds for the charge, and requesting him to send all writings received concerning it, and the names of his informants

In obedience Sir Richard wrote as follows .—

"That my duty was my only ground for what I writ concerning Sir Edward Hyde As for my authors Colonel Wyndham said to myself at Boulogne in June, 1653, that Sir Edward Hyde had been in England, and that there he had private speech with Cromwell 'Also,' said he, 'Mr Robert Long was in Holland, he can and will give more certain information of its particulars,' and that therefore I did desire Mr Long to certify the truth of that report

That on July 28, 1653 I received his answer wherein he appeared to confirm what I writ was said of Sir Edward Hyde by Colonel Wyndham, which letter I send because so commanded, but greatly against my will

Since which letter Mr Robert Long sent me another containing thus—

'I will assure you it will be verified that the person named did positively and constantly affirm before two witnesses, whereof one is on this side of the sea and the other in England, that that person brought Sir Edward Hyde to a Conference with Cromwell, and described him so particularly that it was evident he was known, and did as particularly describe a person that was there with him '

And lastly concerning Sir Edward Hyde's Pension for Intelligence, that it was so said by divers persons. so commonly and in divers places, that I did not charge them to my memory, therefore I could not possibly at certainty name many authors for it, but I did well remember Mr Campbell said it sundry times in my hearing at Paris, so also did the Bishop of Derry speak it to me at Flussing, July 1653

The King considering that the charges had not been proved, refused, by the following Order in Council, dated 13th February. 1653, to allow Sir Richard to appear at Court, or come into his presence - ·

Tuesday the 15th January 1654.
Present

The King's Majesty.
The Queen's Majesty.   .
The Duke of York.
The Duke of Glocester.
Prince Rupert.
Lord Keeper, Sir Edward Hubert.
Lord Chamberlain, Lord Piercy.
Lord Inchequin
Marquis of Ormond, Lord-Lieutenant of Ireland.
Lord Jermin
The Chancellor of the Exchequer

" Whereas upon complaint made the 22nd day of December
last by Mr Chancellor of the Exchequer of certain discourses
spread abroad to his prejudice, as if he was under an accusation
for High Treason , and upon his humble desire that His
Majesty would examine the grounds of those discourses, His
Majesty, after other inquiries, caused a letter to be read which
had been written to himself in August last past by Sir Richard
Grenville, in which he informed His Majesty that Mr. Chancellor
of the Exchequer had made a step into England before his last
coming to Paris, and that he had there private Conference with
Cromwell, and that he had a pension paid him a long time out
of England for intelligence.

For justifying which information the said Sir Richard being
required by His Majesty to send him the grounds thereof, had
sent a letter written to him by Mr Robert Long, which was
there likewise read.   Upon which matter, after His Majesty had
examined the allegations made by Sir Richard, which He found
to be untrue, and some whereof His Majesty knew to be false,
His Majesty had formerly declared His judgment to the said Sir
Richard, forbidding him to come into His presence.

And moreover His Majesty examined Mr. Peter Massonet at
the Board, the 12th of this instant, in regard he had been
mentioned as one of the authors of that report, and likewise
caused a paper written by the said Mr Robert Long dated
January 13th, in justification of what he had formerly written
to Sir Richard Grenville, to be read, which paper His Majesty
looks upon as a libel derogatory from His own honour and
justice, as well as full of malice against the Chancellor, and will
hereafter take further consideration thereof   And upon the
whole matter declares That the Accusation and Information

against the Chancellor is a groundless and malicious Calumny, and that he is well satisfied of his constant Integrity and Fidelity in the service of his father and himself, and moreover that he will in due time farther examine this unworthy combination against him, when it shall be made in his Power to Punish the Persons who shall appear to be guilty of it And in the meantime His Majesty further declares his former Judgment that the said Sir Richard Grenville shall not presume to come into His Presence"

This enforced banishment from the Royal Presence was the crowning misfortune of Sir Richard Granville's life; it broke his heart

Early in 1654 he printed and published his "Vindication" in Holland, which concludes with these sad words "I must confess Truths After sight of his Majesty's Displeasure it gave me for some Days a most hearty sorrow and grief for myself as having lost that Royal Countenance which loyal duty made me love Now also I'll confess, I am not less sorry for the King's Loss of so faithful a servant, that has freely sacrific'd both his estate and life for him Such he wants, and such he will want, but that's not valued Hyde must be conceived injur'd by Common Fame He may not be taken guilty of any Disloyalty But Sir Richard Grenvile for his Presuming Loyalty must be by a Publick Declaration defamed as a Banditto and his very Loyalty understood a Crime

"However, seeing it must be so, let God be prayed to bless the King with faithful Councillors, and that none may be prevalent to be anyway hurtful to him, or any of his relations. As for Sir Richard Grenvile, let him go with the reward of an old soldier of the King's. There is no present use for him, when there shall be, the Council will think on't—if not too late. Vale"

It is said that he let his beard grow and never allowed it to be shaved again

The year of his death is uncertain, but in May, 1658 he had permission to travel with a testimonial from Charles II, then at Brussels (Egerton MSS. 2542, fol. 261), and on 10th May, 1659 his daughter, Elizabeth, petitioned the King to prevent his agent, Sir Henry de Vic, from interposing in the suit she is compelled by her father's debility (he suffered from ague, and had fallen downstairs—letter from Sir R.G to Sir B Hyde—Clar MSS) to carry on before the Privy Councill of His Catholic Majesty. This petition has an indorsement in Sir Edward Nicholas' writing —

"R (received ?) 17 June 1659 Pet of Mtrss Eliz Greenville

to ye Prince, to forbid Sir H de Vic, his Majtie's Resident to medile in the suit of her father."

How long after this he lived we cannot tell, but the probability is that he died just when the exiled Court was full of thoughts and hopes of the return to England

Cromwell was just dead, and the Restoration was no longer a dream but an imminent reality, in which Sir Richard's two nephews, Sir John Granville and Bernard Granville, were taking so prominent a part   And amid the general excitement the death of Sir Richard, who had made himself so many enemies and so few friends, was passed by without comment

He died it is supposed at Ghent, where his great nephew Lord Lansdowne states a monument existed to him in one of the churches with the simple inscription .—

"HERE LIES SIR RICHARD GRANVILLE THE KING'S GENERAL
IN THE WEST '

No such monument can now be discovered, nor any entry of the burial, though careful search has been made.

The whole history of his life is a marked contrast to that of his chivalrous brother, and indeed he seems to have had little in common with the long line of his illustrious predecessors, excepting then just pride of ancestry and their aptitude for fighting

"My former life spent has been as a soldier," he wrote in 1654 "as were all my ancestors since the Conquest of England, 1066, ever constantly for services of the Crown of England "

His character was perhaps aspersed with unnecessary severity by Lord Clarendon, yet it cannot be denied that he was frequently actuated by the dictates of a violent and revengeful temper, and the admission, which he himself made in his own defence, of conduct which had caused him the heavy displeasure of the exiled King, goes far to prove that the descriptions that have been handed down to us of his intriguing, high-handed and unscrupulous disposition are anything but un-just   He represented the worst type of the Cavalier

His daughter Elizabeth soon afterwards married Captain William Lennard, a gentleman who had occupied himself in capturing English ships, on the principle that all who did not fight for King Charles were against him, and therefore fair prey.

He was taken prisoner February 8th, 1659-60 (S P. Dom) as a pirate of Ostend and brought from Dunkirk to Devon at an expense to the Country of £2.

But fortunately for him, this happened in 1660, and he was

soon set at liberty and given the post of Captain of the Block Houses at Tilbury and near Gravesend (July 12th 1660)

He did not long enjoy this place, for in 1664 or 1665, his widow petitions the King for a Privy Purse pension of £100 for herself and her infant son, referring to her father Sir Richard Granville's services to the King, and especially in Jersey in 1650, and her own virtuous conduct in giving up the Earl of Suffolk's goods without compensation after her father s death (S. P. Dom)

Sir Richard's widow, Lady Howard, as she called herself, lived on at Fitzford, her ancestral home, with her illegitimate son George Howard, whose premature death on the 17th of Sept, 1671, proved so great a shock to her, that she only survived him one month.

In the Register of Tavistock parish church her burial is thus recorded

The Hon Lady Mary Howard als Grenfield ob 17 Oct & bur 10 Nov 1671.

Before her death she made a will leaving the whole of her property, with the exception of some legacies, to her first cousin Sir William Courtenay.

To her daughter Mary she left only £500 to be paid within four years of her decease, provided that the said Mary or her husband do not in any way clayme, etc, any of the estate or inheritance of which she was heretofore seized, and to her daughter Elizabeth she left £1,000, to be paid within two years and £20 within one year, and if she protested, then she was only to receive the £20.

The will is signed,

MARY GRINVEL

Probably the first time for many years she had used that detested surname

After her death Fitzford was partially dismantled, and remained in a more or less ruinous state till 1750, when all the Fitzford estate was sold to John, fourth Duke of Bedford, and now only the old gateway exists to mark the site of this fine mansion.

About 1656 Sir John Granville and his family seem to have returned to Stowe after a long absence, since there was formerly a letter from Sir John's youngest sister, Joanna, the wife of Colonel Richard Thornhill, dated " Olantyh July ye 6th 1656 " in which she congratulates him " yt he with her honored sister, his lady, and all ye family are settled at Stow," where she hopes they may live without disturbance. Probably, therefore, Stowe

had not been regularly inhabited since Lady Grace's death.   At
any rate, it must have been to a small remainder of their former
fortune that the new generation of Granvilles returned.   The
country was now divided into ten military governments, each
with a major-general at its head, who were empowered to disarm
all papists and royalists and to arrest suspected persons.   Funds
for the support of this military despotism were provided by an
Ordinance of the Council of State, which enacted that all who
had at any time borne arms for the King should pay every year
a tenth part of their income, in spite of the Act of Oblivion, as
a fine for their loyalist tendencies (*cf.* Green's "History of the
English People," bk vii, ch xii , pp 289 290)

Sir John's pecuniary position therefore must have been much
straitened at this time, and it is not surprising to find letters
from him like the following .—

August the   . . .
16 . .

. .
I have sent the bearer Andrew Cory purposely to treat wth you and to
offer you ye best expedient I may concerning ye satisfaction of y^r debt uppon
ye morgage of Stowe and Kilkhampton, for ye effecting whereof and certaine
paym^t of soe great a summe if y^u please to afford me some convenient time y^u
will lay a very great obligation uppon mee & in some measure reape ye benefitt
y^t selfe in receaving y^r money much sooner that way then otherwise possibly
y^u can by ye rigor of ye lawe, against wch I shall be nesisetated to crave reliefe
in chauncery, unlesse y^u are pleased to prevent mee by having one in y^r noble
breast according to ye rules of hono^r & justice wch I conceave will be a much
better course & effected wth lesse trouble & expence & wth more certaine &
speedy advantage on both sides wch I defer to y^r consideration, & have ordered
ye bearer more particularly to conferre wth y^u about ye busines to whome I
desire y^u to give creditt on my behalfe and to favour me wth a speedy answer
wherin y^u will very much oblige

Sir
Y^r affectionate fiende and servant
J GRENVILE

There are also the remains of a letter signed " Will Grosse,
Morwenstow Oct 26 1656," and directed "ffor the right worf^{ll}
Sir John Grenvile at Stowe, these " entreating the payment of
money due

Bernard Granville, Sir John's brother, after he left Scilly,
had been educated at an academy in Angers, and afterwards
stayed with his uncle Sir Richard in France, who had written
from St Malo on his behalf to the Duke of York requesting him
to be pleased to receive him into his family and service near his
person   This the Duke promised to do when he had a vacancy,
but apparently young Bernard was soon after this made a

Gentleman of the Bed-chamber to the young Duke of Gloucester, who died in 1660 at the early age of twenty.

Dennis, the youngest brother, was educated probably at Eton, as he is stated, on the authority of Archbishop Sancroft, to have afterwards (1662) been a fellow of Eton College (*cf.* "Athenæ Oxon ed Bliss," iv., 497) The following letter from him at this period is extant —

DENNIS GRANVILLE TO SIR JOHN GRANVILLE

Cadleigh March 1 1656

Honoured Brother

We being all come safe unto oʳ journeys end, I thought fitt that my penne should give yᵘ an accompt thereof and allsoe present my service unto you and my honoured sister. I beleeve I shall make here a fortnight or three weekes stay, & after that tyme hasten to retourne (or sooner if should bee yᵒʳ pleasure) about wᶜʰ tyme if yoⁿ could spare Chinge for twoe or three days I should bee very glad of that conveniency to retourn, otherwise I'le take an opportunity wᵗʰ some other person. Wee did meet upon the way (by one that came from Exon) a report of a great navy of Spaniards that did appeare upon oʳ coasts, (though I thinke nott much to bee credited) wᶜʰ if should bee true, cann bee noe newes to yoᵘ by this tyme, for they say this appearance to bee upon the Cornish shore neare Famouth There is likewise another reportt (wᶜʰ I can noe more affirme than yᵉ former, having nott had time to enquire yᵉ certainty of either) that major Blackmore hath sent, or intends to send, some of his troops for Sʳ James Smith & Sʳ Charles Trevanion But I have itt from such ill hands that I scarsely beleeve itt I will say noe more concerning newes, having none certaine, soe yᵗ it is only fitt for Chings relason (?) itt being onely wᵗ I heare nott wᵗ I beleeve, therefore I shall conclude, desiring yoᵘ to accept of my hearty acknowledgmᵗˢ for yoʳ great affection and kindnesse for wᶜʰ, in testimony of my gratitude, I will always continue as now I expresse my selfe

Yoʳ most affectionate Bro
and Servantt
DENNIS GRENVILE

(Superscription)
For his honoured Brother
Sⁱ John Grenvile
these
at Stowe

The following letter shall conclude this chapter The writer is John Basset, eldest son of Arthur Basset of Umberleigh, and a contemporary of Sir John's, his mother was one of the Leighs of Northam —

Mʳ JOHN BASSET TO SIR JOHN GRANVILLE

Sʳ

Since my recovery out of that unhappy sickness you intimate I have had little or noe converse with Doctor or phisicke And have noe receipt by mee worthey to bee sent you Fror what I tooke for the removinge my malady waspurge, pills, and powders, off what nature (I must confesse) I know not

U²

But my physition was Doctor Davies who I am confident vunderstands the
cure of that disease as perfectly well as any Doctor can doe   I presume hee
will readily wayte upon you and contrybute the best off his skill   In the In-
trim give mee leave f¹ to acknowledge yor oblinge favor to mee that you
daygne me worthey yor Comands in arry thinge   you cannot more freely impose
them then ffaythfully and readily they shall bee obayed by

S^r

Yo^r most affectionate

Umberly the 2nd of   ffaythfull humble
    Sep^tr 57   Servant
(Superscription)   Jo Bassett

Ffor my worthey and much
honored Friend
Sr John Grenvile att
his house att
Leigh
These
I pray

GEORGE MONK, FIRST DUKE OF ALBEMARLE.

From an Original Portrait in the possession of Sir George S. Studley, Bart.

CHAPTER XV

WE now come to that very interesting period of Sir John Granville's life when, in conjunction with his cousin, George Monk, he proved very instrumental in effecting the restoration of Charles II.

At the outbreak of the Civil War Monk had hesitated for some time between the King and the Parliament, but finally decided on joining the forces which had been sent over from Ireland by Ormond to Charles' assistance. As major-general of these troops, Monk took part in the battle of Nantwich, where he was taken prisoner, and committed to the Tower. Here he received offer after offer from the Parliamentarians to desert the royal cause and accept a command in the new Model Army, which Cromwell at this time was forming. But they all mistook their man. He still held the King's commission. The war for which he had engaged was still raging, and the most brilliant offers that could be made him he only regarded as insults. Pressure was even brought to bear on him, it is said, by a more rigorous confinement, but it was useless, and he indignantly refused his liberty except by a regular cartel.

Attempts were made on the King's part to exchange him for another prisoner for service in Ireland, but Parliament had no intention of allowing so valuable an officer to get back to the royal camp, nor did they even allow Monk to hear of these efforts of his friends. He consequently began to think himself forgotten and forsaken. His money was gone and a penniless prisoner in those days was the most miserable of men. Of his annuity fifty pounds was all he had had, and on Nov. 6th, but four months after his committal, he sat down to write an urgent appeal to his brother for another fifty, concluding with a pathetic cry for his release. The letter which is still preserved among the Coham MSS., is as follows:—

GEORGE MONK TO THOMAS MONK.

Deare Brother,

I wrote unto you by Chaptaine Bley in which letter I did desire you, to send mee some monies. I have received 50 poundes by your order long sence for which I returne you manie thanks. my necessities are such that they inforce mee to intreat you to furnish mee with 50 poundes more as soon as possible you maie, and you shall verie much oblige mee in it   I shall intreat you to bee mindfull of mee concerning my exchange for I doubt all my friends has forgotten mee concerning my exchange, but I shall earnestly intreat you if it lies in your power to remember mee concerning my libertie and so in hast I rest

your ffaithfull brother & servant
to serve you
GEORGE MONCK

ffrom the tower
this 6 of November
    1644

(Superscription)
ffor my most affectionated Brother Thomas
Monck Esquir
these ·

There is also a postscript written on the outside by Henry Davey (probably George Monk's servant) requesting Mr. Monk to present his service to all " at Poddridg " and to certify his wife of his welfare.

This interesting letter is indorsed with the words —

"sent my Brother on this letter 50 lb
Anno 1644
THO' MONCK /

The weary months went by and, no exchange being effected, George Monk thought himself indeed deserted.   Once out of the very depth of poverty the King sent him an hundred pounds, an extraordinary mark of esteem as things went at Oxford then. But that was all.   Bitterly he felt the seeming ingratitude, and yet, in spite of all, with obstinate loyalty he refused to desert his colours, and sat himself down to forget, in the pursuit of literature, the fancied wrongs under which he smarted.

While Monk lay thus honour-bound in the Tower the new Model Army had done its work.   The war was practically over and Parliament turned its attention to clearing the prisons.   On the 9th of April, 1646, a return was ordered of all soldiers of fortune, then prisoners to the Parliament, who were desirous of going abroad, with the intention that on taking the negative oath they should be permitted to do so   Under this order Monk must have applied, and on July the 1st he obtained permission to go beyond the seas   Once more an offer was made him by Parliament, namely, the command of the English forces in Ulster, and there was now no reason why he should not accept it   The war for which he had engaged was at an end, and the new service that was offered to him was one which he had been led to think as noble as a crusade   It was against an enemy in open rebellion against England and in secret league with Spain He therefore accepted, and from this time Monk continued very firm to Cromwell, who was liberal and bountiful to him, and took him into his entire confidence, nor was there any man in the army upon whose fidelity to himself Cromwell more depended   Monk remained in command in Ireland till August, 1649   About this time his eldest brother Thomas had died from the effects of a fall from his horse, and George Monk went to Potheridge to take possession of the family estates which fell to him as heir-in-tail.   It was probably at this time that he became fully impressed with the abilities of Mr. William Morice, who was destined to influence his career so profoundly This remarkable man, scholar, historian, recluse, and a man of business, had been managing the Granville property with great skill ever since Sir Bevills death, and Monk found that he could not do better than commit his own property to the same stewardship

In June, 1650, when the new storm broke out in the north, and Scotland welcomed Charles II as its King, an invasion was resolved upon by the English Parliament, and Cromwell, having been voted to the command of the Army, at once sent for Monk to assist him in the organization of his forces, and promised him a regiment.   He accepted, and, excepting the short period of the Dutch war in 1653, when he served as Admiral, and had a share in the great victory off the Texel, he remained in Scotland, successfully quelling the rebellion till his famous march to London on the 3rd of February, 1660

All this time the " Sealed Knot " were plotting and planning to bring about the King's Restoration, but their designs and insurrections were betrayed to Cromwell by a false brother, Sir Richard Willis   The Royalists were secretly persuaded that they had an ally in Monk, though those who knew him best were persuaded that it was to no purpose to attempt to approach him while Cromwell lived, but he was generally regarded as a man more inclined to the King than any other in great authority   His eldest brother had been a staunch Royalist and all his relations were of the same faith, not excepting his wife, who was ever urging him to favour the Royalist plots and adopt the Martyr's cause.   It must be confessed that the General was a little hen-pecked at home and a little afraid of his wife's sharp tongue, so like a wise man he let her talk treason to her heart's content without reply, but told his chaplain Price, who was secretly a Royalist, that he had no sympathy with the cause of a man who had shewn himself

hopelessly incapable of governing   "If the martyr had been
fit to reign," he used to say "he would have taken his advice
and fought the Scots in 1638 "

Monk therefore remained true to the Protector.   He had
taken his commission from him and had promised to support his
dynasty   So when Cromwell died in September, 1658, his son
Richard was duly proclaimed by him at Edinburgh

The new Protector was a weak and worthless man, lax and
worldly in his conduct, and believed to be conservative and even
royalist in heart   The tide of reaction was felt even in his
council   Their first act was to throw aside one of the greatest
of Cromwell's reforms, and to fall back in the summons which
they issued for a new Parliament on the old system of election
It was felt more keenly in the tone of the new House of
Commons when it met in January, 1657   In this Parliament
Sir John Granville and William Morice were elected for Newport,
which had now for several years been unrepresented and Morice
informed the General that in the West the King's Restoration
was so impatiently longed for that they had made choice of no
members to serve for Cornwall or Devonshire but such as would
contribute all they could to invite the King to return

The King's prospects certainly seemed brighter than they
had yet been and he appointed new Commissioners and sent
over to England a blank Commission, dated at Brussels the 11th
of March, in the eleventh year of his reign, which was to be
filled up with the name of Arthur Annesley, afterwards Earl of
Anglesea and Lord Privy Seal, John Mordaunt, brother to the
Earl of Peterborough or Sir John Granville, Sir William Peyton
and William Legg the substance of which was that he appointed
them his Commissioners, giving them, or any one or more of
them, power to treat with any of his subjects of the Kingdom of
England or Dominion of Wales, that were or had been in arms
against him or his father, or that had contributed to the present
rebellion in England, excepting such only as had taken a direct
part in his father's execution, and to assure them in his name
that, if they would forsake the present rebellion and join heartily
and effectually in suppressing it, he would fully pardon them
and recompense such of them as should by any remarkable
service merit of him, and the Commissioners were further empowered to promise in the King's name that he would ratify
whatever engagements they, or any one or more of them,
undertook

"These gentlemen " writes Lord Clarendon, " proceeded with
a great deal of warmness and diligence in the execution of their

commision (and no man more active than Sir John Greenville) to engage the country to take up arms for his Majesty's service" A simultaneous rising of the King's friends in every county was determined on, and on July 5th Monk wrote the following warning to the Council of State, "I make bold to acquaint you that I hear that Charles Stuart hath laid a great design both in England and Ireland, but as yet I hear nothing that he hath written over to this country (Scotland) concerning that business. I am confident if he had I should have heard of it" By a strange irony, almost as he penned the words, Sir John Granville was in consultation with Mr Mordaunt as to the best method of making the General a party to their design Now Monk's favourite brother Nicholas had been sometime previously to this presented by Sir John to the fat living of Kilkhampton on the one only condition that if he should ever happen to have any business with "cousin George" up in Scotland, perhaps Nicholas would not mind making himself useful.

At this juncture, therefore, Sir John, who had obtained from the King a letter for the General, sends for Nicholas Monk to London, and arranges with him to go to Scotland, ostensibly for the purpose of settling his daughter Mary's marriage and the dowry the General was going to provide, but really to carry the King's letter to his brother and negotiate the secret treaty. Nicholas flatly refused to touch the letter. It was far too dangerous. He consented however to carry a verbal message, and was solemnly sworn not to breathe a word of the very delicate affair to anyone but his brother. Nicholas reached Dalkeith on August 8th, and gave his message and disclosed the plot, which was received by the General with discreet silence as to his approval or non-approval of it, but there can be no doubt that he did not regard the proposed rising of the Royalists with disfavour, for, taking into his confidence one or two trusted friends, he was preparing to issue a manifesto to Parliament, reminding them that they had not yet filled up their numbers, nor passed any Electoral Bill, as the very name of Commonwealth required them, and hinting that the army could not in conscience protect their authority unless they forthwith remedied their neglect, when the startling news came that the Royalist plot had failed; the manifesto was burnt, and Monk, and those he had admitted into the secret, thanked Heaven for the narrow escape they had had.

The General's feelings vented themselves in anger against his brother and Granville. He felt he had been deceived and entrapped into a plot which had no more bottom than the rest.

He angrily told poor Nicholas to go back to his books, and meddle no more in conspiracy. He charged him with a similar sharp message to his young cousin, and swore if either of them ever revealed what had passed he would do his best to ruin them both

The course of the next few months, the abdication of Richard Cromwell, and the struggle between the Army and the Parliament, at length determined General Monk to march into England to the help of the Parliament, and he entered London February 3rd, 1660, and the Rump welcomed him as their deliverer.

Perceiving the strength of the Royalist reaction the General determined to restore the monarchy, yet so wily and reserved was he that when the Royalists again and again pressed him to espouse their cause his only answer was that he was in the service of the Commonwealth and could not listen to them All but the most sanguine of the Cavalier agents began now to consider him hopelessly loyal to his trust   Not so, however, his cousin Sir John Granville, who, in spite of his notorious malignancy, was free of St. James's on the ground of his relationship, but for a while he too had no better luck than the rest. Fruitlessly he sought a private interview through their mutual friend Morice   Night after night he stayed till everyone was gone, but " good night, cousin, 'tis late," was all he got for his pains, as the wary old General went off to bed

Such was Monk's position when the Portugese ambassador asked for an audience. The recent treaty of the Pyrenees had left Portugal at the mercy of Spain, and she had sent a special envoy to England to seek assistance   The power of Monk and the now inevitable recall of the King, suggested to the ambassador a brilliant piece of diplomacy, and he resolved to flash a dazzling prospect in the eyes of the General   Morice had been previously sounded and approved. The ambassador began by saying that without wishing to pry into the General's intention with regard to the King, he thought it only right to tell him that Charles Stuart ought at once to get out of Spanish territory, since directly the probability of his restoration was known he would be kidnapped and held as a hostage for the retrocession of Jamaica and Dunkirk , on the other hand if he were restored, the King of Portugal was prepared, in return for military assistance against Spain, to offer the King the hand of the Infanta, and with her a dowry of an unheard of sum of money, together with the towns of Tangiers and Bombay   The advantages of such an arrangement were obvious. It would give to England the command of the Mediterranean and East Indian trade, and enable her to complete the humiliation of her great rival which the heroes of the Armada had begun.

To a man of Monk's hot patriotism, who remembered Raleigh, who had been moulded into manhood while Drake and Granville and Hawkins were living memories, the prospect was too dazzling to resist, and Monk determined to communicate with the King. Absolute secrecy was essential, and the General looked round for a messenger on whom he could implicitly rely Morice could not be spared, and it was clear that Granville was the man. After two ineffectual attempts to induce him to disclose his secret mission to Morice, Monk was convinced of his discretion and promised an interview. Accordingly one night shortly after the dissolution of the Rump Parliament, Sir John was introduced into Morice's private appartments at St James's The General appeared from a secret stairway, and Granville, without preface or apology, thrust into his hands the King's letter, which his cousin Nicholas had refused to take up to Scotland. Monk started back and asked him fiercely how he dared to play the traitor. The Cavalier quietly replied that in the service of the King his Master danger had grown familar to him. Overcome with his young kinsman's coolness and the memories of all he owed to his house, the old General unbent at once and cordially embraced him Then he read the King's letter In flattering terms it assured him of Charles' favour, and of his intention to follow Monk's advice implicitly if he would only espouse his cause Granville added that he had been empowered to promise a hundred thousand a year for him and the offer of any title he chose, and the office of Lord High Constable Monk replied that what he did was for his country's good, and that he would not sell his duty or bargain for his allegiance Sir John pressed for a written answer, but the wary soldier refused ; he had intercepted too many letters himself. Granville was told he must take his reply by word of mouth, and so was dismissed till the morrow.

On the following evening Monk made Sir John learn by heart his answer to the King, which he had prepared, together with the advice proper for the King to follow, and then when he had repeated them to him, so as to prove himself to be fully master of them in his memory, he made him tear the writing in pieces before his face, and swear not to reveal any part of this conference to any man alive but the King himself, and to require the same secrecy of the King also. He also commanded

Sir John not to leave the King till he was out of the Spanish territory, and so dismissed him, and Granville left London that same night,

The King received Sir John with open arms, and there and then, April 2nd, signed the following Warrant, whereby he promised on the word of a King to bestow on him the place of Groom of the Stole and first Gentleman of the Bedchamber. together with the dignity of an Earl of England. He also engaged to pay all the debts that Sir John or his father Sir Bevill had contracted in the service of King Charles I. and likewise to settle an estate of inheritance in good land to the yearly value of three thousand pounds, the better to support his dignity —

CHARLES R

In consideration of the many services done Us by our Right Trusty and Well-beloved Servant Sir John Grenvile (one of the Gentlemen of Our Bedchamber) and his Father, the most valiant and loyal Sir Bevill Grenvile, who most honourably lost his life at the battle of Lansdowne in the defence and service of the Crown against the rebells, after he had performed other great and signal services But more especially in consideration of the late most extraordinary services (never to be forgotten by Us or Our posterity) which the said Sir John hath lately rendered Us in his person in his secret, prudent, and most faithful transactions and negotiations in concluding that most happy treaty which he hath lately, by Our special command and commission, with Our famous and renowned General Monk, and wherein he alone (and no other) was intrusted by Us concerning the said treaty about those most important affairs for Our Restoration, which he has most faithfully performed with great prudence, care, secrecy and advantage for Our service without any conditions imposed upon Us beyond Our expectation, and the commission We gave him, whereof We doubt not but by God's blessing We shall speedily see the effects of Our said happy Restauration We are graciously pleased to promise, upon the word of a King, that as soon as We are arrived in England and it shall please God to restore Us to Our Crown of the Kingdom, We will confer upon Our Right Trusty and Well-beloved Servant Sir John Grenvile, the place and office of Groom of Our Stole and first Gentleman of Our Bedchamber, with all fees, pensions, and perquisites thereunto belonging, together with the title and dignity of an Earl of Our Kingdom of England And the better to support the said title of honour, and to reward, as We ought, those many great services, and to recompense the losses and sufferings of him and his family, We are further graciously pleased to promise, upon Our said Royal word, to pay all the debts that he the said Sir John or his father Sir Bevill have contracted in the late wars in Our service or in Our Royal Fathers of blessed memory And also to bestow and settle in good land in England an estate of inheritance to the value of at least Three Thousand Pounds per annum upon him the said Sir John and his heirs for ever, to remain as a perpetual acknowledgment for his said services, and as a testimony of Our grace and favour towards him and that ancient and loyal family of the Grenviles unto all posterity

Given at Our Court at Brussels
the 2nd of April in the twelfth year of
Our Reign 1660
By his Majesty's Command
EDWARD NICHOLAS

Charles at once acted on Monk's advice, and left Brussels and went to Breda, and Sir John, after seeing him safely upon Dutch soil, hastened back on April 4th with a dangerous burden. Besides official letters for the two Houses of Parliament, the Council, the army, and the city, each containing a copy of the famous "Declaration from Breda," in which he promised a general pardon, religious toleration and satisfaction to the army, he carried an autograph letter from the King to the General, together with a commission for him to be Captain-General of the three kingdoms and a signet and seal for a Secretary of State to be delivered to whomsoever the General chose. The letter Monk accepted, but he had still enough of the true soldier of fortune in him to refuse a Commission incompatible with the one he held. Nor would he take the Seals, but told Sir John to hide himself and his papers till Parliament met and then act according to his instructions.

A plot on the part of the army at this time was likely to ruin all, but Monk luckily discovered it and nipped it in the bud, not however without having first sent word to the King by the hands of Sir John and his brother Bernard to say that, should the revolt spread, he would publish his commission from the King, and raise all the loyal party of the three kingdoms.

Parliament met quietly on April 25th, and the Commons next day passed the General a vote of thanks for his unparalleled services in having conquered the enemies of Church and State without so much as "a bloody nose." The few Presbyterian lords who had met uninvited did the same, and Monk in his acknowledgment bluntly begged them to look forward and not backward in transacting affairs, a hint they were careful to take.

While this was going on in Parliament Sir John Granville presented himself at the Council Chamber and asked to see the Lord-General. Monk came out and received from his cousin's hands, as from a stranger, an official letter addressed "To Our trusty and well-beloved General Monk, to be by him communicated to the President and Council of State and to the officers of the armies under his command." Monk at once ordered his guards to detain the messenger and returned to the Council chamber. There he broke the seal and handed the letter unread to the president. The surprise was complete; no one but Morice had an idea of what had been going on. Still it was clear that the letter came from Charles, and after some debate it was resolved that without being read, it should be presented to Parliament on May 1st, the day they had fixed for the

business of the settlement of the nation. Meanwhile Granville
was to be placed under arrest, but the General interposed, saying
that, although a stranger, he was a near kinsman of his own, and
that he would be responsible for his appearance at the
Bar

Accordingly Sir John, so soon as the Houses met, attended and
having delivered the King's Letter to the Serjeant to be delivered
to the Speaker, withdrew.   " The House immediately called to
have both Letters read, that to the General and that to the
Speaker, which being done the Declaration was as greedily called
for and read ; and from this time ' Charles Stuart ' was no more
heard of, and such universal joy was never seen within those
walls   They immediately without one contradicting vote
appointed a Committee to prepare an answer to his Majesty's
Letter, and likewise ordered at the same time the two letters
and the Declaration enclosed and the Resolution thereupon to
be forthwith printed and published   This kind of reception was
beyond what the best affected, nay even the King himself could
expect and hope, and all that followed went in the same pace. The
Lords when they saw what spirit the House of Commons was
possessed of, would not lose their share of thanks but made
haste into their House without secluding any who had been
sequestered from sitting there for their delinquency ; the Earl
of Manchester was chosen their Speaker, who being acquainted
that Sir John attended at the door with a letter from his
Majesty, the Earl went down to the Clerk and received it "
(Lord Clarendon's History)   In the meantime the Commons
having drawn up, engrossed, and signed a letter to his Majesty,
Sir John Granville was appointed to attend again, and he being
brought to the Bar, the Speaker stood up and delivered the
thanks of Parliament to him in the following terms —

" Sir John Grenvile   I need not tell you with what grateful
and thankful hearts the Commons now assembled have received
his Majesty's gracious letter. ' Res ipsa loquitur   You yourself
have been auricularis et ocularis testis de Rei veritate '   Our
bells and our bonfires have already begun the proclamation of
his Majesty's goodness and our joys.   We have told the people
that our King, the glory of England, is coming home again, and
they have resounded it back again in our ears, and they are
ready and their hearts are open to receive him   Both
Parliament and people have cried aloud in their prayers to the
King of Kings ' Long live King Charles the Second.' I am
likewise to tell you that this House doth not think fit that you
should return to our Royal Sovereign without some testimony

of their respect to yourself. They have ordered and appointed that five hundred pounds shall be delivered unto you to buy a Jewel as a badge of that honour which is due to a person whom the King had honoured to be a messenger of so gracious a message, and I am commanded in the name of the House to return you their very hearty thanks."

The city of London also presented Sir John with three hundred pounds to buy a ring.

Sir John hastened back to the King carrying with him the answer of the Houses of Parliament to his Letters, and the £50,000 that had been voted him for his present use. In Pepys' Diary, under date 16 May, 1660, Pepys writes " This afternoon Mr Edward Pickering told me in what a sad poor condition for clothes and money the King was and all his attendants, when he came to him first from my Lord, their clothes not being worth forty shillings the best of them , and how overjoyed the King was when Sir J. Greenville brought him some money ; so joyful that he called the Princess Royal and Duke of York to look upon it as it lay in the portmanteau before it was taken out."

When all was concluded for the King's Restoration Monk thought it proper to send his last despatch by one whom he could trust, namely Bernard Granville. Sir John's brother who was to inform his Majesty that everything was ready for his reception. Prince says Monk's despatch " was full of duty and obedience and assurance that he would serve his Majesty with hazard of his life and that without the clogs of any previous conditions, so that he should return a free and absolute Monarch to his ancient dominions " As other messengers were crossing to Breda at the same time and in the same ship, Bernard Granville was to take care not to be suspected of being anything more than a common passenger, nor charged with any special business, and he was, above all. to use such diligence as to get first to the King in order that his Majesty might not be surprised or perplexed by any uneasy importunities or disagreeable demands, but be prepared in which manner to receive and content the Commissioners with general assurances

He accordingly arrived first by two or three hours, and found the King at supper Upon sending in his name, his Majesty immediately rose from the table and came to him in another room, and he no sooner read Monk's letter than he embraced the bearer for joy, and told him that " never was man more welcome to him, he could now say he was a King and not a Doge."

Thus pointed out to his country as a principal instrument of the Restoration, Sir John Granville was quickly rewarded with such honours as his services and those of his family might very justly claim.   According to the Patent Roll he was appointed on the 22nd of June, Warden of the Stannaries, High Steward of the Duchy of Cornwall, and Rider and Master of Dartmoor Forest, and on the 22nd of the following month, Keeper of the House and Wardrobe of St. James's, and on the 1st of October, Lord-Lieutenant of Cornwall, and on the 6th of October, he was appointed Groom of the Stole and first Gentleman of the Bedchamber to King Charles II. upon the decease of the Duke of Somerset, (*cf.* Establishment Books of the Household, Lord Chamberlain's Department, Record Office)   His brother Bernard, who had been Gentleman of the Bedchamber to the Duke of Gloucester during his exile, was also promoted to be Gentleman of the Horse and of the Bedchamber to the King.

The following year, three days before the King's Coronation, viz , on April 20th, 1661, Sir John Granville was created Baron Granville of Kilkhampton and Bideford ; Viscount Granville of Lansdowne and Earl of Bath, in accordance with the Warrant which had been signed by the King at Brussels, the preceding year.   The title Earl of Bath had been for some years dormant by the death of Henry Bouchier the last Earl of Bath of that most illustrious family, to which they were first promoted by King Henry VIII.

That he might be the better enabled to support his new dignity the King settled upon him £3,000 a year out of the Stannaries, besides other donations of less value.

In Evelyn's Memoirs, vol. 1, p. 318, under date April 22nd, 1661 (it should have been 20th) we read —

" Was ye calvacade of his Matie from ye Tower to Whitehall, when I saw him in the Banquetting House create 6 Earls and as many Barons, viz , *Edward Lord Hide*, Lord Chancellor, *Earle of Clarendon*, supported by ye Earles of Northumberland and *Sussex ;* ye *Earle of Bedford* carried the cap and coronet, the *Earle of Warwick* the sword, the *Earle of Newport* the mantle.

Next Capel, created Earle of Essex ,

Bendenell,	,	Cardigan ;
Valentia,	.,	Anglesea ;
Greenvill,	,,	Bath ;
Howard,	,,	Carlisle.

JOHN GRANVILLE, FIRST EARL OF BATH.

From an Original Portrait, by Sir Godfrey Kneller, in the Wellesbourne Collection.

The Barons were —
> Denzill Holles ,
> Cornwallis ;
> Booth ;
> Townsend ;
> Cooper ;
> Crew ;

who were all led up by severall Peers, with Garter and Officers of Armes before them , when, after obedience on their severall approaches to ye Throne, their Patents were presented by Garter King at Armes, which being receiv'd by ye Lord Chamberlaine and deliver'd to his Majesty and by him to the Secretary of State, were read and then againe deliver'd to his Matie, and by him to the severall Lords created ; they were then rob'd, their coronets and collers put on by his Matie, and they were plac'd in rank on both sides the State and Throne, but the Barons put off their caps and circles and held them in their hands, the Earles keeping on their coronets as cousins to the King."

General Monk was raised to the peerage by the title of Duke of Albemarle, Earl of Torrington and Baron Monk of Potheridge, Beauchamp, and Tees He also received the Garter, and was appointed a Gentleman of the Bedchamber and Master of the Horse, and by his patent as Captain-General he was granted the extraordinary privilege of entering the royal presence unannounced and remaining there till he was told to go His affection for John Granville Earl of Bath was unabated , at his particular request the King passed a further warrant under the Privy Seal whereby he obliged himself, and recommended it to his successor, that in case of failure of male issue the title of Duke of Albemarle should descend to Lord Bath and be continued in his family, and promised to annex the valuable estate of Theobalds to the Dukedom, which otherwise would revert to the Crown, failing male issue to the Monks

By another writ, dated 6 April, 1661, his Majesty promised Lord Bath the reversion of the Earldom of Glamorgan, formerly enjoyed by his great ancestor Robert Fitzhamon (failing heirs to the Marquess of Worcester, by whom the title was then held, or supposed to be held, since it was conferred by Charles I upon Edward Lord Herbert, somewhere between 16 April, 1643 and 1 April, 1644), and should Lord Bath leave no sons, the latter Earldom was to revert to the right male heirs of his father Sir Bevill.

Neither of these took effect, the contingency (*i e.* the failure of issue male of the then Marquess of Worcester) as to the

Earldom of Glamorgan never arising, and that as to the Duke of
Albemarle not occurring till 1688, after the King's death, whose
warrant, though it " obliged himself," only recommended it to
his successor, that in case of failure of male issue to General
Monk, the title of Duke of Albemarle should descend to the said
Earl of Bath and be continued in the family *cf* Peter
Heylin's " Help to English History," Edit. 1773, 162.

In the meanwhile the Earl of Bath was permitted to use the
titles of Earl of Corboile, Lord of Thorigny and Granville, as
his ancestors had done (*cf* pp 15, 16).

The following words are employed in the preamble to this
permit —

" Whereas it appears to Us that Our right trusty cousin and
councillor John Earl of Bath etc is derived in a direct line as
heir-male to Robert Fitz Hamon Lord of Gloucester and
Glamorgan in the reigns of King William the Conqueror, King
William Rufus and King Henry I, and who was the son and
heir of Hamon Dentatus Earl of Corboile and Lord of Thorigny
and Granville in Normandy, (which titles they held before
Normandy was lost to the Crown of England) whereby he
justly claims his descent from the youngest branch, as We
Ourselves do from the elder, of Rollo Duke of Normandy etc."
So that by an immediate succession from father to son,
beginning at the year of our Lord 876 from Rollo's great grandson, Mauger, first Earl of Corboile, John Earl of Bath was the
twenty-third Earl of Corboile, Lord of Thorigny and Granville
And in all warrants or patents passed there is particular regard
had in mentioning as well the great honour and antiquity of his
family, as the great loyalty, sufferings and services of himself and
his ancestors, more immediately of his father, Sir Bevill, whilst as
the King says in his warrant dated at Brussels, Sir John was
the only man trusted in the negociations with General Monk,
" a transaction that shall never be forgot in history but serve
for an eternal illustration of his family (if indeed it can receive
any) no subjects ever surpassing them in valour, nobleness of
birth, or in loyalty and fidelity to the Crown, which they have
shewn in all ages since the Conquest "

On the 13th of May, 1661, Lord Bath was appointed
Governor of the Town and Castle of Plymouth and of St.
Nicholas Island ; a post which he held till the year 1695, when
he was succeeded by Major-General Trelawney

On the 15th of August, 1661, he accompanied the King and
the Duke of York to the grand entertainment given in their
honour by the Society of the Inner Temple.

On the 25th of July, 1663, he was made a Privy Councillor, and on the 28th of the following September he accompanied the King and Queen to Oxford, when that University conferred on him the honorary degree of Master of Arts

Not long after the Restoration the province of Carolina in North America, was claimed by Charles II, and united to the imperial crown of Great Britain as a Principality or Palatinate The fertile districts between Albemarle Sound (N lat 35° 59') and the river St. John (N. lat 30° 23') were granted to eight of the King's favourite noblemen, their heirs and successors, the terms of the concession making them absolute sovereigns within the limits named   Lord Bath was one of these, the others being the Earl of Clarendon, Lord Chancellor, George, Duke of Albemarle, William Earl of Craven, Lord Ashley Cowper (afterwards Earl of Shaftesbury), John Lord Berkeley, Sir William Berkeley, and Sir John Corinton   The result of this annexation was a mighty influx of emigrants from every part of Great Britain and its dependencies to the fruitful lands. which had long been claimed as their exclusive property by the Spaniards   The original proprietors were literally crowded out by "gay cavaliers" and rapacious planters, who soon made the very name of a white man hateful in the ears of the unfortunate Indians   Under the governorship of the terrible Seth Sothel, a man whose name will live for ever as that of the most infamous of many reckless rulers of Carolina, the natives were hunted down on every side and sold as slaves to West Indian planters, whilst those amongst the emigrants who retained any reverence for the human or divine had their feelings outraged at every turn   Not until the 18th century was considerably advanced did the Carolineans obtain any relief from this terrible state of things, but in 1721 George I. consented to take the government into his own hands, and a few years later, the lands granted to the eight noblemen by Charles II were bought up by the Crown for some £28,000, and from that time the colony grew rapidly in prosperity and importance   (American Discovery. N. D'Anvers, pp. 209-211.)

In the year 1666 Lord Bath laid the foundation stone, which still bears his name, of the Plymouth citadel   This stone is situated at the ground level of the projecting angle of the "Old Saluting Battery," being the most southerly point of the citadel proper   Its inscription is divided into two parts by this angle, the one part being on the south-west face, and the other on the south-east face   It is contained within two panels sunk in the two faces of the stone, so that the letters and figures,

A'

while level with the original surface of the stone, stand out from the sunken surface of the panels as *alto relievo*   On the south-west face is " J° EARLE OF," and on the south-east face. " BATHE 1666 "

The citadel appears to have occupied about four or five years in construction, for over the main gateway is inscribed the date " 1670," as well as the arms of the Earl of Bath, viz., gules, three rests, or, surmounted by the coronet helm and crest, a griffin's head, the supporters being griffins

Upon the completion of the citadel the King came by sea to inspect it, and the following letter (much damaged and scarcely legible) from Lady Bath to her husband is amongst the Wellesbourne MSS, and has reference to the building of the citadel and the King's proposed visit

FROM THE COUNTESS OF BATH TO HER HUSBAND

St Jamses May 23rd

My deare Harte,

I wrot to you by Ching on fryday morning, and that night I went to Dorchistar, the next day I went to Stockbridg, on Sunday I came to Bagshot. Yesterday att 3 a cloke I came hethar (where I found our famelly, I thanke God, all very well) I came extremly weary, hott, and dusty to toune, but your horses came all very well, and I thinke the best in the countrey or they could never have parformd the journey   Everybody here thinkes I flew, but enough of myselfe till our meeting   According to your ardar I sent my Lord Arlington his lettar on Sounday night, but I have heard nothing of him sense. Sr G T and brother Prideux came to mee as sone as ever I came home and began to be very outragus about your stay, but att last when we came to bee serious, I find thar one consensus is that   most.   I am now a gooing to Whithall to delivar your lettar to the King, and will not seale this till my returne that so I may geive you an account how things stand thar, which I hope is very well for I cannot find for all thar talking anything to the contrary.   I gave my brother Prideux . . . lettar . . . which hee plesantly carryed to him, but I have not heerd from the tressurer sense.   I gave Bull Sr J C and Sr H Devie the furs   . delivared but the second is gon to Winsar but I have sent it after him   I have leiwise given him Sr B's gems, which hee says he will delivar this afournone   I sent my Lady . .   . . and the rest I will geive you an account of the delevary by the next post.   Sr G and Bull will both write to you by this post   No newes stirring heere but was alarmed att Dorchistar by Mr .   . . rrig of Bri . .   . how went not from Exeter tell the Monday before   . with Matthewes the carrier and when they came to Dorchistar he mayd himselfe drunck and came into the inn wher wee ley and thar came into the company of on Mr Gold his father being a parliament man and hath they say 100 thossand pound a yeare. He began to be very rude and swore very much   The gentleman severall times asked him why hee did soo, which he tooke for an afront and so struck Mr Gold, and went to draw his sword, but hee disarmed him, and they say beate him soundly   The countabel came in and would have carry'd him to prison but hee say'd hee was yr sarvant, soo they lett him goo, but within an houre after hee was gon, they heerd hee was out of y^r sarvis, and then they ware sorry they had not layd him by the heeles   This is all the account I can geive you of him as yett

I begin to think the time long alliedy sens I see thee, thar for be shure I will make all the dispatch I can of our bisnes   Bull geives me very lettell hopes of anny monny   I have ordered him to bri..g mee his accounts to-morrow, so I hope by the next post to geive you a bettar account of all bisnes   In the meanetime for God's sake make much of y^r selfe and   love mee, for that is no pleasure in this world like a true friend, and I am shure none can or ever shall bee so faithfull to you as my selfe, for I love thee with my soule and will do so to my deth

I am now just come from Whithall and the post I feare will be gon, thar fore I have only time to tell you that I deleuared y^r lettar to the King and to the Duke   The King was very kind to mee and   as you may immagin, and said that I had a great hand in y^r stay—but all bid mee tell you that he would have the worked finished   The Duke was alsoe treu kind and asked mee how you did and tould mee that as he had bine a fiiende to the workes from the beginning—so hee would nevar live till they ware finesshed, and hee would bee the solissetar for them   I find my lord   a very good friend to you   Your intarest in the West hath bine mitelly canvassed, and greet discord about the Knight of the Shire, but lett that pase tell wee meet, and heerafter open y^r eyes wide that you may see who are y^r friends and who otharwis   Euary body semes to ask very keind'y aftar you   M and M^r J, ye furst past by mee senerall times and stept by mee and take no notis of mee at all—the latter aftar a lettel while tould mee I was welcom to towne   I find it is the opinion of most pepell that the King will see Plymouth this sommer, but they do not declare soo, but the Duke sayes hee cannot yett say what he may do, and the K to, when they come to portsmouth or the new forrist

By the next you shall heere from mee more att large—but now I feare the post will be gon   Tharfor my Deare Harte good might & bee confedent that I will ever bee

Your most affectionat
and most faythfull wife and saruant

J   BAIHE

Give my blessing to Henaretta and geive mee leve to tell you that I think I may without vanity say you have as fine cheldoren as evar was bourn.   Pray God blese them when they grow up

The close of the year 1669 had seen the Duke of Albemarle in fast failing health.   Dropsy had declared itself, complicated by an affection of the heart and lungs.   Sometimes at Newhall, his seat in Essex, sometimes, when feeling a little easier, back at his duties at Whitehall, he presented a distressing sight. Lord Bath, whose friendship he dearly cherished, was assiduous in his attendance, and Gilbert Sheldon, the aged Archbishop of Canterbury, who all through the plague had stood unflinchingly by the General's side, prayed with him constantly   Even the laughter-loving King tore himself almost daily from the society of Lady Castlemaine to show his sympathy and affection. Though to the last he could not quite believe that his disease had mastered him, he viewed the prospect of his approaching death with the same quiet resolution with which he had looked it in the face a hundred times before. He thought he might still live to staunch the bleeding wounds of his country, and see its King.a man again But if he might not raise it he at least could leave it with little regret now it was sunk so low. For years his own life had been a pattern of temperance and chastity, and the unblushing sin, with which his great achievement had deluged the country, was the source of real and poignant grief to him

But one desire really bound him to life and that was to see his son married Christopher was now a gallant of about eighteen years old, and ever since his father was first taken ill a marriage had been in course of arrangement between him and Lady Elizabeth Cavendish, grand-daughter of the Duke of Newcastle Now, at the eleventh hour, the business was completed, and on December 30th the young couple were brought to the General's chamber There beside his chair as he sat gasping for life, they were married, and the last faint effort of the arms, that had lifted a king on his throne, was to take the silly girl he had chosen, and place her feebly in the arms of the beloved son she was destined to ruin He died January 3rd and was buried in Westminster Abbey. The funerals of the great chiefs of the Restoration, George Monk Duke of Albemarle, Edward Montagu Earl of Sandwich, James Butler Duke of Ormond, followed the precedent set by the interments of the Duke of Buckingham in the reign of Charles I and of the Parliamentary leaders in the Commonwealth They were all buried amongst the Kings in the Chapel of Henry VIII. At the head of Queen Elizabeth's tomb, in a small vault, probably that from which the body of Dorislaus had been ejected, Monk was laid with Montagu, it being thought reasonable that those two personages should not be separated after death. (Crull, p 107) In the interval between Monk's death and funeral his wife died and was buried in the same vault, February 28th, 1669-70 " This twain were loving in their lives and in death they were not divided " was Seth Ward's text of the funeral sermon

After the General's death Lord Bath became the chief adviser and friend of young Duke Christopher and was consulted by him in all matters. On the 7th of September, 1670, Lord Bath was appointed Keeper of the House and Manor of St James, and his eldest son, Charles, Viscount Lansdowne, though only nine years of age at the time was appointed joint Keeper.

A document, dated 24 June 1670, is extant by which the

Earl of Bath, as Lord-Lieutenant of the county of Devon, appointed twenty-one gentlemen of the county to act as his Deputies Appendant to this Commission is a magnificent circular seal, nearly three inches wide.   On it is represented the Earl in armour on horseback charging the foe   The inscription is

SIGILLUM PRÆNOBILIS JOHANNIS COMITIS BATHONIÆ

The reverse bears the family arms quarterly   (1) Granville; (2) Wyche; (3) St Leger; (4) Bevill, and on a scroll is the expressive motto, " Futurum invisibile "

The following letters belonging to this period are also extant; the first is from one of the above-mentioned deputy-lieutenants, viz, Sir Thomas Clifford, Knight, Treasurer of the Household and a Member of the Privy Council —

SIR THOMAS CLIFFORD K^T TO THE EARL OF BATH

Whitehall, Oct. 27, 1670

My Lord,

I cannot forbeare telling y^r L^dship what an excellent vote pass'd the House of Comons this day, viz, that his Majesty be supplyed proportionably to his occasions, and he demanded in my Lord Keepers speech his debts upon interest to be discharged (wch are thirteen hundred thousand pounds) and eight hundred thousand pounds more to fit out a fleet of 50 saile of ships the next spring the house pass'd the vote without a negative I know this will please you as it doth all his friends We are now adjourn'd till Munday, and there is no Writt yet moved for Devon so that it cannot be in Devon by the next County Court day, wch I learn is upon the 11th of Nov so that noe election can be made till a month after, The Court and Parl^t are both full of the discourse of the contest I hope a good issue as we desire I will write to my friends to be active I kisse my Lady's hands, And am my Lord,

Y^r L^d ships
most humble and most
obedient Servt
J CLIFFORD

To the Earl of Bathe

The next four letters are from Sir Thomas Higgons who had married as his second wife Lord Bath's sister, Bridget, the widow of Simon Leach, of Cadleigh   Sir Thomas Higgons, after serving as envoy to Saxony and ambassador to the Court of Venice, had been Knighted at Whitehall the 17th of June, 1663   He was the son of Thomas Higgons, D.D, Rector of Westburgh, Salop ; his seat was at Grewell, near Odiam, Hants. His first wife had been Elizabeth Countess of Essex, who had been divorced from Lord Essex on the charge of adultery. Mr Higgons (as he was then) pronounced a funeral oration over her grave in Winchester Cathedral, the 16th of September, 1656, clearing her character from the charge This oration is printed in the Miscellanies of the Philobiblon Society, vol III.

SIR THOMAS HIGGONS K^r TO THE EARL OF BATH.

London, Nov ye 12, 1670

My Lord

I have received y'o^r Lord^{hps} of the 8th instant being much satisfyed to know that you are well, and that we shall see you Lord^{pp} shortly, wch all who love you much desire   The Spanyards have a Proverb wch sayes 'Los muertos & ydos no nan amigos' that is, the dead and the absent have no friends   I hope yor Lo^{rpp} will never experiment this in yor own particular, but if it be true in the world in general, it is much more in Courts where all things are more subject to mutation than in other places   The King's business in Parliament hath gone on hitherto very prosperously, for they have voted a supply proportionable to his Maties occasions even when they understood those occasions to require above two millions of money viz 800,000^{lbs} to set out a fleet this sūmer and 1,300,000 to pay off his debts wch lye at interest.   But yor Lord^{pp} will wonder when you shall know that this vote passed without contradiction wch is more than I ever yet saw in the like occasion—tis not but that there were some who had a good mind to oppose it, but finding much the greater part of the House for it, they were so wise as to give way to that wch they could not hinder, so that all they can do now is by artifices to delay and obstruct the wayes of raysing this money a by making all meanes ineffectuall wch we can propose, to throw us upon a necessity of the Land Taxe, wch the House does generally abhorre, as the most unsupportable of all Taxes and that wch will give the greatest discontent to the people   We are endeavouring to find better wayes for raising his Maties supply, and in order thereunto we have voted a week since at the Committee of the whole House (& it was yesterday confirmed by the House) that towards the King's supply there shall be an additional duty of 15 pence a barrell layd upon strong beere and ale, and 6 pence a barrell upon small beere, wch as it is computed will amount to 170,000lbs an yeare   And as it is apprehended that this new duty may hurt the old by making l'eople brew their own beere to save the excise, we have added a clause to be put into the Bill, that no man within any Corporation or fower miles of any Corporation, who hath not brewed in such a time shall be permitted to brew during the time of this new duty unless he pay the same Excise as is set upon the Brewer and retayler   Too day we have gone upon other heads for raysing the Kings supply and having a paper before us wch was delivered in by the Farmers of the Customes of what Comoodityes would beare a greater duty, we began with Tobacco & voted 3 pence a pound to be layd upon all tobacco coming from o^r English plantations and 6 pence a pound on all Spanish, wch hath been made will amount to four score thousand pounds a yeare   Thence we came to Salt & have voted, twopence a Gallon to layd upon all forrein salt with a Proviso of exception for the fishing trade wch is to pay nothing—F^m forrein salt we came to Scotch salt and home made salt & voted presently a penny a gallon upon Scotch salt   But when we came to levy money upon o^r English salt it was mightily opposed and urged against as a home excise & some of the Kings neer servants were against it   But that, after a long debate, was carryed too & a penny a gallon layd upon English salt, so that in every thing yet, they who have been serving the King most expeditely have prevayled   This duty of salt (as it is computed) will amount to thirty thousand pounds per annum   The Treat of the Union is this day adjourned to the end of March, it being very probable tht is will never come to any thing—there are so many difficulties likely to arise   This is all I can send yo Lor^{pp} by this post, if any thing occure to me worthy yor knowledge betwixt this and next week I will advertise you of it & please myself in serving yor Lo^{rpp} in such things as I can since Fortune will

not oblidge me with the occasions of doing you what service I would & showing
you with what passion

I am My Lord

Yo^{rs} Lo^{rpps} most humble

& obedient servant

THOMAS HIGGONS

My humble service
To my Lady

FROM THE SAME TO THE SAME

London Nov 29 1670

My Lord

As soon as I had receaved yor Lo^{rpps} of the 24th instant I spoke to my
Lord St John & S^r G T who shewed me a copy of the letter wch hath made
such a noyse in the House of Comons I was very glad to see that there was
nothing in it but what yor friends might be able to defend, and that the stile
of it was not at all imperative but meerly recomendatory They would have
persuaded us here that it was not a letter, but a warrant to the respective
Constables to choose Mr F & they shewed me a Copy (since I last wrote to
yor Lo^{rpp}) of the said letter wch they had directed to the Constables of the
several Hundreds, and so would have it a Warrant and not a Letter But I
believe they will stir no more in it now they see they can make nothing of it,
and so the report will dye of itself If any man should be so impertinent as
to make a matter of it in the House of Comons I doubt not but yor Lor^{pp} will
be vindicated sufficiently by the friends & servants you have there & that
this proceeding wch they have represented so enormous will appear no more
than what hath been always practiced in the little occasion I wrott yor
Lor^{pp} in my last of one man who gave out that he would complain to the
House of it But since that time I have spoken with his Uncle about it, who
assures me that his nephew hath no such intention, & that he hath promised
him he will never appeare in it And truly I beleeve no man else will How-
ever I will be vigilant and as much in the House as I can, till yor Lo^{rpp} come
to town In my opinion it were well that the election were defered till yor
Lor^{pp} were out of the Country, for if you should be there the Authors of this
Report will take colour from thence to say you stayed to awe the election By
the great preparations that are making it is beleev'd the King of France will
attaque the Hollanders at Spring, though some think that he will invade the
Bishoprick of Triers wch is less able to resist him But we shall see what the
Princes of the Empire will do now Loriaine, wch is a member of it, is taken
from them I have nothing more but to assure yor Lo^{rpp} of the inviolable
respects and service of

My Lord

Yo^r Lor^{pp's} most humble

& obedient Servant

THOMAS HIGGONS

For the Earle of Bathe
at his house at Stow
Leave this at the Port house
at Exeter
franc

FROM THE SAME TO THE SAME.

London Dec 6 1670

My Lord

Since my letter in answer to yor Lor^{pp} of the 24th of Nov from Stow there
hath little occur'd to me worth the sending yor Lord^{pp} The report wch yor

friends here were so concern'd at before they truly inform'd of the business is vanish'd into fume, for I have not so much as heard of it lately—so that yor mind may be in repose for any trouble that is like to arise to you from thence We have now made a good progress in raising a supply for the King for besides the duty wch we have levy'd upon Sugar, Tobacco, Linnen and other Merchandize we have this day passed several votes for charging all Writs, Subpœnas, Charters, Bills and Answers, Declarations, Deeds enrolled, and several other Papers and Instruments relating to the Law, wch though it be estimated but at 40000^{lbs} p ann by those who brought it in, is thought by others will amount to a much greater sum, that we are in hopes to serve his Maj^{ty} with an effectual supply without laying any burden on o^r Lands   There had like lately to have happened a new War betwixt the two Houses upon occasion of a dispute betwixt the Duke of Richmond and the Earle of Newburgh for certain lands in Sutton Marsh in Lincolnshire—for the Tenants of the Lands having lately attain'd to my Lord Newburgh the Duke complained of it to the House of Lords as a breach of Priviledge—whereupon the Lords (though it were earnestly opposed by many of them) without taking notice that my Lord Newburgh was a member of the House of Commons made an order to put the Duke of Richmond in possession, wch was resented by the Commons as a high breach of their priviledge & a violation of the Rights of the People   But before the report could be made from the Committee, the Controversy was determin'd by the death of my Lord Newburgh, who, poore gentleman, after he had endured much payne & misery in his Sickness, departed this life on Saturday last, dying with great resolution and calmness of mind   In his Will he hath recommended his son to the King, who, it is thought, will be so gratious to my young Lord as to enlarge that terme of yeares wch he hath in his father's offices   My wife hath been in Town most of this winter with her son intending to place him abroad at School, but not finding yor Lord^{pp} in Town nor in hope to see you here before the holydays, she is resolv'd to do nothing in that matter without yor approbation   And so we are next week into the country to pass o^r Christmas   If yor Lor^{pp} & my Lady will do us the honor in y^r returne to London to take a bed at Gruell, my wife & I would think ourselves very happy   But if that should fall out to be a convenient stage for you in regard of the shortness of the dayes, if I may have the favor to know when you pass by Bagshot or Hartford Bridge I would wayt upon yor Lor^{pp} to pay you the humble respects and services of

My Lord

Your Lor$^{pp's}$ most humble
and obedient Servt

THOMAS HIGGONS

My Lord St John desires me
to present yor Lor^{pp} his services
and to let you know that he longs to
see you here

FROM THE SAME TO THE SAME

London January 18 1670

My Lord,

      At last the mine hath played, and without hurting any man is evaporated in fume   This morning St John Rolles moved for a writt for choosing of a Knight for the county of Devon which I think had ended there, but that Sr John Northcot opposed the sending of the writt   Whereupon Mr Rolles stood up and sayed that it was strange that they should be against the electing of a new Knight, who had themselves sent warrants for the electing one   At that word a hoat alarum was taken and Rolles produced the copies of the letters which yor Lor^{pp} and yor Deputy Lieutenants had sent to the Constables wch after much opposition were ordered to be read   Hereupon arose a debate concerning the nature of Papers read, some contending that they were warrants sent to awe and intimidate the country, others that they were only letters recomendatory and an effort of yor care for preventing disorders and preserving the peace of the country wth wch you were intrusted   The debate lasted many howers, and as the business was press'd hard by one side, so it was defended by the other, tho' I must needs say it was carry'd with much respect to yor Lor^{pp} even by those who were against you   At last the house without passing any censure upon their members passed a vote to this effect, seeming only to have regard to the future, viz, that the sending of warrants or letters in the nature of warrants to any constables or other officers, when a Knight of the Shire or other members is to be chosen to serve in Parliament is unparliamentary and a violation of the liberty of elections and so the business ended   Those who spoke most concerndly in yor defence were Sr Robert Car, Colonel Sandys, Sr John Trelawney, S^r G Talbot, Mr Treasurer, Sr Charles Harbord, Mr Seymor, and the Speaker himself, who as he rose up to put, declared that far as he could perceave, it was the sense of the house and of every man in it that nothing in all this proceeding reflected upon the Earle of Bathe, who had done nothing to deserve blame   I heartily congratulate yor Lor^{pp} this good success, for it is more than an ordinary felicity to be accused in the House of Comons and to come off without reproche   All the good M Rolles hath done himself is to show that he can speak (wch he never did before) and to give yor Lor^{pps} friends an occasion both to mention yor family and person with honor   Sr John Maynard gave his opinion that this letter was in effect a warrant in as much as it came from persons in authority, but concluded in yor favour that it was done with a good intention, and therefore moved to proceed no further upon it   My Lord Hawley excused Sr John Northcot very pleasantly saying "if this gentleman have written a letter like a warrant you must consider, Mr Speaker, that he is an old Justice of Peace and that he hath made warrants so long that he can write in no other style"   My Lord St Johns, from whom I now parted, presents yor Lor^{pp} his humble service, and seems very glad tht this business is come to so good an issue   He was very attentive during the debate, and assures me that he was prepared to speak, but that there was no occasion for it, you had so many friends to stickle for you   My sister Thornhill enjoyn'd me to present yor Lor^{pp} and my Lady with her humble service and told me she should sleep the better (for she was going to bed) for the good newes I brought her from Westminster   Indeed my Lord, all those who love you are pleased with this day, amongst whom I will presume to reckon

My Lord

Yo^r Lord^{hps} most humble and obed Servant
THOMAS HIGGONS.

After the matter concerning the letter was determined we resumed o^r first debate of sending down a writt for a new K^t wch was at last carried in the affirmative, so that I doubt not but the writt will be quickly in the country I humbly beg the favor of yor Lord that to assure my Lady of my most humble service

The next letter is from Sir George Talbot, a Member of Parliament, between 1670-71, and who was referred to in the previous letter. The year is not given in this letter but the date is ascertained by the reference it contains to the deaths of the Earl of Norwich and Mr. Cavendish, both of which took place on the 3rd of March, 1670-71.

SIR GEORGE TALBOT TO THE EARL OF BATH.

Whitehall, March 5

My L^d,

I have had noe letter from you since you left Stow, yet I heare ye unhappy news of yor Lady's miscarriage, for wch I am most heartily sorry. This morning ye Triumvirat went down to assist ye election (I mean S^r W Courtne', Sr Edwd Seymor, & S^r Jo Rolles) S^r W C sayd ye last night that he would not have stirred in y^r business, if the E of Bath had not appeared in opposition to S^r C B, & if he should receive a baffle in this election, he would sell all his estate in Devonshire and leave the country. He was the last night to take his leave of the S C G and told his Ma^{ty} that he was going down to assist his friend S^r C B in the election. His Ma^{ty} bade him keepe the peace there. He replyed "I hope y^r Ma^{ty} doth not suspect that I shall breake it, if y^r Ma^{ty} hath received or shall receive any story that may induce you to conceive soe ille of me. I beseech you to suspend y^r beliefe till you heare me answere for my self", and thereupon he kissed his hand & took his leave. After he came from the K^g, he visited the Treasurer, and there told the dialogue that had passed betwixt his Ma^{ty} & him, and amongst other discourse sayd he wished y^t the L^d of Bath would appear at Exeter when ye county met, for then, if Bamfield lost ye election, he would make it a voyd one upon pretence of force. Y^e D of Albemarle, when they were feasted at Sr James Smith's at ye wedding, threw 2 glasses in S^r W Courtne's face & being questioned for it the next morning, sayd he was drunk and knew not what he did. Truly, I think, he scarce knoweth at any time what he doth, for he is become the most debauched creature that I ever saw. He oweth much of it to his tutor Armstrong. Y^r worthy friend Sr Courtne' Poole hath bestowed an extraordinary complimint upon him, for wch y^r Lp ought to give him thanks, it is this, "I hope y^r Grace will (when my Lp shall resigne up to you the Ld Lieutenancy of Devonshire) continue me in the comand of my Regiment'. I am going with y^r brother to spend ye shrovetyde at Abs Court and shall not write to y^r Lp on tuesday next. In ye meane time be pleased to know that Savage Fennick & Dunbair are fled & the endictment runneth onely agst them. The rest have (as they flatter themselves) slipped theyre necks out of the halter. The E of Norwich, young Mr Cavendish, & Hatton Rich are dead. I write in haste & disjointedly—excuse this fault in

y^r L^{ps} most obedient
& faythfull Servt

G TALBOT

The next letter is from Sir Robert Cary of Clovelly :—

SIR ROBERT CARY TO THE EARL OF BATH

Clovelly, March ye 29th, 1671

My Lo^d

Could yor Lo^p but truly apprehend my condition or my own pen expresse it, I should then noe way doubt either of yor Lo^{ps} pitty and compassion then be so jealous as I am y^t y^r Lo^p thinks mee both unkind and unciuill in not wayting one you all this time att Stowe where I have never had the good fortune to be since the Princes being there. Now o^r King & your Lo^{ps} maister I resolved to have sent this paper excuse some time sinthe to yor Lo^p, but was prevented by an extream Goutish payne in all the joints of my fingers so that

I could nether hold or use a pen, and comonly att this tune of the yeare I am con fined to my bead, but I thanke God as yet He hath bine pleased to spaie me from those extreame afflictions y⁵ (as I have sayd) doth assault me in the spring wch hath soe much encoraged mee as to hope I may not bee pre-uented in the resolution y⁵ I have taken wch is (y⁵ if the weather change and prove any thing warme, & the wayes passable for such a carriage as I must make use of (a Sedan, for one horse back I cannot) to wayte upon yor Lo^p & my ever honnor'd good Lady I have bine scant downe of my chamber since y^r Lo^ps Noble favour of seeing Clovelly, but yett have hopes to weane myselfe out of it as fayre weather comes one, and then I shall be impatient untill I have assur'd yor Lo^p in p son tht had I a Body answerable to my haste, there's not a person living y⁵ more really affects yor Lo^ps person and desires faithfully to serve you then myselfe Nay I would then be bold to court my selfe into som Imploym⁵ in y^r Lo^ps service, y⁵ might give you a full assurance of it.

Now, my Lo^e, all the Nuse in the Country is y⁵ the act for the subsidy (as its called) granted the King for the supply of his extraordinary occasions in come downe by wch I perseave my Lo Lucas might have spared his Impertinent speech wch was flying about the country, written, not printed as not deserving it I my weake judgem⁵ I never read a more inconsiderate discourse as the state of affairs stand in respect of o^r Nighbours preparations, the Arguments in generall tends rather to the granting of noe more supplyes to y^r King than to his conclasion in redusing the 12^d in the pound upon all land etc unto 8^d. certainly his Lo^p thinks it a fine thing to be poppoler though but amongst the inferiour and low discerning people, enough of wch there are noe doubt y⁵ to save there moneys would be content y⁵ both the Honner of the Nation & the security of it should run a hazard It sayd y⁵ the King intends for Newmarket as soon as the Parlem⁵ is adjourned, w^ch, as its thought, will be speedely And if so, I have a fancy yor Lo^p may inclyne to make some longer stay in the Country then is given out, and that to compleat the settlem⁵ of yor country affairs ere his ma^tie retourne to London And if y⁵ should (be) yor Lo^ps resolu-tion, I hope I may not despayre, but y⁵ both the weather and ways will be good, ere yo^u departe, for a Sick man to put in Execution what he intends—wch is to have the Honnor to kisse yor Lo^ps hands att Stow & after to live & dye in yor Lo^ps good favour, as a person y⁵ is

My Lo^d

Yo^r Lo^ps affectionate kinsman
& most humble & faythfull Servant
Robert Cary

These
flor the Right Hono^ble John Earle
of Bath Ld Leftenaut of Deuons^h & Cornewell
present
att Stow

Then follows one more letter from Sir Thomas Higgons in the autumn of that same year, and written from Torrington after a visit at Stowe :—

SIR THOMAS HIGGONS KT. TO THE EARL OF BATH

Torrington
this 28 of Sept
1671

My Lord

I cannot let Ching returne to Stow without charging him with my most humble service to yor Lor^pp & my Noble Lady & giving both of you a

thousand thankes for the favors & honors which you were pleased to do me
when I was there   I am obliged also to thank yor Lor^pp for giving me so
good a Guide, without whom I believe I had lost my way to Torrington   If I
could have foreseen how the afternoon would prove I had certainly turn'd
back from Kilkhampton to Stow, and ,had the happinesse of yor Lor^pp's company and you the trouble of mine one night longer   But led on by Ching
who spirited with hoat water and Tobacco defyed the weather I got in good
time to this place though so wash'd as I have not been these many yeares   I
should have been more mortifyed with so ill a day but that I consider how
many good ones I have had in enjoying yor Lor^pp wch for anything I have
suffer'd is an ample amends to

My Lord
Yo^r Lor^pp's most humble
& most obedient ser^t
THOMAS HIGGONS

For my Lord
The Earle of Bathe
at
Stow

As a further proof of his affection for Lord Bath, Charles II.
was pleased, by letters patent. 16 August, 1674, to grant him
and his heirs a further annuity of £3000,[1] charged on the
Duchy of Cornwall or on the hereditary excise, and on
the 21st of April, 1679, he was again admitted a member
of the Privy Council   His eldest son, Charles Viscount
Lansdowne, was elected to represent Launceston the 19th of
November, 1680, while still a minor , but, upon the dissolution
of the parliament a few months afterwards, he left England to
take part in the wars of Hungary against the Turks, being
commended to the care and tuition of Count Taff, a younger
brother to the Earl of Carlingford, who had early sought to
make his fortune in foreign parts, and became in time, both in
court and camp, one of the most accomplished persons of that
age   Lord Lansdowne took part in the battle of Kornenberch,
when the Duke of Lorrain defeated 12,000 spahyes in a rase
campaign , he was present at the siege of Vienna, when it was
attacked by 200,000 Turks, under the command of the Prime
Vizier Kara Mustapha, and displayed great bravery at the rout
of the Ottoman army   and following them up again engaged and
defeated them at Baracan, when the King of Poland and his
whole army would have been certainly lost if the Duke of
Lorrain had not come in and turned the day at the very instant
that fortune was declaring for the infidels   He was also present

---

In 1826 one moiety of the above sum was bought up by the Treasury, and 1856 the
other moiety was transferred to the Consolidated Fund   *Cf.* Parliamentary Return, 9 Feb
1881, where the amount £1,200 "now due" appears to be paid to trustees for the heirs of
Captain F. Garth

CHARLES GRANVILLE, SECOND EARL OF BATH.
From an Original Portrait in the Wellesbourne Collection.

at the taking of Gran and several smaller engagements, in all of which he displayed such unwonted valour and intrepidity for one so young, that the Emperor, as a special mark of honour, was pleased by his charter, bearing date at the Castle of Lintz January 27th, 1684, to create him a Count of the Sacred Roman Empire, by the style and title of Earl of Lansdowne "to remain and be continued *ad infinitum*" (as it is expressed in the Patent) "to the name and family of the Granvilles," with the distinction of bearing their paternal coat of arms upon the breast of the Roman eagle. In 1685 he was elected as Knight of the Shire for Cornwall, and in June of that year was sent as Ambassador to the Court of Madrid, where he continued till the Revolution, when he delivered up his credentials to King James at the Court of St Germains, and on reaching England joined his father in espousing the cause of the Prince of Orange.

Lord Lansdowne had married at St Martin's Church in the Fields, the 22nd of May, 1678 (he being about seventeen and she fourteen years of age) the Lady Martha Osborne, fifth and youngest daughter of Thomas, Earl of Danby (afterwards created Marquess of Carmarthen and Duke of Leeds) Lord High Treasurer of England Lady Lansdowne died in childbirth in 1689, and was buried in Westminster Abbey, in the chapel of St. Nicholas The inscription on her coffin-plate, preserved in one of the Funeral Books, reads thus —

THE RIGHT HON^{BLE} MARTHA LADY LANSDOWNE
DAUGHTER OF THOMAS MARQUESS OF CARMARTHEN
DIED 11 SEPT 1689 IN HER 25th YEAR.

She left no issue, but the Funeral Book mentioned above states that her coffin was exposed in 1713 and another found with this inscription —

THE HON MRS ELIZABETH GRANVILLE
DAUGHTER OF CHARLES LORD LANSDOWNE.

Lord Lansdowne married secondly, in February, 1690-1, Isabella, sister of Henry, Earl of Grantham, and daughter of Henry de Nassau, Lord of Auverquerque, Count of Nassau, Master of the Horse to King William III, and afterwards Velt Marshall General of the United Netherland Provinces, by Frances Aersen Van Sommelsdyck, daughter of Cornelius, Lord of Sommelsdyck in Holland She too, died in childbed, 30 January, 1691-2, leaving an only son, William Henry, who eventually became 3rd Earl of Bath.

CHAPTER XVI.

In 1679 Lord Bath pulled down old Stowe and in its place, though on a different site nearer the shore, built a magnificent new mansion, covering $3\frac{1}{2}$ acres of ground, and containing, it is said, 365 windows, out of the monies he had received from the Government as a debt owing to himself and his father for their sacrifices to the royal cause. Dr Borlase describes this new Stowe as "by far the noblest house in the West of England," and in the MS. diary of Dr. Yonge, F R.S., a distinguished physician of the latter part of the seventeenth century, the following entry occurs in the year 1685 .—

"I waited on my Lord of Bathe, then Governor of Plymouth, to his delicious house Stowe. It lyeth on y⁰ ledge of y⁰ north sea of Devon a most curious fabrick beyond all description"

An indifferent picture of this second Stowe is preserved at Haynes Park by the Thynne family, to whom the Cornish property eventually descended, whilst another indifferent one is in the possession of Mrs Martyn, the wife of the rector of Lifton, near Launceston. This new mansion, however, stood for less than half-a-century, being pulled down in 1720 by Lord Bath's daughter, Grace, Countess Granville and Viscountess Carteret. In Polwhele's History of Cornwall it is stated that a man of Stratton lived long enough to see its site a cornfield, before the building existed, and after the building was destroyed a cornfield again The materials were sold piecemeal by auction; the carved cedar wood in the chapel, executed by Michael Chuke, was bought by Lord Cobham and applied to the same purpose at his mansion of Stowe in Buckinghamshire. The staircase, it is said, is at Prideaux Place, Padstow, while a great portion of the stone-carved work was removed to South Molton (where the Town Hall was ornamented with it), to Castle Hill, and other places in the neighbourhood. The stables alone remain and have been converted into a farmhouse; the tennis-court into a sheepcote; the great quadrangle into a rick-yard, and civilization, spreading wave after wave so fast elsewhere, has surged back from that lovely corner of the land, let us hope only for a while.

Referring to this ruined mansion, Edward Moore exclaims—

> Ah ! where is now its boasted beauty fled ?
> Proud turrets that once glittered in the sky,
> And broken columns, in confusion spread,
> A rude mis-shapen heap of ruins lie
>
> Where too is now the garden's beauty fled,
> Which every clime was ransacked to supply ?
> O'er the dread spot see desolation spread,
> And the dismantled walls in ruin lie
>
> Along the terrace-walks are straggling seen
> The prickly bramble and the noisome weed,
> Beneath whose covert crawls the toad obscene,
> And snakes and adders unmolested breed

Here, however, in great grandeur and style, John, Earl of Bath spent the remainder of his days with his large family, consisting of five sons and eleven daughters   Two of the sons and eight of the daughters however died in childhood.   He continued without the least interruption in great favour and esteem with Charles II to the time of the gay monarch's death, 6th February, 1684-5, and although he mixed so constantly with the licentious court his private character was, according to all accounts, strict and moral   A staunch protestant himself, he and Lord Feversham, the Captain of the Guard, were the only officers of state present when the King drew to his end, and the Duke of York secretly introduced the Roman Catholic priest, Huddlestone, into the bedroom to administer the last sacraments of that church, the King having declined the ministrations of the Archbishop and Bishops who had been in attendance upon him (cf Lord Macauley's History of England, vol. 1, civ   Life of James II, p 747   Evelyn's Diary, vol ii, p 545)   A little before the King died, so Le Neve states, he commended Lord Bath to the Duke of York, desiring him to consider him not so much a servant as a friend ; but upon the accession of the Duke as James II he was removed from his office of Groom of the Stole, which was given to Lord Peterborough   According to Le Neve, Lord Peterborough claimed the offices of Groom of the Stole and of First Lord of the Bedchamber as his right, he having occupied them previously in the Duke's household   The two claimants had a hearing before the King and Council, but the matter was finally referred to the Attorney-General, Sir Robert Sawyer, who gave it as his opinion that these offices were at the King's disposal, but that the salary of Groom of the Stole of right belonged to the Earl of Bath, upon which the King told the Earl of

Peterborough that he was to have ' the shell but my lord of
Bath the kernell " However in reality it did not prove so, for
Lord Peterborough had both the salary and the place, and Lord
Bath, finding how the King's favour went, was forced to sit
down with the loss. He continued, however, Lord Warden of
the Stannaries and Keeper of St James' Park, and remained,
so long as he conscientiously could, unshaken in his loyalty to
the King. But James II was a Romanist by religion, and for
this reason had been disliked by the nation for a long time, and
efforts had been made to exclude him from the throne. Indeed
when in the previous reign he had warned Charles of plots
against his life, Charles had wittily replied " Never fear,
brother, they won't kill me to make you king!" This hatred
of the nation had embittered his disposition ; he became stern,
morose and bigoted, and he no sooner ascended the throne than
he determined to make himself absolute, and to restore the
Roman Catholic faith at all costs. One great obstacle in his
path was the Test Act. Unless this was repealed he could not
place Romanists in any office. Parliament would not consent
to its repeal, and so he determined to make use of his
dispensing power and to grant offices in defiance of the Test
Act. Having successfully won a collusive action, the judges
proving subservient to his commands, the King proceeded
to place Roman Catholics in his army and council. He
moreover attempted to win over the Nonconformists to his
side. They, like the Romanists, were severely persecuted
by the penal statutes of the Church of England. Relaxation
from these would have been to their advantage, but, to their
credit be it said, they preferred civil liberty to religious
liberty. Seeing through the King's designs they refused to
be won over, either from a noble patriotism or because they
felt that if once Roman Catholicism should be re-established
in the land, their persecutions would be still more severe.
The Lord-Lieutenants of the different counties were required
to test the sentiments of the county gentlemen, and Lord
Bath, as Lord-Lieutenant of Devon and Cornwall, was dismissed into the West with no fewer than fifteen new charters,
so that he was nick-named " the Prince Elector " (*cf.* Evelyn's
Diary II , 562) Evidently this could have been no pleasing
mission for him, for he had been one of the eighteen Lords who
had drawn up a petition to the King for a free Parliament in
order to redress the grievances of the nation. But the King
had rejected their advice His plans, however, proved an utter
failure, and his proposals met in all quarters with answers

adverse to his wishes Lord Bath returned from the West with gloomy tidings for him   He had been authorized to make the most tempting offers, and particularly to promise that the trade in tin should be freed from the oppressive restrictions under which it lay   But even this lure, which at any other time would have been irresistible, was now slighted   All the justices and deputy-lieutenants of Devon and Cornwall, without one dissentient voice, declared that they would put life and property in jeopardy for the King, but that the Protestant religion was dearer to them than either life or property   "And, Sir," said Lord Bath, "if your Majesty should dismiss all these gentlemen, their successors would give exactly the same answer" (*cf* Van Cittens, April $\frac{10}{20}$ 1688).

It was on the 9th of October in this year that Christopher, Duke of Albemarle, died without issue.   Five years after his marriage he had made a will in which he settled a great part of his estates on Lord Bath, failing male issue of his own body, and repeated his father's request to King Charles that the Dukedom might be given him, his eldest son bearing the title of Lord Monk   This he did, he expressly said, in consideration of Lord Bath being one of his nearest kindred, and out of gratitude due to him for many acts of friendship and good offices done to him and his family, and he especially mentioned that Lord Bath had procured him his father's Garter when he might have had it himself   The unhappy connubial quarrels had commenced , no child blessed the ill-omened union and the extravagancies of the half-witted wife had already driven the young Duke to those evil courses which dragged him down to his untimely end   In 1681, a deed was drawn up by the Duke's solicitor and signed, confirming the provisions of this will in the main; *i e*, it settled the chief portion of the estates, after the Duke and Duchess's deaths without issue, upon Lord Bath ; the other portion immediately after his own death without issue, partly upon Lord Bath, and partly between Bernard Granville, the Earl's brother, and Sir Walter Clarges, the Duke's maternal uncle   The Duke, as he handed the deed, or a copy of it, to Lord Bath, said he wished he could have done more for him.   In 1687, having been appointed Governor of Jamaica the Duke, at the instance of Lord Bath, had a fresh Deed prepared to ratify the former documents, for fear lest the Duchess, who had formed a great dislike to Lord Bath, should prevail upon the Duke in some drunken bout to revoke the former Deed in due form against his will. The existence of this fresh Deed was carefully concealed therefore from the

z²

Duchess and her agents, but was retained by the Duke or his
solicitors Before leaving England the Duke informed some of
his Essex friends that they would have good neighbours at
Newhall in the Earl of Bath and his family, if he should die
in Jamaica, and gave directions that the Earl should be communicated with and given the keys of his writings, if any
mischance should befall him He also handed to Lord Bath
the Will and former Deed under the same cover with the seal
of the Duke's arms upon it Lord Bath's fears were soon
realised. Evidently the Duchess worked upon her husband's
enfeebled will, for at this time he had given way a great deal
to drink, and she caused a new will to be drawn up in 1687,
revoking the Deed of 1681 Although constantly importuned
to sign it, the Duke refused for six months, and, in order to
avoid her importunities, locked himself up in his room, so that
those who wished to speak to him had to do so through the
window At last, however, he was persuaded to sign the will,
the doctor informing him (as was sworn to in the evidence),
that "her Grace would have a violent return of her distemper
and be very bad again if her wishes on this matter were
frustrated" He told the Duchess, however, that she might
"pay the counsel's fee as her own business" By this new Will
some parcels of land were given to Bernard Granville, Sir
Walter Clarges, and others, and a larger provision was made for
the Duchess for her life than she would have had under the
previous will, but the main bulk and residue of the estate was
bequeathed to a very distant cousin, Colonel Thomas Monk,
whose existence had been discovered and the King was petitioned
in this Will to confer a title of honour upon Colonel Monk, and
to create him Baron Monk of Potheridge Now by the last
Deed of 1688, it was provided that the Duke should have the
power to revoke any of the uses in the former Deed and Will
and to limit new ones ; yet no alteration of the provisions were
to be made except by writing under the Duke's hand and seal
witnessed by six persons, of whom three were to be peers of the
realm or without the tender of sixpence to each of the two
Trustees named in the Deed This Jamaica Will was witnessed
by three persons only, none of them being peers, and there
was no tender of money to the trustees Lord Bath, on hearing
of the Duke's death, produced the will of 1675 and the two
Deeds, and the will was proved, but no steps were taken to
recover the title. Charles II , while " obliging himself " to continue it in the Granville family, was only able to " recommend '
it to his successor , and Lord Bath, knowing that he was in but

poor favour with James II, made no application for it, and in
1696 Arnold Joost van Keppel, Lord of Voorst, who accompanied the Prince of Orange to England, and was a great
favourite of his, was created Earl of Albemarle. Meanwhile
matters in England were fast tending to a crisis. William of
Orange and Mary his wife, the daughter of Charles I, had long
been regarded as possible successors to James II, and being
Protestants there was a large party in the English nation on
their side. The trial of the Seven Bishops for refusing to read
the Declaration of Indulgence was the last straw that broke
the camel's back, and negotiations were entered into with
Holland. James first learnt of these proceedings from his
minister at the Hague, and was struck with terror equal to his
former infatuation, and immediately sought to regain popularity
by repealing his obnoxious Acts. All confidence was, however,
destroyed between the King and the people, and William
arrived with his fleet in Torbay, the 4th of November, 1688,
and was at once joined by a number of influential persons.
Fixing his quarters at Exeter, where he occupied the Deanery,
he held Court and gave a public reception to the whole body of
noblemen and gentlemen who had assembled there. The Earl
of Bath, who was still Governor of the Town and Royal
Citadel of Plymouth, where the Earl of Huntingdon was in
command with a regiment of Foot, resolved to secure that
place for the Prince of Orange. Having first taken the Earl
of Huntingdon prisoner, by the help of his kinsman, Lieutenant
Colonel Ferdinando Hastings, he proceeded to apprehend all the
Roman Catholic officers and soldiers in the Garrison, and then,
having assembled the remainder of the troops, he caused the
two Declarations which the Prince of Orange had issued to be
read out before them. They were received with loud and
repeated acclamations, and the officers and soldiers unanimously
declared that they would live and die with the Prince and Earl
of Bath in defence of the said Declarations. Lord Bath then
admitted part of the Dutch fleet into the harbour of Plymouth,
and despatched his own regiment, under the command of his
nephew Bevill, the eldest son of his brother Bernard, to Jersey,
where the Papists were again disarmed and the island secured
to the Prince.

But there was at least one member of the family to whom
Lord Bath's conduct was a source of real grief. This was
Dennis Granville, Lord Bath's youngest brother, who was at
this time Dean of Durham. He regarded his brother's espousal
of the cause of the usurper as having sullied the hitherto

stainless loyalty of the House of Granville   In the autumn
of 1688 the intelligence that the Prince of Orange was preparing an armament for the invasion of England reached
his ears   Anxious to vindicate the ancient reputation for
loyalty of the Bishopric of Durham, the Dean's first care
was to establish, if it were possible, the parishioners of his
country cures in his own high principles of subjection and
allegiance to their Sovereign, showing them that " subjects were,
upon noe consideration whatsoever, neither of religion, liberty,
nor life, to resist or desert their lawfull Soveraigne, tho' he were
no better than such a one St Paul lived under, when he writ the
Epistle to the Romans, not only a heathen, but a cruell
persecutor, a Nero, a Caligula, or a Diocletian, and that subjects
to a Christian prince, and to a prince soe mercifull and gracious as
ours, by consequence would be more guilty, if they should
rebell against or resist him, merely because he professed a
different religion "

He then repaired to his Deanery at Durham and "summoned
his brethren the Prebendaryes together" into the Chapter
house, where he " propounded to them the assisting of the King
in soe sad an exigent with their purses as well as with their
prayers "   All present complied with the Dean's proposition, and
an Act in Chapter was passed granting 700*l* for his Majesty's
service ;   100*l* from the Dean and 50*l* from each of the
Prebendaries, to which all absent from Durham at the time,
with one exception, gave their assent by letter   The Bishop
being absent in London, Dennis Granville next called the
clergy of his Archdeaconry together, to confirm, if it might be,
the loyalty of the wavering, and to do all that in him lay, as he
somewhat pathetically expresses it, "to awaken those out of
their sin whom he could not confirm in their duty "   In the
course of the address he delivered to them, he earnestly set
before them the duty of assisting their Sovereign at the
impending crisis, and of securing their flocks by every means in
their power from being seduced by the arguments of his enemies

The Dean was further anxious that his brethren of the
Chapter and the Magistracy of the County should have united
with him in a loyal address to the King, expressive of their
horror of the invasion with which his dominions were threatened,
but the proposition was coldly received, and he was obliged to
satisfy himself by forwarding to his Majesty his own personal
assurances of devoted allegiance   This address was intercepted
at York and fell into the hands of the Earl of Danby and other
adherents of the Prince of Orange, who had already seized upon

that city and " were some of them advancing northwards to secure Durham and Newcastle" A fruitless attempt was made by Granville to induce the Magistrates and Deputy-Lieutenants to take measures to check this advance, and Durham was entered by Lord Lumley with a small force on the 5th of December whilst the Dean was preaching one of the Advent sermons in the Cathedral No opposition was offered The Dean was summoned to deliver up his arms and horses, and on refusal was confined within the walls of the Deanery during the occupation of the city by the friends of the invader. The Prince of Orange's declaration having been publicly read by Lord Lumley at the Castle and at the Market Cross, and sanctioned by the presence of most of the country gentry, he was encouraged to demand admittance into Newcastle, but meeting with opposition to this farther advance he withdrew to York The Dean now stood alone, or nearly so, as an adherent of James, but mounted the Cathedral pulpit on the following Sunday, with unabated courage, to discharge his conscience by preaching another "seasonable, loyall sermon . . . to persuade the members of that Church and all the auditory, to stand firm in their allegiance in that day of temptation, and never to joyn in the least wayes in that horrid rebellion which was at that time sett on foot in the nation." Matters however wore a hopeless aspect as far as James' cause was concerned, and Granville began to despair of being of any further service to his Sovereign by remaining at his post His personal liberty appears also to have been in some danger, and after much consideration he finally resolved upon flight.

Accordingly at midnight, on the 11th of December, Dean Granville quitted the walls of the Deanery, never again, as it proved, to re-enter them. His journey to Carlisle, his reception there, and the hardships he underwent before he could pursue his way to Edinburgh, are graphically described by him in a letter to his brother, the Earl of Bath, which he afterwards printed together with his Farewell Sermons Soon after his arrival in Edinburgh an opportunity offered of embarking for France, of which he readily availed himself, being anxious above all things to join his Sovereign On the 19th of March he landed at Honfleur, where he had the mortification of hearing that he had arrived the very day after James' departure from Brest for Ireland His stay at Honfleur was of short duration, for on the 25th of the same month he departed for Rouen, where he took up his abode with Mr Thomas Hackett, an English merchant resident in that city, from whom he appears to have experienced no ordinary kindness and attention   In this city he resided at intervals for several years

Dennis Granville's career had been a distinguished one. Educated probably at Eton (see p 337) he was admitted a fellow-commoner of Exeter College, Oxford, on the 22nd of September, 1657, and on September 28th 1660 was, amongst others, created Master of Arts in that University, an honour which he is said to have owed to the ' favour of his great relations," and to which old Antony à Wood seems to have thought he was scarcely then entitled, inasmuch as " he had been no sufferer for the King's cause, nor ejected his college, because entered therein after the Parliament visitors had turned out all the Royalists "

It would appear that he had been designed for the Church from his earliest years   In his letter to the Earl of Bath above mentioned he states the intention of his parents to devote one of their sons to the especial service of God in His Church   The lot, as he expresses it, fell upon him, and he fulfilled their pious intentions by "devoting himself thereto, honestly, with good will to God's service and without designe,"—"in a time of adversity and rebellion, when there was small hopes of being Dean of Durham "   This is proved by the following interesting letter he wrote before his ordination to Mr George Trosse, a college friend, afterwards a Minister of the Gospel in Exeter —

DENNIS GRANVILLE TO MR GEORGE TROSSE

Cadleigh June 28 1660

Dear Friend

I had according to my promise written to you before this time, had I gotten into Devonshire as soon as I imagin'd I should   I met with an obstacle in my journey down, which oblig'd me to go towards London , where I tarried near a month's space and was hasten'd thence upon the sad occasion which I believe you have heard of long ere this, I mean the loss of my brother Leache who is as much lamented in these parts as any man hath been these many years   And truly, I think, very justly, having great ground to conclude th' God hath sanctified his dispensations towards him unto his soul by several passages before and since his death, and th' he would have prov'd a great instrument of God's glory and of good unto his country, had it been the will of God to have granted him a long life   But blessed be God, howsoever he disposeth of us   for his dealings with us are for the best tho' they appear to us otherwise

I do yet, I bless God, hold my resolutions, by his assistance, of under-taking the ministry , and hope th' by his grace I shall continue in them , which that I may do I beg your prayers and the prayers of all good Christians, for I am not insensible of the many difficulties which I have to struggle with, but I praise God, where I feared I might have met with some I have not yet met with any, I mean amongst my own relations , for I'll assure you th' not one of them hath us'd any argument to dissuade me from being a minister I confess some others have occasionally done it, but I trust in God th' the devil and his instruments shall never in this particular, prevail against me though reflecting upon my own infirmities, I may justly fear it, did I not also look to my Saviour at the right hand of God, making intercession for me, who hath promised not to suffer his servants to be tempted above what they are able, but will also with the temptation make a way to escape

Dear friend, pray let me hear from you, for I value nothing more than conference with God's children by letters, if not by personal discourse, and I hope we have a Christian love for each other, though perchance we differ in opinion in some trivial circumstances But it is my principal (and I hope ever will be) th' difference in judgment, when not in fundamentals, is not a sufficient ground (as now it daily is) for breach of charity where there is hope of sincerity. But no more of this at present I do heartily pray th' God by his Holy Spirit would give us both a right judgment in all things, and show us the truth in whatsoever we err or are deceived

I do once more desire your prayers in a particular manner, (you shall not want mine) being often something startled at the difficulties I discern in a Christian course of life, especially in undertaking th' weighty calling which makes the Apostle cry out who is sufficient for these things? Well, friend, farewell I beseech God to preserve you I intended once to discourse further with you but I am prevented.

I shall ever be your friend & servant in the Lord,

DENNIS GRENVILE

Superscription
  For Mr George Trosse
    at his Chamber in
    Pembroke College in
    Oxford

His actual ordination, however, did not take place until after the Restoration, for we learn from a letter addressed to his friend Beveridge that they received Holy Orders together from the hands of Bishop Saunderson in the year 1661 His first preferment was Kilkhampton, where he succeeded Nicholas Monk, promoted for the part he took in the Restoration, to the See of Hereford, 13 January, 1661 As, however, no record of his incumbency appears in the Parish Registers, he, probably, never resided at Kilkhampton, but a letter from Bishop Cosin's domestic chaplain, Davenport, to Sancroft, dated Auckland, October 4th, 1662, sufficiently proves that he was at the time Rector (*cf.* Tanner MSS., xlviii, 55)

Two events, which occurred about this time, gave him no doubt a claim to future patronage, which was scarcely likely to be overlooked Charles II. made him one of his Chaplains in Ordinary, and he married Anne, daughter of Bishop Cosin. But there is no reason to suppose that he was a man who received preferment simply on the ground of family connection. There is abundant evidence that he threw himself gallantly into the work of re-construction which was so much needed in the Diocese of Durham over which Cosin was called to preside, when the Church and the Monarchy were re-established. And Cosin was a man of far too high administrative power to select unfit instruments as his co-adjutors in the task which he so resolutely took in hand.

The earliest preferments which Dennis Granville received from Bishop Cosin were the first stall in the Cathedral, his installation to which bears date September 24, 1662, and the Archdeaconry of Durham with the Rectory of Easington annexed, to which he was collated in the same year. To these was added in 1664 the Rectory of Elwick, which he resigned in 1667 on obtaining Sedgefield. The death of Dr Naylor, who was Rector of Sedgefield, occasioned also a vacancy in the second, or golden, stall of the Cathedral, to which Granville was removed on the 16th April, 1668. These were assuredly great preferments, too great indeed, in some respects, to be given to so young a man as he then was. The consequence was "Jeshurun waxed fat and kicked." The rich young pluralist, instead of staying at one at least of his cures, was constantly careering about at Oxford and in London, to which latter place he was attracted by being chaplain to the King. This, of course, disgusted so strict a disciplinarian as Bishop Cosin, who complains of his son-in-law's non-residence, and still more of the reason he gave for it, which was in truth the strangest ever given for absenteeism, "because his wife had taken physic." "I know not what to do with Mr Grenvyle," writes the Bishop, "who is still at Oxford idling away his time, and suffering his curates to be non-resident at Easington and Sedgefield as hee himselfe is, under colour of his wife's taking physick, who for ought I see never needed any, for from her coming to Durham to this day she was never better in all her life, though she be now thrust up into a coop, and a strait close place which may much endanger her health. But hee is a wilful man and will order her as he lists. In the meanwhile, though I went to visit both him and her a month since, I never saw either of them at my lodgings here, for she dares not go forth of her own without his leave, which leave, it seems, hee left not behind him." Again, in another letter, the Bishop writes, "Mr Grenvyle's priviledge is now out of doors for his privilege lasteth no longer than 20 dayes after the adjournment of the Parliament. I told you in my last that he had carried his wife from Bigglesworth to Oxford, and now I can tell you that he hath left her there (where she is not acquainted at all) with a kinswoman of his there whom I know not, being himselfe come up hither to London to see the funerall of the late Generall,[1] which is this day to pass from Sommerset House to Westminster. Hee tells me his wife is very well, and that the waters were so much out as they journeyed about Newarke, that they were forct to stay 12 dayes by the way which I think was no way to cure her from the lightnes of her head, but rather a certaine way to augment her old, or else to get her a worse and a new disorder."

On the 20th of December, 1670, he took his Doctor of Divinity degree at Oxford, and appears to have spent some months after this in London with his wife—possibly on her account. There can be no doubt that their married life was a time of much domestic infelicity. Mrs. Granville laboured under occasional attacks of mental excitement, of the extent of which the Bishop and his family appear to have been either ignorant or incredulous. John Proud, Dennis' faithful and devoted servant, wrote in after years that he was "the best of husbands to her, and took all imaginable care for her recovery. Shee was a very pious good woman, and the best of all her sisters (that I knew) in the intervalls of her distemper which lessen'd as she grew older. He had noe [issue] by her, which I often heard him bless God for." A further cause of domestic strife was the fact that the marriage portion, which he expected to have received with his wife, had never been paid, and there exists a large quantity of correspondence on the subject which is characterised with much exasperation of feeling on both sides, and not only were the good offices of Lord Bath and of the Duke of Albemarle enlisted by Dennis in the matter, but even the King himself indited the following letter to Bishop Cosin on the subject —

CHARLES II TO BISHOP COSIN

Right Trusty and welbeloved, We greet you well. Whereas We are informed th' our welbeloved servant Denis Grenvile hath yet received no portion with your daughter, though others very largely, at which wee cannott but justly wonder, especially since the Generall (a person so well deserving from the whole Kingdome and th' hath been so greatly instrumentall in Our happy Restauration) hath zealously appeared in his behalfe, and still resents the usage his kinsman hath mett withall. And th' notwithstanding the Preferments bestowed on him (though very good) have (as usually) brought divers and great incumbrances along with them, which hath increased that debt hee was unhappily involved in by the sufferings of his Familly, before he related to yours, you have yet contributed no assistance to alleviate his burthen and present trouble, chiefly occasioned by your invitation of him into the North, which hath prov'd very unfortunate to him in severall respects, and by the disingenuity of some employ'd in the proposall of the match, may be a cause of much further misery to him, as well as posterity, if God send him any,

---

[1] George Monk, Duke of Albemarle.

A

Wee therefore taking his perplex'd condition into our consideration which Wee greatly pity and for whom Wee are so much concern'd that to signifie Our grace and favour unto him Wee are contented to write in this particular and extroardinary manner, being fully satisfied th' hee deserves th' good report which is generally given of him notwithstanding all that hath been said to the contrary to some of Our publick Ministers of State (which might have been forborne to have been said of a servant of Ours whom Wee thought worthy of our Royall Dispensation) cannot but recommend him in most effectuall manner unto you as a person not only well deserving in himselfe, but relating to a Family whose favour you would not doe well to contemne, that have done and suffered so much for Our Royall Father as well as Ourselfe, assuming you th' in bestowing a fortune on him suitable to his present unhappiness and helping him out of his distractions occasioned by his debts (which may now prove very injurious to your daughter as well as himselfe) you will not only doe yourselfe a great kindnesse but a most gratefull and acceptable thing to Us and divers considerable persons who heartily solicits on his behalfe, and will not rest satisfied till you have complied with his desires, which appeare very modest and reasonable not only to Ourselfe but must needs do the like (his quality and condition considered) to all indifferent and unbyassed persons th' truly understand his case   Wee shall say no more at present but mind you that it is for the Churche's honour as well as your owne th' you put speedily to this affaire (without any more adoe) such a period as may give satisfaction to himselfe and relations   Expecting your complyance herein and an account of the same (which for your owne sake as well as his We shall be very sorry you should fail of) Wee bid you farewell

    Given at Our Court at Whitehall the   .   day of   in the
18th yeare of Our Reign

Dennis Granville's imprudent expenditure had resulted in a most humiliating and public exposure of his pecuniary difficulties some three years previously.   On the 8th of July, 1674, as he was "coming from publick prayers and a funerall (where the chiefest of the gentry of the country were assembled) and being in his habitt he was openly arrested within the cloysters at the door of the cathedrall by three bailiffs"   By a high-spirited man like Granville "with a strong dash of the cavalier about him," (as Surtees happily expresses it) this must have been felt as a most galling affront , for the pride of the high-bred gentleman as well as the dignity of the churchman must alike have been most bitterly wounded   The manner in which he more than once refers in his correspondence to his "odeous arrest" sufficiently proves that this was the case   It was in vain that he pleaded his privilege as Chaplain-in-Ordinary to the King   The bailiffs were inexorable   an appeal to Mr Richard Neile the under-sheriff was equally unsuccessful, and Dr Granville was carried off to gaol "with many aggravating circumstances"   The matter however was not allowed to rest there   The appeal, which was made in vain to the under-sheriff and his bailiffs, was brought before the King in Council without much delay, and the result was that 'the King was

LADY JOANNA GRANVILLE.

WIFE OF COL. THORNHILL.

From an Original Portrait, by Wright, in the Wellesbourne Collection.

pleased very much to reprehend Mr Carnabie, a person concerned in it, and to direct his Attorney-General to prosecute him and Mr. Neile But on the submission of Mr Carnabie a pardon was granted to him and also to Mr Richard Neile on the petition of his father Sir Paul Neile, and on expressing his sorrow for his misdemeanour, who declared himself ignorant that Dr. Granville was his Majesty's Chaplain-in Ordinary

This sharp lesson however was not lost on Dennis Granville, who henceforth circumscribed his expenditure within more prudent limits During the year 1678 and 1879 he travelled abroad accompanied by his sister Lady Joana Thornhill and her family, residing chiefly at a small town in Provence called Tours d'Aigues Lady Joana had married in 1653 (as his second wife) to Richard Thornhill son of Sir Timothy Thornhill of Ollantegh, in the parish of Wye, Kent, commander of a troop of Horse which he had raised at his own charge for the service of King Charles the First According to the handsome monument erected to her memory in Wye Church, " she lived with him in the most entire affection near three years being in the twenty-second year of her age at the time of his death. But in a letter from Dorothy Osborne to Sir William Temple a very different account of their connubial felicity is given us.

But in earnest there was one more to be pitied besides us and that was Colonel Thornhill's wife, as pretty a young woman as I have seen She is Sir John Grenvils' sister and has all his good nature with a great deal of beauty and modesty and wit enough This innocent creature is sacrificed to the veriest beast that ever was The first day she came hither he intended, it seems, to have come with her, but by the way called in to see an old acquaintance and bid her go on , but he did not come till next night, and then so drunk he was led immediately to bed, whether she was to follow him when she had supped I blest myself it her patience, as you may do that I could find anything to fill up this paper withal—Adieu

After the Restoration Lady Joana Thornhill was appointed Lady of the Bedchamber to Queen Catherine, consort to Charles II , a post she filled to the time of the Queen's death Apparently she was no exception to the spendthrift character that marked the Granville family, and it is amusing to find her extravagant brother Dennis writing thus about this fault of hers.

" I have condemned many expences of my lad Sp [1] for superfluous since our coming abroad as well as some unreasonable saving, but I never observed any soe exceeding blameable as the giving of this late louis d'or to three or foure men for shewing a masquerade of Hobby

[1] Lady Spirmont the name by which Lady Joana is usually mentioned in his Diary for some reason or other

horses, or *cheveux frustes*, as they terme them in this country   It is as much
as if shee had given £5 in Engl[and]   A crowne had been, as I hinted, a
great piece of generosity   I doe believe it a sin, and yet I dare not tell her of it
lest I doe occasion many more   Such is my state that I am reduced to, God
give me patience, etc   It is not that she is greedy of such sights (her vanity
lies not that way) but that she is over greedy of praise even among such
as are noe judges of true worth   I did never thinke that I should see such a
failing in my   [? sister]   But while I am condemning her let mee not
forgett that this sin of v[ain] g[lory] is the sin of our family and that it is
possible that I have been guilty of it as egregiously   Alas ! my conscience tells
mee that I have, otherwise it had not been possible to have squandered away so
many thousand pounds '

Lady Joana survived her husband fifty-two years, and died
January 7, 1708, and by her last will left many charitable
bequests to Wye Parish, especially founding a school there
" for the poorest sort of children of the town of Wye for their
improvement in learning "

Dennis Granville returned to England in 1679.   His
" Remains," published by the Surtees Society, which give us
almost as racy and naive an account of ecclesiastical as the
immortal " Pepys' Diary " does of civil life at this period, prove
that he was a thoroughly conscientious man   We must not
judge of his pluralities and non-residence by the standard of the
present day. His conscience, "more temporum," was quite easy so
long as he took care to provide proper substitutes, and (*pace* Bishop
Cosin) he *did* take care to do this   His instructions to his curates
at Sedgfield and Easington are most strict in the enforcement of
duty, and it may be added, most amusing.   The curates are to
carry out to the very letter all the rubrics of the church, and
he bitterly complains when they did not do so   He set himself
to establish weekly Communions in all the Cathedrals in the
land, and daily prayers in all the considerable country parishes
in his archdeaconry.   "Through this work" he writes, " will
I go, or I will make a filthy bustle before I dye among the
clergy of the nation, contemptible, mushrump, and silly
ignoramus, as some do make me "   And really he seems to
have had extraordinary success in both attempts.   He also
waged internecine war against " Pulpit prayers," and was
considered generally, as he tells us, " the most exact observer of
rubricks and stickler for conformity."   His directions for the
government of his own household are strict, even to the verge
of asceticism, and so are the rules he lays down for his own
personal conduct   Hammond among the dead, Beveridge
among the living, were the two that he took for his models ;
Gunning was his spiritual father, and Barnabas Oley the object

of his utmost admiration. The standard he set before him was thus a high one, and to judge by the testimony of his contemporaries he did not fall far behind it. "You had an uncle," wrote George Lord Lansdowne in after years to Mr. Bevill Granville, on his taking Holy Orders, "whose memory I ever revere, make him your example Sanctity sat so easy, so unaffected, and so graceful upon him, that in them we beheld the very beauty of holiness He was as cheerful, as familiar and condescending in his conversation as he was strict, regular and exemplary in his piety ; as well-bred and accomplished as a courtier, as reverend and venerable as an apostle" Sir George Wheler, his nephew, bears witness to " his pious and devout temper," and Barnabas Oley, we are told, always spoke of him as that truly pious and devout good man Dr Granville.

He was appointed Dean of Durham the 14th of December, 1684, on the death of Dr John Sudbury, whose health had long been failing The likelihood of a speedy vacancy occasioned somewhat of a struggle for the great preferment which he held The powerful interest of the Earl of Bath had been exerted some time previously to secure the Deanery for his brother, in opposition to the scarcely less powerful interest of the new Bishop of Durham (Lord Crewe), who was equally anxious to secure it for his nephew Dr Montague The Bath interest in the end prevailed, and Dennis Granville was installed Dean of Durham, retaining also his archdeaconry and the rectories of Easington and Sedgefield, and his debts were gradually liquidated out of the revenues of these rich preferments

In June, 1687. we find that the Dean was in London, and he tells us of his having been " sorely attagued at York and all along the road by the voters for *non-addresses* to the King," but he could discern nothing substantial in the arguments by which they sought to bring him to their views In March of the following year the King was on the eve of issuing his second Declaration of Indulgence, that fatal measure which proved how wrongly he had estimated his own strength and his subjects' submission and patience In the midst of much censure the Dean of Durham had nevertheless prepared himself to follow out the principles he had always professed and taught, viz : an implicit obedience to the commands of his Sovereign— "If the King goes beyond his commission he must answer for it to God, but I'le not deface one line thereof Let my liege and dread Soveraign intend to do what he pleases to me or mine, yet my hand shall never be upon him, so much as to cut off the skirt of his garment In this Magna Charta aim'd at by the King for establishing his Declaration, our religion will be established in the first place, and others incapacitated to hurt us as much as we to hurt them   And if we can't be put into better circumstances without resisting the King in lawful commands, there is no remedy but Christian patience"   Consistently with these sentiments, which in his case were not those of a mere sycophantic time-server, like his Bishop (Crewe), the Dean was one of the few clergymen who obeyed the King's order and read the Declaration

After his flight from Durham above recorded, Dean Granville resided in Rouen at intervals for several years, occupying himself during the earlier part of the time in committing to the press the Farewell Sermons and Letter which have been reprinted by the Surtees Society   In February, 1689-90, he undertook "a hazardous journey into England, wherby he got a small sum of money to subsist awhile abroad.   . . . . tho' with much trouble and danger, occasioned him by an impertinent and malitious postmaster, who discover'd him in Canterbury" From a letter addressed to Sancroft after his arrival in England, it is evident that he had entirely withdrawn himself from all communion with those who had taken the oath to the new Sovereigns

His determination on this point was not to be shaken. Through the interest of Lord Bath he is said to have been enabled for some time to retain his revenues   But after his obstinate refusal to take the oath, he was stripped of his preferments on the 1st of February, 1690-1, the day fixed by Act of Parliament for the deprivation of all those clergy who, up to that date, should have refused compliance with the conditions which it imposed   It was a grievous blow to him when his ideal clergyman, Beveridge, submitted to the new *régime* ; but his cup of indignation was full when another old friend, Thomas Comber, took, not only the oaths, but also the deanery from which he himself was rejected.   With a grim sort of humour he addressed Comber as his steward, and directed him how he might safely send sums of money due from the "intruder into the deanery" to himself the true Dean

After the defeat of James II in Ireland Dr Granville repaired to the fallen monarch's court at St Germains, where his devotion to his Royal Master's cause might fairly have entitled him to have looked for a kind reception, seeing he had given up for him "the best deanery, the best archdeaconry, and one of the best livings in England ; " but his firm and unalterable attachment to his " Mother, the Church of England," as he delights to call her, stood in the way. He was " slighted by the bigoted Prince for whom he had forfeited every worldly possession because he would not also abandon his religion."

It is said, indeed, that upon the death of Dr. Lamplugh, he had the empty title of Archbishop of York conferred upon him by James, but this, if true, forms a solitary exception to the ungracious manner in which he and the other members of the Church of England were treated by the master for whom they had sacrificed so much   They were desirous, not unnaturally, of having a chapel assigned to them at St Germains " for the exercise of their worship according to the Church of England, and proposed Dr Granville as a fit person to be their chaplain . they urged the great encouragement such a toleration would give to his adherents in England, and what satisfaction it would be to such Protestants as followed him ; but tho' common policy and his circumstances made everybody believe that this request would be easily granted, yet it was positively denied, and Dr Granville was obliged not only to retire from court, but also from the town of St Germains, to avoid the daily insults of the priests and the dreaded consequences of the jealousies with which they posses't King James' court against him " (*cf View of the Court of St Germains*, p 5)

In 1695, a plan having been set on foot for the relief of the nonjuring clergy, many of whom, like Granville, were reduced to great indigence, he came incognito to England, probably to try and secure pecuniary assistance, but he soon returned After leaving St Germains he retired to Corbeil, one of the old seigneuries of his family, where he appears to have met with respect and attention as the descendant of its ancient lords, as is shown by the following extracts from letters written by him to his faithful servant, John Proud, who, after the Dean left England, appears to have gone into the service of Lord Barnard of Raby Castle .—

Tho' I have little time to write more, (seldome, according to an old evill habit, getting pen to paper till the post is going) I cannot forbeare to add an act of God's goodness to me in conducting me and fixing me in this Province of Bry, where I now live, when I am from my father [James II]   My house is in the Faubourg of Corbeil, a little towne, but of great antiquity, from the antient earles whereof, potent men, I am descended in a right line, and one of my ancestors being a man of great piety and valour, having founded here two Collegiate Churches, is in great veneration, and being buried in one of them, I have lately and very happily discover'd his tomb, which is very magnificent And being now proclaimed to be their founder's kinsman receive many civilities from the people, more than before   I pray when you see my sister enquire for a copy of our pedigree, and bring it over   It was some good angel which lead me here to the place I sought, thinking it in Normandy, where I could never find it, tho' I found there the other places named in the Pedigree. May I never want such a good spirit to conduct and inspire me ' "

And again in another letter to him he writes —

' After living three yeares at Tremblet, alias Tremblay, in the Fauxbourg of Corbeile, alias Corbeile upon the River Seine, with as much quiet and pleasure as a man in my circumstances could expect, enjoying the honor and respect of all the inhabitants with all other conveniences, from my very private devotions to my very divertisement of angling (which I love above all other) I have lately and happily discover'd that this town, a very antient little town and pleasant place in a fine country, in the middle between Paris and Fontainbleau, hath been the seat of my Ancestors   And that this Corbeil sur Seine (as stiled to distinguish it from another Corbeil in the Province of Gatinois) is that Corbeil whereof there were antiently Earles (who were, as many others in France, little Soveraine Princes) from one of whom I have made out my descent in a strait line, by confronting my Pedigree sent me out of England with the written Antiquities and records of the towne, greatly to my honor and satisfaction, which is made beyond all dispute, as was so acknowledged by my Father himself, as he passed by us, by my comparing my armes in my seale with Count Hamon's on his tomb, who sent two sons with his cosen germaine William the Conqueror into England   You have I suppose in your country, at least in the study of Sir G W(heler), a book of verses reprinted and published by Dr Berk(head), in the preface whereof you will find mention made of this famous Hamon Dentatus and his two renowned sons that assisted King William the Conqueror in the year 1066 at the battaile of Hastings to win the crown of England   I pray tell this story to the worthy knight and his vertuous lady (for both whom I heartily pray) and take occasion to give them my hearty service and thanks for a token I received about two yeares since   The making out my descent as above hath made me known to some noble familyes at Court, now flourishing, allyed to the Counts of Corfeil who can do kindnesses in a strait and are likely (in case God takes away my F(ather, i e James II) to get my annuity now allowed me continued by the K(ing) of France."

And yet again he writes —

"I may, by my providentiall discovery to all here that I am not only originally French but descended from a cosen germain even of a Queen of France, sister to the Emperor Otho, be enabled to play a good after game and obtain by a petition to the Grand and most Generous Monarch, back'd with the recommendations of my Father, etc   (who increases in strength dayly) more than my lost salary   And as a step to this project a fresh providence seems to concur   Upon making out publickly my descent from the aforesaid famous Count, in high veneration, almost adored for a saint, I am made known to some noble familys, and received but yesterday from a very noble old Countess of 84 yeais old, but lusty and strong, a kind invitation to her Castle, 4 leagues of, and to stay with her a week or fortnight, to divert my self in her ponde and river that goes thorow her Park "

In a letter written from Corbeil, in 1702 of which only a portion has been preserved, and which was probably addressed to his nephew Sir George Wheler, he acknowledges the receipt of ' a seasonable supply of £20," and recounts with some degree of quiet humour the *desagrémens* attending upon his rheumatic attacks, and the attempts which were made to convert him to the faith of the Church of Rome Controversial subjects were pressed upon him by the priesthood of the place with officious pertinacity, but with unbroken spirit and unwavering attachment in poverty and exile to the Church at whose altars he had served, he refused to be drawn into disputation, and their endeavours were utterly futile, and he died, as he had lived, a true and genuine son of the Church of England

We derive the following account of his last hours from a MS note, written by Dr Rawlinson in his copy of the Farewell Sermons, etc , in the Bodleian Library —

" Dr Granville sicken'd on Thursday the 12th of April 1703 N s , continued ill that night and the next day , (at Corbeil, 7 leagues from Paris upon the Seyne, in the way to Fontainebleau, where he commonly resided, and was much delighted with the place, and the rather because he there discover'd the original of his ancestors) On Saturday the 14th, finding himself some thing better, he went to his lodgings at Paris upon the Fossee St Victoire On Sunday the 15th the ague or fever returned, continued the 16th and 17th and on Wednesday the 18th, at 6 in the morning, he dyed, and was privately bury'd in consecrated ground within the city of Paris, either that or next night [by Dr Taylour, from whom I took this account June 9th 1713] attended by Mr. Thomas Higgins his nephew and some few of his acquaintance of the Church of England "

Another note by Dr. Rawlinson tells us that the place of his interment was the lower end of the Holy Innocents' Churchyard in that city, and that this grave in holy ground was procured through the influence of his Royal Mistress, Mary of Modena,* who rigid and undeviating, as she herself was, in obedience and attachment to the Church of Rome, was yet gentle and tolerant, kind, liberal and openhanded to those who had left all, country and kindred, position and affluence, to follow the adverse fortunes of her Royal Consort

Dennis Granville never had any family His wife apparently

---

* "It is also worthy of observation that he who had burved soe many in gardens and fields in france, had the honour to be buryed himselfe in a church yard at Paris, attended by two mourning coaches which privilege was procured by King James' Queen, Mary, who sent her Secretary and the Deans nephew, Sir Thos Higgins to perform that ceremony at her own charge, and who had alwayes been kind to him giving him many 20 guineys when she had not many to spare for herself He called her his mother, and gave her the character of a most comp----ionate woman "

L.

did not follow her husband into his exile, and was reduced to such distress that she was granted a pension by the Dean and Chapter of Durham, as is clear from the following order taken from the Chapter Act Book.

'Dec 8, 1690. Whereas upon a complaint made to the Chapter on the behalf of Madam Anne Granville, wife of Dr Granville, Dean of this Cathedral that it appears she is left destitute and unprovided for her present subsistence, it was therefore, in compassion to her necessities, ordered that Mr Treasurer for the time being shall allow and pay her twenty pounds quarterly (to be reckoned from Michaelmas last past) out of the Dean's revenues"

And on the appointment of Dr Comber to be dean, this order was renewed, but she did not live many months afterwards, as the Cathedral Register informs us that she was buried at the Cathedral on the 14th of October, 1691. Her frequent attacks of mental excitement bordering on insanity caused great domestic infelicity, which was aggravated by Dr. Cosin's stubborn refusal to pay the marriage portion

A portrait of the Dean after Beaupoille, engraved by the famous Edelinck, is prefixed to the copy of his ' Farewell Sermons," etc. in the Bodleian and is marked as one of the rarest prints in the British series. It is reproduced in this volume.

Upon the debates for settling the Crown upon the Prince and Princess of Orange, the Earl of Bath argued against a Regency, and voted for their being declared King and Queen , whereupon, after their proclamation, he was sworn in a member of the Privy Council, the 14th day of February 1689, and reinstated in his former offices, being re-appointed Lord-Lieutenant for the counties of Devon and Cornwall, Lord Warden of the Stannaries, Governor of Pendennis Castle, as well as Captain and Governor of Plymouth, and Ranger of St James's Park, and his son, Charles, Lord Lansdowne, was summoned to the House of Lords as Baron Granville, of Kilkhampton and had his place there assigned according to the antiquity of his father's Barony and was one of the four Lords who supported the King's train at his coronation   At this time constant reprisals were made by the French and English upon one another's shores, and in one of these the town of Granville, in Normandy, was bombarded by the English fleet   The following verses were written by George Granville, second son of the Honourable Bernard Granville, to his cousin Charles, who had taken a prominent part in the bombardment .—

THE HONBLE. AND VERY REV. DENNIS GRANVILLE.
DEAN OF DURHAM.
From an Engraving by Edelinck, after a Portrait by Beaupoilz.

Tho' built by gods, consum'd by hostile flame
Troy bury'd lies yet lives the Trojan name,
And so shall thine, tho' with these walls were lost
All the records our ancestors could boast
J or Latium conquer'd, and for Turnus slain,
Æneas lives, tho' not one stone remain
Where he arose nor art thou less renown'd
For thy loud triumphs on Hungarian ground
Those arms which for nine centuries had brav'd
The wrath of time, on antick stone engrav'd
Now torn by mortars, stand yet undefac'd
On nobler trophies, by thy valour rais'd
Safe on thy eagle's wings they soar above
The rage of war, or thunder to remove,
Borne by the bird of Cæsar and of Jove

And in a foot-note to these verses it is stated that the Granville arms were still remaining before the bombardment on one of the gates of the town The eagle's wings refer to his creation as a Count of the Roman Empire

When the French made several attempts in the year 1690 to land in the West of England, Lord Granville, with the county militia, guarded the coast so effectively that but little damage was done. He marched with the Stannary troops from Plymouth to Torbay, on the 25th of July, where he found Sir Bouchier Wrey with his regiment of Horse, Sir William Drake the Sheriff, Major Rolle, and several other Deputy-Lieutenants of Devon.

After hearing the next morning that the enemy had sailed towards Teignmouth, he at once proceeded there with all the Horse; but at Newton the news reached him that the French gallies, after having played their cannon for about half-an-hour, had early that morning landed some men there, who set the town and some vessels in the port on fire, and after that returned to the fleet After this demonstration the French appear to have left the coast without any other disturbance, save "firing some cannon on a little town called Torkey," and Lord Granville went back with his troops to Plymouth On the 15th of August in that year, he and those who had been associated with him in the defence of the Western coasts, presented an address to the Queen, the substance of which was that "after Her Majesty's so gracious acceptance of their hearty endeavours for her service on the late invasion of the French, they held it their duty both to express their true sense and acknowledgment of Her Majesty's great goodness and condescension therein, and to return their unfeigned thanks for the same, together with their humble assurances that, as they were ready upon that occasion to have ventured their lives and fortunes, so they would continue with the like duty and forwardness at all times to show their zeal and fidelity to Her Majesty and her present government, in the support whereof they were sensible that both the tranquility and safety of their country, their religion, and interest did consist, etc. In this address he styles himself the Right Honourable Charles Lord Lansdowne, Count of the Sacred Roman Empire, and Baron Granville of Kilkhampton, at present executing the office of Lord Lieutenant of her Majesty's counties of Devon and Cornwall, and Commanding-in-Chief the whole militia in both the said counties, as well Tinners as foreigners "

He was greatly in favour at Court, and this led him to apply for certain arrears due to him on account of the embassy to Spain in the previous reign Finding he did not succeed as he expected, he spoke to the King himself about them as a just debt and burthen upon him, and hoped His Majesty would order the speedy discharge of it, and when the King hesitated and demurred, he is reported to have boldly said to him, "What ! is your Majesty shocked at doing justice '" What the result of this boldness was is not stated, or whether his arrears were paid, but in March. 1692, he was appointed a Gentleman of the Bedchamber to King William III.

Lord Bath's latter years were much embittered by a long and expensive law-suit over the will of Christopher, Duke of Albemarle For two years no appeal had been lodged against the validity of the first will which had been proved by Lord Bath as already stated on page 370 ; but in 1691 it was alleged by the Duchess and Colonel Monk, who would have inherited under the Jamaica will, that the Deed of 1688, by which the Duke bound himself not to revoke the will of 1675, except under certain conditions which were not fulfilled, was either never executed by the Duke at all, or else that it was imposed upon him by surprise and not fairly obtained, and its purport by fraud concealed from him The cause was first heard before the Lords Commissioners on the 8th of July, 1691, who decreed that the personal estate should be accounted for and applied for the payment of the Duke's debts, but before the Court would deliver any final judgment as to the Real Estate they ordered a trial at law to be had in ejectment, in which the Duchess and Colonel Monk were the Plaintiffs, and the Earl of Bath, Bernard Granville. and Sir William Clarges the Defendants, to try the title to the Real Estate The trial came on in the King's Bench in the Michaelmas Term and resulted in a verdict for the Defendants. Thereupon the Lords Commissioners proceeded to decide upon the Real Estate, and after the counsel had been heard for several days the Court took time to consider their judgment and before it was pronounced matters were complicated by the marriage of the Duchess to Lord Montague, who claimed to be considered as a Plaintiff on behalf of his wife On the 12th of December, 1693, judgment was given by the Lord Keeper, the two Chief Justices and Mr. Baron Powell, who unanimously decided for Lord Bath and the other Defendants, and dismissed the Plaintiffs' Bill.

On the 28th of December Lord Montague brought his appeal in the House of Lords against the decree of the Commissioners, and on Thursday, February 1st, the Lords began to hear the great cause. On February 13th the King himself came to listen to the arguments in the case. On the 19th an order was about to be made to affirm the decree for the Earl of Bath, when Lord Nottingham made a motion to suspend entering the same for that there might be some salvo for the Earl of Montague to try the validity of the Deed again at law Accordingly the reading of the order was deferred to the following day, when Lord Montague petitioned the House of Lords for a rehearing, and then Lordships ordered precedents to be searched and a report made. On Friday 24th, Lord Montague's petition was dismissed by two voices, 30 being for Lord Bath and 28 for Lord Montague. The trial however was eventually reheard on the 19th of November, 1694, and lasted till 9 a m. next day, the Court sitting all night, when a verdict was again returned for Lord Bath The following year several minor trials in connection with this case were heard, Lord Bath each time winning his cases, but on the 17th of June, 1696, there was yet another trial between Lord Bath and Lord Montague in the Court of Common Pleas, which again lasted all night and till noon the following day, when a verdict was returned in favour of Lord Montague and Colonel Monk, and on the 23rd Lord Bath appealed, and on the 30th had leave of the Court of King's Bench to indict several persons for perjury, but this trial did not come off till the following May and lasted for several months, but eventually Lord Bath proved perjury and bribery against several of Lord Montague's witnesses. In Luttrell's Diary, under date Thursday, 27th of October, 1698, we read " The Earles of Bath and Montague, who have been many years in law and spent vast summs of money about the late Duke of Albemarle's estate, have now at last agreed the same," but again under date the 15th of August, 1699 . — " The great cause so long depending between the Earles of Bath and Montague about the last Duke of Albemarle's estate is like to be renewed next term by the relations of Mr Pride." Mr Pride married the daughter of Elizabeth Monk, daughter of Sir Thomas Monk, the Duke's eldest brother. and had issue Thomas and Elizabeth Pride, from whom eventually Lord Bath purchased the Potheridge estate   At any rate the law suits over which Evelyn in his Diary (II 55) states £20,000 was spent, ended in a compromise, but Theobalds, which was the Duke's chief seat, annexed by King Charles II to the Dukedom, and which both Dukes, George and Christopher, had petitioned might be given to Lord Bath, was granted to his enemy Lord Montague

Lord Bath did not long survive the worry and vexation of the law suit. He died August 22nd, 1701, at his house at St. James   Lady Bath had predeceased him the 3rd of February, 1691-2, and was buried at St Clement Danes   Lord Granville, his eldest son, shot himself within two weeks of his father's death, viz, on the 4th of September, 1701   He was found dead in his chair in his bed-chamber, wounded in his head, with a brace of pistols by him, one barrel being discharged   Luttrell in his Diary states "'Tis said he had been melancholy for some time past, the honour falls to his son at five years old'   An inquest, however, was held next day, and the jury, having examined several witnesses, brought in their verdict that he shot himself by accident whilst preparing for the journey into Cornwall, to take down his father's body for burial   At any rate the remains, both of himself and his father, were taken down to Kilkhampton together for burial, and were interred in the family vault on the 22nd of September   In consequence of this tragic event arose the saying that "there were three Earls of Bath above ground at the same time"

The following is the will of the first Earl of Bath, dated the 11th of October, 1684, together with the codicil which he made shortly before his death, and which was necessitated by "the many accidents and alterations which have since happened as well in my family as estate ," his wife and his daughter, Lady Henrietta Maria, being both dead

JOHN GRANVILLE EARL OF BATH
SEPT 1701

Dyer
146

T m
Prœnob et
h orandi Vni
Johannis
Comitis Bathe

In the Name of God Amen I, John Earle of Bathe, Viscount of Lansdowne, Baron of Granville, Bideford, and Kilkhampton, &c being in good and perfect health and of good and sound mind, memory, and understanding, praised be God, knowing the certainty of death and uncertainty of the time thereof, doe this eleaventh day of October one thousand six hundred eighty and four, make and declare my last Will and Testament in writing in manner and forme following first and principally I recommend my Soul into the hands of Almighty God my glorious Creator, assuredly trusting by and through the meritorious death and passion of Jesus Christ my blessed Saviour and Redeemer, to receive a glorious Resurrecĉon, my body I leave to the Earth from whence it came to be buryed Item I give and devise to my dear wife Dame Jane Countesse of Bathe All my Plate, Jewells, household stuff, personall Estate, and all and singular my goods and chattells whatsoever, (except what is hereafter by me given and bequeathed) And I make and ordaine my said wife sole execucury of this my last Will and Testament This is the last Will and Testament of me the said John Earle of Bathe, made and declared the day and yeare first above written, touching the disposicôn of all and singular my Boroughs, Mannors, messuages, lands, tenements, and hereditaments, in the County of Cornwall or elsewhere Whereas my said dear wife Dame Jane Countesse of Bathe, at my request and towards the discharge of my proper debts, hath joyned with me the said John Earle of Bathe in a Conveyance of the Mannor of Woodford and other Mannors and Lands in the County of Cornwall (amongst other things) setled on or in Trust for the Countesse my wife before her intermarriage with me for her life for Ioynture, And to the intent that in part of satisfaccôn thereof some addition might be made to the Remainder of the Ioynture of my said wife, In case she shall survive me the said John Earle of Bathe I the said John Earle of Bathe, according to the power liberty and authority to me given and reserved in and by one Indenture Tripartite, bearing date the sixteenth day of October one thousand six hundred fifty and two, made between me the said John Earle of Bathe by the name of John Grenvile Sonn and Heire of Sr Bevile Grenvile late of Stowe in the County of Cornwall Knight deceased, of the first part, The Right Honorable Warwick Lord Mohunn, Baron of Okehampton, George Montague Esqr, one of the sonns of the late right honorable Henry Earle of Manchester deceased, Sr John Myricke of Mounckton in the County of Pembrooke Knight Sithence deceased, and Dame Jane Myricke, and Cyrillees Wyche, and Ffrescanne Wyche, gentlemen, younger Sonns of Sr Peter Wyche and Dame Jane, Andrew Riccard, Citizen and Alderman of London, Anthony Crofts Esqr sithence deceased, and Robert Raworth of Grayes Inne in the County of Middx Esqr, and William Seaman of London gentleman, of the second part, And Henry Ovenden Esqr, Sonn and Heire apparent of Sr James Oxendon of Deane in the parish of Wingham in the County of Kent Knight, and Nicholas Penning of London Lsqr, of the third part, By this present writing purporting my last Will and Testament by me sealed and published in the presence of three and more credible persons, give devise limitt and appoint to the said Dame Jane, my present wife, All that Capitall messuage Barton and demeasne Lands of Dinsmouth, with the Rights members and appurtenances thereof in the said County of Cornwall and all and singular Messuages, Tofts Houses, Mills, Gardens, Orchards, Meadowes, pastures, Woods, Underwoods, Warrens, Commons, Waters, Watercourses, ffishings, Rents, Reverʃions, Services, Mines of Cole, Open and Covert, Courts, Libertyes, Priviledges, and Profitts whatsoever to the said Capitall Messuage Barton and Premisses belonging, All which premisses are scituate lying and being in the Parish of Kilkhampton in the said County of Cornwall, To have and to hold the said Capitall Messuage, Barton, and premisses, from and after my decease, unto the said Dame Jane my wife for and dureing the terme of her naturall life, She yeilding and paying therefore yearely and every yeare dureing her life, to the Heires and Assignes of me the said Earle of Bathe one Pepper Corne only, if it be demanded, with

Sententia lata pro valore Testamenti et Codicilli dicti defuncti 12 Septembris 1701

the ancient usuall and accustomed Service thereto belonging; And whereas I
have found other meanes of discharging those Debts for which those Lands mentioned in the said Conveyance were to be sold towards the discharge of those my
said Debts, And therefore have not sold the same, But are still remaineing in my
possession, I have thought fitt and just to reconvey the same back againe to
the use of my said wife as part of her Joynture in the same manner as was
setled upon her at my intermarriage with her, as appeares by a Conveyance
made to that purpose which I doe hereby ratifye and confirme   And further
I, the said John Earle of Bathe, according to the power, liberty and authority
to me given and reserved in the said Indenture Tripartite, Doe by this present
writing, purporting my last Will and Testament in writing by me sealed and
published in the presence of three and more credible persons, In case I shall
dye leaveing one or more Sonn or Sonns by the said Dame Jane my wife, give
devise limitt and appoint All that the Borrough, Mannor, and Barton of Bideford in the County of Devon, And all Lands Tenements and hereditaments
thereunto belonging, unto the said Dame Jane my wife, Bernard Grenvile,
Dennis Grenvile, brothers of me the said Earle, and Sr Cyrill Wyche Knight,
brother of my said wife, then Executors, Admnrs, and Assignes, for the terme
of fourescore and nineteen yeares, Upon speciall trust and confidence in them
reposed, That they, and the Survivors and Survivor of them, and the Executors
and Admnrs of the survivor of them, shall and may, by and out of the Rents
Issues and Profitts thereof, or by makeing Lease or Leases thereof or of any
part thereof, for any terme or number of yeares under fourescore and nineteen
yeares raise, levy, and receive the sume of three thousand six hundred sixty six
pounds thirteen shillings and fourpence of lawfull money of England, for the
Portion of my daughter Henrietta Maria Grenvile to be paid at her marriage
or within one yeare after my decease, which shall first happen   And further I,
the said John Earle of Bathe, according to the power, liberty, and authority to
me given and reserved for my younger Children In one other Indenture
Quadrupartite. beareing Date the Sixteenth day of May one thousand Six
hundred Seaventy and eight, made between my self and the right honorable
Thomas Earle of Danby and others, at the marriage of my eldest Sonn with
the daughter of the said Earle, Doe by this present writing purporting my last
Will and Testament in writing by me sealed and published in the presence of
three and more credible persons, give devise limitt and appoint unto my two
younger Sonns John and Bevill the Annuity or yearely sume of six hundred
pounds for and dureing their naturall lives, to be equally divided betwixt them
(that is to say) three hundred pounds to each of them dureing his naturall life,
The same to be raised and paid unto them in such manner as by the said deed is
directed and appointed   Item I doe alsoe, by vertue of the same power to me
reserved in and by the said last recited Indenture, give, devise, limitt, and
appoint unto my said daughter Henrietta Maria, being unmarryed, over and
above the sume before menconed, as an addition for her Portion, the sume of
six thousand pounds   Item I doe likewise, by vertue of the same power to me
reserved in and by the said last recited Indenture, give devise limitt and
appoint unto my daughter Katherine, (being alsoe unmarryed', the like sume
of six thousand pounds to be raised and paid unto them at their respective
marriages, or within two yeares next after my decease, which shall first happen
Item whereas there is due and oweing to me, the said Earle of Bathe, the sume
of twenty five thousand pounds principall money besides Interest by and from
the Kings Most Excellent Majesty, and charged upon the Customes by virtue
of a Privy Seal beareing date the ninth day of August in the seaven and
twentieth yeare of his now Majesties Reigne besides severall other great sumes
of money oweing to me from his said most sacred Majesty for my ffee and
wages as Groome of the Stole and first gentleman of his Majesties Bedchamber

My will is that my Debts and Legacyes be paid with all speed after my decease out of the said Privy Seale and the arreais of my pention and other Debts oweing me from his Majestie as aforesaid, if it may be done, and the other part of my Estate freed from the same And when the same shall be fully paid and satisfyed, then I give and bequeath the overplus of the said privy seale and Debts oweing me from his Majestie, unto my eldest sonn Charles Lord Lansdowne, to his owne proper use and behoofe, he paying out of the same unto his two younger brothers, my said sonns John and Bevile six thousand pounds, (that is to say) three thousand pounds to each of them, and one thousand pounds more unto his Sister my eldest daughter Jane wife of William Leveson Gower Esq[r], And one thousand pounds more to his other sister, my youngest daughter, Grace, wife of George Lord Carteret, otherwise the said overplus to remaine to my Executrix for the uses and ends afores[d], not intending that my said Executrix should any wayes be troubled or charged in any other manner with the payment of my debts which are to be satisfyed out of my said Estate Privy Seale and other debts oweing me from his Majestie as before expressed Item in case it shall please God I shall dye without leaveing issue male, and my sonns shall alsoe happen to have noe Issue male, I doe then and not otherwise for the preservation of my name and ffamily give devise limitt and appoint unto my said brother Bernard Grenvile All my Borroughs, Mannors, messuages, lands tenements, and hereditaments whatsoever, within the Countyes of Cornwall and Devon or elsewhere, and to the Heires males of his body lawfully begotten And for want of such issue then to my other Brother Dennis Grenvile, Arch Deacon of Durham, and to the Heires males of his body lawfully begotton And, for default of such issue, Then to the most noble and my ever honoured Kinsman, Christopher Duke of Albemarle, and the Heires Males of his body lawfully begotton, And for want of such Issue Then to me the said Earle of Bathe and my right Heires for ever Item I doe hereby give and bequeath to each and every of Servants one yeares wages over and above what shall be due and oweing unto them at the time of my decease And I doe nominate and appoint my said brothers, Bernard and Dennis Granvile, S[r] Peter Wyche, and S[r] Cyrill Wyche, to be Overseers of this my Will, leaveing to each of them one hundred pounds apeice as a Legacy to buy each of them a Ring, desireing them to be aiding and assisting of my wife, whome I have and doe nominate sole and absolute Executrix of this my last Will and Testament, hereby revoakeing, annulling, and makeing void all former or other Will or Wills, Testam[t] or Testaments, by me made or declared, either by word or in writing, and this to be taken as my last Will and none other In witness whereof I the said John Earle of Bathe have hereunto set my hand and Seale the day and yeare first above written And likewise have Set my hand and Seale to the other two Sheetes annexed, my said will being contained in these three annexed Sheetes BATHE Signed Sealed delivered published and declared by the said John Earle of Bathe to be his last Will and Testam[t] in the presence of WILL HAWARD, THOMAS NIXON, JO TREMAYNE, WM THOMPSON, SCR, RICH GORTION

      Whereas I, John Earl of Bathe, heretofore made my laste Will and Testament in writing beareing date the eleaventh day of October in the Yeare of our Lord one thousand six hundred eighty four, which I doe not intend wholly to revoake, But in regard of the many accidents and alterations which have since happened, as well in my ffamily as Estate, I doe by this my Codicill, which I make and appoint to be taken as part of my Will, revoakeing all other Codicills, ffarther will and devise as followeth viz[t].

I give and devise unto my daughter Katherine Granville All my Jewells as well what were my late wifes her mothers or otherwise The greatest part whereof I have already put into her owne hands and possession, and the rest are to be found in my Cabinett and Trunks at my house at St James's or elsewhere. And I doe also give her the sume of tenn thousand pounds for her portion and in full [discharge] of what she may be entitled unto by or under any Settlement, in marriage revoakeing alsoe all Legacyes by my said Will to her devised, Item I give and devise unto my sonn John Granville All that the Capitall messuage Barton ffarme and Demeasne Lands of Potheridge, And all those the Mannors of Potheridge Cherrubeare and Dolton and the advowsons to them or either of them appendant, And all other messuages lands tenements and hereditaments by me purchased of the Heires of Monke, And all that the Mannor of Kenton in the County of Devon And all my ffee ffarme Rents within the said County which I purchesed from my late most gracious Master King Charles the Second or his Trustees To have and to hold all and every the said messuages ffarme and Demeasne Lands ffee ffarme Rents Tenements hereditaments and premisses unto my said Sonn John Granville for his life, without Impeachment of wast, with power to grant Leases of all and every the antient Conventionary Tenements of the said Mannors under the ancient Rents Suites and Services for any number of yeares determinable upon one two or three Lives, or for one two or three Lives absolute, Soe as there be not upon any one Demise at the same time any Larger Estate then for three Lives or Yeares determinable upon three Lives And after his death unto the first Sonn of my said Sonn John Granville and the Heires males of the body of such first Sonn And for want of such Issue unto every other Sonn of him the said John Granville and the Heires males of the body of every such other sonn, the one after the other as they shall be in Seniority of age and priority of birth, the elder of such Sonns and the Heires males of his body being alwayes to be preferred before the younger of such Sonns and the Heires male of his body- And for want of such Issue unto my dear sonn Charles Lord Granville his Heires and Assignes for ever Item I give and devise all my Castles Mannors Honours messuages lands tenements and hereditaments within the Kingdom of Ireland, And all that my Proprietorshipps Right Title and Interest of in and unto the Province of Caroina and the Bahama Islands or elsewhere in America unto my said sonn John Granville his Heires and Assignes for ever And I doe further will and devise unto my said sonn John one Annuity or Rent Charge of Six hundred pounds a yeare for his life payable quarterly at the four most usuall ffeasts or dayes of payment in the yeare, to be issueing and goeing out of all my Lands by this my Codicill charged with my Debts and Legacyes, with power of distresse for nonpayment, Provided neverthelesse that if my Sonn Charles Lord Granville shall thinke fitt to ease his Estate of such Rent, that then upon payment of Six thousand pounds to my sonn John without deduction of what shall have been received or due before such paym^t, That then and not before the said Annuity shall cease And I doe revoake all Legacyes in my said Will devised to my said Sonn John Item I give and devise unto my Nephew George Granville Esqr one Annuity or Rent of one hundred pounds a yeare for his life to be issueing and going out of the Mannor of Lance to be paid half yearely with power to distraine for nonpayment Item I give and devise unto my said Sonn John all my goods both within Doors and without that shall be at and upon the said Capitall messuage and ffarme of Potheridge at the time of my decease Item I give and devise a yeares wages to every of my Household Servants that have lived with me above a Yeare and shall be liveing with me at the time of my death, and unto every other of my Servants that have not lived with me soe long a half yeares wages a peice Item I give unto my dear daughter the Lady Carterett the súme of five hundred pounds, she releaseing what is otherwise devised to her by my said Will at her eleccõn Item I give and devise unto Edward Tregenna and John Haven gentleman and their Heires one Annuity or yearely rent charge of fifty pounds a yeare during the life of Elizabeth the wife of Nicholas Courtney Esqr to be issueing and goeing out of all my messuages lands and tenements in Saltash and St Stephens near Saltash or elsewhere within the Hundred of East in the County of Cornwall, payable quarterly at the four most usuall ffeasts or dayes of payment in the yeare with power of distresse for non payment under this speciall trust nevertheless That they the said Edward Tregenna and John Haven and their Heires shall from time to time pay into the hand of the said Elizabeth Courtney or permitt to be received by her or such other person or persons as she the said Elizabeth Courtney, notwithstanding her Coverture by any writing by her signed, from time to time shall direct and appoint The said Annuity or Rent of fifty pounds a yeare for her owne private and particular expences with which the said Nicholas Courtney is not to intermeddle without her expresse appointment, and without being subject unto any account to be given unto the said Nicholas Courtney or to the disposall Debts or fforfeiture of the said Nicholas Courtney Item I, give unto Elizabeth Herbert, Ffanor Clarkson and Martha Wynn my late dear wifes Servants of her Chamber attending her at her death and since in my service, the súme of one hundred pounds apeice over and besides the yeares wages above to them devised Item I give and devise unto every of my grand children and great Grandchildren the súme of one hundred pounds apeice And I will that twenty pounds of each of their Legacyes shall be laid out in a Ring or piece of Plate to be kept by them respectively in memory of me And I further give and devise unto John Aleman and Richard Gorton the súme of one hundred pounds apiece over and besides the yeares wages above devised And I recommend them to the care and kindnesse of my two sonns And my will is that my Executor continue all my Servants in my ffamily till after my ffuneralls All the rest and residue of my personall Estate household goods, Stock, Corne, Cattle, Debts, from the King, Money due from the Revenue of the Post Office, and all other my goods and chattells whatsoever, I give and devise unto my dear Sonn Charles Lord Granville, whom I constitute and appoint my so'e and whole Executor in the Place of my late dear deceased wife, desireing him to be carefull to discharge all my lawfull just Debts and Legacyes And my further will is that in case my said Testamentary Estate prove defective for dischargeing of my Debts and Legacyes That then all that the Honour and Mannor of Newhall in the county of Essex, And all other the Honnours Mannors Messuages Lands Tenements and Hereditaments unto which I am entitled by from or under Christopher late Duke of Albemarle, either in possesssion or Reversion, And alsoe all other my Mannors Messuages ffee ffarme Rents Lands Tenements and hereditam^{ts} (except what is herein before devised to my Sonn John) shall stand charged for payment of my said Debts and Legacves and of all Annuityes, (except one Annuity of fifty pounds p Annum charged on Pothcridge for the life of Mrs Sherwin formerly Gibbs)

Vicesimo sexto die mensis Febrij AnnoD n1719 emt Com° Pieuobih et Honorando viro Henrico Comiti de Grantham [na^{to}] maximo et Extori Testi et codicilli Prœnobilis et Honorauds Feminæ Franciscæ Comitissæ Dotissæ de Nassau Dñæ D Averquerque defto dum visit Extricis Testi Prœnobilis et Houdi vni Gulmi Henrici nup comitis de Bath defti dum visit filij et unice prolis Prœnobilis et Houdi viri Caroli nup Comitis de Bath defti dum visit filij Extoris et legatarij Residuarij nominat in Testo dei Prœno vilis et Honorandi viri Johannis nup Comitis de Bath defti ad adstrand bona jura et cred dei Johis nup Comitis de Bath defti juxta tenorem et effectum Testi et codicilli ipsius defti per dcam Franciscam comitissam Dohssam de Nassau Duam D Averquerqy modo etiam do mortuam in adstrata De vene etc Jurat

Concordant cum
Oribus Testamᵒ
et Codicillo dicti
defuncti facta
collatione per Nos
Tho Welham
Regᵘ Depᵗᵘʳᵘ Ri
Eides
　[Ph Tyllott]

13° Septembris
1701

Recepi Testa-
mentum et
Codicillum
originalia dicti
Prenobilis et
Honorandi viri
Johannis Comitis
Bathe in vsum
meum

J. Granville

Testibus
Tho Welham
　Regᵘ Depᵗᵒ
　[Ph Tyllot]

And my will is that my said sonn Charles Lord Granville and his Heires in case of such deficiency of my personall Estate shall by Leaseing Mortgageing or Sale of soe much of the premisses soe charged as will be sufficient raise money to doe and performe the same Whereas John Manley Esqʳ hath faithfully served me as my Steward of the Stanneries and as my Councill at Law I doe in consideration thereof discharge him of all accounts debts and demands And appoint that one Obligacõn wherein he stands bound for payment of one hundred pounds unto me be delivered up unto him to be cancelled Item I give and devise unto Mʳ Christopher Bedford my Chaplaine the summe of one hundred pounds over and besides his yeares sallary in consideracõn of his dilligence and faithfull service In witnesse whereof I have hereunto set my hand and seale this fifteenth day of August in the yeare of our Lord one thousand seaven hundred and one *Bathe* Signed sealed published and declared to be a Codicill to be added to the last Will and Testament of the Right Honᵇˡᵉ John Earle of Bathe by him the said Earle in presence of us underwritten who subscribed our names attesting the same in his presence after the adding of the underwritten Device to the Lady Johanna Thornhill Nicho Courtney Will Mathew Christopher Bedford J Manley. Jo Nicholls Richᵈ Clayton J Haver

Lastley I give and devise unto my dear and loveing sister the Lady Johanna Thornhill the summe of five hundred pounds to be by her disposed unto such charitable uses as she shall think fit *Bathe* Witnesse hereto the day and yeare abovesaid Nicho Courtney, Will Mathew, J Manley, Jo Nicholls, Christopher Bedford, Richᵈ Clayton, J Haver

Decimo die mensis Septembris Anno dni miltimo Septingēmo primo Emanavit Comᵒ Honbli viro Johanni Granville Armñ Patruo et Curatori itime assignato Prænobili et Hoñdo Willimo Henrico Comiti de Bathe filio prænobilis et hoñdi viri Caroli nup Comitis de Bathe defti (aum vixit) filij Extoris et Legatarij Residuaꝭ nominat in Testo et Codicillo Prænobilis et hoñdi viri Johis nuper Comitis de Bathe defti habentis etc Ad admiñstrand bona jura et cred dicti Johis Comitis de Bathe defti juxta tenorem et effectum Testi ipsius

Primo die mensis Julij Anno D'ni 1712 emᵗ Comᵒ prænobili et Honorandæ Fœminæ Franciscæ Dñæ D'Auverquerque Comitissæ Dotissæ de Nassau viduæ Aviæ et Extrici Testi prænobilis et Hoñdi viri Wilhelmi Henrici nup Comitis de Bathe defti dum vixit filij et unicæ prolis prænobilis et honorandi viri Caroli nup Comitis de Bath defti dum vixit filij Extoris et Legatorij Residuarij nominat in Testo prænobilis et Hondi viri Johannis nup Comitis de Bathe defti hentis etc ad adstrand bona jura et credita dicti Johannis nup Comitis de Bathe defti juxta tenorem et effectum Testᵗ ipsicus defti Eo quod deus Carolus nup Comes de Bathe defti anteqnam omis executionis dei Testi in se acceptasset fatis cesserit De bene etc Jurat Lris administrationis cum deo Testo annexo bonorum etc dei dni Johannis nup Comitis de Bathe defti decimo Sexto die mense Martij coram Dno Johanne Stanley Baronetto Curi dei Wilhelmi Henrici Comitis de Bathe concessis ratione mortis dei Wilhelmi Henrici Comitis de Bathe cessatis et expiratis etc

Decimo sexto die mensis Martij Anno Dni 1707° emᵗ Comᵒ Dommo Johanni Stanley Baronetto Administratori bonorum jurium et creditorum prænobilis et hondi viri Caroli nupei Comitis de Bathe defti dum vixit filij Extoris et Legatarij Residuarij nominat in Testo dicti prænobilis et hondi viri Johannis nuper Comitis de Bathe defti hentis etc Ad adstrand bona jura et cred dei Johis Comitis de Bath defti juxta tenorem et effectum Testi et Codicilli ipsius defti in usum et beneficium puobilis et hondi viri Wilhelmi Henrici Comitis de Bathe minoris et donec vicesimum primum ætatis sue annum attigerit De vene etc Jurat Lris Admⁿⁱˢ cum Leo Testo annexo vonore dei defti ult mense Sepᵇʳ ˢ 1701 houdo viro Johanni Dno Granville Baroni Granville de Potheridge patrno et Curi minori pred concessis racone mortis curis pd cessatis et expiratis defti (in usum dicti Willimi Henrici Comitis de Bathe et donec vicesimum primum ætatis Annū attigerit) eo quod dictus Carolus nuper Comes de Bathe antequam onus execucōnis dicti Testamenti in se acceptasset fatis cesserit De bene et fideliter admstiandt eadem ad Sancta Dei Evangelia Jurat

William Henry, Lord Granville's only child, who now succeeded to the Earldom, was a child of nine (not five as Luttrell states), having been born the 30th of January, 1691-2. He was educated and brought up with great care under the wing of his maternal grandmother the Lady Auverquerque, his own mother having died in giving him birth. He soon exhibited the same taste for warlike adventure which had distinguished his ancestors, and was twice engaged in campaigns in Flanders

The two following letters were addressed to him by his cousin George Granville whilst he was serving at the camp in Flanders —

GEORGE GRANVILLE TO THE EARL OF BATH

Sept. 4, 1710

My dear Lord,

Whilst you are pursuing honour in the field in the earliest time of your life, after the example of your ancestors, I am commanded by the Queen to let you know she has declared you her Lord-Lieutenant of the County of Cornwall, the Earl of Rochester to act for you till you are of age You will do well to write your most humble thanks to her Majesty for so graciously remembering you, unsolicited, in your absence You should likewise do the same to my Lord Rochester for accepting the trouble This, my dear Lord, is a preparative to bring you upon the stage with some lustre at your first appearance in the world

You are placed at the head of a body of gentry entirely disposed in affection to you and your family You are born possessed of all those amiable qualities which cannot fail of fixing their hearts You have no example to follow but to tread in the steps of your ancestors 'Tis all that is hoped or desired from you You are upon an uncommon foundation in that part of the world, your ancestors for at least 500 years never made any alliance, male or female, out of Western Counties Thus there is hardly a gentleman either in Cornwall or Devon but has some of your blood, or you some of theirs I remember the first time I accompanied your grandfather into the West, upon holding his Parliament of Tinners as Warden of the Stanneries, when there was the most numerous appearance of gentry of both counties that had ever been remembered together I observed there was hardly anyone but whom he called cousin, and I could not but observe at the same time how well they were pleased with it Let this be a lesson for you when it comes to your turn to appear amongst them

Nothing is more obliging than to seem to retain the memory of kindred and alliances though never so remote, and by consequence nothing more disobliging than a forgetfulness of them, which is always imputed to an affected disdainful superiority and pride There is another particular in my opinion of no small consequence to the support of your interest, which I would recommend to your imitation, and that is to make Stowe your principal residence I have heard your grandfather say that, if ever he lived to be possessed of New Hall, he would pull it down that your father might have no temptation to withdraw from the ancient seat of his family From the Conquest to the Restoration your Ancestors constantly resided amongst their country men, except when the public service called upon them to sacrifice their lives for it Stowe in my grandfather's time till the Civil Wars broke out was a kind of academy for all young men of family in the country he provided himself with the best masters of all kinds for education, and the children of his neighbours and friends shared the advantage of his own Thus he in a manner became the father of his country, and not only engaged the affection of the present generation but laid a foundation of friendship for posterity, which is not worn out at this day

Upon this foundation, my Lord, you inherit friends without the trouble of making them, and have only to preserve them, an easy task for you, to whom nature has been so liberal of every quality necessary to attract affection and gain the heart I must tell you the generality of our County men have always been Royalists, you inherit too much loyal blood to like them the worse There is an old saying among them that 'A Godolphin was never known to want wit, a Trelawney courage, or a Granville loyalty " Wit and Courage are not to be mistaken, and to give these families their due they still keep up their character, but it is the misfortune of loyalty not to be so clearly understood or defined In a country subject to Revolution what passes for loyalty to-day may be treason to-morrow But I make great difference between real and nominal treason In the quarrel of the Houses of York and Lancaster both sides were proclaimed traitors, as the other prevailed Even under Cromwell's usurpation all who adhered to the King were proclaimed traitors and suffered as such, but this makes no alteration in the thing itself It may be enacted treason to call black black or white white, but black will be black and white will be white in spite of all the legislators. There can be no doubt about allegiance unless Princes become tyrants and then they cease to be Kings, they will no longer be respected as God's vice-regents who violate the laws they have sworn to protect

The preacher may tell us of passive obedience, that tyrants are to be patiently suffered as Scourges in the hands of a righteous God, to chastise a sinful nation, and to be submitted to like plagues. famines, and such like judgments from above Such doctrine, were it true, could only serve to mislead all judging Princes into a false security Men are not to be reasoned out of their senses, human nature and self-preservation will eternally arise against slavery and oppression It is therefore not to be supposed that even the weakest Prince would run that hazard, unless seduced by advice wickedly palliated by evil counsellors Nero himself under the influence of a good ministry was the mildest, the most gracious, and best beloved of Emperors, the most sanguinary, profligate, and the most abhorred under a bad one

A Prince may be deceived or mistaken in the choice of his favourites, but he has this advantage, he is sure to hear of it from the voice of the public, if then he is deaf he seems to take upon himself the blame and odium of those actions which were chargeable before but upon his advisers

Idle murmurs, groundless discontents, and pretended jealousies and fears, the effect of a private prejudice and resentments have been and will ever be under the wisest administrations We are pestered with them even now when we have a Queen who is known to have nothing so much at heart as the contentment of her people, these are transitory vapors which scatter at the first appearance of light, the infection spreads no further than a particular set of sour splenetic enthusiasts in politics not worth minding or correcting

Universal discontent cannot happen but from solid provocations Many well-meaning persons, however abounding in zeal, have been often unwarily caught by popular pretences, and not undeceived till 'twas too late Have a care, my dear Cousin, of splitting upon that rock. There have been false patriots as well as false prophets

To fear God and honour the King, were injunctions so closely ticked together that they seem to make but one and the same command A man may as well pretend to be a good Christian without fearing God, as a good subject without honouring the King "Deo, Patriæ, Amicis" was your great Grandfather Sir Bevill's motto In these words he has added to his example a rule which in following you can never err in any duty of life The highest courage and the gentlest disposition is part of Lord Clarendon's character of him, so much of him you have begun to show us already, and the best wish I can make for you is, to resemble him as much in all but his untimely fate

My dear Lord
I am for ever etc etc
GEORGE GRANVILLE

Septem 22nd

My dear Lord,

Every living creature is entitled to offices of humanity, the distress even of an enemy should reconcile us to him "If he thirsts give him drink, if he hungers give him food, overcome evil with good" It is with this disposition I would have you enter into the exercise of that authority (Lord-Lieutenant of Cornwall) with which her Majesty has honoured you over your countrymen Let nobody inspire you with party prejudices and resentments, let it be your business to reconcile differences and heal divisions, and to restore if possible harmony and good neighbourhood amongst them If then there should be any left to wish you ill, make them ashamed and confounded with your goodness and moderation Not that I would ever advise you to sacrifice one hair of the head of an old friend to your family to gain fifty new ones, but if you can increase the number by courtesy and moderation it may be worth the trial

Believe me, my dear Lord, humanity and generosity make the best foundation to build a character upon A man may have birth and riches and power, wit, learning, courage, but without generosity it is impossible to be a great man Whatever the rich and powerful may think of themselves, whatever value they may set upon their abundance and grandeur, they will find themselves but the more hated and despised for the ill use they make of it You should look upon yourselves but as stewards and trustees for the distressed Your over abundance is but a deposit for the use and relief of the unhappy You are answerable for all superfluities misspent It is not to be supposed that Providence would have made such distinctions among men such unequal distributions, but that they might endear themselves to one another, by mutual helps and obligations Gratitude is the surest cement of love, friendship and society

There are, indeed, rules to be observed and measures to be kept in the distribution of favours We know people who have both the power and inclination to do good, but for want of judgment in the direction they pass only for good-natured fools instead of generous benefactors My Lord . will grudge a guinea to an honest gentleman in distress, but readily give twenty to a common strumpet Another shall refuse to lend fifty pounds to his best friend without sufficient security, and the next moment set his whole fortune upon a card or a dye—a chance for which he can have no security My Lord is to be seen every day at a toy shop, squandering away his money in trinkets and Baubles, and at the same time leaves his brothers and sisters without common necessaries

Generosity does not consist in a contempt of money in throwing it away at random without judgment or distinction, though that indeed is better than locking it up, for multitudes have the benefit of it, but in a right disposition, to proper objects, in proportion to the merits of the circumstances, the rank, and condition of those who stand in need of our service

Princes are more exposed than any others to the misplacing their favours Merit is ever modest and keeps its distance   The forward and importunate stand always nearest in sight, and are not to be put out of countenance nor thrust out of the way   I remember to have heard a saying of the late King James "that he never knew a modest man make his way in a Court," David Floyd, whom you know, being then in waiting at his Majesty's elbow, reply'd bluntly, "Pray, Sir, whose fault is that?"   The King stood corrected and was silent

If Princes could see with their own eyes and hear with their own ears, what a happy situation it would be both for themselves and their subjects !   To reward merit, to redress the injured, to relieve the oppressed, to raise the modest, to humble the insolent, what a God-like prerogative, were a right use made of it !

How happy are you, my dear Lord, who are born with such generous inclinations, with judgment to direct them and the means to indulge them Of all men most miserable is he, who has the inclination without the means To meet with a deserving object of compassion without having the power to give relief, of all the circumstances of life is the most disagreeable, to have the power is the greatest pleasure

Methinks I see you ready to cry out "Good Cousin, why this discourse to me?   What occasion have I for these lectures? '   None at all, my dear Lord, I am only making my court to you by letting you see I think as you do

But one word more and I have done   In trust, intimacy, and confidence, be as particular as you please, in humanity, charity, and benevolence universal.

I am, for ever &c,

GEORGE GRANVILLE

Alas ! within eight months of the date of the above letters, the young Earl, in whom so many hopes were centred, died of small-pox, unmarried, the 17th of May, 1711, at the age of nineteen, to the great grief of his noble relations

And with him died this eldest branch of the family, for both his father's brothers had pre-deceased him—Bevill, the younger one, dying, unmarried, of small-pox, the 15th of September, 1706 ; and John, the second son of John, Earl of Bath, dying without issue on the 3rd of December, 1707.   Little or nothing is known of Bevill, but John Granville had had a distinguished career.   Born at St. James' on the 12th of April, 1665, he matriculated at Christ Church College, Oxford, when fifteen years of age (March 12th, 1679-80).   He afterwards entered the Navy, and was appointed Lieutenant of the "Crown," but in what particular year is not known   His second commission was a Lieutenant of the "Adventure," and was dated the 24th of May, 1688   On the 29th of October (or as we learn from other information, on the 22nd of December) in that year he

was promoted by commission from Lord Dartmouth to be
Captain of the "Bristol" Like the other members of his family
he became a steady adherent to those patriotic principles which
suggested and effected the Revolution, and accordingly was
continued in his command by William III. In 1689 he was
promoted to the command of the "Lennox," and took part in the
several naval engagements of that time, behaving with great
bravery and skill, particularly at the siege of Cork in 1690
Besides his naval command, he held the position of a Colonel
in the Guards, and was Governor of Deal Castle.

He had formed a warm attachment to Arthur Herbert, Earl
of Torrington, Lord High Admiral of England, who at one time
was regarded as one of the bravest and most skilful officers in
the Navy But he was also one of the loosest voluptuaries of
the time, and his licentiousness undermined his usefulness and
relaxed his nerves, so that he was utterly incapable of self-
denial or of strenuous exertion The vulgar courage of a fore-
mast man he still retained, but both as Admiral and as First
Lord of the Admiralty he became utterly inefficient Month
after month the fleet, which should have been the terror of the
seas, lay in harbour whilst he was diverting himself in London
The sailors, punning upon his title, gave him the name of Lord
Tarry-in-town. Matters came to a crisis when, in July, 1690,
he was defeated by the French off Beachy Head He had
command of both the English and Dutch fleets, but displayed
such pusillanimity that, after the engagement, he was committed to the Tower and tried by court martial. He was
acquitted, but dismissed the service. John Granville generously
indicated his friend's character at the trial, but at the cost of
his own favour with the King, and he, too, was dismissed, not
only from his naval command, but from every other appointment he held under the crown How far his moral character
was assimilated to the Earl of Torrington's is not known, but
we have a hint given us in a letter from Richard Lapthorne
from London to Richard Coffin of Portledge, near Bideford,
dated the 5th of March, 1691-2, in which occurs this passage—

There was a duell fought lately by the Lord Berclay and Collonel Greenvill
about Madame Temple, one of the mayds of honor, but no great harm don,
saving the last received a slight wound

Le Neve states that being qualified "*tam Mercurio quam
Marti*," John Granville became a great spokesman in the House
of Commons, where he made a very considerable figure, and his
speeches were such as were not always agreeable to the Court
He had already represented Launceston from 1685 to 1687 and

he had sat as a representative for Plymouth from 1689 to 1698,
and for Newport from 1698 to 1700, for Fowey from 1700 to
1701, and for the County of Cornwall from 1701 to 1702.   His
cousins, the sons of the Honourable Bernard Granville, also
represented several Cornish constituencies at this period ; indeed,
as has been said, " for many years after the Restoration there
was scarcely a constituency in Cornwall, from the county itself
to the meanest borough, which did not return a Granville for at
least one parliament, and if happiness is measured by the
possession of parliamentary influence the family would be
reckoned among the happiest of the happy. '

On the accession of Queen Anne, John Granville again came
into royal favour, and every compensation was made to him for
his former ill-treatment.   In the month of June, 1702, he was
appointed, during the minority of his nephew, the third Earl of
Bath, for whom he managed the family estates, Lord-Lieutenant
of Cornwall, Lord Warden of the Stannaries, High Steward of
the Duchy, and Custos Rotulorum of the county of Devon, to
which was soon afterwards added the office of Lieutenant-
General of the Ordnance.   He was also admitted a member of
the Privy Council in 1701   The day after the Queen entered
on the second year of her reign she was pleased to distinguish
by higher titles of honour several persons who had distinguished
themselves by their eminent zeal for the Church of England
and her Majesty's service, and the first person raised to the
rank of a peer was John Granville, who was created Baron
Granville of Potheridge in the county of Devon, he having
succeeded, by his father's will, to that portion of the Monk
property which had been acquired by purchase at the termination of the long law-suit.   Lord Granville was Lord Palatine of
Carolina and, being very desirous to exert his zeal for the
Church of England, had procured an Act to be passed in the
Assembly there for the establishment of religious worship
according to the rites of the Church of England, and for erecting churches and parsonages, and for raising an endowment
fund ; but the House of Lords having been petitioned by
several inhabitants, who objected, the Act was afterwards repealed.

Lord Granville was married by licence on the evening of
the 15th of April, 1703, to Rebecca, Marchioness of Worcester,
mother of the second Duke of Beaufort. and daughter of Sir
Josiah Child of Winstead in the county of Essex, first Baronet
(by his second wife, Mary, daughter of William Attwood),
and sister of Richard, Earl Tylney.   In 1705 political parties
changed, and on the 3rd of April, the Lord Treasurer was
made Lord-Lieutenant of Cornwall in Lord Granville's place ,

Mr Godolphin succeeded him as Lord Warden of the Stannaries, and Lieutenant-General Earle as Lieutenant of the Ordnance On the 12th of October, 1706, Lord Granville's horse won the Queen's plate at Newmarket, so Luttrell informs us in his Diary, and under date, Tuesday, 29th of July, 1707, we read.—

Yesterday the Lord Granville was taken with an apoplexy and is dangerously ill

But he lingered till the 3rd of December, when he died at the comparatively early age of forty-two, and was buried on the 16th in St Clement Danes' Church His wife died on the 27th of July, 1712. Lord Granville had been made a D C L. of Oxford, the 26th of April, 1706, and in Christ Church, Oxford, there is a monument to his memory, which bears the following inscription —

𝔐 ☙

HON^ISSIMI DNI JOHANNIS BARONIS GRANVILLE DE POTHERIDGE
Ex perantiqua ac prænobili Granvillorum de Kilkhampton
In agro Cornubiensi familiâ
oriundi
Viri, ob amplitudinem tam illustris prosapiæ, merito spectabilis ob egregia
virtutis et ingenii ornamenta,
Etiam absq, generis splendore insignis
Qui landabili famæ ardore perculsus
Majorumq, Gloriæ piè æmulus,
ab hâc Æde,
Cujus celebritatem auxerit togatus,
In Militiæ disciplinam profectus est.
In Præliis
Terrâ Mariq, commissis versatus,
Utroq, bellandi genere inclaruit
Militis asperitatem Aulicarum artium Eligantiâ
Ita feliciter temperavit,
Ut non linguâ minus quàm patriâ inserviret
In utroq: Parliamenti Domo
Et populi jura, et Principis Prærogativam
Summâ fidelitate atq Eloquentiâ propuguavit
Senator integerrimus
Ab augustissima Principe Annâ Titulis splendide exornatus,
Rerum gestarum gloriâ et honoribus florens,
A molestâ hâc vitâ ad alterius tranquillitatem
Tanquam ab Urbe in Rus
Evolavit
Hujus ut recens usq vigeat fama,
Honoratissima D^na Vigorniæ Marchionessa
Uxor ejus dilectissima
Huic Ædi, quam ille egregie charam habuit,
Trecentas libras munifice legavit
Quorum impensis
In perennem Viri memoriam
Et Cenotaphium hoc positum,
At Atrii Peckwaterensis Latus Orientali
ad optatum finem
Feliciter perductum est.

CHAPTER XVII

AFTER the Restoration all Sir Bevill's younger children had been granted by special warrant the privileges, honours, and precedence enjoyed by the sons and daughters of an Earl The Honourable Bernard Granville, who had played no unimportant part in the Restoration as messenger between Monk and Charles II, was appointed Gentleman of the Horse and of the Bedchamber to the King In Marvell's Tract he is described as "a bedchamber man who had received in boons the sum of twenty thousands pounds." The University of Oxford conferred upon him the honorary degree of M A the 28th of September, 1663. He served his country in Parliament, and sat for Liskeard in the first Parliament of Charles II and again in 1677, whilst he was three times entrusted with the confidence of the electors of Saltash, viz, in 1679, 1681, and 1689, though on the first occasion he preferred to sit for Launceston, which had also chosen him for its member, and in 1695, when his son Bevil deserted the electors of Lostwithiel for those of Fowey, he was elected in his place by the former constituency And besides these Cornish boroughs, he also represented Plymouth in Parliament in the first year of James II. He married Ann, the only child and heiress of Cuthbert Morley of Hawnby in Cleveland, in the county of York, by the Lady Catherine Leake daughter to the first Earl of Scarsdale of Marr, near Doncaster The marriage licence runs thus —

1663-4 Feb 25
    Bernard Grenvile of St Martin in the Fields Middlesex, Esquire, Bachelor, about 30 and Anne Morley, Spinster about 20 daughter of James (?) Morley of the same, Esquire, who consents, at St Bennets Paul's Wharf London or St Martin's aforesaid

Mrs. Delany, his grand-daughter, mentions in one of her letters (*cf* her Life and Correspondence, v. 325) that Mrs. Granville "lost our family £2,000 a year in Yorkshire by throwing away that estate in hopes of doubling it by a copper mine"

The Marr property, which she inherited from her mother, was occasionally the residence of the Bernard Granvilles, and especially of their son George, afterwards created Lord Lansdowne, who dates several letters from Marr. Apparently

THE HONBLE. BERNARD GRANVILLE.
(BROTHER TO JOHN, EARL OF BATH.)

From an Original Portrait, by Sir Godfrey Kneller, in the Wellesbourne Collection.

there was a law suit over a portion of this property, as in Luttrell's Diary, under date 29th of April, 1699, we read—

The Lords this day decreed the case depending between the Earl of Scarsda'e and Bernard Granville Esq about an estate of £600 a year in favour of the latter.

As already stated, Bernard Granville also inherited under the will of Christopher, Duke of Albemarle , Mote Park, adjoining the Great Park at Windsor, being a portion of his legacy. Apparently, however, from the number of his petitions in the Calendar State Papers to the Lords of the Treasury, he had great difficulty in securing the rent of this property, owing to a counter claim to it set up by Lord Montague on behalf of the Duchess of Albemarle, and under date the 1st of November, 1700, we have a proposal he makes to my Lords, viz , that the King should carry out the contract he had entered into with the Duke for the purchase of the estate for £7,000, with the interest at 6 per cent for the past twelve years since the Duke's death in 1688 over and above the rent (£300) which he had received He proposed further that the large house and grounds, etc , at Mote Park should be exchanged for the house and grounds at the Bird Cage in St James' Park, where he lived   " He flattered himself that this would be so agreeable to their Lordships that they would not only approve, but would report it with convenient speed to his Majesty, and that they would be induced to incline the King to consider the payment of his arrears and annuity, and that the King would direct a present supply of £1,000 upon the said arrears and annuity, as he owed all his necessities and misfortunes to the interruption of these payments, although purchased by the hazard of his life upon several occasions, by the loss of his liberty for many years, by the ruin of his estate and by forty years' constant and faithful service."

My Lords, however, did not entertain his proposals, and on the back of the petition is the following indorsement :—

" Mr G's mem⁴ re Mote Park read   The King will goe no further than the agreement with the Duke of A "

Again on the 17th of November in the same year Bernard Granville wrote " presuming to entreat their Lordships that they would order him £100 out of the royal bounty as it would be Christmas before there was an order for his year's rent."

This Petition is indorsed.

Mr G's Mem⁴ read   The K. gives him £100 bounty, but orders my L⁴ˢ to finished the old bargain for Mote Park

Apparently from the above Petition the house in which Bernard Granville lived in Bird Cage, St James', was allowed him by the King In Evelyn's Diary, under date September 17th, 1673, we read—

I went with some friends to visit Mr Bernard Grenville at Abs Court in Surrey, an old house in a pretty park.

Abs Court was at Walton-on-Thames, and was evidently his country residence

He died the 14th of June, 1701, in the seventieth year of his age and was buried at Lambeth, as was also his wife who died on the 20th of the following September. There was originally a very handsome monument to their memory in Lambeth Church but at the so-called restoration of the church about sixty years ago it was pulled down from its position in the chancel and mutilated, all the fine ornamental work that formerly surrounded it having been taken away, and merely the white slab with the Latin inscription left, and this was erected again in a dark corner at the very top of one of the Church walls, where it is practically out of sight Thus was the memory of one of the restorers of our Monarchy treated by the Rector and Churchwardens of Lambeth Parish Church in those days !

The Honourable Bernard Granville left issue three sons and two daughters viz. Sir Bevill, George created Lord Lansdowne, and Bernard. Anne the eldest daughter was Maid of Honour to Queen Mary, and was particularly favoured and distinguished by her, and "early attained all the advantages of such an education under so great and excellent a princess without the least taint or blemish incidental to that state of life so dangerous to young minds" A seal given her by Queen Mary is still preserved in the family. It has the head of Minerva in a helmet, engraved on an amethyst, with the crown and M in the corner, also a motto round it, which unfortunately has become illegible from use, and having been cut in the part of the stone which projected beyond the gold setting. After the Queen's death Anne Granville was married to Sir John Stanley, Bart. (so created 14th April, 1699), of Grange Gorman, Ireland, who at that time was acting as Secretary to the Lord Chamberlain, the Duke of Shrewsbury. He was afterwards one of the Commissioners of Customs. King William, who bestowed the usual addition to the Maid of Honours' portion on her marriage, also granted her the apartments in Whitehall that were afterwards the Duke of Dorset's, and she was subsequently appointed housekeeper of Somerset House. Somerset House was built by John of Padua, a celebrated Italian architect, for Edward, Duke

ANNE GRANVILLE (LADY STANLEY).
From an Original Portrait, by Hopsmous, in the Wellesbourne Collection.

of Somerset the Protector in the reign of King Edward VI At the Duke's death it was forfeited by his attainder to the Crown, and assigned as a residence to the Princess Elizabeth, who was afterwards Queen Subsequently this palace was successively the residence of Anne of Denmark, wife of King James I of Henrietta Maria, wife of Charles I, and of Catherine of Braganza, the wife of Charles II. It belonged also to each succeeding Queen as an appurtenance until Buckingham House was by Act of Parliament settled on Queen Charlotte in its stead in the year 1775 Here Lady Stanley died March 1st, 1730 Her husband survived her till December, 1744, having spent the remainder of his days at their country seat North-end, Fulham, which he had purchased in 1718 Mrs Delany, who lived here a great deal with Sir John Stanley, describes it as possessing " all the beauties of Arcadia—the trees, the water, the nightingales, the flowers, all now are gay and serene—only now and then a gentle breeze serves as a thorough bass to the singing birds " After Sir John's death it was sold by his nephew, Mr Monck, and it passed through several hands It was eventually sold for £11,000, the house pulled down, and the gardens converted into brick fields !

Mr. Bernard Granville's other daughter, Elizabeth, was Maid of Honour to Queen Anne She lived chiefly with her brother, Lord Lansdowne, and died unmarried

Bevill, the eldest son, appears to have inherited all the courage, candour, and generosity of his grandfather, whose name he bore After being educated at Trinity College, Cambridge, he entered the army, and served with distinction in his uncle's regiment in Ireland and Flanders On the 22nd of May, 1686, he was Knighted at the head of his uncle's regiment (of which he was captain) on Hounslow Heath, where the King had formed, within the circumference of about two-and-a-half miles, the celebrated camp, consisting of fourteen battalions of foot and thirty-two squadron of horse, amounting in all to 13,000 fighting men He afterwards rose to the rank of Major-General, and again served with distinction in Flanders When his uncle, the Earl of Bath, revolted to the side of the Prince of Orange Sir Bevill was despatched to Jersey to disarm the Papists and secure the Island, a mission which he carried out with complete success He represented Fowey in Parliament from 1685 to 1689 * In the Parliament of 1689 he was chosen representative for Lostwithiel. But

* Fowey was incorporated mainly through his influence in 1688, and he presented the borough with two Gilt Maces, of which a record may till be seen in the Town Hall

his leanings were towards a military rather than a political life Accordingly, we find him next taking part in the Continental Wars, and behaving with conspicuous bravery at the battle of Steinkirk, the 3rd of August, 1692. The army of the Allies was commanded by King William, and that of the French by the Marèchal Duc de Luxemburg. The vanguard being oppressed by numbers, and Count Solmes neglecting to support them, out of envy to the English and distaste to the Prince of Wurtemberg, who commanded, and having at last sent horse instead of foot, expressly contrary to royal orders, to their relief, his Majesty, who foresaw the consequences of this ill conduct, exerted himself with the utmost vigour to repair it, though by this time the foot were a mile distant from the troops that were engaged, and had already suffered severely. However, the King made all possible diligence to get the infantry up, ordering a brigade to march to the wood, and forming a line of battle in the plain with such foot as could come up The eagerness of the soldiers to follow and engage the enemy was such that they put themselves in some disorder and took more time to form their battalions than could now be spared ; so that before they could reach the wood, the vanguard and infantry of the left wing being overpowered by thirty battalions of the enemy, who charged them continually one after another, and by a fresh body of dragoons brought up by Boufflers, they were forced to retreat in great confusion and to leave the wood in the enemy's possession

Five fine regiments were entirely cut to pieces in this battle, and no part of the devoted band would have escaped but for the courage and conduct of Auverquerque and Sir Bevill Granville, who commanded the Earl of Bath's regiment, and who came boldly to the rescue in a moment of extremity with two fresh battalions These regiments received the enemy's fire in their faces before any one of their platoons discharged a musket The gallant manner in which Sir Bevill brought off the remains of the vanguard and captured the Baron de Pibreck, who was in command of one of Luxemburg's divisions, was long remembered and talked of with grateful admiration by the British camp fires. The ground where the conflict had raged was piled with corpses, and those who buried the slain remarked that almost all the wounds had been given in close fighting by the sword or the bayonet

On the death of his father Sir Bevill petitioned the King for the arrears of his father's annuity of £500 a year (amounting to £8,000) besides a bounty of £300 a year on account of his great sufferings for the Crown He prayed the King in consideration of his family and his own early and faithful services to grant him the same marks of his bounty as were intended for his father, and for a present supply

In the Treasury Books the following Minute with reference to this Petition states —

" Read 23 June 1701   My Lord will speak with him and give the King an account next time "   " 27 June 1701   £100 bounty paid "

Shortly after the accession of Queen Anne Sir Bevill Granville was rewarded with the Governorship of the Barbadoes, with a fixed salary of two thousand pounds a year   He was accompanied by his younger brother Bernard, who had also served with him in all the wars in Flanders.   He presented his Letters Patent to the Council on the 11th day of May, 1703, and took the oath as Governor of the Islands   He was extremely welcome to the inhabitants on his first arrival, but he had not been there long before disputes arose, which were gradually carried to a very great height, and an attempt was made to assassinate him.   The Council on this occasion presented him with the following address .—

TO HIS EXCELLENCY Sᴿ BEVILL GRANVILLE Kᴺᵀᵀ, CAPTAIN GENERALL AND GOVERNOR IN CHIEF OF THIS AND OTHER CARRIBBE ISLANDS TO WINDWARD OF GUARDALOUPE

The Humble Address of the Representative Body of this Island of Barbados

May it please your Excellency

The Letter which our Speaker lately received Importing that as yᵒʳ Excellency was sitting in a window of yᵒʳ own house you heard a Bullett to pass by, which was Discharged from a Pistoll by some Person who was in the High Road, hath, together with some late indecencyes offered to yʳ Excellency's Person as well as severall contriveances to render the ignorant and unthinking people disaffected to your Government ministered unto us, just causes of suspition that ye Malice of some ill designed men may att last vent itselfe in greater degrees of violence to your Excellencyes Person and Governmᵗ   And to ye end that the House which is a considerable Part of ye Constitution may not on such occasions bee wanting in their allegience to her Majesty and Duty to your Excellencyes Person and Governmᵗ

Wee, the Generall Assembly of this Island think ourselves bound to express our Gratitude to her Sacred Majesty for haveing constituted a Person in all respects soe well qualifyed for ye Administracon of Government in this her Island as is Your Excellency, and to Assure her Majesty tht Wee are and undᵉ all circumstances whatsoever will approve ourselves to be her most Loyall and Dutifull Subjects, and more especially as a Naturall consequent to such an Allegience   That Wee will on this & all other occasions stand by and suppoit yor Exc^y in this Your Governm^t with our uttmost efforts, as for the Prservacon of your Peison fiom all Indignities & to secuie Itt from Violence And Wee doe fuither and moie particulaily declare our utter abhorrence and destatacon of an Act soe Stupendiouslye Villmous as that of attempting through youi Exc^{yes} Sides to Wound and Destioy her Majestyes Regallity heic, and Begg Leave to assure y^r Exc^y that if any Persons whatsoever shall be soe haidy as to oppose themselves to your Legall Authority We will, from a Just Sence of Oui Allegieuce as well as a Necessary Security for Our Rights and Libeityes, Maintaine tht just balance of Powei in your Exc^{yes} Administracon as may iend this Place Safe and Secuie fiom the attempts of her Majestye's Enemyes as well Foreigne as Domestick

Read and Passed ye Assembly

Nominee contia-Dicente

ye 27th day of June, 1704

W^M Rawlins

Cl of ye Assembly

These disputes and the unhealthiness ot the climate had such an effect upon Sir Bevill that he solicited his recall, and, having obtained it, embaiked on board an infected vessel, H M.S "Kinsale," and died on his passage home, the 15th of September, 1706, in the flower of his age, unmarried, and universally lamented By a curious fatality his cousin, the Honourable Bevill Gianville, third son of John, Eail of Bath, died the very same day of small-pox. Sir Bevill's will is dated the 16th of January 1701-2. In it he bequeathed all he possessed to his biothei Geoige, whom he appointed his executor, and who proved the will the 6th of November, 1706

George Granville was boin at Abs Court about the year 1667 As a boy he was sent to Fiance under the tuition of Sir William Ellis, a gentleman who was eminent afteiwaids in many public employments, and from whom he not only in-herited a taste for classical leaining, but by whom he was also instructed in all other accomplishments suitable to his rank When but eleven years of age he accompanied his elder biother Bevill to Tiinity College, Cambiidge, where he iesided five yeais, but at the age of thirteen he was admitted to the degiee of Master of Aits, having, before he was twelve yeais old, recited the following verses of his own composition to the Duchess of York on the occasion of a visit paid by Hei Royal Highness to the University —

> When joined in one, the good, the tan, the gieat,
> Descend to view the " Muses " humble seat,
> Though in mean hnos, they then vast joys declare,
> Yet foi sincerity and tiuth, they daie
> With youi own Tasso's mighty self compare
> Then bright and meiciful as Heaven, receive
> Fiom them such piaises as to Heaven they give,

GEORGE GRANVILLE, LORD LANSDOWNE.

From an Original Portrait, by Sir Godfrey Kneller, in the Wellesbourne Collection.

Then praises for that gentle influence,
With those auspicious lights, your eyes dispense,
Those radiant eyes, whose irresistless flame
Strikes envy dumb, and keeps sedition tame,
They can to gazing multitudes give law,
Convert the factions, and the rebel awe,
They conquer for the Duke, where'er you tread,
Millions of proselytes behind are led,
Through crowds of new-made converts still you go
Pleased and triumphant at the glorious show
Happy that Prince who has in you obtained
A greater conquest than his arms e'er gained
With all war's rage, he may abroad o'ercome,
But love's a gentler victory at home,
Securely here he on that face relies
Lays by his arms and conquers with your eyes.
And all the glorious actions of his life
Thinks well rewarded, blest with such a wife.

Upon the accession of King James II, George Granville addressed three poems to the new monarch, which Johnson describes as being " the first profane, and the two others such as a boy might be expected to produce " But he was commended for them by old Waller, who, perhaps, was pleased to find himself imitated in six lines, which, though they begin with nonsense and end with dulness, excited in the young author a rapture of acknowledgment—

"In numbers such as Waller's self might use "

Panegyric, in prose and in verse, was in fashion in those days Louis XIV. had introduced and rewarded it in France, and from thence, with the other modes of that court it spread over all Europe and very early into England, where Waller, Dryden and Otway distinguished themselves in this way and therefore it was the more excusable for young Granville, prompted alike by inclination and ambition, to tread in the same path.

Unlike his cousins, George Granville remained true to James II amid the public distractions occasioned by the king's efforts to re-introduce Popery. He had early imbibed the principles of loyalty, and as his grandfather, Sir Bevill, had fallen in the cause of Charles 1, so he thought it was his duty to sacrifice his life also for the interest of his sovereign, and upon the expected approach of the Prince of Orange's fleet, he addressed the following letter to his father, which he wrote from his mother's house, Marr, near Doncaster, and which expresses the most ardent desire to serve the King in person and to enter his army as a volunteer —

GEORGE GRANVILLE TO THE HONBLE BERNARD GRANVILLE.

Marr near Doncaster
Oct. 6. 1688.

Sir

You having no prospect of obtaining a Commission for me, can no way alter or cool my Desire at this important Juncture to venture my Life in some manner or other for my King and my Country

I cannot bear living under the Reproach of lying obscure and idle in a Country-Retirement, when every man who has the least sense of Honour should be preparing for the Field   You may remember, Sir, with what Reluctance I submitted to your Commands upon Monmouth's Rebellion, when no Importunity could prevail with you to permit me to leave the Academy, I was too young to be hazarded, but give me leave to say it is glorious at any Age to die for one's Country, and the sooner the nobler the sacrifice

I am now o'der by three years   My Uncle Bathe was not so old when he was left among the slain at the Battle of Newbury, nor you yourself, Sir, when you made your escape from your Tutors to join your Brother at the Defence of Scilly

The same Cause is now come round about again   The King has been mis-led, let those who have mis-led him be answerable for it   No Body can deny but he is sacred in his own Person, and it is every honest man's Duty to defend it   You are pleased to say it is yet doubtful if the Hollanders are rash enough to make such an Attempt   But be that as it will, I beg leave to insist upon it that I may be presented to his Majesty as one whose utmost Ambition it is to devote his life to his Service and my Country's, after the example of my Ancestors

The Gentry assembled at York to agree upon the Choice of Representatives for the County have prepared an Address to assure his Majesty they are ready to sacrifice their lives and Fortunes for him upon this and all other Occasions, but at the same time they humbly beseech him to give them such Magistrates as may be agreeable to the Laws of the Land, for at present there is no Authority to which they can legally submit

They have been beating for Volunteers at York and the Towns adjacent, to supply the Regiments at Hull, but no Body will list

By what I can hear every Body wishes well to the King but they would be glad his Ministers were hanged

The winds continue so contrary that no Landing can be so soon as was apprehended—therefore I may hope with your Leave and Assistance to be in Readiness before any Action can begin   I beseech you, Sir, most humbly and most earnestly to add this one Act of Indulgence more to so many other Testimonies which I have constantly received of your Goodness, and be pleased to believe me always, with the utmost Duty and Submission

Sir
Your most dutiful Son
and most obedient Servant
GEO   GRANVILLE

(Superscription)
To the Honourable Mr Bernard Granville
at the Earl of Bathe's, St James's

During the whole of the reign of King William he retired into private life, enjoying the company of his Muses, and employing his time in celebrating in verse the beauties of that age, as Waller, whom he strove to imitate, had done those of the preceding. He resided at this time a good deal at Mari, where he became enamoured of the Countess of Newburgh, the "Myra" to whom a great number of his amatory poems were addressed She was the daughter of Francis, Lord Brudenell, son and heir-apparent of George, Earl of Cardigan, and married Charles, the 2nd Earl of Newburgh. Her mother was a Savile, a family celebrated for its beauty.

George Granville wrote verses to her before he was three-and-twenty, and may be forgiven if he regarded the face more than the mind Many passages in his poems are of a somewhat licentious character We have also several dramatic pieces written by him at this time The comedy, "The She Gallants," was acted in 1696, at the Theatre Royal, Lincoln's Inn Fields He afterwards (in 1728), altered this comedy and published it among his other works, under the title of "Once a Lover always a Lover," which, as he observed in the preface, is a new building upon an old foundation It is in a great degree indecent and gross. He could not admire without bigotry He copied the wrong as well as the right from his masters, and may be supposed to have learned obscenity from Wycherly, as he learnt mythology from Waller

Partaking of the presumptuous folly of some of his betters he altered Shakespeare's Merchant of Venice, under the title of "The Jew of Venice," in the year 1698 The character of Shylock is made comic, and we are prompted to laughter instead of detestation. It was acted with applause, the profits were designed for Mr Dryden, but, upon the poet's sudden death, were given to his son "Heroic Love," a mythological tragedy was written in 1701, and was praised in verse by Dryden, and in prose by Pope, while "Peleus and Thetis" a masque, was written about the same time, to accompany "The Jew of Venice" "The British Enchantress," for which Addison wrote the Epilogue, was, as George Granville himself tells us, "the first essay of a very imperfect Muse, being rather a task of hours free from other exercises than any way meant for public entertainment." But, Betterton the actor, having had a casual sight of it many years after it was written (1706), begged it for the stage. "where it found so favourable a reception as to have an uninterrupted run of at least forty nights"

These literary pursuits were his only pleasure at this time. "He was," as one of his biographers has observed, "the younger son of a younger brother," a denomination by which our ancestors proverbially expressed the lowest state of penury

and dependence   He is said, however, to have preserved himself at this time from many difficulties by economy, which he
forgot or neglected to do in more advanced life, and when
fortune smiled upon him   ·

At the accession of Queen Anne, having had his pecuniary
position improved by bequests from his parents, he was chosen
in Parliament for Fowey, and soon afterwards was engaged in a
joint translation of the Invectives against Philip with a design,
surely weak and puerile, of turning the thunder of Demos-
thenes upon the head of Louis XIV.   His estate was further augmented in 1706 by an inheritance from his brother, Sir Bevill,
at whose death the guardianship of the family estates during
the minority of the young Earl devolved upon him, and his
letters of advice to the young Earl have already been given.

George Granville continued to serve in the Parliaments
called in the fourth and seventh years of Queen Anne's reign; and
in that called in the ninth year, he was elected for the borough
of Helston, but having been also returned for the county of
Cornwall, he chose to represent the latter.   The celebrated trial
of Dr Sacheverell for the sermons he had preached in order to
create alarm for the safety of the Church, and to excite hostility
against the Dissenters, was exercising the public mind at this
time, and in this Parliament he was impeached in the House of
Commons   Mr John Trevanion had been elected at the same
time as Mr. George Granville, and the election cry had been—

Trevanion and Granville as sound as a bell
For the Queen and the Church and Sacheverell

At the memorable change of Ministry in the autumn of
1710 he was made Secretary of War in the place of Robert
Walpole, afterwards Earl of Orford, an office which he filled
with great ability.

Next year when the Treaty of Utrecht came before the
House of Lords it was found necessary to strengthen the Tory
interest in that assembly, consequently, twelve Peers were
created in one day (31 December, 1711), and George Granville
became Lord Lansdowne of Bideford by a promotion justly
remarked to be not invidious, inasmuch as he was at that time
the heir of a family in which two peerages, that of the Earl of
Bath and Lord Granville of Potheridge had recently become
extinct, for the young Earl of Bath had died of small-pox on
the 17th of May, 1711.

At this time he married Lady Mary Villiers, daughter of
Edward Villiers, Earl of Jersey, and widow of Thomas Thynne,

son of Henry Frederick Thynne, one of the Clerks of the Privy
Council, and grandson of Sir Henry Frederick Thynne, of
Kempsford, Bart. Mr Thynne had died in 1710 and his only
child, Thomas, became 2nd Viscount Weymouth, in 1714, on the
death of his great uncle, Thomas, 1st Viscount Weymouth.

George Granville was honoured by the Queen's especial
favour, and in 1712 was appointed Comptroller of her Household, a Privy Councillor, and in the following year he was
advanced to be Treasurer of her Household, a post which he
retained during the remainder of her reign.

But with the accession of George I. in 1714, the Whigs
gained the ascendancy, and the Tory party fell into disgrace,
being supposed to be in favour of the exiled Stuarts rather
than of the House of Hanover. Many of them were impeached
for high treason and fled the country, but Lord Lansdowne,
having been ousted from the offices he held in the former reign,
stood his ground, and, true to his principles, protested with such
of his political friends as were still likeminded with himself
against the Bill for attainting the Duke of Ormonde and his
life-long friend, Lord Bolingbroke, who afterwards joined Charles
Stuart, the *Pretender*, and became his Secretary of State. He
even entered deeply into the scheme for raising an insurrection
in the West of England, and, if we may believe Lord Bolingbroke, was at the head of it, "being possessed now with the
same political phrenzy for the Pretender as he had shewn in his
youth for the father." The plot having been detected, Lord
Lansdowne was seized as a suspected person, and on the 26th of
September, 1715, was committed, along with Lady Lansdowne,
to the Tower, where they were confined as close prisoners until
the scare was over.

It was, probably, in consequence of his political proclivities
that Lord Lansdowne never succeeded, as he, apparently, ought
to have done, under the will of John, Earl of Bath, to the
Granville estates, though the following letter, written years
afterwards, would seem to point otherwise —

LORD LANSDOWNE TO HIS NEPHEW, BERNARD GRANVILLE.

Dear Bunny, July 17th 1726,

Your Aunt Lansdowne having got perfected some writings for the
settlement of my affairs according to my direction it is possible that for forms
sake the lawyers may desire your signing with me, having made you my heir,
in case of failure of sons from myself.

If I had had the same fair play from my uncle it would have been better
for us all. This is therefore to desire you to comply with what she shall
advise you upon this occasion, and to believe me ever, my dear nephew,

Your most affectionate uncle,
LANSDOWNE.

Certainly from the above, Lord Lansdowne seems to have
accepted the fact that his uncle, Lord Bath, had not settled the
property upon himself, and in a letter to Lord Gower, dated
November 3rd, 1714, he writes, " I shall mention nothing more
but what relates to the honours of the family, which, I think,
ought to be insisted upon to be restored.   My Lady Carteret,
having the Cornish estate, should be created Countess of Bath,
and I am entitled, by virtue of King Charles's Warrant, to
assume the Earldom of Corbeil, as the direct male descendant
from Sir Bevill   I cannot think a patent would be refused me
for it, if it was represented to the King as an article that would
give peace to the family.   I would not have you indifferent in
either of these articles nor look upon them as vanity , you will
find them of use   It is likewise my opinion that the Granville
name should go along with the estate " (5th Report of the
Historical Manuscripts, p 188) In the 5th Report of the
Historical Manuscripts, p. 190, occurs a letter from Lord
Carteret to Lord Gower   He mentions that the King has
created his mother Countess Granville and Viscountess Carteret,
which is a title that he (Lord Gower) could not have taken,
having two surnames already ; by this means the title of Bath
is open to him (Lord Gower) and he (Lord Carteret) does not
doubt he may get it.

The fact is that upon the death of William Henry, 3rd Earl
of Bath, the Granville property was laid claim to by his two
aunts, the two surviving daughters of John, 1st Earl of Bath,
viz , Lady Jane Leveson Gower and Lady Grace Carteret , their
other sister, who was alive at the time of their father's death,
namely, the Lady Catherine Peyton, wife of Craven Peyton,
Esq , Warden of the Mint, and who had inherited all her
father's jewels and £10,000, having died without issue. Another
family law suit was the result of this claim   In a letter from
Mr. H Doughty to the Rev. James Hope (one of Dean
Granville's former curates) dated London, 21st Feb , 1712, is
the following passage, the purport of which it is not easy to
comprehend, as the Dean, being Lord Bath's youngest brother,
would not have inherited before Bernard Granville's sons, even
if he had been alive.—

" I hear nothing yet of Dr Taylor's arrival here as was expected, upon a
lycence which was granted him on the account of being an evidence that the
good Dean of Durham was dead, he having administered the Holy Sacrament
to him on his death-bed and buried him in France   This point of his death
decides a law suit between the ofsprings of the Earl of Bathe's daughters and
the Lord Lansdown (as they call him) a son of Barnard Greenvil's, who has got
possession of the estate   He managed so in Trenity Term as that the jury

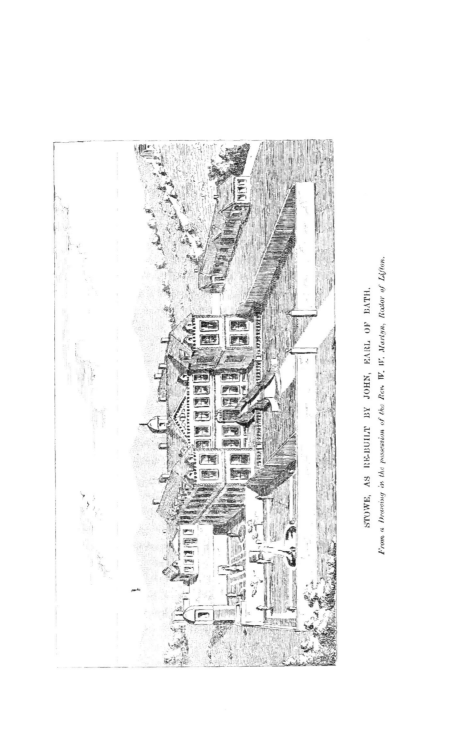

STOWE, AS RE-BUILT BY JOHN, EARL OF BATH.

From a Drawing in the possession of the Rev. W. W. Martyn, Rector of Lifton.

brought him in alive, tho 5 witnesses swore they were in France when he died And this same gentleman and his near relations also went into mourning for him here

It was, probably, while Lord Lansdowne was still a prisoner in the Tower, that he compromised the law suit for £30,000, and thus the property, instead of descending in the male line, as John, Earl of Bath, had expressly willed that it should, descended in the female line, and Lady Jane Leveson Gower succeeded to the Devonshire property, and Lady Grace Carteret to the Cornish

Lady Jane Granville had married Sir William Leveson-Gower, fourth Baronet, who was adopted by his great-uncle Sir Richard Leveson, K B , and thus acquired the Trentham property the well known Staffordshire residence of his descendants the Dukes of Sutherland Lady Jane left two daughters and an only son viz —Catherine, who married Sir Edward Wyndham, ancestor of the Earls of Egremont, and Jane, who married Henry Hyde, Earl of Clarendon, the ancestor of the present Earl of Clarendon Her son was created Baron Gower of Sittenham in the county of York, the 16th of March, 1702, and her grandson, John, was created the 8th of July, 1746, Viscount Trentham of Trentham and Earl Gower. Her great grandson, Granville Gower, became Marquess of Stafford in 1786 Her great-great grandson, George Granville, became Duke of Sutherland in 1833 The grandson of the 1st Marquess of Stafford was the late Earl Granville, the celebrated statesman and diplomatist, whose father, the youngest son of the 1st Marquess, was created Viscount Granville of Stone Park, 12th August, 1815 and advanced to the Earldom the 10th of May, 1833

Lady Grace Granville had been married at the early age of eight to George Carteret, grandson and heir of Lord Carteret, a bridegroom of the mature age of five years ' She was created Countess Granville and Viscountess Carteret Her son was the famous John, Lord Carteret, the statesman of the reigns of George I and George II , and who succeeded his mother in her title, the 18th of October, 1744, and became Earl Granville He was succeeded in the Earldom by his only son Robert, who died without issue in 1776, when the title became extinct in that branch of the family. He left five sisters, namely, 1., *Lady Louisa*, married in 1733 to Thomas Thynne, 2nd Viscount Weymouth Their son was created Marquess of Bath. Lady Weymouth inherited the Granville property in Cornwall, which is still possessed by the Thynne family, 11 , *Lady Grace*.

F 2

married in 1729 to Lionel, 3rd Earl of Dysart, iii., *Lady Georgiana Caroline* married first, in 1734, the Honourable John Spencer—their son was created Baron and Viscount Spencer in 1761, and Viscount Althorpe and Earl Spencer in 1765—she married secondly, William, 2nd Earl Cowper; iv., *Lady Frances*, married in 1743 to John 2nd Marquess Tweeddale, and v , *Lady Sophia*, married in 1765 to William, Earl Shelburn, 1st Marquess of Lansdowne

Thus the two Ladies Granville who succeeded as co-heiresses to William Henry, third Earl of Bath, were the ancestresses of some of the most distinguished and illustrious representatives of the English nobility of the present day.

On being at last liberated (8 Feb., 1717) from the Tower, Lord and Lady Lansdowne appear to have resided for several years at Longleat during the minority of the 2nd Viscount Weymouth, Lady Lansdowne's son by her first husband

Two years after his release from the Tower, we find Lord Lansdowne as warm as ever in the defence of his political principles, and the first time he spoke in the House of Lords in the debates about repealing the Act against occasional conformity, he did not scruple openly to charge the Rebellion in 1715 to the misconduct of the administration   He told their lordships that he " always understood the Act of Toleration to be meant as an indulgence for tender consciences, not a licence for hardened ones, and that the Act to prevent occasional conformity was designed only to correct a particular crime of particular men in which no sect of dissenters was included, but those followers of Judas who came to the Lord's Supper for no other end but to sell and betray Him   It is very surprising," he continued, " to hear the merits of Dissenters so highly extolled and magnified within these walls   Who is there amongst us but can tell of some ancestor either sequestered or murdered by them ? Who voted the Lords useless ? The Dissenters   Who abolished Episcopacy ? The Dissenters   Who destroyed freedom of Parliament ? The Dissenters   Who introduced governing by standing armies ? The Dissenters.   Who washed their hands in the blood of their martyred Sovereign ? The Dissenters   Have they repented ? No, they glory in their wickedness to this day   He then proceeds to remark the turbulency of the Dissenter from the time of Charles I. to Queen Anne, and with regard to the then present reign he observes, " that they have remained, as had been said, not only quiet, but appeared jealous in supporting the present establishment, is no wonder, for who but themselves or their favourers have been thought worthy of

countenance ? If there be a universal discontent among the
people at this time the reason is plain, is flagrant, is notorious
The early impatience and presumption of the Dissenters,
their insolent undissembled expectations, their open insults
of the clergy, then affixing bills upon our very Church doors
with this scandalous inscription, ' a House to be lett,'
their public vindications of the murder of Charles I., and their
vile reflections upon the memory of Queen Anne, for ever dear
to the people of England, besides many other indecent and
arrogant provocations, too many to enumerate, too much to bear.
The violences that ensued let the aggressors answer for   Their
acting all this not only with impunity, but with reward out of
the public treasury, was more than sufficient reason for jealousy,
a jealousy for which this new attempt to break down all the
fences and boundaries of the Church at once will indeed be no
remedy."

In 1721 Lord Lansdowne, upon some discontents, occasioned by political affairs, went with his family to France,
and continued abroad about eight years   His affairs had also
apparently become embarrassed through his wife's somewhat
extravagant mode of life   Mrs Delany states in her autobiography that Lady Lansdowne had been indiscreet   She
was very handsome and gay   she loved admiration—a most
dangerous disposition in an agreeable woman, and it proved a
most ruinous one to her   The libertine manners of France
accomplished what her own nature was too prone to   No
woman could less justify herself than she could   "Lord
Lansdowne, whom she married for love, had every agreeable
quality that could make a husband amiable and worthy of
the most tender and constant affections ; he was fond of her to
excess, generous to extravagance, allowing her the command of
all his fortune.   He had learning and sense, far beyond her
capacity and wit, with the greatest politeness and good-humour
imaginable , in a word, he was as fine and finished a gentleman
as, in his own or any other age, ever adorned his country "

"Lord Lansdowne, had he married a woman of prudence,
sense and virtue, would have made a shining figure in the world
to his last moments ; and Lady Lansdowne, had she married a
man of a resolute arbitrary disposition, might have made a
decent wife , but she was extravagant and given up to
dissipation, and her husband's open, unsuspecting temper gave
her full liberty to indulge the unbounded vanity of her heart "

Whether he still kept up any connection with Charles
Stuart the Pretender is not known, though it has been stated

that in 1721 he was created Duke of Lansdowne by the titular
James III., just as James II. had created Jacobite Peerages
after he was declared to have abdicated the English throne
He appears to have spent this time of retirement in resuming
his literary pursuits.   Burnet's History of His Own Times had
just been published and was attracting great attention, and
finding the characters of the Duke of Albemarle and the Earl
of Bath treated in a manner he thought they did not deserve,
he formed the design of doing them justice.   This led him to
look into the works of other historians, more especially those
of the Earl of Clarendon and Archdeacon Echard, when finding
his great-uncle, Sir Richard Granville, "the King's General in
the West," more roughly handled than he considered, he deserved,
and having in his possession memoirs capable of setting his
conduct in a fairer point of light, he "resolved to follow the
dictates of his duty and his inclination by publishing his
sentiments upon these heads and giving the world those lights
which in respect to them they had long wanted."

Being now desirous to conclude his labours and enjoy his
reputation he returned to England in 1729, and published in 1732,
in 2 vols. quarto, a very beautiful and splendid edition of his
works, in which he omitted what he disapproved and enlarged
what seemed deficient.   He now went to Court and was kindly
received by Queen Caroline to whom, and to the Princess Anne,
he presented his works with verses on the blank leaves   These
concluded his poetical labours   The remaining years of his life
were passed in privacy and retirement.   He died on the 30th
of January, 1735, at his house in Hanover Square, his wife
having predeceased him by a few days only.   They were buried
in St Clement Danes Church   No tomb or tablet of any kind
marks the site of their sepulchre, and when inquiries on this
point were made in 1859, it was found that a short time
previous to that date an order to close the vault under the
church had been put in force.   The coffins were placed in the
centre of the chamber, a quantity of quicklime was thrown in,
and the whole then filled up with rubbish   Previous to this
there were two bodies in the vault which had always been
called "My Lord and My Lady," and which were in an extraordinary state of preservation.   They were not skeletons,
although the skin was much dried, and they were very light
They were set upright against the wall, and it had always been
the custom, whenever a new clerk was appointed, to take him
down into the vault and introduce him to "My Lord and My
Lady."   It seems not at all improbable that these were the

corpses of Lord and Lady Lansdowne, and that this remarkable preservation was due to their having been embalmed, and that after the coffins had decayed and the plates lost, or (if silver) stolen, they might have retained the appellation of "My Lord and My Lady," till all trace of any other name had disappeared

The following is the bill for Lord Lansdowne's burial, which is interesting —

St Clement Danes in the County of Middlesex   A Bill of Dues for the Burial of the R^t Honble the Lord Lansdown

	£	s	d
Chancell Vault ..	15	0	0
Minister . .	1	0	0
Clerk		15	0
Mason		5	0
Light and Charcoal for ye Vault .		8	0
Sexton		3	0
Bearers		12	0
Lights in the Church .		10	0
Bell	1	0	0
Register		1	0
Late Attendance		10	0
	£20	1	0

ffebruary the 3 day 1734
then received the ffull of this bill
    By me   Robert Cocks
               Parish Clerk
on the back   Mr Thos Blackwall Rector of St Clements.

Lord Lansdowne's niece, Mrs Delany, thus sums up his character —

No man had more the art of winning the affections where he wished to oblige, he was magnificent in his nature and valued no expense that would gratify it, which in the end hurt him and his family exceedingly

Of his character, as a man and a poet, Anderson thus writes in his "Poets of Great Britain" —"The character of Granville seems to have been amiable and respectable. His good nature and politeness have been celebrated by Pope and many other poets of the first eminence The lustre of his rank, no doubt. procured him more incense than the force of his genius would otherwise have attracted, but he appears not to have been destitute of fine parts, which were, however, rather elegantly polished than great in themselves There is, perhaps, nothing more interesting in his character than the veneration he had for some, and the tenderness he had for all, of his family. Of the former his historical performances afford some pleasing proof, of the latter there are extant two letters, one to his

cousin, the last Earl of Bath, and the other to his nephew, Mr.
Bevil Granville, on his entering into Holy Orders. written with
a tenderness, a freedom, and an honesty which render them
invaluable.

"The general character of his poetry is elegance sprightliness
and dignity. He is seldom tender and very rarely sublime. In
his smaller pieces he endeavours to be gay, in his larger to be
great. Of his airy and light productions the chief source is
gallantry, and the chief defect a superabundance of sentiment
and illustrations from mythology. He seldom fetches an
amorous sentiment from the depth of science. His thoughts
are such as a liberal conversation and large acquaintance with
life would easily supply. His diction is chaste and elegant, and
his versification, which he borrowed from Waller, is rather
smooth than strong."

"Mr. Granville," says Dr. Felton, "is the poetical son of
Waller. We observe, with pleasure, similitude of wit in the
difference of years, and with Granville do meet at once the fire
of his father's youth, and judgment of his age. He hath rivalled
him in his finest address, and is as happy as ever he was in
raising modern compliments upon ancient story, and setting off
the British valour and the English beauty with the old gods and
goddesses."

"Granville," says Lord Orford, "imitated Waller, but as
that poet has been much excelled since, a faint copy of a faint
master must strike still less."

The estimate of his poetical character, given by Dr. Johnson,
is, in some respects, less favourable —

"Writers commonly," he says, "derive their reputation from
their works; but there are works which owe their reputation to
the character of the writer. The public sometimes has its
favourites whom it rewards for one species of excellence with
the honour due to another. From him whom we reverence for
his beneficence we do not willingly withhold the praise of genius;
a man of exalted merit becomes at once an accomplished writer,
as a beauty finds no great difficulty in passing for a wit."

Granville was a man illustrious by his birth, and thereupon
attracted notice, since he is by Pope styled "the polite," he
must be supposed elegant in his manners and generally loved.
He was in times of contest and turbulence steady to his party,
and obtained that esteem which is always conferred upon firmness and consistency. With those advantages, having learnt the
art of versifying, he declared himself a poet; and his claim to
the laurel was allowed. But by a critic of a later generation,

who takes up his book without any favourable prejudices, the praise already received will be thought sufficient; for his works do not show him to have had much comprehension from nature or illumination from learning. He seems to have had no ambition above the imitation of Waller, of whom he copied the faults and very little more. He is for ever amusing himself with the puerilities of mythology, his King is Jupiter, who, if the Queen brings no children, has a barren Juno. The Queen is compounded of Juno, Venus, and Minerva. His poem on the Duchess of Grafton's laws suit, after having rattled awhile with Juno and Pallas, Mars and Alcides, Cassiope, Niobe, and the Propetides, Hercules, Minos, and Rhadamanthus, at last concludes its folly with profaneness.

His verses to Mira, which are most frequently mentioned, have little in them of either art or nature, of the sentiments of a lover or the language of a poet: there may be found, now and then, a happier effort, but they are commonly feeble and unaffecting, or forced and extravagant. His little pieces are seldom either sprightly or elegant, either keen or weighty. They are trifles written by idleness and published by vanity. But his prologues and epilogues have a just claim to praise.

The Progress of Beauty seems one of his most elaborate pieces, and is not deficient in splendour and gaiety; but the merit of original thought is wanting. Its highest praise is the spirit with which he celebrates King James's consort, when she was a queen no longer.

The Essay on Unnatural Flights in Poetry is not inelegant or injudicious, and has something of vigour beyond most of his other performances: his precepts are just, and his cautions proper; they are indeed not new, but in a didactic poem novelty is to be expected only in the ornaments and illustrations. His poetical precepts are accompanied with agreeable and instructive notes.

The Masque of Peleus and Thetis has here and there a pretty line, but it is not always melodious, and the conclusion is wretched.

In his "British Enchanters" he has bidden defiance to all chronology by confounding the inconsistent manners of different ages: but the dialogue has often the air of Dryden's rhyming plays; and his songs are lively, though not very correct. This is, I think, far the best of his works; for if it has many faults, it has likewise passages which are at least pretty, though they do not rise to any high degree of excellence.

Pope, in a courtier-like passage in his "Windsor Forest"

—a poem which he dedicated to Lord Granville—says of him —

> Here his first lays majestic Denham sung,
> Here the last numbers flowed from Cowley's tongue.
>
> Since fate relentless stopped their heavenly voice,
> No more the forest rings, or groves rejoice,
> Who now shall charm the shades where Cowley strung
> His living harp and lofty Denham sung?
> But, hark! the groves rejoice, the forest rings—
> Are these revived? or is it Granville sings?

adding,

> The thoughts of gods let Granville's verse recite
> And brings the scenes of opening fate to light

With one more extract from the praises of his contemporaries, and this, the weightiest and most poetic of them all, we will conclude Dryden said of him—*àpropos* of his " Tragedy of Heroick Love '—

> Auspicious poet, wert thou not my friend,
> How could I envy what I must commend?
> But since its Nature's law, in love and wit,
> That youth should reign and withring age submit,
> With less regret these laurels I resign,
> Which, dying on my brow, revive on thine

Lord Lansdowne left four daughters but no son, and, failing male issue, the greater part of his money descended to his brother's son, Bernard Granville of Calwich Abbey, it having been so settled that he could not touch it.

The second daughter, Mary, had been married in 1730 to William Graham, Esq, of Platten, near Drogheda, twenty miles from Dublin, and died in the same year as her parents (November, 1735) Dean Swift wrote after Lord Lansdowne's death to tell Mrs Delany (or Pendarves, as she was then), that " Graham is ruining himself as fast as possible, but I hope the young lady has an untouchable settlement." The other daughters were left in great pecuniary distress, having only £100 a year each to live upon Their half-brother, Lord Weymouth, had promised to support and protect them, but his great extravagance and licentious mode of living ruined his character and made him callous to their necessities The eldest one, Anne, seems to have possessed an excellent tone of mind and her complete resignation under her trials, as evidenced in her letters, is very touching, *e g*, the following beautiful letter to her cousin, Mrs Pendarves —

THE HON^BLE ANNE GRANVILLE TO MRS PENDARVES

Old Windsor ye 8—1740

I received yours, my fair and amiable cousin, full of sweets to me, for every fresh mark of your friendship adds to my happiness, though I could almost find in my heart to huff you for flattering me Your goodness of heart makes you glad to hear from your friends, but when my dear Pen talks of *my instructing her,* I could almost think you laughed at me I look on my keeping up my spirits in our present situation as no merit of my own, but a gift and blessing from the hand of Providence which *never* sends us more distress than that at the *same time* His Divine power enables us to bear I speak by experience, who receive daily marks of His blessing by bestowing on us, unworthy mortals, a fortitude of mind to support our worldly disappointments, which did we make a proper use of, ought to instruct us not to set our hearts "on any child of man," but build our hopes on a much surer foundation Although my thoughts since I began writing to my dear Pen have been more celestial than terrestial, still I think whilst we are in this world (though not with too much anxiety) that it is a duty incumbent on us to endeavour to be as happy as we can , and if our affairs succeed let us thank our great Benefactor, if not " His will be done," whose wisdom directs everything for our good Could we bring ourselves to acquiesce without grumbling we should contribute much to our present happiness By this time I hope you have received my letter with Lady Jersey's answer I wrote last post Mrs Dewes word my conversation with the Duchess of Portland, and should be obliged to you if you would write your opinion on the subject to her, which must have weight on everyone that you will speak your mind to, for as you were the person that was so good to apply to my brother about a pension, you are better able to judge what method will be most likely to succeed Now as to Lady B 's, you know whatever offer is made one in distress, let it be ever so small, is still an obligation, and I believe I shall convince you at present it is *better* being *there* for a little time than at your house in town, and less expensive, and I do not know in what situation your house stands, though I am told it is *not made over* to the trustees But my brother *may imagine* we want to intrude on him, and a thousand things that may be put in his head, for I *can't give him up,* but really believe he has been ill-advised, and being so much reduced himself, has made him more easily comply with his later behaviour to us But, my sweet Pen, I know your heart . *you think* that if Weymouth had your house still in his hands he might be persuaded to let us have it, but *if it is* still his, I hope those will remain in it that make the ornament of the place, and never take in your head that I could bear to be the occasion of your leaving a place that I know is convenient to you, which would vex me much more than having a house rent free would do me good

I have wrote two letters to my brother , in my last I mentioned everything in as civil a manner as I was capable of, and put him in mind of our arrears , but when we go to London, which please God will be one day this week, I shall see Sir Robert Worsley and then shall tell him the situation of everything He has shown more feeling for us than any of the rest—I mean of the *trustees* As to Mrs Petite she will live with her friend Mrs Favor , as for poor Mrs Bourgois she says she can't bear the thoughts of leaving us, she *will have no wages* but says shall be happy in doing anything, let it be *what it will,* to serve us I know the tenderness of your heart that you would not know what to say to anybody you find so affectionate ; but I am sure I do not, for I am surrounded with many difficulties God guide me in whatever I do for the best ! I always think of Mr Pope's prayer ("Teach me to feel another's woe") I sincerely do for those that suffer at present with my fall of fortune .

G^d

and wish I alone was the only sufferer, but let my pocket be ever so low, my heart will always be great in affection to my dearest cousin this I beg of you to believe, as likewise that I am

Ever your obliged humble Servant,

A GRANVILLE

Betty is your humble servant and desires hers and your humble servant's compliments to Mr & Mrs Dewes I have wrote to my sister Foley about lacing strait, she assured me she *does not* Her jumps (stays) will go next Sunday and I dare say she'll put them on Mr & Mrs Foley come to London when the Parliament meets, which is the 18th of November

The third daughter, Grace, was married, on the 28th of March 1740, to Thomas Foley, Esq (afterwards, in 1776, created Baron Foley) Mrs Delany writing to her sister thus describes the wedding —

This moment we are returned from Audley Chapel, where we have been witness of the union of two people that seem made for the happiness of each other It has at last been concluded in so great a hurry that I hardly think I am awake, but I fear I shall start and rub my eyes, as out of a dream, before I can finish my letter. The writings were signed this morning, and at twelve all the company assembled in the vestry, Lord Foley and my brother were the bridemen Miss Granville and our Miss Foley the bridemaids My Lord's sister is not well and can't come among us, the bride and bridegroom look modest but well pleased Lord Weymouth gave her away, at night all the company meet at the Bedford Head Tavern, where my Lord Weymouth gives a very fine supper, there is to be the harper, and we are to play at cards Lord Wey Sir John Stanley, the bride and bridegroom, Miss Granville and my brother dine with me, that is with my brother, for *he* gives the dinner, which is a very handsome one I think I have told you abundance, considering the engagements of the day At night Gran and I put the bride to bed at her father's house, she has behaved herself excessively well and so has he in every particular They go out of town to-morrow morning, and propose being at Gloucester on Tuesday night or Wednesday noon I shall envy them the pleasure of seeing you and dear mama Your new cousin very readily and thankfully accepts of her kind invitation

Mrs Foley died very suddenly the 1st of November, 1769, leaving a large family to mourn her loss Her eldest son Thomas, eventually became 2nd Lord Foley, and the eldest daughter, Grace, was married, 21st May, 1774, to James, last Earl of Clanbrassil, and Anne, the youngest, to Edward eldest son of Sir Edward Winnington, Bart.

Lord Lansdowne's fourth daughter Elizabeth, or " Daisy," as her friends called her, was appointed a Maid of Honour in 1742. She was celebrated for her beauty.

Mrs Delany, in describing a fashionable dinner party and the dresses of the ladies there, writes thus —

But our fair Maid of Honour outshone them all, clad in rich pink satin trimmed with silver, more blooming and dazzling than anything there except her own complexion she was perfectly well dressed and looked so modest and unaffected that I think I never saw a more agreeable figure

She was a great friend of her cousins the Carterets, in so much that some people thought that Lord Carteret, who was then the leading minister of the day, was making too great a "fuss" with Daisy, and that his kindness to her was excessive But there was nothing more than kindness in it. Speculating gossipers, as well as the world of fashion and of politics, experienced the bewildering pleasure of a total surprise when it was suddenly announced that the leading English minister was to marry *the* leading English beauty of the day, Lady Sophia Fermor, daughter of Lord and Lady Pomfret Whether Daisy herself had cherished hopes of becoming Lady Carteret herself fame does not say At any rate she became very ill and her life was despaired of

They call it a consumption but it is of a singular nature The pain on her breast is constant and violent, and at times she is so oppressed that if not constantly bled they say she would expire, and yet it is not an asthma The physicians *talk learnedly* about her, but in truth, though they all give her up as *irrecoverable*, they don't well know what her distemper is Pray God give them all consolation

Daisy, however, seems to have been one of the most marvellous instances of vitality, in spite of human art, that ever existed, for she not only gradually recovered but survived till 1790, forty years after Mrs Delany had thus written about her! In 1756 she resigned her place of Maid of Honour for that of Bedchamber-woman to the Princess of Wales. "She is young and handsome enough," writes Mrs Delany, "still to grace a Court, but has not health to support the fatigue of so public an appearance, for which reason she is very discreet in desiring the change, which was granted very graciously; and the Princess told her she liked to have her so much nearer her person The salary is the same, and the advantage of the clothes · and not being obliged to dress, will be an equivalent to house-rent and board-wages which was nearly two hundred pounds a-year, besides her salary "

The Honourable Anne Granville, the eldest sister, struggled on with her small pittance. She was a frequent and welcome visitor at Bulstrode with the Duchess of Portland, who in February, 1750-51, succeeded in obtaining a pension of £200 a year for her from the King, and Lord Weymouth had also about this time allowed her £100 a year, and on his death each of his

three sisters had a legacy of £400 from him   Mrs Delany did
her utmost to find her a suitable husband, but in vain   In 1745
she was appointed Bedchamber-woman to the Duchess of
Cumberland, a post, however,. that brought in but a small
increase of salary, but Mrs Delany hoped it might bring her
into the way of something better in time.   In February, 1756,
she had a very narrow escape   Crossing the Strand, by
Northumberland House, a hackney coachman (though called to
by her footman to stop) drove full against her chair, and over-
turned it with great violence   Had the pole come against the
glass instead of the leather, it must have bruised her to death
" She was hurt a little, and blooded for it."   Whether from the
effect of a blow or not is not known, but she died from a
cancer in the breast, after much suffering, the 18th of October,
1767.   Mrs Delany writes of her, " She was always good in
spite of bad example. and is now, I do not doubt, amply
rewarded."

CHAPTER XVIII

BERNARD, the third son of the Honourable Bernard Granville, served with his eldest brother, Sir Bevill, in the wars in Flanders, and also accompanied him to the West Indies, when he went out as Governor of the Barbadoes. He was appointed a Colonel by commission from Queen Anne, and on his brother's death was made Lieutenant-Governor of Hull. He married Mary, daughter of Sir Martin Westcombe, Baronet, Consul-General of Great Britain at Cadiz, in the Reign of William III. Her brother, Sir Antony Westcombe, was Deputy-Judge, Advocate-Commissary of the Musters at Minorca, and finally Deputy-Muster-Master-General of the forces till his death in 1752. He married Anna Maria, daughter of Josias Calmady, Esq., of Leawood and Langdon, by his wife, Jane daughter of Sir Thomas Rolt of Milton, in the County of Bedford, and left all his property to his sister's son.

Colonel Bernard Granville was member of Parliament for Camelford in 1710, and for Fowey in 1712. He had four children · Bernard, afterwards of Calwich Abbey, Staffordshire; Bevill, in holy orders; Mary, the celebrated Mrs Delany, Queen Charlotte's friend: and Anne, wife of John D'Ewes of Wellesbourne.

The Bernard Granvilles lived first at Coulston in Wiltshire, and afterwards in London; but London not agreeing with Mrs. Granville they settled at Little Chelsea * Being a younger son, Colonel Granville's chief dependence was on the favour of the Court; but the death of Queen Anne made a considerable alteration in the affairs of all the Granvilles, who lost their public employments on the accession of the Whigs to power at the commencement of the reign of George I. When his brother, Lord Lansdowne, was committed to the Tower for the part he took in the Jacobite plots, Colonel Granville, who then resided in Poland Street, determined, as a measure of safety, upon retiring into the country. He ordered two carriages to be at his door at six o'clock in the morning, and gave a charge to all his people not to mention his design as he did not wish to

* Now West Brompton

take a solemn leave of his friends upon an absence of such uncertain duration   The man from whom the horses were hired, and who proved to be a spy, immediately, in hopes of a reward, gave information at the Secretary of State's Office of these private orders, affirming that it was his belief that the Colonel and his family were going secretly out of the Kingdom   Mrs. Delany adds, "I was sleeping in the same bed with my sister, when I was suddenly awakened by a disturbance in my room. My first idea was of being called to rise early, in order to sit for my picture, which was then painting for my father, but the moment I looked round me, I saw two soldiers by the bedside with guns in their hands   I shrieked with terror and started up in my bed.   'Come, Misses,' cried one of the men, 'make haste and get up for your going to Lord Townshend's' (then Secretary of State)

'I cried violently ; they desired me not to be frightened My mother's maid was with difficulty admitted into the room to dress us.   My little sister, then but nine years old, had conceived no terror from this intrusion, but when the maid was going to put on her frock, called out 'No, no, I won't wear my frock , I must have my bib and apron I am going to Lord Townshend's'

"When we were dressed we were carried to my father and mother, whom we found surrounded by officers and messengers, two of each, and sixteen soldiers being employed in and about the house.   My father was extremely shocked by this scene, but supported himself with the utmost composure and magnanimity ; his chief care being to calm and comfort my mother, who was greatly terrified, and fell into hysteric-fits one after another Here, before any removal could take place, while we were in the midst of our distress and alarm, my aunt 'Varina' (Lady Stanley) forced her way into the room.   Intelligence having reached her, by means of one of my father's servants, of the situation we were in, she instantly came, but was refused admittance.   She was not, however, to be denied , she told the officer that she would be answerable for everything to Lord Townshend, and insisted on passing, with a courage and firmness that conquered their opposition.   I can never forget her meeting with my father   she loved him with the extremest affection, and could never part from him, even for a short absence, without tears ; they embraced one another with the most tender sadness, and she was extremely good in consoling my poor mother.   She entreated that the messengers would at least suffer her to convey them to their confinement herself in her own coach, but this they peremptorily refused.   She then

protested she would positively be responsible for carrying her
two young nieces to her own house, instead of seeing them
conveyed to the messenger's, and in this point she conquered,
and, being forced to separate from my father, she had us both
put into her coach and carried us to Whitehall."

Colonel Granville does not appear to have been committed to
the Tower himself, but having been offered by Lord Lansdowne
a retreat in the country, together with a small addition to the
remains of his fortune, he retired with his wife and two
daughters (the sons being, the eldest at the academy and the
youngest at a public school) to Buckland, near Campden, in
Gloucestershire, where he lived till his death, the 8th of
December, 1723. He was buried in Buckland churchyard,
where there is a raised tomb to his memory with this
inscription —

> COLL. BERNARD GRANVILLE, SON TO BERNARD
> GRANVILLE, ESQ, AND GRANDSON TO SIR BEVILL
> GRANVILLE, WHO WAS KILLED IN LANSDOWN
> FIGHT, LYES HERE INTERRED. HE DEPARTED THE
> FIFTY-THIRD YEAR OF HIS AGE ON THE EIGHT
> OF DECEMBER, 1723.

There is a scutcheon on the tomb Party per pale, 1, Three
clarions; 2, obliterated The tomb was formerly enclosed with
rails but now tomb and all are fallen to decay

Mrs. Delany describes her father as having "an excellent
temper, great cheerfulness and uncommon good humour," but
Mrs Granville was very dejected in spirits in consequence of
the disappointments her husband had met with in his fortune,
and the not being able to give her children all the advantages
in their education she wished to Indeed she became so
dejected that her health was seriously injured. After they had
lived at Buckland a little time, Lord Lansdowne had decreased the
allowance he made to his brother, "supposing that by this time
he was fallen into a method of living in the country, and did
not want so large an income as at first setting out." After her
husband's death Mrs Granville, feeling unable to bear to remain
in a place where she had gone through so melancholy a scene,
removed to Gloucester, where (as her tombstone in Gloucester
Cathedral yard, which has been recently restored, relates) ' she
passed a long widowhood, leading a most exemplary life, doing
all the good to her poor neighbours that her income allowed of. '
Mrs Granville and her daughters were, all three of them,
celebrated spinners both in flax and in that preparation of wool

called Jersey   Mary Granville's wheel and a piece of purple poplin of her spinning, as well as several damask napkins of the finest texture spun by Mrs. Granville and her daughter Anne, are still in existence   Mrs Granville was a great friend of John Wesley's, who was then a Fellow of Lincoln College and leader of the Oxford Methodists.   The following letter from him is still extant —

JOHN WESLEY TO MRS GRANVILLE

Linc Coll Dec 12ᵗʰ 1730

Madam

Were it possible for me to repay my part of that debt wᶜʰ I can't but be sensible is still growing upon me, your goodness would give me a still greater pleasure than I have yet experienced from it   To be the instrument of some advantage to a person from whom I received so much, as it would be the truest instance of my gratitude, is the utmost wish I can form   But a view of my own numerous failings checks the vanity of this hope, and tells me that though He, in whom I move and speak, does not always require wisdom and prudence, yet some degree of purity He does always require, in those who would move or speak to His glory.   I have therefore little reason to expect that He will direct any motion of mine to that end, especially when the particular end proposed relates to one who is far advanced in the great race wᶜʰ I am but lately entered upon, if indeed I am entered yet   What shall I say to such a one as is almost possesst of the crown which I dimly see afar off ?   To another I could recommend those assistances wᶜʰ I find so necessary for myself   I could say, that if our ultimate end is the love of God, to wᵗʰ the several particular Christian virtues lead us, so the means leading to these are to communicate every possible time and whatsoever we do   To pray without ceasing , not to be content with our solemn devotions, whether publick or private , but at all times and in all places, to make fervent returns 'by ejaculations' and 'abrupt intercourses of the mind with God,' to thrust 'these between all our other employments' if it be only by a word, a thought, a look, always remembering

If I but lift my eyes, my suit is made !
Thou canst no more not hear than Thou canst die !

To account what of frailty remains after this, a necessary incumbrance of flesh and blood , such an one as God out of His mercy to us will not yet remove, as seeing it to be useful tho' grievous ; yet still to hope that since we seek Him 'in a time when He may be found' before the great water-flood hath overwhelmed us. He will in His good time 'quell the raging of the sea and still the waves thereof when they arise ! '   To you who know them so well, I can but just mention these considerations which I would press upon another , yet let me beg you to believe, that though I want the power, I have the most sincere desire of approving myself

Madam
Your most obliged and
most obedient humble servant
JOHN WESLEY

My brother joins with me in his best respects both to yourself, and those good ladies whom we love to call your family
Addressed to
Mrˢ Granville, at Great Brickhill
near Stony Stratford

John Wesley was a friend of the Kirkhams, who introduced him to Mary Granville, who was then a widow, Mrs Pendarves, and a correspondence extending over four years ensued, in which Mrs. Granville and her daughter Ann were included (*cf* Tyerman's Life and Times of Wesley. Hodder and Stoughton, 1860, vol. 1., p. 78) Certainly some of the passages are very tender in tone, *e q*., Wesley, who signs himself " Cyrus," writes

> Every line of your last shows the heart of the writer, where, with friendship, dwells humility Ours, dear Aspasia, it is to make acknowledgement, upon us he the obligations of gratitude If it be a fault to have too harmonious a soul, too exquisite a sense of elegant, generous transports, then, indeed, I must own there is an obvious fault both in Selina and Aspasia

A little later :—

> Should one who was as my own soul be torn from me, it would be best for me Surely, if you were called first, mine eyes ought not to overflow because all fears were wiped away from yours ' But I much doubt whether self love would not be found too strong for a friendship which I even now find to be less disinterested than I hitherto imagined. . . Tell me, Aspasia—tell me Selina—if it be a fault that my heart burns within me, when I reflect on the many marks of regard you have already shown

Then Aspasia asks if she may go to " a concert of music " on Sunday evenings, and Cyrus replies somewhat diplomatically —

> Far be it from me to think that any circumstance of life shall ever give the enemy an advantage over Aspasia To judge whether any action be lawful on the Sabbath or no, we are to consider whether it advances the end of which the Sabbath was ordained Whatever, therefore, tends to this end is lawful on this day Whatever does not tend to advance this end is not lawful on this day

In another letter he tells her that he has been accused of being

> too strict, carrying things too far in religion, and laying burdens on myself, if not on others, which are neither necessary nor possible to be borne

By return of post, Aspasia replies :—

> The imputation thrown upon you is a most extraordinary one But such is the temper of the world When you have no vice to feed their spleen with, they will condemn the highest virtue O Cyrus, how noble a defence you make ' and how are you adorned with the beauty of holiness ' How ardently do I wish to be as resigned and humble as yourself '

When some of these letters were written Mrs Pendarves was a frequent guest at the house of John Wesley's relation, Richard Colley, who assumed the name of Wesley on suc

H

ceeding to the Meath estates of his cousin, Garrett Wesley,
and was afterwards created Baron Mornington. John Wesley
greatly admired the fascinating young widow, and Mr Tyerman
evidently considers that his hero had a narrow escape from
the fair worldling, and that her influence would have gone
far to extinguish the shining light of Methodism   But the danger
was probably never very great; John Wesley was always (with
due apologies to the Connexion be it spoken), fond of what was
then called "philandering," and given to cooling down when a
matrimonial crisis seemed imminent; and Mrs Pendarves,
though she was sincerely interested by his undoubted goodness
and talent, and his already distinguished position as head of
the great evangelical revival, was never likely to have adopted
even a modification of his ascetic views   Before long she wrote
to her sister about him thus —

'Cyrus' by this time has blotted me out of his memory   or, if he does
remember me, it can only be to reproach me   What can I say for myself in
having so neglected so extraordinary a correspondent   I only am the sufferer,
but I should be very sorry to have him think my silence proceeded from
negligence   I declare it is want of time

Mrs. Granville died, after a very short illness, in August,
1747   There is a tradition in the family that she died on her
knees in the act of saying her prayers, and that she had often
expressed a wish that she might thus die.   The stool at which
she was kneeling is still preserved   It is high   the legs are
black, like ebony, of a curious ancient form, and it is covered
with needlework, the pattern of which is still perceptible

Her second son, Bevill, had given her great trouble.   He
was born in 1705 and educated at Westminster   In a letter
from his aunt, Lady Lansdowne to his father, dated July 10th,
1721, she writes to inform him that Bevill had written to Lord
Lansdowne to say he thought he had been long enough at
school; "indeed, everybody is of his mind for what he learns
there I believe he would be as well anywhere else   I was in
hopes he would have gone through the school, as my brother
Villiers had done before him, but you must now let me know
your opinion about him   You know your brother has got £500
of his, which we can pay him £50 a year   Bevill is at Sir
John Stanley's and has been there for some time.   The holidays
being almost over makes me write to you, for I suppose he will
not return to school   I wish that it were in my power to serve
both your sons, but the world is so altered that I do not know
anybody that will help one another."   The next we hear of
him is in a letter from his sister Mary Mrs Pendarves. to her

sister, Anne, dated 14 July, 1722. " My brother, Bevill, walked in the park with me last night. I left him well in Stable-yard, but suppose you will have a letter from him this post " Ten days afterward he was married in the Fleet Prison to Mary Ann Rose of Weedon ! He could not have been more than seventeen at the time As his marriage is never alluded to in any of the family letters of this period, we can only conclude that it was contracted against their consent, or, more probably, without their knowledge. The next we hear of this young scapegrace is decidedly startling He contemplates taking Holy Orders ! Writing to his father, on the 15th of February, 1722-23, Lord Lansdowne says —

> I have had a very grave and serious letter from my nephew Bevil, to acquaint me that he has at last taken the resolution of devoting himself to the Church. I cannot say but I am heartily glad of it There is nothing like choosing some profession or other for young men, otherwise they must necessarily fall into idleness without any hope of being ever useful in any kind to their families or country A man of quality, provided he maintains his character (for without that there can be nothing expected) cannot fail of making his way some time or other, and more readily this way than any other He informs me that he designs to enter himself at Trinity College, Cambridge, because I was of that College, which he means as a compliment to me, but I should have him well consider of that In my time indeed it was a most flourishing College, but of late years it has been disturbed with a civil war between the masters and fellows, which is carried on with so much warmth and animosity on both sides that it cannot be comfortable living amongst them I should think he had better choose some College at Oxford which is nearer to you at Buckland, which neighbourhood would make that choice more convenient and agreeable to you all, and besides you would have his conduct and behaviour more under your inspection There is a College in Oxford particular to Western gentlemen My uncle, the Dean, was, I believe, of it, and so was my grandfather whose death the University so much honoured Christchurch I have heard is as much divided as Trinity ; the same reason subsists against going there When one is to choose a retreat one would choose a quiet one There is no studying in the midst of quarrels and disturbance I have answered his letter and given him my opinion in all but this article I would fain have him do well and establish such a character as may give him higher views in time than barely remaining a country parson

Lord Lansdowne's letter to Bevil upon his entering into Holy Orders is printed in his " Works " It is as follows —

> When I look upon the date of your last Letter, I must own myself blameable for not having sooner returned you my thanks for it
>
> I approve very well of your Resolution of dedicating your self to the Service of God You could not choose a better Master, provided you have so sufficiently searched your Heart as to be persuaded you can serve Him well In so doing you may secure to your self Blessings in this World as well as a sure Expectation in the next There is one thing which I perceive you have not yet thoroughly purged your self from, which is Flattery You have

bestowed so much of that upon me in your Letter that I hope you have no more left, and that you meant it only to take your Leave of such Flights of Fancy, which however well meant, oftener put a man out of countenance than oblige him

You are now become a Searcher after Truth   I shall hereafter take it more kindly to be justly reproved by you than to be undeservedly complimented

I would not have you understand me as if I recommended to you a sour Presbyterian severity, that is yet more to be avoided   Advice, like Physick, should be so sweetened and prepared as to be made palatable, or Nature may be apt to revolt against it   Be always sincere, but at the same time always polite   Be humble without descending from your Character, reprove and correct without offending good manners, To be a Cynick is as bad as to be a Sycophant   You are not to lay aside the Gentleman with your Sword, nor to put on the Gown to hide your Birth and Good-breeding, but to adorn it

Such has been the Malice of the World from the beginning that Pride, Avarice, and Ambition have been charged upon the Priesthood in all ages, in all Countries, and in all Religions   What they are most obliged to combat against in their Pulpits they are most accused of encouraging in their conduct   It behoves you therefore to be more upon your guard in this than in any other Profession   Let your Example confirm your Doctrine, and let no Man ever have it in his Power to reproach you with practising contrary to what you preach

You had an uncle, Dr Denis Granville, Dean of Durham, whose memory I shall ever revere   make him your example   Sanctity sat so easily, so unaffected, and so graceful upon him that in him we beheld the very Beauty of Holiness   He was as cheerful, as familiar, and condescending in his Conversation as he was strict, regular, and exemplary in his Piety, as well-bred and accomplished as a Courtier, as reverend and venerable as an Apostle   He was indeed in everything Apostolical, for he abandoned all to follow his Lord and Master

May you resemble him !   May he revive in you '   May his Spirit descend upon you as Elijah's upon Elisha's '   And may the great God of Heaven in guiding, directing and strengthening your pious Resolutions, pour down his best and choicest Blessings upon you '

You shall ever find me, dear Nephew, your most affectionate Uncle and sincere Friend   etc   LANSDOWNE.

Mrs. Pendarves writes to her sister Ann .—

Somerset House 11 Nov. 1727

I am very glad my brother Bevil is in France, it is what I advised him to long ago, and the only secure step he could take   For, as he has managed his affairs I doubt he could not have staid in England with any security.

And again 29 Feb., 1728 —

I have this moment had a letter from my brother Bevil.   He has had a bad cold but is now much better

And again 14 March, 1728 .—

Yesterday my Aunt Stanley received a letter from my brother Bevil. I am sorry he has an ague although it is in the spring

The next reference to him contains also the first allusion to his wife. The letter is dated 11 May, 1728 :—

> I had a letter from Bevil last post, but have heard nothing of his wife lately I suppose she is gone back to Weedon

He apparently returned to England soon after this, and wrote plays, for on the 5th of December, 1728, Mrs. Pendarves writes —

> I have not seen Bevil this fortnight, but hear he is well and very busy about his play, which I fear he will manage simply, and he does not care to be advised He has long promised me a copy of it for you, but I cannot yet get it

Apparently his sister's fears were well grounded, for in her next letter (8 March, 1729) she writes :—

> My brother Bevil has met with great disappointments in his play, which is not to be acted, but he is going to print it, and wants to dedicate it to the Princess Royal I am going this morning to Lady Fitzwilliam's to see if I can get the Princess's leave

Meanwhile interest in another quarter was being used to advance his career, for his sister writes, " From my fireside, 14 March, 1729 " —

> Interest is making to get Mr Horatio Walpole to let my brother Bevil go over with him to Soissons where he is going Plenipo, and I fancy it will be obtained It must be a secret

The next reference to him is in a letter dated Somerset House, 9 Oct , 1729 —

> My brother Bevil is as well as he can be I suppose you may have had a letter from him by this time, for he said he would write I will take care of yours to him.

The following month (20 Nov) Mrs Pendarves writes —

> My lady Sunderland told me the other day, without my asking her, that she would speak to my Lord Sunderland and make him promise her the reversion of Altrope living for my brother Bevil, which is a very good one, a fine house for him to live in, and the advantage of a patron that will have it in his power to promote him It was very kind and obliging.

The following day (21 Nov) Lord Lansdowne writes to Mrs. Pendarves .—

> I hope your brother (Bernard) will find his account by the journey he has taken he is, at least, in the road of preferment I wish I could say the same of poor Bevil.

Evidently Bevil was at this time a very heavy drain upon his sister's resources. Looking back upon this time, she wrote some years afterwards (1740) —

I had not then a turn for saving, or management, so as to make the best of my fortune, but I endeavoured to act prudently and not run out, and now, had it not been for the misfortune and misconduct of my youngest brother, I should have been very happy, but I suffered infinite vexation on his account for some years

And in her Diary she mentions Lady Lansdowne's anxiety lest " the perplexity I labored under on my brother's account would prejudice my health"; and again, " My whole attention and time was given up to her and my unfortunate youngest brother on whose account I have been in distress for some years "

However, an opening presented itself shortly afterwards in a new country   Mrs Pendarves obtains a berth for him in Maryland. Writing from New Bond Street, 5th August, 1731, to her sister, she says —

I believe by this time my brother Bevill is embarked—he only waited for a fair wind   Mr Benedict Calvert, that was Governor of Maryland, is come home on the account of his health and a brother of Mr Ogle's is going in his place   I desired Mrs Donnellan to ask his interest in favour of my brother, and he has in the handsomest manner promised to do everything for him that lies in his power   He has now the fairest opportunity in the world to mend his fortune, and what is past may serve as a very good lesson to him and prevent his splitting on the same rock

On the 7th March, 1732, writing to her eldest brother from Dublin, she adds the following postscript to her letter .—

I had almost forgot to tell you of my brother Bevil's good fortune   He arrived at North Carolina very well

The next tidings we hear of him is in a letter from Lord Lansdowne to his niece, Ann Granville, dated Old Windsor, June 23, 1732 —

The last news we had of your brother Bevil was that he was settled, at the time of his writing to his satisfaction in Carolina, where he found the Governor an old acquaintance and schoolfellow at Westminster, who immediately put him in an advantageous way of preaching the Gospel and converting infidels   If he could but have been steady but a very little longer in his pious fits in this old world, he would soon have been under no necessity to seek his fortune in the new, but I hope that is not irretrievable   Time and patience bring about many unexpected events

He appears to have continued to do well there, for writing from Killala, 7 August, 1732, to her sister, Mrs. Pendarves ends her letter with these words —

I have not had any letter from my brother Bevil, but my Lord Lansdowne has had an account since I heard of him, that confirms the news of his extraordinary good fortune

The climate, however, disagreed with his constitution, and he died in 1736   Mrs. Pendarves writes thus of his death in her Diary :—

Though he had occasioned me much sorrow, his death was a most sensible grief to me

Eleven years afterwards, she writes to her sister the following report of his widow .—

Yesterday D[r] Carmichael and the Bishop of Down and his sister dined here , D[r] Car   and his lady are two good-humoured prating people who were in raptures with Delville. They gave me a long account of my sister Granville who lives within two miles of them in Buckinghamshire , she is very well, fat, and handsome   Her mother, and brother, Dick Rose, are dead, Tom just married, and they give him the character of a very honest good-tempered man , his sister lives with him and is neither "mad " nor "married," though both were reported of her

Whether, however, there were not some grounds for the rumour of her re-marriage is an open question, or rather whether she had not a child which must be regarded as a blot on her fair fame.   In the Autobiography of Augustus Bozzi Granville, M.D., F R S , he describes his parentage thus   " My mother, Maria Antonietta, was one of the four daughters of the Chavalier Rapazinni, who filled an important post under Government in the Secretary of State Department (in Milan).   Rapazinni, in 1761, took for a second wife a very young English lady, born in Italy, whither her father Bevil Granville, a Cornish gentleman, implicated in some political troubles, had withdrawn, and where his wife, Rosa Granville, had presented him with a daughter   This daughter, also named Rosa, grew up and was educated in a convent, which she left at the age of fifteen to become the wife of Rapazinni, and the mother of his daughter, Maria Antonietta, who in due time married Carlo Bozzi, and was my mother "   Augustus Bozzi afterwards, 1806, added to his paternal name that of his mother's maternal ancestor, and was known henceforth as Augustus Bozzi Granville
Now as Bevil Granville died in Carolina in 1736, and Rosa Granville was not born until 1746, and as there was no other Bevil Granville alive at that time, and as, moreover, the name Rosa or Rose was chosen as a christian name, it is at least suspicious that Bevil's widow, Mary Ann (Rose), was the mother of Dr Granville's mother, and hence the rumour of her

re-marriage as alluded to in Mrs. Delany's letter   The girl's
education in a convent also tends to confirm the suspicion

Within the Parish Church of Wingrave, in the county of
Bucks, is a mural tablet, somewhat in the shape of a heart,
placed between the east window of the north aisle and the arch
dividing the aisle from the nave, with the following inscription .—

Mrs.

Mary Ann Granville

Of Weedon in this Parish

relict of

Bevill Granville, Esqr

Died the 8th of Sepr 1779

Aged 76 years

To whose Memory

This monument

is erected

Weedon was a hamlet formerly in the parish of Wingrave
but is now annexed to the parish of Hardwick.   Above the
inscription is a small lozenge-shaped shield, but if the arms
were painted upon it they are now entirely obliterated

Bernard Granville, or "Bunny" as he was usually called in
the family, the eldest son, was the heir to his uncle, Lord
Lansdowne, and proved the last of the male line of this ancient
and distinguished family.   After leaving the University he
entered the Army, but on his uncle's death he quitted that
profession and took a house in Hollis Street   The same year
(1734) he received a further addition to his fortune by the
death of the Duchess of Albemarle,* whose property was
divided between Countess Granville, Lord Gower and Bernard
Granville, as the heirs of John, Earl of Bath.   In 1738 he
purchased of the Fleetwood family the estate of Calwich Abbey
in Staffordshire, close to the Derbyshire border and the pretty
town of Ashbourne.   The Abbey was built on the site of an
Hermitage, which belonged to the Priory of Kenilworth.   To

---

* She died according to the Funeral Book at Westminster Abbey, where she was buried,
at Newcastle House, Clerkenwell, 28th August, 1731 aged 80 , but the journals of the day,
still quoted, stated her age to be 96   She was known as 'the mad Duchess," and her
history is too familiar and too painful to require rehearsing   She survived the Duke of
Albemarle 46 years, and thus kept the Granvilles waiting for the property, in which she had
a life interest, nearly half a century

that religious house it had been given (says Tanner in his 'Notitia Monastica) before the year 1148, by Nicholas de Gresley Fitz Nigell, and therein was placed a small convent of Black Canons (Carthusians)   This house was given (17 Henry VIII.) to the monastery of Merton, Surrey, in exchange for the manor of East Molsey, and as a parcel of the same was again granted (34 Henry VIII) to John Fleetwood, a member of the ancient Lancashire family of that name, and it continued in the possession of his descendants till purchased by Bernard Granville   The mansion was of modern date when he bought it, standing at the base of a lengthened woody knoll, which, stretching east and west, formed the right boundary of the vale of the Dove   A rich screen of fine forest trees sheltered it on the north, and beneath was a fine verdant expanse of ornamental grounds, which Bernard Granville soon enlivened by a broad sheet of water fed from a branch of the serpentine Dove.

On the 6th of December, 1752, Sir Anthony Westcombe died and left the whole bulk of his property to Bernard Granville, who was his nephew and godson, including a library that comprehended a valuable selection of the best works in British, Continental, and Classical literature, and a valuable collection of fine prints and drawings by the old masters, amongst which may be named two landscapes of Rembrandt and several smaller ones by Ruysdael Segers, Vandort Poussin, and Wynants   A "St John in the Wilderness ' by Ludovico Carracci ; " A Sleeping Child " and "Boys with Fruit" from the pencil of Murillo.

In addition to these the walls at Calwich were hung with the splendid collection of family portraits by some of the best painters, which he inherited from Lord Lansdowne and his brother Colonel Granville

Here he lived, a high-bred and accomplished person, but somewhat stern and unloving in his character   He never married   There is a family tradition that a disappointment in love, whilst a young man staying with his sister, Mrs Pendarves, in Cornwall, soured his disposition, and caused him to desert that county to which all his family had belonged for so many centuries, and to settle, when he came into his wealth, in far-off Staffordshire, a stranger among strangers, breaking off, to a great extent, all family habits, and caring little latterly to see any of his relations, except the children of his sister Anne (Mrs Dewes), who were dreadfully afraid of him.   His sister Mary he never forgave for marrying Dr. Delany, a man who had no claim of

J³

ancestry to bring forward, or anything to offer in excuse for what he doubtless considered unparalleled presumption, and though after the marriage there was a certain appearance of amity it was very clear that there was a great change in the feelings and conduct of Mr Granville, which made Mrs. Delany very unhappy.

One of Bernard Granville's few friends was Jean Jacques Rousseau, who, a victim to imaginary terrors, fled from his native country and his friends, and taking refuge in England settled down in 1766, at Wootton Hall, close to Calwich, where he became very intimate with Bernard Granville, who was said never to have been the same after his acquaintance with his theoretical opinions of religion To young Mary Dewes the presence of "Monsieur Rousseau," who used to write notes to her "*à ma belle voisine*" was a relief to her long visits to her formidable uncle, and her partiality for him rather shocked Mrs Delany, who wrote to her, "I always take alarm when virtue in general terms is the idol without the support of religion, the only foundation that can be our security to build upon."

Another constant visitor at Calwich was Handel the composer, and Mr. Granville, who was devoted to music, had an organ built in 1756, under Handel's personal supervision, by Father Smith which is still in the family On this instrument Handel used to play for hours together, and doubtless composed many of his eternal symphonies upon it There was also at Calwich a valuable collection of Handel's MS music in thirty-eight volumes, copied under the great composer's personal superintendence by his amanuensis, Smith In November, 1784, King George III, who with Queen Charlotte had frequent communications and conversations with Mrs Delany on the subject of Handel's music, expressed his wish that Mrs Delany would procure from her nephew the catalogue of her late brother's collection The following letter was written to Mrs Delany by Queen Charlotte on returning the catalogue, inclosing one from the King on the same subject —

FROM QUEEN CHARLOTTE TO MRS DELANY

I have the pleasure of returning dear Mrs Delany the catalogue of Mr Granville's collection of music with a note from the King, which will sufficiently prove how much he is satisfied with the manner in which she has executed his commission I avail myself with pleasure of this opportunity of assuring one of the worthiest of our sex of my sincere regard and esteem

CHARLOTTE

Windsor the 7th Novbr 1784

FROM KING GEORGE III TO MRS DELANY.

The King is much pleased with the very correct manner in which Mrs Delany has obligingly executed the commission of obtaining an exact catalogue of Mr Granville's collection of M$_r$ Handel's music, and desires she will forward it to Dr Burney, at the same time, as Mrs Delany has communicated Mr Granville's willingness of letting the King see those volls that are not in the list of his original collection, he is desired at any convenient opportunity to let the following ones be sent to town, and great care shall be taken that they shall be without damage returned —

No 19   Opera of Amanets
   22   Teseo
   25   Amadisce.
   35 and 36   Vols of Duets
   87   Miscellanies and Water Musick.

As also the Quarto manuscript of a song composed by that great Master in eight parts, beginning, "Still I adore you, tho' you deny me"

Mrs. Delany procured the music the King asked for, and received the following acknowledgment of it from him :—

FROM KING GEORGE III TO MRS. DELANY.

The King has just received the copies of the three operas Mrs Delany so obligingly borrow'd for him He therefore returns the three scores, the two other books that accompanied them, as also the terzetto in the unrivalled author's own hand, and the *beautiful song* in eight parts, and desires Mrs Delany will express everything that is proper to her nephew for communications that have been so agreeable The King hopes when the spring is far enough advanced that he may have the pleasure of having that song performed at the Queen's House to the satisfaction of Mrs Delany, not forgetting to have it introduced by the overture of Radamistus

GEORGE R

Queen's House, Feb 11, 1785

The Granville collection of Handel's MS music in 38 vols. it is believed, were *all* sent by Mrs Delany to George III. but from some carelessness on the part of those entrusted with their return, only 37 vols were ever received back, among which "The Song in eight parts" was not included, to which the King so especially alluded in his letter. Mrs. Delany never was able to trace the missing music, which was the cause of much vexation to her, though it is probable the King and Queen were never made aware of its loss before her death.

This valuable Collection is still in the possession of the family, in perfect preservation, original calf bindings It comprises—

1	Messiah	20	Hymeneus
2	Sampson.	21	Rodelinda
3	Joseph	22	Otho
4	Saul	23	Deidamia
5	Esther	· 24	L'Allegro ed il Pensieroso
6.	Athalia	25	Ricciardo
7	Deborah	26	Liroe
8	Il Trionfo (Italian words)	27	Tamerlane
9	Te Deums and Jubilate	28	Admetus
10	Fifty Cantatas	29	Guilio Cesare
11.	Israel in Egypt	30	Anthems
12	Acis and Galatea	31	Anthems
13.	Amadigi	32	Anthems.
14.	Teseo	33.	Anthems
15	Lotharius	34	Duetts.
16	Scipio	35	Organ Concertos
17	Ariodante	36	Instrumental Concertos
18.	Alexander	37	Miscellanies, viz, Concertante in
19	Rinaldo		nine parts, Water Music

Besides these there is a Trio, " se tu non lasci amore," in 3 movements, in Handel's autograph, 29 pages, oblong 4to, signed on the last page, " G. F. Hendel, li 12 di Luglio 1708 Napoli."

This MS, written, doubtless, from the great care bestowed on it, for presentation, is supposed to be unique   On the last page, in the handwriting of Mr. Bernard Granville, is the following —

This original is of M^r G F Hendel's handwriting, given by him to Mr Bernard Granville, and is the only copy extant, as Mr Handel told him when he gave it him as an addition to his collection of Musick

The collection also contains a curious Book, thus entitled —

Krieger (Johann) Organisten und Chori Musici Directore in Zittau, Anmuthige Clavier Ubung. Oblong 4to, Nurnberg 1699

Mr. Granville has written the following memorandum with regard to this work .—

This printed book is by one of the celebrated organ-players of Germany Mr Handel in his youth formed himself a good deal on his plan, and said that Krieger was one of the best writers of his time for the organ and, to form a good player, but the clavichord must be made use of by a beginner, instead of organ or harpsichord

There is also a Presentation Copy to Mr Granville of Handel's " Suites des Pieces," vol i , on which are these words in Mr. Granville's handwriting .—

This book not published by himself, but full of mistakes in the copying.

and the following —

1 *Early edition* of Suites de pieces pour le Clavicin by G F Handel
2 Early edition Six Fugues or Vo'untarys for the Organ or Harpsichord by G F Handel
3 *Ditto* Semele Opera set to Musick by Mr Handel
4 MS Il Meghor d'ogni Amore by Francesco Gasparin
5 MS Oratorio, San Filipponeri by Alexandro Scarlatti
6 MS Kyrie et Gloria by Sig Aut Lotti
7 MS. Cantate a voce sola

Handel died in April, 1759, and in the codicil to his will left many legacies to his friends, including two pictures by Rembrandt to Mr Granville, which Mr Granville had formerly given him as presents

Early in January, 1775, Bernard Granville was seized with his last illness   Mrs Delany, writing to her niece, Mrs Port, describes his ' present situation as deplorable as to all that regards this world, unable to give or receive pleasure and struggling with pain and sickness   I endeavour to cast a veil over that sad scene, and to hope he has, *in the main*, made a good use of his tryals, and that when it pleases God to finish his sufferings He will receive him into His holy habitations—this I earnestly pray for and submit to His blessed will   My poor brother's errors have been owing to a temper never properly subdued   it has clouded many good and agreeable qualities , it has corroded his spirit with suspicions, and it has made him and his friends unhappy ; but I must own, though I have suffered at times *inexpressibly* by its cruel effects, and tho' they have in some degree abated, they have by no means extinguished my affection.   I am afraid I have said too much on the subject ! My heart was full—and is now reliev'd   I think by his last letters there is a great alteration "

He lingered till the 2nd of July   Mrs. Delany was not allowed to be with him, and personally administer to his comfort   At one time he appeared anxious for frequent letters from her, especially on religious subjects ; at others, all inter-course on his side ceased, and it appears that her offer of going to Calwich was not accepted.   Hopeless of his recovery, Mrs. Delany admitted to her niece that his release from a state of continued suffering would be a blessing and relief, but yet the trial when it came was very painful.   She had ever retained her attachment to the remembrance of what he *once* was to her, and as long as life lasted hope lingered, and she evidently caught at every little trait of kindness that the " *Bunny* " of the " *past* " would re-appear.

Bernard Granville left his own epitaph, and over it the following words were written –

The inscription for the monument that is to be at Elaston

Under the epitaph was a pen and ink sketch which was intended to show in what part of Ellaston Church his vault was to be made and his monument erected, and he directed his vault to be full nine foot deep, and lined with a good brick or stone wall. He was buried in Ellaston Church (the parish Church of Calwich), and the inscription on his monument is as follows —

HERE LIES INTERRED THE BODY OF
BERNARD GRANVILLE
WHO TRUSTED IN THE MERCY OF ALMIGHTY GOD
FOR THE FORGIVENISS OF HIS SINS
THROUGH THE MERITS AND MEDIATION
OF
JESUS CHRIST, THE SAVIOUR AND REDEEMER
OF MANKIND.
HE WAS THE SON OF BERNARD GRANVILE
AND GREAT-GRANDSON OF SIR BEVILL GRANVILLE
WHO WAS KILLED IN THE CIVIL WARS
FIGHTING FOR KING CHARLES THE FIRST,
ON LANSDOWN, NEAR BATH, IN SOMERSETSHIRE.
HE DIED AT CALWICH, JULY THE 2ND 1775
AGED 76.

The above epitaph is nearly the same as the one found among his papers, but in the MS instead of the " civil wars," the words were —

The wars between King Charles I and the Rebbells

He left the bulk of his property to his nephew, the Rev John Dewes, the third son of his sister Anne It had always been anticipated that Bernard the second son, would have been his heir, but he received a very small share only of it However, the result was eventually the same, as Court, the elder brother dying unmarried, Bernard succeeded to his father's estates, and John of Calwich fully justified the opinion entertained of him by Mrs. Delany and was one of the most benevolent, liberal and kind-hearted men that ever lived Moreover, his only child, John, dying in 1800, aged twenty, the Calwich property eventually passed, in 1826, to Bernard's only son Court.

CHAPTER XIX

Six thick volumes containing the autobiography and letters of Mary Granville, Mrs Delany, Bernard Granville's eldest sister, were published by Lady Llanover in 1862, and since then an epitome of these has been published by Mrs. Townshend Mayer in her "Women of Letters," 1894, so that these pages will only contain a brief outline sketch of her life, culled mainly from the latter source.

Mary Granville was born at Coulston, in Wiltshire, the 14th of May, 1700. When she was eight year old, her father and the rest of his family having settled at Little Chelsea, Mary was taken to Whitehall to live with her aunt, Lady Stanley, who had no child of her own. Here she remained till Colonel Granville removed into Gloucestershire whither she was summoned to join them. She was now fifteen years of age, handsome, lively, accomplished, and of an impetuous temper. She had been brought up in the expectation of being, as so many of her female relatives had been before her, a Maid of Honour, but the death of Queen Anne and the accession of the Whigs to power at the commencement of the new reign, and the ill-favour the Granvilles fell into at this time at Court, dashed these hopes to the ground, and her lamentations at being torn from the delights of London and plunged into the wilds of Gloucestershire in winter-time, found utterance in Pope's verses

> Thus from the world fair Zephalinda flew,
> Saw others happy, and with sighs withdrew .
> She went to plain work, and to purling brooks,
> Old-fashioned halls, dull aunts, and croaking rooks
> To part her time 'twixt reading and bohea—
> To nurse and spill her solitary tea
>
> Some Squire, perhaps, you take delight to rack,
> Whose game is whisk whose treat a toast in sack .
> Whose laughs are hearty, though his jests are coarse,
> And loves you best of all things—but his horse !"

However when Spring came round Buckland proved a much more endurable abode than she had anticipated, and she soon found a lover, whom she called "Roberto," supposed to have been a Mr Twyford, who, however, being provided with nineteen brothers and sisters, and a stony-hearted stepmother unfavourable to his settlement in life, could not bring his love affair to a happy conclusion

In the Autumn of 1717, Lord and Lady Lansdowne, released from the Tower, invited their niece to join them at Longleat, where she found herself once more in the gay world of fashion, the house being constantly filled with visitors, who danced every night to an excellent band. Amongst the guests was Mr Alexander Pendarves, of Roscrow, Cornwall, a Squire of sixty winters, who was attracted by her beauty, and Lord Lansdowne, rejoiced at an opportunity of strengthening his interests in Cornwall, insisted upon her accepting his offer of marriage, pleading her father's altered circumstances and the duty and gratitude she owed to all her family Her parents were at once sent for, and a very grand wedding was arranged without loss of time.

Never was woe drest out in gayer colours, she says, and when I was led to the altar I wished from my soul I had been led, as Iphigenia was, to be sacrified I *was* sacrificed. I lost, not life indeed, but all that made life desirable

After a very bitter honeymoon spent at Longleat, Mr Pendarves carried his reluctant bride to his castellated mansion near Falmouth The house was guarded by high walls that hid it from view It had been uninhabited for thirty years, and had rotting floors, falling ceilings, and windows high above all possibility of looking through them Here she lived with her ugly, gouty, jealous snuff-taking, heavy-drinking husband for seven years, the dullness of it being, however, occasionally relieved by short visits to town and Windsor Mrs Pendarves attracted, wherever she went by her youth and beauty, admirers of a more or less ardent description. On one of these brief emancipations from dreary Roscrow, a presentiment of evil made her return earlier than usual from her friend Lady Sunderland's house, where she had been spending the evening, whilst her husband was away " with his usual set." He had reached home before her, and said many kind things to her, and wished he might live to reward her, and told her to ring the bell that he might sign his will This, however, she persuaded him to defer until the morrow, but early next morning she found him, to her horror, lying dead by her side ! The will not having been signed, the fortune on which Lord Lansdowne had counted, when he compelled her to marry Mr. Pendarves, was reduced to a slender jointure, and the Cornish estates passed to her husband's niece.

The young widow took up her abode with her aunt, Lady Stanley, and, after the first shock of Mr Pendarves' death, appears to have led a very happy life, and to have been once more the centre of admiration In 1731 Mrs Pendarves was invited to Ireland Dublin society at this time was very brilliant and she ' fluttered" at all the vice-regal entertainments, besides assiduously cultivating the friendship of the wits and scholars. Amongst these was Swift, Dean of St Patrick's, with whom she formed a life-long acquaintance, and many of his amusing letters to her are extant. With all her gaiety of heart and love of every harmless amusement, Mrs Pendarves found plenty of time and inclination for study. She became a proficient in painting and drawings in crayons Her portraits were admirable She also drew all the patterns for the immense quantity and variety of artistic needlework with which she furnished her own and her relations' houses She was also very fond of botany and, in her old age, excelled in making paper imitation flowers. The first she attempted was in her seventy-fourth year, and this formed the principal recreation of her latter years, and her collection is still extant, and is the marvel of all who behold it. Horace Walpole, in his "Anecdotes of Painters," mentions Mrs. Delany, who " at the age of seventy-four *invented* the art of paper mosaic, with which material (coloured) she executed in eight years within twenty of 1,000 various flowers and flowering shrubs with a precision and truth unparalleled ," and Sir Joseph Banks used to say that Mrs Delany's mosaic flowers were the only representations of nature from which he could venture to describe a plant botanically without the least fear of committing an error. In June, 1734, she writes —

I have got a new madness I am running wild after shells This morning I have set my little collection of shells in nice order in my cabinet, and they look so beautiful that I must by some means enlarge my stock The beauties of shells are as infinite as of flowers, and to consider how they are inhabited enlarges a field of wonder that leads one insensibly to the great Director and Author of these wonders

In 1740, her passionately-loved sister, Anne, married Mr. D'Ewes, a country gentleman of good family and fortune, after about six months' acquaintance, made with a most business-like view to marriage, and without consulting Mrs Pendarves, who naturally regarded the match with some coolness and mistrust at first, but Mr D'Ewes' very high character seems to have

h '

won the regard of all his new relations, though the outspoken
comment of one of them, on hearing of the marriage, was,
"Lord, have mercy upon us! She was very sly to carry it
off so!"

In April, 1743, Mrs. Pendarves received another offer, and
many of her friends and relations were inclined to think that,
like the girl in the fairy tale, she took the crooked stick at last,
For Patrick Delany, Chancellor of St Patrick's, was a widower,
in his fifty-ninth year, of moderate fortune and obscure birth.
But he had some repute as a theologian, a spotless character,
tastes very similar to Mrs Pendarves' own, and great popularity
in the cultured circles in which she was such a favourite
Like her sister, she promptly made up her mind when the right
suitor appeared, and was married very quietly in June, afterwards visiting her mother at Gloucester, her sister Mrs Dewes,
and some of her friends, many of whom however frowned on the
bride and bridegroom. Her brother, Bernard Granville, as
stated in the previous chapter, never became thoroughly cordial
to Dr. Delany, and "the old Countess,"* she writes, "looked so
cross and cold that I stayed but one quarter of an hour, and she
received 'D D' in the same way"

There is every indication that they were a very happy
and sympathetic couple, but one cannot avoid a dark suspicion
that 'D D.' was sometimes rather formal and heavy, and, as
the letters proceed, a moralizing and didactic tone occasionally
qualifies their natural vivacity, which would seem to have been
caught from Mrs Delany's "worthy, sensible friend" She was
much on the alert when bishoprics were vacant, but in 1744
the Duke of Devonshire offered her husband the Deanery of
Down, which they agreed in thinking "a better thing than any
small bishopric," and in June they sailed from Chester for
Ireland to take possession

Mrs Delany was delighted with Delville, her husband's
miniature estate, with its picturesque gardens and lovely view
of Dublin harbour, where she spent the happiest possible life,
entertaining rich and poor alike and being loved by all   In
1752, however, a cloud gathered over their peaceful home in
the shape of a long and harassing law suit brought by the
Tennisons, the family of the first Mrs Delany, which lingered
on for nearly six years, and was at last concluded by an appeal
to the House of Lords, where Lord Mansfield, "after an hour
and a half speaking with angelic oratory pronounced the decree
in our favour" Dr Delany was to pay £3,000 and some other

* Countess Granville

comparatively trifling sums—but "the Dean's character is cleared," writes his wife joyfully, and set in the fair light it deserves."

From 1760 onwards frequent visits were paid to England, Dr. Delany, in whom rapidly increasing signs of age were showing themselves, being ordered to the Bath waters. He lived till 1768. After his death Mrs Delany lived much with the Duchess of Portland, under whose loving care she recovered health and serenity, and again entered into society, where, as heretofore, she was regarded as an ornament and leader. Edmund Burke, for example, describes her as "a *truly great* woman of fashion, not only the woman of fashion of the present age, but the woman of fashion of all ages, and the highest bred woman in the world."

It was not until 1778 that the Duchess of Portland presented Mrs Delany to George III and Queen Charlotte at a breakfast given to them at Bulstrode. They inspected and admired her needlework and her "book of flowers," requesting her to go to Windsor next day to see "all their children together." They received her there with the utmost kindness, and she says :—

Though age and my long retirement from Court made me feel timid on being called on to make my appearance, I soon found myself perfectly at ease

This was the beginning of the really close and genuine friendship which the King and Queen manifested for Mrs Delany. They took an interest in all her pursuits, sent for her to any entertainments which they thought would interest her, supplied her with flowers to copy from the houses at Kew, and often gave her little souvenirs, made more valuable by kind inscriptions.

After the death of her bosom friend, the Duchess of Portland, in 1785, and knowing how greatly she would miss the change afforded by her long and frequent visits to Bulstrode, the King and Queen gave Mrs Delany a house at Windsor and £300 a year with which to keep it up. This sum the Queen herself brought her quarterly in a pocket-book, "that it might not appear as a pension or be diminished by taxation." The King and Queen went daily to the house while it was being got ready for Mrs Delany, personally directing all improvements and additions, and taking great pleasure in furnishing it. When it was at last ready the King's special message to Mrs Delany was to desire her only to take herself her niece (great-niece, Miss Port), clothes and attendants, as stores of every kind would be laid in for her.   Mrs Delany arrived at her new home on the evening of September 20th, and found the King waiting to receive her and express his hope that she would find the house comfortable and agreeable.   The Queen walked over (Mrs. Delany's garden joined that of the Queen's Lodge) next morning, and repeated in the strongest terms their wish that she should be as easy and happy as they could possibly make her, saying that they desired to visit her "like friends."

Thenceforward some of the royal family drank tea with her every day, unless she was at the Castle, to which she was carried in a very elegant new chair, a present from the King.   The Queen sent her a beautiful spinning-wheel, and asked for some lessons in spinning, and sometimes unattended and unannounced would join her at her early dinner and praise her "orange pudding."

In the autumn of 1787, Mrs Delany had an illness, during which a favourite bird, which had belonged to the Duchess of Portland, and which she kept in her own room, died.   The Queen had one of the same kind which she valued extremely, and fearing that the bird's loss would distress her old friend, she took her own bird to Mrs Delany's house and placed it in the empty cage, cautioning everyone not to let her discover the change.   The Queen had but few more opportunities of showing this thoughtful affection.   In the following January Mrs. Delany removed to her house in St James's Place, and early in April she was seized with inflammation of the lungs, for which her doctors ordered bark.   "She looked distressed," her waiting-maid says, and told them "she always had a presentiment that if bark was given her, it would cause her death," giving her reasons for the fear.   But the doctor said there was no alternative, it was the only medicine that would remove the fever.   "Seeing the dear old lady so averse to taking it," Mrs Astly continues, "I offered to keep her secret and to put it away," "Oh, no!" she said "I never was reckoned obstinate, and will not die so."   She took the medicine, and some hours afterwards she died, in her eighty-eighth year.

She had given directions in her will, that as little expense should be incurred in her burial as decency would permit, "no matter where," she was accordingly interred in in a vault in the church of St James's, Piccadilly, in which parish her house was situated, and on a column in this church

MARY GRANVILLE MRS. DELANY.
From an Original Portrait, by Opie, in the Wellesbourne Collection.

there is a tablet to her memory, with an epitaph written by
Dr Hurd, Bishop of Worcester :—

NEAR THIS PLACE LIE THE REMAINS OF
MARY DELANY,
DAUGHTER OF BERNARD GRANVILLE,
AND NIECE OF GEORGE GRANVILLE, LORD LANSDOWNE
SHE WAS MARRIED, 1st TO ALEXANDER PENDARVES OF ROSCROW,
IN THE COUNTY OF CORNWALL, ESQ,
AND 2ND TO PATRICK DELANY, D D, DEAN OF DOWN, IN IRELAND
SHE WAS BORN MAY 14, 1700, AND DIED APRIL 15, 1788.
SHE WAS A LADY OF SINGULAR INGENUITY AND POLITENESS, AND OF
UNAFFECTED PIETY
THESE QUALITIES ENDEARED HER THROUGH LIFE TO MANY
NOBLE AND EXCELLENT PERSONS,
AND MADE THE CLOSE OF IT ILLUSTRIOUS BY PROCURING FOR HER
MANY SIGNAL MARKS OF GRACE AND FAVOUR FROM THEIR MAJESTIES

Anne, Mrs Delany's only and dearly-loved sister, was seven
years younger than herself, having been born in 1707   Unlike
her sister, she had lived principally with her parents, and after
her father's death had removed to Gloucester with her mother
The offer of a place at Court—which would have entirely separated her from her mother, but for which she evidently had
had a great inclination—she had unselfishly relinquished for her
mother's sake   She was not like her sister, living in the world
and able to choose her own society   She languished in the old
town of Gloucester, from whence her occasional escapes to a
more congenial atmosphere enabled her to strike the balance,
and decide in favour of a country home of her own with a
companion she could esteem and love, and where she would
still be within reach of that mother, to whom both daughters
were devoted   Such a home and such a husband seemed in
time to offer themselves   and the following letter is a curious
instance of the way matches were arranged one hundred and
fifty years ago, and how gentlemen were *assisted* by being
"*recommended*" to the lady of their fancy, by a mutual friend,
before they were made personally known to her.   Miss
Granville's correspondent is her bosom friend Lady Throckmorton, (*neé* Catherine Collingwood), whose husband Sir Robert
Throckmorton's seat was at Coughton Court near Alcester —

I have a question to ask you, my dearest Kitty, that requires all your
secresy and prudence (which I depend upon,) and for your truth I cannot
doubt it, therefore without any preamble I desire you will inform me what
Sir Robert's real opinion is of Mr D'Ewes and yours, if you know him   There
is a person he is recommended to, but she is quite a stranger to him, and is
my friend, and therefore I make an inquiry about him, that I

that not a word of it be mentioned to anybody, because the thing is an entire secret   The person I speak of has no notion of happiness in a married life but what must proceed from an equality of sentiments and mutual good opinion , and therefore she would be glad to know if Mr. D—— has agreeable conversation, generous principles, and is not a lawyer in his manners   I remember Sir Robert told me something about him at Bath, but I have forgot what   Once more, my dear friend, be secret and never by word, look, or gesture discover what I have said to you   when I am allowed to say more I will , and answer my letter as soon as you can

Mr John D'Ewes, of Wellesbourne, near Stratford-on-Avon, about whom Miss Granville thus secretly enquires, and whom she married the following summer (August, 1740) was descended from Gerard (or Geeradt), son of Adrian D'Ewes, who, with Alice Ravenscroft his wife, was buried under the fine monument in the church of St Michael Bassishaw, London, mentioned in Weever's "Antiquities"   He was the son of Court D'Ewes of Maplebury, and grandson of Richard D'Ewes of Coughton, who married Mary, daughter and co-heir of Edmund Court of Maplebury.   The family was descended from Otho des Ewes, of the duchy of Guelderland, who was ancestor of Gerard des Ewes, Lord of the territory of Hessel, who married Anne, daughter of Prince de Horne, and whose descendant Adrian, above-mentioned, younger brother of the Lord of Hessel, came into England, in the reign of Henry VIII , when that duchy had been depopulated in the wars by intestine discord   He died of the sweating sickness, 5th Edward VI   His grandson, Sir Paul, was the father of the famous Sir Symond D'Ewes, the antiquary, who wrote "The Journal of the Parliaments during the reign of Elizabeth "   The last baronet was Sir Jermyn d'Ewes of Stow Hall, Suffolk, who died at Thetford in Norfolk, April, 1731.   He was named after his maternal grandfather Thomas Lord Jermyn, whose title became extinct in 1703.

The younger branch of this family, from which Mr John D'Ewes was descended, had been settled for many generations in the counties of Warwick, Gloucester, and Worcester, and the manor of Wellesbourne Mountford, came into their possession about the beginning of the eighteenth century   Thurston de Mountford probably received this manor in the time of Henry I Through failure of heirs, it had passed to the Botelers in the ninth year of Richard II , and Sir John Mobley, by marriage, became possessed of it in the reign of Henry II.

Thus it was that the beautiful and gentle Anne Granville married Mr. D'Ewes, whose descent was as ancient, though not quite so illustrious, as her own, and whom she preferred with a

COURT D'EWES AND BERNARD D'EWES.
CHILDREN OF JOHN AND ANN D'EWES.
From an Original Picture in the Wellesbourne Collection.

JOHN D'EWES (AFTERWARDS GRANVILLE),
MARY D'EWES (AFTERWARDS PORT),
CHILDREN OF JOHN AND ANN D'EWES.

From an Original Picture in the Wellesbourne Collection.

moderate fortune to numerous admirers who had previously been rejected because their principles did not keep pace with their estates.

Mrs. Delany was a constant guest at Wellesbourne, the two sisters, who were truly devoted to each other, enjoying what they called "days snatched out of the shade" of the rest of their lives. But in 1760 Anne's health began to fail, and she was ordered to the Bristol hot-wells, the prospect of a perfect cure being held out to her. Mrs. Delany and her husband joined her there, but she gradually grew worse, and expired on the 16th of July, 1761, to the inexpressible grief of Mrs. Delany. She left behind her some very touching prayers, which prove how through long years she had prepared herself for death while in the full current of life. Dr. and Mrs. Delany did not inhabit the same house at Bristol as Mrs. D'Ewes, and the latter, who was seized quite suddenly at the last, would not have them sent for, desiring to spare her sister the last awful scene of parting. She well knew that no assurances were required by her sister of the affection which had been mutually proved through their lives, and that her last moments had better pass in silent communion with that God in Whom they both had ever trusted, and in that Saviour through Whose merits they would hope to meet again in heaven. Her husband Mr. D'Ewes was at Wellesbourne when she died, where no doubt he had returned, at her request, to attend to the welfare of their children. She was buried in the family vault at Wellesbourne church, and the stone which marks the spot, bears the following inscription —

To the Memory of
ANN, THE BELOVED WIFE OF JOHN DEWES,
OF THIS PARISH, ESQ.,
WHO DEPARTED THIS LIFE THE 16TH OF JULY, 1761,
IN THE 54TH YEAR OF HER AGE.
SHE WAS DAUGHTER OF BERNARD GRANVILLE AND NIECE TO
THE RT HON GEORGE GRANVILLE LORD LANSDOWN.

HERE ALSO LIE THE REMAINS OF
JOHN DEWES ESQ.
WHO DESIRED TO BE BURIED BY THE SIDE OF HIS WIFE AND
TO BE REMEMBERED ON THE SAME STONE.
A MUCH LARGER ONE WOULD NOT SUFFICE TO ENUMERATE
THOSE VIRTUES WHICH ALL WHO KNEW THEM WOULD
MOST JUSTLY ALLOW THAT THEY POSSESSED.
HE DIED AUGUST 30TH, 1780, IN THE 86TH YEAR OF HIS AGE.

They left issue three sons, Court, Bernard, and John and an only daughter, Mary, who lived with Mrs Delany after her mother's death, and to whom Mrs Delany transferred all the boundless affection she had felt for the sister she had lost Henceforth the education and happiness of little Mary D'Ewes was the chief object of her life, till in December, 1770, she was married from Bulstrode (the Duchess of Portland's place) at Upton church, to Mr John Port of Ilam in Derbyshire, who had changed his name from that of Sparrow on succeeding to the property of a maternal uncle The ancient and loyal family of Port had been settled at Ilam for several generations It was a picturesque old family house, which has been thus described by one who visited it in the summer of 1820 —" The principal entrance, agreeably to the fashion that once generally prevailed, was a square hall in the centre of the building, which communicated with the adjoining apartments a massy, old-fashioned fire-place, admirably adapted for winter, with a huge unlighted log of wood, and some faggots of wood in the grate, occupied nearly one side of the room in a niche opposite hung a Chinese gong whose loud and sonorous sound summoned the company at Ilam to dinner bows, arrows, and targets, a fine old organ, and some antique chairs completed the remaining part of the furniture of this apartment" (Rhodes's "Peak Scenery.") Owing to embarrassment of his pecuniary circumstances, increased by the expenses of a large family, Mr Port was obliged to let Ilam, and afterwards in 1807 his son sold it to Mr Watts Russell, who pulled down the picturesque old family house, and built the present overgrown castellated building, that ill-suits the lovely scenery by which it is surrounded

Their eldest daughter, Georgina Mary Ann (born 1771), succeeded her mother as the favourite of Mrs. Delany and the Duchess of Portland, and eventually married Mr Waddington of Llanover, by whom she was the mother of Frances, Baroness Bunsen, and of Augusta, Lady Llanover.

Court D'Ewes, the eldest son of John and Anne D'Ewes, was born in 1742. He too was a great favourite with Mrs Delany, and to his care she bequeathed little ' Portia," as she called her great-niece, Georgina Mary Ann Port But he had naturally a cold and ungenial nature, and a dislike to young people, and treated her with positive coldness and harshness as well as with neglect of her worldly interests. He was never married, and travelled a good deal abroad in search of health. He succeeded his father in the Wellesbourne property, but only survived him thirteen years, and died in 1793, aged fifty-one

COURT D'EWES, ESQ.,
OF WELLESBOURNE.

From an Original Portrait in the Wellesbourne Collection.

His brother Bernard succeeded him He was born 1743, and is described as of Hagley, Worcestershire He had married in December, 1776, Ann, the daughter and co-heiress of Mr. John De la Bere of Southam, near Cheltenham, and two years afterwards his brother John married her other sister, Harriet Joan. The De la Beres were an ancient family, and among the pictures at Wellesbourne is one painted on wood representing Sir Richard De la Bere presenting to the Black Prince the arms taken from the King of Bohemia at the Battle of Cressy Southam, then a curious old-fashioned residence near Cheltenham, was purchased by Lord Ellenborough after his return from his government of India

Mrs Bernard D'Ewes was considered a great beauty. She died in her third confinement, the child only living a few hours. (August, 1780) She left issue a son, Court, born 1779, who eventually succeeded to the Calwich and Wellesbourne properties, and a daughter Anne (Nanny) whose beauty excelled even that of her mother. Mr D'Ewes married, as his second wife, Judith, daughter of Richard Beresford, Esq, of Newton Grange, Staffordshire, a member of the ancient family of Beresford, which had been settled in Staffordshire and Derbyshire for many generations The present Marquess of Waterford is descended from Humphrey, seventh son of Thomas Beresford, a warrior who resided at Fenny Bentley, Staffordshire, in the time of Henry VI. Two sons were born of the second marriage, viz Bernard D'Ewes, who died at Malvern Wells, November 19th, 1800, in his sixth year, and is buried at Wellesbourne, and John D'Ewes, born 1804, and died 1861 Judith, Mrs D'Ewes, "ruled all around her with the absolute power usually exercised by second wives" "I remember," adds Baroness Bunsen, "with great pleasure her charming singing and her duets with her lovely step-daughter Anne D'Ewes This cousin. Nanny D'Ewes, was most attractive in my eyes, and not in mine only, for she was the admired of all beholders and the darling of her elder relations, while her contemporaries could not help forgiving her the homage she received, from the absence of all pretension on her part Her countenance and demeanour were the effusion of the purest and the most perfect feminine modesty, without shyness. She seemed not to fear or mistrust her fellow creatures any more than to presume over them. Her voice, in speaking as in singing, seemed to pour forth the melody of the whole being, and each syllable dropped from the lips and the pearls within, as if the purpose of speaking was to show their perfection. Her look seemed to ask everyone to be kind to her

1.*

without making demands as of a right " She married G. F.
Stratton, Esq , of Tew Park, Oxfordshire, whom she survived
many years, ending her widowhood at Barnard's Green,
Malvern, the 20th January, 1861, " having to the last fulfilled
the bright promise of her youth " She is buried in the Abbey
Church of Great Malvern There is a very fine cartoon of Mrs
Stratton at Wellesbourne, by Sir Thomas Lawrence, as well as
an oil picture with a Newfoundland dog, by the same master
Her step-mother died the 27th of November, 1814, in the
forty-ninth year of her age, and is buried at Wellesbourne.
Mr Bernard D'Ewes died in 1822

John D'Ewes, his younger brother, took Holy Orders in
1769, and was appointed chaplain to the Countess of Cowper,
fourth daughter of Lord Carteret, afterwards created Earl
Granville After having served in Warwickshire for three years,
his uncle, Mr Bernard Granville of Calwich Abbey, obliged him
to give up his work, and come and live with him on account
of his failing health.

Lady Cowper writes thus to Mrs. Port, 22nd December,
1771 —

I imagine you have heard of the extraordinary step Mr Granville has
insisted upon your brother John's taking, of throwing up his chaplainship   I
conclude he means by it (if he has any meaning left) to make him more
dependent on him, and he will, I suppose, make *him* his heir   Alas, poor
Bernard !   Some people contrive to make their family unhappy even after
they are dead !   Your brother wrote me as proper a letter upon the occasion
as such an unprecedented step could produce ' but I am not displeased *with
him*, and I shall supply his place with my old acquaintance who said to you
I was "*the* sweetest woman ''—he will then think me sweeter than ever

Lady Cowper was more correct in her surmises than his
relations, who all along concluded that Bernard D'Ewes would
succeed to Calwich on Bernard Granville's death ; but when the
end came it was found that the last male heir of the Granvilles
had chosen the youngest of his sister's sons to succeed him.
Mrs Delany writes, the 29th of July, 1775, to their sister
Mrs Port —

I have had the company of your dear bro[rs] 3 times to dinner and
tomorrow they are engaged to me   The *more* I converse with them the
greater is my esteem of them   John stays purely out of kindness to Bernard,
whose little employm[t] has obliged him to stay in town   They are impatient
to return into Staffordshire, as you may believe, and to see their friends at
Ilam   I hope, tho' the disappointment has been very great to my dear
Bernard, that time will reconcile him to an event so unexpected by him   He
has no corroding passions to deal with , he is neither avaricious nor envious ,
his resentment arises from sentiment to be dealt with unkindly when he must
be conscious he did not deserve it, and this must hurt a generous nature , but

ANN D'EWES,
WIFE OF G. F. STRATTON, ESQ.
From an Original Portrait, by Sir Thomas Lawrence, in the Wollesbourne Collection.

he does not say a murmuring word, and his brother John seems, in the midst of his own great acquisitions, to feel so sensibly what must pass in Bernard's mind that I am sure he will do all he can to soften the disappointment, but there must be time to consider what can be done or what he may have in his power, but they seem quite satisfied with one another

The enclosed letter from Mr. Granville about John D'Ewes, recommending him for preferment, which he wrote to the Duchess of Portland, asking her to show it to the Archbishop of York, and to request his Grace to petition the Bishop of Lichfield for the first vacant prebend that fell in, shows what a high opinion he had formed of John's character. —

his character and behaviour in his vocation, as well as in his private life, have been unexceptional   . After having served in Warwickshire for four years I was obliged to recall him in consequence of my own severe illness, during which time he has served the cure of this parish in such a manner that the parishioners adore him   He found an abandoned church, it is now so crowded that there is scarcely room for the congregation, as people come four or five miles round to hear him, and his attendance on the sick, with every other part of the duty of a clergyman, cannot be exceeded   His character and conduct in Warwickshire are well known

Yet John had deeply resented living with his cross old uncle and was very unhappy at Calwich. Mrs Delany, writing to Mrs Port (27th January, 1772), says —

I have had a most disconsolate letter from John about his present confinement, and beseeching me most earnestly *to get a call* for him : meaning, I suppose, a living   Had that been at *my* call he would have had one long ago, and those who I thought might have answered favourably have been reminded, but when people are to bestow favours they will do it at their own time   I do most sensibly feel his painful situation   I have experienced it often and attended with aggravating circumstances, and for a much longer time than he is likely to. But his good principles will support him while he is performing an act of duty, and his being able at the same time to improve himself in French and music are advantages that make some amends   An ingenious mind is never too old to learn, besides there is another mitigating circumstance that the worst part of the winter is over, that is the shortest days, and time flies fast, a consideration which he is young enough to avail himself of, and when the trial is over will it not be a lasting consolation to reflect on having sustained it patiently, and at the same time given any comfort to age and infirmities

Bernard Granville died in 1775, and in 1778 John D'Ewes married Harriet Joan De la Bere, and the following year a son and heir was born, and named John after his father, and subsequently a daughter named Harriet, who died in infancy   In 1783, he was instituted to the living of Ham, which he held for his nephew, Bernard Port, who succeeded him in 1801, but from the Registers it would appear that he only very occasionally officiated there himself. In 1785 he assumed by royal command the surname and arms of Granville This was done at the instigation of Mrs. Delany, as is evident from the following postscript to a letter which has been lost .—

P S —Time runs on and our glass is spent before we are aware of it, even in old age, it is prudent in me not to suppress what has been for some time on my mind I have always thought that it was laudable and proper that names of respectable families should be kept up, especially by a direct descendant of so worthy and so great a man as Sir Bevil Granville (who died for his king and country) and not let his name sink in oblivion I sometime ago mentioned this, you apprehended it was not particularly my brother's desire you should take his name, but such reasons have started since as I am sure would have convinced my brother Granville that it ought to be done These urgent reasons, which I cannot explain in a letter, and must be quite between ourselves, are relating to Earl Temple's family, and though it may be a matter of indifference to yourself, it may prove of consequence to your descendants Upon the birth of your son I thought it more incumbent for you to take it into consideration The D^{ss} of Portland, Lord Guilford, Mr F Montagu, and many other friends by all means think it a very becoming step for you to take, and this has been often urged to me without my leading them at all into the subject, which is a sanction to my own opinion, and I shall be happy if it agrees with yours
I have said nothing to any of your family about this affair, only have always in general terms wish'd it

On the 9th of November, 1785, Mrs. Delany writes thus to Mrs. Frances Hamilton —

It gave me a pleasant opportunity of presenting Mr D'Ewes (Court) to their Majesties, the King took gracious notice of him, and having heard that his youngest brother wished to take the name of Granville, said to Mr D'Ewes that he "desired he might from that time be called by that name," and gave orders that his sign-manual should be prepared for that purpose, which has accordingly been done

And in her Diary, under date 29th October, 1785, Mrs Delany writes thus —

The King in the most gracious manner told Mr D Ewes that he was informed that his youngest brother Mr J D'Ewes, and the rest of the family were desirous that he should take the name of Granville, and that His Majesty was very well pleased it should be so immediately.

The following letter is also extant from Court D'Ewes to his brother John, bearing on the subject —

Court D'Ewes Esq to the Rev John D'Ewes
Windsor, Oct 29, 1785.

Dear Brother *Granville,*
For, after having his Majesty's commands to call you so for y^e future. I don't know whether it would not be a misdemeanour in me to do otherwise !

THE REV. JOHN GRANVILLE,

OF CALWICH.

From an Original Portrait, by Barber, in the Welleshourne Collection.

To be serious I think from y⁰ time you receive this letter you may assume the name The King was here last night, he called me to him, he said he heard yᵗ Mˢ Delany and yᵗ family wished you sᵈ take y⁰ name of Granville, and yᵗ you desired it yʳself Y⁰ King said "he thought it was very proper," and bid me for y⁰ future call you 'Granville," and y⁰ Queen in a conversation afterwards with Mˢ Delany about your family called your wife "Mˢ Granville," and I will, if you think proper, write to Pardon to prepare yʳ instrument, and get it sealed and registered

I have been here since Tuesday Their Majesties have spent two afternoons here I have had a good deal of conversation with the King I defer particulars till we meet wᶜʰ I hope will be early in the winter I return home on Monday y⁰ 7ᵗʰ Mˢ Delany is wonderfully well, Mary Ann quite so, we all join in kind love and congratulations to yʳself and Mˢ Granville I hope a second visit to Buxton has had a good effect upon Miss De la Bere For myself, I think I mend, but not quite so quick as I should wish

I am always

Yours affectionately,

C D'Ewes

Mr. and Mrs Granville were much beloved and esteemed at Calwich, and he is described as "one of the most benevolent, liberal and kind-hearted men that ever lived" They were especial favourites with their nephews and nieces the Ports, who rejoiced at every opportunity of a visit to Calwich, indeed the youngest niece, Frances Anne (born April 18th 1783) lived entirely with them, and was adopted by them (they having no daughter of their own, but an only son) till her marriage with Mr Ram of Clonolten, co Wexford

Baroness Bunsen was also a frequent visitor at Calwich in her childhood and in some *records*' thus describes it —

The small river of Calwich had been widened by Bernard Granville so as to have the appearance of a lake with buildings in questionable taste in the Italian villa style, those at each end serving the purpose of concealing the entrance and exit of the natural stream, and keeping the water high and smooth, while a central building contained a picture gallery and music room in which my uncle Granville would occasionally practise the violoncello, both he and his brother D'Ewes having fortunately attained the consciousness (so rare amongst *dilettanti*) that their life long passion for music was, as related to performance, unfortunate, and thus best exercised out of hearing The older part of the house was of bachelor dimensions, the library, very spacious sunny and sheltered, showed dark rows of venerable books little used by the modern world since the death of Mr Bernard Granville who had been a man of studious habits, and containing besides a collection of MS works of Handel, who often passed his summer leisure at Calwich and played on the organ in the dining-room, upon which his bust was erected

My uncle Granville had added much to make the house complete as a residence, and I believe with much taste He had just finished his improvements, which were to be all ready for his beloved son's coming of age, when in June, 1800, the desolated dwelling opened to receive the funeral procession on its way to Ellaston Church.

In the previous summer he (young John Granville) had spent a few days at Llanover, and was as engaging to us children as to all the older members of society—beautiful in person, intelligent in mind, everywhere showered upon with golden opinions, commended at school, adored at home, having just entered upon his twenty-first year, so that the whole mass of our relations were full of the anticipations of his coming of age. He had gone to Clifton with a cough to have recourse to the two nostrums of the Hot-Wells and Dr Carrick. His mother was watchful but not anxious, when in a moment before her eyes the precious life was closed to all earthly consciousness. Immediately on receiving the grievous news my mother went to Clifton and brought back the bereaved parents to Llanover. I remember how she would walk up and down the gravel in front of the house with her uncle, who was soothed with the tones of her voice, and for whom she always seemed to find conversation by the hour, alternating with long sittings in the little morning-room with Aunt Granville, whose calm and patient endurance of her lot inspired deeper sympathy than the more aggressive grief of her husband.

The following lines were written by the bereaved father and engraved on a slate which was kept in a wooden case at the back of a seat under an old beech tree at Calwich, on which young Granville had carved his own initials, in the centre of a row of trees leading to a romantic spot known as " Cabin Knowle "

> When Lycidas, intent on rural fame,
> Grav'd on the smooth rind of this spreading beech
> The dear initials of his fleeting name,
> He stretched his fancy to its utmost reach
> Of pious resolution, both to guard
> And nurse these groves, as his fond sire had done.
> Ah, me ! how great then gain had he been spared !
> How great then loss now Lycidas is gone !
> Yet shall a future master of these trees,
> Of kindred blood and kindred mind the same,
> Struck by the record which he passing sees,
> Protect their honour and respect his name,
> For they survived that storm and ruin wide
> Which sunk poor Calwich when her darling died.

J G   1800.

There is a very beautiful oil painting of young John Granville, who was thus cut off on the very threshold of his manhood, by Hoppner, and it is one of the gems of the Wellesbourne collection of family portraits. It is easy to understand the deep grief and crushing sorrow which his early death caused his loving parents and friends, as one gazes at a face that indeed seemed almost " too beautiful to live "

In the north chancel aisle of Ellastone Church is a Tablet to his memory bearing the following inscription —

JOHN GRANVILLE,
ONLY SON OF REV. JOHN GRANVILLE, OF CALWICH.
From an Original Portrait, by Hoppner, in the Wellesbourne Collection.

𝔖acred to the 𝔐emory of

JOHN GRANVILLE,

ONLY SON OF JOHN and HARRIET GRANVILLE

OF CALWICH,

WHO

WAS SUDDENLY CUT OFF IN THE PRIME AND PRIDE

OF YOUTH AND EXPECTATION BY A RAPID

CONSUMPTION

THIS MARBLE IS NOT ERECTED TO REMIND HIS AFFLICTED PARENTS AND SORROWING FRIENDS WHAT MANNER OF YOUNG MAN HE WAS, FOR THAT WILL EVER BE REMEMBERED BY THEM, BUT TO INFORM POSTERITY THAT RELIGIOUS AND MORAL INSTRUCTION, AIDED BY AFFECTIONATE CONFIDENCE, AND ENFORCED BY GOOD EXAMPLE, WILL, AND DID IN THIS INSTANCE, COUNTERACT THE DANGERS OF A PUBLICK EDUCATION AND EARLY INTRODUCTION TO THE WORLD TO ENUMERATE AND ENLARGE UPON THE DISTINGUISHED GOOD QUALITIES OF HIS HEART AND MIND, HIS LOVE OF TRUTH AND VIRTUE, HIS ATTAINMENTS, THE AMIABLE POLISH OF HIS MANNERS AND BEHAVIOUR, WOULD EXCEED THE LIMITS OF A BRIEF MEMORIAL LET IT BE RECORDED, HOWEVER, THAT HE WAS HONOURED BY THE NOTICE AND APPROBATION OF THOSE OF THE HIGHEST RANK, AND GRATIFIED BY THE LOVE AND ESTEEM OF ALL IN INFERIOR STATION, DOWN TO

> The humble tenants of his native vale,
> Who marked with pleasure his increasing years,
> And with prophetick eye were wont to hail
> The dawning prospect   Stay, O! stay your tears
> While you now comtemplate his dark, cold grave
> He is not there, blest Spirit!   He stands among
> Th' innumerable multitudes, that wait
> Before the High Throne and before the Lamb,
> Cloathed in purest Robes and bearing Palms,
> Freed and exulting in Eternal Day

HE DIED AT BRISTOL HOT WELLS, ON THE 7TH,

AND WAS

INTERRED NEAR THIS PLACE ON THE 12TH OF JULY, 1800,

IN THE 21ST YEAR OF HIS AGE.

PARENTAL GRATITUDE, AS WELL AS AFFECTION FOR THE

BEST OF SONS, PLAC'D AND INSCRIBED THIS

The Reverend John Granville died the 14th of November, 1826, in the 83rd year of his age, his wife having predeceased him on the 25th of April, 1825, aged 71 On the Tablet to their memory in Ellastone Church are the words—

THEY DID JUSTLY, AND LOVED MERCY, AND WALKED HUMBLY WITH THEIR GOD

Their portraits were painted by Barber of Derby, and the following lines were composed on seeing them by their great-nephew, the Rev Brownlow Layard, grandson of Mary Port —

> The pictures are like both in form and in face,
> And the emblems about them well show every grace
> Of this excellent pair, whose conjugal love
> In a still flowing stream, like their own silver Dove
> Dispensing its blessings to thousands unseen,
> Keep their friends, like its meadows, continually green
> As the marble she leans on, so polish'd her mind,
> Not a flaw or a roughness upon it we find
> And the pillar so firm, so correct, and so true,
> No doubt will her temper present to our view
> A fit emblem of candour the curtain this shown,
> By which she hides everyone's faults but her own
> Like the leaves of the rose when they dry and are shed,
> Her virtues a fragrance will give when she's dead,
> And those who survive her with pleasure will find
> In her bodily likeness a touch of that mind,
> Which the painter with judgment and pencil so true
> In this beautiful picture presents to our view
> When I turn to the other, O Barber, for shame !
> It's our own uncle Granville you've placed in that frame
> 'Tis himself ! 'tis his chair, 'tis his stick, 'tis his box,
> I believe you are playing upon us a hoax
> With his good-natured look 'tis himself every inch,
> And the snuff-box will show he's a friend at a pinch,
> Not a doubt of the wig could anyone harbour,
> I believe they're both made by the very same Barber !
> But let me be merry and wise, if I'm able,
> For a Bible I see he has placed on the table ,
> That Bible his guide from the first to the last,
> By its aid thro' each passage of life has he pass'd,
> Stemmed the torrent of sorrow, and fitted his mind
> To enjoy every bliss which in future he'll find
> In the regions above—*this* we all must believe,
> Though his fulness of joy there we cannot conceive

Count D Ewes, eldest son of Bernard D'Ewes by his wife Ann De la Bere, succeeded to the Calwich property. He was born in the year 1779, and had married, in 1803, Maria, daughter of Edward Ferrers, Esquire, of Baddesley Clinton. co. Warwick, the head of an ancient family, than which few could claim higher or more illustrious descent, and which had been settled at

MRS. GRANVILLE,

OF CALWICH,

From an Original Portrait, by Barber, in the Wellesbourne Collection.

Baddesley Clinton since the fifteenth century, when Sir Edward Ferrers married the heiress of that property On succeeding his uncle, Mr Court D'Ewes assumed the name and arms of Granville After a few years possession, becoming seriously embarrassed by the mismanagement of his property, and by unfortunate speculations in mines, Mr Granville was unhappily compelled to part with Calwich, and passed the remainder of his days at York House, Leamington, where he died the 16th of July, 1848, aged 68, and he and his widow (who died the 16th of November, 1852, aged 78) were both interred in the family vault at Wellesbourne Calwich Abbey was purchased by the Honourable and Very Reverend Augustus Duncombe, Dean of York, who pulled down the old mansion, and rebuilt one on a higher level, formerly occupied by stables and farm-buildings and by an ancient walled garden, which dated from the time of the monastery.

Mr. and Mrs Court Granville left issue four sons and three daughters viz :—

(*I*). BERNARD GRANVILLE OF WELLESBOURNE, born the 4th of February, 1804 and educated at Rugby He married first Mathewana Sarah, second daughter of Captain Matthew Richard Onslow, of the Coldstream Guards, and granddaughter of Admiral Sir Richard Onslow, Baronet, K C.B She died at Calwich Abbey, on the 3rd of August, 1829, in the twenty-first year of her age, three months after giving birth to a daughter, Joan Frederica Mathewana, who was married, in 1850, to the Honourable and Reverend Lord Charles Paulet, second son of Charles Ingoldsby, thirteenth Marquess of Winchester. Lord Charles Paulet was forty years Vicar of Wellesbourne, and a Prebendary of Salisbury Cathedral He died 23rd July, 1870, aged 67. They had issue —

> ERNEST INGOLDSBY ; born, 22nd August, 1851 ; died, 5th February, 1853
>
> ADELA ; married 5th June, 1886, Frederick Thorne, Esq , of Leamington, and died 15th July, 1893.
>
> ELEANOR MARY , married, 1st June, 1889, Lieut -Col E. H T. Hutton, C.B , King's Royal Rifles.

Mr. Bernard Granville married, secondly, in 1830, Ann Catherine, younger daughter of Admiral Sir Hyde Parker (second son of Admiral Sir Hyde Parker, Baronet, of Melford Hall, Suffolk, who attained the rank of Vice-Admiral of the

M³

Blue, and was Commander-in-Chief of His Majesty's ships in the action of St Lucia in 1780 , and also in the memorable action with the Dutch at the Doggerbank, in 1781), by his second wife, Frances, daughter of Admiral Sir Richard Onslow, Baronet   Admiral Sir Hyde Parker commanded at the battle of Copenhagen (2nd April, 1801), when Nelson was second in command   His reputation as a naval commander has suffered in the eyes of the world by what may be called the incident of · the Telescope and the Blind Eye "   It should be known however, that the Rev Dr Scott, who was Sir Hyde Parker's chaplain on the *'London*," bears witness, in his "*Recollections*," p 70, that 'it had been arranged between the Admirals (Parker and Nelson) that should it appear that the ships which were engaged were suffering too severely, the signal for retreat should be made to give Lord Nelson the option of retiring if he thought fit '   Sir Hyde, after Nelson s squadron had been exposed for three hours to the most severe cannonade that the hero of the Nile had ever undergone, deeming it impossible for his junior officer to hold out any longer, and desirous of relieving him of the responsibility of a retreat, hoisted the permissive signal that had been agreed upon   It was really an act of magnanimity.   He was aware of the consequences," he said, " to his own personal reputation , but it would be cowardly in him to leave Nelson to bear the whole shame of the failure, if shame it should be deemed '   There was no need, therefore for Nelson to have pretended not to see Sir Hyde Parker's signal to retreat, because that signal was not absolute , and if Nelson wished to go on fighting (as when did he ever wish to stop ?) he was at full liberty to do so, without any such performance as legend has attributed to him   Nelson was deservedly made a Viscount for the battle of Copenhagen   The Commander-in-Chief himself was passed over unhonoured. although a peerage was at one time under consideration

By this second marriage Mr. Bernard Granville had a large family, namely ·—

(*I.*) BEVIL , born at Wellesbourne, 20th January, 1834 ; educated at the Royal Military College, Sandhurst , entered the Army in 1851, when he joined the 23rd Royal Welsh Fusiliers in Canada, and served there two years   He embarked with his regiment on the 4th of April, 1854, for the East , served in Bulgaria, and landed in the Crimea on the 14th September, 1854 , was present at the affair on the *Boulganac*, at the battle of Alma, at the taking of Balaclava, at the

WELLESBOURNE HALL, CO. WARWICK.

battle of Inkermann and the Siege of Sebastopol He served
as A D C. to Major-General Lord William Paulet, commanding
the Light Division, and returned to England at the conclusion
of the war with his regiment, and received the Crimean medal
with three clasps, and also the Turkish medal On the 17th
of June, 1857, he sailed for China, but on reaching the
Cape of Good Hope, the regiment was ordered to Calcutta
the Indian Mutiny having broken out He landed at Calcutta
on the 18th of September, 1857, and was present with his
regiment, which was part of the relieving force under General
Sir Colin Campbell, at the relief of Lucknow, the battle of
Cawnpore, and the taking of Lucknow He commanded the
rear guard of his regiment at the withdrawing of the forces
after the relief of the Garrison from the Residency on the
23rd of November, 1857 He was given a Brevet-Majority at
the end of the Mutiny for service in the field and a medal with
two clasps Major Granville retired from the Army in 1863,
and was appointed Major of the 2nd Warwickshire Militia, in
which he served till 1865 He was appointed by His Royal
Highness the Duke of Cambridge to the Royal Body Guard in
1863 on his retirement from the Army, in which he had served
twenty-three years, and had the Jubilee Medal sent him in 1887.
He also served for twenty years as Adjutant of the Herts Royal
Volunteers, retiring on a pension and the officer's decoration
for long service Major Granville is a Magistrate for the
Counties of Warwick and Herts He married in October, 1865,
Alice Jane, 2nd daughter of the Rev. Nathaniel Wodehouse
(*see* Kimberley) and Georgina his wife, daughter of the Hon.
and Rev William Capel, and has by her—

> BERNARD, born 21st July, 1873, a Lieut 3rd Batt
> Royal Welsh Fusiliers
>
> VIOLET married Walter Mandsley, Esq, of Cadogan
> Square, London, S W
>
> MARY OLIVE, married Arthur E Wood, Esq, of
> Newbold Revel, Warwickshire
>
> MURIEL, married Frederick C Blomfield, Esq of
> Colne Cottage, Herts
>
> GRACE, married Harold McCorquodale, Esq. of the
> Grange, Shenley, Herts
>
> MORWENNA, unmarried

(*II*) RICHARD DELABERE, born 7th July 1835 entered

the Royal Navy as a Naval Cadet in 1847 and served in the
Meander, on the Pacific Station, under Captain the Honorable
Henry Keppel (now Admiral of the Fleet) until 1851, when he
returned home as midshipman ; he was appointed to the
Bellerophon in 1852, and served in her under Captain Lord
George Paulet in the Black Sea Fleet against the Russians,
being present at the storming of the Forts at Sebastapol, and
serving in the trenches at Eupotoria   For these services he
received a medal and a clasp   After the battle of Alma he
went in search of his brother Bevil, whose regiment had been
cut to pieces   Finding he was not with the survivors he searched
the battle field and found him lying on the ground unwounded,
but utterly prostrate from the exhaustion and privations he
had undergone   The following touching verses on the meeting
of the two brothers were composed by Mr. T R J. Langharve,
and are thought not unworthy of insertion in these pages ·—

THE BROTHERS

A youth went forth to the battlefield
  At the close of an autumn day,
If his brother haply he might find
  Surviving from the fray

The champion of the oppressed had sent
  Her armaments to war,
The weak to aid against the might
  Of Russia's tyrant Czar

Forth from one home two brothers went
  Amid the warriors brave ,
One serving on the tented field,
  One on the dark sea wave

With beating heart and anxious gaze,
  Perch'd on the top-mast's height,
From burning noon till dewy eve
  One watched the bloody fight

Where the volleying storm was thickest
  Of the murderous shot and shell,
Where, like corn before the reapers,
  Britain's gallant heroes fell

Where the carnage raged the fiercest
  Near the Alma's crimson sand,
Well his eye could trace the progress
  Of his brother's daring band

The fight is done, the field is won,
  Ceased has the cannon's roar,
From the frigate's side there is seen to glide
  A boat to the Alma's shore.

A sailor lad from the boat has sprung,
And with step as quick as thought
His foot speeds on to the deadly spot,
Where his brothers band had fought

Full many a form of the young and brave
Lay there in a warrior's rest,
Where o'er mangled corpse and quivering limb
His hurrying footsteps pressed

But he finds not there the face that he seeks,
Yet the face that he dreads to see,
The face that has given him smile for smile
In their hours of boyish glee.

He turns, for a voice on his anxious ear
In well-known accents falls,
'Tis his brother's self before him stands,
His brother's voice that calls

All spent with fatigue, tho' unscathed by a wound
He has passed through the dreadful strife,
But a brother is near to support and cheer
And restore his fainting life.

Oh ! for a limner's hand to paint,
For a poet's pen to write,
The scene where those youthful brothers met
On the Alma's bloody height

Alas ! on the voyage home Richard Delabere Granville was struck down with Maltese fever and died, and was buried at sea, three days from Malta, 11th February, 1856, aged 19

(*III*) GEORGE HYDE, born 22nd February, 1837 , joined the Madras army, H E I C S in 1856, and in 1857 was chosen as one of the officers of the Madras Rifles, a regiment composed of different Madras Regiments, and sent to the Mutiny in Bengal He served in this regiment during the whole of that eventful time, and received a medal He retired in 1866 He married, 18th June, 1862. Henrietta, sixth daughter of Edward Bolton King, Esq , of Chadshunt, co Warwick, by his wife Georgiana, daughter of Robert Knight, Esq , of Barrels in the same county. and has by her—

> DENNIS, born 14th April, 1863 , Captain Royal Warwickshire Regiment , married 31st July, 1895, Margaret Beatrice, daughter of Lady Waller and the late Major-General Sir George Waller, Baronet, of Woodcote, Warwickshire.

> ROBERT, born 26th October, 1864 , Lieutenant in the 95th (Derbyshire) Regiment, died at Jubbulpore, India, 24th May, 1892, aged 27.

MABEL GEORGIANA LUCY, unmarried.

(*IV*) FREDERICK JOHN, born 14th October, 1839 ; joined the Madras Fusiliers at Lucknow in 1857, having previously been attached to the 23rd Royal Welsh Fusiliers for a short time He served with his regiment at the taking of Lucknow, and received a medal and one clasp. Having been invalided home, he exchanged into a regiment at home, but retired from the service in 1859 He married, 2 id July, 1864, Cecilia Anne (who died 7th February, 1877) only child of Robert Hook, Esq , by Katherine his wife, widow of the late Sir Henry Cooke Knight, and daughter of the late Vice-Admiral William Windham, of Fillbrigg co Norfolk, and had issue —

> CHARLES DELABERE, born 21st July, 1865, a lieutenant, R N.
>
> CECIL HORACE PLANTAGENET, born 4th February, 1877
>
> MARIAN FLORENCE, unmarried

(*V*) ROGER, born 6th February, 1848, educated at Wellington College , late Pemberton Scholar of University College, Durham B A (2nd Class) 1869 , M A 1874 , ordained deacon 1871 by the Bishop of Exeter (Temple) and priest 1872 by the Bishop of Worcester (Philpotts) , Curate of Huish and Merton, Devon, 1872, Wellesbourne, 1872, Charlecote, 1872-75 ; Vicar of Charlecote, 1875-76 , Rector of Bideford, 1878 , married 20th September, 1870, Matilda Jane, daughter of Alexander Liebert, Esq , of Swinton Hall, Lancashire, and by her has issue —

> COURT, born 6th May 1872, formerly lieutenant in the 4th battalion Royal Warwickshire Regiment
>
> ELEANOR MORWENNA, unmarried.

(*I*) ANNE died an infant, 1832

(*II*) FANNY (twin with above) married 22nd April, 1858, the Rev Wellesley Pole Pigott, Rector of Bemerton, Fovant, and Fugglestone, Wilts (4th son of Sir George Pigott, first Baronet, of Knapton, Queen's County, Ireland) who died 27th February, 1890, leaving issue —

> WELLESLEY GEORGE, Captain and Adjutant in the Rifle Brigade , born 20th April, 1861 , married 7th July, 1891, Helen Louisa, widow of Captain Frederick Ind, R A , and only daughter of Captain Thomas Donaldson, 3rd Hussars

HENRY A'COURT, born 25th February, 1870 ; educated at Wellington College and Christ Church, Oxford, B A

FANNY ADA, married, 25th May, 1886, her cousin, Major Charles Berkeley Pigott, D S O , only son of Sir Charles Pigott, third Baronet, of Knapton

(*III*) CAROLINE died, unmarried, 10th Sept , 1883 and is buried at Wellesbourne

(*IV*) LOUISA married in 1872, Sir George Stucley Stucley, Baronet, of Hartland Abbey, Affeton Castle and Moreton, in the county of Devon and has issue —

HUGH NICHOLAS GRANVILLE born 22nd June 1873 a Lieutenant R N

HUMPHREY ST LIGER, born 7th June, 1877

(*V.*) AMY, married 4th December, 1861, to Captain Henry Bathurst, late 23rd Royal Welsh Fusiliers (only son of Col Henry Bathurst (*see* Earl Bathurst) of the Scots Guards by Emily his wife, daughter of Henry Villebois, of Marham, Norfolk), who died 5th September, 1886, and has issue —

HENRY VILLEBOIS, born 30th October, 1862

GRANVILLE FREDERICK VILLEBOIS, born 5th February, 1864

LAUNCELOT VILLEBOIS, born 23rd April, 1870

LAURENCE CHARLES VILLEBOIS, born 4th June, 1871

EMILY VILLEBOIS

FINETTA VILLEBOIS

AMY VILLEBOIS.

GRACE VILLEBOIS

(*VI.*) HARRIET married, in 1869, to Henry Compton, Esq , of Minstead, Hants (who died 5th July, 1877) and has issue —

HENRY FRANCIS, born 16th January, 1872 , married 12th June, 1895, to Dorothy Ann, daughter of the late Sir Richard Musgrave, Baronet, and of Lady Brougham and Vaux, of Edenhall, Cumberland

GEORGE, born 4th February, 1873

EDWARD BATHURST, R N , born 14th August, 1875.

HARRIET

ELEANOR

Mr. BERNARD GRANVILLE was a kind-hearted and generous gentleman, a lover of hospitality, and a fine sportsman. The " Old Warwickshire Hounds " were under his management, jointly with several other gentlemen, in 1836 and 1837, and were celebrated for the fine quality of the horses He was a magistrate and deputy-lieutenant of Warwickshire, and died at Leamington, 6th January, 1869, and was buried at Wellesbourne. His widow, who resides at Bideford, still survives him, aged 90.

2 GRANVILLE JOHN GRANVILLE , educated at Rugby ; entered 12th Lancers in 1824 , exchanged into 53rd Foot in 1830; sold out in 1833 and went to Downing College, Cambridge was ordained by Bishop Kaye of Lincoln for the Bishop of Lichfield in 1836 , was curate of Norbury-cum-Snelston, 1836-1839 ; perpetual curate of Chelford, in the diocese of Chester, 1839-1852 ; curate of Charlecote, 1853-1855 , vicar of Stratford-on-Avon, 1855-1867 , rector of Pleasley, 1867-1871.   He died 21st April, 1871, and was buried at Pleasley.   He married, in 1839, Marianne, 5th daughter of Sir Gray Skipwith, Baronet, of Newbold Revel, co Warwick   She died 27th October, 1878, and is buried at Ilam.   They had issue —

> GRAY, born 1843   Educated at Christ Church, Oxford, B A 1867, M A 1876 ; was ordained deacon by Bishop Trower, for the Bishop of Lichfield, 1868 , was curate of Ashbourne, 1868-69 , of Pleasley, 1870-71 of Lighthorne, 1871-73 , Rector of Blore Ray, Staffordshire, 1873-75 , Vicar of Ilam, Staffordshire, 1875 and was appointed Rural Dean of Alstonfield, 1886 He married, 1st March, 1881, Josephine Dora Lawrance, who died 11th February, 1884.

> GRACE married, 1st August, 1871, Henry Leigh Bennett, Vicar of Mansfield, and Prebendary of Lincoln Cathedral, and has issue .—   .

> GERTRUDE, married 30th April, 1878, the Right Reverend George Richard Mackarness, Bishop of Argyle and the Isles, who died 20th April, 1883, and was buried at Ilam

3. COURT GRANVILLE, born 23rd April, 1808, educated at Trinity College, Cambridge, B A 1832, M A 1835; ordained deacon by the Bishop of Lichfield and Coventry, 1835, and priest by the Bishop of Worcester for the Bishop of Lichfield and Coventry, 1837, curate of Norbury-cum-Snelston, 1835; vicar of Matherfield, 1837, appointed rural dean of Uttoxeter, 1838; vicar of Mayfield, 1844; vicar of Alnwick, 1846; domestic chaplain to Hugh, Duke of Northumberland, 1846; to Algernon, Duke of Northumberland, 1847, appointed an honorary canon of Durham Cathedral, 1851, vicar of Thaxted, Essex, 1854, vicar of Alnwick, 1851, rural dean of Alnwick, 1859, honorary chaplain to the 2nd Corps of Northumberland Artillery, 1860, proctor for the Diocese of Durham in the Convocation of York, 1866; domestic chaplain to George, Duke of Northumberland, 1865, and to Algernon George, Duke of Northumberland, 1868 vicar of Chatton, 1869 He married, in 1847, the Lady Charlotte Augusta Leopoldina Murray, eldest daughter of James Lord Glenlyon, and sister to George, Sixth Duke of Athole She died 2nd May, 1889, aged seventy-two, and was interred with the Rev Court Granville (who had died 13th March, 1871, aged sixty-three) in the family vault at Wellesbourne

4. FREDERICK GRANVILLE, born 3rd February, 1810, formerly Major in the 23rd Royal Welsh Fusiliers and Colonel of the 2nd Warwickshire Militia. He died at Ivybridge, co. Devon, 15th October, 1885, and was interred at Wellesbourne He married, in 1854, Isabel. only surviving daughter of Edward Sheldon Esq, of Brailes, co. Warwick, M P His widow married, secondly, Vincent Pollexfen Calmady, Esq, of Tetcott, Holsworthy.

1 HARRIET JOAN GRANVILLE died, unmarried, 1857.

2 MARY GRANVILLE, married, in 1858, to Col David Forbes, late of the 91st Regiment, and died at The Holmes, St Boswells, N B, 28th October, 1886.

3 LUCY GRANVILLE died, in a Convent at St. Leonard's, 22nd November, 1887.

A Royal Descent of the Granville Family.

Edward I., King of England ⊤ Eleanor, dau. of Ferdinand III. King of Castile, 1st wife

Edward II., King of England ⊤ Isabella, dau. of Philip *the Fair*, King of France

Edward III. King of England, founder of the most Noble Order of the Garter, *d* in 1377

Lady Elizabeth Plantagenet 5th dau of Edw I ⊤ Humphrey de Bohun, Earl of Hereford

| Lionel of Antwerp Duke of Clarence, K G, *d* 17 Oct 1368 ⊤ Elizabeth, dau and heir of William De Burgh, Earl of Ulster, *d* 1363 | John of Gaunt, Duke of Lancaster, King of Castile and Leon, K G *d* in 1399 ⊤ Catherine, dau of Sir Payne Roet Knt & relict of Sir Otho Swinford, Knt *d* in 1403 | Eleanor eldest dau and coheir of Hum phrey de Bohun, Earl of Hereford, &c ⊤ Thos Plantagenet, of Woodstock, Earl of Buckingham, Duke of Glouces ter, K G *d* in 1399 | Lady Eleanor de Bohun dau of the Earl of Hereford ⊤ James Butler, Earl of Ormon de. |

| Philippa, only dau and heir, *b* 16 Aug 1355 ⊤ Edmund Mortimer, Earl of March &c *d* at Cork, 5 Rich II 1382 | Joan, dau of Johnof Gaunt, Duke of Lancaster, *d* in 1410 ⊤ Ralph Neville Lord of Raby created Earl of Westmoreland, Earl Marshal of Eng land *d* in 1426 | John Beaufort, Mar quess ofDorset, Earl of Som erset, K G *d* in 1410 ⊤ Mar garet, dau of Thos Holland, Earl of Kent | Edm Stafford, Earl of Stafford, K G ⊤ Anne, dau and coheir of Thos Duke of Glou cester | James 2d Earl of Ormonde, *d* 1382 ⊤ Eliza beth, dau of Sir John D'Arcy |

| Elizabeth, dau of Edmund, Earl of March ⊤ Henry Percy the renownedHotspur, son of Henry Earl of Northumberland slain in 1403 | | | | James 3rd Earl of Ormonde, *d* 1405 ⊤ Anne dau of John, Lord Wells |

| Hen Per cy, Earl of Northum berland, slain at St Albans 22 May, 1455 ⊤ Eleanor, dau of Ralph, Earl of West more land | Eleanor, dau of Richard Beau champ, Earl of War wick *d* in 1467 ⊤ Edmund Beaufort, Duke of Somerset, Marquess of Dorset, K G, *d* in 1455 | Anne, dau of Ralph Neville Earl of West moreland ⊤ Humphrey Stafford, Duke of Bucking ham K G | | James, 4th Earl of Ormonde, *d* 1452 ⊤ Joan, dau of Gerald 5th Earl of Kildare |

| Hen Percy, Earl of Northumber land, slain at Towton field, 1460 1 ⊤ Eleanor, dau & heir of Richard Poynings, *d* in 1474 | Margaret, dau of Edmund, Duke of Somerset ⊤ Humphrey Stafford, Earl of Stafford, slain at St Albans, *s p* | | Thomas, Earl of Ormon de, *d* 1515 ⊤ Anne dau & heir of Sir Rich Hank ford |

| Hen Percy, 4th Earl of Northum berland, *d* in 1489 ⊤ Maude dau of William Earl of Pembroke | Catherine dau of Richard Widville, Earl Rivers, K G and sister of Elizabeth, Queen of Edward IV ⊤ Henry Duke of Buckingham, Constable of England K G, be headed in 1483 | Lady Ann Butler, dau and coheir of Thomas, 7th Earl of Or monde ⊤ Sir Ja St Leger, Knt |

Eleanor dau of Henry Percy, 4th Earl of Northumberland ⊤ Edward, Duke of Buckingham K G, beheaded on Tower Hill, in 1524

a   *b*

a
Mary =George, Lord
　　　Abergavenny

b
Sir George St Leger, Sheriff=Anne, dau of Edmund Knevyt
of Devon, 22 Henry VIII　　of Buckingham

Catherine dau of George,=Sir John St Leger of Annery,
Lord Abergavenny　　　　　Devon, High Sheriff, 1562

Mary St Leger, eldest=Sir Richard Granville, Knt, of Stow, Admiral in the reign of
dau and coheir　　　　ELIZABETH representative of Richard de Granville, Earl of
　　　　　　　　　　　Corben, a descendant of Rollo the Dane.

Sir Bernard Granville of Bideford,=Elizabeth, dau and heir
M P. for Bodmin　　　　　　　　of Philip Bevil, Esq

Sir Bevil Granville, Knt of Bideford,=Grace, dau of Sir George Smith,
the gallant Cavalier Commander　　　Knt, of Exeter

Bernard Granville, Esq, 4th son was Master of=Anne, only dau and heir of
the Horse and Gentleman of the Bedchamber　Cuthbert Morley, Esq, of
to CHARLES II　　　　　　　　　　　　　　Haunby, co York

Colonel Bernard Granville, of Buckland,=Mary, dau of Sir Martin
co Gloucester, 3rd son, d 1733　　　　Westcomb, Bart

Bernard Granville, Esq, eldest son and heir,
purchased the estate of Calwich Abbey, co
Stafford d unm 1775

Other
issue

John D'Ewes, Esq,=Anne Granville,
of Wellesbourne,　d 1761.
co Warwick

Bernard, D'Ewes, Esq 2nd son of John=Ann, eldest dau of John De la Bere,
D'Ewes, Esq, of Wellesbourne, died 1822　Esq, of Southam, Cheltenham

Court D'Ewes Esq, of Calwich and Wellesbourne,=Maria, dau of Edward Ferrers,
eldest son of Bernard D'Ewes assumed the name　Esq, of Baddesley, Clinton, co
and arms of Granville, 1827, d 1852　　　　　Warwick

Bernard Granville, Esq of Wellesbourne, eldest=(2nd wife) Ann Catherine younger dau
son of Court Granville, died 1864　　　　　　of Admiral Sir Hyde Parker

Major Bevil Granville, of Wellesbourne 19th m=Alice Jane dau of Rev.
a direct descent from EDWARD III, King of　Nathaniel Wodehouse
England

INDEX

CORRIGENDA

Page 5, line 37, *for* Acquitaine *read* Aquitaine
Page 13, line 32, *for* fendality *read* feudality
Page 13, line 35, *for* are *read* is
Page 14, line 9, *for* Manger *read* Mauger
Page 15, line 18, *for* eldest *read* eldest surviving
Page 16, line 21, *for* Bramlly *read* Bremily
Page 18, line 22, *for* Abselm *read* Anselm
Page 19, line 39, *for* Rhy's *read* Rhys's
Page 20, line 22, *for* Melmesbury *read* Malmesbury
Page 40, line 15, *for* was *read* has been
Page 40, line 19, *for* wordly *read* worldly
Page 18, line 37, *for* Rigister *read* Register
Page 18, line 10, *for* quotaton *read* quotation
Page 48, line 43, *for* Apaiently *read* Apparently
Page 61, line 45, *for* Philipa *read* Philippa
Page 68, line 5, *for* Jane daughter of   Jous and widow of Hills of Taunton *read* Joan daughter of   Combes and widow of John Towse (whose daughter married Roger Hill of Taunton)
Page 72, line 9, *for* cousin *read* uncle
Page 82, line 11, *for* Sir John Carew *read* Sir George Carew
Page 110, line 24, *for* pent *read* peut
Page 135, line 24, *for* Tremeer *read* Lanteglos by Fowey
Page 133, line 19, *for* Them *read* Thiem
Page 157, line 13, *for* illand *read* island
Page 162, line 29, *omit* present at the christening to stand as
Page 174, line 35, *for* 1620 *read* 1630
Page 184, line 22, *should read* the Granvilles and the Arundells frequently intermarried The father of John Arundell
Page 188, line 2, *for* Grenville *read* Granville
Page 197, line 29, *for* tittle *read* title
Page 197, line 32, *for* Tywndreth *read* Tywadreath
Page 197, line 37, *for* His *read* The
Page 200, line 13, *for* it *read* them
Page 290, line 12, *for* Waller *read* Wilke
Page 316, line 19, *omit* had
Page 322, line 8, *for* 1664 *read* 1646
Page 350, line 39, *for* Bondeuell *read* Bardencll
Page 351, line 19, *for* was *read* had been already
Page 439, line 21, *for* Chavaher *read* Chevalier
Page 441, line 32, *for* brother *read* father

EXETER

WILLIAM POLLARD AND CO, PRINTERS, NORTH STREET

CPSIA information can be obtained
at www.ICGtesting.com
Printed in the USA
LVHW101718071118
596305LV00014B/299/P